GIRLS AND WOMEN IN CLASSICAL GREEK RELIGION

It has often been thought that participation in fertility rituals was women's most important religious activity in classical Greece. Matthew Dillon's wide-ranging study makes it clear that women engaged in numerous other rites and cults, and that their role in Greek religion was actually more important than that of men.

Women invoked the god's help in becoming pregnant, venerated the god of wine, worshipped new and exotic deities, used magic for both erotic and pain-relieving purposes, and far more besides. While traditional scholarship has seen such involvement in religion as escapist, Dillon's skilful presentation of the evidence proves that this denigrates women's religiosity and the real importance they attached to their relationship with the divine.

Clear, coherent and comprehensive, this volume challenges many stereotypes of Greek women and offers unexpected insights into their experience of religion. With more than fifty illustrations, and translated extracts from contemporary texts, this is an essential resource for the study of women and religion in classical Greece.

Matthew Dillon is Senior Lecturer at the University of New England, Armidale, Australia. He is also the author of *Pilgrims and Pilgrimage in Ancient Greece* (Routledge 1997), co-author (with Lynda Garland) of *Ancient Greece; Social and historical documents from archaic times to the death of Socrates* (2nd ed, Routledge 2000), and editor of *Religion in the Ancient World: New themes and approaches* (1996).

GIRLS AND WOMEN IN CLASSICAL GREEK RELIGION

Matthew Dillon

Routledge
Taylor & Francis Group

LONDON AND NEW YORK

First published 2002
by Routledge
2 Park Square, Milton Park, Abingdon, Oxon OX14 4RN

First published in paperback 2003

Simultaneously published in the USA and Canada
by Routledge
270 Madison Avenue, New York, NY 10016

Reprinted 2008

Routledge is an imprint of the Taylor & Francis Group, an informa business

© 2001, 2003, Matthew Dillon

Typeset in Garamond by
Keystroke, Jacaranda Lodge, Wolverhampton
Printed and bound in Great Britain by
Biddles Ltd, King's Lynn, Norfolk

All rights reserved. No part of this book may be reprinted or
reproduced or utilised in any form or by any electronic,
mechanical, or other means, now known or hereafter invented,
including photocopying and recording, or in any information
storage or retrieval system, without permission in writing
from the publishers.

British Library Cataloguing in Publication Data
A catalogue record for this book is available from the British Library

Library of Congress Cataloging in Publication Data
Dillon, Matthew, 1963–
Girls and women in classical Greek religion / Matthew Dillon.
p. cm.
Includes bibliographical references and index.
1. Women and religion—Greece—History. I. Title.
BL795.W65 D55 2001
292.08´082—dc21
2001019956

ISBN 978-0-415-20272-5 (hbk)
ISBN 978-0-415-31916-4 (pbk)

CONTENTS

List of illustrations	vii
Preface	x
Introduction	1

PART I
Public religious roles for girls and women   7

1	Women as dedicators	9
2	The public religious roles of girls and adolescent women in Athens	37
3	Women priests	73

PART II
Segregated and ecstatic religious rites   107

4	Women-only festivals	109
5	Women at the margins of Greek religion	139
6	Prostitutes, foreign women and the gods	183

PART III
Sacrificial and domestic rituals   209

7	From adolescent girl to woman, wife and mother	211
8	Women, sacrifice and impurity	236

CONTENTS

9 Women and the corpse: mourning rituals   268

Epilogue   293

Notes   301
Glossary   369
Abbreviations   372
Bibliography   380
Index   403

ILLUSTRATIONS

1.1	Marble statue of the goddess Artemis, dedicated by the woman Nikandre	10
1.2	A bronze statuette of Athena, dedicated by the woman Meleso	16
1.3	Xenokrateia's dedication to the river god Kephisos, for the upbringing of her son	24
1.4	A family group, with sow, before the goddess Athena	33
2.1	A young woman holding a basket pours a libation onto a flaming altar	40
2.2	A young girl carries a basket on her head as part of a sacrificial rite	42
2.3	Young Athenian women (korai) taking part in the Panathenaic procession, from the Parthenon frieze	44
2.4	Young Athenian women (korai) taking part in the Panathenaic procession, from the Parthenon frieze	45
2.5	The woman priest of Athena Polias with the two arrephoroi and their secret bundles; a male figure, perhaps the king (basileus) archon, receiving the peplos from a girl, from the Parthenon frieze	46
2.6	Young Athenian women (korai) taking part in the Panathenaic procession, from the Parthenon frieze, with two men (marshals) directing them	48
2.7	Young Athenian women (korai) taking part in the Panathenaic procession, from the Parthenon frieze	49
2.8	The marble caryatids of the south porch of the Erechtheion, the acropolis, Athens; from an old photograph	51
2.9	Caryatid in the form of a young woman (kore) from the porch of the Erechtheion	52
2.10	Caryatid from Hadrian's Villa (Tivoli, near Rome), which stood with others along the Canopus pool; copied from the caryatids of the Erechtheion	53
2.11	Samian temple water basin (perirrhanterion)	55
2.12	Girl with offering tray of cakes and fruit	61

ILLUSTRATIONS

2.13	The 'Anzio Girl': a young woman and her tray with sacrificial items	62
2.14	Two young women wreathing bulls before the animals are sacrificed	64
2.15	Women perfuming clothes for the Choes festival	70
3.1	Bronze temple key in the shape of a serpent, temple of Artemis at Lousoi, Arkadia	81
3.2	Grave-stele of Polystrate, possibly a woman priest, with temple key	82
3.3	Grave-stele of Polyxena, possibly a woman priest, showing her holding a cult statue	83
3.4	A woman priest, before Athena, leading a sacrificial procession	88
4.1	Woman 'watering' four phalloi in the ground, possibly a representation of the Haloa	123
4.2	Women in lines, holding wreaths and each other's hands; so-called *frauenfest* (women's festival) scene	129
5.1	Maenad with thyrsos, bare feet, panther-skin shawl, panther, and snake headband	141
5.2	Serene women before a mask of Dionysos	150
5.3	Maenads dancing before a statue of Dionysos	151
5.4	Maenads dancing (reverse of 5.3)	151
5.5	Grave relief of Nikomache with her tympanum (kettle-drum)	157
5.6	The Great Mother–Cybele, with lion, and Attis in their temple, approached by a worshipper and her servant	158
5.7	Eros hands a Garden of Adonis to Aphrodite	162
5.8	Women at the Adonia, or a bride and attendants with her wedding gifts	168
5.9	Medea with her drugs rejuvenates a ram, while Jason watches	173
5.10	Medea with the daughters of Peleus (the Peliades) about to attempt to rejuvenate Peleus, their father	174
5.11	Deianeira hands Herakles a cloak which she believes is imbued with a love potion	176
6.1	Lawrence Alma-Tadema, *Pheidias and the Frieze of the Parthenon*, 1869	187
6.2	Aspasia, portrait herm	188
6.3	The 'Ludovisi Throne': Aphrodite arises from the sea-foam from which she was born, assisted by two attendants	204
6.4	The 'Ludovisi Throne': a flute girl, probably a prostitute, plays the double pipes for Aphrodite	204
6.5	The 'Ludovisi Throne': a respectable citizen woman burns incense for Aphrodite	204
7.1	Woman presenting offerings to Persephone; terracotta plaque (pinax) from Lokris	223

ILLUSTRATIONS

7.2	Procession scene; terracotta plaque (pinax) from Lokris	224
7.3	Pregnant woman and attendants sacrificing to the nymphs for a successful childbirth; painted wooden plaque from Pitsa	229
7.4	A woman presenting a baby to the goddess Artemis in her temple, marble relief from Echinos, Greece	232
8.1	A woman with a basket sacrificing a puppy to the goddess Hekate	247
8.2	Auge and other maidens worshipping before a statue of Athena	259
8.3	Hippodameia clings to a statue of Artemis	261
8.4	A warrior leaving home performing a libation ceremony to the gods	265
9.1	Women rending their hair at the bier of a deceased woman; terracotta funerary plaque (pinax)	276
9.2	Mourning women seated, probably within a house, with a small child; funerary plaque (pinax)	278
9.3	Mourning women in a funeral procession; funerary plaque (pinax)	278
9.4	Women mourners at the bier	280
9.5	Two terracotta figurine women mourners	281
9.6	Two women, one weeping, and one (partly visible) carrying a basket of tomb offerings, at a tomb	284
9.7	Man, and woman with tray of funeral offerings, at a tomb	286

PREFACE

This book has been many years in the writing, frequently interrupted by teaching commitments. My hope is it represents a serious start on my study of girls and women in classical Greek religion. I have many debts. I would like to thank Professors Deborah Boedeker and Kurt Raaflaub who allowed me use of the library facilities at the Center for Hellenic Studies at Washington DC while my wife held an eight-month fellowship at Dumbarton Oaks (1997–8), where also I was allowed access to the library. These libraries were far superior to anything available in Australia, and since Washington DC I can hardly have kept pace with recent publications. To those museums which supplied me with photographs, I am deeply indebted. Many colleagues have commented on versions of this book given as papers, and their criticisms have been valued. An especial thanks for those close friends who politely asked, especially over the last few months, whether 'the book' was finished: I am grateful for their encouragement. To my wife, Lynda, who read several drafts and commented upon them, I am very indebted, especially for her patience in allowing me to spend so much time on this project while the grass in the garden grew longer and longer and the weeds flourished as this last summer progressed. As a final note, if I have unwittingly employed patriarchal language or expressions, or employed a train of thought that reveals a misunderstanding of the 'female race', or overlooked observations that would seem self-evident to women, I apologise.

February 2001
Armidale, Australia

INTRODUCTION

> And in matters concerning the gods, for I consider these matters to be the most important, we women have the greatest share. For in the temple of Phoebus [Apollo] women prophecy the thoughts of Loxias [Apollo], and around Dodona's holy foundations by the sacred oak it is the female sex which conveys the thoughts of Zeus to any Greek who seeks them. Also, as to those rituals which are performed for the Fates [Moirai] and the Nameless Goddesses [Eumenides], it is not holy for men to participate in them: all of them flourish in the hands of women. This is how the case for women stands in their dealings with the gods.[1]

That this, the only explicit statement concerning the importance of women in the religion of ancient Greece, comes from a play (which survives only in quotations from other ancient writers) by the fifth-century BC tragedian Euripides is perhaps no surprise, given his sympathetic attitude towards women. Here, the speaker is probably Melanippe herself, after whom the play is named, defending herself and other women against their (male) detractors. As well as stating the case for their importance in religion, Melanippe, in the lines just before the passage quoted above, also stresses their domestic importance: a household could be neither clean nor prosperous without a woman. Euripides specifically points to the role which women have as prophetic priests at Delphi and Dodona, and their participation in the worship of the Fates and Nameless Goddesses. At Delphi and Dodona, women were the oracular mouthpieces of gods, providing advice on a variety of matters, both personal and public. At Athens, women played the most important role (even if imperfectly known) in the worship of the Fates and Nameless Goddesses. What is interesting here is that modern scholarship emphasises the role which women played in fertility rites over which the goddess of agriculture, Demeter, presided, such as the festival of the Thesmophoria: their fertility made them conduits of the soil's fecundity. But Euripides stresses very different roles: in one of these, the oracular, their role was very publicly 'on show' (at Delphi and Dodona), and in the case of their worship of the Fates and Nameless Goddesses at Athens their involvement was, as will be seen, spectacular and solemn, and entailed secret rites.

Euripides has, in fact, chosen some rather sombre aspects of Greek religious practice, but, for evidence of women's mass participation and enthusiasm, Aristophanes in the *Lysistrata* (produced in 411 BC at Athens) livens up the cultic scene:

> But if the women were summoned to some rite of Bacchus, or shrine of Pan, or of [Aphrodite] Kolias, or of Genetyllis, you wouldn't be able to get through, what for the number of drums [tympana].[2]

Lysistrata, in trying to organise a meeting of the women of Athens to discuss how to bring the Peloponnesian War to an end, complains of their tardiness in attending it, contrasting this with their religious zeal if a celebration were in the offing. Aristophanes seems to think that women were enthusiastic about joining in religious rites. But what cults did they participate in, and why? Of the deities mentioned here Bacchus' (Dionysos') rites at Athens, as will be seen in Chapter 5, were represented on vases, which show women dancing, playing musical instruments, and enthusiastically worshipping the god Dionysos. The drums – tympana – which Lysistrata says could be apparent in great numbers, were particularly associated with the worship of Dionysos and the Great Mother–Cybele. Tympana, sometimes translated as 'kettle-drums', can be seen in Figures 5.5 and 5.6; they were round but shallow, and accompanied dancing. The god Pan obviously had marriage connotations: a mother dreaming of the marriage of her son dashes into the countryside to worship and perform a sacrifice at a shrine of Pan and the nymphs.[3] Kolias should be taken as a reference to a shrine of Aphrodite, goddess of love, at Cape Kolias near Athens; here Aphrodite Kolias was worshipped, and may have had shrines in Athens itself. Aphrodite Kolias is linked here with the female deity Genetyllis, as elsewhere in Aristophanes.[4] Genetyllis, less well known to us but familiar to Aristophanes' audience, was celebrated in a festival held by women, and apparently had kourotrophic (child-rearing) attributes. Hesychius in the fifth century AD says that she was a deity of procreation to whom women sacrificed dogs, as they did to Hekate, goddess of sorcery, with whom he connects Genetyllis.[5] These then are four deities – Bacchus, Pan, Aphrodite and Genetyllis – which were favourites with women in classical Athens and for whom they would gladly get out their drums and participate in religious worship. The scene is obviously meant to be familiar but strikes the modern reader as exotic, and challenges preconceptions about the lives of wives in classical Athens: Aristophanes presents crowds of women beating on drums for deities whose responsibilities were largely for love, marriage and wine.

Euripides and Aristophanes sketch a broad picture of women's religious activities, concentrating on women's rituals from which men were excluded,

INTRODUCTION

hinting at the sedateness and ecstasy of which women were capable in their relations with the divine. The philosopher Plato in the fourth century BC was rather more critical, and in giving the details for his ideal state decided that there would be no private shrines in houses, complaining that,

> It is not easy to establish temples and gods and to do so correctly needs a great deal of thought. Yet it is customary both for women especially – all of them – and for sick people everywhere, as well as for those in danger or difficulties, whatever the problem is, and on the other hand whenever they meet with some good fortune, to dedicate whatever is at hand, and vow sacrifices, and promise the establishment of shrines to the gods, daimones, and children of gods. And through fears caused by daytime apparitions and dreams, and similarly as they recollect many visions and make remedies for each of them, it is customary for them to establish altars and shrines and fill with them both every house and every village and open spaces too, as well as the spots where they had these experiences.[6]

What is interesting here, and in Aristophanes' account, is an apparent freedom of expression in divine matters. Women are not alone in their shrine-building but it is a peculiar weakness of women that they engage in this, according to Plato, and he considers that all women are susceptible to such expressions of belief. If his details can be trusted, it must be imagined that women were prone to set up shrines to the gods when certain circumstances arose. Aristophanes has the women in eager outdoor worship of deities; Plato mentions the home. If women could not get out and about, home provided ample scope – too much for Plato – for private worship. Yet Plato also stresses women's outdoor religious foundations as well: their religiosity did not find material expression merely within the home but outside, too, they commemorated their religious experiences. Theophrastos in the fourth century BC complained of the superstitious man that if he sees a sacred snake he establishes a hero-shrine on the spot.[7] But Plato and Theophrastos point to a particular weakness (in their estimation), respectively, of women and the superstitious, that they were too prone to give a material expression to their religious beliefs.

Women's involvement in rites and cults in classical Greece was much more 'liberal' than that of their sisters across the Adriatic, the matrons of republican Rome. Dionysios of Halikarnassos compared features of Greek and Roman religion, and while Greek men did engage in most of the activities he mentions below, the references to Persephone, Dionysos and ecstasy point clearly towards Greek women:

> And no festival is observed among the Romans by the wearing of black garments or as a day of mourning and with the beating of breasts and lamentations of women because of the disappearance of deities, in the

way that the Greeks commemorate the rape of Persephone and the
experiences of Dionysos. . . . And one will see among the Romans no
ecstatic possession, no Corybantic frenzies, no begging rituals, no
bacchanals or secret mysteries, no all-night vigils of men and women
together in the temples, nor any other trickery of this kind.[8]

One of the plays by Platon the comic poet had the title, *The Women Returning From Worship*; unfortunately only a few lines, irrelevant to the theme of this book, survive. But an important idea is raised here: women would proceed to the temples in groups to worship the gods, without their menfolk. It would be interesting to consider whether Platon had them encountering danger, perhaps of a sexual nature, on their way home.[9]

Women participated in many religious roles, public and private. They did so while carrying out duties as wives and mothers, or if girls their roles often presented them to society as ready to take on the role of wife and subsequently mother. What has been attempted in particular in this book is to stress the iconographies of girls' and women's religious experiences, which elucidate the literary and epigraphic (inscriptional) evidence but which also provide a new insight into their activities. Even the magnificent description of the Theban maenads in Euripides' *Bacchae* cannot convey the excited and ecstatic behaviour of the women on the red-figure vase shown in Figures 5.3 and 5.4. The respectable citizen women, Athenian counterparts of the maenads of the city of Thebes, dance, clang their clappers, and dip their heads, all in honour of the mask of Dionysos on its robed pillar, which they have previously adorned with offerings of round cakes. In other artistic media, women pull at their hair and draw blood from their faces at funerals, throw puppies into crevices, make dedications to the gods, and take part in solemn processions. The male world of politics which excluded them is left behind as women make public statements of their piety, though much of their religious behaviour was also private and guarded from the eyes of men, when women met in groups to ensure fertility, both agrarian and human. The provision of a representative range of the iconographic evidence and its relationship to the literary and epigraphic evidence for girls' and women's cult activities has been attempted here, though it has not always been possible to obtain photographs of some of the items which it would have been useful to discuss in more detail. It has also been difficult to find all the relevant details for individual pieces, but as many as possible have been given here. In citing the artistic evidence, several references to the standard modern works on Greek art are given, so that most readers, even those with access to a fairly basic library, should be able to find photographs and discussions of the pieces which are referred to. The dates for vases, reliefs and inscriptions are as given in the relevant publications; occasionally a comment is made when a different date seems called for.

In the following nine chapters, several aspects of women's roles in classical Greek rituals and rites are examined. The study is by no means exhaustive, and spatial constraints prevent many points and pieces of evidence being pursued in greater detail. But the roles played by girls and women both in their private and communal relationships with the gods are stressed. This is not a book about goddesses or heroines,[10] though they of course play a part, but about the girls and women of the classical period, and how and why they worshipped the gods. What has been attempted above all is to identify women as individuals wherever possible. Women, of course, fell into several 'categories', and these illustrate the ways in which classical Greek men constructed the societies in which they lived. Numerous oppositions in the ways in which women were categorised, often determined by their role in society, and also their ethnic origin (in itself a definition of identity in Athenian society), are reflected in the various dichotomies of citizen wife/foreign woman, slave/free, prostitute/wife, girl/woman, and woman priest/woman sorcerer, to name some, all of which could overlap, and influenced how, why, when and where they gave expression to their religious beliefs.

There is much more to say on the topic than space in this book permits. In many ways, the conclusions are kept brief, as the major consideration has been to set out the evidence for various forms of religious activity by the women of classical Greece. It has been fruitful to look backwards at the archaic period to some extent, but while comparisons with the hellenistic period might have been useful there has not been the time or space to do such comparisons justice. Hopefully the diachronic limitations of the book will not prove too constraining. This book is also intended as a concrete gathering of some of the data; too many articles and books deal with topics about Greek women with the barest of facts and substitute semantic flourishes and imaginative conclusions for solid facts and discussion of the women themselves. Naturally, there are various methodological pitfalls in such a study. In some ways, this book looks at women 'in a vacuum', so to speak; there has not been scope to compare in detail the degree to which their participation matched that of men. To compare, for example, men priests with women priests is impossible within the confines of a single chapter, and there is clearly room for a monograph on boys, men, and their involvement in cult. Despite the attempt here to look at women other than those at Athens this is extremely difficult, and the tantalising scraps about the maenads of Boeotia or the festival of the Thesmophoria in Sicily hint, it seems, that the religious life of the women in these places was as complex and varied, and perhaps even more so, than that of the women at Athens. This study attempts to engender one aspect of Greek religion, and the girls and women themselves stand – as on the Parthenon frieze – at the core of this treatment.

Part I

PUBLIC RELIGIOUS ROLES FOR GIRLS AND WOMEN

1

WOMEN AS DEDICATORS

Of the nearly 900 inscribed dedications from throughout the Greek world collected by Lazzarini, ranging from the early archaic period (eighth century BC) to the end of the fifth century BC, eighty, or nearly 10 per cent, were dedicated by women.[1] Some of the more important examples of these are discussed below in order to consider what dedications by women can reveal about the role which they played in Greek religion, and the way in which their offerings differed from dedications made by men, in expense, the wording of dedications, type and aim; in addition examples from the fourth century BC, mainly from Athens, also need to be considered. Several dedications by women are well known, such as those by Nikandre of Naxos, Telestodike of Paros, and Iphidike at Athens. Inscribed dedications often took the form of korai (singular: kore): statues, usually life-size or larger of female figures, generally goddesses. Other statues were dedicated and placed on top of inscribed columns. In addition, pins, mirrors, and the like were dedicated; there were other types of dedications as well, which have not survived but which are recorded in inscribed lists of temple possessions. Into this category in particular fall the lists of dedications, by both men and women at Athens, to the deities Asklepios and Athena. All such dedications, but in particular the ones which would have been expensive, such as the korai, raise several socio-economic questions. Did the women who dedicated these, such as Nikandre with her votive offering of a 1.75-metre kore, actually pay for these dedications from their own resources, or do these indicate that the women only dedicated the votive in name, with a male relative or husband meeting the expense? Before considering these questions, a representative selection of women's dedications will be examined.

A statue of Artemis dedicated by Nikandre of Naxos

A well-known dedication by a woman is that of Nikandre of Naxos, who presented to Artemis a larger than life-size statue on the sacred island of Delos (Figure 1.1). It is possibly the earliest dedication in the archaic period by a woman; its date is only approximate, c. 650 BC. The statue, at 1.75 metres, was

Figure 1.1 Marble statue of the goddess Artemis, dedicated by the woman Nikandre, on the island of Delos; marble; one piece; 650 BC; overall height: 200 centimetres, statue itself: 175 centimetres; greatest thickness of statue: 17 centimetres (courtesy, ©National Archaeological Museum, Athens: inv. 1).

discovered in the sanctuary of Artemis on Delos, and clearly represents the goddess. Her peplos is belted at the waist and is tight-fitting, rather than being loose with numerous folds. Careful attention has been paid to the hair, most of which falls down her back, but with four plaits arranged each side of her face and falling over the front of the body. Traces of paint in rectilinear patterns could once be seen on the front of the statue, indicating that her dress was patterned. The whole effect of the statue is formal but pleasing.

Usually described as being 'plank-like' the statue is not 'in the round' but rather is carved from a long thin piece of island marble and is almost rectangular in character. The inscription recording the dedication is on the left side of the statue, in three vertical lines not heavily incised. The statue speaks to the reader:

> Nikandre dedicated me [the statue] to the goddess [Artemis] the far-shooting rainer of arrows, Nikandre, the pre-eminent daughter of Deinodikes of Naxos, sister of Deinomenes, and now wife of Phraxos.[2]

As a larger than life statue it represents the goddess rather than Nikandre, with 'far-shooting' referring to Artemis.[3] The hole in each hand means that the goddess was represented holding objects, probably cult attributes, such as her bow and arrows.

The Ionian island of Naxos is close to Delos, and Ionian women and children accompanied their husbands to Delos for the festival which the Ionians celebrated together on the island in honour of the god Apollo.[4] Nikandre herself presumably went to Delos for the dedication of the statue, probably with members of the family listed on the inscription. Commentators have not picked up on the force of the 'now': this could indicate that Nikandre is dedicating this statue to Artemis in thanks for her marriage, as women did pray to this goddess for husbands, and the dedication would be appropriate at this time of transition in her life, with marriage bringing the promise (and danger) of childbirth.[5] It has been suggested that Nikandre mentions her brother in addition to her father because the father is dead and the brother is now the head of the family.[6] It is just as possible that both father and brother were well-known figures and are mentioned for that reason; certainly the dedication of this monumental statue of the goddess and its presence in the sanctuary attest to the wealth and importance of the family. A priesthood for Nikandre is sometimes suggested, but in this case the dedication might more properly have been made on Naxos, and she might well have been expected to mention such in her inscription along with her other personal details. What is clear is that this is a very large and public dedication made at the least in the name of if not actually by a woman, and apparently a recently married one; by it, Nikandre openly asserts her religiosity, and uses the dedication as a way of expressing her status and perceptions of herself.

'Artemis, to you Telestodike dedicated this statue'

Telestodike, over a century after Nikandre, appears to have made two offerings to Artemis, if the woman Telestodike in the two following inscriptions is one and the same person, as is usually assumed. The first is on a small marble column probably from Paros, of about 500 BC. Telestodike identifies herself by reference to her father and son,

Artemis, to you Telestodike dedicated me, this statue,
Mother of Asphalios, daughter of Therseleos.
I [the statue] boast that I am the work of Kritonides of Paros.[7]

In another inscription, from Paros, on a statue base also from about 500 BC, a Telestodike (the same?) refers to her husband:

Demokydes and Telestodike having made a vow
Together erected this statue to the virgin Artemis
On her sacred ground, the daughter of aegis-bearing Zeus;
To their family and livelihood give increase in safety.[8]

That in one she refers to her father and son and in another her husband suggests that these are two different women, or perhaps that she has simply identified herself in different ways in each. Once again, as with Nikandre, women's concern with Artemis is made clear. The goddess is to be imagined as having had a special place amongst women's religious interests not simply as a goddess of childbirth but also as a major deity.

Dedications of kore statues

Statues of young women, life-size or larger, are known today as korai statues, and their male counterparts, those of young men, as kouroi statues (singular: kore and kouros respectively). The dedication of Nikandre, for example, was a kore statue, and here the kore represents a goddess. But some kore statues were funerary in nature, as in the case of the well-known Phrasikleia, over whose grave (c. 540 BC) a kore was placed which acted as a grave marker; the kore clearly represented her: 'The marker (sema) of Phrasikleia. I shall always be called kore ("girl"), having been allotted this name, instead of marriage, by the gods.'[9]

Most of the korai are from Athens, where many were dedicated on the acropolis from about 570 to 480 BC, when the Persians sacked the acropolis and the korai were damaged. Some of them have inscriptions, like that of Phrasikleia, indicating that they were dedicated by both men and women, but in non-funerary contexts; however, many of them have no inscription at all. Nearchos the male potter dedicated a statue of a kore to Athena (and in this sense it is obviously Athena that is being represented). Alkimachos, also a male, dedicated a kore to Athena.[10] When there is no inscription, it has been suggested that the korai could represent young girls, in particular the arrephoroi, the 7-year-old girls chosen each year to serve Athena on the acropolis. But, when there is no inscription, it seems best to interpret these statues along the lines of those with inscriptions: the korai are for the goddess Athena, dedicated to her by grateful worshippers, both male and female.

Dedications of mirrors

Korai were but one form of dedication; expensive, they were limited to the well-to-do, and clearly not all of them were dedicated by women. In fact korai went out of fashion at the beginning of the classical period. Mirrors, as a feminine item, were particularly appropriate as a dedication by women, and were also relatively inexpensive; despite this, very few have survived as inscribed dedications, and most of these consist of mirror handles, with the bronze mirror itself having been long since melted down for another purpose.[11] Large numbers of mirrors are recorded in the inscribed lists from the Athenian acropolis of the dedications made to Artemis Brauronia in the fourth century BC. A well-preserved inscribed bronze mirror found at Brauron itself reads: 'Hippylla, daughter of Onetor, dedicated (this) to Artemis at Brauron.'[12]

The mirrors recorded in the inscribed lists of dedications to Artemis Brauronia were usually grouped together, and one entry simply reads: 'bronze mirrors: 119',[13] indicating how common these dedications were. In another list which records garments dedicated to Artemis, an entry in 347/6 BC concerning a mirror has slipped in: 'Aristodamea dedicated a mirror . . . with an ivory handle'.[14] This mirror with its ivory handle was more elaborate than most and considered worthy of individual mention.

A bronze mirror handle from Athens bears an inscription that it was dedicated as a dekate ('tenth', or tithe) by Glyke.[15] Another dedication was made on the Athenian acropolis by a Glyke of the same period, about 480 BC, as a dekate to Athena,[16] and this might even be the same woman. Phila dedicated a bronze mirror (handle and disc both survive, cast as one piece): 'Phila dedicated to Elythia (i.e. Eileithyia, the goddess of birth-pangs)'.[17] 'Charias dedicated to Athena' reads an inscription on a bronze disk, probably a mirror, found on the Athenian acropolis.[18] Women dedicated mirrors at places other than Athens. Aristeia dedicated a mirror at the sanctuary of Hera, the Heraion, in Argos.[19] Similarly, at Delphi, Archippa dedicated a bronze disc, almost certainly a mirror, to Eileithyia.[20] A handle of a bronze mirror from the sanctuary of Hera at Perachora near Corinth has the inscription, 'Chrysanthis dedicated to Hera'.[21] 'Euonyma dedicated to Athena' reads a mirror handle from the sanctuary of Athena Chalkioikos (Athena of the Bronze House) at Sparta.[22] Another well-known dedication is an early fifth-century BC bronze woman statuette on an Ionic capital, part of a mirror stand, from Poseidonia (modern Paestum): 'Phillo, daughter of Charmylidas (dedicated this as) a tithe to Athena.'[23] Also in Italy, Xenodoka at Lokris in the sixth century BC dedicated a mirror to Persephone, wife of Hades.[24] All the mirrors are dedicated to goddesses, as might be expected, as items which women could afford, or would have possessed.

Dedications to the goddess Hera at Corinth

Small domestic items were clearly preferred by many women, because these fell within the scope of their private expenditure and/or because they had personal relevance or were appropriate to their gender, and could be dedicated at rites of transition (such as marriage, or the birth of a child) which were important for women; many were cheap household objects. At the coastal sanctuary of Hera at Perachora, near Corinth, terracotta spindles were favoured dedications. While the Demeter sanctuary at Corinth presumably attracted women worshippers in large numbers, the archaeological record there is ambiguous, and the many thousands of Demeter statuettes might have been dedicated by either men or women, but presumably mostly by women as Demeter was a favourite deity of theirs. But at the sanctuary of Hera, there is clear evidence for women worshippers of the goddess Hera, patron of marriage. The sanctuary's origins have been dated to the early eighth century BC, and from that period on there was increasing activity at the sanctuary.[25] The evidence comes in the form of women's items found, and so obviously dedicated, within the sanctuary. About sixty terracotta spindle-whorls were excavated there, as well as some bobbins and loom-weights. The largest number of ivory 'spectacle-fibulae', used in fastening dresses, from any site in the Greek world were found at this sanctuary.[26] These decorated pins were of bone or ivory with two circles either side of a 'bridge', and usually decorated with incised designs. These were particularly appropriate dedications for women to make.

Particularly associated with fertility rites are cakes (koulouria) of various sorts, and terracotta models of these have been found at Perachora, indicating Hera's role as a kourotrophic (child-rearing) deity. These were dedicated from the geometric period onwards. Cakes were offered to other kourotrophic deities as well, and women were presumably the main if sole dedicators of these.[27] Such domestic dedications reveal women's domestic concerns, and their need for goddesses' assistance and favour as they went about these tasks, especially as spinning and weaving were tasks which might be of economic importance to a family. They are not matched by similar male dedications of items used in their livelihoods, indicating a gender difference along property lines: many women would have 'owned' only household implements, and from this meagre store of belongings nevertheless sought to honour goddesses, whom they obviously considered would be pleased with these offerings.

Women dedicators from the Athenian acropolis

'Polemon the Periegete wrote four books on the dedicatory offerings on the [Athenian] acropolis alone';[28] most of these dedications were by men, but a significant proportion were by women. Raubitschek listed nine dedications made by women on the acropolis who give only their first name and do not mention a husband or a father; all but one of these dates to before 480 BC. After that, it became normal to mention one or both of these, and this must reflect a shift in emphasis in the attitude to women suggesting that in the classical period they were not so much individuals in their own right but adjuncts of their fathers or husbands.[29] Sometimes the dedications are on what are clearly statue bases, or pillar monuments on which a statue or other item (such as a marble basin) would have stood; the bases and pillars survive but the statues do not. Sometimes the goddess Athena is specifically mentioned, as is the fact that a dekate or aparche ('first-fruits' offering) is being rendered; when Athena is not referred to, either because of the brevity of the inscription or its fragmentary nature, it is presumably to Athena because of the find spot, the Athenian acropolis.

Ergokleia dedicated as an aparche a marble pillar monument on which a bronze statue (presumably of the goddess Athena) would have been placed, in the last quarter of the sixth century BC. This appears to be the earliest surviving dedication by a woman on the acropolis.[30] Another early dedication by a woman on the acropolis was that of Iphidike, in c. 510–500 BC, to Athena Poliouchos ('Protector of the city'). An inscription makes the dedication speak to the passer-by: 'Archermos the Chian made me. Iphidike dedicated me to Athena Poliouchos'. This inscription, on a column, does not indicate what the actual dedication was.[31] Also towards the end of the sixth century BC, [Ph]sakythe made a dedication, to 'Athena Guardian of the City'; this was inscribed on a statue base; there were three cuttings in this for statues, and the dedication states that Hermippos had made it.[32] The mention of the artists, and in one case his foreign origin, indicate that these are not simply ordinary items, but specially commissioned and expensive. The women mention no male relatives, and so assert a right to be viewed as independent dedicators.

Smikythe the washer-woman (plynteria) also needs consideration here.[33] The simple inscription from her acropolis dedication of 500–480 BC reads, 'Smikythe the washer-woman dedicates a tenth', and appears on the fully preserved pedestal base on which a marble basin would have rested. The 'tenth' of her income, from washing clothes, paid for the basin. A dedication to Athena from around the same period inscribed on a statue base by a Smikythe, a Phyrne, and a person (man or woman) whose name is lost can also be mentioned here; perhaps this is the same Smikythe as just mentioned.[34]

Other dedications can be mentioned, to indicate the sort of offerings made, though in the following cases the dedicatory inscriptions reveal little information about the donors. Empedia dedicated a dekate, as a column dedication, to Athena.[35] Kalikrite dedicated an aparche to Athena, in this case a marble basin (presumably an expensive item), with the dedication inscribed around its rim.[36] Pheido made a dedication of a pillar monument.[37]

Mikythe dedicated a pillar monument to Athena as a dekate for herself and her children, and specifically refers in the inscription to the statue, the agalma, on the pillar. The monument was made by the sculptor Euphron (of Paros) and here surely once again a statement of wealth and prestige is being made by this woman.[38]

There were also bronze dedications for which the inscription was on the bronze piece itself. A woman called Meleso in c. 480–470 BC dedicated a dekate to Athena in the form of a bronze statuette of the goddess which is nearly 1 foot high, found on the acropolis and presumably dedicated there (Figure 1.2): 'Meleso dedicated this as a tithe to Athena'. The dekate, tenth, was probably the profits from her work, such as weaving or selling goods.[39] Athena obviously wielded a spear in her right hand, and has a particularly striking helmet, and is usually imagined to be striding towards a giant threatening her. The bread-seller (artopolis) Phrygia as her dedication on the acropolis to Athena gave a small bronze shield with a gorgeion, Athena's special attribute, on it; the inscribed dedication runs around the rim of the shield. While citizen women

Figure 1.2 A bronze statuette of Athena, dedicated by the woman Meleso, from the Athenian acropolis; c. 480–470 BC; height: approx. 28.8 centimetres; National Archaeological Museum, Athens: inv. 6447 (courtesy, ©Deutsches Archäologisches Institut, Athens, neg. NM 4742).

did sell produce and goods in the market place, the fact that Phrygia gives herself no other designation besides her name (such as a patronymic (father's name) or husband's name), and that her name is eastern has suggested, though not conclusively, that she was a metic, a foreigner (i.e. non-Athenian) living and working in Athens.[40] Athena here is not venerated as a patron of arts or handicrafts but as Athens' most important deity: the martial goddess who protected the city.

But if personal name and lack of any other identification are equivalent to metic status, then that many of the acropolis dedications are by women and do not all mention their father's name (of course, some of them are damaged and it is impossible to know whether the father's name was given) would consign too high a proportion of the dedications to metics. And trade or occupation should not mislead, as there is no reason why an Athenian woman could not have been a bread-seller, as is the citizen woman Myrtia in Aristophanes' *Wasps*. Lysilla dedicated on the acropolis a small discus of bronze to Athena.[41] Of interest is that two sisters, Aristomache and Charikleia the daughters of Glaukinos the Argive, dedicated a pillar monument on the acropolis, *c*. 470–450 BC. The circumstances of their doing so are lost.[42] What is important to note is that the women are not restricted to dedicating domestic items if their socioeconomic status permits, and their range of dedications encompasses Athena and her warlike attributes. Women, either citizen or foreign, make dedications, displaying their piety in a material form. Presumably most women, if they had the means, would have made such dedications; they were not less pious if they could not do so, though that in the eyes of their contemporaries such dedications were very real manifestations of piety must not be overlooked.

As noted, women dedicators of the archaic period were much more likely not to describe themselves according to their relationship with a man. In the period after the Persian Wars (from 479 BC on), a designation by father or husband is typical. Aristomache and Charikleia have been mentioned already and gave their Argive father's name. Kallisto the daughter of Naukydes dedicated a marble basin (with the dedicatory inscription around the rim) as an aparche to Athena.[43] The wife of Prepis (her name would need to be restored) dedicated a pillar monument to Athena.[44] Eumelides, wife of Sphettios, made a dedication, possibly of a marble basin.[45] In mentioning their fathers and their husbands, these women were defining themselves through their relationship with men in a way in which the previous dedicatees did not, and this must surely have some significance for their social status. A father might make a dedication on behalf of his daughters: Kynarbos made a dedication which, from the two bronze plinths still on the inscribed statue base, must have consisted of two bronze statuettes dedicated for his daughters Aristomache and Archestrate.[46]

After about 450 BC, actual public dedications by women are no longer found on the acropolis as such, though men's continue; from now on, dedications by women took place within the main temples on the acropolis when these were completed, the Parthenon and Erechtheion, and it is in inventory lists of items dedicated in these temples that dedications by women, which now take on a standard form largely of phialai (shallow libation bowls, which could be of silver, but otherwise terracotta), jewellery and the like, are to be found. Women and their piety to the gods become much less public in nature. These lists of dedications were inscribed by the Treasurers of Athena whose task it was to keep track of precious objects in the temples of the acropolis and whose lists survive from the fifth and fourth centuries BC. The Parthenon inventories date from 434/3 BC onwards, and shed light on what women dedicated, but not why.

Harris in her study of the inventory lists of the Parthenon notes that there were gender distinctions amongst the dedications, just as Aleshire has observed for the Asklepieion (the sanctuary of Asklepios; see below). Similarly, it is interesting that of the ten silver phialai (libation bowls; singular: phiale) dedicated in the Erechtheion, women dedicated eight. Perhaps this in fact needs to be put in the architectural context of the Erechtheion and the six maidens of its porch who carried phialai in their hands (see Figures 2.8–2.10). Moreover, while men and youths could carry the sacrificial basket and phiale, phialai are much more generally associated with young women before marriage, and wives afterwards. A woman usually held the phiale before a man took it, and then the woman poured wine into it, which the man would pour out onto an altar or the ground as an offering to the gods; women poured such libations much less frequently than men. In addition, Harris notes that in the acropolis inventories dedications by women indicate their relationship to a male: father or husband. However, twelve women – a minority – who made dedications in the Parthenon and Erechtheion according to the preserved lists are identified only by their name. In this period of Athenian history, this presumably means that they are not from the elite, but are either foreigners or women of lower socio-economic origins than the women with elite status.[47] In a typical entry, from the beginning of the fourth century BC (it was not necessarily made at this time, but could record a dedication earlier than the compilation of the list), a dedication is recorded for Glyke, the daughter of Archestratos, who presented earrings, two gold rings, and a gem set in gold, presumably from her own jewel collection.[48]

In the archaic period, women are more likely to have made dedications in their own right, and for these to have been out in the open air; in the classical period, votives were interior items, but the lists recording them were set up, outside, on the acropolis. In this sense, the dedications by the women as recorded in the lists were publicised, but certainly not in a conspicuous manner. Women made these dedications through piety, often as thanksgivings, and presumably, in the case of the more expensive dedications, to show their status and that of their families.

Some prominent non-Athenian women immediately after the classical period are worth mentioning. Roxane, Alexander the Great's wife from Bactria, as recorded by the Parthenon inventory lists dedicated an unspecified number of gold necklaces and a golden rhyton to Athena on the acropolis. Married to

Alexander in 327 and dead in 310 BC, she must have made the dedication when she visited Athens in 319 BC. She almost certainly viewed her son, Alexander, as the legitimate successor to his father, and the dedication may well have been a public statement of her position as Alexander's wife and her hope that his son would succeed him.[49]

Perhaps Roxane was imitating her husband, who had dedicated 300 shields in the Parthenon from the Battle of Granikos. Olympias (Alexander the Great's mother) too, was a dedicator, and had received booty from Gaza; she made dedications of golden crowns at Delphi, and *c.* 300 BC she dedicated a gold phiale to the statue of Hygieia (Health) on the acropolis at Athens, which act apparently did not go uncriticised at Athens. She and Athens were in dispute at about this time concerning Dodona, an oracular shrine in northern Greece: twice the orator Hypereides had, in the Athenian assembly, responded to complaints from her ambassadors that the Athenians had refurbished the statue of Dione at Dodona. The Athenians argued that they had done so in response to an oracle from Dodona, while Olympias argued that Molossia, where Dodona was situated, was in her control, and the Athenians had no right to interfere there. Hypereides argued that the Athenians should allow Olympias' dedication to Hygieia to go uncontested, so that she have no ground for their actions concerning the statue at Dodona.[50]

Dedications of clothing to Artemis Brauronia

From the sanctuary of Artemis Brauronia on the Athenian acropolis come several inscribed inventories of the years 355–336 BC recording offerings made to Artemis.[51] According to the traditional interpretation of these Athenian lists, they record the dedications made at Brauron, and it is argued that the same records were inscribed and displayed both at Brauron and at Athens,[52] and that the Athenians presumably felt that these records had to be made public both for greater scrutiny (to avoid items going 'missing' over the years) and to advertise the piety shown towards the goddess. The main interest in these inventories lies in the large number of clothes dedicated by women: the dedicatees are named, sometimes with a male designation ('daughter of –', or 'wife of –'). That some of the items are described as having no label indicates that many women when dedicating the clothes obviously tagged them; another way of identification, found several times, was for the name of the dedicatee to be sewn into the clothing.[53] A shawl of Theano had 'sacred to Artemis' embroidered on it.[54] In addition other items, such as Aristodamea's mirror (discussed above), and bronze, gold and silver objects were also dedicated. As with any other deity, her worshippers felt that the goddess would appreciate fine objects, as well as clothes. There is also literary evidence: a father dedicated sandals and the mother woollen garments to Artemis for the birth of a son.[55]

In the fourth century BC, when there are inventories of dedications made to both Asklepios and Artemis Brauronia, in addition to the Parthenon inventories, it is dedications to Artemis and Asklepios which outweigh all other dedications made by women. This is not simply a reflection of the fact that lists were kept for these two deities, but also because these two were deities – more so than Athena or even Aphrodite – of particular concern to women:

> You, Iphigeneia, by the holy meadows of Brauron, must serve as keybearer to this goddess [Artemis]. You will die and be buried there, and they shall dedicate as an offering to you dresses of finely woven materials, which wives when they die in childbirth leave behind in their homes.[56]

Iphigeneia, a local mythical heroine, was the object of a cult at Brauron, and associated, sometimes to the point of identification, with Artemis in protecting women in childbirth. From the inventory lists for Artemis Brauronia on the acropolis it appears that living women also dedicated clothes to Artemis, presumably by way of thanksgiving. Those who had suffered and recovered from physical symptoms and hysteria during menarche also dedicated clothing to Artemis.[57]

Menarche – an adolescent girl's first menstrual flow – was a concern of the Hippocratic Corpus, and the short Hippocratic treatise *On Virgins* (*Peri Parthenion*) is taken up with this aspect of women's health. It notes that when parthenoi (virgin girls and young women before marriage), who have been suffering during menarche (the first period) from abnormal blood flow, leading to delirium, visions and suicidal tendencies, recover their senses, they make offerings on the instructions of manteis (diviners), especially of valuable clothes to Artemis, not realising – the author of the treatise comments – that the cure has a biological rather than divine origin. While the Hippocratic treatise scorns this recourse to thanksgiving, clearly offerings to Artemis were thought appropriate both by those who had suffered and by her relatives.[58] The treatise might criticise beliefs about Artemis but could not in reality vie with them: classical Greece was not ready for science to replace the divine.

Like the lists of dedications in the Parthenon, each inventory of Artemis Brauronia covered the items which were in the sanctuary in any one year, so that the same dedication turns up year after year, and in this way the inventories served the purpose of keeping a running record of the dedications. The dedications were listed under archon years, with each of the items listed according to the year in which they were given. For example, in the inscriptions of dedications to Artemis Brauronia from the acropolis, the shawl of Theano, dedicated in the archonship of Euboulos (345/4 BC) appears in several surviving lists.[59] As each new board – the epistatai – in charge of the dedications came into office it could check the offerings which were listed against what was actually in the sanctuary, and in turn have its records scrutinised when it left office. Unfortunately, the prescripts (introductory clauses) of the inventories are not preserved, which could have shed light on the procedures involved.

The items, judging from the passage in Euripides and the *Peri Parthenion* (13–14), were often for those who had died in childbirth or made by women on behalf of those who had undergone menarche. The lists themselves provide no guide as to the motivation for these gifts, but presumably the clothes were dedicated for other reasons as well: surely women who had undergone successful pregnancies, or who had asked for a particular gender of child made their offerings to the goddess. It is clear from the *Peri Parthenion* that the clothing dedicated was valuable, and this is reflected in the lists which reveal many quality items described as polutelestata ('expensive' or 'costly'), the same word being used in the *Peri Parthenion*. But also the range of clothing items dedicated does need to be noted: chitons (tunics), belts, himations (outer garments), robes, shawls, 'a many coloured Median upper garment with sleeves',[60] and textiles. Unlike dedications for Asklepios and Athena, as well as other gods, which were in most if not all cases manufactured specifically for dedication, these items of women's clothing may well have been in a woman's wardrobe already: one can imagine a woman (or her relatives in the case of the deceased woman) going through her wardrobe and picking out a favourite and valuable item. But perhaps a scenario in which a woman sat down and specifically wove or purchased a new item for the goddess should also be considered. In addition, there are a few references to krokotoi (saffron coloured dresses), which the young girls who were arktoi – bears – wore as part of the ritual at Brauron; it would be natural for these to be dedicated to the goddess, though perhaps it is surprising that not more of these were recorded in the inventories as dedications.[61]

On the Echinos relief in which a child is being presented to Artemis (Figure 7.4), clothes can be seen in the background of the relief. Whether this indicates that the clothes were affixed along the walls is unclear. The sheer bulk of clothing dedicated to Artemis Brauron must have called for a special method of display and/or storage. Some of the clothes are recorded as being kept in oblong boxes, which could easily have then been kept on shelves, the method apparently used in the Parthenon for storing at least some of the dedications there. Theano's shawl is described consistently in several lists as being 'around the statue'. Similarly, Nikoklea's dedication of a linen chiton from Amorgos is described as 'around the old statue'. Various other items of clothing are described as 'around the statue' and presumably there were several statues of Artemis Brauronia upon which women placed or draped the clothing which they were dedicating, and there such clothing remained. Archaeologists claim to have found at Brauron the place where the women's garments were placed on racks.[62]

While modern historians cannot resist conjuring up the image of a used clothing shop, it is more probably a Parisian boutique which should be imagined at both Brauron and the Athenian acropolis – clothes draped over statues, some in boxes, some hanging in racks, all meticulously recorded from year to year in the inventories published at Athens. The expensive nature of the offerings suggests that it was not so much the average woman who made dedications but the wealthier. This is confirmed by prosopographical studies of some of the women, who can be identified as coming from 'high status' and wealthy families.[63]

When several identical names appear with different dedications, it is hard to avoid the assumption that the same woman has made more than one dedication to the goddess. For example, in the best preserved of the Artemis inventories, a Phile dedicated a belt, a Phile a garment with a border, and a Phile a 'double' krokoton in a plaision (box), all in the same year (345/4 BC), and she is surely one and the same woman.[64] Clothing would have been an intimate item for a Greek adolescent girl and woman, something which belonged to her and which was valued. Judging from the descriptions of the items dedicated, and from the dresses actually worn by women on special occasions (Figures 1.4, 2.1–10, 2.13, 2.15, 7.3, 9.3), dress could be elaborate, and obviously expensive judging from the sumptuary legislation from some states and cults.[65] Dedicating it to the goddess, either by the woman herself or her family if she died in childbirth, displayed piety, especially when exhibited in the sanctuary where other devotees could see it.

Although outside the period under discussion here, the inscribed list of clothing dedications from Tanagra in Boeotia (central Greece) is worth noting because of the similarity it provides with classical Athenian examples. The inventory of dedications to Demeter and Kore appears to date from the first half of the third century BC. Various women dedicated items of clothing, both men's and women's, girls' and boys', including chitons, tunics, robes, and shawls (including 'a yellow chiton having six Sardian buttons'). No rationale is made clear, and the fact that male clothing is included indicates that these are not clothes intended for the goddesses' 'use'. Are these simply valuable items that the dedicatee hoped would please the goddesses? The list concludes with dedicated gold items, amounting to 3.5 staters (700 drachmas) and 2 obols.

The obverse side of the inscription, probably dating to c. 230 BC and so later than the inscribed list of clothing, is a decree calling upon women to make contributions to rebuild the sanctuary of Demeter and Kore, in response to a Delphic oracle which gave permission to move the location of the sanctuary. Women are recorded as making contributions of 5 drachmas each (it is interesting to note that the women are called upon to make donations of not more than 5 drachmas), and are recorded by their name and patronymic (their father's name). Six women in fact made contributions of as little as 3, 2, or even just 1 drachma in one case; nearly a hundred women in total made a contribution.[66] The group dynamics are important here: all the women, even those giving small amounts, are listed, indicating how the community of women as a whole showed their piety, and how those who had the lists inscribed wanted to publicise their contribution.

Dedications of clothing to the goddess of childbirth, Eileithyia, were made in her sanctuary at Delos.[67] A catalogue of clothing – listed as 'old and useless'

– from Miletos in Asia Minor must surely fall into the same category as the lists from Tanagra and the sanctuary of Artemis Brauronia on the Athenian acropolis: clothing dedicated to a goddess, though not necessarily Artemis, given that the Tanagra garments are dedicated to Demeter and Kore. However, Cole notes the large number of belts (the zoma or zone) in the Milesian list, and that the belt (or 'girdle') was dedicated to Artemis upon marriage.[68]

Dedications of temples and altars by women

While it is perhaps true that women's euergetism (benefaction) in religious matters begins on a large scale in the hellenistic period after 323 BC, particularly because queens became benefactors of religious cults, this can be discerned already in the classical period, and its existence even at Athens must reveal something about the social structure there.

Chairigenes and his daughter Eudeine dedicated an altar near Eretria on the island of Euboia, in the fifth century BC.[69] Lysistrate, the daughter of Stephanos, in about 450 BC, 'does not spare her belongings, but is ungrudging to the gods within her power', and presented Demeter and her daughter with an agalma (offering, perhaps a statue) to beautify the forecourt of her sanctuary; the inscription was found in Athens, and presumably refers to the Eleusinion (the sanctuary of the Eleusinian deities) there.[70]

There was a sanctuary of Aphrodite Pandemos ('The Whole People') on the south-west slope of the acropolis. Within it was a small temple building (an aedicula), probably dating to 350–320 BC, of which the foundations, and of the building itself the upper part, the frieze and peristyle, survive. The peristyle carries an inscription indicating that the small shrine was dedicated by Archinos, son of Alypetos of the deme Skambonidai, and his mother, Menekrateia, daughter of Dexikrates of the deme Ikarion, to Aphrodite Pandemos. Menekrateia is referred to as a woman priest, obviously of this goddess. On the frieze above the epistyle, doves (Aphrodite's sacred birds) hold in their beaks a string of knotted woollen sacrificial fillets, with which beasts were adorned prior to sacrifice.[71] The mother and the son are joint-dedicators, but the son's name appears first, and Menekrateia, given that the son but not the husband appears as co-dedicator, could well be a widow. Did the son pay the entire cost of the construction for Aphrodite Pandemos of whom his mother was the priest, and include her as co-dedicant to indicate the reason (that his mother was the priest) why he was erecting this small temple? It is also possible that if a widow Menekrateia might have had her own money (such as her dowry), which she used to help defray the expenses of the construction.

An altar, of the middle of the fourth century BC, was dedicated at Athens by a woman priest of Artemis Agrotera ('Of the Fields'). The actual name of the dedicant is missing from the dedicatory inscription, but it states that she was the mother of Dionysios' children, and a priest (propolos) of the city shrine of Artemis Agrotera. This deity had a sanctuary in the Ilissos region of the city, so the woman was presumably priest there. But this altar was found at Kephissia, and the inscription in fact states that the altar was dedicated to the goddess in the fields, so for whatever reason the woman priest erected this altar not in the Ilissos city region where it might have been expected, but in the country.[72]

Chrysina at Knidos (Asia Minor) in the second half of the fourth century BC on a base of blue marble had the following inscribed:

> Chrysina, mother of Chrysogone and the wife of Hippokrates, dedicated a house and statue to Kore and Demeter, after seeing a holy vision in the night, for Hermes commanded her to be a priest to the goddesses at [the place called] Tathne.[73]

Since Chrysina was now to serve the goddesses, the 'house' might refer to a building in which she could stay while serving the goddesses, just as the Pythia had a house at Delphi. But more probably it refers to the building of a new cult place, a shrine, for the goddesses. Chyrsina mentions her daughter, Chrysogone, clearly wishing her to be associated with her mother in this foundation.

Xenokrateia at Athens at the end of the fifth century BC dedicated a votive relief showing eleven deities, and herself and her little son, whom she commends in the accompanying inscription to the god Kephisos, to whom in the relief the little boy raises his right hand; the god bends forward to the mother and son (Figure 1.3):

Figure 1.3 Xenokrateia's dedication to the river god Kephisos, for the upbringing of her son; Athens; marble; 405–400 BC; height: 57 centimetres (courtesy, ©National Archaeological Museum, Athens, inv. 2756).

WOMEN AS DEDICATORS

> Xenokrateia has founded the sanctuary of Kephisos, and has dedicated this gift to him and the gods who share his altar, for the upbringing of her son; [Xenokrateia] daughter and mother of Xeniades, from Cholleidai.[74]

The relief was found at the mouth of the Kephisos river at Neon Phaleron, the Piraeus. Xenokrateia is a particularly interesting case because in the middle of the classical period when it was the greatest glory of a woman, according to Thucydides, not to be talked about by men for either praise or censure,[75] she dedicates a shrine to the river god Kephisos. This phenomenon is much more common in the hellenistic period and is less usual for Xenokrateia's time.

The kourotrophic powers of Kephisos are unknown; for some reason, Xenokrateia was attracted to the worship of this deity. A list of deities,[76] found in the same vicinity as Xenokrateia's relief, is probably to be connected with those depicted, and aids in their identification. Two of those listed, Artemis Lochia and Eileithyia, both goddesses of childbirth, are surely on Xenokrateia's relief, especially the third figure from the right, which once clearly held something, possibly a torch, a common attribute of Artemis Lochia. One of the figures on the relief, the fifth from the right, facing right, is usually identified as Eileithyia, and on the basis that she is 'holding her peplos' can be viewed as Eileithyia lysizonos, girdle looser;[77] the nymphs on the list are also probably there, being often connected with child-bearing and child-rearing. What is of importance here is that Xenokrateia describes herself as the daughter of Xeniades of the deme Cholleidai (she is obviously a citizen), and as the mother of the young boy; a husband is not mentioned; it is the boy's maternal, rather than paternal, grandfather who is mentioned.[78]

In all of the above cases, women with access or joint access to finance are found not just simply making dedications in temples, but actually founding altars and shrines to divinities. As noted in the Introduction, Plato complained about this very activity.[79] In doing so, women are often named in their relationship with men, which identifies them but does not necessarily imply that their religious activities were financed by men, though of course in some cases they probably were. Women thereby establish places where worship – by both men and women – could take place. Poverty might force women out of doors to work or fetch water, but wealth could enable a woman (with the qualification that the evidence is for only quite a small number of women) to worship at their very own altars and shrines.

The socio-economic status of women dedicators in the cult of Asklepios

> Andromacha of Epirus, on account of children. She slept in the temple and saw a dream. It seemed to her that a beautiful boy

embraced her, and after that the god [Asklepios] touched her with his hand. And because of this a son was born to Andromacha by (her husband) Arybbas.[80]

Children, men, and women sought the healing god Asklepios' assistance in times of sickness. The records for women consulting healing sanctuaries fall largely into two categories. At some sanctuaries, the authorities inscribed accounts of the cures performed there, sometimes based on a record which an individual had already inscribed on a tablet (pinax). The account of Andromacha's night in the healing sanctuary of Epidauros comes from one such engraved list of cures. The healed might also leave behind votive offerings in the form of the parts of the body which were healed: for women, there are numerous examples of breasts, and some pudenda. Representations of the uterus do not necessarily refer to childbirth but could refer to uterine medical conditions.[81] Terracotta figurines of women in labour are presumably votive in nature to give thanks for a safe delivery.[82] Depictions of pregnant women found in sanctuaries will also have been votive in nature.[83] Women, but more usually men, sometimes dedicated carved pictorial representations of their cure in stone. Both men and women might dedicate a silver relief of their cure. Medical conditions peculiar to women appear prominently, and indicate that women sought divine assistance for problems peculiar to their biology and physiology.

A very typical type of relief from Athens, quite similar to the reliefs from Brauron which show family groups of worshippers approaching Artemis, are the numerous reliefs in which a group consisting of a man and woman, with children, and a female servant carrying on her head a kiste (a round chest), approach the god Asklepios. In one such relief from Athens, now in the Berlin Museum, a male figure is seated on a chair under which there is a snake; this snake, and the way in which the figure has his left hand raised indicates that this is Asklepios; the female figure behind him could therefore be the goddess Hygieia (Health). A man and woman stand in front of them, a female figure (probably a servant) carries a huge kiste, and five smaller figures are also present (there seem to be four girls and a boy). The family has come to worship the healing god.[84]

A woman, cured of an eye illness, looked over the range of silver eyes at the silversmiths' booths outside the Asklepieion below the acropolis, and settled for a pair which weigh 3 obols, and paid that price and the smith's fee for his workmanship. He also carved her name on the eyes for her. She took them to the sanctuary, and she or the priest if he was present placed them in the temple. In the third century BC, the decision was taken to melt down all of the offerings to make new cult equipment, and inventories were drawn up of the mainly silver dedications (there were a few gold pieces) with their weights, so that the weight of the finished products could be compared with the original sum of metal. So Demetria's silver eyes, worth a mere 3 obols, were consigned to the melting pot.[85]

At the Asklepieion at the foot of the acropolis in Athens, such inscriptions (referred to as inventories) recorded the dedications which were made by men and women in the sanctuary, founded sometime between 422 and 420/19 BC.[86] In addition, numerous marble votive reliefs showing Asklepios and worshippers were discovered at the site, and are now housed mainly in the National Museum, Athens. An Ionic stoa at the Asklepieion with four rooms was presumably the abaton (healing place) where incubants would have sought cures.

Women made dedications to Asklepios, but how did these compare with those of men in quantity, quality and type? Nine inscribed inventories, not all complete, of dedications made in the Askepieion at Athens survive, but only cover certain years and there is no complete record of all the dedications made. Enough survives, however, to give some indication of the range and nature of the dedications and dedicators.[87] Listed for the Athenian Asklepieion are silver body parts, typoi (votive plaques), amounts of money, crowns, jewellery, medical equipment, vases and the like; body parts and typoi were the most frequent dedications listed in the inventories.

Conclusions based on gender are difficult because of the incomplete nature of the inventories. Aleshire notes that in the inventories now numbered as (iii), (iv) and (vii) women are recorded as dedicating twice as many typoi as men (24 versus 11), but (v) has roughly equal numbers of men and women (56 women to 59 men). Overall, women slightly outnumber men in the number of dedications recorded in the inventories. Women dedicated more anatomical pieces than did men, but only just; the typoi are offered by each sex almost equally. Men, of course, dominated in categories such as the dedication of costly crowns, and also of medical equipment. As might be expected, the offerings of jewellery and vases were largely those of women.[88] Where men markedly outnumbered women was in stone dedications,[89] which would never have cost a mere few drachmas, and would reflect the generally greater access of men to finance. Asklepios cured both men and women but was thanked unequally by them, with men yielding costlier dedications for his attentions.

These rather interesting, if incomplete data, prompt a few suggestive comments. Here is a cult in which men and women participated – at the level of worshipper – on what appear to be the same terms (the priesthood, however, was reserved for males). The women dedicated as frequently as men – perhaps even slightly more frequently than men – and these dedications were recorded alongside those of men, and (leaving aside stone reliefs) were not generally intrinsically inferior in worth. No dedication was apparently too small to escape the notice of the compilers of the inventories. Anatomical dedications worth only one obol are recorded, such as the eyes dedicated by the woman Kallistomache; Mika dedicated eyes worth a mere 2 obols.[90] The woman Aristagora dedicated 20 drachmas' worth of coins.[91]

The social status of the dedicators as revealed by surviving dedications and entries in the inventories is also important. Was the cult of Asklepios a lower socio-economic phenomenon for those who could not afford doctors? What has attracted attention and affected the interpretation of the identity of the dedicators is that many of them are not given a patronymic or demotic, or sometimes only a demotic (the name of the deme where they came from; only citizens had a demotic). The modern assumption is that in Athens, the citizen woman was meant to articulate her identity through her father or husband; the women in the inventories and dedications who lack these identificators were therefore non-citizens: slaves, metics and prostitutes (who could fall into either of the two previous categories).[92] Reinforcing these assumptions is the fact that some of the dedications are quite low in value, as little as one obol.

Aleshire's analysis of the inventories indicates that the percentage of dedicators – male or female – without patronymics or demotics is quite high (in inventory (iv), 72 per cent, and in (v), 86.4 per cent, of dedicators were recorded by name only), and observes that this is also the case with the inventories of Artemis Brauronia. But clearly the cult of Asklepios, and that of Artemis Brauronia, could not have drawn such a high percentage of its clientele from non-citizens.[93] The lack of identificators could have originated either in the original inscriptions of the dedicators (perhaps owing to a lack of space on the item), or in the record which the authorities decided to keep of them prior to their being melted down (lack of space in the inventories, and the fact that they were being recorded not as part of a temple treasure but because their value was being ascertained before their destruction, could have been factors).

However, the lack of real value for many dedications cannot have been a cause of lack of identification as even some very expensive dedications were not inscribed with the name of the dedicant, which may have been attached in some way and later lost, or simply not recorded by the dedicant for whatever reasons. It is clear that of all dedications given a weight one-third were for less than 1 drachma, nearly one-half come in under 2 drachmas, and about two-thirds were less than 4 drachmas.[94] But some of these dedications are made by individuals who are given demotic and patronymic, and so are citizens. In fact, for the majority of citizens at Athens, a dedication of one drachma of silver – a day's wage – was not a slight outlay.

Dedications of breasts, vulvae, and uteri to Asklepios

Of the anatomical body parts dedicated by women, breasts (none of which are dedicated by men) and female genitalia (one of the three being dedicated by a man)[95] raise the question of what these votives represent. The suggestion that the breasts are 'in the hope of plentiful food supply' for a baby is not without its attraction.[96] But generally Asklepios dealt with cures, and the kourotrophic deities dealt with hopes. Unless a category of kourotrophic power is conjectured for Asklepios, it seems best to view these as offerings for some illness affecting the breasts: Asklepios is a god who causes pregnancies or brings them to successful conclusions, and here too the women have presumably suffered some problem: perhaps even trouble with milk-flow after birth. While no individual cure accounts are available for the healing sanctuary of the hero god Amphiaraos at Oropos, midway between Thebes and Athens, he clearly had women clients, and the inventory list which survives from there includes dedications of breasts by women.[97]

By way of example, Phile dedicated a pair of breasts to Asklepios in Athens in the fourth century BC, and numerous dedications of breasts are recorded in the Asklepieion inventories; one votive breast was found in the sanctuary of Amynos (see below). A pair of breasts of the imperial age dedicated at Athens to Artemis Kolainis might indicate that she received such offerings earlier; there are some examples of votive breasts of the second and third centuries AD from the sanctuary of Zeus Hypsistos in the assembly place, and there is a pair of third-century BC marble breasts offered to (Artemis) Kalliste, who had a temple in Athens.[98] Similarly, at Corinth, Asklepios' interest in women's problems is indicated by the votive breasts dedicated at the Asklepieion there, amongst the hundreds of body parts (dated to 425–325 BC) which grateful men and women dedicated to the god in return for cures.[99]

Vulvae are amongst dedications to gods, but interpretation is difficult. These may refer to successful conceptions or successful conclusions of pregnancies, or perhaps even a cure for thrush. Conceptions and births, as seen, were both reasons why women travelled to Epidauros. At the shrine of Aphrodite along the Sacred Way, mid-point between Athens and Eleusis, grateful Philoumene dedicated a vulva to Aphrodite, with an inscription: 'Passers by, praise (the goddess).'[100] Various other vulvae were found in this sanctuary, and as seen above, they were dedicated in the Asklepieion below the acropolis. A vulva discovered on the acropolis perhaps made its way there from the Asklepieion.[101] There are also votive uteri, but the authenticity of any votive uterus is apparently in question. Two uteri are listed as offerings in the inventories of the Syrian gods from Delos in the second century BC; there may be two other examples from ancient Greece.[102]

Women at the Asklepieion at Epidauros

> Agameda from Keos. She slept in the temple on account of children and saw a dream. It seemed to her that in her sleep a snake lay on her stomach. And because of this five children were born to her.[103]

Epidauros provides material of a more detailed and personal nature than at Athens. Many individual testimonies such as Agameda's, as well as oral traditions of cures, were compiled by the priests and inscribed on large blocks of stone (stelai), set up where subsequent worshippers could see them. Many of the cures – the iamata – are of a fantastic and imaginary nature, but clearly others are more realistic and credible. The numbers of cures recorded for men clearly outnumber those for women. About half of the cures for women concern gynaecological problems; this could reflect the reality but might also represent a deliberate process of selection by the priests responsible for compiling the records. Asklepios' sanctuary at Lebena in Crete was similar to that at Epidauros in that here, too, records of cures were made, and the range of problems for which women sought the god's assistance was similar. In displaying the cures effected on women, Epidauros encouraged other women to seek the god within its sanctuary walls. Clearly fathers and husbands allowed their daughters and wives to seek divine assistance, and they presumably had little other choice.

The god's sacred animal, the serpent, played a role in securing pregnancies; women claimed that they dreamt of sleeping with a serpent or serpents and fell pregnant subsequently; the phallic connotations of the serpent, needless to say, have fascinated scholars but need not detain us here. The mother of the third-century BC general Aratos from Sikyon claimed to have become pregnant with Asklepios' assistance – a woman riding a serpent on the roof of Asklepios' temple at Sikyon was identified as Aristodama, and Aratos was publicly known as the son of Asklepios to the Sikyonians.[104]

Women might travel long distances to visit Epidauros: Andromacha, wife of Arybbas, king of Epirus in the fourth century BC, visited distant Epidauros in order to become pregnant; her cure inscription is the one quoted above,[105] and there is other evidence that women undertook pilgrimages to Epidauros, both from nearby cities and those further afield.[106] In fact, religious motives provided one of the few times when women travelled away from their home town or city. Many local centres had Asklepieia (sanctuaries of Asklepios), but the most important were panhellenic in character: Epidauros, Kos and Pergamon, though little is known of the presence of women at the latter two.

Asklepios and Amphiaraos were not the only healing deities. Finding out why one was childless and what to do about it was also an oracular question. Enquirers at Delphi were expected to have come 'about crops or children', both questions of fertility.[107] One woman after experiencing miscarriages asked at Delphi if she would ever successfully conclude a pregnancy; she soon had two children, and set up an inscription at Delphi to commemorate her enquiry and the births.[108] Women in the fifth century BC could consult the oracle, and the only obstacle was financial: to pay the cost of the pelanos, the sacrificial cake offered before a consultation, and a beast as well; travelling there and waiting for the monthly day of consultation would also have caused the women to incur expenses.[109]

Herakles–Pankrates attracted sick women's attention at Athens.[110] Also in that city a shrine of Zeus Hypsistos was used from at least the first to third centuries AD in the assembly place on the Pnyx, and several dedications from that period which were placed in niches in a rock face near the speaker's platform survive, including breasts. It is possible that the cult dates to much earlier.[111] The precinct of the hero Amynos, also at Athens, dates to the sixth century BC, and amongst the votive offerings found here is a breast dedicated by a woman in the fourth century BC, but inscribed 'Hedeia to Asklepios', with whom

Amynos is linked in inscriptions found in the sanctuary.[112] On the south slope of the Areiopagos, it is therefore in close proximity to the later Asklepieion, and one wonders what factors contributed to its continuing popularity after the foundation of the latter. But within a stone's throw of each other, Asklepios, Amynos and Zeus Hypsistos all made healing contributions to women, who chose one deity over another for reasons which elude us; preference and perceived efficacy must have played their role.

At Athens' port, the Piraeus, there was another Asklepieion, established a little earlier than the one in Athens itself and probably its founder. A relief of about 400 BC shows a sick woman lying on a couch, while the bearded Asklepios lays both of his hands on her right shoulder; a female deity, presumably Hygieia (Health) stands behind him. Three adult figures line up at the foot of the bed: a man followed by a woman, with their right hands raised in adoration to the god. Another woman, possibly a servant, follows, and there is a small child, presumably the couple's.[113]

While women were the dedicators of these objects – and the items mentioned in the iamata from Epidauros and the inventories from the Athenian Asklepieion and the Amphiaraion at Oropos – it is impossible (once again) to decide whether their male relatives may not have actually financed the dedication. What is important is that with women subject to a greater degree of medical risks than men, especially considering the medical conditions of the time, healing deities assumed a significance alongside that of the deities of love, marriage and kourotrophia. In worshipping healing deities, it was not a question of women preferring divine intervention over medicine. But it may be a question of access: for many women Asklepios or Herakles–Pankrates was probably more readily available than a doctor, particularly if there was a nearby shrine, and there is no reason to believe that women had a choice as to whether to consult a doctor rather than a healing deity. And a deity could be more efficacious than a doctor. The relationship which women had with Artemis and often but not always with Asklepios was different from men's in being based on gynaecological suffering; moreover, Dionysos and Aphrodite were celebrated by women with joy and dancing, but Artemis and sometimes Asklepios with pleas derived from daily suffering and childbirth.

A family at worship on the Athenian acropolis

Family groups, husband, wife and their children, clearly went together to shrines in order to worship and make dedications as a family, the basic societal unit. In the cases of the groups who are depicted in dedications worshipping healing gods, they must do so for the benefit of a sick family member, but other deities are worshipped as well by the family group as a whole for the benefit of all those concerned.

A votive marble relief of the early fifth century BC from the Athenian acropolis shows a family worshipping Athena. The goddess, larger than her mortal worshippers, displays her martial characteristics as the defender of Athens by wearing a helmet; the crest was painted on. Her hair is in the tresses common to korai statues; some of the tresses fall over her pointed left breast. Although not altogether clear because of the break in the stone, she holds her chiton (dress) in her left hand. Immediately before her stand two boys, one awkwardly superimposed upon the second (and difficult to see in the photograph), whose facial profile and hands are alone visible; perhaps they are meant to be twins. The first boy holds a disk in his hand: this could well be the phiale for pouring a libation to the goddess; but the presence of this in a child's hands would be iconographically unusual. The boys stand immediately before the man who is presumably their father; another tall figure is presumably the mother; the arms of these adults cannot be seen in the lower part of the relief that survives so presumably they were raised in a gesture of adoration. The girl immediately before her mother appears to be older than the boys, and is probably their sister; she has her left hand by her side, with the right raised. Everyone including Athena is barefoot. The sow who is part of the procession and is clearly intended for sacrifice has full hanging teats: she is either pregnant or has recently given birth (Figure 1.4).[114]

Aristonike dedicated a relief in the second half of the fourth century BC at Brauron. It is of four couples each with a child; a male leads an ox to the altar at the head of this procession; Artemis with a bow holds a phiale as she stands behind the altar. At the very end of the group, a woman, presumably a servant, carries a large kiste. While Aristonike dedicates the relief, she is not put in front of her husband. This could however be a ready produced relief, simply with Aristonike's name placed on it.[115]

Earlier, in the middle of the sixth century BC, on the island of Samos, a group of six life-size marble statues set into a marble base was dedicated. The names of some of the statues are still preserved: three are women; at the far left end is the seated statue of Phileia, which also bears the name of the sculptor, Geneleos, giving the modern name for the dedication, 'the Geneleos group'. Then there were four standing figures, as indicated by the holes in the base of the monument; two of the statues survive, young women or adolescent girls, who are named (Philippe and Ornithe). Fragments of a third statue, another girl, also survive. There is no real reason to assume that the fourth, lost, statue was a kouros as opposed to another girl.

At the end of the statue base is a reclining figure, who is described as the dedicator of these statues to Hera but whose name itself does not fully survive; there is some dispute about whether it is a man or a woman. The figure is fairly rotund and clothed, but this would be an acceptable rendering of a man in the eastern Greek sculptural tradition. If a man, the group could represent a mother and father, one at each end, with their four children in between – at least three of whom are girls. If a father, he could well have dedicated a 'family portrait' to the goddess, and his wife and daughters – if that is their identity – are sufficiently important to him to dedicate representations of them to the goddess.

32

WOMEN AS DEDICATORS

Figure 1.4 A family group, with sow, before the goddess Athena; Athenian acropolis; marble; 490–480 BC; height: 66.5 centimetres; width: 65.5 centimetres; thickness: 8 centimetres (courtesy, ©Acropolis Museum, Athens: inv. 581).

In fact, he may well have been particularly pleased to dedicate statues of his virgin daughters to the goddess. But if the reclining figure is a woman – and she might well have been holding a bird, a woman-only attribute – it might be possible to see in the group six women and girls dedicated to the service of Hera in her temple, with the group presented by the seated figure, reading -arche, the ending for a woman's name. She could, then, be the main priest, making a substantial and expensive offering to the goddess, in company with the deity's votaries.[116]

Families worshipping heroes

A particularly fine relief from the first half of the fourth century BC from Cumae (Italy) depicts a family of six worshipping an unidentified (generic) hero. On the left side of the relief a hero sits astride his horse, with three of its legs off the ground; to one side of the rear of the horse stands an obviously divine woman, perhaps the rider's wife. In front of the horse, both a man and a woman who is behind him raise their right hands. Their four children, first three girls and then a boy (the boy plays with a hare which is standing upright, touching his right hand), appear after them in descending size, making room in the top right-hand corner for a large shield, with a helmet above the wife's head. This is clearly meant to depict the hero's shrine.[117] Other examples of reliefs which show the hero on his horse being worshipped by men and women worshippers are from Hyettos (Boeotia) and Amorgos.[118]

In another hero-relief dedication, from Tanagra in Boeotia, the hero stands next to his horse and an altar, while a woman of the same size, presumably his wife, pours from an oinochoe into a phiale which he holds. They are worshipped by a family of four: a man, a woman, and two apparently male children. There is an inscription indicating that the relief is dedicated to Aleximachos: 'Kalliteles dedicated to Aleximachos'.[119] The hero also stands next to his horse and is worshipped by a man, two women and two children in an example from Thebes; other examples of the hero next to his horse with male and female worshippers are from Lakonia, Epirus and Pergamon.[120] These hero-reliefs invariably show men, women and their children worshipping a hero.

There are several such hero-reliefs from Sparta in the second half of the sixth century BC. The example usually illustrated is the one from Chrysapha, Lakonia.[121] A pair of deities, heroes rather than gods owing to the snake that is shown, are seated on a chair from under which a snake arches itself along the full height of the chair until its head is just behind the hero's. The male deity holds a kantharos (a broad cup, about 10–15 centimetres wide, with two vertical handles), while the female holds a pomegranate and in the other hand pulls up her veil. The two worshippers who approach are rendered very much smaller than the divine figures. The man holds a rooster and an egg and the woman a pomegranate flower and a pomegranate. There is another example, almost identical to this, with a couple holding the same objects worshipping a similar pair of deities.[122] The enthroned deities being worshipped could represent heroes, or perhaps the heroised dead ancestors of the worshippers. The snake has clear chthonic connotations; the kantharos indicates that the hero is to receive libations. The families worship the heroes for benefits which elude us.

A relief from Mytilene on the Aegean island of Lesbos shows a woman with what appears to be an offering basket in her hands, at one end of a table beside which two much larger female figures are standing; a snake coils up from beneath the table. These two are probably heroines and receive an offering from the woman devotee, unless she is simply a semi-divine attendant, similar to the male attendant frequently present on hero-reliefs who pours the wine.[123] Similarly, another example from Mytilene shows a single woman in attendance upon the usual heroic pair, and she is holding some sort of offering in her hand; there is no snake present, but a horse's head is on the wall.[124] These examples of a single woman in attendance upon heroes, and heroines, might indicate that women could go to the hero-shrines and worship, pouring libations and bringing offerings.

There are numerous votive reliefs which depict a male figure reclining on a couch, with a female figure sitting on the couch with him. In a relief from Athens, a snake rears up underneath the couch of the reclining hero and heroine, with a horse's head in the far left top corner of the relief. A male nude attendant on the far right in front of a large krater (a wide bowl used for mixing wine with water) holds a phiale. A man and a woman and their three children are present; the couple and two of the children venerate in usual solemn style, but the rest of the scene is somewhat lively; a small servant figure in front of the parents hangs onto a pig, while behind the two children and next to a servant with a large kiste on her head a boy, the third and smallest child of the couple, makes a grab with both hands for a bird, perhaps a duck or goose.[125] From Gallipoli comes a late fourth-century BC example with a dog under the hero's table; a man places something on the altar, then there is a man, two women, two children, and a sheep being led by a small figure but probably meant to be an attendant rather than another child.[126]

Other examples are similar, and throughout the Greek world (except for the western Greeks) there are numerous examples of families worshipping reclining and dining heroes: from the Piraeus, Megara, Corinth, Sikyon, Argos, Thespiai (Boeotia), Delos, Mytilene, Melos, Tenos, Samos, Chalkis, Pergamon, Erythrai, Tralleis, Thebes and Ephesos. These reliefs show women accompanying their husbands, with their children, to worship these heroes.[127] Sacrificial animals are sometimes shown, while in some reliefs a female servant carries a large kiste on her head, presumably with offerings. In most cases the male figure leads, but occasionally a female does.[128]

These dedications by families point to the social integrity of the family, reinforced by religious practice. While sacrifice might occur without the presence of women, or without men, the family was an important religious unit. It could be upheld and sustained by its communal experience of the divinity through family sacrifices. There seems to be little discrimination on the family's part, and several divinities received family delegations with a sacrificial offering. But at Athens, it is Asklepios and Athena, followed by Artemis, who are best represented iconographically, though Herakles–Pankrates was also not inimical to the family. The children are usually shown behind their mother, following the father. In this sense, families at worship reflected societal norms and the patriarchal structure of the classical Greek family.

These family dedications are only part of the overall pattern of dedications. Women dedicated in their own right items to the gods in both the archaic and classical period. From the smallest spindle whorl to the 1.75-metre statue of Artemis dedicated by Nikandre, women ensured that they came to the notice of their gods, and often their contemporaries. They advertised their piety, and in some cases their wealth (in others their poverty). They recognised the gods, and their society gave recognition to the concept that women had a role to play in making cult offerings to the gods. Fathers, husbands and sons joined with daughters, wives and mothers in the dedicatory procedure. In fact, if some or all of the money for a dedication came via a man, he might well wish this to be advertised, though clearly women in the archaic period were much less concerned with identifying themselves through a man, whereas this became more routine in the classical period. The dedication process for women (as for men) was episodic, and occurred when and as the need arose. There was no concept of regular dedication – sacrificial offerings were the normal religious practice occuring at routine intervals – but rather dedications were made as required. A crisis (such as sickness) provoked a need for divine assistance; the dedication supplied the thanks and was insurance if further assistance was required.

Men definitely dedicated to the gods more frequently than women, reflecting socio-economic realities. But for the individual woman, for all the women like Demetria with her 3-obol offering to Asklepios, or the woman of Tanagra with only one drachma to spare for the goddesses Demeter and Kore, this giving was important, and crucial for their relationship with the gods. What should not be understated is that women through their dedications – which are sometimes anonymous (the spindle whorls) but are often marked – emerge as individuals. The inscribing of their religious devotion publicised their society's acquiescence in a material display of religious feeling. Women's role in Greek religion was not simply collective or purely adjunctive to men's role. Their men allowed them to be named as dedicators, and probably in many cases encouraged them to be so identified. In some cases the women may have been independent enough to do so without permission. In this way, the very real anonymity of women in other areas of Greek religion – such as the hundreds of nameless girls who served Athena at Athens in the archaic and classical periods – is somewhat tempered.

2

THE PUBLIC RELIGIOUS ROLES OF GIRLS AND ADOLESCENT WOMEN IN ATHENS

The chorus of women in Aristophanes' *Lysistrata* sing of their religious duties when they were girls and young unmarried women:[1]

> When I was seven years old
> I was an arrephoros,
> then I was a 'corn-grinder' at ten
> for the Archegetis [Artemis],
> and then wearing the saffron-coloured robe
> a bear at the Brauronia,
> and as a beautiful girl I was a basket-bearer
> wearing a necklace of dried figs.

Parthenoi – unmarried virgins – obviously had important religious roles at Athens, serving Artemis and Athena in various capacities. They were often the ones who in religious processions carried various items needed for cult rituals, particularly baskets (the kana; singular: kanoun). Kanephoroi – basket-bearers – are prominent in Athenian iconography, and they fulfilled this role in other cities as well. Young girls were also singers and dancers for the gods, as will be seen in Chapter 7. These roles were open to girls and adolescent women partly because as they were unmarried they had no other responsibilities; once married, public roles such as these, particularly in a city such as Athens, were presumably thought inappropriate for them as wives of Athenian citizens. But the virgin status of girls must have been a factor in their filling these roles: in serving as attendants bringing the sacrificial items their purity was doubtless important.

Kanephoroi: basket-bearers

In the period immediately before marriage a girl might act as a kanephoros at a religious festival or at a sacrifice. These basket-bearers were drawn from the eugeneis, the well-born, and this is reinforced by the case of the sister of the aristocrat Harmodios; the latter refused the Athenian tyrant Hipparchos' advances and so he in turn countered by turning Harmodios' sister away as a kanephoros for the Great Panathenaia of 514 BC.[2] A kanephoros was a girl not yet wedded but on the point of being so, as is indicated in the myth of the basket-bearer Oreithyia, who was abducted and raped by the North Wind, Boreas, while she was participating in a procession to the acropolis, in honour of Athena Polias.[3] The insult to Harmodios' sister (who is significantly not named) was not simply that of turning her away and so affronting the dignity of the family, but implied that the would-be kanephoros was not a parthenos: a slight on her virginity and so an insult to her brother and family.

The Panathenaia (Great and Annual) was the most important Athenian festival at which young unmarried women carried the baskets.[4] In these baskets they carried 'the things for the sacrifice',[5] in particular the sacrificial knife, which the kanephoros carried in the basket but did not wield in the sacrificial act, as well as the barley which was needed for dousing the victim's head, to make it nod, yielding to its own destruction voluntarily, and the fillet (the stemma, ribbon) with which to adorn the beast.[6] Baskets were of wicker work or metal. They came in a variety of shapes, from simple shallow trays to more elaborate trays with high handles – open or closed – which sometimes look like horns. The kanephoroi – the adolescent girl basket-bearers – are shown carrying them on their heads, or with them in their hands. Not all basket-bearers were young women, and male youths are also depicted on vases in this role at sacrifices, with no women portrayed; girls probably performed the basket-carrying function at public festivals, and male youths at private sacrifices at which women were not present.[7]

Athena and Artemis were divine prototypes of the kanephoros; both are sometimes depicted as a kanephoros:[8] the kanephoroi reflect the purity of these two eternally virgin goddesses, and participate in a pure sacrifice to the gods. The parthenos acting as kanephoros is frequently shown leading the sacrificial procession, as in the main Pitsa pinax (Figure 7.3). Similarly, in Aristophanes' *Birds*, Prometheus follows the kanephoros, pretending to carry the parasol and be a chair-bearer (diphrophoros) too.[9] In the *Ekklesiazousai*, Chremes instructs his household possessions to come out: first the flour-sieve, like a kanephoros to start out first in the procession, and she is 'powdered' (referring presumably to the kanephoros' face), and then he asks where the diphrophoros is.[10] Similarly in the *Acharnians*, the kanephoros leads off.[11] The fifth-century BC Athenian comic poet Hermippos referred to the white-powdered kanephoroi, and to the diphrophoros,[12] and Nikophon, also a fifth-century Athenian comic poet, mentioned the diphrophoros.[13] At Athens for the Panathenaia the duties of carrying the parasol and chair for the kanephoroi, but not the basket itself, were given to the daughters of the metics, the foreigners resident in Athens.[14] The kanephoroi provided enough interest for Athenian comedies to be written featuring them by Anaxandrides and Menander.[15]

From the mid-sixth century BC, the kanephoros appears on Athenian vase-paintings, later than her Corinthian counterpart, but no doubt she had been present at sacrifices earlier than the vases indicate. On an Athenian mid-sixth-century BC black-figure kylix (cup) a sacrificial procession for the benefit of Athena Promachos is depicted. A kanephoros is behind a man who stands at an altar; this man clasps hands over the lit altar fire with a woman, who stands in front of the goddess; this woman is presumably a priest. The kanephoros' basket appears to be woven, and has the three-horned appearance which is common. Sacrificial animals, pipe-players, hoplites (heavily armed infantry) and a man on horse make up the procession, which is suggestive of that of the Panathenaia.[16] There is a kanephoros with very elaborate dress on one red-figure volute krater of the third quarter of the fifth century BC in a procession to Apollo; he sits on a tripod and this appears to depict a sacred pilgrimage to Delphi, perhaps the Pythais (see below).[17]

A woman holding an elaborate basket of 'crown' shape, which will have held offerings of some kind, and pouring a libation from an oinochoe (jug) is shown on the interior of a very fine late-archaic (c. 480 BC) red-figure cup by the painter Makron (Figure 2.1).[18] She pours wine onto the altar, on which a fire has been lit; the blood stains on the side of the altar, painted in red, are clearly visible: a sacrifice has already taken place here, perhaps recently. She is barefoot, but her dress is very elaborate: she wears a chiton, with a himation on top, draped over her shoulders, both front and back, but falling further to the ground at the back. It has a border, and its numerous folds attest to the fineness of her dress and indicate that it is made of a heavier rather than a lighter material. The tassels hanging from her belt are added in red. This style of mantle is seen on many women engaged in religious duties, such as on the terracotta kanephoros from Rhodes, to be discussed below. She has a fillet in her hair, which is bound, except for a single curled lock which escapes from behind her ear, which emphasises rather than detracts from the orderliness of her hairstyle, and wears a simple hoop earring. The incense burner behind her is smoking. That she pours a libation herself is unusual: this was normally a task reserved for men. The exterior of this cup has scenes which have been interpreted as men negotiating with prostitutes on the price of sexual intercourse. The drinker could see these scenes on the exterior, but only when he drained the cup of red wine was he confronted with the image of pure, virgin, Athenian womanhood, with whom marriage and intercourse provided legitimate offspring.

Individual named girls – not from the classical period but several centuries later – who were basket-bearers are known for several Athenian festivals: for example, the Panathenaia, Epidauria, Dionysia, the festival for the Mother of the Gods, the Eleusinia, for Dionysos Lyaios at Eleusis, for Isis and Sarapis, and for the Pythais of Apollo sent to Delphi, indicating that parthenoi went from Athens to Delphi for this purpose.[19] But the honorary decrees and dedicatory monuments naming these girls are all after the classical period, and it would have been unthinkable to name or honour girls in this way in the fifth and

Figure 2.1 A young woman holding a basket pours a libation onto a flaming altar; interior of Athenian red-figure kylix (cup); *c.* 480 BC; painter: Makron; diameter of cup: 29 centimetres; diameter of painting (including frieze): 14 centimetres (courtesy, ©Toledo Museum of Art, Toledo (Ohio), inv. 1972.55).

fourth centuries BC. Outside the classical period, the boule and demos erected statues for some of these kanephoroi.[20] Some inscriptions indicate that a girl could serve in this role in several festivals, and this may have held true for the classical period as well. Athenian kanephoroi were involved in the annual sacred delegations known as the Pythais sent to Delphi; two of these are known from statue bases erected by the state.[21]

As discussed below, no young women with baskets are depicted on the Parthenon frieze, and in fact Roccos has noted that depictions of the kanephoros with basket became less frequent on vases from about the middle of the fifth century BC at Athens. She argues that after this time the kanephoros is not indicated by her basket but by her elaborate ritual dress alone.[22] An Attic red-figure volute krater shows a mature girl with basket and elaborate dress,[23] and it is in this dress that young girls are sometimes depicted, but without a basket, after this time.

The best-preserved example of a kanephoros statuette, terracotta in this case, is from Rhodes; she wears a long-sleeved chiton with a himation over it and has both hands holding the elaborate kanoun on her head, with the handles on the basket clearly rendered. The kanephoros steps forward with her left leg, and wears a mantle over her peplos which extends down to her footwear so that her feet are hardly visible, with her sleeves extending down to her hands. The folds of the dress and the billowing of the mantle in conjunction with the extended leg convey the idea of walking in a procession. Her peplos (elaborate upper garment) has a belt, and her visible hair is neatly arranged. She carries a basket on her head, using both hands to support it (Figure 2.2).[24] Such statuettes will have been votive in nature, dedicated by the kanephoros to the deity of the sacrifice which she was attending.

The importance of kanephoroi at Athens is indicated by the distribution of meat at the annual festival of the Panathenaia in honour of Athena; a fourth-century BC decree provides that the prytaneis (serving sub-committee of the council) were to receive five shares of the meat, the archons three, the treasurers of Athena and hieropoioi (sacred officials) one, the strategoi and taxiarchoi (generals and commanders) three, while the participants and kanephoroi were to receive shares 'as customary', with the rest of the meat being distributed to the Athenians.[25]

The statesman Lykourgos as part of his financial measures in the 330s and 320s BC provided ornaments of gold for 100 kanephoroi.[26] Some baskets were dedicated as votive offerings, and kana (baskets) are listed in the accounts of the Treasurers of Athena and the Other Gods amongst the dedications to Asklepios, and in one of the inventories of items dedicated at the Asklepieion itself below the acropolis.[27] Those in the accounts were heavy: one was 2,406, one 3,596, and another 3,690 drachmas; one has a restored weight of 2,906 drachmas, 4 obols; an Asklepieion inventory lists one at 945 drachmas. With 6,000 drachmas to one talent of silver (about 26 kilograms), these are too heavy to be carried on the heads of kanephoroi, and they must have been intended purely as dedications. Kanephoroi in the cult of Asklepios are attested from about 300 BC on, but presumably they are not a late development in the cult.[28]

From Corinth come the earliest representations of the kanephoros in Greek art. A middle-Corinthian (600–575 BC) amphora shows a kanephoros carrying a huge basket on her head, with jugs and a rectangular structure with items inside, upon which rests a smaller tray, also with two jugs flanking a rectangular container of items.[29] Another depiction is that of three kanephoroi in a line on a middle-Corinthian amphoriskos (a small amphora); this sort of line-up must often have been the case at Athens but this Corinthian depiction is unique. The three kanephoroi, with flat baskets, are followed by a large bull, by a figure which could be a man or woman, and by a woman pipe-player and two more women.[30] From Boeotia there is the well-known mid-sixth-century BC black-figure cup which shows a series of figures approaching an altar behind which stands an armed goddess with shield and spear, presumably Athena Promachos; a kanephoros leads the procession.[31]

Figure 2.2 A young girl carries a basket on her head as part of a sacrificial rite; Lindos (Rhodes); mid-fourth century BC; height: 13 centimetres; hollow-moulded; terracotta with slip (courtesy, ©Department of Classical and Near Eastern Antiquities, National Museum of Denmark; inv. 10780).

The parthenoi of the Parthenon frieze[32]

As the ancient Athenian approached the Parthenon, the temple of the virgin goddess (parthenos) Athena on the Athenian acropolis, the metopes (sculptures running around the architrave above the outer columns) and pediment sculptures were visible above the first row of columns, while inside there was a frieze above the inner central block of the temple, above the columns at the east and west ends, and the walls of the north and south, forming a 160-metre-long frieze that ran the four sides of the temple, which was not visible from the outside. The frieze is discussed in terms of the direction each side is on: east, north, west, south. Each of the figures appearing on the frieze has been individually numbered by scholars with Arabic numerals, so that a reference to a particular frieze (i.e. east) and a figure number (i.e. §6) allows the identification of particular individual figures.³³ In a clockwise direction, the east frieze is at the front of the temple, then the south, west and north (as one comes up through the gateway of the acropolis (the propylaia), the west side of the Parthenon is encountered first).

Young women appear on the east but not on the other sides of the frieze. They are clearly intended to be young mature women on the verge of marriage; once married, a public role such as they are shown performing on the frieze would have been considered inappropriate for them. This east frieze was seen as one approached the east door which gave access to the chamber where Pheidias' massive statue of Athena Parthenos stood. Interpreting and understanding what these young unmarried women are doing is linked with what the frieze represents. It could be a festival procession, either the Panathenaic procession as celebrated in the second half of the fifth century BC when the frieze was carved, or a mythical Panathenaic procession – perhaps the inaugural one celebrated by King Erichthonios. It may be the procession arriving on the acropolis, or it may be composed of scenes of the procession as it made its way along the Panathenaic Way (the Sacred Way) from the Dipylon Gate up to the acropolis. Whatever the frieze represents, it had to convey themes and depict practices which the fifth-century BC Athenian viewer would understand. Any cult items, for example, must be explicable in terms of contemporary cult practice and worship of Athena.

The procession on the frieze is in two lines, converging on the body of gods in its centre. Of the young women, the first two, on the left hand side of the frieze (those numbered §§2–3), are represented by only a few fragments, though Carrey's drawings, made before the explosion of the acropolis in the seventeenth century AD, show them carrying phialai (libation bowls); women §4 to §6 are on a slab of the frieze now in the Acropolis Museum, Athens (Figure 2.3);³⁴ adolescent women §5 and §6 each carry a phiale, and according to Carrey's drawings, figures §§2–4 did so also. The pleated sleeve of §4, and the florets on the sleeves of §§5–6 should be noted, as should the heavy drapery which falls in numerous folds on all of the young women of the frieze.

Women §§7–17 are on a slab of the frieze now in the British Museum (Figure 2.4);³⁵ §§7–11 each carry an oinochoe (these phialai and oinochoai were for pouring libations of wine onto altars, or onto the ground). Women §§12–13 and 14–15 as a pair carry between them a trumpet-shaped object each, tapered end up (women §§16–17 carry nothing). Various suggestions as to what these two objects are have been made: incense burners, stands for roasting spits, or parts of the loom used for weaving the peplos.³⁶ Figure §57 does in fact carry an incense-burner (thymiaterion), and the objects held by the pairs §§12–13

PUBLIC RELIGIOUS ROLES FOR GIRLS AND WOMEN

Figure 2.3 Young Athenian women (korai) taking part in the Panathenaic procession, from the east frieze (slab II, §§ 4–6) of the Parthenon, Athens; marble; frieze carved: 447–432 BC; height: 105 centimetres; length: 79 centimetres (courtesy, ©Acropolis Museum, Athens inv. 877).

and 14–15 are similar to its base. The shapes of these objects are also very much like an incense-burner which a winged Nike (Victory) holds on an Attic red-figure lekythos, having a similarly flared base.[37] Thymiateria were amongst the precious items recorded in the inventories of the Parthenon: ten silver and six gilt incense-burners,[38] which were presumably the ones used for the Panathenaic procession and seen on the east frieze of the Parthenon.

Following are six men (§§18–23; the first two of whom can be seen in Figure 2.4), probably some of Athens' ten eponymous heroes (after whom the ten political divisions, tribes, of Athens were named), then a group of seated gods and goddesses (§§24–30). One of these, Hera (§29), holds out her veil, a marriage custom, indicating her patronage of weddings, and perhaps significant given the proximity of so many unmarried young women. There is then a group of five figures (§§31–35), and then more seated gods (§§36–42), facing the

44

Figure 2.4 Young Athenian women (korai) taking part in the Panathenaic procession; from the east frieze (slab III, §§7–15) of the Parthenon, Athens; now in London; marble; frieze carved: 447–432 BC; height: 105 centimetres; length: 308 centimetres (courtesy, ©The Trustees of the British Museum, inv. BM 109.161).

opposite direction, toward the procession coming along the right side of the frieze.

Figures §§31–35, on another slab now in the British Museum (Figure 2.5),[39] have occasioned much discussion. Figures §§32–33 are in the very centre of the frieze; it is not surely a case of applying modern perceptions of the importance of centrality to assume that this is the single most important part of the east frieze, and of the frieze as a whole (in that the north and south friezes fan out from the eastern, and it is these figures which were over the actual door of the Parthenon). The two female figures §§31–32 are often interpreted (incorrectly) as diphrophoroi, stool carriers. A third, taller, woman (§33) extends a hand onto the object the second figure (§32) on the right is carrying.[40] If they were diphrophoroi, they could represent metics, as metic daughters were said to carry diphroi (stools) for the Athenian daughters in the Panathenaic procession. The objects which the two girls in the frieze carry have flat bases and a rounded top, like a high cushion. These might be stools, as is often stated; but who would they be for: perhaps for the woman priest and the bearded figure (§§33–34)?

Figure §31 carries something badly damaged in her left hand. It is sometimes argued that this is a footstool, to go with the conjectured stool, with a visible projection at its base taken as a leg of the stool.[41] This, however, is not the case, and the object is actually tilting up at an angle to the flat 'stick' taken to be a

Figure 2.5 The woman priest of Athena Polias with the two arrephoroi and their secret bundles; a male figure, perhaps the king (basileus) archon, receiving the peplos from a girl; from the east frieze (slab V, §§31–5) of the Parthenon, Athens; now in London; marble; frieze carved: 447–432 BC; height: 105 centimetres; length of slab V: 442 centimetres; length of illustrated section: 190 centimetres (courtesy, ©The Trustees of the British Museum, inv. BM 115.161).

leg.[42] This is not a footstool but some other, indeterminate, object, perhaps another shrouded, secret item which the woman priest has given her to carry.

As for the objects on the girls' heads, these can only be made into diphroi if legs are attached to them, and as what is seen as a leg on the object carried on the head by §32 is carved in stone the other legs, if there were any, would also have been so carved, but of this there is no trace. Nor do the so-called stools have folding legs (a feature of many Greek diphroi), as there is no trace of this either. Stools – diphroi – are in fact shown on the east frieze of the Parthenon, but it is the gods who sit on them (as they do on the frieze of the Siphnian treasury at Delphi).[43]

In fact, these girls are clearly carrying on their heads flat baskets with contents which are tightly shrouded or covered over with cloth. The young woman §32 in fact, as is often overlooked, is clearly carrying a lighted torch (though one can understand why some have been tempted to see a chair leg).[44] At the arrephoria festival the arrephoroi at night received from the woman priest of Athena Polias items which they carried on their heads; presumably they needed the torch for their nocturnal rite (see below); these two girls, younger than the other women, are clearly two arrephoroi.[45]

The central element of the frieze is the five figures who divide the gods into two sets, each set receiving the head of the two processions of young women. The very middle of the frieze, in fact, is an imaginary vertical line which can be drawn through the right arm of the woman (§33) assisting the first arrephoros (§32).[46] The most important event connected with Athena is the presentation of the peplos, woven by the arrephoroi, and this is what is being depicted here. The older woman (§33) is obviously a woman priest, and, if these are arrephoroi, she will be the woman priest of Athena Polias, from whom the arrephoroi received their bundles.

The male figure §34 requires a word of interpretation. He and a smaller figure (§35) are handling, each with both hands, a piece of cloth which judging from the visible lines on its edge has already been folded several times. The adult male (§34) is usually interpreted as the archon basileus, the chief religious official of ancient Athens, taking over the religious duties of the abolished monarchy. The smaller figure has a cloak over it that leaves its buttocks naked and exposed. This and its weathered face have led to questions concerning its gender.[47] Ancient Greek depictions of bare buttocked children of either gender exist and mean that no parallel can be drawn. However, figure §136 at the very end of the north frieze, clearly a boy with bare buttocks, has a garment which only reaches half way down his thighs, rather than all the way as with §35, and is portrayed very differently from §35.[48] There is no evidence for any temple servant-boy for the Parthenon or the Panathenaia, meaning that attempts to identify him as one in Athena's cult are fruitless.[49] The full length of the peplos, and the fact that it is not girt, indicates that §35 is a girl who does not need to be modest, that is, a girl not yet approaching puberty, and clearly the artist rendered her in this way to emphasise her tender years.

Mythology can perhaps be of service in understanding the east frieze. Pandrosos was the only one of the three daughters of King Kekrops who, entrusted by Athena with the chest in which the infant Erichthonios was, did not open it; the other two sisters, Aglauros and Herse, did so.[50] Aglauros and Herse saw Erichthonios and a snake (or two) inside and threw themselves to their deaths off the acropolis. It is possible to see in §§31–32 two girls chosen as arrephoroi to live on the acropolis for a year and weave the peplos for Athena as a ritual of atonement for these two mythical virgin girls, Aglauros and Herse; the third girl is their obedient sister.

It has also been pointed out that the procession of the north frieze, which continues the procession of the east frieze and to which figure §35 belongs, consists of both sheep and cattle, while the other procession, of the south side of the east frieze and its continuation on the south frieze, has bulls only. Whenever a sacrifice of a cow was made to Athena, one of a sheep was to be offered to Pandrosos.[51] The third daughter, Pandrosos, the obedient one, received a cult on the slope of the acropolis, and it is possible to argue that she is depicted in the Parthenon frieze as a young girl, receiving Athena's peplos from her father, King Kekrops, the archetypal basileus archon.[52] The taller woman (§33) is clearly the priest of Athena; in mythical terms she would represent Praxithea, the wife of Kekrops. This, then, is the Athenian royal family of myth, the two parents and the three daughters, with the disobedient ones depicted in the role which Athenian girls would take on for them in a ritual of atonement, while the youngest girl handling the peplos, §35, does not actually represent any member of the cult personnel in fifth-century BC practice as it is known.

The next group of young women (§§50–51, 53–56) appear on a slab of the frieze now in the Louvre, Paris (Figure 2.6).[53] Two of these young women in particular, §§50–51, are sometimes described as kanephoroi because of the male figure §49, the first figure on the left of this particular slab, who stands immediately in front of them; he is probably a 'marshal' of the procession. He is holding in his hands, and apparently handing to one of the two figures a flat object which is sometimes described as a kanoun, basket.[54] There are certainly flat baskets which could be seen as being similar to the Parthenon object. But the indented base of the object seems to point to it being a phiale, a libation bowl. There are, then, no parthenoi actually carrying baskets, either in their hands or on their heads, among all the adolescent women of the east frieze. Presumably some of the young women are basket-bearers, but they are yet to receive their baskets.

Another marshal, §52, follows; he is pointing at two young women who are standing side by side (§§53–54); nine young women follow in single file (§§55–63); figures §§57–61 are on a slab of the frieze (Figure 2.7), now in the British Museum which immediately adjoins the Louvre slab.[55] Figures §53, §54, and §56 hold nothing in their hands, while each of the following women do carry objects; §55 appears to be carrying a bowl.

Figure 2.6 Young Athenian women (korai) taking part in the Panathenaic procession, with two men (marshals) directing them; from the east frieze (slab VII, §§49–56) of the Parthenon, Athens; now in Paris; marble; frieze carved: 447–432 BC; height: 105 centimetres; length: 207 centimetres (courtesy, ©Musée du Louvre, inv. Ma 738).

RELIGIOUS ROLES IN ATHENS

Figure 2.7 Young Athenian women (korai) taking part in the Panathenaic procession; from the east frieze of the Parthenon (slab VIII, §§57–61), Athens; now in London; marble; frieze carved: 447–432 BC; height: 105 centimetres; length: 160 centimetres (courtesy, ©The Trustees of the British Museum, inv. BM 124.161).

Young woman §57, the first in Figure 2.7, carries what is correctly interpreted as an incense-burner; nearly all of the relief is lost but the outline on the stone is clear. A similar incense-burner is shown on the cup by the Makron painter (Figure 2.1).[56] Figures §§58–59 carry jugs (the details are not quite clear), while §§60–61 carry shallow bowls (phialai), just as §55 does. The long sleeves of §§57, 60–61 should be noted. That is the end of the east frieze procession as it now survives; two more figures (§§62–63) followed, according to Stuart's drawings carrying bowls like the previous figures.

Some of the adolescent women in the processions of the east frieze hold items, bowls and oinochoai, and one at least an incense-burner which will be used during the sacrifice. Others do not carry anything, but the marshall (§49), about to hand out a phiale to one of the women (§§50–51), indicates that what the frieze is representing is the procession in preparation: some girls have received their phialai, oinochoai and thymiateria, others are about to. The gods chat, waiting for the procession to start. These young women stand ready to play their role in the procession and consequent sacrifice; the animals are coming up behind, and soon the women will play their role in pouring libations; some may soon be involved in dousing the victims' heads with water or barley, others in wreathing the beasts for sacrifice.

The Lokrians in Italy had a parthenos as a phialephoros to lead their processions. Persephone had an important sanctuary outside the city, which according to Diodoros was the most famous temple in Italy, where quantities of phialai have in fact been discovered, indicating their importance as items for dedication. Anaxandrides and Poseidippos each wrote a comedy, the *Lokrian Women* (Lokrides) which perhaps concerned the Lokrian maidens; Anaxandrides' *Phialephoros*, however, need not relate to the girl phialephoros at Italian Lokris, but may concern a girl with this cultic role at Athens.[57]

The Erechtheion parthenoi

Six statues of maidens, with something on their heads but with their hands now missing, held up the porch of the Erechtheion on the Athenian acropolis, built after the completion of the Parthenon in 438 BC, probably *c.* 420–415, with four figures in a line at the front and one behind each corner figure. In the inscribed building accounts of the period, they are referred to simply as korai (and never as caryatids). The ones now on the acropolis are copies, but Figure 2.8 shows five of the six original korai still in place; the sixth on the right hand rear of the porch is only just visible in this photograph. The 'blackened' caryatid is an even earlier copy of the one removed to the British Museum (Figure 2.9); the other five originals were also removed, in the 1970s, to the Acropolis Museum, Athens, and copies put in their place.[58] They clearly carry something on their heads: elaborate baskets.[59] Their hair is carefully arranged, braided and wrapped around the top of the head, then styled to fall in two main parts down the neck, and tied at the base of the neck to form a single wide plait.[60] The peplos carved in many folds which each is wearing goes down to their feet. Although their hands are now lost, the way in which the drapery is carved at the back in radiating lines clearly indicates that each kore held her peplos in her left hand; this was also a typical pose for archaic korai. Their faces are those of young girls, and as far as can be seen, the korai all differ in facial looks, the arrangement of the folds of their clothing, and their hairstyles, though their demeanours are alike, with a steady and serious gaze. The breasts of each of the korai are well defined, and visible through the opaque material clinging to them. These are mature parthenoi, in their last cultic activity prior to marriage. They move in a line, the first two advance their left leg, the second two their right. As one walks past the porch it is not difficult to imagine the figures – despite being copies – to be walking in procession. On them are clearly visible features, such as the so-called 'Venus-rings' around the neck.[61] The young virgins holding up the Erechtheion porch belong to the same age-group and class as the ones on the Parthenon frieze, and they too are engaging in religious activity.

The two caryatid korai from the Forum of Augustus in Rome have baskets on their heads, and are also clearly based on the Erechtheion prototype. While their hands are badly damaged, fragments of the phialai (libation bowls) which

RELIGIOUS ROLES IN ATHENS

Figure 2.8 The marble caryatids of the south porch of the Erechtheion, the acropolis, Athens; 420–415 BC; from an old photograph (courtesy, ©Deutsches Archäologisches Institut, Athens, neg. Acropolis 644).

they held survive.[62] Four caryatids which are obviously copies of the Erechtheion ones lined the Canopus pool at the villa of the Roman emperor Hadrian (reigned AD 117–38) at Tivoli near Rome; the four in a line mirror the four at the front of the porch of the Erechtheion. Two of the korai have phialai in their right hands; the one illustrated here shows how closely they approximate to the Erechtheion korai (Figure 2.10); the other two have damaged hands but presumably would have carried phialai as well. These Roman copies of the Erechtheion korai allow it to be said with confidence that the Erechtheion caryatids also held phialai.[63] Other Roman statues clearly copied the Erechtheion korai, but did not include the phiale, such as the Vatican Kore, which has a basket on its head but an empty right hand.[64] The Florence Kore adds an apparently Roman touch by placing a small lighted torch in the kore's right hand.[65]

Figure 2.9 Caryatid in the form of a young woman (kore) from the porch of the Erechtheion, the acropolis, Athens; 420–415 BC; marble; height: 231 centimetres; it originally stood in the front row of four, the second from the left (courtesy, ©The Trustees of the British Museum, inv. BM 407).

Figure 2.10 Caryatid from Hadrian's Villa (Tivoli, near Rome), which stood with others along the Canopus pool; copied from the caryatids of the Erechtheion, Athens; *c.* AD 125; marble; height: 230 centimetres; (courtesy, ©Deutsches Archäologisches Institut, Rome, Hadrian's Villa no. 2233, neg. 57.1102).

Caryatids at Delphi

The treasury of the Cycladic island of Siphnos at Delphi, constructed *c.* 520 BC, consists of a single room with a porch; the walls of the building form the three sides of the porch, with just one side left open, which is supported by two caryatid figures between the antae (the projecting walls). These two female caryatids, each carrying a cylindrical basket (a kalathos) on her head, are somehow connected with cult, and they might well represent two women who participated in celebrations at Delphi when Siphnos sent delegations to Delphi for the four-yearly Pythian festival, or perhaps when the state consulted the oracle.[66] One can imagine the young women boarding ship, taking their baskets with them, and arriving in Delphi to participate in solemn religious occasions. The earlier sixth-century BC Knidian treasury also had caryatids, presumably affixed to the building in the same architectural manner. There is a cylindrical basket (kalathos) on the head of one of the pieces of the caryatids which survives, and presumably these Knidian caryatids represented a similar type of young maiden to the Siphnian, performing a comparable cult role.[67] Under the Sacred Way (Delphi), a bronze statuette of a young woman holding up an incense-burner is further testimony to the role of women as incense-burner carriers.[68]

Perirrhanteria

From the Heraion (temple of Hera) at Samos in the third quarter of the seventh century BC comes the oldest of the Greek perirrhanteria, water basins, which were placed outside temples in sanctuaries and used in purification ceremonies. The interest of these perirrhanteria, of which the two main examples are from Samos and Isthmia, but fragments of which survive from Rhodes, Sparta, Olympia, the sanctuary of Apollo at Ptoion in Boeotia, Delphi, Athens and Selinounte (Sicily), lies in the water bowl being frequently supported by figures of females, similar to the caryatids just discussed. In the Samian example, three figures of the deity 'Potnia Theron', the Mistress of the Animals, supported the bowl, now missing. Each holds the tail or leash of a crouching lion in her hand (Figure 2.11).[69]

The perirrhanterion from Isthmia which stood before the temple of Poseidon there is similar; three young female figures (korai) support a water basin; the remains of tails and leashes held by the korai, as well as of two lions' heads, indicate that it is of the Potnia Theron variety.[70] The most intricate of all the perirrhanteria, the Isthmian example, dates to the same period as the construction of the archaic temple of Poseidon on the Isthmus of Corinth, and so was presumably dedicated as part of this building process. Some other perirrhanteria with women also included lions, but not the later ones. Most of the perirrhanteria date to 660–580 BC, but they are more popular and better executed in the earlier part of this period. The lions were presumably left out as their exotic appeal faded; initially they were clearly influenced by Neo-Hittite sculptural forms in Syria and Near Eastern patterns in general. Samos clearly acted as a conduit, through Cyprus, of Syrian and Egyptian influences on Greek art. But by the classical period, Greek perirrhanteria were much simpler, usually without caryatid figures.

The Potnia Theron of the Greek perirrhanteria was presumably Artemis, and placed outside Hera's temple on Samos or Poseidon's temple at Isthmia she

Figure 2.11 Samian temple water basin (perirrhanterion); three women (probably goddesses) holding lions by their leashes and tails; grey–white marble; 650–625 BC; preserved height: 52 centimetres; dimensions of base: 35 centimetres by 37 centimetres; the water basin itself which the female figures supported is no longer preserved (courtesy, ©Antikensammlung, Staatliche Museen zu Berlin, Preussischer Kulturbesitz, inv. 1747).

acted as a tutelary (protective) deity. Presumably these korai (which are clearly divine) carrying a water bowl inspired the human caryatid figures which, unlike those of the perirrhanteria, were not divine figures. The caryatids at Delphi or those of the Erechtheion of the classical period, and so later in date than the Samian and Isthmian perirrhanteria, may have copied the idea of korai supporting a burden, but with the divine element left out; the divine korai protecting the temple are diminished in stature and become mere mortal girls carrying water. But the question remains: to what extent were the korai of the perirrhanteria goddesses, and to what extent were they making a transition to the human female caryatids at Delphi and Athens which carry baskets on their heads? For the lion-restraining korai of the perirrhanteria are also water-bearers, with the water bowl on their heads, and they could well represent, not just the goddess, but the hydrophoroi, the virgin girls who carried water and who were essential participants in many Greek sacrifices.[71] Similarly, the thymiateria (incense-burners) which have stands in the shape of women point to the role which women had as incense-burner carriers.[72]

The role of girls in ritual is also made clear by the small hollow terracotta moulded statuettes of the second half of the sixth century BC from the Greek city of Paestum (ancient Poseidonia) in Italy, in the shape of adolescent women; these are described as 'balsam-containers' (perfume vessels). Fourth-century BC terracotta pieces from Paestum consist of an adolescent woman's bust and head with lily petals emerging from their heads; one of the surviving examples has traces of burning within the petals, suggesting that these are thymiateria; the so-called 'balsam-containers' might need to be interpreted in the same light.[73] A water jug from the Kerameikos, Athens, has women supporting its lip: clearly a reference to the role of women as water carriers (though probably not cultic in this case but referring to their domestic roles).[74]

At the Athenian Dipolieia festival, at which the Bouphonia rite took place, parthenoi served as hydrophoroi, bringing the water for the whetstone to sharpen the axe and sacrificial knife (machaira);[75] water could also be sprinkled around the altar to purify it, and to wash the participants' hands.[76] The water used at sacrifices was called the chernips, and the basket and the chernips could be mentioned together as the main paraphernalia of the sacrifice.[77] When Orestes is to be sacrificed, the woman priest refers to herself as the sacrificer – though she will not do the actual killing herself – and says that she will sprinkle his hair with the chernips.[78] There were thirty maidens (korai) at Athens who were responsible for carrying water to the Lykeion,[79] a gymnasion adjacent to the shrine of Apollo Lykeios. In a unique representation on a grave-stele from Athens, a young woman is shown with her left hand raised in a gesture of adoration, and in her right hand she carries a small hydria; a fillet binds her hair. It has been plausibly suggested that she is a hydrophoros. She has presumably been depicted in this role as it was the most important in her life.[80]

A fifth-century BC statuette of a young woman from Syracuse shows her holding a hydria in her right hand, and her raised left hand appears to have held some sort of offering. She is valuable evidence that cult activity in the Greek cities of Sicily was much the same as in Greece, with an important role for young women. Similar statues with damaged hands were presumably of the same nature.[81]

Carved kistaphoroi, young women with kistai (chests) on their heads, in a similar fashion to the Erechtheion caryatids, were part of the Eleusinian Lesser Propylon (monumental gateway) of the sanctuary at Eleusis, Attica. Here, two marble kistaphoroi bore kistai, which represent the kistai which were taken from Eleusis to Athens, and returned in the great Eleusinian procession in the month Boedromion (on the nineteenth), and which contained the secret items displayed to the mystai by the hierophant during the initiation ceremony.[82] The propylaia and caryatids were constructed in the second half of the first century BC, but reflect the ritual, and perhaps the architecture, of the classical period.

A woman with a cylindrical kiste on her head is shown on the calendar frieze from the church Hagios Eleutherios, Athens, for the month Pyanopsion: she therefore must represent a woman participating in a festival in this month, and the women-only fertility rite of the Thesmophoria is the most likely candidate. Her kiste may well have contained secret items connected with the Thesmophoria, as is usually suggested.[83]

In his *Hymn to Demeter*, Callimachus describes a festival procession in which married women (gynaikes) liknophoroi, bear likna in a procession to Demeter's temple. Likna (singular: liknon) were baskets in the shapes of scoops, used for measuring grain. Here, they are full of gold to be presented to the goddess, in the hope that in return the worshippers would receive gold (i.e. prosperity) in plenty.

Naturally, these various representations of young women in cult roles, whether they be pictures on vases, terracotta statuettes, the virgins of stone on the acropolis or the caryatid figures of Delphi, are clearly crafted with some purpose in mind. The societies which produced these artistic versions of their virgin daughters carrying out religious roles valued the activities of the girls as participants in procession and sacrifice. Most of these representations in fact are not authored by single families but by the community, desiring to stress that its purest members were employed in the worship of the gods. Both the individual families and the community as a whole valued the role which these adolescents fulfilled.

The arrephoroi and weaving Athena's peplos

> What god, then, is to protect our city?
> For whom will we weave the peplos?[84]

The two arrephoroi,[85] shown with the woman priest of Athena Polias on the east frieze of the Parthenon, were chosen to commence the weaving for the peplos of Athena's ancient statue. The chorus of women in Aristophanes' *Lysistrata* mention that being an arrephoros was their first religious duty, at the age of seven.[86]

Lexicographers state that the girls were between seven and eleven, wore white, that any gold they wore became consecrated, that they commenced the weaving, that there were four arrephoroi of whom two worked on the peplos and had a part in a nocturnal rite, and that they set the warp in the loom for

Athena's peplos during the Chalkeia festival in the month Pyanopsion.[87] The extra pair of arrephoroi might well have been 'in reserve', for clearly whoever performed the nocturnal rite had to have undergone this period of preparation on the acropolis first. This was some nine months before the Panathenaia itself, when the peplos would be presented. The Chalkeia was primarily Athena's festival, as Athene Ergane was the patron of works and workers in this festival of bronze (chalkos). But Hephaistos, god of metallurgy, also played a role in the festival.[88] The arrephoroi were chosen by the basileus archon.[89] A relief from the acropolis which has a female figure (not necessarily a young girl) who looks upwards and appears to adjust something, with a pole on the right, could well be a depiction of the setting up of the loom for Athena's peplos.[90] In the classical period, the expenses of the arrephoria were not apparently met by the parents, but rather this was a liturgy, a compulsory financial activity organised by the state; a speaker in a lawsuit boasts of many liturgies, including amongst them the arrephoria.[91] The girls lived on the acropolis for their period of service, not far from the temple of Athena Polias, and here they had a playground which they used for ball-games; after all, they were just little girls.[92] The place where they lived has been identified as a large, substantial square building with a single room and porch west of the temple of Athena Polias.[93]

Several statue bases and capitals dedicated for arrephoroi have been found on the acropolis. None of these belong to the classical period; four belong to the third century BC, the others to later.[94] At Athens, the parthenoi involved in one Panathenaic procession in the first century BC were honoured: the fathers of the parthenoi who had 'worked the wool' for Athena, taken part in the procession, and who dedicated a silver phiale of 100 drachmas to Athena brought this to the attention of the boule, and at the fathers' request the parthenoi were honoured by a public decree. Each girl is named, and listed according to her tribe. This decree, long after the classical period, does not reflect classical practice. The arrephoroi, of course, were girls not women, but in the classical period even girls were not named, like the kanephoroi. This particular dedication reinforces the anonymity of so many women in archaic and classical religion.[95]

The weaving itself was not completed by the arrephoroi but by others. For the classical period the number is unknown, but the honorary decree just mentioned and one other of the first century BC honour the parthenoi who worked on the peplos;[96] one decree preserves fifty-six names from at least five tribes, and one preserves thirty-five names from four tribes, so that these numbers could easily be doubled to give the number of parthenoi involved in weaving any one peplos. They do the hard work of the weaving, which the arrephoroi do not, who were, after all, only seven or so. It was appropriate that virgins weave the peplos for the virgin goddess. The second decree was to be erected next to the temple of Athena Polias. A lexicographer refers to ergastinai as the weavers of the peplos, and presumably they are to be identified with the parthenoi honoured in these inscriptions, even though they are not specifically referred to as ergastinai.[97]

RELIGIOUS ROLES IN ATHENS

But this commencement of the weaving was not the main ritual duty of the arrephoroi. Pausanias writes that when it was time for the festival, and by this he means the arrephoria rather than the Panathenaia,[98] the arrephoroi performed nocturnal rites. They carried on their heads what the woman priest of Athena gave them; the items were so secret (and so extremely sacred) that neither the woman priest nor the girls knew what they were;[99] their destination, via a natural subterranean passageway, was a place 'not far away' from the sanctuary of Aphrodite in the Gardens in the city. Pausanias mentioned a sanctuary of Aphrodite in the Gardens when dealing with the Ilissos area.[100] For many scholars the chasm the girls descended is the cleft in the rock on the north slope of the acropolis which opens into the so-called 'cave of Aglauros', not far from which is an area identified as a sanctuary of Aphrodite and Eros.[101] But Pausanias, who is describing the temple of Athena Polias and refers to a chasm 'in the city', cannot possibly mean the north slope of the acropolis. It is important to note that the arrephoroi began their descent into the earth only when they arrived at the chasm; there is no need to invent a tortuous route down the acropolis via the steep stairway that had originally led to the Mycenaean well and out through the so-called 'cave of Aglauros' and down the north slope of the acropolis to the Eros and Aphrodite sanctuary. In fact, the actual sanctuary of Aglauros, the Aglaurion, has now been identified as on the other side of the acropolis slope, and a nocturnal route down the steps to the well and out through the cave to the sanctuary of Eros and Aphrodite can be safely jettisoned: the girls descended not here, but elsewhere.[102]

The myth concerning the two prototype arrephoroi Aglauros and Herse reminded the little girls of what happened to those who looked at what was entrusted to them. Athena is said to have been approached by the god Hephaistos who desired her. She rebuffed him, but he ejaculated on her thigh; she wiped off the semen with wool which she threw to the earth, from which Erichthonios was born. Athena gave Aglauros and Herse, King Kekrops' daughters, the infant Erichthonios in a chest or basket into which they were not to look, but they did so and saw him and the snakes guarding him; horrified, they threw themselves – to their deaths – off the acropolis. Erichthonios grew up, became king of Athens, and instituted the Panathenaia.[103]

Erichthonios is shown on a red-figure stamnos being handed to Athena from out of the ground by a female figure, presumably the goddess Ge – Earth. A male figure, usually identified as Hephaistos, stands on the other side, while winged Erotes (Eros figures) flank the scene. Athena has draped her aegis over her front, and uses it as a swaddling garment with which she will wrap the naked (precocious) child, who reaches out for her. The fact that the male appears to have one leg longer than the other would be an indication of his lameness and support his identification as Hephaistos. His presence at the 'birth' of Erichthonios might appear incongruous, but no more than that of the winged Erotes.[104] It is possible that the chasm which the arrephoroi descended could be the very chasm from which Erichthonios was said to have emerged. Among the secret items which they carried could be Athena's aegis in which he was swaddled, and perhaps even the wool itself. A scholiast on Lucian writes of the *Arretophoria* (sic) in connection with the Thesmophoria, and writes that the secret things the girls carried were images of snakes and phalloi made of dough.[105] This does not fit in with our impression of the arrephoroi, concerned with weaving and imitating Erichthonios' carers, nor their virginity, and is obviously a confusion with the fertility worship undertaken at the Thesmophoria.

The rite of the arrephoria was not initiatory in any sense; certainly the girls are too young for a rite of sexual passage. But they do represent girls chosen from the well-born, and so they were the 'best' which the community had to offer as substitutes for the girls who disobeyed Athena at the cost of their lives.

Other duties for girls at Athens and elsewhere

Young girls also appear as tray-bearers, to be interpreted in a sacrificial context. A bronze statuette of about 450 BC now in the Boston Museum shows a girl in a full-length Doric chiton, which leaves her arms exposed; her neckline has a patterned border. Some traces of gilding remain on the statuette. Her hair is shoulder length but neatly arranged, with a circular hair tie above the forehead. She is carrying a tray, on which there are cakes and fruits which she will present to a deity; she appears to be probably the same age as the kanephoroi, post-pubic but not yet married. This is presumably a dedication made either by a girl who was a tray-bearer, or by someone on her behalf (Figure 2.12).[106]

The Boston statuette can be compared with the third-century BC larger-than-life marble statue of a girl with an offering tray with some of the necessities for a sacrifice, the so-called 'Girl from Antium' or 'Anzio Girl' (Figure 2.13). She is sometimes considered to be a copy of a statue no longer itself surviving called the *Epithyousa* ('Woman making a sacrifice') by Phanis, one of the pupils of Lysippos, as mentioned by Pliny.[107] The young girl (note the very immature breasts, and that the tunic although tied up in two places and actually bundled up under the second tie nevertheless trails behind her and so is too big for her) looks intently at a tray, on which there is a slightly unrolled length of cloth for a fillet to tie onto the sacrificial beast, and a small branch of laurel, as well as what appears to be a small incense-burner. She is completely absorbed in her task; although her right hand is lost, the position of its stump suggests that she was touching or handling something on the tray. The unusual arrangement of the hair is not of a particular style, but indicates that it has been untidily pushed into a bun at the front of the head to keep it out of the way while she performs her tasks.

Amongst the duties of the women of the chorus of the *Lysistrata* when they were girls was that of being an aletris (plural: aletrides) when they were ten years old. The fifth-century AD lexicographer Hesychios explains the duty as being an honour, commenting that the aletrides ground the corn for the cakes used at sacrifices; the scholiast explains that they were 'well-born', and that they had sacred molones ('mills' or 'querns') for this purpose.[108]

Figure 2.12 Girl with offering tray of cakes and fruit; bronze, now green patina; 450 BC; height: 13 centimetres; said to have been found at Corinth (Henry Lillie Pierce Fund, courtesy, Museum of Fine Arts, Boston: inv. 98.668. Reproduced with permission. ©1999 Museum of Fine Arts, Boston. All rights reserved).

Elsewhere, nine parthenoi – agretai – were chosen each year on the Aegean island of Kos to 'care for Athena', presumably involving service in her temple and care for her statue and vestments.[109] There were also agretai in the cult of Apollo: Kos sent an embassy (theoria) and choruses of agretai and boys to Delos.[110] On Rhodes, at Kamiros, the anthestrides (flower-girls) sacrificed a lamb to Artemis in the month Dalios; lexicographers describe them as girls before marriage.[111] The sacrifice to Artemis will have been particularly

Figure 2.13 The 'Anzio Girl': a young woman and her tray with sacrificial items; marble; found at Anzio, in southern Italy, early Roman imperial, probably a copy of a Greek bronze original of the first half of the third century BC; height: 170 centimetres; marble (courtesy, ©Rome, Museo Nazionale Romano, inv. 596).

appropriate for these girls on the verge of such an important transition. One aspect of the Persephone myth that is often overlooked is that Hades produced a field of flowers as part of his plan to abduct Persephone. While she was gathering the flowers, Hades came up out of a chasm and carried her off. Pollux records an Anthesphoria ('flower-bearing') festival of Kore amongst the Sicilians. If the festival followed aetiology, parthenoi will have played a role, for according to Euripides Persephone was abducted from amongst 'the circular choruses of parthenoi'.[112] Hera at Argos had anthesphoroi, 'flower bearers', who were presumably girls.[113]

In the basket of the kanephoros there was, along with the grain and sacrificial knife, the fillet (stemma; plural: stemmata).[114] This ribbon-like piece of cloth, or knotted cord, was used by young women to adorn the sacrificial beast at the altar prior to its sacrifice. Several Athenian vases show young women placing a fillet or wreath with fillets around the sacrificial beast, in several cases bulls. The best example involves a scene on one side of a vase, in which two young women, back to back, each place tasselled fillets (stemmata) over the horns of two cows, one of which obligingly bends its head to receive its fillet. Behind each beast there stands a large tripod. Both women wear crowns in their hair, and their peploi hang down to their bare feet; they are obviously young women, prior to marriage. This tranquil scene indicating the role of parthenoi in sacrificial ritual belies the death of the beasts that will have taken place within minutes (Figure 2.14).[115]

Similarly, on a vase from Italy and attesting to practice there or simply deriving from Athenian motifs, a Nike (Victory) places a wreath onto a bull from which a knotted fillet hangs, with a priest waiting with the sacrificial knife poised above the bull's head; behind the priest a young woman holds an oinochoe and a basket with two sprigs.[116] On a red-figure lekythos a youth alongside a lively bovine attempts to place a red fillet on its head; he is succeeding but the result is untidy.[117] Presumably it is only when women are excluded from a sacrifice that a boy rather than a maiden would perform this task, unless it is rather a case that when the animal was rowdy, a male would undertake this role. The women 'Victories' (Nikai) shown restraining a bull from the temple of Athena Nike on the Athenian acropolis also attest to this role.[118] A winged Nike pours water into a bronze cauldron for a bull to drink while a young woman approaches from behind the beast with a ribbon; the bull already has a tasselled cord around its neck; here watering the beast before sacrifice is added to the duties of young women, if the Nike represents a young woman.[119]

The two Lokrian maidens sent to Ilion

> At any rate the people of Ilion despite so much time having passed and all their preparations are still unable to prevent the Lokrian maidens entering their city, despite their great efforts and precautions. But a few men, making sure that they are not seen, have gone undetected each year for many years in bringing in the maidens.

Aeneias the Tactician of the fourth century BC is the first source for a practice which involved the Lokrians of mainland Greece sending two maidens (Lokrides, or parthenoi, depending on the source) to Ilion (Troy); despite the attempts of the Ilians to prevent this, he writes, a few men escaping detection

Figure 2.14 Two young women wreathing bulls before the animals are sacrificed; red-figure Athenian amphora; 450–425 BC; Nausicaa Painter; overall height of vase: 44.5 centimetres (courtesy, ©The Trustees of the British Museum, inv. E284).

bring the maidens to the city *ana etea*. The precise meaning of this expression is unclear: it could mean every year, or once in a period of years.[120] But Strabo[121] writes that the parthenoi had been sent every year and this would accord with Aeneias' statement that a few men succeed in getting the girls, two at a time, into the city. Other sources state that if the maidens were caught outside the temenos (sanctuary), they would be killed (this is why the men sneaked them in), with stabbing or stoning amongst the methods for this.[122] But Aeneias notes that the maidens were always brought in successfully, and clearly no deaths occurred: like the pursuit of the maenads at the Agrionia, the pursuit was only a pretence.[123]

Aias, the son of Oileus of Lokris, had – in some versions of the myth – raped Kassandra in the temple of Athena at Ilion after dragging her from the Palladion (the archaic statue of Athena) to which she was clinging. Aias had died at sea; nevertheless, Athena struck Lokris with a plague and Delphi instructed the Lokrians to send Athena two maidens to Ilion to propitiate the goddess.[124] Of course, Strabo noted that Troy was completely destroyed in the Trojan War (no matter what the current inhabitants thought), and that the practice of sending the maidens began when Persia held sway in Asia Minor.[125] The first oracle requiring the dispatch, arising out of a plague in Lokris, would then have been sixth century BC in origin, but with tradition giving it a much more antique origin.

Entries in the Suida, which are gathered together as a fragment of Aelian, give a version that the practice ceased at some stage but that when Lokrian women gave birth to cripples and monsters, the oracle at Delphi commanded that it be resumed. The Lokrians consulted King Antigonos as to which city should send the two girls; he told them to use the lot to decide.[126] Antigonos Gonatas in the early third century BC may well be meant here.[127]

The so-called Lokrian maidens' inscription of the third century BC concerns this practice, but there are some difficulties of interpretation. It is an agreement between the city of Naryka, located in western Lokris, and the Lokrians as a whole; it is apparently separate from Antigonos' decree, and in fact his provision that the girls be chosen by lot is apparently overturned by the undertaking of the city of Naryka, in return for various privileges, to provide the two Lokrian maidens to be sent to Troy. The inscription refers to Naryka taking over the responsibility for sending two maidens each year. In return, the city receives various privileges, of a political and legal nature. The parents of the girls are to receive tropheia (sustenance money), and the two maidens themselves are to receive fifteen mnai for their clothing and sustenance (line 10). Girls who had served in the past are mentioned, perhaps with respect to seeing that justice is done to them (the sense is uncertain); girls who have returned from service in Ilion might be retrospectively compensated as well.[128] The reference to past girls indicates their return at the end of their year's service. The inscription cannot be dated precisely, but 270–230 BC has been suggested on the basis of the lettering.

The difficulty is sorting out poetic fiction from what actually occurred. Aeneias and Strabo indicate an annual tenure of office. Lykophron in his early second-century BC *Alexandra*, however, has an account with the maidens selected by lot and staying in Ilion until death, when a replacement would be sent for the one who had died. They are denied proper burial, being cremated with 'uncultivated wood', and their ashes are cast into the sea.[129] This poetic licence is also reflected in lines by another author quoted by Plutarch, to the effect that the girls were treated like slaves, with no cloak and going barefoot, sweeping and purifying the shrine until they were very old.[130] But an annual service is indicated by Aeneias, Strabo, Aelian and the scholiast on the

Alexandra; and the girls' return is vouched for by the inscription from Naryka. The strange story that, in order to avoid the girls being killed, the Lokrians started sending 1-year-olds with their nurses is bizarre simply on the grounds of the one-year tenure; moreover, like other girls dedicated to a goddess, they would have had specific ritual duties to perform.[131]

Some sources say that the obligation lasted 1,000 years, dating it from the third year after the end of the Trojan War, and that the Lokrians ceased sending the maidens after the Phokian War in the fourth century BC.[132] The service was later resumed. There was therefore a period of a 'lapse', as scholars call it, and poetic details might easily have grown up in this period. One of the notices in the Suida has two of the girls growing old in Troy because the Lokrians had failed to send their replacements, and Lykophron's details about the girls serving until death and then their ashes being cast into the sea could both be an embellishment on this. The Lokrians almost certainly would have brought these last two girls home when the first period of service ended, but later what would have appeared as a logical consequence of the lapse – that the last two were left behind – allowed for some licence.[133]

To sum up, a rationalisation of the various accounts suggests that around the sixth century BC, perhaps because of an oracle, the Lokrians sent two virgin girls every year to Ilion to serve the goddess Athena, and the Ilians in a ritual act attempted to deny them entry. Sometime, possibly in the late fourth century, the practice lapsed, but was soon recommenced; Antigonos adjudicated and instituted the lot, and shortly afterwards Naryka took up the responsibility in return for various privileges. Polybios in the middle of the second century BC apparently writes of it as a past practice, while Strabo in the first century BC definitely consigns it to the past.

The metopes from the temple of Hera at Sele, Italy

Five metopes from the temple of Hera at Sele, a few miles north of Paestum in southern Italy, each show two young women in profile, one superimposed on the other. These pairs of women have been interpreted as either a pair of young dancers from a chorus, or as Nereids fleeing. Each girl in a pair dances (or runs) towards her left, with her left hand stretched out in front of her, and the one in front holds the hem of her chiton in her right hand. Their hair is shoulder length, bound at the top, and they wear short-sleeved but many-folded garments which reach almost to their ankles, with a mantle over a dress arranged so that the dress over the left breast, with its different pattern, can be seen; in one example, the right leg is exposed, helping to convey the idea of rapid movement. Five metopes each with a pair of dancers makes up a chorus of ten, as in the chorus of Alkman's longest surviving partheneion;[134] so the interpretation that they are fleeing Nereids – of whom there were according to Greek mythology at least fifty and sometimes one hundred – is unlikely. A similar pair appears on a metope from the sanctuary of Demeter Malophoros at

Selinounte in Sicily. A damaged terracotta piece from Reggio also shows a pair of dancers and may also be a temple metope.[135]

The Proitides – daughters (parthenoi) of Proitos sent mad by Hera for boasting in her temple (surely the Heraion in Argos is intended) of their father's power – were cured by Artemis, and so they established a temple, sacrifice and choruses of women in her honour. Maddened, the daughters had run through the countryside and the mountains; one version of the myth has them disfigured by a wasting disease. Boasting of the power of their father in Hera's temple represents a rejection by the parthenoi of the power of Hera, goddess of marriage. This rejection leads to their wildness in the wild countryside – the parthenoi the opposite of tamed domesticity. Artemis, the principal conduit of the transition from maidenhood to marriage, saves them, and married women in Argos sing in choruses in honour of Artemis as a consequence.[136] Hera herself was worshipped at the Argive Heraion by Argive parthenoi at a sacrifice.[137] These choruses celebrated the transition from the relatively free and untamed state of girlhood to the domesticity of the married woman.

In all periods and places, girls and women are found dancing in honour of the gods. An archaic relief (c. 540 BC) from Branchidai in Asia Minor shows several women in a line dancing, and vases of similar date (550–540 BC) from Clazomenai show several women holding hands in a dance.[138] Parthenoi danced at the pannychis – all-night celebration – before the Panathenaia, making ritual cries (ololygmata).[139] The interior circle of an Athenian white-ground phiale is decorated with seven young women holding hands by the wrists around the central sunken knob. They appear to be moving slowly in a stately dance; another young woman plays the double aulos in front of a burning altar.[140] The sculptor Kallimachos in the classical period carved a relief which does not survive of dancing Spartan women, and imperial reliefs could derive from his work. Such reliefs show topless girls dancing; on their heads they have a kalathiskos hat (a small basket widening at the top), after which they were named. The kalathiskos dancers performed at the Karneia (celebrated throughout the Doric world but particularly important to the Spartans). Their skirts whirl around them.[141] Girls and women certainly danced as part of the marriage ritual, as did young men. On a lebes gamikos, a bride leads fifteen women, perhaps all young virgins, in a dance. A black-figure lekythos with a detailed wedding scene has three groups of three dancing women, and two seated musicians, and must be associated with the wedding dance.[142]

On the island of Samothrace, from a gateway (propylon) to the sanctuary comes a frieze of young maidens dancing. Dating to c. 340 BC, the frieze survives in many fragments, and its main details are clear, with several surviving sections of groups of young women dancing in lines. Each dancer is about 25 centimetres high. Reconstructed, the frieze extends to a length of 36 metres, possibly wielding a total of 200 or so maiden dancers. The dancers, on tiptoes, and wearing polos crowns (a headdress, as worn by the goddess Cybele in Figure 5.6), appear in profile. Although they appear in a single line, it is clear that they in fact form two separate single lines, with half of the dancers moving to the right and half to the left, converging on a single point. On the best-known fragment, the maidens are arranged in facing pairs, each dancer holding the right-hand wrist of the dancer in front of her, forming a continuous line. The dancers wear a short-sleeved chiton of Ionic style, over which they wear a mantle. Every second dancer, the ones turning backwards to face their immediate dancing companion, wears a shawl-like (or scarf-like) garment draped over the shoulders and billowing out at the elbows. Their hair is carefully arranged under the polos. What is clear is that care has been exercised in carving the women to show the stateliness and grandeur of their clothing. Three women musicians, possibly cult personnel, each playing the kithara (harp), aulos (flute) and tympanum (drum), are interspersed amongst the dancers, and presumably in the lost portions of the frieze there were other musicians.

These young women could be interpreted generically as Muses or Samothracian nymphs. But the best interpretation is that they are maidens dancing in honour of the deities worshipped in the annual Samothracian Mysteries. The polos is an attribute of a goddess, and here the maiden dancers are assimilated with the goddess worshipped in the Samothracian Mysteries, perhaps Demeter or a Cybele-like goddess. The maidens will have danced at some stage in the performance of the Mysteries, which attracted initiates (mystai) from all over the Greek world. The dancing must have been a spectacular part of the rites. Dressed in their ritual garb and performing in front of the hundreds of mystai who converged annually on the island, dancing on their tiptoes in the swirling lines must have been the high point of the religious life of the Samothracian maidens involved.[143] On the whole, the artistic evidence from archaic and classical Greece seems to show a predilection for young women before marriage dancing in honour of the gods, a role obviously considered to be particularly appropriate for them, and one which it was important to depict them fulfilling.

Seven boys and seven girls

Seven boys and seven girls chosen from aristocratic Corinthian families spent a year in the temple of Hera Akraia at Corinth (that is, at Perachora); during this time, they wore black clothes in mourning, and cut their hair, dedicating it to Medea's children. The lament sung for the dead children may have been part of the fourteen children's duties. Their service came to an end at the festival of the Akraia, when a black goat was sacrificed with a knife which had been buried in the precinct and which the goat itself dug up. The children went home to be replaced by another fourteen; the sacrificial knife would be reburied for the next performance of the rite. The aetiology involved the murder of Medea's children: they had been killed with this very knife at the altar in this sanctuary, and were buried, like the knife, in the sanctuary where their tombs could be seen; with their murder, newborn Corinthian infants were killed by the spirits of Medea's children, until an oracle (probably from Delphi) gave the ritual advice about establishing these rites.

Dead children received sacrifices elsewhere, particularly at the Nemean and the Isthmian festivals,[144] and the Akraia rite was clearly an act of atonement. This was not an initiation rite: the limited number (fourteen) of children and the mixed sexes involved mitigate against this interpretation;[145] the girls and boys propitiate the children of Medea killed at the altar.[146] It is the affinity in age which countenances the propitiatory role of the children.

The seven-and-seven combination is most familiar from the Athenian tribute of seven boys and seven girls to the Minotaur, which ended when Theseus slew the beast. He had formed the fourteen into a chorus at Knossos and praised the gods; on his way back to Athens, he stopped off at Delos, and there they danced before the statue of Aphrodite which Ariadne had given to Theseus and which he now set up on this island. The Delians kept up the tradition and annually wreathed the statue, and danced the 'Crane Dance': the girls beat the ground with their feet while the boys sang.[147] The annual theoria from Athens to Delos commemorating the safe return of the fourteen presumably consisted of a chorus of fourteen youths and maidens, although there is no direct evidence for this.[148]

Swinging girls

A curious rite is represented on some Athenian choes vases (jugs). A girl is shown in several scenes on a swing, pushed by a man or even a satyr.[149] In one example, an adolescent girl swings above a pithos set in the ground, with a woman pushing her.[150] The vase does not show what the swing is suspended from. One scene is more elaborate. A little boy on the far left stands behind a woman who is pouring something from a jug onto a small fire under the swing, possibly in order to perfume the clothes (perfuming clothes is an attested Greek practice). Several garments have already been placed on the swing; a woman with her right hand hovering over the swing with its clothes stands in front of a chair on which there is a patterned dress similar to the one worn by the woman on the left. The clothes are being fumigated, purified; soon a girl will mount the swing as part of the Aiora rite (Figure 2.15).[151]

The myth behind the rite is clear. Ikarios, killed by those who were drunk with the first taste of wine (and so 'new' wine to them), was sought by his daughter Erigone; when she found his corpse buried under a tree, she hanged herself from it. Struck by a plague, the Athenians consulted Delphi: they were both to hang images and to swing their maidens from trees. The depictions of swinging show an open pithos, wine jar, and Callimachus has a rite, which he otherwise does not describe, at which the Athenian women lamented Erigone during the festival of the Anthesteria; this rite of mourning was presumably the Aiora.[152] The Aiora rite was one of atonement, a 'purificatory' rite in that it purified Athens of the plague and the death of Erigone; the clothes are being

Figure 2.15 Women perfuming clothes for the Choes festival; red-figure Athenian oinochoe; *c.* 420–410 BC; attributed to the Meidias Painter; overall height of vase: 21.4 centimetres (courtesy, ©The Metropolitan Museum of Art, New York, Gift of Samuel G. Ward, 1875, inv. 75.2.11).

purified in the scene above as part of this ritual. Girls approaching puberty were viewed as suicidal, and the Erigone myth has Athenian girls following her hanging example; the Aiora rite was to circumvent this loss of life and ease the transition to puberty and womanhood. As seen in Chapter 1, the Hippocratic Corpus noted this malady amongst parthenoi undergoing puberty: there was a tendency towards suicide as the worst of a number of other problems, such as delirium.[153] The Hippocratic Corpus noted that when parthenoi recovered from this transitional illness the women (gynaikes) made dedications to Artemis; this was one approach to the problem, the other was the Aiora rite, 'swinging' the hanging tendencies out of the girls.

But one example shows a small garlanded boy being placed in a swing by a man; there are two wreaths of vegetation on the swing; the ropes are high, and presumably hang from a tree (not shown). An elaborate garment is hung over a chair, and could well be the priestly robes of the male figure, shown on the vase as dressed only from the waist down (perhaps he is the basileus archon). A large pithos, for wine, is to the left of the swing. But this is the only time a boy on the swing is depicted, and in fact a girl is seen waiting with a youth on the left. She, in fact, seems rather timid and he appears to be comforting her; it is probably she who will be swung (the man has perhaps placed the little boy on the swing to show her that no harm will befall her).[154]

In Sophocles' *Oedipus at Kolonos*, blind Oedipus and his two daughters, Antigone and Ismene, sit down in the shrine of the Eumenides at Kolonos in Attica, where they are told by a passing stranger that it is not holy to tread (36–43). The chorus advises performing a purification, and, as Oedipus cannot, Ismene undertakes the task (466–507). This involves drawing water from a flowing stream, with clean hands, crowning kraters, tops and handles, with a fleece of a newly shorn sheep, and pouring a libation from the kraters; the libation is to be of water and honey, but with no wine added. Ismene is to face the 'first light', and place three times nine twigs of olive wood before uttering the words of a prayer on Oedipus' behalf. After this, she must depart without turning around. If Ismene needs anything, there is a man who lives there who will instruct her. This sounds very much like an actual ritual and a specific cult place. Whether women would ordinarily carry out these rites or whether Ismene only does so because her father cannot is uncertain, but Sophocles does not hint that there is anything unusual here. The scene aptly conveys the beauty of a virgin's religiosity.

The Parthenon was a celebration of the virgin goddess Athena, and the marble adolescent women taking part in her processions on the east frieze and Erechtheion porch offer their virginity to her. It is soon to be lost in marriage, but in the meantime their purity has served the goddess, just as a very few of them will once have served her as arrephoroi. But these girls are aristocrats, and while representing the polis are not representative of it. There are thirty-two young girls on the frieze, including the two arrephoroi and the young girl with the peplos. They are but a small portion of the Athenian girls who every year became young women and were married. Even the names of the elite group of girls serving the goddess go unrecorded until after the classical period.

But nevertheless it is difficult to speak of the young virgins on the east frieze as purely anonymous, precisely because many are faceless in the most literal sense: few of them still have their faces or part thereof (a few of the heads are separate from their bodies in the Acropolis Museum, Athens). Most apparently held their heads erect, some with a slight bent. They could be said to be static, but they are waiting for some reason, possibly to be equipped for the procession. They do not simply stand at order but at ease, with one leg in front of the other, knees bent; hands are loose by the sides or casually holding their jugs and dishes. One holds onto a fold of her peplos. Figure §56 (Figure 2.6) is headless, but the twist of her upper body suggests that she is turning to talk to the one behind her holding the incense-burner (figure §57; Figure 2.7).[155] This is obviously a deliberate touch by the artist. Some have hair which flows down their neck, others have it in a bun; where it is possible to see their heads, they have a ribbon around the middle of their hair. Breasts which are not fully mature are clearly seen in some cases. No two young women, as far as can be determined, are identical, and all are 'individual', if only in a limited sense. There are differences in their dress which might simply be for artistic reasons of variety, or perhaps have a meaning which is lost. Some have their arms covered, others are bare from the shoulder down, some are covered to the elbow. The few surviving faces seem 'expressionless', or it should be said, silent and intent. While it does not seem likely that these are individual portraits of adolescent virgins, they are nevertheless not generic. In this the girls find parallels in male figures §3 and §4 of the north frieze, with their heads inclined, and figure §4 with his neck swathed with his cloak. Every year a similar group would serve the goddess at her procession and festival but, for the parents and many of the spectators, these girls were still individuals and their individual participation had value for those who organised their role in this procession.

These aristocratic young women offer their virginal status to Athena; their pure hands can carry jugs, bowls and incense-bearers for use in the sacrifices to the goddess and the company of gods. Dressed in their finery, they must have been the pride of their families, and they are in a sense at their 'coming out': soon marriage will find them no longer virgins, and never to repeat the public role they played in the procession. Their role in the procession publicly affirmed their virginity, social status and desirability as marriage partners. In fact, despite what might seem to be a variety of roles, the number of girls in Greece who had such religious roles was small. Yet in a very real sense they symbolised all the city's young womanhood. This final public role as carriers of baskets, incense stands and libation jugs and bowls underscored that while the virginity of Athena was permanent, their own was transient, fleeting, ready to be destroyed like Oreithyia's. But this was necessary and crucial: becoming women they would undertake other important roles on behalf of the polis, not just as mothers but as celebrators of vital festivals such as the Thesmophoria. This transition was also underlined by the fact that the only other major sanctuary besides Athena's on the acropolis was that of the virgin goddess Artemis Brauronia, into whose care as mothers these young adolescent women would soon be placed. Athena herself was eternally virgin but ever vigilant in the transition of these girls to womanhood; the Panathenaic festival both celebrates her and the city's parthenoi. Boys, with a relatively simple transition from puberty to manhood, and whose heterosexual purity and virginity were of no value or consequence, do not require or merit the celebration with which the daughters of the polis were fêted.

3

WOMEN PRIESTS

From the temple of Artemis at Ephesos in Asia Minor and dating to about 560 BC comes an ivory statuette of a woman, about 11 centimetres high, originally the handle of a wand; the woman's head is topped by a hawk, and she appears to be a woman rather than a girl. One hand holds a jug, and the other a shallow bowl; both hands rest by her sides. Known as the 'hawk-priestess', she carries items of a ritual nature and is presumably a woman priest of the goddess Artemis at Ephesos. With her fine dress, which has a vertical frieze at the front, disc earrings and spiral clips in her hair which has long and elaborate tresses, she is wearing her ceremonial best for the ritual duties she is no doubt about to perform for the goddess.[1]

Women priests in classical Greece were not just the women's equivalent of male priests; nor were they women who primarily served the religious needs of other women.[2] There were features which set the two – priests and women priests – apart. Girl and women priests tended to serve female deities, and male priests male deities, though the distinction was not always preserved, and the most important cult of Apollo, the male god of prophecy, at Delphi had women priests. However, while women did serve very important goddesses, such as Athena Polias at Athens, arguably the most important cult in that city, men's priesthoods on the whole were more prestigious than women's priesthoods elsewhere in Greece, particularly in Asia Minor where priesthoods were offered for sale: men's priesthoods were generally much more expensive than women's.

Women priests attracted the interest of ancient writers: Aeschylus wrote a play entitled *Women Priests* (*Hiereiai*), Menander a *Woman Priest*, and Hellanikos a book on Argive women priests using his list of them for chronological purposes. Thucydides might be using Hellanikos' text when among a list of chronological indicators for the year of the outbreak of the Peloponnesian War (431 BC), he gives it as the forty-eighth year of the priesthood of Chrysis, woman priest of Hera, at Argos.[3] A woman priest's name and office might occasionally be used as a dating criterion at Athens, such as the woman priest of Artemis Aristoboule in the deme Melite, while the woman Kallisto's priesthood was used by one Sostratos to indicate when he dedicated a marble throne to Nemesis at her temple at Rhamnous in Attica.[4] While many girls at Athens in the capacity of kanephoroi and sacrificial attendants performed public roles, these ceased upon marriage, after which transition women found a public and formal role in state cults only as women priests. Classical Athens in particular was chauvinistic in terms of perceptions about gender, and women priesthoods gave adult women a public role not allowed in other avenues of life.

Greek women priests were generally referred to as hiereiai (sacred women), and a general word amphipolos ('attendant') was also used. But there were more specific titles as well. Each woman priest of Apollo who sat on the tripod at Delphi was known as the Pythia; the women attendants of Dionysos at Athens were the gerarai, venerable ones. Women priests of Artemis were melissonomoi, 'bees', which embodied the principal women's virtues of chastity and hard work, and the term melissa was also used for the prophetic women priests at Delphi. The prophetic women priests at Dodona were peleiai (doves); in addition there were various other individual titles for women priests in particular places.[5]

'Healthy and sound' women priests

The woman who purchased the priesthood of Aphrodite Pandamos on Kos in the third century BC was to be physically healthy and sound of body.[6] As is sometimes the case, the sale of a priesthood was made according to certain stipulations concerning the physical well-being of the person purchasing the priesthood. Just as the offering to a god had to be holokleros, unblemished,[7] so too did the priests and women priests in any cult. Inscriptions prescribe that priests, both women and men, be 'healthy and sound' of body: they were to be free of sickness and without physical deformities. For example, the purchaser of the woman's priesthood in the cult of Dionysos Thyllophoros on Kos was to be both 'healthy and sound' of body.[8]

The comic poet Anaxandrides raised a laugh (presumably) by comparing Greek and Egyptian customs, joking that while it was the custom that Greek priests be whole, Egyptian priests were castrated (which was not the case, and he might be referring to the Egyptian practice of circumcision). Plato in the *Laws* prescribes that priests had to be sound of body and also legitimate, probably a reference to the fact that only citizens could be priests, and bastards (nothoi) as is clear from Kos could not participate in priesthoods. A lexicographical entry claims that at Athens the basileis (the basileus archons; there was one chosen each year and they had important religious duties) and the priests were examined to ascertain whether they were unblemished and sound of body.[9] The physically disabled at Athens were debarred from holding political office, and presumably this also reflected an inability to carry out religious duties.[10] These regulations concern physical 'purity', and it is interesting to note that at Athens a male citizen who had prostituted himself was debarred from holding priesthoods because he was not pure of body,[11] and adulterous Athenian women could not take part in religious rites.[12]

The age of women priests

Several of the women priesthoods mentioned by Pausanias had to be filled by girls before marriage. At Sikyon, only two people could enter the sanctuary of Aphrodite, and everyone else had to stay outside to pray and worship: the two exceptions comprised a woman who was never to sleep with a man again, and so committed herself to a particular lifestyle, and a virgin woman priest serving for a year. The priest of Poseidon on the island of Kalaureia was a virgin and held office until her marriage. This was also the case at the shrine of Artemis Triklaria at Patras, where the priest was a parthenos and also held office until she married. Also at Patras, the festival of Laphria in honour of Artemis involved the parthenos priest riding last in the procession in a cart pulled by deer, Artemis' animals. The priest of Artemis at Aigeira (Arkadia) served the goddess until her marriage, and Athena Alea's priest in the large temple at Tegea served the goddess until the time of puberty.[13] The woman priest of Artemis Hymnia in Arkadia was a woman who 'has had enough sexual intercourse with men'; the priest and woman priest of Artemis Hymnia in Mantineia were, unusually for Greek practice, lifelong virgins.[14] At Phigalia in Arkadia, there was a woman priest of Demeter, assisted by three female 'sacrificers', the youngest of whom – presumably a parthenos – is present with the woman priest at sacrifices.[15] In Temesa in Italy, a parthenos was given each year in 'marriage' to a divine hero, until 476 BC when an Olympic victor challenged him and took the current parthenos for his own.[16]

In inscriptions on Kos specifying the sale of priesthoods, the requirements of health and wholeness are usually accompanied by a specification concerning age, usually a minimum age requirement. Purchasers of priesthoods needed to be over 8, 10, 12, 20 or 40 years of age, depending on the individual cult; two of the ages specified are for a woman priest.[17] The degree to which virgin adolescent women priests were women priests in the full sense, with a range of religious responsibilities, is unknown. Whether they presided over sacrifices and received the sacrificial offerings is not clear. Some degree of adult supervision must surely be assumed for girl and young women priests.

Inscriptions often record that the purchaser of a priesthood was to hold the office for life, which presumably relates to the fact that many of the priesthoods were so expensive, and priesthoods were often paid in instalments. The woman priest of Aphrodite Pandamos on Kos in the third century BC paid for her priesthood in four instalments over two years, and she was 'to be woman priest for life'.[18]

Moreover, there are some individual women priests from Athens who can be named who held office for life. Lysimache was woman priest of Athena Polias at Athens for sixty-four years.[19] Thucydides points out that when the Peloponnesian War broke out in 431 BC, Chrysis had been woman priest of Hera at Argos for forty-eight years, and was woman priest for another eight and a half years after that, ending her priesthood when she put a lighted lamp near the garlands which caught fire; the temple burned down, and she fled. The Argives appointed (how is unknown) another woman priest in her place.[20] Euamera at Athens who made a dedication in the first century BC to Artemis at Athens describes herself as 'woman priest for life' (presumably in Artemis' cult).[21]

The epitaph of Myrrhine, a woman priest of Athena Nike at Athens, in which she proclaims that she was the first woman priest of Athena Nike, is usually dated to c. 405 BC. The inscription establishing the priesthood of Athena Nike is dated to either c. 448 or c. 424/3 BC, depending on the dating adopted for Athenian decrees. She could either be a woman priest serving for about forty or for twenty years. She is of further interest in that she is sometimes identified as the Myrrhine in Aristophanes' *Lysistrata*.[22] Women priests at Athens, once appointed, clearly served until death, and as Myrrhine's epitaph indicates, were very proud of their positions.

Becoming a woman priest

As will be discussed below, the woman priest of Athena Polias came from the Eteoboutadai genos, and the woman priest of Athena Skiras came from the genos of the Salaminioi. In contrast, the woman priest of Athena Nike was chosen from out of 'all' of the Athenian women by lot (though presumably there was some sort of 'short-list'), and the priest and woman priest of the Thracian goddess Bendis were also chosen out of all the Athenians.[23] Here there is a distinction between gentilician priesthoods from aristocratic families and a publicly introduced priesthood in democratic Athens (gentilician or gentile priesthoods, terms used by modern scholars, were ones where the holders of the priesthood were drawn from a specific genos, an aristocratic family, or clan).[24] Elsewhere, that Theano, woman priest of Athena at Troy was 'chosen' by the Trojans to be woman priest reveals little, except that perhaps the community did choose her, presumably through some form of election. At Athens, there is no evidence for sale of priesthoods, but in Asia Minor and the islands this was a typical way of becoming a woman priest. Inherited male priesthoods are known from elsewhere, but not many, and they are outside the classical period.[25] No inherited women's priesthoods are known outside of Athens, but these could well have existed. When men and women's priesthoods were sold, the price for men's priesthoods was typically higher than for women's ones. This indicates the greater importance attached to men's priesthoods in these places and presumably also reflects the way in which society viewed women's priesthoods: important but not as important as the male ones. However, to men for whom status and public appearances were important, particularly as adjuncts to political involvement in their cities, the higher prices need not reflect the greater importance of these priesthoods but greater competition for them: men's priesthoods carried higher status than women's, simply because they were filled by men, and the actual nature of the cult itself need not have been of primary significance.

Cult requirements: virginity, chastity and diet

The Pythia at Delphi could be married, but had her own house and lived away from her husband and so kept free of sexual intercourse while she was serving the god. In this way the woman priest was pure, and the requirement was consistent with her role as the mouthpiece of the god. The aetiological myth for the fact that she had to dress as a virgin was that originally the Pythia had been chosen from amongst virgins but that a rape led the Delphians to choose an older woman, while retaining the same dress.[26] Virginity for women priests was usually a temporary requirement, and young virgin girls appointed as priests ordinarily relinquished their roles when the time for marriage came, emphasising that marriage was the role allocated by society to the adolescent woman. The priest of Herakles Misogynes was meant to be chaste while in office,[27] and Athenian priests had to remain chaste for a prescribed number of days for some duties.[28] Temporary chastity for the male hierophant at the Eleusinian mysteries is attested,[29] a similar requirement as for the Pythia, but clearly the Greeks did not think that the gods required vows of virginity: a fixed period of chastity was sufficient, when and if required, with the majority of priests and women priests not having to observe such requirements.

At Sikyon, only a woman neokoros ('guardian'), who after appointment could not have intercourse with a man, and a virgin who held the post of loutrophoros (bath-bearer) for a year, could enter the sanctuary of Aphrodite. In Achaea, the sanctuary of Ge had a woman priest who had to be chaste after taking up office, and to have slept with only one man before then; the test was to drink bull's blood. This obviously did not deter women seeking office, for if there was more than one candidate for the position lots were cast; the old woman who tended the cult of Sosipolis at Elis lived in chastity.[30] Herakles had a virgin woman priest at Thespiai, who served until death. The rationale for this was the myth that Herakles slept with forty-nine of Thestios' fifty daughters in a single night, but one refused him, so he condemned her to be his virgin woman priest for life. Pausanias does not believe the aetiological myth, and in fact argues that the temple predated Herakles.[31] Whatever the case, this is an unusual example of a parthenos who had to remain ever-virgin: as noted, in most cases virgins relinquished priesthoods at the time of marriage, or women remained chaste for a period of time, or simply were allowed to be married and to rear children while women priests.

The woman priest of Demeter at Eleusis could have children, as too could the woman priest of Aglauros at Athens. The women priests of the Mother of the Gods were married. Artemis, the virgin goddess, had a married woman priest at her main Athenian sanctuary at Brauron, whose daughter had a role in the rituals there. The woman priest of Nemesis at Rhamnous was married with children.[32] This does not indicate whether they might not, like the Delphic women priests, have given up sexual activity while they were women priests; they could easily, in fact, have had these children in office if they were appointed early enough. The gerarai who served at the Athenian Anthesteria swore that they were pure from intercourse with a man, but there are no grounds for assuming that they were aged women. In the *Lysistrata*, the women swear an oath that they will be sexually abstemious, and this could be a parody of the oath which the gerarai had to swear.[33] No celibacy was required of the woman priest of Athena Polias serving this most virgin of goddesses; the statue base for Lysimache, who served the goddess for sixty-four years, mentions that she had four children. Other women priests of Athena Polias at Athens certainly did have children.[34] For Lysimache, the honour of being allowed to erect a statue of herself on the acropolis was considerable. In another instance, a decree praises the husband of a woman priest of Athena Polias and awards him an olive crown.[35] Chairestrate, woman priest of the 'All-bearing Mother' had a granddaughter (see below). In Messenia, if a child of a priest or woman priest died, they had to relinquish their office;[36] the premature death of a child was obviously considered particularly polluting, rendering the parents impure for service to the gods.

In a well-known anecdote, children of Hera's woman priest at Argos are attested. This woman priest had to make her way at the time of the festival from the town to Hera's sanctuary, the Heraion. Herodotos has a charming story that the oxen had not returned from the fields and were not available to draw the cart on which the woman priest travelled to the sanctuary; so her sons took the place of the oxen and pulled the cart 6 miles to the Heraion. Everyone, men and women, congratulated her on having such sons, and she prayed to Hera that they receive the greatest blessing of mortal men. After this prayer, the sacrifice and festival took place: the two sons fell asleep, never to wake, and Hera had answered the mother's prayer. This is clearly a procession and major festival of Hera, perhaps the same as the Heraia festival described by Pindar.[37]

Besides the Pythia's house, houses were provided for the women priests at Eleusis, and the male dadouchos (torch-bearer) and Kerykes (one of the two priestly families with hereditary jurisdiction over the mysteries) also had houses.[38] The house of the woman priest of Demeter may have been for use on such occasions as the Haloa festival and the several nights of the Greater Mysteries. As seen, the hierophant had to observe chastity during the Mysteries, and perhaps the fact that he had a house in the sanctuary is a sign that the woman priest of Demeter had to do so as well. The existence of such houses may be explained by reference to abstinence requirements, or the need to be in proximity to their cult place. The girl arrephoroi lived on the Athenian acropolis, near the temple of Athena Polias, clearly to be near their place of duty.[39] Presumably someone must have supervised these young girls during their stay on the acropolis (but the house may simply have been for daytime use, with the girls going home to their parents at night, except for the occasion of the nocturnal festival). It is sometimes suggested that the woman priest of Athena Polias had a house, with her two assistant women priests, on the acropolis,[40] but there is no specific evidence for this.

Dietary restrictions for members of certain cults are well known.[41] The woman priest of Athena Polias was not allowed to eat cheese made in Attica. Nor was she allowed, according to Athenaeus, to preside over sacrifices of ewes.[42] Some have found the prohibition on ewes difficult to comprehend, as sheep are listed as sacrifices to be made to Athena Polias on the acropolis.[43] In fact, Athenaeus refers to his own time, and makes this clear by referring to a similar ban in the past, when cows could not be sacrificed in Attica, because of a shortage.[44]

Women priests, citizenship and public life

The idea that only citizens were to hold priesthoods associated with the state cults of a city is evident. At Halikarnassos, the woman priest of Artemis Pergaia was to be born from two citizen parents, with citizens on both sides for three generations.[45] Similarly, in 21 BC when the priests of Apollo at Halasarna were listed, they had to be patriastei (having a citizen father) and there is a similar case from Rhodes.[46] A decree in Demosthenes states that the Plataians granted citizenship in 428 BC were, however, to be barred from the nine archonships, and priesthoods and rites belonging to a particular family, but their descendants would be eligible.[47] Aristotle in the *Politics* notes that priests should be drawn from the citizen class.[48]

By virtue of taking part in sacrifices, both public and private, women priests had a public role. But it is unclear how far this public role extended. For example, it was Aristophanes, the son of the woman priest of the heroine Aglauros, who in 247/6 BC reported to the boule (council) 'concerning the sacrifices which she had made', and this is in a period when the classical norms of a woman's seclusion were breaking down. On the other hand, the decree is concerned with praising and honouring her, and perhaps bringing her conduct of her office to the boule's attention was a task best suited to someone other than herself.[49] Similarly, in 287/6 BC a relative reported to the assembly on behalf of the woman priest of Aphrodite Pandemos.[50]

But elsewhere, the woman priest of Demeter at Arkesine in the fourth century BC reported directly to the boule there about public sacrifices at the goddess's shrine, and also complained about women entering the shrine, clearly while she was absent. The point was probably, as in the case of the Thesmophorion at the Piraeus, that the women were sacrificing without the woman priest and she was missing out on her perquisites as a result. In a third-century BC inscription from Mylasa in Asia Minor, 'the women resolved' in a cult of Demeter, and one is immediately reminded of the decision-making of the women at the Athenian Thesmophoria in Aristophanes' *Thesmophoriazousai*.[51]

Greek women priests, unlike the Roman Vestal Virgins, did not escape guardianship, and women priests clearly, like all other Greek women, had kyrioi (guardians). On fourth-century BC Kos, an inscription concerning women priests provided that women who could not be present for the drawing of lots were to send their kyrios along in their place: importance was attached to the physical presence of the women, as the lot indicated the will of the gods about the suitability of the choice of a particular woman for the priestly office.[52]

Keys and cult images

A few grave reliefs from Attica show women with keys.[53] These are probably women priests with keys to temples, indicating that they were entrusted with the key(s) to the temple where they served. This responsibility for the temple, which often had the cult statue and valuable dedications inside, reveals something about the way in which these women priests were viewed. A very good example of an actual temple key is the 40-centimetre-long bronze key of the fifth century BC with an inscription indicating that it belonged to the temple of Artemis in Lousoi (Arkadia), and was thus probably in the custodianship of a woman priest there. It is in the shape of a serpent which has a protrusion under the head, usually described as either a beard or tongue, but more probably simply the locking mechanism. The top of the head is incised with a pattern (Figure 3.1).[54]

Polystrate's fourth-century BC grave-stele (in stone) from Athens shows her carrying a large key; it is in the shape of a long rod, which has two right angles in it to form a lightning-bolt shape; the actual key mechanism can be clearly seen, and Polystrate holds the key just beneath this. She is dressed elaborately in a peplos with himation and styled hair with fillet, and the sheer fact of the gravestone and its elaborate palmette design points to her high status: she is presumably a woman priest, of an indeterminate cult (Figure 3.2).[55] Similarly, Choirine on her fourth-century BC grave-stele is shown holding a key by its short end. As the stele was found at Eleusis, and because her name evokes the Eleusinian piglet – choiros – it has been suggested that she was a woman priest at Eleusis.[56] Another gravestone shows a woman with the key on her shoulder; this stele was found in the temple precinct at Rhamnous, so this woman was probably a woman priest and the key shown is that of the temple.[57]

Chairestrate, a woman priest of the 'All-bearing Mother' at Athens, is shown seated on her chair on her grave-stele. There is a long rod held vertically at an angle in her hand. While the depiction is awkward, this does seem to be a key, and to have a shape like the key of the previous example, from Rhamnous. Chairestrate describes herself as a woman priest, and a young girl – described in the accompanying inscription as her granddaughter – standing in front of her holds a large tympanum. Presumably the key is that of the Great Mother's temple where Chairestrate was woman priest.[58] Gravemarkers of some women have a key below the name of the deceased, doubtless as an indication of priestly office. Three simply give the names of the women without specifying a particular priesthood, with the key below their names.[59] In two other cases, the key has tainiai (ribbons) around it, and in both cases the woman is known to have been a woman priest of Athena.[60] The role of tainiai in funeral rites is clear.[61]

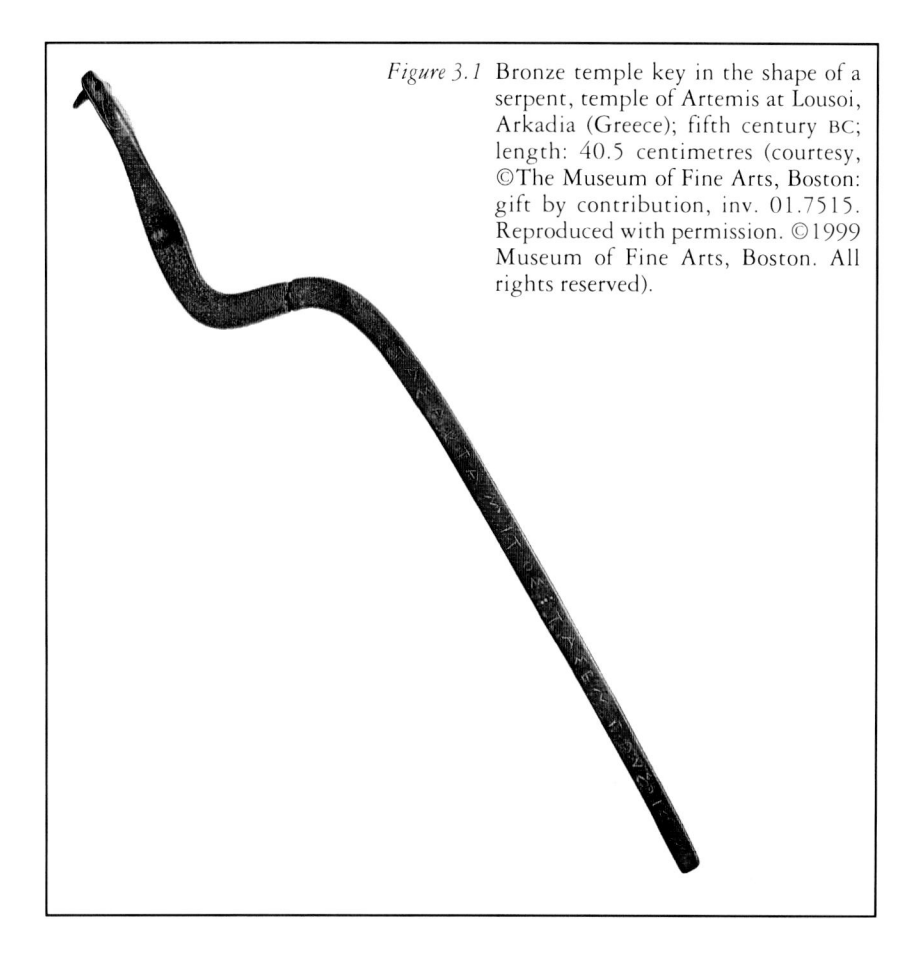

Figure 3.1 Bronze temple key in the shape of a serpent, temple of Artemis at Lousoi, Arkadia (Greece); fifth century BC; length: 40.5 centimetres (courtesy, ©The Museum of Fine Arts, Boston: gift by contribution, inv. 01.7515. Reproduced with permission. ©1999 Museum of Fine Arts, Boston. All rights reserved).

Priests are not shown with keys, not because they did not have custody of them but because showing a woman with a key was a way of indicating her role, whereas for priests the iconography was different; for example, some priests are shown on their grave reliefs holding a sacrificial knife,[62] whereas women priests would not usually carry out the killing at a sacrifice. The chorus in Euripides' *Iphigeneia in Tauris* describe themselves as parthenoi who serve the kleidouchos (key bearer) Iphigeneia, the woman priest of Artemis.[63]

The responsibility of women priests for cult images is apparent from epigraphic evidence. The fifth-century BC grave-stele of Polyxena (her name can just be seen inscribed along the lintel which supports two columns, probably an idealised rendering of a temple), discovered in Boeotia (in central Greece), shows her holding a statuette of a goddess in the palm of her left hand, and she is perhaps a Boeotian woman priest, judging from her clothing and veil; she wears a peplos, which has an overfold with a pointed end at the front, and the

Figure 3.2 Grave-stele of Polystrate, possibly a woman priest, with temple key, Kerameikos cemetery, Athens; c. 380–370 BC; marble; height: 102 centimetres; breadth: 42 centimetres; Kerameikos Museum, Athens, inv. I.430 (courtesy, ©Deutsches Archäologisches Institut, Athens, neg. Ker. 6164).

veil is shown as part of this. Her feet are shod, and the peplos hangs low to the ground. She looks at the statuette of the goddess, with what appears to be a smile (though this part of the face is damaged). Her right hand is held along her side; a hole has clearly been bored through the gap between her thumb and other fingers, presumably for some sort of metal attachment, possibly even a bronze key; if so, this would definitely signify her role as a woman priest (Figure 3.3).[64]

What is relevant is that Polyxena or whoever commissioned her grave-stele thought it important to show her in the role of caring for a cult statue. Whether the statue she may well have cared for was a small one like the one depicted is unknown, but more probably this is an idealised rendering of a large cult statue in a temple. The goddess's identity is irrecoverable; she stands with her left foot

Figure 3.3 Grave-stele of Polyxena, possibly a woman priest, showing her holding a cult statue, Boeotia; marble; *c.* 420 BC; height: 112 centimetres (courtesy, ©Antikensammlung, Staatliche Museen zu Berlin, Preussischer Kulturbesitz, inv. 1504).

forward; her right hand looks as if it might have held something, and seems to be veiled; her peplos is girdled, her veil appears to join with the upper garment (as does Polyxena's), and her arms are bare; the traces of stone above the head suggest that she wore a polos headdress. It would not be surprising that woman priest and goddess were dressed similarly, though the correspondences are not exact. Athena is a very real possibility because of her importance in Boeotia. At the Argive Heraion, before the entrance, Pausanias saw statues of women priests, which seem to have been erected in the lifetime of the incumbent woman priest, for when the temple burnt down during Chrysis' priesthood and she fled to Tegea, the Argives nevertheless did not remove her statue.[65]

The woman priest of Athena Polias at Athens

There were several women priests at Athens, and a complete survey of all the evidence is not possible here. They had lifelong tenures, and most of them reflect the rituals of pre-democratic Athens: women priests were drawn from specific gene (singular: genos), the ancient aristocratic groups which could loosely be described as clans. The woman priest of Athena Nike is the major exception to these woman priesthoods of Athena, being chosen in a democratic fashion.

The woman priest of Athena Polias (Athena of the City) was arguably the most important priest of either gender in archaic and classical Athens. It is difficult to ascertain whether any priest was more important than her, and it is she who, time and time again, is shown presiding over sacrifices at Athens. Of course, she owes her importance to the fact that the tutelary deity of Athens was a goddess. Presiding over Athena's sacrifices, this woman priest's official point of duty could have been the Erechtheion, the 'old temple', on the acropolis, where the archaic cult statue of Athena Polias which the Praxiergidai genos cared for was housed, or later the altars which must have stood outside the Parthenon.[66] The responsibility for Pheidias' statue of Athena Parthenos is unclear; this statue-goddess in fact appears to have had no separate woman priest, or washing and dressing rituals.

Athena Polias' woman priest was drawn from the Eteoboutadai genos, which also provided the priest of Poseidon Erechtheus; she held this priesthood, Athena's most prestigious, for life.[67] She had two assistant women priests, the Kosmo and Trapezophoros (sometimes referred to as Trapezo), who 'manage everything' for her, and these might well have been drawn from the junior women or girls of the genos.[68] The name trapezophoros implies something to do with a trapeza, 'dining table' or perhaps altar, probably in the context of a sacrifice. One woman priest of Athena Polias is praised for her care over the trapeza, indicating its importance.[69] In a dedicatory inscription, Syeris in the third century BC describes herself as the diakonos, 'servant' or deaconness, of Lysimache in the temple, who set up a statue of Syeris, surely not a classical practice; Lysimache can be identified as a woman priest of Athena Polias (a different Lysimache from the one discussed above), and Syeris' patronymic and demotic appear to be given in the inscription, so she is a citizen woman, as would be expected.[70]

The woman priest had to perform preliminary sacrificial rites whenever burnt offerings were made at Athena's altar, which implies that her presence was required whenever a sacrifice was made to Athena Polias on the acropolis.[71] What share she received of any sacrifices is nowhere made clear. According to the *Oikonomika* attributed to Aristotle, Peisistratos in the sixth century BC prescribed that she receive one choinix (roughly a quart, or 2 litres) of barley, one of wheat, and an obol for each citizen who died (presumably from his family), and similarly from a father when a child was born. Whether this information is reliable, and whether it reflected a classical practice, is unknown. Being a woman priest chosen from a genos, it is very unlikely that she received a salary from the state, whereas the woman priest of Athena Nike, a priesthood newly instituted in the second half of the fifth century BC, and appointed from amongst the citizen women, received an annual payment of 50 drachmas and perquisites (of legs and hides) from the sacrifices. In a fragment of a religious calendar, often associated with Nikomachos' revision of the law-code at the end of the fifth century BC, the woman priest of Athena Polias is to receive a certain amount of money for apometra, but what this means precisely is unclear, and possibly it is expenses for conducting sacrifices.[72]

Other women priests, like their male counterparts, received perquisites. At Athens, the women priests of the Heroines, of Dionysos Anthios, Hera, Demeter Chloe, and other women priests for deities whose names are missing from the relevant inscription, all received hides, meat, wheat, honey, oil and firewood from the sacrifices at which they officiated, with the quantities specified.[73] Naturally this was their reward for attendance at these sacrifices, as they were not in any other sense 'paid' for their work. When men's and women's priesthoods were sold, particularly in Asia Minor, the relevant decrees spell out what the priests and women priests were entitled to. In addition to perquisites arising from sacrifices, there might be other revenues. For example, the woman priest of Aphrodite Pandamos on Kos in the third century BC was paid, according to custom, the fines levied on the merchants and sea-captains who did not sacrifice to the goddess when setting out on their journeys, clearly compensating her for lost perquisites. This woman priest also, once a year, received half the proceeds of the goddess's treasury. A fourth-century BC inscription from Miletos concerning the woman priest of Artemis provides for fines for those not giving the woman priest her lawful share of the sacrifice. But any possible greed on the part of a woman priest was held in check on fourth-century BC Kos: the woman priest of Demeter was to charge only the fees allowed by law.[74]

The woman priest of Athena Polias had charge of the arrephoroi, as noted in Chapter 2. She was involved in the procession of the Skira festival on the twelfth day of the month Skirophorion, from Athens to Skira, in company with the priest of Poseidon. An obscure allusion in a speech states that this woman priest was required by decrees to affix her sign to the registers.[75] Perhaps this is connected with the provision mentioned by Aeschines whereby priests and women priests were subject to an audit (euthyna), both individually and collectively, and not only individuals were accountable, but the entire priestly clan such as the Eumolpidai, Kerykes and 'all the others'.[76] And this was despite the fact, Aeschines states, that they received perquisites only (payments in kind, rather than money), and had to pray to the gods on behalf of the city. The euthyna, presumably annual as for state officials, will have been an accounting of their cult-related actions, and while Athena's monies were not handled by the woman priest but by the goddess's treasurers, nevertheless she presumably had access to where dedications were stored, and would need to give an account of any dedications she received or handled on behalf of Athena Polias.

In fact, she had responsibility for certain items, and at least in one year handed over some items to the treasurers.[77] In one list of offerings to the goddess, there is the enigmatic phrase, 'the woman priest said', and then the stone breaks off; perhaps she said something about a dedication or dedications, and what is interesting is that her comment was recorded. This could be one of the few occasions, such as when the woman priest refused to curse Alkibiades, when a woman's voice comes down to us (but not quite in this case) directly from the classical period.[78] Similar procedures may have applied to all other Athenian women priests. For example, the woman priest of Artemis Brauronia, despite the fact that the cult had male officials (epistatai), came into contact with dedications and handed items over to the epistatai; it is possible that she had the initial responsibility when dedications were made at the sanctuary.[79] No one was to make dedications in the Thesmophorion at the Piraeus, nor sacrifices or purifications, nor to come together as thiasoi (groups meeting to worship), or go to the altar or megaron (innermost room of the shrine), without the presence of the woman priest, but at the festivals of the Thesmophoria, Plerosia, Kalamaia, Skira and on other days the women were to gather there, according to ancestral practice.[80]

In the archaic and classical periods, individual women priests at Athens are little known. The name is not known of the woman priest of Athena who in 508 BC told Kleomenes, one of the two kings of Sparta, who had come to install Isagoras as leader of an oligarchy, and attempted to gain entry to the temple on the acropolis, that Dorians were not permitted, which led to his laconic quip, 'I am not Dorieus, but an Achaean', referring to his half-brother (Dorieus) who had felt that he rather than Kleomenes should be king. In 480 BC, when Themistokles had persuaded the Athenians to abandon their city and to trust in the wooden walls of the ships in the face of the Persian invasion, the woman priest of the time reported that the snake which guarded the acropolis and received a honey-cake to eat each month, which was always consumed, had left it on this occasion untouched, with the consequence that the Athenians thought that the goddess Athena herself had abandoned the acropolis, and so were more eager to leave the city. To what extent she, or someone else, was collaborating with Themistokles (or whether this was a coincidence) is unclear.

Lysimache, as noted above, served for sixty-four years, and was honoured by the state with a statue. Her exceptionally long service to the state explains this.[81] A woman priest whose name is missing (another Lysimache?), the daughter of Lysistratos of the deme Bate, has a statue base found on the acropolis, dedicated by the son of a Polyeuktos.[82] In the hellenistic period, such honours became more frequent. A woman priest of Athena Polias, whose name is also missing in the relevant decree but who was the daughter of a different Polyeuktos of the deme Bate, was honoured.[83] Similarly, Penteteris, daughter of Hierokles of Phlya, was similarly honoured, in the first half of the second century BC.[84]

Known or possible women priests of Athena Polias are listed by Lewis and Aleshire.[85] How the priesthood was transmitted is uncertain. But there is no evidence that it was transmitted directly through the female line, and it is more than likely that when a woman priest died, the eldest surviving daughter of the eldest surviving male relative inherited the priesthood.[86] Lykourgos mentioned the Plynteria in his speech, 'Concerning the Woman Priest', which almost certainly concerned the woman priest of Athena Polias, and it would not be surprising if she had some role in this rite (the Plynteria) concerning the statue of Athena Polias. This speech might perhaps have been concerned, according to a suggestion by Davies, with the succession to the priesthood.[87] That the priests for the priesthoods of the Eumolpidai, Kerykes and Eteoboutadai were chosen by lot is asserted by a lexicographer on the authority of [Aristotle's] *Athenaion Politeia*; this would mean that the woman priest of Athena Polias was chosen from amongst the Eteoboutadai by lot. There is not enough evidence to accept or reject this. Aleshire suggests that if there were enough candidates equally eligible for a priesthood, sortition may have been used to determine the successor.[88] It is also possible that a lawsuit would have been used to determine who should succeed.

While priests were honoured in classical Athens, usually with laurel but sometimes with gold crowns (worth 500 or 1,000 drachmas), the only case when a priest or woman priest holding office because of membership of a genos (i.e. a gentile or gentilician priesthood) was honoured by the state was the long-serving Lysimache, the woman priest of Athena Polias. The erection of a statue in Lysimache's honour on the acropolis, near the temple of Athena, must have been with the permission of the state and presupposes an honorary decree for her.[89] The lack, otherwise, of honours for gentile priesthoods could be explained by a democratic reluctance to praise individuals holding priesthoods by virtue of coming from ancient aristocratic families. When priests were honoured, it was for some extra service to the state, and gentile priesthoods might not have afforded the same potential for coming to the attention of the demos through benefactions. The priest of Poseidon Erechtheus had a reserved seat in the theatre of Dionysos (the privilege of proedria), and just as other women priests and a kanephoros also had this right, so did the woman priest of Athena Polias.[90]

In the third century AD the arrival of the sacred objects (hiera) and their military escort from Eleusis in Athens (where they were housed at the Eleusinion) on the thirteenth of the month Boedromion was announced to the woman priest of Athena Polias. How long this arrangement had been in place is unknown, though the reference 'according to ancestral practice' could indicate that this was also the case in the classical period. Athena had nothing to do with the Mysteries, but she was the goddess of Athens, and the arrival of the hiera of the Eleusinian goddesses Demeter and Persephone-Kore in her city and the announcement of this to her woman priest was one way in which the Athenians integrated the Eleusinian cult into the Athenian festival calendar.[91]

Leaving aside the literary and epigraphic sources, vase paintings frequently indicate the woman priest carrying out what must have been her main duty, presiding over sacrifices. A woman stands near the goddess Athena in scenes of sacrifice, and is obviously her priest. Sometimes the woman wears flowing robes, but sometimes a blouse with short but wide sleeves and a long tight skirt. Presumably this woman, despite the martial appearance of the statue which conjures up the epithet 'promachos', is the woman priest of Athena Polias, and the goddess Athena Polias (at any rate, Athena Promachos did not have a separate woman priest).

On one sixth-century BC Athenian black-figure vase, a woman priest has three sprigs or branches of vegetation in each hand; holding one hand up in adoration, she is in front of an altar behind which stands Athena, with a patterned dress, poised spear and crested helmet (Figure 3.4). The goddess's rigid and formal poise suggests that this is a cult statue, standing behind the altar, the courses of which are shown, but on which the sacrificial fire has yet to be lit. The woman priest wears a decorated dress (belted at the waist) extending down to her bare feet; the dress has a double border at the bottom, and she is

Figure 3.4 A woman priest, before Athena, leading a sacrificial procession; Athenian black-figure vase; c. 540 BC (courtesy, ©Antikensammlung, Staatliche Museen zu Berlin, Preussischer Kulturbesitz, inv. 1686).

clearly wearing her best clothes; her upper garment has wide stripes with some florets. The woman priest is followed by a bearded older man, and then by two young men with the sacrificial beast; on the reverse of the vase, not shown here, the men are followed by two flautists (auletai) and two harp (kithara) players, playing their instruments and rounding off the procession which the woman priest has led to the altar.[92]

The woman priest of Athena Skiras

This woman priest was important because of her role in the state festival of the Oschophoria (in the month Pyanopsion), which involved a procession from the city to the shrine of Athena Skiras, at the old harbour of Phaleron. Bunches of grapes still attached to vines were borne in this procession by two young men – oschophoroi – who are described as being dressed as women; they probably wore the male Ionian garments which were traditional when the festival was inaugurated, and which appeared 'feminine' to much later generations. These youths were drawn from the Salaminioi genos, like the woman priest of Athena Skiras herself (and a single woman priest of the three deities Pandrosos, Aglauros and Kourotrophos). The Oschophoria commemorated Theseus' return from Crete, when he himself on his return on 7 or 8 Pyanopsion, with two youths, led a procession to the nearest shrine at Phaleron – that of Athena Skiras.[93] After the woman priest of Athena Polias, she was probably Athens' most important woman priest. On the sixth day of the month Mounychion, the Athenians sent their daughters (korai) to the Delphinion to supplicate Apollo, according to Plutarch, just as Theseus in setting out with the victims for the Minotaur had made his way to the Delphinion. This seems a false aetiology, as one would expect both girls and boys.[94]

The settlement by arbitration of a dispute between the two branches of the Salaminioi (i.e. the Salaminioi of the Heptaphylai and the Salaminioi in Sounion) is known from an inscription of 363/2 BC (which was to be set up in the temple of Athena Skiras); a second dispute in the third century BC was also arbitrated.[95] Various provisions were made concerning such things as the filling of priesthoods, property and distribution of the meat of sacrifices, indicating that these items had been matters for arbitration.

The priesthoods of Athena Skiras (she is mentioned first), Herakles at Porthmos, Eurysakes, and 'Aglauros and Pandrosos and Kourotrophos', were to be common to both branches, and when a priest or woman priest died, a successor was to be chosen by lot from both groups combined. The other woman priest of note here is that of Aglauros, Pandrosos and Kourotrophos mentioned in the Salaminioi decree: she is to be appointed by lot from both branches of the Salaminioi.[96] The women priests' shares of sacrifices is also dealt with. Each group in turn selected by lot an archon to appoint the oschophoroi ('vine-branch bearers') and deipnophoroi ('dinner-bearers'), in consultation with the woman priest and the herald, as was customary.[97]

The women priests of Athena Skiras took part in the procession and joined in the sacrifices of the Oschophoria: according to legend, the mothers of the seven boys and seven girls chosen to go to the Minotaur brought bread and meat for their children while they were shut in the shrine of Athena waiting to leave (these mothers were the archetypal deipnophoroi), and the mothers told tales (mythoi) to comfort the children. For this reason myths were told at the Oschophoria.[98]

There were several women priests at Athens, notably those of Athena Polias, Athena Skiras, Athena Nike, and probably Artemis Brauronia, on the acropolis. The Hekatompedon inscription (*c.* 485/4 BC) refers to 'women priests and zakoroi (attendants)', and provided a heavy fine of 100 drachmas if they did either of two forbidden things; if the treasurers permitted them to do these things they would be fined the same amount. Interpreting what these two things were is difficult because of the vocabulary of the inscription. One of these things was perhaps 'not to make a storeroom on the acropolis', which might be a prohibition against setting up a temporary booth that would detract from the sacredness of the acropolis. The second is more difficult: the women priests and zakoroi are not on the acropolis hipne[uesthai]. Jordan has discussed the possible meanings of this. Of these the most interesting prohibition and the least likely to be true is the one enjoining them not to have sexual intercourse on the acropolis; the etymology does not support this, though intercourse and birth were not allowed on the acropolis. A prohibition against fires is possible, but as fires were lit on the acropolis for the many sacrifices that took place there, Jordan suggests that a prohibition against profane fire and the preparation and consumption of non-sacrificial food is intended; or perhaps the injunction is that the women priests were not to sleep on the acropolis. Whatever the precise nature of the prohibition, the fine is severe, both for the woman priest and the treasurers who permit her to do wrong (100 drachmas in both cases).[99]

The zakoroi are associated with the woman priest, but mentioned after her, and so clearly in an inferior position to her. But how inferior is unclear. The position of zakoros could be important, and a former woman priest of the Great Mother was appointed as zakoros for life in that cult in the second century BC.[100] Lexicographers define zakoros as equivalent to neokoros, temple guardian, but as having responsibility for keeping the shrine clean and sweeping it, which as Jordan says might simply be a false etymology based on koreo, to sweep. But they also mention a responsibility for 'the fire', presumably the sacrificial one, citing Menander's *Leukadia*, and one lexicographer describes it as a 'holier' position than that of neokoros.[101] The word could also be used in a less technical sense, as the hetaira Phryne was described as a zakoros and hypophetis (attendant and expounder) of Aphrodite – simply because she had such a magnificent body.[102]

Eleusinian women priests

Other women priests at Athens are less well known, but the women priests at Eleusis were obviously important.[103] It is interesting to note that while this purely Eleusinian cult attained a panhellenic character under Athenian patronage after the incorporation of Eleusis into Attica, the most important official of this cult of Demeter and Kore–Persephone was of course the male hierophant, rather than a woman priest. The chief woman priest was the woman priest of Demeter; there were also other women priests of Demeter and Kore, about whom little is known.

The cult officials of the Eleusinian mysteries were entitled to receive 'fees' from each of the initiates, mystai. The important inscription concerning the mysteries which dates to c. 460 BC indicates that the woman priest of Demeter was to receive 1 obol from each mystes (initiate) at both the Lesser and Greater Mysteries; the previous entry has the hieropoioi (sacred officials) receiving a half-obol each day, and this 'per day' requirement may have applied to the women priests as well. The priest of the altar, the phaidyntes ('washer'), and another priest received a sum, lost from the inscription. The Eumolpidai and the Kerykes (the gene responsible for organising the Mysteries) received 5 obols and 3 obols from each man and woman initiate respectively. All of the money paid to the goddess was to go to 'the goddess' except for a total of 1,600 drachmas, presumably to be used for expenses.[104] In the law-code of Nikomachos, the woman priest of Demeter is to receive apometra (probably expenses for sacrifice) of 100 drachmas annually.[105] The priests and women priests of Eleusis who received proceeds from the sale of grain 'according to ancestral practice' from the harvest of the Rarian field must include this woman priest.[106]

The office of Demeter's woman priest was at least occasionally filled by women who were aware of their status, position and prerogatives. One hierophant conducted a sacrifice to Dionysos at the Haloa festival but as this was the prerogative of the woman priest he was found guilty of impiety. It is probable that the woman priest had a hand in the case.[107] But a case in which an actual woman priest initiated the prosecution of a hierophant in the late fourth century BC did take place: attributed to Deinarchos, the title of the speech is preserved, 'Diadikasia (Lawsuit) of the woman priest of Demeter against the hierophant'. What the speech was about is unknown. But the fact that two hierophants somehow interfered with the woman priest's prerogatives (one imagines that the Deinarchos lawsuit was a dispute along these lines) could indicate some difficulty in differentiation of duties, and perhaps hierophants had a tendency to intrude into the sphere of influence of the woman priest.[108] Similarly, another woman priest of Athena Polias called Lysimache is recorded by Plutarch as having an exchange with the muleteers who had brought the sacred vessels to her; they asked for a drink (i.e. from the sacred vessels), but she hesitated, 'lest this became customary'. She was clearly concerned that ritual practice not be changed in any way.[109]

Athenian women priests, like priests, prayed for the good of the city.[110] When Alkibiades was condemned to death in his absence for his involvement in the profanation of the Eleusinian Mysteries in 415 BC, and had his property confiscated, it was decreed that he be cursed by all the priests and woman priests. It was a woman priest of Demeter, Theano, daughter of Menon of the deme Agryle, who alone of all the priests refused to curse him, declaring that she was a praying rather than a cursing priest.[111] There do not seem to have been any repercussions for her, but to stand out in this way against the state is remarkable.

The main duty of the various other minor women priests of Demeter and Kore might have involved the carrying of the kistai in the procession from Athens to Eleusis on 15 Boedromion. An inscription refers to 'the women priests' carrying the kistai across the Rheitoi streams, over which a bridge had been built so that they could carry them across 'most safely', but does not specify which women priests.[112] The woman priest of Demeter might have been one of these. In addition, women cult officials known as hierophantides, one hierophantis for Demeter and one for Kore, are known from the third century BC on.[113] Along with the hierophant, in 352/1 BC the woman priest of Demeter was to make a sacrifice at the time of the dispute concerning the charge that the neighbouring Megarians were cultivating sacred land belonging to Eleusis.[114] It has been suggested that she impersonated Demeter at the Eleusinian Mysteries, if indeed there was a sacred drama as part of the ceremonies.[115]

The two gene, the Kerykes and Eumolpidai, provided most of the sacred officials for the Eleusinian Mysteries (Kerykes: dadouchos; Eumolpidai: hierophant, exegetai ('expounders'), phaidyntes (washer)), but Photios has this woman priest of Demeter chosen from the Philleidai genos; as with other gentile priesthoods, tenure was for life.[116] Several women priests who held this office are known.[117] Lysistrate, describing herself as the 'servant (propolos) of the unspoken rite' of Deo and her daughter, made a dedication.[118] A woman priest of Demeter and Kore in the second century BC repaired the shrines of the Eleusinion and was given the privilege of setting up her portrait on a tablet in the temple of Demeter and Kore as other women priests had, but whether this privilege extended back from the second to the fifth and fourth centuries BC is open to very real doubt, though Lysimache's statue on the acropolis could perhaps dispel any scepticism about this.[119]

The 'child of the hearth'

No child was initiated into the Eleusinian Mysteries,[120] except for the 'child of the hearth', who propitiated the goddess on behalf of all the initiates. He or she was selected by lot each year for the Greater Mysteries, and the expenses associated with his or her initiation – for the sources speak of myesis (initiation) – were met by the state. Several statues or parts thereof of boys, some of them with a pig, found at Eleusis have been interpreted as these hearth initiates. No individual hearth initiates are known from the classical period, and records of names, of both boys and girls, first appear in the second century BC. These known individuals all came from prominent families, and 'none is known not to have been a child of a member' of the Eumolpidai or Kerykes gene.[121]

However, in the fourth-century BC inscription giving regulations for the Eleusinian Mysteries,[122] anyone who wishes could submit a name of a child to be the 'child of the hearth'; after the classical period – with its emphasis on democracy in as many things as possible, including religion – had ended, this practice ceased. Whether girls were permitted in the classical period, as they were clearly in the second century BC and beyond, to serve as the child of the hearth is not made clear.[123]

Which hearth is meant is unclear, and the hearth of the prytaneion at Athens has been suggested: the child propitiated the Eleusinian goddesses on behalf of the city. But surely this hearth should be at Eleusis, and the one which springs to mind is the hearth in which Demophoon was laid each night in the coals of the fire by Demeter; he grew quickly and was like the gods. His mother saw this one night, and shrieked for the safety of her child; the goddess was angered, took the child from the fire and threw him from herself. It is in fact because of her anger over *this* incident that the goddess commanded the Eleusinians to build her a temple, in return for which the goddess taught them rites to appease her. Metaneira had deprived her child of immortality, now he cannot escape death.[124]

The woman priest of Artemis Brauronia

The woman priest of Artemis Brauronia[125] is of interest because of the ceremonies for pre-pubescent girls over which she must have been the main presider. There was a sanctuary of Artemis Brauronia at Brauron where these rites occurred, but also one on the Athenian acropolis, possibly a sixth-century BC foundation of the tyrant Peisistratos, who came from the region near Brauron.[126] The relationship between the Athenian and Brauronian shrines is unclear, as is whether they shared a woman priest. In myth, Artemis' first woman priest was Iphigeneia, 'strong in birth', and presumably this was originally a cult title of the goddess; Iphigeneia may have been a goddess perhaps local only to Brauron, or Attica in general.

Two of the fourth-century BC inventories of dedications to Artemis Brauronia from the acropolis mention a woman priest, who had jurisdiction, along with the epistatai (superintendents), over the dedications to Artemis Brauronia.[127] Hierokles, the son of the woman priest of Artemis Brauronia, was brought before the ekklesia (assembly) in the fourth century on a charge of hierosylia – temple robbery – because he had been seen carrying clothes, marked in gold letters with the names of dedicators. Hierokles defended himself, saying that he had been sent by his mother to take the clothes to the shrine. Aristogeiton proposed that Hierokles be put to death without a trial, but Hierokles' father indicted the decree as an unconstitutional proposal and Aristogeiton was fined 5 talents by the demos; Aristogeiton had also made unspecified accusations against the woman priest of Artemis Brauronia.[128] The father and son are named but the mother, typical of classical Athenian practice, is not. The father of a woman priest of Artemis Brauronia is mentioned as having urged on someone who was beating a man up (so badly that he died; the woman priest's father was exiled for his part in this), and in another case the daughter of another woman priest was involved in a transgression involving the theft of dedications.[129] In addition, a fragment of an inscription attributed to an inventory of items dedicated to the goddess has a reference to women priests, but the context is too uncertain to attribute more than one woman priest to this cult.[130]

Other duties presumably included presiding at the penteteric (four-yearly) festival of the Brauronia in the month Mounichion, which must have somehow involved women invoking Artemis, and also the procession from the Athenian shrine to the one at Brauron, as part of this penteteric festival, perhaps involving the young girls who would serve as arktoi – bears – in that particular year (the rite itself, known as the arkteia, was, however, annual).[131]

The attendants of the Semnai Theai

> I Athena will send you [the Eumenides] by the light of flaring torches to your home below the earth, escorted by attendants who guard my image as is proper. For the eye of the whole land of Theseus shall come forth, a glorious company of girls and wives, and a throng of elderly women. Honour them [the Eumenides] with purple-dyed garments and let the flare of the torch come forth so that the well-disposed band of Eumenides may make its presence felt for the future through circumstances prosperous to men.[132]

Women priests were chosen from the Hesychidai genos at Athens – the land of Theseus – to pour wineless libations over offerings of honey cakes to the Semnai Theai, the 'revered goddesses'. The women priests appear to have been known as the Hesychides or Leiteirai. There was an annual procession to their shrine (see below), involving male cult officials (the hieropoioi), and at least in the third century BC the ephebes (a corps of 18- to 20-year-olds involved in military training) were involved in the cult.[133] The Semnai Theai are included with Zeus Olympios, Athena Polias, Demeter and Kore, and the 'Twelve Gods' in a decree of alliance with the Arkadians, Achaeans, Eleans and Phleiasians in 362/1 BC; the company the Semnai Theai keep in this decree illustrates the importance of these goddesses to the state.[134]

The Semnai Theai are the Eumenides, or Furies, also the Anonymous Goddesses, those without names, a collective group of deities with no individual personalities; Euripides[135] mentions them in conjunction with the Fates with whom they must have been associated. The Eumenides are best known from their pursuit of Orestes (who had killed his mother Klytaimnestra for murdering her husband and his father, Agamemnon) to Athens in Aeschylus' *Eumenides*, in which play they are granted a state cult at Athena's command. The torch-lit procession at the end of Aeschylus' *Eumenides* and described in the passage quoted above is part of the ritual associated with this cult. Athena commands that the Eumenides be escorted with torches to their place beneath the earth, clearly some sort of subterranean shrine, with girls, wives and a throng (stolos) of old women, all dressed in purple, the colour of the underworld, as their prospoloi (attendants). The chorus of the procession at the very end of the play in fact sings to the Eumenides, probably reflecting a hymn sung by the girls and women during the nocturnal procession. Clearly a very important rite and a crucial role for the girls and women of fifth-century BC Athens is being hinted at here, to propitiate the Eumenides for the prosperity of the state.

These Eumenides are also the Nameless Goddesses of Euripides' *Melanippe*.[136] It is this role of women, along with women's prophetic roles at Delphi and Dodona, which Euripides argues indicates that women were important in Greek religion. But as little is known of the cult of the Semnai Theai, despite the procession, its importance cannot be assessed, unless Euripides' comment – and Aeschylus' role for women in the procession – hints at a much more elaborate celebration and a ritual significance for the women that cannot be otherwise vouched for.

The women priests of Bendis and of Cybele

Introduced in the late fifth century BC, Socrates himself saw the festival of the Thracian goddess Bendis with its torchlight race on horseback at the Piraeus.[137] Various details concerning the introduction of the cult are dealt with by an inscription, which mentions a woman priest and possibly a provision (similar to that for the woman priest of Athena Nike) to select her from all the Athenian women.[138] Nothing definite is known of the women priests of the shrines of the Great Mother (Cybele) in Athens (the Metroon, Agrai at the Ilissos river, and in the Piraeus at Moschato).[139] The tombstone of Chairestrate, the august and dignified servant of the 'all-bearing mother', shows her holding the key to one of the Great Mother's three known shrines in Athens.[140]

Begging women priests and begging women

At Athens a woman priest of Athena set out from the acropolis with the aegis (in this case made of woollen fillets),[141] begging at shrines and from new brides.[142] It is the woman priest of Athena Polias who will have had possession of the aegis. Robertson argues that as it was from this begging practice that the proverb 'aegis around the city' was used to describe 'those who go around helter-skelter', the latter can only be described in this way if the woman priest *shook* the aegis as she went, whereas the traditional interpretation is that she wore the aegis during her begging.[143] As she went begging from the acropolis to the shrines, new brides presumably would have given money to her in the hope that Athena would grant them children. The only other collections at Athens seem to have been for the 'oriental' cults: collections in the second century BC are attested in inscriptions concerned with the cult of the Great Mother, and collections were apparently also made for Bendis.[144]

There are several examples of begging women priests from ancient Greece, and their main role seems to have been to solicit money in return for women's fertility. While ritual begging is sometimes described as non-Greek and outside the world of the polis,[145] and in fact is so in the case of the collections in the cults of the non-Athenian Bendis and the Great Mother–Cybele at Athens, the begging woman priest of Argos was well-known to Aeschylus, Herodotos mentions ritual begging as a widespread phenomenon, and the woman priest of Athena begged at Athens, so that 'begging' for women's fertility was a normal part of traditional Greek religion.

In a fragment of Aeschylus' *Xantriai* ('The Women Carding Wool'), Hera appears disguised as a begging woman priest of the Inachid nymphs (they are the daughters of the river Inachos in Argos). The nymphs are referred to as 'life-giving', and the fragment makes it clear that they are associated with marriage and birth: there is (probably) a reference to marriage songs, but also to the bridal bed and to the labour of childbirth. The woman priest would presumably beg from the newly-wed who had reason to fear childbirth; Robertson sees wool-carding as the particular preserve of young women, who will have been the woman priest's particular concern.[146] Presumably the presence of a begging woman priest in an Athenian tragedy reflects not simply a myth but cultic reality, and therefore this particular priestly begging was not only well known but explicable within the Athenian context.

Herodotos reports that the women of Delos 'beg' for the heroised virgins Arge and Opis, and the other islanders and Ionians also begged for them, learning this practice from the Delian women;[147] a woman priest is not mentioned. To beg for heroised virgins was to seek their aid in assisting virgins to make a successful transition to motherhood. A begging rite on Kos in the cult of Demeter has long been known, but recently published inscriptions from Kos provide more evidence for collections in other cults on this island. The cult of Demeter at Antimacheia, Kos,[148] concerns rites to be conducted for the betrothed and the married. There was a collection (agermos) involved in this cult, and so it seems that ritual begging was carried out on behalf of these two categories of women, probably for the benefit of child-bearing.[149] Another inscription indicates that in the cult of Aphrodite Pandamos, which was a cult the state had charge of, there were revenues deriving from 'collections', and sacrifices are to be paid for from these;[150] and collections are similarly mentioned in two other inscriptions from Kos.[151] In one of these, the woman priest is to beg each year on the first day of the month Artamitios, in the same manner as prescribed for the cult of Artemis Pergaia on Kos;[152] unfortunately the division of the proceeds is not dealt with. The begging of the woman priest of the cult of Artemis Pergaia at Halikarnassos was regulated by a state decree which restricted the number of days on which she could beg: perhaps not surprisingly as the proceeds of the begging, the agermos, were to belong to the woman priest in their entirety.[153]

At Miletos the degree to which collections were important is made clear in a decree of the demos concerning the agerseis, the 'money collections' made for Artemis Boulephoros Skiris. A delegation was to go to consult Apollo's oracle at nearby Didyma concerning whether the collections were to be made in the traditional manner or in a new way. Neither the old nor the new proposed way of making the collections is the subject of any detail, and the outcome is also unknown. Presumably women undertook the begging, given that it was for Artemis.[154]

Women as cult proselytisers

> They [the Sikyonians] say that the god Asklepios was introduced to them from Epidauros in the form of a snake on a carriage drawn by two mules, and that it was Nikagora of Sikyon who brought him.

Just as Asklepios was brought to Athens in *c*. 420 BC by Telemachos, so too did the woman Nikagora of Sikyon introduce Asklepios to her home town from Epidauros, where she had been cured.[155] Strabo records a story that when the Phokaians sailed to Massilia, they received an oracle that they take with them a hegemon ('guide') from Ephesian Artemis. Some of the Phokaians sailed to Ephesos and asked how to fulfil this oracular request; the night before their arrival, the goddess had sent one Aristarcha (one of the women held in honour by the Ephesians) a dream, commanding her to go with the Phokaians and to take one of the sacred images with her; this will have been a cult statue of Artemis Ephesia. This she did; upon arrival at Massilia, the Phokaians made her the woman priest of the cult for the temple they built to the goddess at Massilia. Whether this story is legendary or not is difficult to say: Aristarcha is the cult epithet of Artemis, and so the story could be seen as purely aetiological and Aristarcha as unhistorical, unless perhaps, as Malkin argues, the woman priest was named after the goddess. But the story seems simply to be explaining the existence of a priesthood of Artemis at Massilia. What Strabo's account does indicate is that there was presumably a woman priest of Artemis Aristarcha at Massilia, and that like Aristarcha from Ephesos, she was chosen from the women 'held in honour'.[156] Women, as will be seen in Chapter 5, were prominent in new cults, such as that of Adonis and Sabazios, and while not actively proselytising for these cults probably encouraged their women friends to participate in them. It is apparent that women played greater roles in the informal introduction of new and exotic cults than men did.

Apollo's prophetic women priests

The temple servant Ion tells the chorus of Athenian women who have come to Delphi with his mother Kreousa:

> If you have made a sacrifice of the sacred cake before the temple and wish to seek an oracle from Phoebus Apollo, go to the altar, but do not go into the innermost chamber of the temple unless you have slaughtered a sheep.[157]

Women could consult the oracle of Delphi, Apollo's most important and Greece's most prestigious centre of prophecy. What was required was the sacrifice of the pelanos, a sacred cake, later commuted to a monetary payment, and the sacrifice of a beast. Women will have primarily been concerned with items nearest to their heart and the role assigned to them in Greek society: children. Ion asks in the play of his name of Kreousa whether she has come 'concerning the earth' or children; fertility of the soil and of the woman are linked here as often in ancient Greece.[158]

As noted, women priests mainly, but not exclusively, served goddesses, and the main exceptions were women priests in Apollo's cults. Here the main focus of attention is the women priests at Delphi, responsible for giving oracles to those who came to the god for advice.[159] Euripides, as noted in the introduction, has a chorus of women claim that they have the greatest share in the rites of the gods because, amongst other things, women were the prophets of Apollo at Delphi and of Zeus at Dodona.

Apollo's women priests at Delphi answered enquiries, on one day once a month, from consultants from all over the Greek world and beyond. A woman priest – the Pythia – would mount the tripod in Apollo's temple, and receive consultants, who might have questions of either a personal or political nature. In the classical period, there were three women priests, who took it in turns to answer questions on the same day, which would have been necessary if there were numerous consultants.[160] The Pythia was chosen from amongst all of the Delphian women, presumably by lot with some belief in divine inspiration in the choice.[161] A hereditary woman priesthood for the Pythia might have led to an uninspired choice. Although she did not take drugs, chew laurel leaves or hallucinate, the Pythia did have to prepare herself. Once a month before prophesying, she bathed in the Kastalian spring, and drank from it.[162] The enquirers had to make their questions known to the male priests of the sanctuary in advance, so that the Pythia had prior warning of them. To what extent the Pythia was guided in her replies by the priests is a matter for conjecture only. How diviners in most if not all human societies provide an answer to the questions being put to them seems clear.[163] The Pythia would have known in advance the question which she was going to be asked, and in various ways the enquirers would have made clear what sort of answer they were expecting. This is to simplify matters to some extent, as there must have been cases when enquirers were genuinely uncertain as to which course of action to take. But in cases where the approval of the god was being sought, or some problem which could be dealt with by reference to prescriptions for slaughter and sacrifice, the Pythia's advice would have been, in a sense, formulaic, or more precisely, 'prescriptive', to make a particular sacrifice to a specified deity. Many of the questions were of the formula, 'which god should I/we pray to?', so that it was not specific advice which was being asked for but rather direction as to which deity needed to be worshipped in the particular circumstances.

Old-fashioned scholarly notions that the woman priest was influenced by some form of narcotic or inhalations simply arise from later Roman fantasies.[164] For the Greeks, she was the simple mouthpiece of the god Apollo, who in turn served Zeus' will.[165] Her answers were delivered clearly; but ambiguity sometimes arose when her reply had a riddling quality. Most of the Pythias delivered their prophecies in prose, though some were clever enough to deliver them in poetic hexameters; many oracles were probably turned into hexameters by their recipients if the oracles were considered particularly important. Certainly not infallible, errors of prophecy were ascribed to misinterpretations of the oracle by the recipient.[166]

But the Pythia was corruptible, or at least there were allegations that she had been bribed; and in one case, these allegations resulted in her dismissal.[167] Demosthenes could accuse the Pythia of 'philippising', of serving the needs of Philip II, king of Macedon (382–336 BC). More difficult to ascertain is the Pythia's role before the Persian War of 480–479 BC, in which she, either genuinely or perhaps advised by the priests, gave a series of oracles which hardly recommended resistance to the invader. The Athenians were very unhappy with their first oracle, but managed to bully the Pythia into giving them a more favourable response by taking up positions as suppliants and threatening to remain until they died. The oracle they received was still a little ambiguous but gave Themistokles what he needed to pursue his policy of resistance. Of course, the question of the authenticity of both oracles has been raised.[168] What the Pythia made of these goings-on is unclear.

Many matters came before the Pythia, the most horrific of which was war. Apollo was consulted through the Pythia at Delphi by the Spartans in 432 BC about whether or not to go to war against the Athenians: they received the memorable answer that if they fought hard the god would support them.[169] Similarly, king Agesipolis consulted both the oracle at Olympia and then Delphi as to whether he should reject the holy truce of the Argives and invade their territory; Zeus at Olympia said he could, so he asked Delphi if Apollo had the same opinion as his father Zeus.[170] The Pythia's decision in such matters – to support the disruption of the peace of the land and send men inevitably to their death, and women and children into slavery, and consign fields and orchards to destruction – is almost disturbing, but Agesipolis had been a little unscrupulous here in the way in which he framed his question. However, warfare was an extremely common topic for divination, as indicated by the examination of entrails on battlefields before the clash of arms or the consultation of omens before crossing their own borders by the Spartans on the way to war. The role of the premier form of divination, inspired utterance at Delphi, concerning warfare is not surprising.

Interestingly, despite Euripides' comments about the importance of the women priests at Delphi and Dodona, the Athenians themselves had little recourse to these oracles for important matters after the Persian Wars.[171] Delphi had played a part in earlier Athenian history, when the Alkmeonidai used the Pythia to press for a Spartan invasion of Athens. A little later, the Pythian woman priest chose the ten names of the Athenian tribes in 508 BC from a list of 100 presented to her, perhaps at the behest of Kleisthenes the Alkmeonid.[172] Later, she was consulted in 351 BC about the cultivation of the sacred plain of Eleusis, but given a choice of two answers, inscribed on tin, which hardly gave her scope for inspired utterance.[173]

As noted, childlessness was one field of enquiry, and a woman in the fourth century BC inscribed a record of how the Pythia had prophesied that she would have children;[174] war, as noted, was another concern, but famine, pestilence and drought were problems for which Greeks also sought ritual prescriptions from the Pythia.[175] But what is important is that above all the Pythia frequently gave advice where it is clear that the consultants had come to seek approval for their actions. This was not trivial, a mere rubber-stamping of their decisions, but rather the enquirers were anxious to be reassured that the gods would approve of what they were doing. Before a colony was established, Apollo's approval could be sought.[176] A new constitution for Sparta had the support of the Pythia.[177] While Plutarch could complain that in his time the most serious questions asked by states were to do with crops, herds and health, these were nevertheless questions also posed in the classical period and for which the Pythia would, in the case of famine or pestilence, be asked to provide a ritual prescription.[178]

Dodona, despite Euripides' placing of it on the same footing as Delphi, clearly never had the same panhellenic distinction. The numerous inscribed lead tablets discovered there on which consultants recorded their questions attest to public enquiries, but the overwhelming majority are private matters, including the choice of wife, and whether one's wife was bearing your child or someone else's.[179] There were three women priests here, known as doves, and Herodotos had talked to them,[180] but the mechanism by which they answered enquiries is unclear. Many of the questions ask to which god the consultant must pray and sacrifice, so that as at Delphi, the women priests were probably largely concerned with ritual prescriptions, such as to which god to sacrifice, for winning over the gods.

A woman priest of Apollo is also known from Epirus, and here she had a mantic if not oracular role. Once a year, all the people of Epirus and the xenoi (foreigners) would come to Apollo's sanctuary where there were serpents sacred to the god. The woman priest entered the enclosure alone, taking food for the serpents. If they eagerly ate the food which she brought, a year of plenty, and without sickness, would occur; the opposite applied if the serpents did not take the food. Also prophetic, the woman priest of Athena of the Pedasans, east of Halikarnassos, would grow a 'great beard', whenever misfortune threatened them or their neighbours, and she had actually done so three times.[181]

Amongst the honours awarded by the Delphians to one Chrysis and her descendants for her role in the Pythais (the Athenian pilgrimage) to Delphi was that of asylia ('safety'), probably here a reference to safe passage from Athens to Delphi for the journey.[182] While heralds were clearly inviolable, much less is known about the status of priests and women priests in wartime. Only the priests and women priests were spared enslavement when Alexander the Great sacked Thebes in 335 BC. Alexander was probably more scrupulous than others, though freeing priests and women priests without ransom is heard of.[183] On the other hand, it was Alexander, and Philomelos before him, who forced the Pythia to prophesy on days other than those for consultation. When Alexander forcefully dragged her to the temple to prophesy, she forestalled the need to mount the tripod by crying out that he was 'invincible'.[184]

The basilinna's marriage to the god Dionysos

In a fourth-century BC Athenian law speech attributed to the orator Demosthenes, it is alleged that the woman Neaira was a prostitute living with the citizen Stephanos who attempted to pass her off as his citizen wife. She had a daughter by one of her many clients, whom Stephanos pretended was his own, and he persuaded Theogenes who was basileus archon (king magistrate) to marry her. In this position, as the wife of the basileus archon, Neaira's daughter fulfilled several important religious duties, which the speaker alleges she should not have performed because she was not a legitimate Athenian.

> And this woman [Neaira's daughter] offered for you the not-to-be-spoken-of sacrifices on behalf of the city, and she saw the things which it was not proper for her to see, being a foreign woman, and although being such a woman she entered where no other of the Athenians, though there are so many of them, enters except the wife of the basileus archon, and she administered the oath to the gerarai, who preside at the sacrifices, and she was given as a wife to Dionysos, and she carried out on behalf of the city the ancestral rites for the gods, rites many in number, and sacred, and which cannot be spoken of.[185]

This is a veritable catalogue of the duties of the king archon's wife, the basilinna,[186] but none of the items are very specific; they include much that was secret and unmentionable, and the jurors would not have known what these duties were. The rites must have been ancient, going back to when Athens had a king whose wife would have been equivalent to a high priest.

The qualifications of a basilinna are quite clear from the accusations against Neaira and her daughter: the basilinna is to be born of Athenian citizen parents. To prove his point the speaker cites the law which prescribed that the wife of the basileus be of Athenian birth, and that the basileus was to marry a woman not previously married, but a virgin (parthenos), so that the 'unspoken' sacrifices could be sacrificed on behalf of the city according to ancestral practice, and the established sacrifices be made to the gods piously, without any omissions or innovations. This law was inscribed on a stele and set up in the sanctuary of Dionysos, by the altar in Limnai; it was an ancient law, but the stele still stood there in the speaker's time, with the letters nearly effaced with age. This sanctuary of Dionysos in Limnai was opened only once each year, on the twelfth day of the month Anthesterion.[187]

Thucydides refers to the shrine of Dionysos in Limnai, noting that the more ancient Dionysia was celebrated there during the month Anthesterion, and that the Ionian descendants of the Athenians also celebrate the Anthesteria, but gives no clues as to any precise similarities.[188] Certainly the name of the month, evoking flowers and spring, was celebrated wherever there were Ionians.[189]

The wedding ceremony between the god and the basilinna did not take place at this sanctuary, but at the Boukoleion, near the Prytaneion, and the *Athenaion Politeia* states that the symmeixis and marriage (gamos) of the wife of the basileus with Dionysos took place there.[190] The basilinna wed the god: this was a sacred marriage.

Although the speech does not give a date for the ceremony, it appears that this was one of the chief duties, if not the main responsibility, of the basilinna. As the stele recording this (and her other duties) was set up in this sanctuary, opened once a year only on the twelfth, the middle day of the Anthesteria festival, the day of the Choes seems appropriate for the ceremony (the first day, the eleventh, was the Pithoigia, the twelfth and second day were the Choes, the third day, the thirteenth, the Chytroi).[191] The Choes was so named after the drinking vessels, the choes (singular: chous) which were used during the festival; the chous was a type of oinochoe; it had a single handle, a trefoil mouth (i.e. three curves, not unlike a shamrock shape), with a curved shape from lip to base. Myth relates how Theseus, king of Athens, gave his wife in marriage to Dionysos. A vase showing the reclining god under a 'tree' of grapes, with revellers behind him, receiving a woman (who is painted white) probably represents this.[192] This is depicted on a choes, so presumably the marriage should be assumed to have taken place on the day of the Choes; if at night, this will have been after sunset on the eleventh, when the next day, the twelfth and the day of the Choes, commenced.[193] On another vase, a well-dressed young woman walks shaded by a parasol held by a satyr. This is generally assumed to represent the basilinna being led off to her marriage with the god.[194] The satyr, her demeanour, and the 'swinging' scene of the Anthesteria on the other side of the vase (for which see below), point towards this conclusion.

The speaker continues that after the rites had taken place, the Areiopagos, the council of archons with lifelong membership and jurisdiction over various religious matters, learned of what had happened.[195] The council enquired into who the woman was, and found out that she was the daughter of a prostitute; concerned about the rites, the council wanted to fine Theogenes the greatest amount within its competence, but also wanted to keep the matter secret and with due regard to appearances. When Theogenes convinced the council that he was unaware of her background, and promised to divorce her (which he did), they let him off.[196] It can also be noted that, in keeping with the Athenian custom in the classical period that generally women were not to be named, no basilinna is known: the only one mentioned is Neaira's daughter (originally called Strybele, but later given the more respectable name Phano, according to the speaker).[197]

In addition, the basilinna administered the oath to the gerarai, which is referred to twice in the speech against Neaira (§§73, 78). The basilinna was assisted in administering it by the sacred herald when the gerarai, who served at the sacrifices, swore on their baskets in front of the altar, before they touched the sacrificial victims. The speaker then had the oath which the gerarai swore read out in court (§78), or at least as much as it was possible for them to hear, indicating that the gerarai said other things which were not for anyone else's ears. The oath has been inserted into the text of the speech by a later ancient editor, and so its details are suspect, but states that each of the gerarai swore that she was living a pure life, holy from all the things that are impure, and from intercourse with a man, and that she would be a gerara at the Theoinia and Iobakcheia for Dionysos according to ancestral practice and at the appointed times. But who are these gerarai? The term is sometimes translated as 'venerable women priests', and the connection of gerara with 'venerable' and the emphasis on non-sexuality with the specific exclusion of sexual acts, might imply older, mature women, but ones who are still sexually active (and so not necessarily old). Lexicographers number them at fourteen, one for each of the fourteen altars to Dionysos (it is not made clear if all fourteen were in the sanctuary), and have them appointed by the basileus archon.[198]

The basilinna apparently had at least one other duty. The Choes (12 Anthesterion) was a day of drinking and celebration in which each celebrant had a choes, a jug from which he drank the new wine (women's role in drinking at the Anthesteria is discussed in Chapter 5). Generally at festivals, when the drinking had ended, the revellers dedicated the wreaths which they had been wearing by taking them to a temple and placing them on a statue. But on the Choes, all temples except that of Dionysos in Limnai were closed. So the drinkers put their wreath around their choes and took them away to this shrine, where the woman priest received them and performed sacrifices. This woman priest, since at all other times the shrine was closed, can only have been the basilinna. At the end of the day, she is to be imagined receiving hundreds of wreathed choes from presumably rather drunk revellers. The choes and wreaths were for Dionysos alone as a further thanks for the gift of wine.[199]

Many choes survive, depicting scenes of children, almost all boys, and at any rate only boys are shown on choes holding a chous; the boys are often garlanded with a wreath of flowers or wear amulets. They are frequently shown at play, with rollers on a stick, balls, lyres, go-carts and chickens; this may reflect a sportive atmosphere on the day. Young boys are often shown crawling towards a chous, and they may have been allowed to taste the wine.[200] Girls seem to be excluded from the festivities, and if the boys were allowed wine it seems certain that the girls were not.

Impious women priests

The people of the island of Paros wanted to execute Timo, the woman underpriest (hypozakoros) of the chthonic goddesses (Demeter and Persephone) whose advice led Miltiades in the early fifth century BC to attempt unlawful entry to the Thesmophorion there. But when the Parians consulted the Pythia at Delphi, she commanded them not to kill Timo, as she had merely been the instrument of Miltiades' undoing. That the Parians sought divine sanction for the execution indicates the sacred status of the woman priest and a reluctance on their part to take the initiative and responsibility for her death.[201] The Pythia women priests who accepted bribes will have been viewed as impious, such as Periallos who was deprived of her office.[202]

Demosthenes in 343 BC referred to Aeschines and his mother Glaukothea, the assembler of thiasoi, for organising which another woman priest had been put to death. One scholiast on the passage gives the name of this other woman priest as Nino, executed on account of drugs (pharmaka), for performing 'other rites', and prosecuted for making 'magic potions' (philtra) for young men (or young people generally), which is presumably a reference to love potions. Another scholiast comments that Nino was executed because the rites she celebrated were a mockery of the mysteries; presumably the Eleusinian Mysteries are meant. In two other speeches, Menekles is referred to as the prosecutor who had the woman priest Nino convicted, but the charges are not mentioned.

The second scholiast adds that Apollo in an oracle commanded that they accept the rites, and the Athenians chose the mother of Aeschines (Glaukothea) to celebrate the mysteries and carry out initiations. This oracle is doubtless fiction; what Demosthenes is attempting to say is that Glaukothea and Aeschines were engaged in activities for which another woman had been put to death, and so is trying to establish a link between the activities of Glaukothea and of the executed woman priest, but a link which did not really exist. Demosthenes is making a passing comment; while trying to smear Glaukothea with the same crime as the executed woman priest, he is clearly not doing so very seriously. The scholiast is trying to explain why Glaukothea can be accused, but there is no need to take Demosthenes literally in this way, as the scholiast does.[203]

Josephus has a report about a woman priest whose name has dropped out of his text, possibly Nino, whom the Athenians put to death, accused of initiating individuals into mysteries of foreign gods, which he states was forbidden by law on the penalty of death. Whether there was such a specific law has been doubted, but it might have been more a case that any worship of a foreign god not sanctioned by the state could draw accusations which might lead to death for the organiser: in Nino's case, drugs, mysteries involving thiasoi, and accusations of parodying the Eleusinian Mysteries are all combined.[204]

Women priests and sacred fire

Plutarch reports that wherever a perpetual fire is kept burning in Greece, including Athens and Delphi, its care is entrusted to women past the age of sexuality – not to virgins; these women were the hestiades.[205] The oil lamp made by the fifth-century sculptor Kallimachos for Athena at Athens only needed filling once a year, and was refilled on the same day each year. Pausanias gives no details of any rituals, but what he says is suggestive of an annual ritual act, and just as the sacred flame was entrusted to older women, perhaps this duty – of refilling the lamp – was carried out by them as well.

A marble piece of the last quarter of the seventh century BC from Selinounte, Italy, an oil lamp with a woman's head carved into its front, recalls the responsibility of women for oil lamps in temples throughout Greece. A terracotta lamp from the Heraion at Foce Sele is supported by four women, with four similar heads around the rim of the vessel. The women's hands clasp their breasts and give an oriental touch with perhaps the Near Eastern goddess Ishtar as the ultimate model. A small Athenian marble lamp of the end of the seventh century BC discovered on the Athenian acropolis has four heads of women alternating with four ram heads.[206] Every day a woman (possibly a woman priest) put fire on the altar of Iodama at the sanctuary of Athena Itonia and said three times in Boeotian that Iodama, a mythical woman priest turned to stone by Athena, still lives and asks for fire.[207]

Why did the classical Greeks obviously think it important to entrust certain rites to women priests? There is no apparent reason for women deities such as Athena and Artemis to have women priests, apart from the identical gender of woman priest and divinity. Indeed, Demeter's chief cult officials at Eleusis were men, even though her cult there was basically a celebration of a local Thesmophoria and of the fertility of the soil. But this is a feature of Greek religion: Artemis, Athena, Hera and Aphrodite were accorded women priests, while Zeus, Poseidon and Asklepios, to give just a few examples, had men to minister to their needs; the Pythia at Apollo's oracle at Delphi was a notable exception, probably to be explained by the myth that the original oracle belonged to Ge, the earth goddess. Athena's importance at Athens allowed her woman priest a public role, and the names of various woman priests of Athena Polias even in the classical period are known. But virgin goddesses at Athens did not even require virgin hands to tend to their statues and preside over their sacrifices; identical gender, perhaps, but not identical sexual experience, was required; the identification of goddess with woman priest was not complete. Adult women's virginity was not prized; without exception, the role of the parthenos was to become a gyne, the girl a woman, and even for the handful of women's priesthoods involved at Athens, families did not consecrate their daughters to sexless lives. It was impossible to do so given the way in which the priesthoods were inherited, with almost certainly the eldest surviving woman of the eldest surviving male taking over when the woman priest of Athena Polias died. For example, after sixty-four years of service, who was to succeed Lysimache would be unclear, surely, and a virgin might not even have been 'available' within the family, if that had been required. The Athenians did not require virgin priests to mediate for them with virgin goddesses.

The woman priest of Athena Polias attracted more attention than any other priest or woman priest in Athens; it is difficult to see which priest came anywhere near to her in importance, and even the priest of Poseidon chosen from the same family hardly seems a candidate. Numerous vases, but particularly black-figure ones of the archaic period, show her presiding over sacrifices. The theme becomes less popular afterwards, not because her importance declines but because of changing artistic fashions, and perhaps the growing male chauvinism of Athenian society in the classical period. Yet the importance of this woman priest, her public role, and the fact that the name of the woman priest of Athena Polias at any one time was surely known to everyone in Athens and that to her all had to come to make sacrifices to the city's most important deity at the site of the city's most important cult place, the acropolis, serve to emphasise the lack of prominence otherwise publicly enjoyed by women in classical Athens. This surely applies to the rest of Greece as well, though not probably to the same extent. At the time of the Olympic festival, all women had to leave Olympia: only the woman priest of Demeter could stay, sitting on an altar of white marble opposite the umpires as a spectator of the contests.[208]

The Pythia could be chosen from amongst all the women of Delphi though generally her origins were probably aristocratic, while nothing is known about the 'doves' of Dodona (but very little is known about anyone at Dodona). Both the women who mounted Apollo's Delphic tripod and those who were 'doves' had a unique role as prophetic priests. Euripides, as seen in the Introduction, saw these two particular groups of women priests as partly warranting the claim that women had the most important religious roles in Greece, and in so far as the Pythia and the 'doves' of Dodona gave approval to the establishment of new cities, shrines, the declaration of war, the institution of new law-codes and the like, his claim is reasonable enough.

Part II

SEGREGATED AND ECSTATIC RELIGIOUS RITES

4

WOMEN-ONLY FESTIVALS

Throughout the Greek world there were various festivals which were for women only, and from which men were strictly excluded. These rites ensured agricultural fertility, a facet of religion in which the role of women, in worshipping the goddesses Demeter and her daughter Persephone, was particularly appropriate. In this regard, a fourth-century BC decree from the Piraeus at Athens mentions the festival of the Thesmophoria, as well as the Plerosia, Kalamaia and Skira, and 'whatever other day the women assemble together according to ancestral practice'.[1] There were obviously several days of the year when citizen women of the Piraeus assembled together to worship in connection with agricultural fertility. The various Demeter festivals at Athens were part of the official calendar and central to the polis's construction of its religious identity, whereas that other all-women's festival, the Adonia, was not: agricultural concerns were at the heart of the polis's interests, not private ones. Athens promoted these festivals, not simply by accepting them into the religious calendar (the Adonia was not), but by providing the sacred architecture, the Thesmophorion and other shrines, in which women performed these rites. In addition, by organising the financial arrangements, the city's concern that the festivals would be held and conducted in appropriate 'style' is indicated.

The Stenia festival

The Athenian Stenia was held two days before the Thesmophoria festival, on the ninth day of the month Pyanopsion (September–October).[2] The prytaneis of the boule offered a sacrifice to Demeter and Kore (Persephone) on this day, indicating that these were the two deities worshipped at this festival.[3] Women assembled to celebrate the festival, and blasphemed and abused each other.[4] This will have been part of the general aischrologia[5] of Demeter rites, but otherwise the specific purpose of this rite is unclear. Presumably some of the abuse could have been sexual in nature, particularly if directed at younger women for the promotion of fertility. Secrecy, exclusion of men, and the Stenia's proximity to the Thesmophoria point towards its concern with agrarian and women's fertility.

Thesmophoria: the rotting pigs of Demeter

One of the festivals mostly widely celebrated throughout the Greek world was the Thesmophoria, in honour of the goddess Demeter Thesmophoros. The best-documented celebration is for that held in Athens, though there is some information for other places, such as Paros, Sicily and Eretria. The main features were secrecy, pig sacrifice, and, above all, rites for promoting agricultural fertility.[6]

A myth has Battos, king of Cyrene (in modern Libya), castrated by the women celebrants of the Thesmophoria because he intruded on the secret part of the rites; against the wishes of the women priests he insisted that he view the Thesmophoric ritual, and at a given signal the 'women slayers' with the blood of the sacrificial victims on their swords castrated him. Pausanias relates that the women celebrating the Thesmophoria at Aigila in Lakonia were captured by the Messenian Aristomenes; in turn, they attacked him with the knives which the women used for sacrificing, and the spits which they used to roast the sacrificial meat.[7] Miltiades' fate was also instructive: when attempting to capture the island of Paros, he was approached by the woman Timo, the 'under-priest' (hypozakoros) of the chthonic goddesses on Paros. She gave him advice on what to do if he wished to capture the island. Taking her advice, he jumped over the fence around the sanctuary of Demeter Thesmophoros, and went towards the shrine, but when he got to the doors he was overcome with terror. Turning back, he sprained his thigh in jumping over the sanctuary wall (some said he struck his knee); he developed gangrene from which he died.[8] Like all such ceremonies, the rites of the Thesmophoria on Paros involved secret rites not to be revealed to men. Miltiades' death is presented by Herodotos as an outcome of his intrusion into the sanctuary of Demeter Thesmophoros.

In dealing with the Thesmophoria, one immediately thinks of Aristophanes' play, *Thesmophoriazousai* [*The Women at the Thesmophoria Festival*], produced at Athens in 411 BC, which, however, reveals next to nothing about the rites, because they were secret. It does make clear that men were not supposed to be involved, and also the sorts of jokes which men might make about women's rituals. Aristophanes' Mnesilochos, the male spy who invades the Thesmophoria, has to do so dressed as a woman, and he notes that the women are by themselves. The effeminate Kleisthenes, who has come to inform the women that there is a male spy amongst them, is first thought to be a woman as he approaches to seek out the spy amongst them. Even he – effeminate as he is – is told to withdraw while Mnesilochos is questioned about last year's rites because he is nevertheless a man. It was not lawful for men to see the rites, or to hear about them.[9] Kritylla will test whether Mnesilochos is a woman or not by asking him about the previous year's ritual, and the sacred things that were shown.[10]

At Athens, the Thesmophoria festival was spread over three days of the month Pyanopsion (September–October): the eleventh, twelfth and thirteenth. The first day was the Anodos (also Kathodos), the second the Nesteia (also Mese, middle-day), and the third day was the Kalligeneia. Elsewhere, Pyanopsion was called Demetrios (of Demeter), and the Thesmophoria may have taken place in other cities in this month.[11] The anodos is the 'going up', the nesteia is the fast and lamentation, while the kalligeneia is 'she of the beautiful birth'. At Thebes, the Thesmophoria was celebrated therous ontos, and this is sometimes translated as 'summer', but the reference would have to be to the very end of summer and onset of autumn, with the task of planting the seed not too far in the future; the beginning of Pyanopsion (September–October) can still be quite hot in Attica–Boeotia.[12]

Plutarch refers to a celebration of the Thesmophoria by the leading women of Athens (whom the Megarians specifically wanted to capture during the period when Athens and Megara were at war in the sixth century BC) at Cape Kolias in the deme Halimous on the tenth of Pyanopsion,[13] the day before the three-day Thesmophoria festival started in Athens itself; the presence of these women points to a local celebration which had become of greater significance and was probably now to be classed as a state festival because of the interest of these women in the rites there. This celebration by aristocratic women who travelled the distance from Athens to Kolias was performed by them for the benefit of all the Athenians. The next day, the aristocratic women were back in Athens, celebrating the Thesmophoria for three days, just as they had celebrated the Stenia in Athens the day before going to Halimous: these aristocratic women were both busy and mobile. If the announcement (proagoreusis) on the fifth day of this month at Eleusis of the proerosia, preliminary ploughing, also entailed a commitment by these same women, then this was a very full time of the year for them (and there were several such proerosia ceremonies in Attica), as a counterpart to the physical labour of the farmers, landowners and those with estates to manage in this labour-intensive agricultural season. But after the third day of the Thesmophoria, these women's festival commitments came to an end until just over two months later, when the Haloa was celebrated.[14] Significantly, there were at Athens five festival days which women could attend at this time of year from which men were barred.

At Syracuse, the Thesmophoria lasted for ten days, and commenced with the first sowing of the corn; Pyanopsion at Athens was also a sowing month. At Delos, the Thesmophoria took place in the month Metageitnion, August–September, a month or so earlier than at Athens.[15] Both times coincide roughly with the time of autumn planting, putting the seed into the ground in preparation for spring. Demeter's role in this process is clear from the *Homeric Hymn to Demeter*; when grieving for her daughter Persephone the hymn says she 'hides the grain under the earth', that is, it does not germinate. It is this goddess who is propitiated at the Thesmophoria.

Fertility celebrations were spread over at least these five days in Attica (the Stenia at Halimous, and the Thesmophoria at Athens), and in addition, the Thesmophoria was not only celebrated in the city of Athens itself, but throughout the various demes of Attica. Two wives presided at the Athenian deme (Pithos) Thesmophoria mentioned by Isaeus. A deme inscription of Cholargos in Attica gives instructions for the archousai, women officials, who were to deal with the woman priest and together were to provide her with various items for the Thesmophoria, including grain, wine, oil and money.[16] The Thesmophorion in the Piraeus was in the charge of a woman priest and the demarch, a male deme official. That such women presided indicates that they had a good deal of authority in the conduct of the festival. While the deme decree of Cholargos setting out what the archousai had to provide for the Thesmophoria was proposed and voted for by men, it deals with financial matters, and it is not concerned with ritual.

The women have their own 'assembly' in Aristophanes' *Thesmophoriazousai* (295–570); the meeting of the women concerned with how to punish Euripides for slandering them parodies meetings of the Athenian ekklesia. A cult law from Mylasa in Caria prescribes that rites are to be carried out as decided by the women, and, as a cult of Demeter is attested at Mylasa, the rites referred to are plausibly (but not absolutely certainly) attributed to Demeter; women's jurisdiction at the Thesmophoria celebrations at Athens strongly supports this.[17] Men, of course, are the ones who pass decrees about Demeter sanctuaries; the women's power centres on the celebration, but not on aspects such as finance, or what they may wear on such occasions.[18]

The women who preside over the Thesmophoria were citizen wives; the speaker of Isaeus 8 states that if his mother was not a legitimate daughter of the citizen Kiron she would not have been chosen by the demeswomen to preside, with another wife, over the deme's celebration of the festival.[19] In Aristophanes' *Thesmophoriazousai*, Mnesilochos 'sends away' his imaginary slave-girl Thratta (who he pretends has carried the kiste and sacrificial cake, the popanon) just as he is about to enter the Thesmophorion. Lucian, however, has a hetaira complaining about her lover's new bride, that she is not very attractive; she knows, as she saw her with her mother at the Thesmophoria. But this could probably be simply a literary device, or the hetaira may well have seen the Thesmophoria in the sense that there was a public gathering of the women as they made their way to the sanctuary where they would celebrate the rites. It is a safe assumption that the celebration of the Thesmophoria, both at Athens and in the non-city demes, was for citizen wives only. Moreover, Callimachus has parthenoi ineligible to attend the Thesmophoria, and the unmarried young woman would have been a parthenos.[20] The citizen women invoke the goddesses' aid for the fertility of the city; the fertility of the parthenos is an unknown quantity, and she who has not proved her fertility cannot participate. When with Artemis' aid she has made this transition, she can join in Demeter's rites. The opening prayer of the women in the *Thesmophoriazousai* mentions several deities, but the first are the Thesmophoroi Demeter and Kore, then Ploutos, Kalligeneia, Kourotrophos Ge, Hermes and the Graces (295–300).

Scholars usually explain the term 'ascent', Anodos, by the fact that women ascended to the Thesmophorion shrine (which they take as being either on the Pnyx or on the acropolis) at Athens. Similarly at Thebes the women celebrated the Thesmophoria on the Theban acropolis, the Kadmeia, and so 'went up' to it.[21] Mnesilochos refers to how Euripides sent him up (1045) to where the women were to celebrate the Thesmophoria. However, in a fragment of Lykourgos' speech *On the Priesthood*, there is a reference to a festival called the Procharisteria, the most ancient sacrifice celebrating the ascent – Anodos – of the goddess Kore (from Hades), for the growth of the fruits of plants. This is a more likely explanation of the term Anodos, and it is this sacrifice which in particular would have occupied the women on the first day of the Thesmophoria.[22] No other details are known about this first day, and perhaps this was the day of the pig sacrifice, as the second and third days seem to have been otherwise occupied.

The second day was the Nesteia, a day of fasting, and the gloomiest day of the three-day festival; fasting was a common enough purity rite in Greek religion, but particularly associated with Demeter and her fasting after the disappearance of Persephone.[23] The women put hagnos ('pure') plants on their pallets on which they sat and rested during the Thesmophoria, which were thought to repress sexual desire; this would have been on the second day. The Lucian scholiast gives three days' sexual abstinence specifically for the 'Bailers', without mentioning the other women. The women at the Thesmophoria were termed 'bees': the 'bee' was not simply the ideal woman as in Semonides, but above all was sexually chaste,[24] so perhaps two nights of abstinence before they returned at night to their husbands was to be imagined.

It was on the third day, the Kalligeneia, the day of the beautiful birth, that the women called on the goddess Kalligeneia for the fertility of their own wombs. The anti-aphrodisiacism of the day before is laid aside. This aspect with its emphasis on the fertility of the citizen wives would have been just as important in men's eyes as the rituals guaranteeing the fertility of the crops. At Eretria during the Thesmophoria, the women cooked meat in the sun rather than using fire, and they did not invoke Kalligeneia. That Kalligeneia is so important a part of Thesmophoria rites is made clear by Plutarch's pointed reference to its absence at Eretria.[25]

Part of the rite of the Thesmophoria appears to have involved the women jesting and jeering amongst themselves. Diodoros refers to the obscenities uttered at the Thesmophoria in Syracuse. Without specifying particular places, Apollodoros notes that women jeer at the Thesmophoria, just as Iambe with her jokes cheered up Demeter in the Homeric Hymn. Epicurus' language was harshly criticised by the Stoic astronomer Kleomedes, who complained that some of it was like the talk of prostitutes, and resembled remarks made at Demeter festivals by women holding the Thesmophoria.[26] These jokes, obviously lewd, played an important role in Demeter festivals, and promoted and presumably celebrated and encouraged women's sexual desires and hence fertility.

As the second day was one of gloominess, the aischrologia would have occurred on the first or third days; the latter is the best possibility, with the fasting and gloom over, and the promise of women's fertility promoted by bawdiness and lewdness appropriate then, on the day of the 'Beautiful birth', the Kalligeneia. Another element general to Demeter festivals was the use of the morotton, an object plaited from bark with which the women struck each other 'for Demeter'. This fertility rite is not specifically attested at the Thesmophoria, but could well have taken place there.[27]

Moving on from the *Thesmophoriazousai*, the main source of information about the Thesmophoria at Athens is a scholiast on Lucian who seems to be relying on classical sources, so that despite what appears to be some confusion in what he relates, the broad details provided can be accepted.[28] In outline, he states that at the Thesmophoria piglets were thrown into pits, megara (singular: megaron). The decayed remains of the piglets were later brought back up out of the pits, by women known as 'Bailers' (Antletriai). They maintained a state of purity for three days before descending into the megara. Noise was made when the women went down to bail up the remains, and again when the pigs and dough were thrown in, due to snakes in the megara. The bailed-out mixture was then spread on altars; the belief was then that whoever took this and scattered it with seed on his field would enjoy a good harvest. This was of course not compost, the amount would not be sufficient, but was a 'fertility mix'.

Clement of Alexandria and the scholiast write that the explanation given for the casting of pigs into megara – pits – at the Thesmophoria was that this practice recalled the herd of pigs which was swallowed up in the chasm in the earth which opened when Hades and Persephone went down to the underworld. But obviously the aetiology was the other way around: for some reason pigs were thrown into pits, and the myth sought to explain why. The scholiast notes that piglets are symbolic of fecundity. The multiple births of a sow became a generic representation of animal and human and presumably even agricultural fertility. These megara are found in Demeter sanctuaries throughout Greece; excavated megara are seen to be not just pits, but lined structures in the ground.[29]

On Thasos, dozens of small terracotta piglets have been discovered; terracotta substitution for the real thing being reasonably common in Greek religion, such as in the cult of Asklepios where clay chickens could replace real ones as thanks-offerings. These model clay piglets from Thasos, and also some examples found on Naxos, have their stomachs slit lengthwise, from head to thigh, with the organs exposed and depicted.[30] Several Thesmophoria sites from throughout the Greek world, especially at Syracuse, yield statuettes of women carrying piglets – often the woman has a torch in one hand and a piglet in the other, and in most cases a goddess, presumably Demeter, is intended; she is synonymous with the women worshippers.[31] Dough models of snakes and phalloi, both fertility icons, were thrown into the pits as well. Pausanias notes that at the sanctuary of Demeter and Kore outside Thebes piglets were released into megara, and were said to later turn up at Dodona; he does not, however, believe the story himself. Obviously Pausanias knew that the animals at Thesmophoria rites were not cast alive into pits, which would delay their decay, not simply because of the time it took for the piglets gradually to die of hunger and thirst but because the full bodies would take longer to decompose than if they were mutilated with their internal organs exposed, particularly since there does not seem to have been much of a time interval between casting the pigs in and bringing up their remains.[32]

The scholiast does not date the 'mucking out' by the 'Bailers'. If the pigs were thrown in at the Thesmophoria, the remains would have come out at a later date, when they had decomposed; after all they are said to be 'decayed', but *when* is not made clear. Whether last year's offerings were left there for a year and then brought up at the Thesmophoria before the next throwing in of piglets is possible. But as the rotting mixture was to be spread on the fields to yield a good harvest, a date compatible with the sowing of seeds is needed; the Thesmophoria occurred before the sowing. It might only have been a matter of weeks after the Thesmophoria that the 'Bailers' went to work, bailing out a mess of partly decomposed pigs and old dough.[33]

But who killed the pigs? As noted above, Battos of Cyrene was said to have encountered 'women slayers' at the Thesmophoria, with the blood of the sacrificial victims on their swords. Aristomenes was confronted by women celebrating the Thesmophoria who had knives used for sacrificing, and spits for cooking with. It is easy to rationalise both stories as just that, stories, and to dismiss them as evidence that women sacrificed victims in Demeter's Thesmophoric cults.

But Pausanias who writes about Aristomenes evinces no surprise that women should slay animals in this women-only cult, and while too much credence should not perhaps be placed on Aelian's use of the word sphaktriai – women slayers – for the women who slaughtered the pigs and then turned so handily on Battos, there is nothing in the stories that mitigates against believing that women could slay animals except for the notion that women should not do so.[34] At the Thesmophoria in Lakonia clearly the women ate some of the pigs, and one presumes women also did so at Athens, although there appears to be no direct evidence for this. If the evidence of a scholiast in fact is to be trusted, the women at the Thesmophoria not only ate the meat of the pigs but were themselves the sacrificers.[35]

In the stories of Battos and Aristomenes the women have the sacrificial implements, knives and spits, but this is usually interpreted as reflecting an aberration rather than the norm. However, this is not the case; it is not a case of ritual inversion that women have the means to kill here, with the stories being didactic in nature about the dangers of women and sacrificial instruments, but rather these stories reflect that women were 'slayers'. In Aristophanes it is a man who in comic jest delivers the fatal blow to the wine cask while a woman hastens to catch its 'blood', but it is a man who should not be there, and it was a woman's knife he used.[36] Mnesilochos' 'sacrifice of a child', in which he seizes Mika's baby, threatens to stab it at the altar and then does so, reveals the 'baby' as a full wineskin Mika has been clutching (690–764, cf. 564–5). This could simply be comic fun: women and drink being a stock motif as other lines in the play reveal (393, 420). But the skin of the flask will be given as a perquisite to the woman priest (758), as in sacrifices, and the 'blood' of the 'child' will be caught: Mika calls for the 'blood-vase' (sphageion) with which to do this (754). This must be a parody of the pig sacrifices at the Thesmophoria, which men knew occurred and which Aristophanes could joke about in this way.[37] The obvious conclusion is that women carried out pig sacrifices themselves. A woman could surely kill a piglet with little trouble. The women priests at the Argive Heraion used the river near it to draw water for purifications and 'secret sacrifices': what animals they slew will never be known.[38]

Not all evidence, of course, points in this direction. The Delian temple accounts which concern the Thesmophoria on Delos provide for certain sums of money for the sacrifice in the Thesmophoria: a pregnant sow is purchased for Demeter, and pigs for Demeter, Kore and Zeus Eubuleus, and for purifying the Thesmophorion itself. There is money provided for wood, charcoal, fruit, oil, food (trophe) for the sacrificial animals (until they are sacrificed), and also money to pay for the services of the mageiros, the sacrificial butcher.[39] But this is a rite for women only, and so it has to be imagined that the mageiros slips into the Thesmophorion, makes the sacrifices and leaves again; if so, the situation was different from that at Athens. At Methymna, on the other hand, the gynaikonomos ('supervisor of the women') is to wait outside while the women celebrate their all-night festival; he is to be over forty and a citizen of Methymna; the gynaikonomos is to ensure that no other man enters the shrine; if there was any sacrificial activity here, it would be women's business to carry it out.[40]

One text, the decree from Mylasa possibly concerning rites of Demeter, is very suggestive and as restored has a man carrying out a sacrifice and leaving the rites immediately afterwards.[41] But the restoration could be based on the conception that women could not slay. If correct, it appears to be a case such as at Delos with a male butcher dealing with the victims. Women are kept clear of the axe, the knife, the spits, Detienne argues; they are the cookers of bread, biscuits, and the like, and the purpose of these stories, about Aristomenes but especially Battos, makes clear the danger to men when women are armed. Women, according to Detienne, did not usually wield the sacrificial implements.[42] But there is nothing incongruous about women having sacrificial implements, and the myths of Battos and Aristomenes do not illustrate the danger of women being armed, and so point to the practice that they were not, but rather indicate the danger of men intruding where they should not, and becoming potential sacrificial victims themselves.

A sacred calendar for the deme Eleusis, in Attica, lists costs for several festivals, including the Thesmophoria. The inscription mentions the Thesmophoroi (i.e. Demeter and Persephone), a basket, and an expense for the wood for the altar. This could well be for a local celebration of the Thesmophoria, but Mikalson suggests that this is for the celebration of the festival at Athens, as other festivals in the calendar, the proerosia (ploughing ceremony, see below) and the Pyanopsia, are for these celebrations in Athens, and the whole Eleusis calendar would then be a list of expenses incurred by the demesmen for festivals held in Athens. Against this, there is no reason why the proerosia being referred to should not have been at Eleusis: there was a proclamation of this on 5 Pyanopsion, which the hierophant and the Keryx (herald) announce. The proerosia itself was probably on the same day as it was announced, or surely soon after; it would be strange if it was after the Thesmophoria, i.e. the fourteenth or later.[43]

Other evidence could be interpreted in a similar way to Mikalson's suggestion, but wrongly, as I will argue below.[44] The Cholargos decree in which the deme Cholargos required that the archousai ('women in charge') provide the woman priest with the necessary items for the Thesmophoria need not necessarily refer to a deme celebration.[45] Similarly, the speaker of the lawsuit Isaeus 8 refers to the fact that his mother and another woman, the wife of Diokles (i.e. both married women), were chosen by the wives of the demesmen of the deme Pithos to preside (archein) at the Thesmophoria, and to carry out the prescribed ceremonies. These have been interpreted both as deme celebrations or as arrangements by the deme for when the deme's wives celebrated the Thesmophoria in the city. The deme Melite in the second century BC honoured Satyra, wife of Krateas of Melite, who was priest of the Thesmophoroi, who had 'repaired all the shrines' and given 100 drachmas for annual sacrifices, and Broneer argued that this related to the Thesmophoria celebrated in the city.[46] Another speech by Isaeus refers to the celebration of the Thesmophoria as a liturgy, with someone having a property worth 3 talents being obliged on behalf of his wife to pay for the expenses of the Thesmophoria festival for the wives of his demesmen (the deme is not specified).[47] There must have been other expenses as well, met by husbands, for a man with two wives would need to pay twice the expense at the Thesmophoria and the Stenia,[48] and the archousai of Cholargos also make contributions in kind and money.

Other evidence is less unequivocal. There was a Thesmophorion in the deme Piraeus, and a local celebration here consequently seems certain. The women therefore celebrated their own Thesmophoria, even though the centre of Athens was only some 4 kilometres away; even if they celebrated their Thesmophoria on a different day or days from the Athenian celebration, they nevertheless apparently felt it appropriate to hold their own festival. If women from the Piraeus did not make the trip to the centre of Athens to celebrate the Thesmophoria there, a journey of several kilometres but nevertheless within walking distance, women from outlying demes would not have done so: the deme decrees from Eleusis and Cholargos, and the evidence for Pithos and Melite, as well as Isaeus' speech, surely point to local Thesmophoria celebrations in the demes. At the Piraeus, in the inscription referred to above, the women were to come together, according to ancestral practice,⁴⁹ and the women in the demes surely convened to seek the blessings of the Thesmophoroi for both the farm fields and for the sowing and fertility of their own or other women's bodies. It seems clear, then, that the various celebrations of the Thesmophoria mentioned in connection with demes took place there, not in the city itself.

In the *Thesmophoriazousai*, Euripides sees the sign for assembling outside the Thesmophorion: 'the sign of the ekklesia (meeting) in the Thesmophorion is showing' (278–9). There was a similar sign for when the ekklesia, boule and lawcourts met.⁵⁰ This is the middle day of the Thesmophoria, which Aristophanes terms the mese (middle; the fast). Euripides leaves Mnesilochos, who talks to his imaginary slave girl, Thratta, commenting to her on the number of women coming to the Thesmophorion and the number of their lit and smoking torches. They are to hold their meeting about Euripides at sunrise (275), so the women are to be imagined arriving just at dawn, making an impressive sight with their torches in the twilight of the new day.

The Thesmophoria at Athens is sometimes described by scholars as involving thousands of women camped out for three nights on the Pnyx, the assembly place, having left their husbands behind and abstaining from sex for the duration of the festivities, carried out during the autumn.⁵¹ That is, it is assumed that several thousand citizen wives left their husbands, took over the place of political assembly, and worshipped Demeter. This assumes that all the houses of Athens were emptied of citizen wives.

When Kleisthenes reveals that there is a male spy in their midst, the women know each other, and Kritylla says of Mnesilochos that 'she' is the only 'woman' that the others don't know (614). This suggests a small or limited assembly. In fact, the women's chorus, who are the women at the Thesmophoria, refer to themselves as the eugeneis, 'well-born', women of Athens (330). But is this an aristocracy of eugeneis, or have all the Athenian citizen wives, through the democracy, become well-born, eugeneis? A lawcourt speech of Lysias has a mother and her daughter-in-law attend the Thesmophoria, but the socio-economic status of the daughter is not aristocratic. She does live in a double-storey house, but there is only one maid, and the wife baths the baby herself, and gets up to do it in the night; if she was typical of the wives who attended the Thesmophoria, a larger group than simply the aristocratic women would have participated.⁵²

The action of the *Thesmophoriazousai* takes place in the Thesmophorion (*Thesm.* 277–8) at Athens; its site is debated. Near the Pnyx or on the slopes of the acropolis have been suggested.⁵³ There is no evidence, archaeological or otherwise, for either, except for the mention of the 'pnyx' in the *Thesmophoriazousai*. The location of the Thesmophorion could help to indicate the number of women involved: the Pnyx able to accommodate thousands, or a shrine, which could accommodate only a limited number, perhaps a hundred or two. The capacity of the Thesmophorion is also relevant: at Paros the Thesmophorion was surrounded by an enclosure, while at Aigila in Sparta the women celebrated the Thesmophoria in Demeter's temple. At Thebes the Thesmophoria was celebrated on the Kadmeia, so that the boule (council) which usually met there was meeting in the agora, in order to make way for the women.[54]

The location of the Thesmophoria is important for a consideration of the number of women participants. While the women open their day just as an assembly of male citizens on the Pnyx would be opened, with prayers, and then a formal motion framed by the boule of the women (295–379), this does not mean that the Thesmophoria was celebrated on the Pnyx, where there would be room for thousands of women. As noted, the women of Thebes celebrated the Thesmophoria on the Kadmeia,[55] but this does not equate with the Athenian Pnyx, but rather with the Athenian acropolis.[56] Just as the Eleusinion is to be located on the north-west slope of the acropolis, the Thesmophorion is probably to be located in or near the Eleusinion.[57]

When Mnesilochos' identity is revealed, the chorus sings that it will search for him through the whole pnyx, through the skenai and the diodoi (658). The pnyx here is often interpreted to mean *the* Pnyx, *the* assembly place of the men, which the women have taken over for their festival. A scholiast on line 658, however, explains the pnyx as the assembly of women (rather than as the Pnyx).[58] The skenai are interpreted as the tents or huts which the women are living in during the Thesmophoria.[59] The diodoi ('passageways') are possibly pathways between the women's tents. But it is much more likely that Mnesilochos will be sought amongst the assembly of women, and then amongst the skenai, the stage and its passageways (the diodoi). Locating the Thesmophoria in a sanctuary on the slope of the acropolis and discounting the idea that the women went to the Pnyx which could accommodate several hundred, indeed thousands, of people, means that the majority of citizen women did not pitch their tents away from their husbands and celebrate the Thesmophoria. Moreover, the women arrive on the second day at the Thesmophorion; they have come to it, indicating that they have not been camped out all night. A much smaller group of women than the thousands of traditional scholarship is to be imagined, perhaps at the most a few hundred: one imagines that these will largely be the aristocratic women, congregating at Athens' premier cult location, the acropolis. But balancing this is the evidence for celebrations in the demes, in which women gathered in their own localities. With 140 demes in Attica, assuming that each deme or most of them held a Thesmophoria, this makes for a considerable amount of participation by the women of Athens.

The main rituals, as they were secret, will presumably have occurred in the Thesmophorion. The Thesmophoria would therefore be much more limited than might otherwise be imagined: not thousands of citizen wives from the city up on the Pnyx, but a small group, possibly largely of aristocratic wives, perhaps only a hundred or so, who sought to win the goodwill of Demeter through the rites of the Thesmophoria, carried out in a modest-sized Thesmophorion. The duty may have been of a hereditary nature, with well-known eupatrid families carrying out the rites, just as the Cape Kolias celebration involved aristocratic women. The women arrived in the dawn light, with their young children (if Mika's 'baby' is any guide) but no slaves. Women's cycles of reproduction mirrored those of the fields: the seed planted in the ploughed, fertile soil being equivalent to the embryonic fertility of the women. They do not farm the soil but their gender and reproductivity mirror that of the land.

Ploughing ceremonies in Attica

Hesiod advises the farmer to pray at the first sowing to Zeus Chthonios ('Zeus beneath the earth') and to holy Demeter that the goddess's sacred yield be 'complete and heavy'.[60] In one of Euripides' plays Aithra (Theseus' mother) at Demeter's temple at Eleusis calls upon this goddess and her priests to pray for herself, Theseus and Athens. She is offering a sacrifice for the ploughed land: she has come from her home in Athens itself to Eleusis, where the wheat first shoots forth from the soil. The sacrifice she offers presumably represents the offering which women would normally make at the festival of ploughing, the proerosia.[61]

Plutarch mentions three ritual ploughings, under the acropolis, at Skiron, and at the Rarian plain, Eleusis.[62] These are presumably the most important ones, and there will have been other ploughings which involved rituals. Ritual ploughings are mentioned in deme documents, going under various names and spellings: plerosia, proerosia, prerosia. The deme Myrrhinous celebrated the plerosia for Zeus on the fifth day of a month which needs to be restored; sometimes the month Posideion is suggested, but Pyanopsion, given the date of the Thesmophoria and Eleusis' announcement of a sacred ploughing in this month, would be better. The sacred calendar of Eleusis has the announcement for the proerosia taking place on 5 Pyanopsion; there is no reason why the festival itself (like its announcement) was not also on this day. This proerosia is probably the sacred ploughing which Aithra presided over and which Plutarch mentions. There was a prerosia at the Athenian deme Thorikos according to the local sacred calendar, which mentions it twice, the second time definitely in Boedromion, with the month lost for the first mention. Similarly, a plerosia was celebrated in the Piraeus, where the festivals Kalamaia and Skira were also held. The deme Paiania held a proerosia.[63] Each deme presumably had some sort of pre-ploughing ceremony and Thesmophoria. Although apart from Aithra women leave no trace in these mentions, it would be very surprising if they had no role in these events, especially as the proerosia and Thesmophoria must have stood in some relationship to each other.

Haloa: the whisperings of adultery

The Athenian Haloa was celebrated on 26 Posideion (November–December), a few months after the women had been so concerned with the crops. As with the Thesmophoria, most of the information about the Haloa festival comes from the scholiast on Lucian.[64] But first, the little contemporary evidence needs examination. In the fourth century BC, Archias, the hierophant of the Eleusinian Mysteries, was found guilty of impiety in an Athenian lawcourt for carrying out an unlawful sacrifice for the hetaira Sinope at the Haloa in the courtyard at Eleusis, as it was illegal to sacrifice on that day in the courtyard; in any case the woman priest ought to have officiated. Why she in particular should have carried out this sacrifice is not made clear; the nature of the victim or its purpose might have provided the reason. The impiety in this case was against the god Dionysos, for the speaker refers to it as an act against 'the same god' that Neaira's daughter has wronged at the Anthesteria (i.e. Dionysos, one of the deities honoured at the Haloa).[65]

In the second century BC, a demarch of Eleusis was honoured for making sacrifices for the Haloa, and for Chloe, Demeter, Kore, and for the other gods, according to ancestral practice; this identifies Eleusis as the location for the Haloa (the sacrifice must be imagined as taking place somewhere other than the courtyard).[66] While part of the Haloa was a secret rite for women, this was apparently preceded by general celebrations. There was a contest (agon) of some sort as part of the overall festivities, and an inscription reports that at one celebration of the Haloa for Demeter and Kore, all the citizens were invited to the sacrifice by a general and he paid for the expenses himself.[67]

In addition to this evidence, the Lucian scholiast provides various details: this festival concerned mysteries of Demeter, Kore and Dionysos (for the cutting of the vine and the tasting of the wine which had been set aside from the previous season). Male genitalia featured prominently at the festival, as a symbol of human procreation, with the god Dionysos' gift of wine causing male erections. The god had given the wine to Ikarios, an Athenian farmer, who was then killed by shepherds who had drunk the wine, ignorant of how it would affect them and blaming him for their drunkenness. They then attacked Dionysos himself, and were driven mad by the permanent erections they received because of the alcohol. An oracle advised that they would no longer suffer if they set up clay model phalloi. They did so, and their sanity and limpness returned; the Haloa commemorated this experience.

But the women also celebrated the Haloa on the same day, at Eleusis, to which they went for this purpose. Much playfulness and jibing occurred; the women priests whispered into the women's ears incitements to adultery. The women handled representations of male and female genitalia; there was plentiful wine; tables were laden with the foods of both land and sea, along with dough genitalia (male and female). The (male) archons set up the tables for the women, but went outside and left the women alone for the festival, and once outside the archons explained to the men who were present for the other festivities that the Eleusinians discovered nourishment for the human race. The Athenian state supported the festival, valuing its function. What was the point of the wine, if women did not drink it? As will be seen in the discussion of maenadism and the Adonia, sacred rites clearly provided women with access to drink, and apparently not just 'samples' but enough for each woman to have a good-sized quantity of it; one recalls the wineskin of the woman in Aristophanes' *Thesmophoriazousai*, discussed above. Tipsy or drunk women would be more open to suggestions of adultery; the Romans, of course, linked women, wine and adultery together.

The obscenities involved, the representations of the genitalia and the suggestions of adultery, i.e. promiscuity, clearly aided by drink, feasting and the absence of restraining menfolk (though note their presence just outside), are more than aischrologia (ritual abuse), and here clearly promote fertility. The Eleusinians took credit not merely for spreading the art of agriculture, but apparently also viticulture, hence Demeter, Kore (Persephone) and Dionysos are all invoked by the women at the Haloa. The encouragement of the fertility of the foods humans need to exist extends into the sphere of human fertility, with the dough genitalia promoting this. Women, as always, have the most important role in promoting this fecundity.

The Haloa might be seen as particularly attractive to prostitutes. Sinope the hetaira brought her victim to Eleusis on that day, and it is unlikely that this was a coincidence. The hetairai in Lucian obviously took part in a celebration of the Haloa, with one asking another in Lucian's *Dialogues of the Hetairai* what her lover had given her for the feast of the Haloa. Alkiphron has them present at all-night festivities of the Haloa, obviously combining business with pleasure in a way citizen wives did not. These are presented as prostitutes' celebrations, and the nocturnal element is missing from the citizen wives' celebration.[68] What attracted prostitutes to the Haloa will have been the emphasis on sexual innuendo and wine; they did not mix with the wives at Eleusis but are to be imagined as celebrating in their own homes.

Some vases are traditionally associated with the Haloa. The best known of these is the one involving a woman 'tending' phalloi: respectfully garbed, she sprinkles something onto four phalloi which are sticking out of the ground; shoots and leaves, perhaps of grain plants, cluster around the phalloi, and the intention seems to be that the phalloi are growing, in the same way as a sheath of corn grows. It is perhaps water (or wine) which she is sprinkling on them (Figure 4.1).[69]

Other phalloi representations, which Deubner associated with the Haloa, are perhaps to be thought of as belonging to phallic processions, such as that at the City (Great) Dionysia. In one such scene which he associates with the Haloa, a naked woman stands to the right of a vertical phallos, the same height as herself. On the left, a dressed woman holds a hem of her skirt bunched up in her right hand, and kicks up her left leg in a dance, with her left hand raised; she is obviously dancing in front of the phallos while the woman holds it.[70] At the Haloa the women played on the threshing floors, presumably those in the sanctuary itself, and this is how the festival got its name, from the word for threshing (haloa). This playfulness might have included dancing, but giant

Figure 4.1 Woman 'watering' four phalloi in the ground, possibly a representation of the Haloa; red-figure Athenian pelike; *c.* 430 BC; Washing Painter (courtesy, ©The Trustees of the British Museum, inv. E819).

phalloi are not heard of in connection with this festival. These scenes in fact might not even be representations of phallophoria celebrations, but the artist's imaginative depiction of prostitutes with their dildos, especially as the scene discussed is from a drinking-cup which would be used in men's drinking-parties.

A fragment of a vase shows a naked woman carrying a pot full of six phalloi, each with an eye.[71] But this should be compared with a scene in which a naked woman – a prostitute – has a leg in a similar basket, and looks as if she is climbing into it, holding one such phallos with two more in the basket, which Keuls interprets as '[a] hetaera leaps into a basket full of dildos'.[72] When is a phallos simply a dildo (olisbos, plural: olisboi), when is it an example of a phallophoria, and when is it part of the Haloa? A naked woman on a vase carries a large model phallos horizontally: perhaps she is part of a phallophoria, or is she a prostitute with an extra-large dildo?[73] The phalloi with eyes in the baskets are identical to the eyed phalloi which prostitutes are seen using in some scenes, as in the red-figure vase in which a prostitute is inserting one vaginally and is about to insert one into her mouth.[74] It seems safe to assume that the woman tending the phalloi is taking part in a Haloa ritual, but naked, cavorting women with small or medium-size model phalloi are prostitutes with dildos, while the naked woman with the mega-phallos is a parody of the prostitute's substitute. The Haloa was primarily a festival of women's fecundity and of the vine. The scurrility and model genitalia of the Haloa were generative in nature, and allowed for and perhaps required 'liberating' behaviour and language, promoting the consolidation of gender identity amongst the citizen wives of Athens.

The Skira festival

The Skira festival came over half a year after the Thesmophoria. What was secret about the women's role in the festival remains so.[75] It was at this festival that the women of Aristophanes' *Ekklesiasousai* hatched their plot to take over the acropolis. In the *Thesmophoriazousai*, it is suggested that the woman who bears a son useful to the state was to have proedria – the first place – at the Skira and the Stenia.[76]

The Skira, also sometimes referred to as the Skiraphoria, started with a procession; it was held on the twelfth of the month Skirophorion (May–June); the month was named after the festival, indicating the celebration's importance. The woman priest of Athena Polias, the priest of Poseidon Erechtheus and the priest of Helios walked from the Athenian acropolis to Skiron; these three were shaded by canopies held over them by male members of the Eteoboutadai genos.[77]

Skiron is near the Kephissos river which divides Eleusis from the rest of Attica; near Skiron was a sanctuary of Demeter and Kore, where Athena and Poseidon were also honoured; at Skiron itself there was a shrine to the hero Skiron.[78] Athena and Poseidon are represented in this rite by their woman priest and priest, but the women's rites are especially bound up with the sanctuary of Demeter and Kore. It is women and the Skira who are associated in the sources and this indicates that Demeter rites were at the core of the festival. Perhaps, with the synoikismos ('unification') of Attica, Athena and Poseidon were installed here as the Athenian counterparts to Eleusinian Demeter and Kore, and the state might have felt it appropriate to send out representatives to honour them and signify Athens' and Eleusis' unity.[79]

The hero Skiron was not honoured as part of this festival, but gave his name to the area and hence the rite. Women will have honoured Demeter and Kore as they did in her other rites, but the only specific information about the festival is that they chewed garlic 'to keep sex at bay'.[80] Amongst Aristophanes' scurrilities against women is that they chew garlic in the morning so their husbands will not realise they have been having sex with other men during the night; i.e. no man could bear to have intercourse with a woman whose breath reeked of garlic.[81] The festival took place at the height of summer, and could well have been looking forward to the harvest, with Demeter and Kore honoured for this reason.[82] One of the three sacred ploughings mentioned by Plutarch took place here (the Skiron, the Rarian plain, and under the acropolis), so obviously it was an important sanctuary and festival. He states that this Skiron ploughing was in memory of the most ancient sowings, and a corresponding women's harvest festival would therefore be appropriate.[83]

Callimachus 'Hymn to Demeter'

> Sing maidens, and mothers sing after them,
> 'Demeter, greatly welcome, feeder of many,
> bringer of many measures [of grain]'.

Callimachus here describes a procession to a temple of Demeter. He provides no locality or temporal context,[84] although a scholiast gives the setting as Alexandria, with Ptolemy Philadelphos in the third century BC establishing the custom of the procession, in which a kalathos (ritual basket) was drawn in a cart by horses in imitation, the scholiast relates, of Athens. Whether there was such a procession at Athens is otherwise unknown, but some sort of scene as described by Callimachus must have occurred in at least one city and perhaps in several.[85]

The women wait for the kalathos to come by in procession, and to return to where it has set out from (Demeter's temple). As it comes by they will call out, 'Demeter, greatly welcome, "feeder of many", and "bringer of many measures (of grain)".' The women also warn that the uninitiated must watch the procession from ground-level: no girl or woman must watch from a roof or 'from above' (and so see the sacred contents of the kalathos, which are for viewing by the initiated only). The women must not do this even if they have unbound their hair (and so carried out one of the requirements of the cult). Men are not mentioned: it is clearly taken for granted that they will not be in the vicinity. The women refer to their spitting from dry mouths, and so they have obviously been fasting, as Demeter fasted while she searched for her daughter Persephone.[86] As part of the procession the women will walk the city, without sandals and with their hair unbound.[87]

The uninitiated may only go as far as the prytaneion, the town hall, while the initiated can go all the way to the goddess (i.e. to her temple), if they are under sixty; clearly the infertile aged women can no longer propitiate the goddess for a plentiful harvest. But for those women who are heavy with child, both the women who stretch out their hands to Eileithyia, the goddess of childbirth, and those who are in pain (i.e. currently in labour), it is enough to go in the procession as far as they can; Demeter will give them all things in quantity, just as if they had come to the temple itself. The women then sing a hymn invoking Demeter and a good harvest.[88] This is clearly a compulsory rite, for all women who can physically participate; the goddess requires the involvement of all fertile women.

Dining in the Demeter sanctuary at Corinth

Dining was a part of various cults, in which sacrifices had to be consumed at the place of the sacrifice, within the sanctuary, and not taken away. When the sacrifice had to be consumed immediately, dining arrangements would need to be made. This could be in tents erected for this purpose, or in permanent dining buildings. The best-preserved dining buildings in Greece are at the sanctuary of Demeter and Kore at Corinth, on the north slope of the Acrocorinth.[89] There were apparently fifty-two dining rooms in total in existence over the period of the late sixth–second centuries BC, each with couches on which the diners reclined; at the turn of the fifth century there were at least thirty rooms being used, which would accommodate between them, according to estimates, 200 to 240 people; there were anything between five and nine couches per room, with seven to eight the norm; each couch was for one diner. By the late fourth century BC, the dining rooms had an adjoining room for washing and cooking. Dining rooms, on average, were 4.5 by 5.0 metres in dimension.[90]

While there is no evidence that these rooms were used exclusively by women, a strong women's presence is indicated at this sanctuary by the types of dedications made, particularly jewellery, mirrors and loom-weights. Thousands of terracotta figurines of women, presumably Demeter, have also been found, and at least a fair proportion of these would have been dedicated by women. It seems reasonable to assume that women made use of these dining rooms, particularly during the celebration of any women-only festivals at Corinth (see the *frauenfest* section below), though men presumably made use of them as well on other occasions.[91] Terracotta model likna (singular: liknon, a tray or flat basket, with modelled fruit and cakes) were found in their hundreds in the sanctuary; most are just a few inches in diameter, given as offerings to the goddess, and that these were mainly women's offerings is more than probable.

A dedication of around the middle of the sixth century BC at Gela, Sicily, of an Attic vase reads, 'Sacred to Thesmophoros, from the skana of Dikaio'. The deity Thesmophoros corresponds to Demeter, and the word skana (i.e. skene) is used in the sense of a group participating in a sacred meal.[92] The woman Dikaio is in some sense the leader of a cultic dining group associated with the cult of Thesmophoros, and perhaps the dedication was made after a celebration of an all-women's rite.[93]

A woman official (the thoinarmostria, 'mistress of the banquet') presided over cult banquets of women at Sparta and Messenia, but is attested only from the third century BC. She had to ensure that the cult regulations of Demeter were observed, to fine offenders (200 drachmas, to be sacred to Demeter), and could herself be fined by the male officials known as the bidiaioi if she connived at the offence or herself broke the rules.[94] At Andania, the thoinarmostria 'for Demeter' and the hypothoinarmostriai (women assistants to the thoinarmostria) were assigned a specific place in the procession of the Mysteries; perhaps they presided at the sacred meal at which various cult officials and the artists and their assistants in the dances dined. The sacrifice of 100 lambs for the initiates might also imply a cult meal for the initiates at which they could have presided.[95]

A private cult at Halikarnassos, founded by Poseidonios, deals with the sacrificial meat and the perquisites of the priest, with the remaining meat to be distributed amongst the banqueters and the women, implying that the latter were not amongst the banqueters, or at least that they dined separately from them.[96] However, at the sanctuary of Demeter at Morgantina in Sicily, there are numerous terracotta figurines of reclining women banqueters, dating to the fourth and third centuries BC, presumably offered as votives to Demeter. The women will naturally have dined without the presence of men.[97]

The Tauropolia

In Menander's *Epitrepontes* (*Arbitrants*), Pamphile, an Athenian citizen girl, fell pregnant at the Tauropolia, a festival in honour of Artemis Tauropolia. She is referred to as a parthenos who was raped, and the man who assaulted her came upon the girls and women at their night revels;[98] he was alone, having sneaked up on the women secretly. He was Charisios; later he married Pamphile, unaware that she was the girl at the Tauropolia (and she unaware that he was the rapist). When Pamphile gives birth to a child just five months after marriage, Charisios leaves her. While men seem to have participated in some aspects of this festival, there were clearly women-only rites at the festival, upon which Charisios has intruded. Habrotonon, although a (female) slave, played an instrument (the psaltria) for some young girls that year at the Tauropolia, and joined in their play; similarly, at the Adonia, amidst the mourning for the youthful lover of Aphrodite there was time for playfulness.

After this, Habrotonon became a prostitute, and Charisios – Pamphile's husband – has hired her, disgusted at his wife's giving birth to what he thinks is a bastard child. So the presence of a slave-girl as an entertainer, who was young enough to join in the games of the citizen girls, is attested, but not that of a prostitute, which she was not at the time. There is no need to assume that this festival involved debauchery of any kind but the situation was presumably similar to the Adonia in Menander's *Samia*: a festival provides the setting for a tryst which has consequences worked out in a play.[99] There was also a chorus of women, at night, indicating singing and dancing at the Tauropolia.

There was a shrine to Artemis, the Tauropolion, at Halai Araphenides, a deme close to Brauron, where this goddess had another cult (that of Artemis Brauronia), the temple and site of which was some 6 kilometres north of that at Halai,[100] and Halai Araphenides is presumably the location of the festival of Artemis Tauropolos being referred to in the *Epitrepontes*.[101] The deme was about 30 kilometres from Athens. Little is known of this cult apart mainly from the references to it in the *Epitrepontes*. There were hieropoioi (cult-officials) of this cult, benefactors of the deme were proclaimed at the festival, and there were contests of some sort, but other features of its organisation are unknown.[102]

Euripides' *Iphigeneia in Tauris* (1449–61) clearly refers to the rites: the cult image of Artemis which Iphigeneia steals from Tauris is, Athena commands, to be taken to Halai in Attica, and set up there in a shrine,[103] with the image to be named for Tauris; for the rest of time mortals will sing of her as Artemis Tauropolos. She ordains a custom that when the people celebrate the festival a sword will be held to a man's throat and blood spilled, as a compensation (to Artemis) for Iphigeneia not carrying out the sacrifice of Orestes and Pylades, who had been consecrated as a human sacrifice to the goddess.[104] The temple of Artemis at Aulis,[105] like the temples of this goddess at Brauron and Halai Araphenides, may well have had women's rites not attested. There was also a sanctuary of Artemis–Iphigeneia at Hermion in Argos.[106]

The Corinthian *frauenfest* scenes

Several sixth-century BC vases from Corinth show scenes of women in a line holding hands. These scenes often occur in isolation, giving no indication of what specific activity the women are involved in; these lines of dancing women and other scenes on Corinthian vases showing women who are clearly engaged in some sort of religious activity are usually referred to as *frauenfest* (women's festival) scenes. For example, a rounded vase of the aryballos type, dating to 600–575 BC, shows two friezes of women; they hold hands and some of them carry wreaths. The artist, with minimal outlines and incised lines, indicates that they are respectably dressed, and with a headband in their hair, which flows down their back (see Figure 4.2).[107] The artist's intention seems to be to show the women dancing; they were probably holding hands in a circle. There is also a woman with a sacrificial basket (she is the middle figure in the lower register; it is a flat basket of tray-shape, and appears to have items in it). Another *frauenfest* scene shows women walking, with one of the women carrying a basket, on which various items such as bottles are visible. Smaller female figures, perhaps daughters, accompany them.[108] Other scenes also include women with children on their laps, as well as walking children, women flautists and women spinning.[109] Many of the *frauenfest* scenes, however, are simply of women holding hands and carrying wreaths. The interpretation of these various scenes

WOMEN-ONLY FESTIVALS

Figure 4.2 Women in lines, holding wreaths and each other's hands; so-called *frauenfest* (women's festival) scene: round aryballos vase, Corinth; 600–575 BC; The Skating Painter; height: 13.9 centimetres (courtesy, ©Walters Art Gallery, Baltimore: inv. 48.192).

is difficult and there is no agreement on their meaning, but clearly the women are participating in a variety of cult activities, which involve dancing, walking in procession and making offerings.

But some *frauenfest* scenes occur on the same vase as depictions of the so-called 'padded dancers' (who are also referred to as komasts), male figures with what can only be described as padded bottoms and bellies. The men are shown dancing, usually with one of their company drawing wine from a large pot, presumably indicating a ritual dancing activity in Dionysos' honour. The lines of dancing women occasionally appear in the same scene as, and face to face with, the padded dancers.[110] This has led some scholars such as Payne to argue that the *frauenfest* scenes as a whole must show women worshipping Dionysos; Juckers, however, preferred to see any *frauenfest* scene as connected with Artemis.

129

The methodological flaw in these interpretations is to assume that the chains of women and their baskets must indicate women in one single form of cultic activity, centred on one deity. This is not necessary. When children, or women spinning or nursing children, are evident, a kourotrophic goddess is presumably called for, probably Artemis. When women dance in company with the padded dancers, cult activity in honour of Dionysos can be assumed. Moreover, the fact that some vases with *frauenfest* scenes of chains of women were found in the sanctuary of Demeter and Kore on the Acrocorinth cannot be without significance.[111] But Aphrodite, who has not been a scholarly candidate, needs also to be considered. She was a major deity at Corinth, and there was no question but that respectable citizen women should worship her, and some of these scenes of dancing women might be intended for this goddess.

The artists who painted these scenes, such as the simple lines of dancing women with wreaths, obviously wished to indicate women at worship, but whether they had a specific cult activity in mind rather than simply a generic scene of women worshipping is unclear. The illustrated *frauenfest* scene (Figure 4.2) provides no clues as to which divinity is being worshipped. There are significant numbers of *frauenfest* depictions, indicating that at Corinth dancing women, sometimes in association with processions, were a central feature of women's worship. The *frauenfest* scenes do not in themselves point to a public venue for the dancing, but the frequency of the depiction of the theme seems to suggest the celebration of a public rite for one or more of Corinth's most important deities.

Elsewhere, geometric vases of Athenian manufacture also show chains of women.[112] At the Argive Heraion, sacred to Hera, late geometric pottery (*c.* 700 BC) shows women in procession, and is probably to be connected with the kourotrophic role of Argive Hera.[113] Girls danced publicly during religious festivals in other Greek states, particularly at Sparta (as will be seen in Chapter 7). Such a public display of women dancing at Corinth and elsewhere is absent at Athens, and presumably *mores* about women and their public appearances were responsible for this. But at Corinth public dancing by women was an important and intrinsic aspect of cult ritual. On Lesbos, the women danced for the goddess Hera, and held a beauty contest, apparently in her honour; the setting appears to have been public.[114]

Frauenfest scenes do not appear to survive into the fifth century BC, when Athenian pottery overwhelmed local manufacturers at Corinth. A small window of opportunity for the historian to glimpse the activities of these women presumably then closed, while the women themselves went on worshipping, unrecorded now in visible media with the major exception of the archaeology of the sanctuary of Demeter at Acrocorinth.

Women and parthenoi at panhellenic festivals

> It is a law of the Eleans to throw down Mount Typaion any women who are detected as having come to the Olympic festival or even having crossed the Alpheios river on the days on which women are prohibited.

Women – but not parthenoi (virgins) – were explicitly prohibited from attending and watching the Olympic festival held every four years, though at other times both parthenoi and women were admitted to the base of the altar of Zeus at Olympia. According to the law of Elis, which hosted the festival, any woman (as opposed to a parthenos) detected at an Olympic gathering or who was even found to have crossed the nearby river Alpheios during the celebration of the festival was to be thrown from Mount Typaion. The only exception to this regulation prohibiting women was the woman priest of Demeter Chamyne who during the festival sat on an altar opposite the hellanodikai, the Olympic umpires.[115] But the exclusion of women does not seem to have been the case at other panhellenic festivals, at Delphi, Nemea and the Corinthian Isthmus, and major sanctuaries and their festivals presumably attracted women of all classes as spectators.

The races of the Heraia for parthenoi were held every four years at the Olympic stadium, but along only five-sixths of its course; the races for men and boys were the original competitions held at the Olympics, and that for virgins might be quite an early rite as well, from the eighth century BC.[116] The victors in the races for virgins received a crown of olive and a portion of a cow which had been sacrificed to Hera, and could dedicate statues inscribed with their names (no such statues survive). The Heraia probably took place immediately before or after the Olympics.[117] Attendance at the Heraia may have been purely local, but, at about the same time as the Olympics, young girls might have been brought along with brothers competing at the Olympic contests themselves; that parthenoi could attend the Olympic festival is relevant.

While there is evidence from other festival sites for parthenoi who competed successfully in athletic competitions, it is not from the classical period. An inscription of the second half of the first century AD records victories for several parthenoi for contests at the Pythian, Isthmian, Nemean, Sikyonian, Athenian (Sebasteia) and Epidaurian festivals. The victories were spread over at least a five-year period, but victories in the Heraia at Olympia are not mentioned.[118]

Spartan girls were notorious for their athletic training, designed to make them healthy for child-bearing.[119] They may have ceased such play when they became wives and mothers, but the Spartan woman Lampito who comes to Athens keeps in training and practises her buttock-jumps.[120] Perhaps this is the origin of the bronze statuettes, from Sparta or of Spartan workmanship, of young girls running, dressed along the lines of Pausanias' description of the girls competing at the Heraia at Olympia: these statuettes could be dedications made after a notable success or victory, or perhaps when the athletic part of their life was over.[121]

Of the other main festivals, the Isthmia, the Pythia at Delphi, and the Nemea, in the absence of specific evidence for exclusion such as is found for Olympia (where in fact it appears that women's exclusion was unusual), it seems that women were probably not debarred from attending sacrifices made to the gods and watching the contests held in the gods' honour. The fifth-century BC Syracusan mime writer Sophron mentions women spectators at Isthmia in one of his pieces, while Pindar has parthenoi watching the local sports' competitions at Cyrene.[122] The *Homeric Hymn to Apollo* has Ionian wives and children on Delos for the festival of Apollo, attesting to a pilgrimage by them, accompanying their husbands and fathers. The *Hymn* also addresses the Delian girls who honoured the god with a chorus, dancing and singing in his honour.[123] Prostitutes, too, were available for hire at some (if not all) festivals.[124]

Women as statue washers

Callimachus describes the washing of the statue of Athena at Argos in his fifth hymn. Whether this is actually a cult hymn commissioned from Callimachus and sung for the occasion in Argos is unclear, but nevertheless the hymn indicates the importance of this ritual.[125] It was perhaps sung by a virgin or woman priest of Athena. 'As many as are the lotrochooi of Pallas, all come out', the hymn commences, the lotrochooi being the 'bathers' or 'washers' of the statue. The sacred horses have arrived, the goddess is ready to go; the women of Argos must all hasten to the temple. This statue is addressed throughout the hymn as Athena: the statue is the goddess. The women are told not to bring perfumes or alabaster jars for Athena does not like scented oils – hurry up, the axles of the wagon are creaking – and the instruction is repeated separately, addressed to the lotrochooi; nor is a mirror to be brought. They are urged to bring 'manly' olive oil, and a golden comb for Athena to use after anointing her hair with the oil.

Athena is then asked to come out, as the daughters of Akestor (an Argive hero) are waiting to bathe her in the river. Water is not to be drawn from the river today for drinking; the women slaves are to take their water from the springs. A clear apposition is set up here between the free women of Argos who take part in the procession, and the slaves who do not.[126] In a similar ritual, Hera, 'the Argives say', washed each year in the spring called Kanathos to renew her virginity. The Eresides, Argive women priests of Hera, drew water for her bath. Clearly this is a plynteria rite, with her statue washed each year to revirginise Hera; the mysteries and secrecy of the rite point to the exclusion of men from the statue bathing.[127]

Pelasgian (i.e. Argive) men are then warned to stay away: whoever looks upon Athena (i.e. her statue) naked looks upon Argos for the last time. Callimachus then inserts a cautionary tale: Teiresias, who accidentally came upon Athena naked, was blinded (lines 51–136). At the river, the goddess Athena will be disrobed, and bathed, just as she bathed naked with her nymphs. The hymn closes: Athena the goddess is coming out now, the speaker says, and the korai (girls) whose task it is to do so are to receive the goddess with acclamations, prayers and ritual cries (ololygai). As the parthenoi are given a special role acclaiming the goddess, the lotrochooi are presumably married women. A lexicographer gives slightly different information, that at Argos the wives of the 'best men' who made up the aristocracy were responsible for washing the statue.[128]

The rite of the washing of Athena's statue at Athens (the Plynteria),[129] involving the disrobing and redressing of the archaic statue of Athena Polias (as opposed to the gold and ivory statue of Athena by Pheidias which did not need to be clothed and was housed in the Parthenon, and (as will be argued below) the statue of Pallas which was washed at Phaleron), was known as the Plynteria. The Athenian genos of the Praxiergidai was mainly responsible for the Plynteria, and most of the details about the role of this genos come from an inscription recording a decree of the boule and demos, dated variously between 460 to 420 BC, in which the state gives the Praxiergidai genos permission to set up its rules on a stele in the 'old temple' on the acropolis. Delphi had been consulted about the role of the Praxiergidai in the Plynteria, and the genos's privileges had been confirmed.[130] The decree arranges that the goddess was to have annually a chiton worth 2 mnai (200 drachmas), and it was probably the responsibility of the Praxiergidai to place the chiton on the goddess's statue.[131]

Hesychius and Photios define the loutrides as two korai or parthenoi, called plyntrides, concerned with the statue of Athena. These 'loutrides' or 'plyntrides' were 'washers'.[132] If the Praxiergidai women clothed the goddess, it seems reasonable to assume that the two girls responsible for washing the statue were also drawn from this genos. In addition, the lexicographers state that there was a kataniptes, presumably a woman, responsible for washing the peplos of Athena,[133] presumably also of the same genos. The aetiology specifically connects the Plynteria with a yearly cycle, because the women went one year without washing their clothes in grief at the death of Aglauros,[134] who had thrown herself from the acropolis after looking into the basket in which the baby Erichthonios was kept (why the other sister who committed suicide, Herse, is not mentioned is unclear).

Alkibiades arrived back at Athens in 407 BC on the day of the Plynteria, which Plutarch dates to 25 Thargelion and states was in honour of Athena, when the Praxiergidai celebrated secret rites, taking the clothes of the goddess and covering up her image. The day was therefore particularly ill-omened (apophras), and no meetings of the ekklesia are attested for it. Some Athenians felt it boded ill that Alkibiades returned then.[135] For the Plynteria and other ill-omened days the temples were roped off, denying access.[136] The Praxiergidai decree seems to refer to the temple being marked off during Thargelion, with the (basileus) archon to give the keys of the temple to the Praxiergidai for this period.[137]

Two later decrees have the ephebes (150 of them) responsible for escorting the 'Pallas' (a statue of Athena) to Phaleron and back again with torches, suggesting the statue had a dusk or evening return to its temple; the ephebes were to act with all eukosmia (good conduct); one of the decrees, of 107/6 BC, mentions that they escorted Pallas 'with the gennetai' (members of the genos).[138] At Phaleron, the city's ancient harbour before the Piraeus took over, a washing of the Pallas statue presumably took place.

Scholars are divided whether the Pallas statue and the statue in the 'old temple' are one and the same.[139] But Xenophon and Plutarch do not mention any trip to the sea to wash the statue of Athena at the Plynteria, and stress that the day was one of ill-omen *because* Athena's statue was covered up in her temple on that day. Clearly this particular statue did not go anywhere. Lexicographers, however, describe a procession for the Plynteria: a cake made of dried figs was borne in the procession, with the woman leading the procession being called the hegeteria, leader or guide. Nothing, however, is stated about the destination of this procession, which could have been a short one within the city, like other festivals, and cannot have involved the statue washed during the Plynteria.[140]

The Pallas statue must be the Palladion, another statue of Athena. The responsibility for this procession lay with the nomophylakes. A myth has King Demophon washing the Pallas in the sea before it was placed in its temple; Demophon belonged to the Bouzygai genos, and the procession to Phaleron re-enacted this, and the gennetai mentioned will have been the Bouzygai.[141] The inscriptions[142] place the procession between festivals to Artemis Agrotera (6 Boedromion), a sacrifice at Eleusis (perhaps the Eleusinian Mysteries of 15–21 Boedromion) and the proerosia there, and the City (Great) Dionysia (10–13 Elaphebolion), so this procession took place between the months Boedromion and Elaphebolion, and so not in chronological proximity to the Plynteria in Thargelion. Where was the Pallas housed? The Palladion, the place of the Pallas, seems to offer a clue. Here, located at either the Piraeus or Zea (another harbour), trials for homicide were held,[143] and perhaps the statue was annually cleansed in this connection. The Palladion was much closer to Phaleron than the acropolis, and this is further indication that the Pallas was not connected with the Plynteria but was washed in a separate rite.

The Kallynteria was associated with the Plynteria, and presumably also took place in Thargelion. Presumably it involved cleaning and purifying the 'old' temple in which the statue was kept.[144] The sacred calendar of the Athenian deme Thorikos mentions a Plynteria in the month Skirophorion, apparently for Athena and Aglauros, indicating that a local statue-washing ceremony was carried out by the demeswomen.[145]

In the third-century BC inscription regulating the procession and sanctuary for Aphrodite Pandemos in Athens, built in the second half of the fourth century BC by a mother and son, the astynomoi were to purify the sanctuary whenever the procession was due to take place. Purification was by means of a dove, and the altar was to be anointed: presumably the blood of the dove was the purificatory agent and the altar was anointed with its blood, the roof was to be smeared with pitch, and the statues were to be washed. Pausanias refers to a sanctuary of Aphrodite Pandemos and Peitho, so the statues being washed must be these deities. A woman priest is referred to in the inscription and presumably she was responsible for the washing. All the arrangements are being made 'according to ancestral practice'.[146]

Euripides' *Iphigeneia in Tauris* has Iphigeneia taking the statue of Artemis to bathe it in the sea. She wants to escape King Thoas, but to do so needs to get to the sea where her brother Orestes' ship awaits her; Orestes, however, with Pylades his comrade is a captive of the king in the temple. They were to be sacrificed, by Iphigeneia, to Artemis, but their identity is revealed, and she determines to help them and escape. To get to the sea, she concocts a plan, taking the statue of Artemis out of the temple. When challenged by the king when he sees her coming out with it, she states that the statue of its own accord turned around and closed its eyes. She claims that the prisoners are unclean, Orestes having killed his mother; this has offended the goddess. Both the statue and the prisoners must therefore be purified in the sea. Significantly, as the statue comes out, people are warned off: all must stay indoors, and those who have come to the temple on account of marriage, or those heavy with child, must go; Iphigeneia stresses that the rite must take place in secret; the henchmen who accompany her must stay out of sight while the rite is performed.[147]

On Kos, when a sanctuary became polluted because of a corpse, the woman priest took the statue of the Kourotrophos to the sea, and purified it.[148] Just as the bride would bathe before her marriage with water drawn from a fountain, so too the wooden image of Zeus' bride at Plataea would be bathed before being burned. In the aetiological myth, the nymphs of the river Triton brought the water for the marriage bath.[149]

At the Tonaia festival, the Samians similarly purified the image of Hera, taking it to the shore of the sea each year to wash it, and made offerings of barley cakes to the statue. In the aetiological myth Admete, who had the care of the temple and statue, purified the statue then set it back on its pedestal, and presumably this purification and replacing the statue on its pedestal would have been the responsibility of the woman priest of Hera, the ritual equivalent of the presumably mythical Admete.[150] At Ephesos, the statue of Artemis was taken out of the temple down to the seashore, laid down on top of celery and other plants, offered food and purified with salt. The aetiological myth explains that Klymene, the daughter of Ephesos' king, originally carried out this rite with korai and epheboi; girls, youths and a woman priest were all presumably involved in the historical version of the rite.[151]

The month Plynterion, 'washing', is attested on the islands of Chios, Ios, Paros and its colony Thasos.[152] Similar festivals of washing statues and clothing probably occurred in these places, and were important enough to name a month after. Women were almost certainly the chief officiants in the case of the celebration involving statues of goddesses. Male gods might well have required men rather than girls and women to wash them. At Olympia, the seated statue of Zeus by Pheidias was washed by the Phaidryntai, the 'cleansers', who were the male descendants (so the people of Elis said) of Pheidias himself; they had charge of making a sacrifice before they cleansed the statue of anything that had settled on it (dirt, dust, probably bird droppings as well), and then they polished the statue.[153]

At Eleusis, there was a similarly named official, the (male) Phaidyntes, 'Cleanser', but of his cleansing functions nothing is known.[154] Other gods had such an official. At Athens, Zeus Olympios 'in the City' and Zeus 'from Perses' each had a Phaidyntes.[155] Statues were cleaned on numerous occasions on which we do not know who was responsible, as in a first-century BC inscription from Galatia in which the statue is washed.[156] A private cult of Poseidon has the statues being purified before a sacrifice.[157]

Goddesses, even in statue form, could not be seen naked by the eyes of men. As goddesses bathed with their nymphs, so their statues entrusted themselves only to women whose privy parts were akin to theirs. Not for men's eyes was the naked image of Athena's statue on the acropolis. They might escort another statue of her to the ancient harbour for a bath, but they would not disrobe or re-dress her. Their qualities were in the masculine sphere of protection, or in organisational matters such as roping off temples on the day of the Plynteria. Both at Argos and Athens, Athena eschewed the company of men for her annual toilette.

Peplos presentation and weaving

> Making the sacred cry (ololyge) all the women raised their hands to Athena
> and the beautiful-cheeked woman priest Theano taking the peplos
> placed it on the knees of lovely-haired Athena
> and prayed to the daughter of mighty Zeus.

The best and earliest example of the presentation of a peplos to a goddess is in Book Six of the *Iliad* in which the Trojan women attempt to placate Athena by presenting her with a peplos. They are led by Hekabe, wife of Priam. When Diomedes is wreaking havoc amongst the Trojans the seer Helenos, son of Priam, tells Hektor to go back to the city and have his mother present Athena with a peplos and a promise of twelve 1-year-old heifers. Hekabe finds the best peplos in her store, 'the most beautiful, embroidered, the largest, glittering like a star' (296), woven by the women of Sidon whom Paris brought back to

Troy, and taking many of the older women of the city with her (which implies a procession) went to Athena's temple where Theano the woman priest let them in. The women made ritual laments, and stretched out their hands to Athena; Theano placed the peplos across the knees of the goddess, and prayed for Diomedes' spear to be broken, for pity for the Trojan wives and helpless children, with the promise to sacrifice twelve heifers. 'But Pallas Athena refused' (311).[158] The seer knows that these women are fit to present the peplos; it does not have to be made by their own hands, but Hekabe knows it needs to be the finest. Athena is not dressed in it, and presumably it was later stored along with Athena's other possessions.

Every four years at Olympia, the 'Sixteen Women' wove a peplos for Hera, for presentation to her cult statue. In addition, they organised two choruses – presumably of girls or perhaps women – in honour of Hippodameia and Physkoa. Hippodameia chose sixteen women to thank Hera for her marriage to Pelops; Physkoa was the first woman in Elis to worship Dionysos, and had a son by the god. The servants – diakonoumenai – of the Sixteen were also women, though whether they helped with the weaving, organisation or just menial tasks is unclear. Both the hellanodikai (the male judges of the Olympic contests) and the Sixteen Women had to purify themselves with a pig, and wash at the spring Piera, on the road from Olympia to Elis. At Amyklai in Sparta, every year women wove a chiton for Apollo in a special room called after the garment, the Chiton. Presumably this was presented to him during the Hyakinthia, and perhaps his statue was dressed in it.[159] The festival of the Endymatia (Robings) at Argos, about which nothing else is known, might well have been something to do with robing a statue.[160] At Athens, as has been seen, a peplos was presented every year to the archaic statue of Athena.

In so far as they are known, women's rituals involved the following activities: women slaughtered piglets and threw them into a pit; later other women, specially purified through abstinence from sexual intercourse, brought out the remains. Women abused each other, listened to suggestions of adultery and promiscuity, and drank wine. Together they plotted against their menfolk and chewed garlic. They ate sacred meals in special dining rooms attached to cults which were particularly their own. Some in their local areas made sacrifices for their local fields, using the money provided by their husbands. Others linked hands, weaving stately processions. Solemnly, women washed ancient statues and laundered clothes for them, re-dressing the ancient and venerable goddesses. Whether ribald or stately all these activities had one thing in common: citizen women celebrated rites without the presence of men, though with their blessing and assistance. Women's role is crucial, not to be gainsaid by men.

Men permit women to engage in scurrilities and abuse, and to leave the household for a day or days to do so. And it is important to note that of the various festivals reviewed here, only the Tauropolia was at night. Demeter is not a prolific child-bearer but it is the Eleusinian myth of her control over agriculture for which she is invoked. It is in fact her daughter's absence with a male – Hades – that interrupts fertility and threatens starvation. So her daughters, the women of Athens, Eleusis, Syracuse, Eretria, Thasos, Paros, and numerous other places, leave their men behind and return to the worship of the mother, who in return provides the gift of fertility, both of field and of body. Women's own fertility is linked with that of the fields, but it is also apparent that their own procreativity enables them to mediate with the goddesses Demeter and Persephone for those very fields. They are, in a very real sense, in an empathetic relationship with the soil.

How women felt about their role is unknown; the only women at a Thesmophoria who speak to us are those of Aristophanes' *Thesmophoriazousai*, and judging by their cranky attitudes they are not enjoying their fasting. Their various complaints about men and sex certainly reflect the ribaldry of the other women-only celebrations. But while Aristophanes does not include the Thesmophoria as one of those rites for which women quickly grab their drums and go,[161] they surely welcomed these various rites, with drinking, feasting, sexual repartee with their peers, and a real 'night out with the girls', except that with one exception the festivals looked at in this chapter were apparently a 'day' or 'days' out, and their husbands and home beckoned at the end of the day and the rites.

5

WOMEN AT THE MARGINS OF GREEK RELIGION

Many of the deities worshipped by Greek girls and women in the classical period were very much a part of mainstream religious beliefs, particularly those dealt with in Chapters 2 and 4. But there were other deities which held a marginal place in classical Greece because of their exotic nature, or whose worship undercut the values of the polis and women's place in it. Of the latter, the most important was women's worship of the god Dionysos, and as part of their worship they were subjected to madness, mania, by the god. But in most senses Dionysos was an 'acceptable' god, admitted into the festivals of the state, with maenads (his women followers) at Athens clearly involved in drawing the wine at the Anthesteria festival. Maenads are nevertheless at the margins, they test the polis' acceptance of rites which are in many ways extraordinary: wild dancing, unescorted journeys into the hills, and clearly some wine drinking. Women in other cults also occupied the fringes of Greek religion. The women followers of Pythagoras were ridiculed, perhaps partly because of the ritual practices of Pythagoreanism but probably because as women taking on a philosophical mantle they were easy targets of ridicule. A picture of women involved in the rites of the foreign god Sabazios could be conjured up in a law speech to damage an opponent's reputation. The worship of Adonis entered Athens sometime in the fifth century BC; women's activities in this cult were tolerated but his festival, informal and somewhat exotic, was never accepted into the state calendar; worshipped by women on rooftops rather than in conventional temples, his rites were marginal and aloof from the polis in the most literal of senses. Hekate, goddess of the crossroads, was liminal in many ways, and worshipped by both men and women, but was considered to be particularly important to women who practised sorcery; spells and incantations were employed in her name, but when a certain boundary was passed, the woman practitioner of the magical arts could face a death sentence.

Dionysos, 'Lord of the Maenads'[1]

> So now I, Dionysos, have driven them (the sisters of my
>   mother) goaded by madnesses [maniai] from home;
> they are living on the mountain, with frenzied wits,
> and I have forced them to wear the equipage of my rites [orgia],
> and all the female seed of Kadmos' people [the Thebans], all of
>   them who are
> women [gynaikes], I have driven mad from their homes.[2]

Euripides depicts Dionysos exulting in the manic possession of his worshippers, maenads, or, as he terms them, bacchae. To visualise a maenad, a follower of Dionysos, one need only look at an Athenian vase by the Brygos Painter (c. 480–470 BC): this maenad has a snake headband, holds her thyrsos in one hand and a panther (or leopard) cub in the other, and she wears a panther (or leopard) skin. The thyrsos was a branch, sometimes of fennel; the end was wrapped with ivy usually with a pine cone – often stylised in artistic depictions – at one end. Barefoot, her unbound hair is flung up as she dances; she is undoubtedly the 'best dressed' and evocative of the numerous depictions of maenads (Figure 5.1).[3] In classical religion, maenads were women devotees of Dionysos, possessed by him and dancing ecstatically in his honour. There were many myths about them, and the maenads of myth and those of reality do not necessarily share the same features. Nevertheless what is clear is that in cities such as Thebes, bands of women during the classical period and later went off by themselves to the mountains to worship the god of wine, while at Athens, women who can be described as maenads are shown drawing wine from jars in the presence of a representation of Dionysos.[4]

Diodoros notes that the Boeotians – where mythically Dionysos' worship in Greece was said to have originated and where maenadism was apparently best represented – and other Greeks had biennial sacrifices to Dionysos, and that every second year bacchic bands (bakcheia, singular: bakcheion) of women collected in many cities.[5] Young girls, parthenoi, carried the thyrsos.[6] Maenads on vases are seen using these to stave off satyrs, mythical creatures sexually aroused by them but never successful in their urge to debauch them. The maenads, Diodoros continues, cry out 'euoi' and join in the enthousiasmos, the state of possession by the god. The women form groups, and sacrifice to the god, as well as 'bakcheuein' (celebrate Bacchus), singing hymns and acting like the maenads of old (i.e. those of myth).

Euripides' *Bacchae*, written probably in 406 BC, immediately springs to mind when considering maenads, as it is the best-known and longest account of Dionysos and the maenads.[7] Semele, one of the daughters of Kadmos of Thebes, gave birth to Zeus' son, Dionysos. Her sisters denied Dionysos' divinity, so he came to Thebes with a band of maenads from Asia and sent the Theban women, including Semele's three sisters, mad with Dionysos worship and they became

Figure 5.1 Maenad with thyrsos, bare feet, panther-skin shawl, panther, and snake headband; Athenian red-figure cup (kylix); white ground; 480–470 BC; Brygos Painter; diameter of painting: 14 centimetres (courtesy ©Staatliche Antikensammlungen und Glyptothek, Munich: inv. 2645).

maenads. Leaving everything behind, including husbands and children, they fled to the mountains, engaging there in maenadic rituals in honour of the god. Dionysos has caused the women to abandon their looms and shuttles, symbolising their domestic tasks, indicating how completely they have abandoned their normal way of life (36, 217, 118, 1236). Pentheus, son of Agaue one of the daughters of Kadmos, has become king and attempts to stamp out Dionysos worship. The god persuades Pentheus, disguised as a woman and a maenad, to spy on the worshippers. Discovered, he is torn apart by them (the sparagmos rite) acting under the delusion that he is a lion.

But Dionysos' maenads are also encountered from the very beginning of Greek literature. The myth of Lykourgos who attacked the maenads who were with Dionysos and was struck blind by Zeus and died appears in the *Iliad*.[8] Herakleitos in the sixth century BC referred to them.[9] There are various myths involving the daughters of Proitos, but Hesiod has a version in which they refused to accept the rites (teletai) of Dionysos, were sent mad, and suffered from machlosyne, apparently a form of indecency in which they shed their clothes, their hair fell out, and they lost their good looks.[10] Bacchylides has the daughters sent mad by Hera for insulting her, and they flee to the mountains, leaving behind the god-built streets of the city of Tiryns. This must be a reference to maenadic behaviour, and Apollodoros has them wandering all over Argos and Arkadia. Other women joined them, leaving their homes and killing their children, a mythical representation of maenadic abandonment of domestic duties.[11] The madness sent by Hera is seen in Bacchic terms.

Another myth has the three daughters – Leukippe, Arsippe and Alkathoe – of Minyas of Orchomenos refusing to leave their domestic tasks when the other women went off as maenads to worship Dionysos; he sent them mad and Leukippe lost her son in a sparagmos rite. It has been suggested that Aeschylus' *Xantriai* ('Carders of Wool') might also have dealt with this myth.[12] Aeschylus also wrote plays connected with Bacchic themes,[13] and other writers, including perhaps Sophocles, also dealt with similar material,[14] indicating a high level of interest in maenads in the classical period.

Probably the most powerful scenes in the *Bacchae* are the ones involving the rending of living human and animal flesh by the maenads. But only once is the eating of raw flesh mentioned, by the Asiatic chorus of maenads in the play who have come with Dionysos to Thebes. 'Omophagos charis', the joy of eating raw flesh, is an attribute of Dionysos (139). Euripides' maenads, however, both Asiatic and Theban, amongst their various 'excesses', do not eat raw meat. Presumably, their historical counterparts did not do so either. In Euripides' *Cretans*, the chorus of initiates of Zagreos, a Cretan deity, lists several initiatory rituals, including 'carrying out feasts of raw flesh', but also that they have abstained from the flesh of living animals; clearly Euripides is here presenting a mish-mash of mystery cults and none in particular.[15] Alcaeus, however, describes Dionysos as Omestas, 'Raw-Eater', in connection with a precinct on the island of Lesbos,[16] while Plutarch makes it clear that this rite was practised widely, and refers to days when the omophagia took place as ill-omened and mournful.[17] From these brief classical allusions, one passes to the Christian writers and a lexicographer, who connect it with Dionysos' own mythical dismemberment and consumption at the hands of the Titans.[18]

A cult rule from Miletos concerning Dionysos worship has a regulation that no one at the sacrifice is omophagion embalein, 'to throw down the raw meat', until the woman priest does so on behalf of the city. Any notion that this inscription refers to the eating of raw meat by the maenads is not correct.[19] Clearly the throwing of raw meat is part of maenadic ritual, as Euripides makes clear when he has Pentheus' various body parts being thrown around; but in cultic reality it occurs within the formal structure of the sacrifice. Cult, at least at Miletos, reflected the sparagmos in a rather prosaic, almost sanitised form. The historical maenads – as far as is known – did not tear sacrificial animals limb from limb; they did so only in myth, as in the *Bacchae*: Pentheus' mother ripped apart a full-uddered cow with her bare hands; ribs and cloved hooves were thrown this way and that, and bits of flesh hung from the pines, dripping blood (735–47). While it is perhaps possible that away from the confines of the ritualised sparagmos of the cultured city some form of dismemberment actually did take place up in the mountains, one wonders what animals the women would have found for such a rite; presumably historical maenads did not chance upon deer or fawns and rip them to pieces. But what can be said is that at Miletos and probably elsewhere, Dionysos unlike other gods accepted sacrifices of raw (uncooked) flesh in his role as a liminal god whose worship often took place outside the civilised world of the polis.

On vase paintings maenads are sometimes but not frequently shown with the limbs of dismembered animals, but are never shown eating them.[20] The earliest depiction (520–505 BC) of the sparagmos of Pentheus, on a fragment of a vase, shows two maenads each grasping one of his arms; his right rib-cage has already been torn away, while another fragment of the same vase shows a maenad holding one of his legs aloft:[21] 'we with our own hands captured this wild beast [Pentheus] and tore it limb from limb', sings the chorus of maenads about Pentheus in the *Bacchae*.[22] Another vase depicts a maenad with a foreleg in one hand and a sword in the other;[23] while in Euripides' *Bacchae* the maenads use their bare hands, there was also a tradition that maenads wielded daggers and swords for dismembering, and the artist is here following a non-Euripidean (and less spectacular) version.[24] In a well-known scene, a maenad dances while holding two halves of a fawn.[25] The baby satyr who appears on one of the vases mentioned above might also possibly be a reference to a sparagmos of the children of maenads, or more probably the mother has not been able to leave her child at home and he has been 'satyrised' in a comical fashion.[26]

Maenads on the mountains

In the *Bacchae*, Dionysos drives the women to Mt Kithairon; they sing of Dionysos rushing to the mountains of Phrygia and Lydia. 'To the mountain, to the mountain', is their ritual cry.[27] This is the oreibasia, the trip to the mountains. When Demeter in the *Homeric Hymn* sees her daughter Persephone returning from Hades, 'she rushed, as a maenad does along the thick-shaded wood on the mountain'.[28]

Anakreon in addressing Dionysos referred to him as whirling on the high mountain peaks.[29] In hellenistic Miletos, the epigram on the tomb of Alkmeonis, the 'holy woman priest' of Dionysos, records that she led the Bacchae to the mountains, and carried the cult's sacred objects in procession through the city.[30] An Athenian red-figure skyphos by the Brygos Painter (c. 480–470 BC) shows a maenad dancing between two high formations of rocks;

Parnassos is possibly intended.[31] A second-century AD inscription from Physkos in Lokris regulating the affairs of a thiasos of maenads stipulates that whoever does not go with the others to the mountains was to pay a fine of 5 drachmas to the association.[32]

Euripides refers to the biennial festivals of Dionysos (133). The Athenian women known as Thyiades went every second year to Mt Parnassos to celebrate rites of Dionysos with the women of Delphi.[33] As in Boeotia, many biennial festivals are attested throughout the Greek world.[34] At Miletos, any woman who wished to carry out rites to Dionysos Bakchios, either in the city, countryside or islands (around Miletos) could do so, but had to pay the woman priest a stater every two years for the privilege of doing so.[35] Such rites may well have been popular: as noted in the Introduction, Lysistrata moans about the enthusiasm with which women would turn out if summoned to worship various gods at their shrines, and she includes a Bakcheion, a shrine of Bacchus (Dionysos).[36]

Snakes appear in the *Bacchae* as attributes of the maenads, being in their hair and licking their cheeks (101–4, 698, 767–8).[37] Historical examples of maenads handling snakes occur in the case of Olympias, Alexander the Great's mother. She provided large tame snakes for the thiasoi (singular: thiasos: a religious group), with the implication that this was not the previous practice; the snakes often crawled out from the ivy and the mystic baskets, and curled themselves around the thyrsoi and garlands of the women.[38] These will have been of the non-venomous sort, like the ones which inhabited Asklepios' sanctuaries, though while the women had no problems with these, the men at the Macedonian court were 'panic-stricken' by the snakes.

The ordered women of the polis keep their hair neat and tidy, and when appearing in ritual roles their hair is often elaborately styled. When the maenads awake on the mountain in the morning in the *Bacchae*, they let down their hair (which they had bound for the night's sleep) onto their shoulders, and adjusted their fawn-skins for the day (695–7). Loose hair is a renunciation of the ordered domestic and social routine of the women, and was a clear rite of liminality.[39]

The maenads had other cult paraphernalia. Dionysos instructs his Asian maenads who have come with him to beat their tympana (drums).[40] A maenad is shown leaning against a large tympanum on an Athenian red-figure pelike.[41] Duris of Samos describes Olympias as going forth as a Bacchant with tympana against her rival Eurydike.[42] The Euripidean Bacchae ululate and cry out 'euai'.[43]

One of the chief ways women worshipped Dionysos was with the dance, which involved tossing the head, and whirling around.[44] A maenad throws back her head while grasping her thyrsos in both hands on a red-figure amphora.[45] Several maenads toss their heads on one of the vases discussed below in connection with the Anthesteria.[46] The Athenian sculptor Kallimachos carved reliefs of maenads on the monument of the choregos for Euripides' *Bacchae*; these were apparently frequently copied in Roman art. The macnads are shown tossing their heads, carrying thyrsoi and halves of animals, and some have daggers.[47] The Athenian Thyiades performed dances along the way when travelling to Parnassos in their biennial ritual.[48] There were clearly similar bands of women in other cities: in 355 BC the Phokian Thyiades in their maenadic wanderings came at night, unknowingly, to Amphissa, allied with Thebes; Phokis and Thebes were at war. The Thyiades flung themselves down in the agora and fell asleep. The women of Amphissa took up guard around them so that they did not come to harm; when they awoke, they each took care of a single Thyias. Having obtained permission from their husbands, the Amphissan women then escorted the Phokian Thyiades safely to the border.[49]

On one occasion the Athenian Thyiades who had ascended Mt Parnassos at Delphi had to be rescued because they had been caught in strong winds and a snowstorm; their mantles were so stiff from the cold that they broke when they were opened out.[50] Clearly this was a freak storm and unusual.[51] That it was abnormal for the Thyiades to be caught in a snowstorm even though they routinely went to the top of the mountain indicates that they went there in spring or summer, or perhaps autumn.

In classical maenadism, women worshipped without the company of men, and there was no male cult leader impersonating the god.[52] In the *Bacchae*, Pentheus accuses the women of both alcoholic and sexual excesses, claiming that the women are putting Aphrodite before Bacchus (i.e. Dionysos) and that the stranger whom he believes to be impersonating Dionysos is violating the women. But Dionysos in company with his maenads is clothed and asexual and in fact Pentheus' messenger absolves them of all these charges.[53]

When asked by Pentheus whether Dionysos' rites are performed at night or day, the god replies that most are held at night, for darkness is holy, which leads Pentheus to comment that darkness is devious and corrupt for women, obviously reflecting at least some men's anxieties and suspicions. The chorus also refers to night dancing. Similarly, Alkman refers to a festival of many torches on the mountain, presumably Dionysiac.[54] The historical incident of the Phokian women ending their night wanderings at Amphissa confirms this.[55]

Worth mentioning are the various vase scenes in which satyrs prepare to rape maenads. No one would suggest any cultic reality for these and they belong to a different world again from Euripides' *Bacchae*, and relate to the role of Dionysos as god of wine which brings sexual arousal; moreover, no satyr is shown as successful in his mission. These depictions might seem to present male fantasies, but rather in fact served to assuage men's anxieties: their wives and daughters while engaging in maenadic activities on mountains without the protection of husbands or relatives will nevertheless be sexually safe.

Maenadic thiasoi at Thebes

In myth, there were three maenadic thiasoi: the three sisters Autonoe, Agaue and Ino, daughters of Kadmos, lead the women in three choruses at Thebes; similarly, the three daughters of Minyas at Orchomenos, and the three daughters of Proitos at Argos, are possessed by Dionysos. An inscription from Magnesia on the Maeander makes this pattern clear, beginning with a Delphic oracle referring to the Theban thiasos:

> 'Go to the holy plain of Thebes to fetch maenads from the race of Kadmean Ino. They will bring you maenadic rites and noble customs and will establish troops of Bacchus in your city'. In accordance with the oracle, and through the agency of the envoys, three maenads were brought from Thebes: Kosko, Baubo and Thettale. And Kosko organized the thiasos named after the plane tree, Baubo the thiasos outside the city, and Thettale the thiasos named after Kataibates.

After their death, these particular maenads were honoured with a public burial at Magnesia. The fact that there were to be three thiasoi each led by a woman 'imported' from Thebes shows the importance of the trithiasic model in mythical and real maenadism.[56] Dionysos in Euripides' *Bacchae* relates how Thebes was the first city in Greece to ululate (make the ritual cry), to wear the fawn-skin and to carry the thyrsos. Diodoros, too, in discussing maenadism specifically mentions Boeotia. It is obviously the case that maenadism was strong here.

Dionysos himself wears the fawn-skin and thyrsos, which he shakes. Pentheus is persuaded by Dionysos to dress as a woman, to don the garb of a Bacchant, and to carry the thyrsos so as to spy on the women.[57] In the exotic world of vases, women occasionally wear leopard (or panther) skins,[58] which presumably the maenads of cult could not aspire to, and even on vases, the fawn-skin is the more frequent accoutrement. Did they kill these fawns themselves, or did men do this and skin them for the women, and were fawn-skins handed down from generation to generation? On the pointed amphora of the Kleophrades Painter, two maenads wear fawn-skins with the heads still attached.[59]

In the third century BC Ptolemy II Philadelphos, probably in the 270s BC, held a Dionysiac procession, possibly as part of the Ptolemaia festival in Alexandria.[60] The statue of Dionysos was adorned, amongst other things, with thyrsoi and tympana, and with ivy and grape vine on the canopy over the statue. There were silenoi (older satyrs) and satyrs, and women impersonated Nikai (winged 'Victories') carrying gold thymiateria (incense-burners). Priests and women priests of Dionysos and thiasoi 'of every kind' were represented, perhaps referring to different types of Dionysiac thiasoi in the city. Interesting are the specific references to the Maketai (Macedonian women), called Mimallones, Bassarai and Lydai, with their hair streaming down, and who were crowned, some with snakes, others with (s)milax (a variety of bindweed), vine and ivy. Dionysos himself was crowned with snakes, as in the *Bacchae* (101–2). Some maenads had daggers in their hands, and others snakes. Whether these were Alexandrian women who belonged to thiasoi named after these groups, or whether they were simply impersonating maenads is unclear; there is always the possibility that Ptolemy imported representatives of these groups for the occasion. The knives are clearly an allusion to the sparagmos rite and once again considerations of whether women carried these simply to represent the myth or did actually slay victims are raised.

But one of the Macedonian kings, Argaios (c. 620 BC), short of men, supposedly had young women (parthenoi) show themselves on a mountain to the enemy; the young women rushed from the mountain, waving their thyrsoi and shading their faces with garlands. The enemy, thinking them to be men, retreated in panic. Argaios established a temple to Dionysos Pseudaner ('False Man'), and ordered that the parthenoi, previously called Klodones, be called Mimallones, as they had mimicked men. This is all quaintly aetiological, but points both to Dionysos' ambivalent sexuality (his effeminacy), and to the man-like qualities of the maenads of myth, who in Euripides' *Bacchae* easily defeat the armed men sent against them.[61]

Aeschylus' play about the Macedonian Bassarai (also Bassarides) indicates fifth-century BC interest in these Thracian Bacchants and about the phenomenon of Bacchants. Next to nothing is known about the Bassarai, except that they apparently took their name from the bassara, a chiton of fox-skins which they wore. Anakreon writes of the 'swaying Bassarides', a reference to their dance. The Macedonian Lydai will have taken their name from the Lydian women who were Dionysos' maenadic companions.[62]

This leads once again to the question of participation. Even putting aside the dictates of space on a vase, the maenads of Athens seem to come in very small groups indeed. Moreover, the travel of the Thyiades from Athens to Parnassos at Delphi, an expedition of several days, requiring leisure and some means, points to women at the upper end of the socio-economic scale. The myth as related by Euripides of the original thiasoi leaders at Thebes points to aristocratic organisation, and this is not surprising. The Oleiai at Orchomenos claimed descent from King Minyas, whose three daughters tore apart Hippasos, son of Leukippe, one of the three. The festival of the Agrionia (see below) involved them, and their descendants may also have organised maenadic groups although there is no explicit statement to this effect.[63] Plutarch addresses Klea as the leader of the Thyiades at Delphi, and she may have been aristocratic.[64] If maenadism was organised by aristocratic women, how many of their poorer cousins were admitted into the thiasoi is not clear. But Diodoros points to fairly widespread participation by women, as Euripides certainly does with all the Theban women driven out of doors: a rite which was celebrated every second year throughout Boeotia and other places such as Miletos and involving large numbers of women involved in daytime and nocturnal activities, with head tossing, snake dancing and ritual cries, involving ecstatic 'possession' by the gods, is to be imagined.

On the other hand, the role of bacchism in women's lives should not be overstressed. Every two years in many but not all parts of Greece, the women went to the mountains. This represented a denial of domesticity and their status and role as wives. They quite literally let their hair down, danced for Dionysos, held rites at night, tossed their heads, sang and ululated (made loud ritual cries). Men were not present at their rites, and Euripides indicates not simply an absence of sex but also even of alcoholic excess. But the messenger who reports this sees the women by day. Dionysos is praised *as* wine in the *Bacchae*, and the earth yields forth wine for the maenads. Wine and the celebration of wine should be seen as important aspects of maenadic mountain ritual: women may have drunk some wine – enough even to get drunk – as part of the celebrations. Women worshipped Dionysos as the god of the wild and nature, but also as god of the vine. This is clearer at Athens, where although women did not generally participate in biennial trips into the Athenian countryside as the women of Boeotia did, the evidence of the vases to be discussed below clearly indicates that the maenads who poured wine in Dionysiac rituals drank wine, and enough to make them at least look rather drunk. For a little while the women are released from the burdens of their societal roles. But as a means of social release, its occurrence was so rare that to discuss it in these terms does not seem valid,[65] except in the broader context of women's religious activities.

In looking at women and Dionysos on vases, it appears impossible to discern historical periods, or a change in the perception of maenads.[66] The maenads of the Athenian vase painter Makron in 490–480 BC are as 'wild' as those of the Dinos Painter at Athens in *c*. 420 BC, but both painters deal with what are obviously indoor ceremonies.[67] Otherwise it can be noted that while in the archaic and early classical period there are representations of the maenads of myth (such as Figure 5.1), in the classical period itself at Athens most of the emphasis is on the actual Athenian maenads who participate in the wine-drawing ceremonies within the polis, as will be discussed below.

But this does not get to the root of the maenadic experience. What did the women experience when worshipping Dionysos? Music, dance, wine, tossing the head, the freedom of leaving the city to head for the hills, letting down their hair, wearing the ritual costume of fawn-skins and ivy and carrying the thyrsos, these let the women be 'sent mad' by their god. Explaining the phenomenon of maenadism in this way is not an attempt to over-rationalise, but on the other hand, it has to be explained in some way. Euripides' *Bacchae* aside, women obviously did experience 'mania'. Maenadism involves so many inversions of the normal state of affairs that it underlines the status quo and the rule of men. The phenomenon reflects the opposition between the mountain as diametrically opposed to the polis and its values, raw meat (the antithesis of civilisation) as opposed to cooked, loose hair as opposed to men's supervision, women leaving behind their looms and husbands, and in the myths, forsaking family life to the extent that they murder their children, loot villages and defeat men in war. But maenadism has features in common with other women's rites, which routinely involved drums, secrecy and the absence of men. Euripides in the *Bacchae* is in effect providing an aetiology for maenadism. Why, in a society in which women were so restricted, should women go out of the polis, without male supervision (and it is undeniable that the Phokian women travel to Amphissa, and arrive there at night, *without* male escorts), and dance and sing themselves into an ecstatic state to the accompaniment of music? Because the god demands this as his due.

Maenads drawing wine at Athens

The so-called 'Lenaea vases' are a small group of vases (about a hundred) produced in Athens which depict a similar scene: a group of women, in a 'mild' state of frenzy and apparently under the influence of mania, who can be termed maenads, appear on one side of the vase, while on the other sedate women draw wine from large vessels into smaller ones. On some vases the women drawing the wine have become less sedate, and the women on the other side of the vase rather more energetic. There are two main interpretations of these vases: that they represent women priests distributing wine to the Athenians at the festival of the Anthesteria, or that the women are the Lenai, maenads at the Lenaea festival.[68]

Several vases have as their central element a mask of the god Dionysos, attached to a column which is partly dressed. In the best-known depiction on a red-figure stamnos (a large vase; plural: stamnoi), a mask of Dionysos is affixed to a draped column, before which there is a table with offerings of cakes; many of these scenes are by the Villa Giulia Painter and date to *c.* 450 BC (Figure 5.2).[69] At either end of the table stand two stamnoi. A woman on the right draws wine with a ladle from one stamnos into a smaller jar, a skyphos; the woman on the left holds a similar skyphos in one hand and her right hand is raised in a gesture of veneration to Dionysos. On the other side of the vase (not shown here) there are three women: two are moving in what is probably a restrained dance, one with a parasol, while a third figure holds a skyphos, similar to those on the other side. There is a figure between each handle: a respectably dressed woman plays the double pipes, and another dances. Other vases also show women drawing wine in the company of the Dionysos mask column.[70] On one depiction, women play the double pipes and lyre while another woman draws wine from a stamnos.[71] A red-figure stamnos of *c.* 420 BC has dishevelled women dancing on one side and equally dishevelled women drawing wine;[72] one is tempted to think that this is a similar group of women as in Figure 5.2 but a little later on, after they have drunk some of (or a lot of) the wine. These depictions of women drawing wine from stamnoi are actually from stamnoi themselves and so are particularly relevant.

A red-figure cup from the period of the Persian Wars by the painter Makron does not parallel the quiet dignity of these women ladling wine in Figure 5.2, and is similar to the example just discussed. On one side of the cup, there is a mask of Dionysos on a column, heavily clothed; four cakes are skewered onto vegetation (probably branches) attached to the column; in front of the god is a low altar; a stamnos stands to one side, under one of the cup's handles. Five

Figure 5.2 Serene ladies before a mask of Dionysos; red-figure stamnos, Athens (Greece), c. 450 BC; attributed to the Villa Giulia Painter, height: 47.4 centimetres, diameter: 33.4 centimetres (courtesy, ©The Museum of Fine Arts, Boston: anonymous gift, inv. 90.155. Reproduced with permission. ©1999 Museum of Fine Arts, Boston. All rights reserved).

women are present on the obverse with the idol, between the two handles (Figure 5.3). They dance, one plays the double flute, another holds a thyrsos. On the reverse are six women, dancing (Figure 5.4).[73] Three hold thyrsoi, of whom one also holds a fawn. Another woman has clappers which she plays. Of the eleven women, only one has her hair bound (she is perhaps a hired flute girl, as she wears a transparent tunic through which her buttocks and the top of her pudenda are visible), the others have short, loose hair. One woman holds a skyphos, a vase into which wine was poured. These are hardly 'frenzied' maenads, but their behaviour is not quite 'refined', and it is quite plausible to see in them citizen women dancing to the sound of flute and castanets before an image of Dionysos, with perhaps the flute girl hired for the occasion. Only

Figure 5.3 Maenads dancing before a statue of Dionysos; Athenian red-figure cup; c. 490–480 BC; painter: Makron; diameter of cup: 33 centimetres; discovered at Vulci, Italy (courtesy, ©Antikensammlung, Staatliche Museen zu Berlin, Preussischer Kulturbesitz: inv. no. 2290).

Figure 5.4 Maenads dancing; reverse of 5.3.

the columned god is shown and no drawing of the wine. But the wreathed stamnos under one of the handles clearly points to the presence of wine, some of which the women must have drunk.

On one red-figure jug (an oinochoe), the mask is shown lying in a basket. A woman stands before it with a basket of fruits, another behind it has a kantharos; a third figure, unfortunately damaged, stands to the left and is apparently a little girl.[74] The intention must be to venerate the god before attaching him to his wooden post for the wine-drawing ceremony. On a red-figure lekythos a woman dances before a mask which has been wrapped with cloth from its neck to the base of the pillar, and which is venerated by a woman whose sleeves extend to the very tips of her fingers; a table with a kantharos stands before the god, with a thyrsos behind the woman. These are the so-called 'wing-sleeves' and are found on other vases depicting maenads.[75]

It is women who pour the wine and dance before the mask of the god, or venerate it in the basket. Apart from women, only satyrs, Dionysos' special ministrants, are shown in company with the mask on the column.[76] There is a uniformity about the vases which suggests a particular ritual occasion.[77] As noted, the candidates for the rite which these stamnoi and drinking cups depict have been the Lenaea or the Anthesteria. The Anthesteria took place at the end of winter, and the first day of the festival, the Pithoigia, celebrated the opening of the new wine, with the second day as the great drinking festival of the Choes. This would appear to be a logical time for women to draw wine in the presence of the god, and to offer libations to him. The woman who is seen drawing the wine could then be the basilinna, the 'wife' of the god, her assistants at drawing the wine being the gerarai. It could be noted that the depiction of women venerating the mask of Dionysos in a liknon (flat basket) comes from a chous,[78] used at the Choes day of the Anthesteria, and perhaps this is relevant as well.

But the Lenaea, celebrated in honour of Dionysos Lenaios, has also been suggested as the occasion for the rite depicted on the stamnoi, because the Lenai were maenads who worshipped Dionysos,[79] with the dancing figures on the vases being referred to as maenads. While these are women dancing in honour of Dionysos and so 'maenadic', to connect these with the Lenai, and so to Dionysos Lenaios, seems tenuous. 'Lenaios' could refer to the wine press, but the Lenaea occurred on unknown dates in the month Gamelion[80] (the month immediately prior to Anthesterion) and grapes would not be being trodden at this time of year.[81] The women ladling wine, dancing, and obviously drinking it (though they are not shown doing so) worship Dionysos; the festival of the wine was the Anthesterion, and this seems the most logical temporal context for the scenes on the vases.

The Agrionia festival: pursuing the maenads

The descendants of the daughters of Minyas who had killed Hippasos, their son and nephew, were known at Orchomenos as the Oleiai, 'Murderesses'. Every year at the Agrionia the priest of Dionysos pursued them with a sword: he could kill any one of them he caught. Plutarch relates that in his own time the priest Zoilos caught and actually did kill one of the women. He became sick from an inconsequential sore and eventually died after it festered. Things also went badly for Orchomenos. It was therefore decided to take the priesthood away from Zoilos' family and to choose the best man from all the citizens for the position. This looks very much like a rite in which there would be a ritual chase, perhaps relating to myths such as that of Lykourgos who pursued the maenads, and that no deaths had occurred in recent or even past times. Zoilos, over-enthusiastic and possibly new at his job, went too far. The Oleiai were clearly maenads; whether they strictly took their descent from the royal Minyads, or whether all the women were maenads at the festival and had this as their generic name, is unclear.[82]

Pythagorean and Orphic women

According to tradition, Pythagoras left Samos because of the tyranny of Polykrates (reigning 532–522 BC),[83] went to the city of Kroton in south-east Italy, and founded the Pythagorean 'group' ('sect' would probably be too strong a word). He was one of the Presocratics, interested in politics, mathematics, music, medicine and religion.[84] Women were attracted to Pythagoreanism: there was a tradition of women students of Pythagoras, with Iamblichus listing seventeen famous Pythagorean women.[85] Timycha, a Pythagorean, bit off her tongue rather than tell the tyrant Dionysios of Syracuse about Pythagoreanism.[86] That women were adherents of Pythagoras is also made clear by the title of some Athenian plays – *Pythagorizousai* – 'the Pythagorean women', and in such comedies these Pythagorean women were perhaps made a point of comic attack, deviating as they did from traditional *mores* about the place of women in society.[87]

An emphasis on sexual 'morality' is also clear in Pythagoreanism. Pythagoras purportedly persuaded the men of Kroton to give up having sex with concubines and to dismiss them.[88] Pythagoras, according to his biographers, said that a woman could go straight from intercourse with her husband to the temples of the gods, but not if the man she had slept with was not her husband, while Theano, Pythagoras' wife, also said that a woman could go from her husband straight to the gods.[89] When Pythagoras descended into Hades, he saw men who had been unfaithful to their wives being tortured, a concept quite alien to mainstream Greek thought.[90]

Iamblichus reports that Pythagoras advised the women of Kroton about making sacrifices: to offer items – cakes and dough models – which they had made with their own hands, and to carry them themselves, rather than letting their servants do this, and not to make blood sacrifices.[91] In the fourth century BC, Alexis at Athens mentioned vegetarian sacrifices: a character in one of his plays says that it was customary for Pythagoreans to offer dried figs, olives,

153

cakes and cheese as a sacrifice.[92] The Pythagorean notion of vegetarianism and metempsychosis is attested in Pythagoras' own lifetime, for his near contemporary Xenophanes mocks the idea that a puppy might once have been a man.[93] As Empedokles (Pythagoras' successor) makes clear, a person might already have been a boy, girl, bird, bush or fish, before her or his present incarnation.[94]

The role of women in Orphism is much more difficult to trace than in Pythagoreanism. It is clear that they were adherents of Orphic beliefs but perhaps, as in Pythagoreanism, they did not have special gender-specific roles. One of the three small bone tablets discovered at Olbia has the words 'life–death–life' scratched on its surface, and another has the words 'psyche–soma', soul and body, indicating a belief in the separation of these two. The tablets have either Dio or Dion, abbreviations for Dionysos, on them. The tablet with 'life–death–life' also has Dio Orphik.. (the two dots indicating letters which are difficult to read) on it, indicating some link between Orphism and Dionysos. Many such tablets have been discovered at Olbia, but nearly all of them are without any writing. Orphics, like Pythagoreans, believed in metempsychosis.[95]

Plutarch also notes that the women of northern Greece were captivated by Orphic and Dionysiac rites from ancient times, and followed the practices of the Edonian and Thracian women, who carried out such rites to excess, but his real interest is in Olympias and her involvement in maenadic practices and he says nothing more about Orphism. This could also indicate that their involvement in Orphism was less spectacular than in maenadism – perhaps this is what would be expected.[96] But whatever Orphic rites Macedonian women engaged in, these are still shrouded in mystery.

The over-superstitious man in Theophrastos' character sketches 'goes to the Orpheotelestai (initiators in Orphism) to be initiated each month, with his wife – if she doesn't have the leisure to do so, he takes the children and their nurse'. Here the wife clearly normally takes part in the Orphic rituals, but apparently since her presence can be substituted with that of the nurse, she appears to be going along more in the capacity of a babysitter: the father clearly wants the children involved in the Orphic rites.[97]

The Great Mother–Cybele

The Phrygian mother goddess Cybele probably came to Greece via Ionia. She was assimilated with the indigenous Greek 'Great Mother', also known as 'The Mother of the Gods' or simply the 'Mother', and while Cybele's iconography – particularly her lion – became well established, the name 'Cybele' itself never appears to have gained widespread use.[98]

Many representations of the Greek Great Mother show her as a Cybele-type goddess, seated on a throne, with a lion or lions; she is often shown with or carrying a tympanum and phiale (libation bowl). She generally wears a specific headdress, the polos (as in Figure 5.6). When her consort Attis is shown with her he wears an oriental, Phrygian style of dress, Phrygian cap, a short belted tunic, and boots, and carries or has with him the pedum (a short staff with a curved end, sometimes referred to as a shepherd's crook).[99] But Attis himself appears to be a case of Greek confusion: in Phrygia there was no Attis, but rather it was a title in the Cybele cult, applied to priests.

The (probably seventh-century BC) Homeric Hymn in honour of the Great Mother refers to her pleasure in clappers,[100] drums and flutes, and associates her with mountains and woods. Pindar in *Pythian* 3 wishes to pray to the Great Mother, to whom (with Pan) the girls sing before the poet's door at night; while in *Dithyramb* 2, he refers to the Great Mother, the beating of the drums and the clappers, once again in a nocturnal context, the 'torchlit night'; he was said to have dedicated a statue of Mother Dindymene ('of the mountains').[101] Diogenes in the classical period, in his tragedy *Semele*, particularly associated the Great Mother with women, referring to the Phrygian women involved in her cult, and her drums and bronze clappers, and here reflects Greek practice as well.[102] Euripides in his *Helen* syncretises the Great Mother, or Mother, with Demeter.[103] Elsewhere her cult is well attested,[104] but the actual role of women worshippers is unclear.

The Great Mother was mentioned in several Athenian tragedies, often invoked in a prayer or a hymn which the chorus, presumably of women, sings.[105] At Athens, the Mother of the Gods was worshipped at the Galaxia festival and the month Galaxion on Delos and Thasos hints at a similar festival.[106] Late sources have a priest of the Great Mother (a metragyrtes) coming to Athens and initiating women into her cult; the Athenians killed him by throwing him into a pit. A plague followed, and the goddess was propitiated by building the Metroon, a temple to the Mother, over the pit into which he had been thrown.[107] Some scholars actually discern in this myth a historical reality,[108] implausibly even identifying the great plague as that which struck Athens in 430–429 BC.

A small marble statue from about 500 BC might depict the Great Mother–Cybele and Parker points to this as perhaps indicating an early date for her presence in Athens.[109] Pheidias' statue of the Mother of the Gods in the Metroon indicates the importance of her cult at Athens by the last quarter of the fifth century BC.[110] In addition to the Metroon shrine, the Great Mother had a shrine at Moschato, half-way between the Piraeus and Phaleron, where a statue of a seated goddess (now headless) with a lion (only the remains of three legs survive) was discovered;[111] there was also a sanctuary in the Piraeus itself.

It is possible to pinpoint some individual women involved in her cult. The tombstone of Chairestrate, wife of Menekrates of the deme Ikarion (and so a citizen woman) in the fourth century BC, proclaims her to have been the august and dignified servant (propolos, also 'attendant') of the 'all-bearing mother'; her granddaughter is depicted before her, with a tympanum; the dedication was found in the Piraeus, and is to be associated with the Great Mother–Cybele's shrine there.[112] The cult will have been passed on through the generations. Citizen women were certainly, then, worshippers at the shrine over which

Chairestrate had jurisdiction. Nikomache on her gravestone is shown seated, clasping a large tympanum (drum) in her left hand, while with the right she shakes hands with her standing husband, who is bidding her farewell (Figure 5.5).[113] Her husband, named and depicted, clearly approved of her involvement in the rites; she or her husband chose to have her shown with her tympanum, obviously her favourite item. Possibly she was a woman priest in a cult of the Great Mother–Cybele; at the least, she is a worshipper who in death indicated what she considered to be her most important role. A fourth-century BC dedication found at the Piraeus was made by Manes and Mika at Athens to the 'Mother of the Gods'. Manes is a Phrygian name, and he is almost certainly not an Athenian, and the lack of a patronymic supports this; Mika (presumably his wife) will therefore have been foreign.[114] The Great Mother appears in the company of other gods in the mysteries at Lykosoura (where she had an altar), in which women were prominent worshippers.[115]

Cybele was also worshipped as Angdistis (or Agdistis), and an Athenian relief of about 300 BC showing Angdistis and Attis was dedicated by a woman, Timothea, 'on behalf of children, according to command', probably a reference to a dream 'sent' by Agdistis and Attis enabling Timothea to bear children. The relief was found in the Piraeus.[116] Here Agdistis appears as a patroness of child-bearing; little evidence for her cult survives in classical or later Greece.[117] There is a reference to her in what is perhaps a fragment of Menander's *Theophoroumene*.[118]

Outside the classical period but worth mentioning is the relief now in Venice, of unknown provenance, dating to about 240–230 BC. The Great Mother–Cybele wears a polos on her head, with a veil over the back of her hair, of which four plaited tresses are arranged over her breasts, and stands with a large tympanum, upturned torch, and a squatting lion with Attis, holding his pedum in his left hand, next to her, facing the viewer. Two mortal figures, rendered about two-thirds and half the height of the gods respectively, a woman and a smaller female figure who perhaps represents a servant or a small girl (perhaps the woman's daughter), stand to the right at a pair of doors, one of which is open. They appear to be just entering, and are probably to be imagined as coming into a temple. The woman raises her right hand in greeting to the gods, and Cybele faces her. The woman appears to be holding a small ball-like object, perhaps a piece of fruit but more probably a small pot of incense, in her left hand; the girl holds a small tray in both of her hands, presumably with offerings on it (Figure 5.6).[119] The Great Mother of the Gods and Cybele, syncretised and worshipped by women, was popular: the Great Mother, as will be seen in Chapter 7, was kourotrophic, as the mother of all her worshippers will have been appropriate for women. She was clearly never as important as Artemis in this respect, but Cybele's arrival and identification with the Great Mother lifted the latter's fortunes somewhat, with the oriental touches of the lion and Attis presumably important. Women (no less than men) could not afford to neglect any goddess who might be of service to them.

Figure 5.5 Grave relief of Nikomache with her tympanum (kettle-drum), bade farewell by her husband; Athenian; marble; 360–350 BC; height: 108 centimetres; breadth: 30 centimetres (Piraeus Museum, Athens 217; courtesy, ©Deutsches Archäologisches Institut, Athens, neg. GR 665).

Figure 5.6 The Great Mother–Cybele, with lion, and Attis in their temple, approached by a worshipper and her servant; marble; 240–230 BC; dimensions: height: 57 centimetres; length: 80 centimetres (courtesy, ©Ministero per i Beni e le Attività Culturali; Venice, Museo Nazionale Archeologico: inv. 17).

Sabazios

Athenian reaction to 'foreign gods' was equivocal. The official acceptance of the Thracian goddess Bendis is quite clear, but the state did not choose to incorporate all foreign deities who attracted worshippers at Athens into the formal state religious apparatus. Sabazios was one such deity,[120] a god from Phrygia who was associated by the Greeks with their own Dionysos.[121] Sabazios apparently arrived in Greece in the fifth century BC, and his cult is ridiculed by Aristophanes in the *Lysistrata*, produced in 411 BC, indicating both a lack of official acceptance and some hostility within the community; divinity, if of foreign extraction, did not necessarily attract respect or acceptance. Cicero states that Aristophanes in one of his plays attacked strange gods and their nocturnal vigils by depicting Sabazios and other foreign gods as being prosecuted and ejected from Athens.[122]

Women were apparently prominent in Sabazios' worship. The orator Aeschines' mother, Glaukothea, was a cult leader of a thiasos which seems to be that of Sabazios: the cult is usually identified with that of this god on the basis of the 'Euoi Saboi' cry made by the worshippers;[123] this seems a reasonable assumption. The old women who cheered Aeschines on when he organised and led the thiasoi through the streets indicate the prominence of women in such cults, though Demosthenes, Aeschines' detractor, might have exaggerated the role of women to denigrate his opponent. What is interesting is Demosthenes' mention of the old women: as in many societies now that they had fulfilled their roles as mothers (and possibly now widows if they had married men fifteen or more years older than themselves, as was often the case) they would have had more freedom, and also a great deal more leisure time. Many, even if some were grandmothers, which might have provided them with a child-caring role, would in a sense have fulfilled the positions of wife and mother which society directed them towards. Participation in such a cult would, even if only occasionally and vicariously, certainly help to fill the need to belong in a society which valued them primarily for their fertility, a reproductive power which they had ceased to possess, passing out of the orbit and interest of Artemis and similar deities.

Theophrastos in two *Characters* refers to male initiates: the Late-Learner when being initiated into the rites of Sabazios goes to great lengths to come out best in the eyes of the priest, while the Superstitious Man if he sees a red snake calls upon Sabazios.[124] Aristophanes refers to a slave devotee.[125] But little is known of the cult; there are four references in separate plays of Aristophanes to Sabazios, and while one refers to the 'wantonness' of the women in the cult, references to women's sexual impropriety are so common in Aristophanes that nothing need be made of this isolated reference.[126] Demosthenes' attack on Aeschines' involvement in a Sabazios cult makes no reference to sexual improprieties. If drum-beating, snake-handling, dancing and marching through the streets with a thiasos of Sabazios devotees to the sound of cult-cries amounts to ecstasy, then perhaps this was an ecstatic cult:

> On becoming a man you [Aeschines] assisted your mother while she performed the rites, reading out the books and helping prepare the other items. At night you robed the initiates in fawn-skins and mixed the wine and cleansed the initiates wiping them with mud and bran and after the purification told them to say, 'I have left evil, I have found the better'. You prided yourself that no one ever raised the festal shout (ololyge) as loudly as yourself (and I believe it; for when you think how loudly he can speechify here, his festal shout would be superb). In the daytime leading the fine thiasoi through the streets, their heads garlanded with fennel and white poplar, squeezing the red-brown snakes and waving them above your head, you shouted the 'Euoi Saboi', and danced to the tune of, 'Hyes Attes Attes hyes', being addressed by the old women as leader and instructor and ivy-bearer (kittophoros) and basket-carrier (liknophoros), receiving as your fee from them crumbly-cakes, and pastry twists and new-cakes.[127]

This account is clearly meant to be derogatory. Aeschines helped his mother when he was a young man (Demosthenes mentions Aeschines' enrolment as a demesman as his next stage of life); in *The False Legation*, Aeschines is said to have been a boy when he read the passages for his mother.[128] The picture conjured up is an exotic one. In the *False Legation*, Aeschines is accused as a child of being in the thiasoi with drunken men; the sleepy slave who attributes his state to Sabazios must be an allusion to supposed drunkenness in the cult.[129] But it has been noted that there is much that is familiar in Demosthenes' description.[130] Dionysiac worship in particular has parallels in the fawn-skins, snake-handling, initiation, ivy, and the thiasoi making a parade, though there were presumably differences in the 'initiations'; the 'books' which are referred to are non-Dionysiac, and find parallels in Orphism. Drum-beating, Sabazios cries, snakes, initations, sacred books and ritual phrases[131] – there was enough here at once familiar but also sufficiently exotic to attract worshippers. Women were the primary worshippers but not the only ones. What particular purpose they had in mind in worshipping this deity is unclear, but the initiations point to soteriological expectations: perhaps the main attraction was a hope for a better afterlife, something in which old women in particular might have an especial interest.

The Ferrara krater

A large red-figure Athenian vase (a krater), discovered at Spina in Italy and now in the Ferrara Archaeological Museum (Italy), probably dating to *c.* 440–430 BC and to a high point – culturally and politically – in the history of classical Athens, depicts a cult scene which arrests the viewer's attention. Two deities on a pedestal are flanked by pillars, indicating that this is a sanctuary. Their identity is disputed, but the woman deity with a lion and crown can be none other than Cybele – the Great Mother. Her companion, it is suggested, might be Dionysos (there are snakes intertwined in his garland); an equally appropriate figure to flank Cybele might be the exotic Sabazios, for whom the snakes are also appropriate. But her actual consort Attis is presumably the best candidate.

But the real interest of the scene lies in the worshippers, an ecstatic and lively thiasos, mainly of women, but also with two men and a boy present. Immediately before the deities, who hold phialai ready to receive libations, there is a figure in line with an altar: on her head she carries something covered with a cloth; from the shape, this is a liknon, a scoop-shaped basket. Behind her a woman plays the double flute, and a smaller girl carries a tympanum, another (as noted above) of the Great Mother–Cybele's attributes. Then there are three other figures: an adolescent girl, woman and a man, dancing ecstatically and brandishing snakes. Behind them, another double flute player facing the opposite direction plays for eight figures, with a male flute player in an elaborate patterned robe at the end of these worshippers. The figures are women and girls dancing energetically; one bangs on a tympanum which she holds by one of its handles. One of the eight is a boy in a short tunic playing the castanets, with a similar snake-head wreath to the male divinity. The women throw back their heads, dance and handle snakes; some of them also have snake headbands.[132]

Is this an Athenian cult? Perhaps one clue lies in the ecstatic male dancer: he is stocky and looks a little un-Greek, almost 'barbaric'. As noted, slaves were involved in Sabazios' cult. But the boy with the castanets and snake headband reminds the viewer of the boy Aeschines. This is either an imaginary scene of ecstatic worshippers in a non-Athenian setting, or of foreigners at Athens worshipping Cybele and Attis, or Athenian citizen women and girls, perhaps their daughters, engaged in ecstatic worship, possibly (but presumably less likely) with foreigners. The vase dates to about a century before Demosthenes' description of Aeschines' involvement in a Sabazios cult at Athens, and to a little before Aristophanes' references to women and their Sabazios cries. On this krater there is probably a pictorial representation of what he, and presumably other Athenian men did not approve: women taking part in a relatively new cult at Athens, one which has arrested the attention of the painter of the Ferrara krater, and which indicates, like the 'Lenaea vases', that religious worship at Athens was not always staid.

Isis

The decree giving the Kitian merchants of Cyprus permission to build a shrine to Aphrodite at Athens did so citing the precedent, 'just as the Egyptians have built the temple of Isis'.[133] Sometime prior to 333/2 BC, then, the date of the grant to the Kitians, Egyptians had built an Isis temple in Athens. The Egyptians, presumably merchants and/or metics who made use of this temple, may or may not have had women with them who also worshipped there. It is possible, too, that these Egyptians were in fact Egyptian Greeks. The grant to the Egyptians and the Kitians should be seen in the light of Lykourgos' measures to ensure Athenian prosperity,[134] and there appears no evidence for any state interest in the cult of Isis. That there was some private interest amongst Athenian citizens is clear from the fact that there was an Athenian male citizen named Isigenes, 'born of Isis', sometime in the early part of the fourth century BC, several decades before the establishment of the Isis shrine.[135] While this shrine to Isis could only have led to an increased awareness of this goddess at Athens, the cult did not become popular in the Greek world until the hellenistic period.[136] Isis' first cult appearance outside Egypt and amongst the Greeks themselves appears to be at Halikarnassos in Asia Minor, in a dedication by a husband and wife and on behalf of their children to Sarapis and Isis; the dedication belongs to the late fourth or early third century BC; all other such dedications are of the third century or later.[137] The funerary monuments from Athens which show the deceased woman dressed as Isis all belong to the Augustan period (31 BC–AD 14) and beyond.[138] Isis was to become extremely popular in the hellenistic period, and not just with women; but amongst her attributes were those of mother, carer and life-giver, which would appeal

SEGREGATED AND ECSTATIC RELIGIOUS RITES

particularly to women. It is not so much a case that traditional goddesses such as Artemis did not satisfy all of women's religious needs, and there is no evidence that after the classical period women paid less attention to 'traditional' deities, but there was always room for devotion to another goddess (or two) who could assist women: after the hellenistic period, Isis found a ready home amongst Athenian and other Greek women.

The Gardens of Adonis: citizen women and prostitutes on the rooftop

In a scene on an early fourth-century BC red-figure vase, a winged Eros hands a large terracotta pot garden to a scantily clad woman with her feet on a ladder. Women, one on each side, raise their hands in adoration: the woman on the ladder is clearly the goddess Aphrodite; there are two more pot gardens on either side of Eros, and presumably these will also be carried to the roof (Figure 5.7).[139] All three pots show sprouting vegetation, and all are upside-down

Figure 5.7 Eros hands a Garden of Adonis to Aphrodite; *c.* 390 BC; Athenian red-figure aryballis, Circle of the Meidias Painter; height: 14 centimetres (courtesy, ©Badisches Landesmuseum, Karlsruhe: inv. R 8057).

amphorai, broken midway. On another vase, Eros hands a terracotta pot to a woman on a ladder; other pots with sprouting vegetation are shown, as well as a seated naked man (perhaps Adonis) at the base of the ladder.[140] These gardens are the 'Gardens of Adonis' (kepoi Adonidos), being taken up to the roof of a house as part of an annual ceremony honouring Adonis in early spring.

Women throughout ancient Greece celebrated the death of the beloved of Aphrodite, the youthful Adonis. Sappho on sixth-century BC Lesbos makes the ritual cry, 'Woe for Adonis' and sings,

> Pretty Adonis is dying, Kythera [Aphrodite]. What are we to do? Beat your breasts, girls, and rip your clothes.[141]

In Greece itself, the Adonia is attested mainly at Athens, and in the hellenistic period at Alexandria, the setting for Theokritos' third-century BC *Fifteenth Idyll*, in which two free Greek women are on their way to the palace of Queen Arsinoe II, sister-wife of King Ptolemy II Philadelphos, where they will hear a woman sing a dirge for Adonis, the same woman who won the prize last year, indicating that there was an annual competition. Both men and women are going to the palace to hear the dirge, and there was a great deal of jostling in the crowd. Before the singing, the two women admire a tapestry at the palace which depicts the dead Adonis lying on a couch. The singer in her dirge makes it clear that the Adonia rite will take place the next day, at dawn by the sea, to which the women will bear Adonis on his funerary couch; they will loosen their hair (as at a funeral), let their robes fall to their ankles, expose their breasts (presumably for beating), and will sing a dirge.[142] Theokritos is obviously describing an actual occurrence of the Adonia as celebrated at Alexandria.

Evidence for Adonis elsewhere in the Greek world is scanty, but it is probably to be imagined that he had similar rites throughout Greece.[143] At Argos, the women mourned Adonis.[144] Praxilla, a woman poet of fifth-century BC Sikyon, wrote a poem in which Adonis described the things which he missed most about life, before he was killed; amongst them were the light of the sun, the stars and the moon, and ripe cucumbers, apples and pears. From this arose the proverb, 'sillier than Praxilla's Adonis'.[145] Hymns to Adonis are known also from Epidauros, Delphi and elsewhere, where they were inscribed on stone. These could well have been performed publicly, as at Alexandria, with women being involved in the women-only rites a little later.[146] Adonis might be represented in the pinakes from Italian Lokris, but this is uncertain.[147]

Adonis was goared to death by a boar while hunting, having aroused Artemis' wrath; depictions of Adonis often show the boar responsible.[148] Women in Athens met once a year in groups and bewailed his death,[149] commemorating it by carrying pots of sprouted seeds up onto the rooftops of their houses, as Adonis had been laid in a bed of lettuce by Aphrodite while he lay dying. The women laid out small images (eidola) of Adonis as corpses for burial and carried them in funeral processions through the streets, conducting mock burial rites

SEGREGATED AND ECSTATIC RELIGIOUS RITES

for Adonis, beating their breasts and singing laments.[150] A line from Pherekrates has a character saying, 'we are holding the Adonia and we weep for Adonis'.[151] The comic poets mentioned Adonis frequently, according to Photios, and he specifically mentions Pherekrates, Platon, Kratinos and Aristophanes.[152] In addition, plays with the titles *Adonis* or *Adoniazousai* were written by several comic poets.[153] Aristophanes has Hermes being promised that the Great Panathenaia, Dipolieia and Adonia will be celebrated in his honour. Why the poet chose to link the three is unclear; the Adonia is probably included as an 'exotic' touch, and not because it ranked in importance with the other two, which would be most unlikely.[154]

Photios states that the Adonia came to the Greeks via Cyprus and Phoenicia.[155] But Adonis was in no sense an eastern dying and reborn vegetation god. The Adonis images laid out as in death, and the seed gardens that never bear fruit, honour him once each year. After the Adonia, he will not make an appearance until the next celebration of the festival (i.e. his death is commemorated each year; only late sources mention a resurrection).[156] Adon has been seen as the Semitic word 'lord'; more decisively, Adonis can be equated to the Near Eastern male consort Damuzi/Damu (Tammuz) of the love goddess Ishtar, and who was bewailed each year by women in the Near East, as Adonis was in Greece; rooftop wailing, it can be noted, is not typically Greek but was a feature of Canaanite religious practice.[157] Why this cult entered Greece is unclear, but its popularity with women, mourning the youthful lover of the goddess of love, would have ensured its spread. Hesiod and Sappho knew of Adonis, so he was apparently an introduction from the east in the archaic period.[158]

In the fifth century, Aristophanes provides evidence for what appears to have been a conspicuous part of the ceremony at Athens. In the *Lysistrata* (411 BC), the women have seized the acropolis, and a magistrate, the proboulos, enters demanding to know what's going on:

> Has the women's dissipation burst forth?
> Their beating of drums (tympanismos) and incessant Sabazios cries,
> and that Adonis mourning (Adoniasmos) from the roofs
> which once I heard in the meeting of the assembly
> when Demostratos proposed – damn him –
> to sail to Sicily, and a woman dancing
> cried out, 'Woe, Adonis', and Demostratos
> proposed to enlist Zakynthian hoplites,
> and then the tipsy woman on the roof
> cried out 'Beat your breasts for Adonis'; but Demostratos forced the
> proposal through.[159]

The woman in *Lysistrata* who celebrates the Adonia and had cried out 'Woe, Adonis' and 'Beat your breasts for Adonis' on the rooftop was 'tipsy' (literally:

'who had drunk in moderation'); this is perhaps not simply Aristophanes once again making disparaging remarks about women and alcohol, but corrolates with Menander's *Samia* (see below), in which women celebrated the Adonia at night and there was much playfulness, paidia.[160] As in the scenes of women drawing wine in the so-called 'Lenaea vases', women obviously drank wine in at least some religious ceremonies, particularly those they held by themselves. However mournful parts of the ceremony for Adonis were, there was the capacity to have a 'good time' in the proceedings, perhaps before the actual 'burials' took place. A hellenistic statue of a drunken woman carved from Parian marble, who sits clutching her wine jug, is sometimes described as a drunken festival woman. Her dress is similar to that worn by the two women going to the Adonia at Alexandria, as described by Theokritos, but this is probably not enough to connect her with this or any other festival.[161]

The cult was not one of the state, but conducted by private individuals, in their own houses, as the *Samia* makes clear. Among citizens only women and not men participated,[162] while prostitutes obviously did so (see below), and evidence suggests that male metics in the city might also have celebrated some form of Adonia festival. There was apparently no particular secrecy involved, as Moschion in the *Samia* sees and hears what the women were doing. Prostitutes celebrated the Adonia, perhaps because they saw Aphrodite as their especial patron. In the *Samia*, Moschion's father has brought a hetaira from Samia, Chrysis, into his house and is living with her; Chrysis and the citizen wife next door have become friends and often visit each other. Their two households have come together, in Moschion's father's house, to celebrate the Adonia (21, 35–40).

The women were making so much noise at their pannychis (all-night rite) that Moschion could not sleep; the woman on the rooftop in Aristophanes is heard during a session of the ekklesia, which must mean during the day unless it was a particularly long meeting which dragged on into the evening. Having carried the pots onto the roof, presumably via a ladder, they danced, and celebrated their all-night festival, scattered about. Moschion was in the house, but could not sleep, and so watched the rites, and had intercourse with a girl.[163] Moschion's reference to there being 'much paidia', which could be translated as 'fun', or perhaps 'jesting' does not mean that Menander's characterisation of the festival is different from Aristophanes' (cf. the wailing and breast-beating woman), but rather that different aspects are being commented on. There was serious wailing, but nonetheless a festive atmosphere prevailed, with women meeting together in the night.[164] Menander makes it apparent that this was an all-women celebration, and in this case nocturnal; Moschion's lovemaking was illicit.

The Gardens of Adonis were pieces of terracotta, in which seeds such as lettuce and fennel were sown; the vase-paintings discussed above have broken halves of terracotta vases being used for the pots. Seeds were allowed to sprout and reach the green stage, and the plants withered because they had not taken root in the shallow soil of the containers;[165] a mock funeral procession through the streets took place for Adonis after the rooftop ceremony, and the Gardens of Adonis, with the images of Adonis laid in their plant beds, were thrown away into a spring or the sea. Just as Adonis died before he reached adult maturity, so too the gardens never reached maturity. In fact, there was a proverb, 'more fruitless than the Gardens of Adonis'.[166] It is widely repeated in the modern literature concerning the Adonia that the Gardens of Adonis withered on the roofs in the heat of midsummer or summer. Detienne, in particular, developed this thesis. But in fact there is no mention in the ancient sources of withering heat causing the Gardens of Adonis to die.

Women's affection for Aphrodite, the goddess of love and marriage, will have been enough to motivate them to mourn her, who has lost her love. But various ideas have been suggested as to why women celebrated the Adonia. Fraser's ideas about Adonis and the dying and reborn vegetation god (note particularly the comparison with the Egyptian god Osiris),[167] have been correctly refuted by Detienne, who argued (but incorrectly) that the Adonia was in apposition to the Thesmophoria: one concerned with fertility and held by citizen wives, one celebrating infertility held by prostitutes, with fertility versus infertility;[168] Winkler argues that women were mocking men's sexuality.[169] Simms argues that the women used the Adonia primarily to weep, particularly in the context of the Peloponnesian War,[170] which laid the war dead to rest in public funerals, at which women's mourning activities would be more than usually proscribed. Solon's attempts to limit the mourning of women, reflected in other states, and Perikles' admonition to the women in his Funeral Oration, clearly intended to restrain their grief, could be noted in this context.[171] But there were plenty of other funerals for women to weep at, even with Solon's restrictions, and tomb visits gave private and unrestricted opportunities for mourning. Burkert reiterates the broad spectrum of sociological explanation used to explain women's festivals: the need to escape from the pressures of the day.[172] Reed restates this position, but claims that the women were in fact impersonating Aphrodite.[173] Segal discusses both Fraser, Detienne and Jung, but concludes that Adonis, who does not reach maturity and failed in hunting, represents the antithesis of polis values: exogamy and reproduction. He is the failed citizen, and his veneration underscores what the male citizen hoplite (the hunter *par excellence*) must be like.[174]

All of these explanations are too ingenious, and dress up the evidence in interpretations too complex for the women at the Adonia to have understood. They celebrated the Adonia because the cult of Aphrodite and Adonis entered Greece, just like those of Cybele and Sabazios. What attracted women to the cult might seem rather banal. Here was a cult of Aphrodite, a goddess attractive by her very nature to women, which gave them a chance to let their hair down in private on the rooftops; one in a sense has to ask not why women participated in this cult, but why they wouldn't. Its popularity must have been reasonably established amongst Athenian women by 411 BC judging by Aristophanes' reference to it. Women empathise with the goddess in her mourning. They are not mourning Adonis as their lost lovers, the love they never found or the like, but because this was the way they found the cult; the goddess mourns and so her worshippers mourn; they do not mourn for themselves or for their deceased loved ones. The Adonia's appeal lay in its establishment, as with other women-only festivals, of temporary communities of women set apart from men, who engage in activities that only they understand. But the informal element and the lack of state involvement in fact points to something particularly important about the Adonia. Plutarch has groups of women throughout the city of Athens celebrating the festival, and taking images of Adonis in funeral processions and wailing, beating their breasts and singing dirges.[175] As in the *Samia*, women could choose with whom they celebrated this rite; while the Thesmophoria and other festivals were women-only festivals, and the women need not have minded the presence of women they did not necessarily know but with whom they came together as part of the official celebrations, the Adonia allowed a freedom to *choose* with whom they would celebrate, to bond further with women they knew and liked, as did the citizen woman and hetaira in the *Samia*.

Does the *Samia*, with the hetaira and a citizen wife celebrating the Adonia together, represent a common or unusual occurrence? What needs to be remembered is that the citizen wife, the mother of Plangon whom Moschion gets pregnant at the Adonia, and the Samian hetaira, have become friends, and furthermore this hetaira clearly has the status of a pallake (concubine): she is living with Moschion's father Demeas and the father is 'in love' with her; he describes her as a 'wife-hetaira' (130). This could well be an unusual case, and one which after all is from comedy.

Diphilos' *Theseus* referred to three Samian girls (korai) solving a riddle the answer to which is 'penis' on the day of the Adonia. They are not referred to as hetairai, but probably are, judging from the subject matter of their riddle, and are celebrating the Adonia. In the *Painter*, Diphilos has a master cook referring to a brothel where a wealthy hetaira had asked 'other prostitutes' (pornai) to come to celebrate the Adonia.[176] Prostitutes are devotees of Adonis and attend his festival in Alkiphron's *Letters*, of the second or third century AD: one prostitute writes to another, inviting her to the Adonia, telling her to bring a garden and a korallion ('figurine'), referring to an image of Adonis on his funerary couch.[177] While commentators see the Adonia as 'much kept' by hetairai,[178] and the evidence supports this, it would not be correct to see the Adonia specifically as a prostitute's festival: citizen women's participation is clear.

The date of the Adonia at Athens continues to be a matter of some dispute.[179] Aristophanes has the festival of Adonis celebrated in the early spring of 415 BC when the Sicilian expedition was being proposed. Unfortunately, Plutarch mentions numerous ill-omens that were said to have occurred at the time of the sailing of the Sicilian Expedition, in the middle of summer. Amongst these omens, he includes the women celebrating the Adonia.[180] Plutarch has placed the omen of the Adonia, not where Aristophanes has it in early spring, but as one of a whole series of omens that took place just before the sailing of the expedition, in midsummer. Plutarch, or his source, has displaced the Adonia in order to give more dramatic effect to the sailing of the expedition, to highlight the mourning the expedition was to cause. Two passages of Theophrastos indicate that the Gardens of Adonis were sown in spring.[181] A vase which shows women, a ladder and grapes has been taken as a reference to the Adonia (because of the ladder) and to a date for the Adonia based on when grapes would be available in Athens (or if they are dried grapes, to a date when fresh grapes would not be available). But no Gardens of Adonis are present in the scene, and this is almost certainly a wedding scene, of no relevance to dating the Adonia or to the festival itself (Figure 5.8); the boxes held by one woman are presumably wedding gifts.[182]

Citizen men kept their distance from the Athenian Adonia. But three decrees of the thiasotai (members of the thiasos) of Aphrodite (302/1, 301/300, and 300/299 BC) found at the Piraeus (so presumably the organisation was based there), honoured Stephanos son of Mylothros, described as a maker of breastplates, for leading the procession of the Adonia according to ancestral practice, which strongly suggests that these thiasotai are non-Athenian men (for

Figure 5.8 Women at the Adonia, or a bride and attendants with her wedding gifts; fragment of an Athenian red-figure lebes gamikos (marriage vase); *c.* 425 BC; Painter of Athens 1454 (courtesy, ©Musée du Louvre, Paris: inv. CA 1679).

Athenian men could not at the end of the fourth century BC claim to be worshipping Adonis according to ancestral practice, though of course 'ancestral practice' could be interpreted as a mere formulation); moreover, Stephanos is given no demotic, and is presumably therefore a metic, as his craft also suggests. These thiasotai are presumably all from the east or descendants thereof; the membership of this metic thiasos will have been discreet, and they will not have made contact with the Athenian women on the rooftops.[183] Similarly, in another inscription from the Piraeus, the Salaminioi honour an epimeletes (cult official) in some respect concerning Aphrodite (apparently for making sacrifices), and the Adonia. These Salaminioi are probably correctly identified as cult members from Salamis, Cyprus, who have brought their cult of Aphrodite and Adonis to Athens (Cyprus was well known as a locale of the Adonis cult).[184]

Another series of vases show women, ladders and incense-burners (thymiateria), and bowls (the thurible) but no 'gardens', but are usually connected by some scholars with the Adonia.[185] One such vase shows a woman descending a ladder, while another respectfully clothed woman plays on the double pipes, to which women are dancing, and a woman with castanets is also dancing. The woman on the ladder is usually interpreted as carrying incense down from the roof, and placing it in the bowl (thurible) held out to her by a woman at the bottom of the ladder. A winged Eros dances near the woman, and she seems to be Aphrodite. A plant with berries is at the right of the ladder.[186]

Another example shows a woman descending a ladder, with a winged Eros next to her, and so probably once again she is Aphrodite, sprinkling incense into a bowl held out by a woman who is perhaps in priestly garb; a large incense-burner is shown. To the right of the ladder a seated woman plays a double pipe, while behind her a woman beats a large tympanum; a woman dancing, and another woman dancing with castanets, are also present.[187] A red-figure lekythos shows a winged Eros descending the ladder, who places incense in a bowl held out to him by a woman (perhaps Aphrodite); there is an incense-burner to the right into which a woman is placing incense.[188] Adonis was the son of Myrrha, and this is possibly the connection here.

Women sorcerers and sorcery

A character in Aristophanes' *Clouds* asks if he should hire a Thesssalian pharmakis (woman sorcerer) to call down the moon at night.[189] The Greek word for sorcery was 'pharmakeia', involving the use of pharmaka ('drugs'), and the woman sorcerer was a pharmakeutria or pharmakis (plural: pharmakides); she could be described as polypharmakos (knowing many drugs).[190] Pharmakeia largely involved the use of pharmaka as well as magic to achieve the desired affect. Women sorcerers were both mythological and literary figures; in addition, there were two historical women accused of being sorcerers who were put to death at Athens.

The goddess Hekate is described by Hesiod as 'kourotrophos', 'child-rearing',[191] and her assistance to Demeter in searching for her daughter Persephone can be noted, but Hekate's main associations were with magic, and she was intimately connected with sorcery. Although particularly involved with women sorcerers, such as Medea, Hekate's cult was not exclusively a woman's one. She was also the goddess of crossroads, of liminal places; cult 'dinners' (deipna) would be left at crossroads, where she was worshipped by people generally. Hekataia, small shrines or statues of Hekate, could be found at crossroads, and also at doors and gates. The dinners could be placed at crossroads at any time, but the new moon was the regular occasion for deipna to be offered. At this time the shrines of Hermes and Hekate, and 'the rest of the shrines' would be crowned and washed; presumably the washing was carried out by women, on the analogy of what is known about the washing of statues in general.[192] Dogs were intimately associated with Hekate, and were sacrificed to her, being sent to the crossroads as a deipnon (supper) for Hekate, and perhaps eaten by the worshippers. An Attic lekythos shows a woman holding a basket (kanoun) and a puppy which she is setting down in front of lighted torches.[193] The dog in Sophron's mime, 'The women who say they will expel the goddess (Hekate)', is presumably to be sacrificed.[194] At Lagina in Caria, Hekate had priests and women priests, as well as eunuch cult personnel. Here there was a special ritual, the kleidos agogia or kleidos pompe, the 'key-procession', in which a woman priest with the title of key-bearer (kleidophoros) bore Hekate's key. This might simply have been the key to her temple, but Hekate's key was the one to Hades, and that might be what is meant here.[195]

Hekate was the patron of women sorcerers; the first encountered in Greek literature is Circe, who makes Odysseus' men forget their homeland by putting drugs (pharmaka) into their drinks, after which touching them with her staff she turns them into swine; later, she anoints them with another drug (pharmakon) to return them to human shape.[196] Also in the *Odyssey*, Helen of Troy put a drug (pharmakon, here probably opium) into the wine which her husband and guests were drinking. Such was its power that it took away all cares; it was impossible to cry on the day the drug was taken – not even if a man's mother and father died, or if he saw someone kill his brother or son. The description of the powers of this drug is like an incantation, and the use of drugs would typically be accompanied by spells.[197]

There were, of course, male sorcerers and herbalists.[198] Men knew of various ingredients which aroused male desire, or caused a woman to fall in love, and discussed these amongst themselves.[199] However, women sorcerers were clearly of more interest as characters in literature than men sorcerers, and it is interesting that in matters of love in literature or quasi-historical tales it is women who use drugs to produce male desire; clearly such spells were thought of as a peculiarly women's speciality.[200] Even Jason, who in some versions of the myth drugs Medea to fall in love with him, has the potion from Aphrodite; the goddess of love also gives him the use of the magical iynx to induce Medea to love him:[201]

> The Lady of the sharpest arrows, the Cyprus-born, bound the variegated iynx bird to the four spokes of the wheel in an unbreakable circle and brought the maddened bird from Olympos to men for the first time; and she taught Jason to be skilful in prayers and charms, so that he might take from Medea her respect for her parents, and that desire for Greece might agitate her burning mind with the whip of Persuasion.

The iynx itself was a magical device consisting of a bird, usually identified as the wryneck, attached to a small wheel. The references to burning and whipping could reflect tortures inflicted on the bird (the wheel itself was an instrument upon which the torture of victims was performed), and Pindar here is describing a process, used in conjunction with spells, to inflame the object of desire: Medea will be whipped and burned with desire for Jason.

Just as Aphrodite teaches Jason the use of the iynx wheel to gain advantage over Medea, she also lends her kestos himas to the goddess Hera so that she can seduce Zeus. The nature of the kestos himas is unclear: it was perhaps a magic girdle, a strap of leather or (less likely) an amulet; what is clear is that in 'affairs of the heart' the goddess of love and her devices were supreme. When Zeus sees Hera, sexually empowered with the kestos himas, he is overwhelmed by a desire stronger than he has ever felt before.[202] Evidence for love amulets occurs in the hellenistic period but whether there were equivalents of the kestos himas worn by women in the archaic and classical periods to attract lovers or husbands is unclear.

In the *Homeric Hymn to Demeter* (227–30), Demeter, disguised as an old woman at Eleusis, offers to look after the infant Demophoon for his mother, wife of the king of Eleusis. The goddess promises that,

> I will nurse him, and I do not expect – through any weak-mindedness of his nurse – that witchcraft or the 'Undercutter' will harm him, for I know an antidote far stronger than the 'Woodcutter' and I know an excellent defence against woeful witchcraft.

The difficulties with this passage are well known, but it apparently refers to incantations and drugs used against pain caused by malevolent forces, perhaps demons or human agents who will seek to cause the boy harm. Demeter, an old woman, is probably representative of old women versed in herbal lore and incantations, who can protect young children with such magic.[203]

The phrase, 'fonder of children than Gello', occurs in a fragment of Sappho, and the proverb-collector Zenobios in the second century AD explains that Gello was a parthenos on Lesbos who died before marriage and whose spirit haunts little children, and she is blamed for the death of those who die young, just as she herself had.[204] In addition to Gello, there were other malevolent virgin and women beings.[205] Outside the classical period, the evidence of lithica (lists of stones and their magic properties) attests to various amulets used to avert the power of malevolent beings such as Gello and other women ghosts, who were believed to harm women in childbirth and to snatch infants out of houses. Women could also wear amulets to aid safe childbirth. The *Cyranides* also contain numerous spells to avert Gello and similar ghosts. Women of the classical period may well have used stones and amulets to ward off virgin and women ghosts preying on parthenoi, pregnant women and babies.[206] In the first-century BC purity regulation of a private cult in Philadelphia, those who entered the shrine were to swear on oath not to administer 'evil' drugs, not to learn or practice spells, nor to administer potions (philtra) or abortive or contraceptive drugs.[207] Magic may well have been a literary topos, as will be seen below, but it was also very much a part of everyday belief, and was clearly a concern.

Sophocles in his play *Root-cutters* has Medea of Kolchis cutting the roots of poisonous herbs with bronze sickles, and catching the juice as it seeps from the cut: 'These bark baskets shield and hide the ends of the roots that [Medea] cut with bronze sickles while she was naked, shrieking and wild-eyed'. How Medea averted her face from the herbs as she cut them is similar to the fourth-century BC advice to root-cutters mentioned by Theophrastos that they should exercise care in cutting roots. This suggests that the cutting of deadly herbs for making drugs was familiar to Sophocles' fifth-century audience.[208]

Medea, the niece of Circe, was skilled in pharmaka; in Apollonios of Rhodes' version of the Argonauts' myth, she advised Jason how to make a midnight sacrifice to Hekate, and then to steep a drug which Medea gives him in water, advising him to anoint himself and his weapons with it so that he could capture unharmed and yoke two fire-breathing bulls. He must not turn around at the sacrifice if he hears footsteps or barking dogs (this will be the goddess and her hounds) or the spell will be broken, and he will not return to his comrades alive. Medea's knowledge of midnight rituals invoking Hekate and drugs is clear. A similar invocation of Hekate took place in Sophocles' *Kolchian Women*,[209] and such Hekate rituals were clearly associated in the popular mind with women.

Medea – the woman sorcerer *par excellence* – used spells and drugs to overcome the ever watchful serpent that guarded the Golden Fleece. She knew how to rejuvenate the old, and persuaded the daughters of Pelias (who was Jason's enemy) that they could make their aged father young again: she placed a ram which she had dismembered into a cauldron of boiling water and pharmaka, and it emerged rejuvenated; there are numerous depictions of this in art. The daughters attempted this procedure on Pelias, but only ended up stewing him. But Medea *was* capable of rejuvenation of humans: she rejuvenates Aison (Jason's father), and in other versions, Jason himself; once more, boiling and pharmaka are involved.[210] On an Athenian vase of about 470 BC, Medea with a skyphos (a small pot, presumably containing her drugs) in one hand shows Jason, whose name appears on the vase to identify him, how she can rejuvenate a ram. Jason appears here white-haired and with a cane, so that his rejuvenation is appropriate (Figure 5.9).[211]

Figure 5.9 Medea with her drugs rejuvenates a ram, while Jason watches; Athenian red-figure hydria; *c.* 470 BC; height: 56.2 centimetres; The Copenhagen Painter (courtesy, ©Trustees of the British Museum, inv. E163).

In a stone neo-Attic relief which is probably a copy of a fifth-century BC carving, Medea is shown with her container (a skyphos) of drugs which she is about to open in front of the cauldron with the daughters of Pelias, presumably just before the attempt to rejuvenate Pelias will begin. The middle figure, one of the daughters, is just setting down a large cauldron in which the rejuvenation process will take place. The second of the daughters holds a sword and its scabbard, ready to carve up first the sheep for the experiment to prove that Medea's magic will work, and then her father. Medea wears a foreign cap and cloak to convey her outside, barbarian and exotic status.[212] A Renaissance copy of this relief reveals more modern sensibilities: the sword is replaced with a sprig of vegetation, and the second daughter takes on a dream-like expression (Figure 5.10).[213]

In the fifth century BC, Sophron of Syracuse wrote a mime entitled, 'The women who say they will expel the goddess (Hekate)', and it can be presumed that the magical processes involved here were ones which were recognised and carried out (if perhaps exaggerated for literary effect here) throughout the Greek world:

WOMAN SORCERER: Put down the table as it is. Grasp a lump of salt in your hands and laurel behind your ears. Now go over to the hearth and sit down. You, give me the sword: bring the dog here. Where's the pitch?
ASSISTANT: Here it is.

Figure 5.10 Medea with the daughters of Peleus (the Peliades) about to attempt to rejuvenate Peleus, their father; marble; *c.* AD 1550; height: 116.5 centimetres; length: 89–96 centimetres (courtesy, ©Antikensammlung, Staatliche Museen zu Berlin, Preussischer Kulturbesitz, inv. SK 925).

SORCERER: Take the little torch and the incense. Come, let me have all the doors open! You watch over there. Put the torch out as it is. Let's have silence, while in these ladies' name I do my sparring. Lady Goddess, your banquet and faultless gifts . . .

The woman sorcerer acts in the company of those who must think that they are in some way afflicted by this goddess. The ritual is probably performed at night, and after the doors are opened the torch is extinguished. Presumably the goddess is thought to come in the dark for her offerings. Propitiated, she will cease to be malevolent.[214] Another fragment of the mime refers to a triad of alexipharmaka, sometimes translated as magic spells but as the alexipharmaka are 'in a cup', and mean 'warding-off drugs', an antidote against Hekate is being referred to.[215]

Theokritos in the early decades of the third century BC in his *Second Idyll*, the *Pharmakeutria* ('The Woman Sorcerer'), describes how Simaitha, with her assistant Thestylis, resorts to magic to restore the attentions of Delphis. She had seen him and been smitten with desire; she had sought the aid of old women to get rid of her infatuation, but failed. Presumably there were drugs or spells to do away with love, as there were ones to cause it; old women, as often elsewhere, are the special repositories of such knowledge. Eventually she propositioned Delphis; he had been visiting her regularly, but now has not visited Simaitha for eleven days; she learns that he has another lover. In particular, Simaitha calls upon Hekate to make her pharmaka as powerful as those of Circe, Medea and the obscure Perimede, obviously another practitioner of the magic arts.[216] She employs magic: at Simaitha's order, Thestylis strews barley groats on the fire while she (Thestylis) says, 'I scatter the bones of Delphis'. Various other types of magic are involved; for example, a thread of Delphis' cloak is burned on the fire, so that he may burn with desire for Simaitha; similarly, wax is melted, so that Delphis will melt with love. The iynx wheel is invoked several times: 'Iynx, draw the man to my house'.

When the centaur Nessos was dying, killed by Herakles as he attempted to rape Deianeira, he gave her the blood from his wound supposedly to use as a love charm to ensure that Herakles always loved her. The tip of Herakles' arrow had been dipped in the blood of the hydra and it was the blood tainted with this poison which Nessos gave to Deianeira. When Herakles took another lover, Deianeira used the blood, 'so that I might in some way with philtra (potions) and charms (thelktra) overcome this girl'. But of course the monster had deceived her; Deianeira dyed a robe with the poisoned blood, and the flesh of Herakles was consumed when he wore it. He blamed his wife, but was told that she thought that it was a love charm. Herakles asks who the pharmakeus (poisoner or sorcerer) in Trachis is, and is told about Nessos.[217]

Several artistic representations show Herakles, Nessos and Deianeira, but none show Nessos giving her the 'love charm' or Herakles receiving the tunic, except perhaps an Athenian red-figure pelike which has traditionally been interpreted as Deianeira holding out a cloak, the poisoned robe, for Herakles. Vollkommer, however, argues that this cannot be so: in Sophocles' play, it is not a woman (as here) who handed Herakles the tunic, but a male messenger, and the cloak was offered to Herakles in a box, as the poison began to work once the cloak was exposed to the light (Figure 5.11).[218] But of course, there were probably other versions of the myth besides the Sophoklean, or the artist might have used some licence in order to convey the myth in one scene.

Medea, in considering how she will kill Jason's new wife, Glauke, daughter of the king of Corinth, for whom he has forsaken her, swears by Hekate, the goddess she worships 'above all others' (Eur. *Medea* 396), that she will have vengeance. She sends the princess a peplos and golden crown anointed with

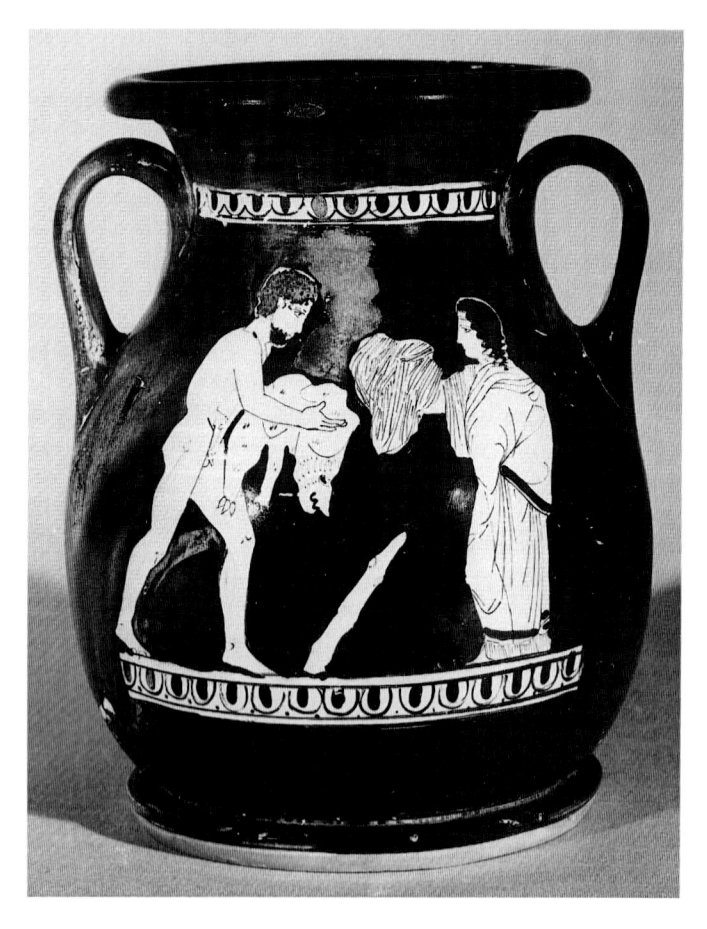

Figure 5.11 Deianeira hands Herakles a cloak which she believes is imbued with a love potion; Athenian red-figure pelike; *c.* 440–430 BC; Manner of the Washing Painter (courtesy, ©Trustees of the British Museum, inv. E370).

pharmaka; both the princess who puts it on and her father who touches her die. Fire consumed the princess's flesh:[219]

> Blood mingled with fire dripped from the top of her head, and flesh from her bones like pine resin, decaying through the unseen jaws of the poison: a terrible sight.

A last example from literature is that of Hermione, wife of Neoptolemos, who believed that her sterility was caused by his concubine Andromache poisoning her womb by using drugs; childless, Neoptolemos will hate her and prefer the concubine. Presumably Hermione thought that the drugs were administered through foodstuffs and drinks. Medea too promised to help Aigeus' childlessness with drugs (pharmaka).[220]

The historical woman sorcerer

In the fourth century BC the woman priest Nino at Athens was put to death 'for assembling thiasoi or on account of drugs (pharmaka)'; she was prosecuted by Menekles for making 'magic potions' (philtra) for young men (tois neois might also refer more generally to young people), apparently a reference to love potions.[221] The woman priest mediated with the gods for the community; the woman sorcerer invoked other powers; there was an opposition between the two roles, and Nino fatally combined them. Women in particular might have been vulnerable to the charges of making potions, and another lawsuit mentions love charms.[222] Aesop has a story of a woman magician (magos) who made charms for laying aside the wrath of the gods, made great profits thereby, and was accused of innovations concerning the gods.[223] Theoris the Lemnian was put to death at Athens in the fourth century BC with all her family because she was a pharmakis, dealing in drugs and charms.[224]

Wives employed drugs and magic (goeteia) to ensure their husbands' love. In Antiphon's speech for the prosecution of a stepmother for poisoning, the son alleges that his father told him that he had caught his wife (the son's stepmother), putting something into his drink, but when challenged she had said that it was only a love potion. Later, when the wife heard that her husband's friend was going to sell his concubine (pallake) into prostitution, she approached the concubine saying that her husband no longer loved her either, and gave her a love potion to administer to the two men: in reality it was a poison which killed both of them.[225] There is much material by way of erotic spells in the magical papyri from Greco-Roman Egypt of the second century BC to the fifth century AD, but it is outside the chronological parameters of this discussion.[226] Sappho's prayer to Aphrodite reads like a magical incantation for erotic purposes, to attract a young girl to her.[227]

Men were using curse tablets (*defixiones*) for amatory purposes in the fourth century BC, and presumably the fashion caught on in turn amongst women, though apparently slowly. Usually inscribed on a strip of lead, though sometimes on a figurine of the person cursed by the inscribed spell, these curse tablets were a form of magic. Men employed curse tablets from the fifth century BC on for matters such as judicial proceedings in order to harm opponents; the extension of their use to harm 'opponents' in love affairs is natural and understandable. The numerous curse tablets from the ancient Greek world indicate one thing of importance: women in the classical period did not on the whole make use of curse tablets to bind lovers to them. It can only be assumed that when and if they had need of magic to attract or retain lovers, women in the classical period generally made use of magic incantations or philtra, or a combination of both. The only known example of a curse tablet definitely used by a woman in the period under discussion comes from the fourth century BC, from Pella in Macedonia. A woman, Thetima, asks of the daimones: 'May he indeed not take another wife than myself but let me grow old by the side of Dionusophon.'[228] Women, particularly in cities such as classical Athens, had little say (if any) in whom they married, and little scope for romantic interests prior to marriage; they had to accept that their husbands might use prostitutes or have concubines, and erotic magic, either by way of philtra or curse tablets, was not an option for many or most of them in obtaining a husband, though the option to use magic and drugs to retain one was open to them.

Spells and childbirth

Plato mentions that women become midwives only after their period of having children has passed, and that barren women do not become midwives; Artemis was childless and so gave midwifery to those who are past child-bearing (and in this sense virgins), but they were women who had given birth to children and so had experienced what it was like and had good practical sense. Midwives through drugs (pharmakia) and incantations (this could also be translated as 'magic spells') were considered to be able to bring on a woman's labour pains and lessen the pain of the contractions; in addition, they could bring on miscarriages if they thought this necessary.[229] It is presumably the drugs which bring on birth and abortions; the incantations, however, will have been important, and both Helen's words, and those of Demeter, have an incantatory character, and whenever possible, the use of pharmaka would have involved ritual words.[230] The use of the herb pennyroyal to bring on contractions was well known and not purely 'women's business', so that midwives' use of certain drugs was not always secret knowledge but rather it was the case that they were the ones in a position to administer such drugs.[231] Considerations of the availability and cost of doctors might also have been important here; but it is easy to imagine that women – as often in many cultures, past and present – preferred the presence and assistance of women.

Women and divine possession

Women, at least in Greek tragedy, were more inclined to 'possession' by a god or goddess than men were.[232] A comedy of Menander's bears the title, *Theophoroumene*, 'The Girl Possessed', or 'The Demoniac Girl'. The play is unfortunately fragmentary, but the action centres upon a free girl who is either mad, or, as one character accuses, simply pretending to be mad. To test to see whether she is mad or not, one of the characters proposes that a piper play the tune, 'Mother of the Gods', but then suggests a Corybantic tune. The girl begins to sing what is obviously a hymn in honour of the Mother of the Gods, mentioning the Corybantes, demons (daimones) associated with Cybele, who danced to the music of flutes (cult devotees who went into ecstatic trances were thought to be possessed by the Corybantes); she also mentions Angdistis. The Corybantes sent people mad, but they also healed them, and people possessed would become ecstatically involved in Corybantic music as a means of healing.[233]

In Menander's play, the girl is possessed (theophoroumene); elsewhere a person experiences an orge (frenzy), or is entheos, 'in the god', possessed by it. When Glauke in Euripides' *Medea* (1163–75) put on the poisoned peplos and diadem, she pranced around the room admiring herself; then as the poisons worked she staggered, and then collapsed onto a chair:

> An old woman, one of the servants, thinking I suppose that a frenzy [orge] from Pan or one of the other gods had come upon her, raised a festal shout [ololyge] to the god, until she saw white foam coming from her mouth.

Similarly, in Euripides' *Hippolytos* (141–7) the chorus asks Phaidra (who through love sickness has kept to her bed and not eaten for three days),

> Are you possessed [entheos] by Pan or Hekate, dear girl? Is your mind wandering under the spell of the revered Corybantes or the Mountain Mother? Are you being consumed for some fault against Dictynna of the wild beasts,[234] you being unholy for having failed to offer her the holy cake [pelanos]?

The chorus is interested in which god is responsible because then that deity can be placated as part of a healing ritual for Phaidra. The nurse asks Phaidra if it is not the spell of an enemy that troubles her (*Hippolytos* 316–19). Similarly, in the Hippocratic Corpus, it is recorded that purifiers saw the Mother of the Gods, Poseidon, Enodia, Apollo Nomios, Ares, Hekate, and heroes as responsible for epilepsy. Women, of course, do not alone suffer because of the gods: the chorus in Sophocles' *Ajax* ask if Ajax's madness is a punishment from Artemis or Enyalios (i.e. Ares). Pan could send panic amongst men.[235] But despite the paucity of the evidence, it does not seem to be stretching it too much to argue that at least in literature and therefore probably the popular imagination, it was women who were more susceptible to possession by the gods.

Mania and 'belly-talkers'

'Mania' is often translated as 'madness' but does not necessarily have this connotation. It was closer to 'possession', a state causing unusual behaviour, though not necessarily frenzy or madness as such; mania affects normal behaviour. Plato defined four types of mania:[236] prophetic mania came from Apollo, mystic madness (telestike mania) from Dionysos, poetic mania from the Muses, and erotic madness from Aphrodite and Eros. Men as well as women were subject to such varieties of mania, but in the case of Apollo and Dionysos women were particularly affected.

What is important to note is that the gift of prophecy which came from Apollo often fell on women, but certainly not always. The classic example, of course, was Kassandra, who received the gift of prophecy from Apollo. There were women priests of Apollo at Delphi, the most important oracular site in Greece; women priests of Zeus gave out the oracles at Dodona, while at Didyma and Klaros, males undertook to give responses to enquirers in Apollo's name. The Pythia was in a state of being entheos when prophesying.[237]

The position of mantis, or seer, does not seem to have been held by women; this art involved the interpretation of signs and omens, and already in the archaic period was developing into a technical, precise art. But amongst the 'free-lance' prophets, women had their place. There were the engastrimanteis ('stomach' or 'belly' manteis) or engastrimuthoi ('stomach' talkers); they were called the Eurykleis (after the most famous practitioner of the art, a man called Eurykles), but in Plutarch's day, Pythones (after the Pythia at Delphi); Sophocles refers to sternomanteis ('chest' manteis). The Hippocratic Corpus compares the heavy breathing of a patient suffering from heart disease to that of women known as 'belly-talkers', probably implying that a large number of belly-talkers, if not the majority, were women. They talked 'through the belly' with a voice other than their own, prophesying the future, and apparently under the auspices of Apollo.[238]

In myth, Dionysos sends women 'mad'. He inflicts them with mania, which drives them to the mountains to worship him. The daughters of Proitos and the other women of Argos are afflicted with mania by Dionysos.[239] Lykourgos in one version of the myth is sent mad, inflicted with mania, for attacking Dionysos.[240] In Diodoros, the women imitate the maenads who had accompanied Dionysos on his travels, and they enter into a state of enthousiasmos – enthusiasm – for the god.[241] Nowhere is this clearer than in Euripides' *Bacchae*. The god himself states that he has stung the women of Thebes with maniai, madnesses, and has made their minds frenzied. Dionysos drives Pentheus out of his mind in order to lead him to destruction.[242]

Women dancing in the street and following a boy acolyte brandishing snakes in the worship of Sabazios provide a glimpse of an unfamiliar classical Athens, and one of which Demosthenes did not approve. The Ferrara krater perhaps shows a moment of an Athens rather remote from the Olympian gods. But the husbands and relatives of these women who were adherents of Sabazios presumably countenanced their activities. In worshipping this relatively new god, women lacked the security of tradition, which permitted rather energetic behaviour on the part of women in the worship of deities, such as Dionysos, who could not be denied. But it is important to stress that much of this marginal religion and behaviour was in many ways familiar and that foreign deities such as Cybele, Sabazios and Isis became 'assimilated' within the framework of traditional polytheism. Such gods would never really gain entry to the polis calendar and festival programme, but that these gods could enter the city, and women could join their cults, indicates that while the state could at Athens, through its jury system, rouse itself to condemn certain religious practices, there were public religious opportunities for women, and they made the most of them, in cults not authorised by the state.

Women's maenadic behaviour was clearly accepted, and in a sense traditional; but in Athens there was apparently no equivalent to Boeotian maenadism in which large numbers of women took to the hills. Dionysos' strong association with Thebes and Boeotia was crucial here; he was welcome in Athens but the maenadic tradition was different, limited to the aristocratic Thyiades who journeyed to Delphi, and the women who broached the new wine from the stamnoi jars. The Boeotian maenads had myth on their side: each husband could potentially meet the fate of Pentheus if he denied the god his due. Moreover, myth made it clear that there was danger to women: if they did not worship the god their mania would not be restricted to a single celebration every two years but they would be sent mad on a scale which was violent and dangerous – the god would not be denied. His particular appropriation of women was presumably owing to societal beliefs that women were more susceptible to madness and possession; the wild, uncontrollable nature of women as viewed by the Greek male was in a sense personified in the god of nature and possession. Participation in Dionysiac ritual was in no sense an 'escape' valve for women. It was not thought that unless women had their 'break' from home they would go mad. After all, it was only every two years that Boeotian women got out in this way, and the average Athenian housewife apparently did not engage in maenadic behaviour of this variety. The Athenian wife might go to a shrine of Bacchus with her drum, or draw wine in the company of the mask of the god, but the freedom of the wilderness was not open to her. The extraordinary liminality of the maenads of Boeotia and their abandonment of domesticity every two years underlined the reality of their roles as wives and mothers.

Various cults involving women, such as these of Cybele, Sabazios, Isis and Adonis, took women to the very margins of accepted worship in classical Athens. The Adonia was not an 'official' festival. The evidence indicates that groups of women – citizen wives and hetairai – could gather together or separately (presumably the presence of the hetaira Chrysis with the citizen women of Menander celebrating the Adonia was not necessarily common) at a particular house for the celebration; it was a 'private' festival. It then became 'public' when the women took their model funeral couches and lamented in the streets. While clearly many citizen husbands did allow their wives to participate, Adonis was always on the fringes of the polis, just as the rooftops were physically separate from the city's ancestral shrines and sanctuaries.

The literary woman sorcerer such as Medea might find no parallel in Greece, but the lovesick woman who employs magic in Theokritos brings us closer to reality. In seeking divine assistance in difficult matters such as childbirth, prayers and dedications to Artemis afterwards were absolutely crucial. But other avenues were not left unexplored; spells and incantations were both employed and clearly accepted. The non-Olympic power being tapped in this way might be personified as Hekate, or more generally as the daimones, but often it is not; however, the 'Undercutter' of the Homeric Hymn presumably points to chthonic powers. Plato does not criticise midwives, but accepts their practices as normal. But Nino and Theoris went to their deaths at Athens for providing love charms and using drugs; they were clearly thought to be abetting adulterous practices by selling these potions to young men for amatory purposes, and undermining the legitimacy of children, citizenship, and hence the state. They operated at the margins of Athenian religion but crossed the boundary into unacceptable practices. Nino also crossed the line into the unacceptable with her thiasoi and a new god, whereas for some reason Glaukothea and her Sabazios thiasos did not – this god, known at Athens for almost a century, was presumably almost acceptable in comparison with the new Isodaites.

6

PROSTITUTES, FOREIGN WOMEN AND THE GODS

Women in general appear to have been marginalised in many ancient Greek societies – though this has been exaggerated by many scholars – but even amongst women some groups were more marginalised than others. These include poor but free women, slave women, free but foreign women, and prostitutes, who could be poor and wealthy, free and slave, and were generally foreign, though occasionally citizen girls must have fallen into this profession. These prostitutes were arguably the most marginalised girls and women in classical Athens (hardly anything is known about prostitutes in other Greek cities, except for Corinth), being primarily non-Athenian and often slaves.

Prostitution was very much a fact of life in classical Athens. The prosecutor of Neaira says that hetairai are kept for pleasure, concubines (pallakai) 'for the daily care of our bodies', and wives for legitimate children.[1] Both hetairai and pornai were considered to be normal adjuncts of Athenian society. There was no 'moral stigma' attached to a male citizen's involvement with prostitutes – either hetairai or pornai – and there was no 'moral' significance to the status of prostitutes: they were not ritually impure, for example, because of the fact that they had sexual intercourse with numerous men. This is a significant point to bear in mind when looking at the religious activities of these girls and women. Two terms were usual for female prostitutes: pornai or hetairai. Hetairai were 'high-class' prostitutes with perhaps some education, wit or conversational skills, suitable as dinner-guests, while the less favoured pornai, prostitutes, were available to all comers and engaged in activities including fellatio and anal intercourse. There were also pallakai, concubines, who could easily lose pallake status if their lover became tired of them, and be sent to a brothel as a prostitute.[2] Flute girls (auletrides) presumably also ended their entertainment at drinking parties by having sexual intercourse with the men present.

Hetairai could command high prices for their favours, and it is these prostitutes who are found in religious contexts, because so much of Greek religion was a monetary affair. A worshipper needed money to buy a cow to sacrifice or to purchase something made of precious metal to dedicate in a temple. So amongst prostitutes the religious life of the less well off is unknown (as is that generally of most poor women in Greece), except that in a general way they must have prayed, attended festivals, and perhaps made cheap dedications. Certainly they were not banned from festivals, sacrifices or temples because of their profession.

Several ancient authors wrote works specifically about prostitutes which are now lost. What survives are quotations, excerpts of these works, in Athenaeus, a Greek living in Naukratis, Egypt, in the late second and early third century AD. He describes a symposium – banquet – which lasted several days and which ranged widely over numerous topics, including prostitutes and prostitution. During the discourse, the speakers quote numerous works on prostitutes, such as those by Aristophanes of Byzantium, Apollodoros, Ammonios, Antiphanes, Gorgias of Athens, and Kallistratos. Athenaeus in a long section quotes or cites the evidence of these ancient authors, and provides some valuable material about prostitutes and religion, especially at Corinth. Machon in the third century BC wrote of Athenian prostitutes in his *Chreiai* ('Bright Sayings'), large sections of which are also quoted by Athenaeus.[3] In addition, there were other writers who dealt with prostitutes, who were clearly a popular stereotype in literature,[4] and there were several plays with the titles of the names of prostitute characters.[5]

Prostitution was simply a fact of life in ancient Greece. At Athens, prostitutes were seen in fact as being a safeguard against adultery: what sexual lusts citizen men had, even if married, could be taken up by access to prostitutes or concubines, rather than with other citizens' wives. The ready availability of female prostitutes was a hallmark of Athenian society. The fourth-century BC poet Philemon comically ascribed to Solon the Athenian reformer (archon at Athens in 594 BC) the establishment of state-owned brothels where a visit to the prostitutes cost just 1 obol – about one-sixth of a day's wage, so extremely cheap – his aim being to prevent young men from becoming adulterers. The fourth-century BC poet Xenarchos made a clear connection, as had Philemon, between the availability of prostitutes and the way in which this should restrict the number of adulterous liaisons. Nikander of Kolophon, in fact, taking these comic notices too literally, imagined that Solon set up the cult of Aphrodite Pandemos at Athens, financing it from the profits of brothels.[6]

Timarchos, the impious male prostitute

Even in the early twenty-first century AD, the mention of prostitutes and prostitution will lead readers to think first of girls and women who engaged in this profession. But in classical Athens, there were male prostitutes called (amongst other terms) hetairoi and pornoi, the masculine form of the words hetairai and pornai, used for female prostitutes. Aeschines accuses Timarchos of being such a male prostitute in his speech *Against Timarchos*, the most detailed source for attitudes to male prostitution.[7]

At Athens, there was a great deal of aversion to a male citizen submitting to anal intercourse – sodomy – with another male citizen, or even worse, a foreigner, particularly if the act involved a transfer of financial favours, i.e. was prostitution. In Athens, pederastic relationships between an older, usually bearded man, and a young boy, just approaching or having experienced puberty, were socially acceptable. But intercourse was meant to be of an intercrural kind, in which the elder male had an orgasm while rubbing his erect penis between the legs of the boy. Touching of the youth's genitals did occur, and is often shown on vases, and in many cases youths who reject unwelcome advances stop the hand of the courter as he reaches for their genitals.[8]

There were numerous laws to prevent boys being left alone in the company of older men in the dark, so that there was a clear fear that such pederastic relationships had the potential to involve sodomy.[9] The cultural norm was phallic sexual penetration of social inferiors: women, prostitutes, slaves (boys, girls, men or women) and foreigners; one did not sexually penetrate one's peers or those who would become one's peers. Accordingly, pederastic relationships with young male citizens could occur but were meant to take place without anal penetration, which would detract from the boy's maleness and social standing when he became an adult.

The younger man was expected to look up to and admire the older man. They were erastes and eromenos, lover and beloved. The lover gave sexual attentions, and the younger received but did not sexually reciprocate them. But there was also a tension here, that such relationships could also be viewed as prostitution, particularly when the giving of gifts, such as a rooster, knucklebones, or something more elaborate, occurred.[10]

Aeschines in his speech against Timarchos in 345 BC portrays him – a citizen – as a male prostitute, and mentions the law that prohibited male citizens who have prostituted themselves from serving as priests, holding political office, or being a herald or ambassador; nor were they allowed to speak in the political assembly or the council. Solon himself, Aeschines notes, was said to have laid down the law that male prostitutes could not speak in the assembly because if they sold their own bodies they would by extension sell the state. Aeschines objects that Timarchos, who had been pressed into prostitution as a boy – through no fault of his own, Aeschines says – chose to continue in this profession when he became an adult, and yet has been on embassies sent to other states. As an ambassador Timarchos wore a garland (i.e. was wreathed), a symbol of sacrosanctity and associated with religious festivals. Male citizen prostitutes could not perform priestly functions, as they were considered to be impure of body and therefore not fit to serve the gods.[11] Men and women priests had to be 'holokleros', free of blemish. Male prostitutes also could not enter temples.[12] Timaios wrote that Demochares the Athenian was such a male prostitute that he wasn't even fit to blow the sacrificial flame, in order to start the fire.[13] But such pejorative connotations did not spill over into attitudes towards girls and women who were prostitutes, where citizenship was not an issue. These were attitudes to male citizen prostitutes which were based not on any ideology of normative heterosexuality but on the construction of citizenship at Athens, and male sexual dominance over those who were not males and/or citizens. Girl and women prostitutes and their religious activities were not affected by the considerations that 'polluted' Timarchos and Demochares.

Aspasia: an impious prostitute?

Wearing a saffron outer garment and her hair modestly veiled, Aspasia stands with Perikles and admires the Parthenon (west) frieze where Pheidias points out relevant details. So did Lawrence Alma-Tadema depict Aspasia in 1869 in his oil painting, *Pheidias and the Frieze of the Parthenon* (Figure 6.1).[14] She is not depicted here as a hetaira but as Perikles' mistress; she is a respectable woman (with veiled hair), except that perhaps the saffron dress – the colour of sexuality for the ancient Greeks – hints at her status. And she is not portrayed as out of place in what is – or will become – the temple of Athens' virgin goddess, Athena herself. Whether this painting accurately reflects the historical situation or not remains to be seen.

Aspasia was from the Greek city of Miletos on the Asia Minor coast, probably coming to Athens in 451 BC or the following year. In the surviving ancient portrait of her, she is respectable, with her hair partly covered; it has been suggested that this herm is a copy of a funeral monument, which could account for her serious expression (Figure 6.2). She was said to have been involved in the philosophic discourses of her time,[15] and Perikles' admiration and attraction to her may well have been primarily (though not necessarily exclusively) intellectual rather than sexual.[16] Routinely, modern historians describe her as a hetaira, but there are no real grounds for this description, as she is not once described by the ancient sources as such. She was a free non-Athenian woman, who lived with Perikles at Athens after he divorced his wife, by whom he had had two sons (Paralos and Xanthippos). By Aspasia, Perikles had Perikles (Junior), who was made a citizen by special decree in 430/29; his father's citizenship law of 451/0 provided that only those with two Athenian parents could be citizens.[17] It is highly probable, on the basis of a funerary inscription, that the elder Alkibiades was married to Aspasia's sister, whom he may have met in Miletos during his period of ostracism from Athens.[18]

Antisthenes and Aischines (not the orator), pupils of Socrates who was sentenced to death in 399 BC, each wrote a Socratic dialogue entitled *Aspasia*.[19] Antisthenes wrote that Perikles went in and out of Aspasia's house twice a day to greet her, and wept more when speaking on Aspasia's behalf in the courts when she was prosecuted for impiety (asebeia) than when his own life and property were in danger, and brought about her acquittal through his tears.[20] Plutarch also gives the charge as that of impiety, with Hermippos the comic poet as the prosecutor, who further accused Aspasia of procuring free women for Perikles' sexual gratification. This charge is reflected in the previous gossip that he had his way with the citizen women who came to the acropolis to admire the work of the artist Pheidias on the Parthenon.[21]

Figure 6.1 Lawrence Alma-Tadema, *Pheidias and the Frieze of the Parthenon*, 1869 (courtesy, ©Birmingham Museums and Art Gallery, Birmingham: inv. 118.23).

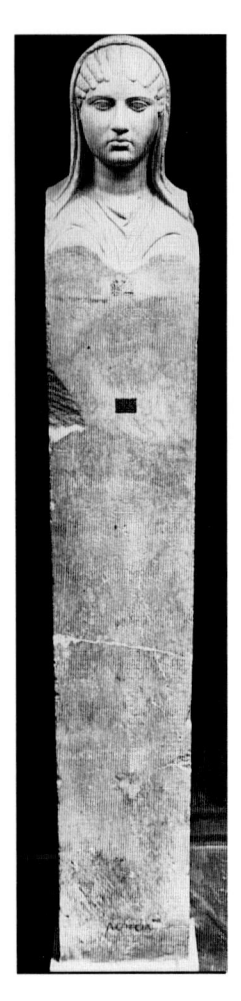

Figure 6.2 Aspasia, portrait herm; marble; late fifth century BC (?); overall height: 170 centimetres, height of head: 25 centimetres (courtesy, ©Vatican Museums: inv. 272).

The motivation behind her trial for impiety was presumably political in nature, in line with the prosecutions of another two of Perikles' associates – Pheidias for embezzlement, and Anaxagoras for impiety. Plutarch dates the trial of Aspasia to about the same time as the prosecution of Pheidias, *c.* 438–436 BC,[22] and it probably occurred at approximately the same time as Diopeithes' decree that those who didn't believe in the gods or who taught scientific theories about the heavens were impious, which was obviously aimed at Anaxagoras.

Simply because Hermippos was a comic poet does not mean that there was an imaginary scene in a play in which Aspasia was prosecuted for impiety, and that later authors reading this play thought that there had been a real trial for impiety.[23] The evidence for an impiety trial is quite contemporary: Antisthenes and Aischines. Her involvement in numerous philosophical discourses with the Socratic circle and the extremely strong tradition of her as a Socratic interlocutor make it probable that Aspasia was tried about her notions concerning divinity, whatever these might have been: perhaps they were similar to Anaxagoras'. That she was tried for impiety because she had entered the Parthenon is unlikely (see below). In addition, the inscribed lists of dedications from the Parthenon list a woman named Aspasia as having dedicated a gold tiara; and this is probably (but not certainly) Perikles' Aspasia.[24]

Thucydides, a great admirer of Perikles, does not mention her once, and the first literary reference to her is in a play (written c. 440–430 BC) by Kratinos, who refers to her as a 'dog-eyed' pallake (pallake kynopis), a concubine; as a metic and non-Athenian woman, her status as Perikles' sexual partner could be nothing else.[25]

Aspasia was said to have influenced Perikles' political decisions, such as Athens' war against Samos, the enemy of Miletos, Aspasia's hometown, this anecdote being first found in the writings of Duris of Samos.[26] She was also (in Aristophanes' *Acharnians*, produced 425 BC) the cause of the Peloponnesian War that convulsed the Greek world from 431 to 404 BC.[27] Eupolis referred to her as Helen, a clear reference to Helen's role in causing the Trojan War and Aspasia's in the Peloponnesian.[28] The Athenian ideal of the decorous wife, encapsulated by Perikles' own advice in his Funeral Oration as recorded by Thucydides, meant that Aspasia could not have been popular in Athens.[29] In Eupolis' *Demes*, produced in 411 BC, Perikles asks, 'Is my nothos (illegitimate son) alive?' and is told, 'Yes, and he would have been a man long ago, except for the evil of having a porne as a mother.'[30] After Kratinos' probably correct reference to her as a pallake, Eupolis, his younger contemporary, referred to her after her death as a porne. As we have seen, this was a pejorative term for a low-class, cheap prostitute, and clearly was used posthumously to attack Aspasia's reputation. Aspasia, in modern parlance, was Perikles' '*de facto* wife' but could never aspire to legitimate marriage. There is no reason to doubt that she made a dedication to the virgin goddess in the Parthenon; and her reputation (and/or Perikles' position) led to an impiety trial, not because of her sexual status, but as an attack on her lover.

Aphrodite Hetaira

Philetairos in a play referred to there being a shrine (hieron) to 'the Companion' (Hetaira) everywhere, but that there was none to 'the Wife' (Gamete) in all of Hellas. This 'Companion' was Aphrodite Hetaira as she was called by the Athenians. But Apollodoros in his *On the Gods* argued that Aphrodite Hetaira referred to the less specific meaning of hetairoi and hetairai, as 'friends', and that Aphrodite Hetaira brought friends of both sexes together; Athenaeus adds that

Sappho called her friends hetairai.[31] Hesychius mentions a shrine at Athens where male and female hetairai, friends, went; Philetairos is limiting the meaning of hetaira in order to make a comic point, and this cult was not one concerned with prostitutes. The Magnesians celebrated the Hetairideia festival, because Jason, when he had formed the band of Argonauts, sacrificed to Zeus Hetaireios (Zeus of the Companions); the Macedonian kings also celebrated the Hetairideia.[32] Ephesos also had a temple dedicated to Aphrodite Hetaira.[33] But Aphrodite Porne – Aphrodite the Whore – did have a shrine at Abydos: the legend was that a porne, common prostitute, had brought freedom to the city, and in gratitude the city founded the temple to the goddess.[34]

Prostitutes and temples

It is sometimes suggested that the charge against Aspasia was that she had visited temples, and that prostitutes were not allowed to do so; Derenne cites three passages to the effect that prostitutes could not enter holy places.[35] But the evidence cited is unconvincing. Male prostitutes in Athens could not enter temples, or go on embassies requiring the wearing of wreaths, but girl and women prostitutes were not similarly debarred.

The speaker of [Demosthenes] 59 indicted Neaira, alleging that although she was a foreign woman who had been a prostitute at both Corinth and subsequently Athens, she was living with the citizen Stephanos as his wife, which was against the law, as only an Athenian woman born of two Athenian parents could be the wife of a citizen. Stephanos gave Neaira's daughter, previously called Stybele but now Phano, as wife to Phrastor, an Athenian citizen, who soon ejected her from his house when he discovered that she was not Stephanos' daughter but Neaira's. Stephanos next gave Phano in marriage to Theogenes, a poor man, selected by lot to be the basileus archon, who had important religious rites to perform. As the wife of the basileus archon, Phano offered the sacrifices 'which cannot be spoken about' on behalf of the city, saw what she should not have seen being a xene (foreigner), went where only the wife of the basileus archon should go, and administered the oath to the gerarai. She was even given in marriage to the god Dionysos himself, carrying out the ancestral rites on behalf of the city, which were sacred and unnameable. But he stops short of saying the daughter is a prostitute; in fact, while the speaker has a good case that Neaira the mother was a prostitute, he doesn't make a case for the daughter being such. Rather, what he stresses here is that a woman who was a xene, a foreigner, performed these sacred rites and that Stephanos passed her off as his citizen daughter when she was not. The speaker pursues his theme further, noting the law that the wife of the basileus archon who performs these rites had to be an Athenian and a virgin at her marriage and that the Athenians showed piety towards the god by making this law (§§85–6). Another passage (§73) makes it clear that as a xene Neaira's daughter should not have partaken in the rites conducted by the wife of the basileus archon.

In case his points that Phano was a xene and not an Athenian do not convince the jurors, the speaker offers another line of argument. Even if Phano is an Athenian, then she must be an adulteress, because her 'father' Stephanos has claimed that he found a man in the act of adultery with her. He then points out that adulterous women are debarred from public sacrifices, which a slave or a foreign woman (xene) could attend to watch and offer prayers (§§85–6).[36] Barring adulterous women from shrines kept the holy places free of miasma and asebeia. It is only if prostitutes were classed as adulterous that they were debarred from temples at Athens under this particular prescription. This could not be the case as there was a law that sex with prostitutes was not adultery (§67). If Phano is a xene, she should not have been the wife of the basileus archon; if she is an Athenian then she is an adulterer, by her father's own testimony, and therefore not allowed to attend – let alone perform – sacrifices. This part of the speech proves two things: that a foreign woman could not be the wife of the basileus archon, and that while adulterous Athenian women were barred from public sacrifices, foreign women could attend these.

In another section of this speech which is relevant (§§113–14), the speaker argues that if Neaira as a prostitute is allowed to pass herself off as a citizen, then no one will marry the freeborn poor women, who will have to become prostitutes in order to have a livelihood. The prostitutes themselves will have the rank of the freeborn women, and the poor freeborn women will give birth to children to whomsoever they please, and still join in the rites and ceremonies of the city. But the speaker is not saying that the involvement of prostitutes at sacrifices and prayers would be unusual. Rather he is stating that the poor free Athenian women will become adulterers – they will bear children to whoever they please – and *nevertheless* take part in the rites, even though they are adulterous and no longer respectable.

A speech by Isaeus indicates that slaves and prostitutes were debarred from entering a particular, unnamed, temple and seeing rites – which are not specified – that only Athenian citizen women were meant to see at that temple.[37] This passage is sometimes cited as evidence that prostitutes could not attend the Thesmophoria, but while women-only rites at Athens were largely in honour of Demeter, there were several such rites – for example, the Stenia, Haloa and Skira – and so it is not necessarily the Thesmophoria which is being referred to here. In this case, the slave involved (who had been a prostitute) was passing herself off as a citizen's legitimate wife, and her two bastard sons by two clients as the sons of her aged 'husband'. Her crime is that of impersonating a citizen wife and of having taken part in rites that she should not, as a xene, have participated in.

Clearly, adulterous women could not attend sacrifices or visit temples, and non-Athenian women were barred from certain rites. But that is as far as the evidence goes. It would help if there were evidence for prostitutes at temples, but there is not, except for their presence at temples of Aphrodite. Prostitutes are described as leaving a temple of Aphrodite at Athens in a third-century BC work by Machon, and they prayed in her temple at Corinth in 480 BC. As this goddess relates to their occupation, it is not particularly persuasive evidence for the presence of prostitutes at temples. But prostitutes did make dedications in temples (see below), and perhaps this is relevant. Moreover, they were initiates in the Eleusinian Mysteries, which means that they entered the telesterion at Eleusis. In addition, Sinope, a hetaira, made a sacrifice at Eleusis in the fourth century BC. Moreover, when Stephanos and Phrynion (the latter had helped to contribute to the price of Neaira's freedom) were arguing about who had sexual rights to Neaira, they met 'in the temple' with arbitrators *and* Neaira, with an agreement made that Stephanos and Phrynion would share her on alternate days.[38] A man might also take his pallake, concubine, to a private sacrifice. Given that prostitutes and sexual intercourse with them were not generally considered polluting in classical Greek thought (see below), it is not surprising that prostitutes were not debarred from temples. At Maionia they were specifically allowed into a shrine which required men who had recently had intercourse to purify themselves: the peculiarity of this last measure indicates how unusual it would have been for prostitutes not to enter temples.[39]

The whores of Demetrios Poliorketes

Demetrios Poliorketes in 307 BC liberated Athens from the regime of the pro-Macedonian Demetrios of Phaleron, and numerous honours were granted to him, such as the use of the opisthodomon (rear chamber) of the Parthenon as accommodation; there he had intercourse with free youths and free women to such an extent that when he introduced (women) prostitutes there he was thought to have purified the place in comparison. The comic poet Philippides referred to Demetrios in the following lines:

> He took over the acropolis as his inn,
> and introduced his hetairai to the virgin goddess.

These hetairai (prostitutes) were obviously lodged in the opisthodomon of the Parthenon. This is not actually referred to as impiety by Philippides or Plutarch, but Plutarch writes that by his activities with youths and free women Demetrios did not behave as was fitting towards the goddess, and his treatment of the Parthenon is obviously included in the 'shocking and lawless things' that he did.[40] Sexual intercourse in temples was always considered unlawful in Greek thought.

Prostitutes and looted temple treasures

The Phokian commanders Phayllos and Onomarchos were fond respectively of women and boys; when the Phokians plundered the treasures of Delphi to pay for their mercenaries in the Third Sacred War (356–346 BC), these two gave away to their lovers some of the dedications which had been made at Delphi. Phayllos gave to the flute girl (auletris) Bromias a silver drinking cup, dedicated by the Phokaians (of Asia Minor), and a golden ivy-wreath, dedicated by the Peparethians. She would have played the flute at the Pythian festival at Delphi had she been allowed, but the crowd prevented her from doing so (because she was a prostitute): this was one line she was not allowed to cross, and so there were apparently some scruples about prostitutes and the divine. But her presence itself was permissible, as long as she did not act the flute girl. On another occasion, Philomelos, strategos autokrator (supreme general) of the Phokians in the fourth century, gave a gold laurel crown, dedicated by the city of Lampsakos, to Pharsalia, a dancing girl from Thessaly; later she travelled to Metapontion in Italy, where according to two different accounts, the manteis (soothsayers) tore her to pieces because of the god's golden wreath, and in another, when she was near the temple of Apollo – the god of Delphi – in Metapontion, young men each trying to take the crown from her tore her to pieces. It was said that she was killed because the wreath belonged to the god. It is not her status as a prostitute which is the problem here: Pharsalia met the fate of temple-robbers which the ancients thought she deserved.[41]

Sacred laws dealing with prostitutes

Sacred laws occasionally mention prostitutes, and while there is only one from the classical period, they are relevant nevertheless in that they indicate that the prostitute was presumably not unwelcome in shrines that did not have such rules, unless unrecorded social conventions prevented their entrance to these shrines. In a fourth-century BC purity inscription from Metropolis in Ionia, two days' purity was required after sex with one's wife, and three days after sex with a prostitute, before a worshipper could enter the shrine. Here the idea is presumably that sex was impure, and that sex outside marriage more so – by a day. But the contrast is much stronger at third-century AD Lindos on Rhodes (some 600 years or so later): sexual intercourse with a prostitute meant a wait of thirty days before entering the shrine, but intercourse with another woman simply required washing to obtain purification.[42] But this is so long after the classical period that this regulation indicates by contrast that in the classical period such lengthy purification periods did not apply. As to prostitutes themselves, a cult in Maionia specified that a prostitute (hetaira) had to abstain from intercourse for two days before entering the shrine, and had to 'purify herself all over', probably by washing; a man was able if he had intercourse with a woman to enter the same shrine that day after washing.[43] Clearly cults which saw intercourse as polluting included prostitution in this category, but this was clearly far from the general formulation of pollution in classical ritual practice. The presence of prostitutes at some panhellenic festivals was obviously normal: one brothel-keeper took his prostitutes to the Delphic amphictyonic gathering at Pyloi and other festivals.[44] A spectator marking out a site for his tent at the

Isthmian festival makes a lewd reference to sexual activity, and is probably hinting at the presence of prostitutes.[45] The presence of prostitutes at festivals and their access to shrines need not be doubted.

Phryne, an impious prostitute

The state might choose to adopt a new divinity for worship, as it did in the case of the Thracian goddess Bendis.[46] Or foreign merchants could apply for permission to build a shrine for their favourite deity, as in the case of the Egyptians for Isis and the Kitians for Kitian Aphrodite.[47] But at Athens, the introduction of a new god by an individual could become the subject of an impiety trial: Socrates, in 399 BC, provides the best example.[48] There were at least three other cases. Demades was fined for proposing a decree that Alexander (the Great) be worshipped as a god at Athens.[49] The other two cases involved a prostitute (Phryne) and a woman priest (Nino); the latter has been discussed in Chapter 3.

Phryne, a prostitute originally from Thespiai, was prosecuted at Athens by Euthias for impiety (asebeia) in about the middle of the fourth century BC for introducing the worship of Isodaites (later equated with Dionysos);[50] his case was that: 'I have shown that Phryne is impious, she has celebrated shameful revels, she is the introducer of a new god, she has assembled illegal thiasoi of men and women.' The unofficial character of some cults and their bands of devotees, thiasoi, at Athens is made clear by a deme decree from the Piraeus that forbade thiasoi to assemble in the deme Thesmophorion.[51] There were bands of worshippers who came together of their own initiative; the city itself did not forbid this practice but could (and did) take action if individuals brought a lawsuit about it or related matters. Phryne, a prostitute and a woman, had organised bands of men and women to worship a new god. The comic poet Poseidippos in the third century BC mentions that Phryne was acquitted in her trial because of her tears, when she clasped each of the jurors by hand.[52] According to Athenaeus, it was a capital charge and she was defended by the orator Hypereides. As he was not convincing the jurors of her innocence, he brought her out where all the jurors could see her, tearing off her chitoniskoi (short tunics) so that her breasts were exposed, and he broke out into lamentations at the sight (of the breasts that were to be deprived of life). The jurors became superstitious of the 'expounder and attendant' of Aphrodite, and acquitted her, concerned that Aphrodite's wrath might fall on them for executing a piece of her handiwork like Phryne.[53] This story of the chitoniskoi appears first in Athenaeus, and, while it might be earlier, it is significant that Poseidippos does not mention it, and it might well be apocryphal.[54]

Phryne's body was most beautiful in the 'hidden parts', such that at the festivals of the Eleusinia and Poseidonia[55] in the presence of all the Greeks she took off only her cloak, let down her hair and walked into the sea: in fact, according to Athenaeus, she was the model for Apelles' painting *Aphrodite Rising from the Sea* and Praxiteles' sculpture, the *Knidian Aphrodite* (or the *Knidia*). Praxiteles' Phryne as Aphrodite was the first three-dimensional nude statue of a woman to be created in the Greek world. It was eventually housed in a special building at Knidos in Asia Minor, and became a tourist attraction. There was a front and back entrance, and a woman was entrusted with the keys to the doors and opened them for those who wished to view the statue.[56] While it is possible to argue that the connection between Praxiteles and Phryne is entirely fictitious,[57] Praxiteles' connection with her is a very strong element of the tradition, and some woman or women served as the model/s; a prostitute would in no way have been an inappropriate model for a goddess who was after all their especial patron.[58]

The reference to the Eleusinia might well be to the day of the Eleusinian Mysteries on which the mystai took their piglets down to the sea to purify them; 'all of Greece' was invited to participate in the Mysteries. Phryne apparently became an initiate of the Great Mysteries at Eleusis, along with other prostitutes, such as Metaneira, Lysias' friend (see below). At Thespiai, her home, Phryne dedicated the statue of Eros which Praxiteles had carved for her. Her clients paid for Praxiteles to make a golden statue of her and set it up on a column of Pentelic marble at Delphi; it was inscribed with her name: 'Phryne, daughter of Epikles, of Thespiai'. Athenaeus saw it there, centuries later, between the statues of Philip II of Macedon (Alexander the Great's father), and Archidamos, the Spartan king.[59] The Cynic Krates commented, however, that the statue was a monument to the akrasia ('incontinence') of the Greeks.[60]

In the case of Phryne, it was not necessarily her status as a prostitute which led her into what the Athenians regarded as impiety, but rather her status as a free foreign woman with more freedom than the average Athenian housewife. However, her status as a metic may have made her more vulnerable, and the Athenians less tolerant, than might otherwise have been the case, though Socrates, also tried for impiety, was both a male and a citizen.

Prostitutes as initiates in the Eleusinian Mysteries

Phryne was arguably an initiate at Eleusis, but other evidence is unequivocal. Lysias was the lover of Metaneira, one of seven girls purchased for prostitution by Nikarete who ran an establishment for this purpose at Corinth. At the time of the Mysteries at Athens, Lysias invited Nikarete to Athens and asked her to bring Metaneira as well, so that Metaneira could be initiated with him. They came and Metaneira was presumably initiated. The Mysteries were open to Athenian and non-Athenian, slave and free. Prostitutes, along with others, desired a blessed afterlife.[61] And presumably Lysias wanted Metaneira in his happy afterlife with him. After this, Simos the Thessalian brought Neaira, with Nikarete, to Athens for the Great Panathenaia; she drank and dined with many men, as hetairai do, the speaker says. No mention of religious activity is made; she was there as part of the festivities to entertain the men. But there was nothing to prevent her from seeing the procession and sacrifices, if she chose to do so.[62]

In the fourth century the hetaira Sinope, as mentioned in Chapter 4, brought a victim to be sacrificed at Eleusis, and the hierophant Archias duly offered it. Prostitutes, like everyone else, had specific religious needs. Sinope had enough money to purchase a sacrificial beast, and the hierophant himself, the chief priest of the Eleusinian Mysteries, carried out the sacrifice for her.[63] Themistios the Athenian was punished with death because he treated a Rhodian lyre player (she is unnamed) violently at the Eleusinian festival: she was probably part of the entertainment at a symposium at the festival, and Themistios was punished with the extreme penalty for violating the sacrosanctity of the festival.[64]

The tombs of prostitutes

Tomb monuments for prostitutes are apparently not classical. Harpalos, Alexander the Great's treasurer who embezzled funds and fled to Athens in 324 BC, fell in love with Pythionike, a prostitute at Corinth and then Athens, and when she died constructed a monument to her costing several talents on the Sacred Way between Athens and Eleusis at Hermos, which Pausanias describes as the tomb (mnema) most worthy of note of all the ancient tombs of Greece; there was another tomb monument for her in Babylon.[65] In the satyr play *Agen*, there was a reference to 'the famous temple (naos) of the prostitute (porne)' built by Harpalos, in his satrapy on the Indus river, where some barbarian magoi (magicians) persuaded him that they could call up the spirit of Pythionike.[66] There was a shrine and sanctuary, and Harpalos dedicated the temple and the altar to Pythionike Aphrodite; Pythionike was the embodiment of the divine Aphrodite.[67] Such a cult could only come with the hellenistic period, and the weakening of the divide between mortals and immortals. On Pythionike's death, Harpalos took up with the prostitute Glykera; summoned by Harpalos to Tarsos, she was honoured there as queen (basilissa), and people did obeisance to her; a bronze statue of her was set up at Rhossos.[68] Stratonike, one of the prostitutes of Ptolemy II Philadelphos of Egypt, had a monument (mnema) near the sea at Eleusis; why is not stated, but perhaps she was an initiate of and devoted to the Eleusinian cult.[69]

Lais the prostitute claimed that Aphrodite Melainis ('of the Dark') would appear as an epiphany in a dream, and tell her of the coming of extremely wealthy lovers. Pausanias mentions Lais' tomb at Corinth, near the shrine of Aphrodite Melainis. She had another monument in Thessaly: she fled there with her lover Hippostratos of Thessaly, from her numerous other lovers and 'the great army of prostitutes' in Corinth. In Thessaly the local women were jealous of her, and luring her into a temple of Aphrodite stoned her to death; the temple came to be called 'Homicidal Aphrodite'. The epigram on her Corinthian tomb as quoted by Athenaeus does indicate that she was buried in Thessaly,[70] and while the historicity of all this is perhaps questionable, it does indicate that in death prostitutes were the equal and sometimes more than so of their citizen women counterparts in being honoured by funerary monuments, given the resources of their patrons and the consequent tombs erected in their memory.

The dedications of prostitutes

Just as citizen men and women, and foreigners of both genders, made dedications to the gods, prostitutes also did so, and the main beneficiary of their dedications was Aphrodite, as might be expected.[71] Prostitutes will have felt little need to call on Athena in her capacity as goddess of weaving (though note Kottina's dedication to her discussed below),[72] or Demeter, the goddess of agriculture, from whose agricultural rites the city of Athens seems to have debarred them. Prostitutes did have children, but any dedications which they might have made to Artemis or other deities associated with child-bearing have left no trace.

Doriche the prostitute from Naukratis dedicated the 'much-talked-of obeliskoi' (roasting spits) at Delphi, which were mentioned in a play by Kratinos. Athenaeus takes Herodotos to task for confusing Doriche with Rhodopis: Herodotos reports the story current amongst the Greeks in Egypt that one of the pyramids was built by the hetaira Rhodopis, who lived at Naukratis during King Amasis' reign. She was born in Thrace and had been brought to Naukratis by a Samian; Sappho's brother while in Egypt paid for her freedom. She continued her trade and spent a tenth of her money on as many iron roasting spits as this would buy, and sent them to Delphi. Herodotos writes that they could still be seen there in his day, behind the Chian altar.[73] This prostitute was apparently known by both names; perhaps Rhodopis was her 'professional' name.

Delphi clearly did not refuse this or other offerings, such as that of Phryne, made by professional sex-workers. Prostitutes had no especial attachment to Delphi or the god Apollo but it was the most important panhellenic sanctuary and a dedication there was an especial mark of piety (and advertised the success of their careers). Perhaps more surprisingly, Polemon wrote about the hetaira Kottina of Sparta in his work *Concerning the Dedications in Lakedaimon*.

> There is a small statue of the hetaira Kottina, because of whose fame a brothel is called after her even today, very near Kolone, where the temple of Dionysos is; the brothel is easy to spot and known to many in the city. Her dedication, on the other side of the statue of Athena of the Bronze House, is of a small bronze cow and the small statue [of Kottina] just mentioned.[74]

Kottina dedicated the statue perhaps not because of any especial affinity with Athena (the deity could hardly have been her patroness) but rather because

Athena was one of Sparta's most important deities and the Bronze House one of its most prestigious shrines. While Plutarch could write that Sparta was not visited by any 'rhetoric teacher, vagabond seer, keeper of hetairai, or any craftsman of gold or silver ornaments, because there was no coinage', clearly there were prostitutes active at Sparta, presumably slaves or drawn from the perioikoi, the people of the neighbouring cities.[75]

The hetairai from Athens who accompanied Perikles during the siege of the island of Samos in 440 BC dedicated the statue 'Aphrodite in Samos', which some called 'in the reeds', and others 'in the marsh', when they had earned enough money from their labours. Presumably it was housed in Aphrodite's temple on Samos.[76] The scene as the prostitutes embarked and disembarked from the boats that took them from the island, the discussions amongst the prostitutes about the dedications, and what sums were able to be contributed by individual prostitutes are all details that have to be left to the imagination of the historian, unless the story is subjected to unnecessary scepticism. The dedications of prostitutes, earned as they were through their profession, were not in any way 'tainted' or 'impure' and this is in accord with what is known about ancient attitudes towards sexuality and prostitutes. Women prostitutes were not in any way unclean or morally impure; Aphrodite, but also Athena and Apollo, received the rewards of the prostitutes' labours.

Prostitutes and festivals

Prostitutes were also apparently regular participants at the Adonia, as well as the Eleusinian Mysteries and various panhellenic festivals. The Athenian comic poet Alexis in his *Philouse* ('The Girl in Love'), referred to a festival of hetairai at Corinth, which was different from the one for 'free-born women'; clearly the free-born women and the prostitutes celebrated separate and probably quite different festivals for Aphrodite, the goddess of the city. Alexis notes that at their festival it was the practice for the prostitutes to revel in the company of men.[77]

The third-century poet Machon had several short pieces on individual prostitutes, including one each on Gnathaina and her prostitute granddaughter Gnathainion. Gnathaina celebrated the Aphrodisios, a festival of Aphrodite (presumably similar to the festival of the Corinthian prostitutes) at Athens, feasting in the company of clients; with her prostitute granddaughter Gnathainion she came out of the temple of Aphrodite (the Aphrodision), which happened to be the same day as the festival of Kronos, and Gnathainion then travelled down to the Piraeus for a festival (perhaps that of Kronos) in order to meet a client.[78] Machon also has prostitutes swearing in jest an oath by Artemis, and by the two goddesses (Demeter and Persephone);[79] what the goddesses would have thought about any such oath has to be left to the imagination.

Athenaeus mentions that Nemeas the prostitute at Athens in the fourth century BC had taken the name of a festival (i.e. the panhellenic Nemea in the

Peloponnese, perhaps because she had done well there), but cites Polemon *On the Acropolis* to the effect that this was forbidden to prostitutes and slave women. However, prostitutes with the names Anthea, Isthmias and Pythionike are known.[80]

Women, often naked but sometimes clothed, are shown on some vases carrying huge phalloi. These were borne aloft in processions at the Country Dionysia and the City Dionysia, but it is unlikely that these representations are of citizen women acting as bearers of phalloi. In fact, men are known to have carried the giant phalloi in processions, and these vase representations must be male fantasies of prostitutes with giant dildos.[81]

The sacred prostitutes of Corinth

Herodotos provides details about prostitution at Babylon, where every woman before marriage had to prostitute herself once in the sanctuary of Mylitta (according to Herodotos, the Assyrian name for Aphrodite) at Babylon – clearly a rite of passage. Herodotos notes that this practice existed also in some parts of Cyprus,[82] and that in Lydia girls earned their dowries through prostitution; but nothing sacred is mentioned about the transactions.[83] According to Justin, the Cypriots sent their virgin daughters before marriage down to the seashore to prostitute themselves (presumably to sailors and other strangers), dedicating their earnings to Aphrodite to ensure that in marriage they would remain chaste to their husbands.[84] At Byblos in Syria women who did not take part in the Adonia festival had to have sexual intercourse in the agora, once, with a stranger, by way of a fine, with the price paid for their services dedicated to Aphrodite.[85] But such rites are absent from mainland Greece in the classical period.

Corinth was renowned for its prostitutes, both secular ones and those who belonged to Aphrodite, more so than any other Greek city. 'Not for every man is the sea voyage to Corinth' went the proverb: Corinth, on the Isthmus and between two seas, became a great trading city.[86] The ship captains and sailors squandered their money on the Corinthian prostitutes, who had a reputation for their expensiveness, hence the proverb.[87] The first indication of the practice of sacred prostitution in Greece comes from no less an authority than Pindar himself. In 464 BC, Xenophon of Corinth competed at Olympia and vowed that if he was victorious he would dedicate hetairai, prostitutes, to Aphrodite at Corinth, his hometown. Pindar wrote both an ode, *Olympian* 13, to commemorate Xenophon's victory in the stade (180 metres) and pentathlon, and also a skolion ('song') which was sung at Corinth. Athenaeus, in dealing with Xenophon's vow, notes that at Corinth individuals made such vows of hetairai to Aphrodite; that is, it was not uncommon practice.[88]

Pindar opened the skolion, sung at the sacrifice made to Aphrodite at which the hetairai were present, by addressing Xenophon's hetairai themselves. Pindar calls them young girls (korai), servants of Peitho (Persuasion) in rich Corinth, burners of frankincense on the altars of Aphrodite Ourania (Heavenly Aphrodite), granted without reproach 'to have the fruit of your soft bloom plucked in lovely beds':[89]

> O mistress of Cyprus, here to your grove
> Xenophon has brought a hundred-bodied herd of grazing girls [korai]
> Rejoicing in his fulfilled vows.[90]

The meaning of the words usually translated as 'one-hundred-limbed' is uncertain. Does it denote twenty-five or fifty girls, as is usually suggested? A better translation is rather 'hundred-bodied'; i.e. Xenophon vowed and dedicated 100 young girls. The mechanics of the vow are unknown: did Xenophon make a public declaration before going to Olympia, warning the temple of what he planned to dedicate? Or did he inform the temple after his victory? Presumably he went to the slave market at Corinth and purchased his 100 prostitutes, and clearly the temple would have had to make some provision for their accommodation, as well as other arrangements. Xenophon was from Corinth, and he would certainly have known about the temple and its prostitutes, as well as the relevant organisational details.

Strabo, writing many hundreds of years later, notes that there was a large number of hetairai sacred to Aphrodite in Corinth, with numerous merchants and soldiers coming to this city to spend their money on them, and that the shrine owned more than 1,000 hierodouloi ('sacred slaves') who had been dedicated by both men and women: because of these hierodouloi the city was crowded and wealthy.[91] Presumably the money for their services – for Pindar makes it clear that they do not simply become temple functionaries but practise the art of sex – went directly to the goddess. In addition to the hierodouloi there were of course many other (i.e. 'secular') prostitutes in Corinth.

Chamaileon of Herakleia noted the ancient custom that when Corinth prayed to Aphrodite on important matters, as many prostitutes as possible were invited to join in the supplication; the prostitutes prayed to the goddess and were later present at the sacrifice to her.[92] So when the Persians invaded Greece in 480 BC, the prostitutes entered Aphrodite's shrine and prayed for the safety of the Greeks.[93] Clearly both hierodouloi and non-sacred prostitutes are meant, joining the citizen wives. The Corinthians dedicated a pinax to the goddess, recording the names of the prostitutes who had made supplication and who later joined in the sacrifices.[94] Simonides wrote an epigram to commemorate the prayers and the pinax:

> These women on behalf of the Greeks and their fair fighting fellow citizens
> Were set up to pray with heaven-sent power to Kypris
> For the goddess Aphrodite did not choose to hand over
> The acropolis of the Greeks [Corinth] to the bow-carrying Persians.[95]

Herodotos is criticised by Plutarch for not mentioning this prayer which the Corinthian women made to Aphrodite to inspire their men with passionate love (eros) for the fight against the barbarian.[96] Plutarch writes that the praying women of this epigram were statues set up in the temple of Aphrodite, and it is easy to understand how he makes his mistake: in the epigram reference is made to 'these women . . . were set up to pray' and Plutarch obviously took this as a reference to a common type of dedication, statues. But in Athenaeus' account, the writing of the epigram is linked to the dedication of the pinax on which the names of those who prayed were recorded, and so the pinax presumably had a painting showing women praying.[97]

The inscription of the epigram could be seen according to Theopompos on the left as one entered the temple.[98] Whether the praying women were the Corinthian wives or the prostitutes or both is sometimes debated.[99] Chamaileon as cited by Athenaeus makes them prostitutes, while Plutarch has the Corinthian women praying for their husbands and Simonides writing the epigram about the wives. The scholiast to the Pindar passage, like Plutarch, has the women as the wives of the citizens.[100] Chamaileon is certainly to be followed here not simply as the earliest authority, but also because Chamaileon was commenting upon the role of the prostitutes in praying to the goddess in times of crisis. After all, it would be particularly appropriate for the prostitutes to invoke Aphrodite's aid in consuming the warriors with lust (eros) to annihilate the enemy; that prostitutes had 'heaven-sent power' from Aphrodite, their especial goddess, which they use while praying, also makes sense.

Pausanias saw the temple of Aphrodite at Corinth, and the statue of armed Aphrodite (Aphrodite Hoplismene) within.[101] Aphrodite is shown on Roman coins in her Acrocorinth temple with a shield.[102] If Aphrodite is an eastern import, as is often argued, then she could easily have had martial characteristics, just as Ishtar, the Babylonian goddess of love and war. At Corinth she is not the Aphrodite of the *Iliad*, wounded and driven from the battlefield by the Greek hero Diomedes,[103] but rather a warlike, powerful deity who can protect the city against a powerful foe.

There is also evidence from cities other than Corinth for sacred prostitutes. At Eryx in Sicily there was a temple of Aphrodite, which Strabo states in 'ancient times' was 'full' of sacred women slaves (hierodouloi gynaikai), dedicated in fulfilment of prayers not only by people in Sicily but from elsewhere as well. No specific reference to prostitution is made,[104] but this seems so like Corinth that the conclusion that these were prostitutes is plausible.

Strabo mentions at Akilisene in Armenia that men and women slaves were dedicated to Aphrodite. Prostitution of these is not mentioned, but he notes the local custom that the leading men dedicate their daughters for a long time to the goddess before marriage for the purposes of prostitution. But the parthenoi are choosy and take on men only of their own social standing. They were paid for their services, but as they were themselves wealthy the girls gave gifts (sometimes of greater value) in return. It would be difficult under these circumstances to accept that the temple slaves were also not engaging in prostitution.[105] It is possible that here the male slaves who were dedicated also served as prostitutes.

At Komana, also in Armenia, there was a great number of women in the city 'working their bodies'. Most of these women were sacred to Aphrodite (they were hierai, 'sacred women'), so that the city was a 'lesser Corinth', and men from all around would come because of the prostitutes and enjoy themselves.[106] At a very basic level, the slaves became the property of the goddess, but they had to earn their keep, 'working their bodies', as at Corinth. Aphrodite owned slave prostitutes, dedicated to her by men and women. Gods, after all, owned livestock, lands, olive trees, rivers and springs, all of which could be leased for the god's benefit. Aphrodite hired out her sacred slaves, just as another god might lease land for the financial benefit of a sanctuary.

According to Justin, when Epizephyrian (western) Lokris in Italy was threatened in war by Leophron, tyrant of Rhegion in 477/6 BC, the Lokrians vowed to prostitute their virgin daughters to Aphrodite; they were saved but did not fulfil the vow. Pindar refers to the relief of the virgin in front of her house at Lokris, thanking Hieron for releasing her from the dangers of war: this is sometimes taken as a reference to the vow, but, having been saved, the virgin ought to have been prostituted. Pindar, therefore, could be referring to the relief of the young girl at not being sold into slavery or concubinage.[107]

Klearchos recorded that the Epizephyrian Lokrians, like the Lydians, Cypriots and various others, prostituted their daughters. The mention of Lokris is probably a reference to the vow of the Lokrians.[108] But while Justin has the prostitution as something vowed as a one-off event (which in any case did not take place), Klearchos treats it as an ongoing practice; perhaps he has confused a single event and written sloppily as if it were a regular occurrence. Certainly nothing in the iconography of Lokris hints at prostitution of daughters: in fact, it is Persephone who seems to be the most important goddess here (as will be discussed in Chapter 7). About a century later, Dionysios II, according to the same passage in Justin, reminded the Lokrians – who were having little success against the Lucanians – that they had not fulfilled their vow, and the girls went to Aphrodite's temple to supplicate the goddess, where Dionysios took the opportunity to lay claim to their jewellery, but the prostitution of the girls did not take place.[109]

Aphrodite and the Ludovisi throne

Aphrodite can be approached by women both of the citizen and of the prostitute class at Corinth, and the duality of her worshippers is seen best in the so-called Ludovisi Throne (Figures 6.3–6.5).[110] Cut from a single piece of marble and hollowed out to give three sides and a base, this piece may have served as a windbreak at one end of an altar (the description 'throne' is inaccurate). The central panel shows two women attendants (probably nymphs) helping

Aphrodite out of the sea and covering her (Figure 6.3). They stand on pebbles, and presumably Aphrodite is to be imagined as emerging from the sea, as in her birth myth. On either side of the marble piece there are two carvings of women worshipping the goddess. On the left side a naked young woman sits on a cushion and plays the double pipes; her curves are sensuous and the cushion is moulded around her buttocks and lower back; her right leg is crossed over the left at the knee; her breasts are exposed to view. Her nudity is relieved only by the cap which tightly binds her hair; a hole in her visible (left) ear was presumably intended for an earring (Figure 6.4).

On the right-hand panel is a contrasting woman, who is fully clothed with a cloak covering her head and arms, leaving only the face and hands exposed to view; her dress is long, revealing only her sandalled feet (Figure 6.5). In her left hand she holds a small object, probably an incense holder, and, while her right hand is damaged, she appears to be taking incense and placing it in a small incense-burner (thymiaterion) immediately before her. Her modesty complements the voluptuousness of the flute player. The contrast is surely that between the prostitute who worships Aphrodite with music, and the citizen wife who reverently burns incense for the goddess. Aphrodite is here not the goddess of adultery threatening to undermine marriages, but presents two roles: the goddess of sexuality as worshipped by the prostitute, and the deity who brings love to the marriage bed. The dichotomy of her roles is encapsulated in the reverence of both these very different women, a paradigm of the situation on the Corinthian acropolis.

Epicurean hetairai as dedicators to Asklepios

The names of seven hetairai who were members of the philosophical school of Epicurus (341–270 BC) during his lifetime are known; while the Pythagorean school had strict notions about prostitution,[111] this was apparently not the case with Epicurus. The names of four of the hetairai, Mammarion, Hedeia, Nikidion and Boidion, also appear in inscriptions of dedications made to the healing god Asklepios at Athens. These names may well represent the same women, and the inscriptions are contemporaneous with the school at Athens, founded by Epicurus in c. 307 BC. An inventory of dedications to Asklepios from the shrine on the south slope of the acropolis has the names Mammarion and Hedeia appearing within some fifteen lines of each other, which would seem too much of a coincidence for them not to be the Epicurean hetairai.[112] Mammarion's dedication is lost, but Hedeia's was of 4 drachmas. Hedeia, Nikidion and Boidion are recorded – again in close proximity – in an inventory of dedications to Amphiaraos, another healing deity, at Oropos.[113] Nikidion and Hedeia at Oropos each dedicated a typion (a small model of some part of the body), and Boidion a model of eyes, reflecting her particular medical need. But hetairai did not constitute a large proportion of the Asklepieion dedicators, as scholars in the past have assumed. Aleshire has studied the inventories and concluded that

SEGREGATED AND ECSTATIC RELIGIOUS RITES

Figure 6.3 The 'Ludovisi Throne': Aphrodite arises from the sea-foam from which she was born, assisted by two attendants; actually a corner piece from an altar, probably a windbreak; length of front: 140 centimetres; height at left corner of central panel: 84 centimetres; original height probably about 102 centimetres; marble; fifth century BC: 470–460 BC?; discovered in Rome; Greek work (courtesy, ©Rome, Museo Nazionale Romano: inv. 8570).

Figure 6.4 The 'Ludovisi Throne': a flute girl, probably a prostitute, plays the double pipes for Aphrodite (courtesy, ©Rome, Museo Nazionale Romano: inv. 8570).

Figure 6.5 The 'Ludovisi Throne': a respectable citizen woman burns incense for Aphrodite (courtesy, ©Rome, Museo Nazionale Romano: inv. 8570).

most of the women dedicators are in fact Athenian citizen women.[114] But if prostitutes were cured of illnesses, then they, like everyone else, had to thank the gods when they were cured. If these women in the dedicatory lists were hetairai, it has to be imagined that they spent a night or more in the sacred healing building, the abaton, at the Asklepieion at the foot of the acropolis, and that they travelled to the Amphiaraion on the Athenian border with Thebes and spent some time there. The rule that men and women slept on different sides of the altar in the sleeping chamber of the Amphiaraion might have had to be more strictly enforced on such occasions.[115]

Women foreigners worshipping in Athens

There were large numbers of metics, foreigners or 'aliens', in Athens, and both men and women metics paid a special tax to the state.[116] Metic participation in Athenian state cult was limited, and the metics must have had their own cults, some of which are known.[117] Non-citizens were excluded from priesthoods; when the people of Plataea were made Athenian citizens after the destruction of their city in the Peloponnesian War, they were not to be eligible to be selected by lot for the nine archonships or for the priesthoods, but their descendants were to be eligible if born from citizen wives (i.e. Athenian women).[118] Non-citizens would be automatically debarred from any rites to do with phratries and gene, and hereditary priesthoods, of course, would be closed to them. Metic women could not become women priests in Athenian cults. That resident foreigners in cities, generally known outside Athens as paroikoi rather than metics, could be involved in the religious life of cities other than Athens is clear,[119] but metic women's role in these cities is largely unascertainable.

A decree of the deme Skambonidai in giving details of sacrifices provides that metics were to share in the sacrificial meat; it is possible that the sacrifice in question is to the tribal hero, Leontis.[120] At the Hephaistia festival at Athens, there were to be 100 beasts for the citizens in the sacrificial carve-up, and the metics were also to receive three.[121] These examples could point to a much more widespread phenomenon, or they could indicate the exceptions rather than the rule. Metic women may well have shared in these festivals and received some of the sacrificial meat allocated to the metics.

In the classical period, the daughters of metics carried hydriai and skiadia (urns of water and sunshades), the latter for the benefit of citizen daughters, in the annual Panathenaic procession.[122] Stools were carried for the kanephoroi,[123] and as the metic daughters carried the skiadia for the kanephoroi, it is possible that these diphrophoroi were also metic daughters. On the Parthenon frieze, four hydriaphoroi – bearers of hydriai – are shown: but they are male.[124] This has led scholars to assume that this task at the time of the carving of the frieze was performed by citizen males but that it was at a later date transferred to the metic girls.[125] However, it is difficult to accept that girls could have carried the rather large hydriai that the youths are carrying.[126] Male metic youths in purple gowns carried skaphai, long rectangular metal troughs; the north Parthenon frieze depicts three such youths.[127] The skiadaphoroi and diphrophoroi are absent from the Panathenaic east frieze, which shows a large number of young girls, but all of them citizens; the two girls sometimes claimed as diphrophoroi are in fact arrephoroi, citizen girls (see Chapter 2). No metic daughters are depicted on the Parthenon frieze, and in a way, this is not surprising. Metics, then, at Athens had some clearly defined participation in Athenian religious life, but would largely have been excluded from the official religious life of the polis, and would have pursued their own religious practices, which in the case of many metics would have involved worshipping the same gods as the Athenians, sometimes at state festivals such as the Panathenaia, and presumably also at festivals celebrated only by metics, involving foreign deities, such as Isis in the case of the Egyptians.

It would not be surprising if metics – both men and women – made dedications in Athens, both to 'Athenian' and to 'non-Athenian' deities. In 333/2 BC, merchants from Kition in Cyprus were given permission to found a sanctuary of Aphrodite in Athens, on the precedent of the grant previously made to the Egyptians to establish a shrine of Isis. A dedication in the fourth century BC by a Kitian woman to Aphrodite Ourania should be connected with their new sanctuary.[128]

A mid-fourth-century BC relief inscribed, 'The washers dedicated to the Nymphs and all the gods', with a list of twelve names of the dedicators following, provides a possible example of a joint dedication by metics and citizens. Pan, Acheloos and the Nymphs, the divine recipients of the votive, are carved on the relief. As the relief was discovered not far from the shrine of Pan, Acheloos and the Nymphs on the Ilissos stream, these 'washers' presumably worked nearby. Ten of the twelve dedicators are men, and of these only four give a patronymic, assigning them to the citizen class. The other six are presumably metics or perhaps slaves; their names include Manes, which also appears as the name of a dedicant of another votive (see below). The names of two women, Leuke and Myrrhine, without designations, are probably those of non-citizens as well.[129] Occupation and a similar interest in the same deities allowed these citizens and non-citizens to cross both gender and ethnic boundaries in dedicating this thanksgiving offering. One fourth-century BC dedication was made by Manes and Mika at the Piraeus to the 'Mother of the Gods'. Manes is a Phrygian name, and he is probably non-Athenian, which the absence of a patronymic strongly supports; Mika (presumably his wife) was probably also a metic.[130]

Little is known about slave women and the gods, but many prostitutes would have been slaves. Foreign women and slaves could, as seen above, attend public sacrifices, either to watch or to supplicate the gods. But that a slave woman attended secret rights intended only for citizen women was a scandal.[131] With pre-pubescent girls, the distinction between slaves and free could apparently be slightly relaxed, and so the slave girl Habrotonon in Menander's *Epitrepontes* played a small harp, but also joined in the fun with the free girls at the night festival of the Tauropolia.[132]

Obviously the Athenians of classical Athens and the rest of Greece did not attribute particular 'moral' (or 'immoral') qualities to prostitutes. Their routine sexual practices, even the sometimes hereditary nature of the occupation, did not exclude these women from religious rites. In fact, it is clear that Greek men placed value on women's participation in religion: it was presumably considered that the gods expected women to worship them and that women were important mediators of the divine. At Athens, no particular importance was attached to prostitutes' worship, but at Corinth their collective religious activity was believed to be powerful enough to avert crisis and disaster from the state through the special affinity they had with Aphrodite, the protector deity of Corinth. Prostitutes visited temples, made dedications and worshipped in their own private groups; a prostitute like Phryne could in fact be seen as the handiwork of the goddess. Their religious activity could be collegial, involving their coming together with other prostitutes and their clients, to celebrate festivals and drink wine as well, though here religious piety and business were obviously mixed. There was no reason to circumscribe their religious activities; prostitutes were not offensive to the gods.

These women who lived by and through sexual intercourse with numerous men are the most visible of the non-Athenian women at Athens. In some ways they had more freedom than citizen wives, particularly the free hetairai, though the position of the slave porne and flute girl cannot have been enviable. Other foreign women leave a few traces but little is known of their religious activities. The participation of metic girls in the Panathenaia, however, suggests that their involvement was welcomed and considered important for the state as a whole. The city could not overlook such a large body of girls; they had to be integrated into the community's worship of the gods. Although excluded from the political community metics were nevertheless viewed as part of the overall body of worshippers, and were allowed some participation in state cults, while also having their own rites, brought from their home cities.

Impious prostitutes were no more numerous than impious women priests or impious citizens, on the evidence of surviving references to prosecutions of women for impiety. This could well indicate that they were not particular targets, despite their vulnerable nature, for prosecution. It might also indicate that prostitutes did not have a great many opportunities to be impious, which suggests that the temples were open to them: i.e. if they were not allowed to enter temples it might be expected that there would be some firm evidence about this and instances of them being charged with this offence. Restricted in their religious activities by the fact that they were non-citizens, prostitutes nevertheless could participate in many religious activities, especially and naturally the rites in honour of Aphrodite. But primarily, it is important to note that it was their status as outsiders, foreigners, rather than any impurity brought upon them by the nature of their profession that excluded prostitutes from roles that, as seen in previous chapters, citizen girls and women performed. In general, citizen women and prostitutes must be seen – in some contexts – as worshipping the same deities side by side in Greek cities.

Part III

SACRIFICIAL AND DOMESTIC RITUALS

7

FROM ADOLESCENT GIRL TO WOMAN, WIFE AND MOTHER

For many aristocratic girls, particularly at Athens and perhaps elsewhere, the last religious role before marriage will have been to act as a kanephoros; an adolescent girl's thoughts must then have turned to marriage, if this was already not a matter of concern. Much more is known about the religious roles of adolescent girls from Sparta, where thanks to the poetry of Alkman and the interest of the ancient sources, it is clear that groups of girls in their adolescent years, largely from aristocratic families, worshipped their gods in very prominent roles before marriage and the acquisition of a husband. After marriage, pregnancy, childbirth and their attendant difficulties found many wives at the altars of various gods, through their own desire for assistance, but also, at least at Cyrene and Kos, because they were required by specific legislation to observe various rites in their new societal roles.

Parthenoi in choruses at Sparta

> Now leaving lovely Taygetos come, Lakonian Muse, come to glorify the god of Amyklai [Apollo], whom we revere, and the Lady of the Bronze House [Athena Chalkioikos], and the brave Tyndaridai [Castor and Pollux], who sport beside the Eurotas. Come, come quickly, come, jump lightly, so we can celebrate Sparta, who loves the choruses of the gods and the sound of feet, where the maidens, like fillies, beside the Eurotas dance, with their feet often bounding, and their tresses waving like those of the Bacchae when they brandish the thyrsos and play. The daughter of Leda [Helen] is at their head, a pure and comely leader. But come, bind your hair with a fillet, and dance hand and foot like a stag; at the same time make a noise to help the dance along, and celebrate again in song the almighty, all-conquering goddess [Athena] of the Bronze House.[1]

In ancient Greece, the role of singing and dancing in rituals belonged largely to virgins, parthenoi, on the brink of marriage. Various poets – Alkman, Pindar,

Simonides and Bacchylides – wrote many Doric partheneia, songs for maidens, and these seem to be a feature of Peloponnesian rites; Anakreon of Teos also wrote partheneia – maiden songs – for nocturnal rites.[2]

In various cults, girls of marriageable age in groups danced and sang as a chorus. The parthenoi of Sparta formed choruses to sing and dance in honour of deities (Amyklaian Apollo, Athena Chalkioikos and the Tyndaridai), and at Athens Aristophanes knew of these and penned the above well-known lines in his conclusion to the *Lysistrata*. The public displays of Spartan girls in festivals were known to the rest of Greece, and what is important here is the very real contrast with Athens. At Sparta, where girls and women enjoyed a degree of freedom compared with their Athenian cousins, and where girls and women were much more in the public sphere, girls danced in several cults. At Athens, aristocratic girls served the gods in rather static roles, carrying phialai, incense-burners, wreaths and the like, but did not perform publicly except by participating in processions. At Sparta, their role in cult was one of a transition rite, when they were ready to shed their maiden status for marriage, and their public worship of deities such as Artemis and Helen was part of this process.

Helen had a cult at Sparta, which Theokritos' *Eighteenth Idyll* describes. Four bands of sixty korai (girls) anointed themselves by the Eurotas river and took part in running competitions; peerless Helen has been amongst their number, but can no longer join in the choruses now that she is married to Menelaos. So the girls dedicate wreaths to her and make a libation of oil at a plane tree which will become Helen's tree. This tree cult was not simply Theokritos' imagining: there was a plane-tree grove at Sparta with a nearby shrine of Helen. She – an adulterer – seems an unusual figure for a cult of parthenoi, but the myth of Paris and Helen is secondary here. What matters is that Helen was once beautiful, young and virgin, a princess of Spartan birth, and then wife of the hero Menelaos, and so is an object of cult for the choruses of adolescent girls who seek her assistance in attracting a husband.[3]

Herodotos tells the story of a Spartan girl born ugly: her nurse took her every day to the shrine of Helen at Therapne, laying the baby before the statue of Helen, and praying about the child's ugliness. As the nurse left the shrine one day, a woman (an epiphany of Helen) touched the baby's head, and said that it would grow up to be the most beautiful of women. And so she did. The girl's parents – who were wealthy – had been distressed at the ugliness of the baby: clearly they were worried that no one would want to marry her. At Sparta, as at Athens and elsewhere, it was of vital importance for girls to wed. This cult was not a kourotrophic one, despite the presence of the nurse, but one of marriage: Helen at Therapne, as at the plane tree, was worshipped in order to ensure that girls would marry.[4] The woman who did not get married grew old, constantly looking for omens that she would in fact marry; a woman who did not wed had no role in society.[5]

Helen is also associated with the cult of Artemis Orthia, through a myth relating that she – before the age of marriage – had been dancing in the sanctuary of this goddess at Sparta when she was abducted by the mythical Athenian hero Theseus. Dancing, the cult of a goddess and girls on the brink of marriage again come together. Two Athenian vases show Helen being abducted from amongst dancing girls, clearly the chorus of maidens dancing in honour of the goddess.[6] Public dancing was seen to be a prominent feature of the lives of adolescent girls in Doric communities.

At Sparta, parthenoi served in two groups called the Leukippides and Dionysiades and sacrificed to the hero (Leukippos) who showed Dionysos the way to Sparta, as well as to Dionysos himself. The eleven Dionysiades ran a race, in honour of Dionysos; Pausanias has them taking the custom from Delphi, pointing to similar races there. The races will have been part of the pattern of virgin races in Greece, as at the Heraia at Olympia.[7]

At Karyai (the 'walnut-trees'), a statue of Artemis Karyatis stood outside in the open air, and the Spartan parthenoi danced there every year, and were known as karyatides. Klearchos in the fourth century BC gave Ktesias a ring on which the karyatides were shown dancing. The myth involved Karya, daughter of the Spartan king Dion; beloved by Dionysos, he turned her into a walnut-tree (Karya), and Artemis revealed this to the Spartans.[8] Aristomenes of Messenia in the sixth century BC captured the wealthiest and noblest of birth of the Spartan parthenoi performing the dances – during the day – in honour of Artemis Karyatis. He had to kill some of his men who attempted to violate the parthenoi. The story reveals that the karyatides were on the verge of marriage, and presumably seeking Artemis Karyatis' assistance in this transition. There was also a similar story that the women celebrating the Thesmophoria at Aigila in Lakonia were also captured by Aristomenes.[9]

In myth, the Pelasgians when they lived at Lemnos seized the wives and daughters of the Athenians at Brauron, where they were celebrating the festival for Artemis.[10] Artemis at Limnai (near the Spartan border with Messenia) is best known for the story that the Messenians attacked the sanctuary while Spartan maidens were celebrating a festival there, and that the girls were raped by Messenians and subsequently committed suicide; so the Spartan story. The Messenians had a different version, that the Spartans laid a plot against high-ranking Messenians who had come to worship at the sanctuary: Spartan lads yet without their beards were dressed up in girls' clothing with concealed weapons. The Messenians defended themselves and killed the youths. These stories indicate that the parthenoi at the cult of Artemis Limnatis were involved in transition rites.[11] These girls were 'ripe' for marriage and stories of their abduction serve as a reminder of this.

At the sanctuary of Leukothea (apparently in Sparta), young women prayed to 'the fair-flowing river' (unnamed, but possibly the Eurotas) that they be married. It was a custom for the parthenoi of the island of Keos to go to the public shrines and spend the day together; their suitors would watch them playing and dancing, in what was obviously a form of pre-nuptial rite.[12]

One of the main festivals of the Spartans was the three-day Hyakinthia, celebrated annually in honour of Apollo and his male lover Hyakinthos, and indicates that while choruses of girls largely sang in honour of female divinities this was not always the case. During the Hyakinthia, boys sang (as did men) and danced; but girls had particularly important ritual roles. They went in special chariots (kannathra, singular: kannathron) for a procession, presumably from Sparta to the sanctuary of Apollo Amyklai, the Amyklaion, some 5 kilometres along the 'Road of Hyakinthos'. It is specifically recorded that King Agesilaos' daughter went to Amyklai in a kannathron which was no better decorated than anybody else's. Some of the girls rode in two-horse chariots, which they raced. In Euripides' play about her, Helen, returning to Sparta, is told that she might find the maidens (korai) at the temple of Pallas (Athena) joining in the choruses, or in the komoi ('revels') of the nocturnal Hyakinthia.[13] Apollo, the brother of Artemis, is associated with girls' choirs as a kourotrophic deity.[14]

Alkman at Sparta in the late seventh or early sixth century BC wrote several songs – partheneia ('maiden songs') – for the parthenoi of Sparta. In the largest extant fragment of these, a song which was performed at dawn and therefore probably for Artemis Orthria (Artemis of the Dawn), the main interest centres around what are contemporary concerns. The chorus sings of Hagesichora ('chorus leader') and apparently other members of the chorus, and the girls express homoerotic attractions (to what extent is unclear) towards each other. They appear to be dedicators of a peplos as well:

> For as we carry a robe to the Dawn Goddess [Orthria] the Pleiades rise through the ambrosial night like the star Sirius and fight us.

The Pleiades might be an astronomical reference to the coming of dawn, or possibly another chorus group to which Hagesichora's is opposed. What seems clear is that Alkman has apparently written this – and presumably the other partheneia – for a particular chorus, the names of whose members he knows, probably being commissioned to do so. This implies an elite group. But there may well have been traditional partheneia as well, sung annually in cults such as those discussed above.[15]

Theokritos' parthenoi who sport beside the Eurotas consist of four groups of sixty. But Theokritos wrote at Alexandria not Sparta, and may not be giving an accurate reflection of numbers. In Alkman's partheneion discussed above, the chorus members say that they, ten, sing as well as eleven girls. The limited artistic evidence available apparently suggests numbers not above the teens in Sparta. The story about Aristomenes capturing the wealthiest and noblest-born of the Spartan parthenoi while they were performing the dances in honour of Artemis Karyatis takes on new significance. If the numbers of parthenoi singing for the goddess Artemis were limited they were clearly drawn from one group: the wealthiest and noblest-born.[16]

Outside Sparta, on Ionian Delos, girls (the Deliades) sang and danced in honour of Apollo, as they did at Delphi and Thebes. The island of Delos was kourotrophic in its nurturing of Apollo, and the god assumes the same character for the girls singing and dancing in his honour there.[17] Artemis was worshipped by choruses of girls and boys at Samos.[18] Maidens were involved in a cult of Aphrodite at Delos, and they formed the rite of a chorus in washing Athena's statue in Argos. Similarly, adolescent girls danced to Artemis at Ephesos:[19]

> As lovely virgin girls the daughters of the Lydians play, their feet lightly leaping, clapping with their hands at the temple of the fairest Artemis in Ephesos, at one moment sinking down upon their haunches and then jumping up again, like the bobbing wagtail.

Customary pre-marital offerings and sacrifices

Toys would be dedicated to Artemis by adolescent girls prior to marriage,[20] as a prelude to finding a husband and having children.[21] More significant as a rite of passage before marriage was the ritual of the cutting and dedication of a lock of hair. Generically, Artemis received the maiden locks of girls prior to marriage.[22] But instead of Artemis, heroised virgins, who had not married because they had died, received an offering of hair in some parts of Greece. As with Artemis, this act was a propitiatory one: those who had not crossed into the married state would nevertheless aid those who were about to do so.[23] The cutting of the girl's 'maiden's hair' signified her transition to marriage and ultimately (through childbirth) womanhood. Mourning was also an occasion for shearing hair, and a lock of hair could be placed on a tomb.[24]

At Megara, girls before marriage brought pitchers, presumably for pouring libations, to the memorial of Iphinoe, who had died a virgin, and placed a lock of their hair on it. Similarly on Delos, girls cut their hair prior to marriage as an offering to the divinised virgins who had brought the first gifts to the island from the mythical Hyperboreans; girls cut off a lock of hair and wound it around a spindle and laid it on the memorial which was inside the Artemision, the sanctuary of Artemis. At Sparta, the bride's hair was shorn close to the skull by the nympheutria (bridal attendant), but with no mention of dedication.[25]

A lock of hair could be dedicated to another virgin goddess, Athena, in gratitude for finding a husband, or to Hera when a girl married.[26] But Hippolytos, Artemis' male votary and male virgin who renounced Aphrodite and marriage, was also the recipient of hair offerings: as he is dying, through Aphrodite's wrath, Artemis promises him that unmarried girls prior to marriage will cut their hair for him. Like heroines, he was a virgin cut off in his prime; punished for his singular loyalty to Artemis, he can mediate on the virgins' behalf with Artemis. Boys would also cut their hair in a public ceremony when they made the transition to adulthood.[27]

Xenophon of Ephesos in a second- or third-century AD work wrote a love story involving Anthia and Habrokomes: during the festival of Hera the former led the maidens (parthenoi) and the latter the youths (epheboi) in the procession; the crowd honoured Anthia as if she was the goddess Hera. Anthia's hair was mainly loose, but a little of it was braided and her hair was blown by the wind. At this festival the parthenoi and epheboi found their marriage partners.[28]

This point about the hair is deliberately made and presumably all the parthenoi in the procession in the festival wore their hair in this way; that this has ritual significance is clear from Samos. Duris of Samos (340–260 BC) quoted verses from the early epic poet Asios to show that the Samians (i.e. the men), when they celebrated the Heraia, processed with their long hair loose over their breast and shoulders, with gold hairbands (they also wore golden armbands). Accordingly there was a proverb, which Athenaeus quotes, 'To go to the Heraion with braided hair'; i.e. go against custom, or do what is not done.[29]

Before leaving Anthia, it can be noted that the couple become separated, but at Rhodes, during the festival of Helios, Anthia dedicated some hair in Helios' temple with an inscription: 'Anthia dedicated this hair to the god on behalf of Habrokomes'. The inscription was seen by friends and the lovers were reunited.[30]

There were other ceremonies of dedication which indicate the deities invoked for marriage.[31] The girdle of a parthenos was dedicated as part of the transition from girl to married woman and girls could dedicate girdles before the wedding.[32] The girdle, worn since puberty, was taken off on the wedding night;[33] Plutarch specifically notes that this was the case at Sparta: before the bridegroom took the bride to the marriage bed, he released her girdle.[34] More significantly, one Athenian red-figure lekythos vase shows the goddess Artemis with torch, bows and arrows; before her a young woman is loosening her girdle. This is probably a reference to the dedication of the girdle by a bride before marriage. Similarly, a bride and mother approach a statue of Artemis seated in her temple, presumably for the same ceremony, on a red-figure pyxis.[35] On one Attic red-figure loutrophoros, depicting the groom grasping the bride's left hand in the standard matrimonial gesture,[36] a belt is conspicuous on the bride's dress: this detail is deliberate as the loosening of this belt was synonymous with marriage. At Troizen, girls dedicated a girdle to 'Deceitful' Athena before marriage.[37] But a woman could also dedicate a girdle to Artemis or Eileithyia for the successful completion of childbirth.[38]

In addition, various deities were sacrificed to as part of the marriage ceremony. Photios defined the proteleia as the sacrifice before marriage; in Athens the woman priest of Athena Polias presided over it. On an Athenian black-figure vase of c. 520 BC, a woman wearing the aegis with its tasselled fringe of snakes on which their heads are clearly visible sees off the bride and groom in the wedding cart, alluding to a role for the woman priest of Athena Polias.[39] The popularity of scenes showing the earth goddess handing the newly born Erichthonios to

Athena might partly be explained by a role for the woman priest of Athena, who received a payment from the father for the birth of a child.[40]

According to the Suida, on the day of the proteleia the parents of the girl about to be married led her to the acropolis and made sacrifices to the goddess (Athena). First-fruits would also be offered. Several deities received sacrifices before marriage, in order to invoke their goodwill. Admetos found the bridal room full of the coils of serpents because when making sacrifices for his marriage, he had forgotten to make a sacrifice to Artemis. The Athenians sacrificed and prayed to the 'ancestors' before marriage for the birth of children. Ge and Ouranos (earth and heaven) also received a proteleia for marriage at Athens.[41] Athena tells the Erinyes that at Athens they will receive sacrifices on behalf of children and of marriage, and the Fates also received offerings. The people of Praisos on Crete sacrificed a pig as a preliminary sacrifice before marriage, as a sow gave suck to baby Zeus and her grunting drowned out his cries.

Aphrodite Ourania ('Heavenly Aphrodite') was clearly associated with marriage at Athens. An early fourth-century BC inscription on a thesauros (treasury box) at Athens reads: 'Thesauros, first-fruits to Aphrodite Ourania as proteleia for marriage: one drachma'.[42] The thesauros needs to be considered in this context: a first-fruit of a drachma is presumably being offered to Aphrodite Ourania in order to secure her blessing for the fertility of the marriage. Pausanias relates that Aigeus instituted her cult and built this sanctuary because he and his sisters were childless, and he considered that this was because of a curse of Aphrodite Ourania.[43]

At Hermion in Argos, girls before marriage and widows who intended to remarry sacrificed to Aphrodite. Artemis Eukleia had an altar and image in each marketplace in Lokris and Boeotia, and she received sacrifices before marriages from both brides and bridegrooms. Young men having sacrificed to Aphrodite Kourotrophos (nurser of youth) led their brides from their homes.[44] At Haliartos, girls before marriage sacrificed the proteleia to the nymphs at the Kissoessa spring. Because the girl in Menander's *Dyskolos* cares for the shrine of Pan and the nymphs at Phyle, Pan causes a rich young man to fall in love with her (lines 37–41). Diodoros notes that even though Aphrodite was given the youth of maidens, in which time of youth they have to marry, and the care of other things connected with marriage, and the sacrifices and libations which men make to this goddess, nevertheless all men everywhere make their first marriage sacrifices to Zeus Teleios ('Married Zeus') and Hera Teleia ('Married Hera'). At Plataea there was a temple to Hera with a statue of Hera Teleia and another statue of Hera which was called nympheuomene, the bride. Hera also received offerings as Hera Gamelia, 'Hera of the Wedding'. Hera Teleia was worshipped at Erythrai on Euboea, and Zeus Teleios (mentioned in conjunction with Hera) in the deme Erchia, Attica.[45] Hera Teleia could be invoked as the guardian of the keys to marriage: she will protect the sanctity of each individual marital union.[46] Hesiod considered there to be specific days which were ill- or good-omened to beget a child, for the birth of male or female children, or for a wedding.[47] It was crucial to win the goodwill of the gods in such a hazardous undertaking as marriage.

The festival of the Great Daidala held at Plataea every sixty years (there was also a Little Daidala celebrated every six years or so) had an aetiology which had Zeus and Hera quarrelling; he pretended to be taking a bride, which was actually a wooden statue, clothed in wedding gear. Hera came to see her, took off her veil, and laughed at Zeus' ruse, and they were reconciled. In the actual celebration, a wooden image of a bride was escorted by a nympheutria, bridal attendant, on a wagon. Taken to the river Asopos, it was washed, obviously a task for women, just as the original wooden bride had been washed by the Tritoneian nymphs. This was a celebration of the divine marriage of Olympos' two most important deities. In the Daidala ceremony, the wooden bride, and various other wooden images, one carved at each celebration of a Little Daidala, were taken to Mt Kithairon and burnt.[48]

The sacrifice of virgins was sometimes referred to as a proteleia: virgins in myth could normally expect marriage; when they are sacrificed, their death is a type of marriage to Hades, and they are themselves the proteleia. Aeschylus has Iphigeneia referred to as a proteleia for the ships which cannot sail to Troy without her death. In Euripides' *Iphigeneia in Aulis* the metaphor is more developed, with Agamemnon pretending that Iphigeneia is to be married rather than sacrificed; Iphigeneia is the proteleia to Artemis, for a successful voyage.[49]

Plato intended that men should consult the exegetai ('interpreters') about the form this proteleia should take. Plutarch refers to the ancestral rite performed by the woman priest of Demeter for the nuptial couple before they went to the nuptial chamber; he may be referring to a Boeotian rite or to a generally Greek one. Finally Plutarch notes that the nuptial pair had need of five deities: Zeus Teleios, Hera Teleia, Aphrodite and Peitho (Persuasion), and lastly Artemis, whom women call upon in the labour of childbirth.[50]

The Theogamia, 'sacred marriage' festival, was celebrated in Gamelion, the month sacred to Hera, on the 27th; it commemorated the marriage of Zeus and Hera.[51] In the deme Erchia, the sacrificial calendar specified sacrifices to Kourotrophos, Hera Erchia, Zeus Teleios and Poseidon on this day. The first three of these at least are directly concerned with marriage, and this will represent a local celebration of the Theogamia festival.[52] The Athenians did not seem to choose this as a month or date for marriage, for although Olympiodoros mentions Gamelion as a time for marriage, no evidence indicates that it was particularly preferred.[53] According to the Suida, Kourotrophos at Athens received a sacrifice whenever a sacrifice was offered to any deity, indicating the importance attached to the rearing of children.[54] At Sparta, a mother would sacrifice to Aphrodite Hera when her daughter was married, a deity combining the virtues of marriage and love. The Athenians sacrificed and prayed to the Tritopatores – the ancestors – for the birth of children whenever they married.[55] Alkestis on the point of death prayed to Hestia, goddess of the hearth, to look after her children, to give her son a wife, and daughter a husband.[56] On an Athenian vase, Hestia carrying a lighted torch in each hand accompanies the married couple to their house.[57]

Wedding vases

Two types of vases in particular were associated with wedding rituals: the loutrophoros, and the lebes gamikos. The loutrophoros is the older of the two types, known at Athens from the late eighth century BC, while the lebes gamikos came into use in the second quarter of the sixth century BC. Another development was that while the black-figure loutrophoroi depicted mainly the wedding procession, red-figure vases (which had superseded black-figure by 470 BC) show other details of the wedding preparations and ceremony as well. The loutrophoros, an amphora or hydria vase, with one or two handles, was used in the drawing of water for the pre-wedding bath of the bride at Athens,[58] and was decorated with wedding scenes, many in fact depicting the procession which carried the loutrophoros to the bride's house. For example, one loutrophoros actually depicts a loutrophoros being carried in a procession away from a fountain-house to the bride's door, which is shown. Several Athenian red-figure lebetes gamikoi show an attendant during the bride's preparations holding the loutrophoros.

Other types of vases, of course, represent wedding scenes, especially mythological ones, but the majority of wedding scenes are found on these loutrophoroi and lebetes gamikoi. The lebes gamikos was a glazed pottery bowl; it had handles on its shoulders, and rested on a base. These are often shown in wedding scenes as being given, presumably as a present, to the bride, or placed at the door of the room where she is being prepared for the wedding, or sometimes on the floor near where she sits.[59]

A horos (boundary) inscription on the south slope of the Athenian acropolis reads: 'Horos: the shrine of Nymphe' – Nymphe is the 'Bride'. Numerous fragments of loutrophoroi were discovered, with the deity's name, Nymphe, scratched on them by the dedicant. The remains of the ellipsoid building serving as the shrine date to the second quarter of the fifth century BC but loutrophoroi of the mid-seventh century have been found here, pointing to an ancient shrine long connected with wedding rituals.[60] Just before or after marriage, brides will have made their way to this shrine to dedicate the loutrophoros in which the water for their bridal bath had been carried.

Loutrophoroi are found in several caves, associated with the nymphs, who were kourotrophoi. The cave at Vari in Attica with its spring sacred to the nymphs was used for the dedication of loutrophoroi, and perhaps brides in the vicinity drew water for their wedding baths from here. Loutrophoroi are also found in Attic caves associated with the nymphs (sometimes in conjunction with Pan) on the slope of the Athenian acropolis, and on Mt Parnes, and at Daphni and Eleusis, indicating that there were several caves throughout Attica where the nymphs were invoked in marriage.[61] Loutrophoroi, however, had another use, and were often put on the graves of girls who had died before marriage: the girls were said to be married to death, which had cheated them of marriage. It must be noted, however, that loutrophoroi were also placed on the graves of unmarried men.[62]

At the enneakrounos, the fountain with nine outlets, the Athenians drew water for marriage and other rites. Herodotos writes that the quarrel between the Pelasgians and the Athenians arose, according to the Athenians, because the Pelasgians were in the habit of leaving Mt Hymettos, where they were dwelling, and raping the daughters of the Athenians fetching water at the enneakrounos.[63] Men too bathed in preparation for marriage, and Aeschylus refers to the singing of the wedding song at the bath of the groom and at the marriage bed.[64] But the bride's bath involved the loutrophoros and the procession in which it was carried, with dedication of the vase afterwards, so it was she and not he who was the focus of ritual.

At Thebes, water for the bridal bath was drawn from the river Ismenos,[65] and Porphyry notes that water drawn from springs, streams or fountains is used for the bridal bath.[66] In the Troad, parthenoi about to marry bathed in the Skamander river, saying as they did so, 'Take my maidenhood, O Skamander', and apparently girls also did so at Magnesia on the Maeander river.[67]

Transvestism in ancient Greece largely occurred in ritual contexts, and was particularly associated with initiation rituals.[68] Heroes, for example, are frequently feminised before their emergence as warriors. The classic example is Achilles, who was dressed as a girl so that he would not be taken to Troy as a warrior; while on Crete, the passive sexual behaviour of the youth who goes into the country with his male lover but then returns to the city and takes up his warrior role and ends his passive sexual liaison provides a 'historical' example.[69] Rites of sexual inversion are known. The nympheutria (bridal attendant) at Sparta dressed the bride in a man's cloak and sandals as part of the wedding night, and the bride was left alone on a pallet without a light until the husband came in. It has been suggested that this could simply be a ritual of inversion, or perhaps because the bridegroom had until this time spent most of his time in company with males, it was an attempt to make the bride 'manlike' so that he felt more comfortable with her.[70]

'Let them all sacrifice a sacrifice to the goddess within the year after marriage'[71]

All of the above examples deal with customary pre-nuptial rites. While there might have been social pressure on brides to undergo these rituals, they were ones ordained by tradition but not required by the state. Athenian 10-year-old girls acted as bears for Artemis at Brauron, but it is only late sources which claim that participation at the Arkteia was compulsory for Athenian girls before marriage.[72] Four ritual roles for young girls are mentioned in the *Lysistrata*: arrephoroi at 7 years, substitute bears at 10, grain-grinders, and kanephoroi.[73]

But none of these activities were compulsory for Athenian girls, and in fact, there would not have been enough religious roles for them all to fulfil. Only four girls each year were arrephoroi, while only certain girls acted as basket-bearers (kanephoroi) in processions. About the grinding of the corn little is known, but this does not sound like a duty all girls performed, and presumably involved a few girls grinding grain for sacrificial cakes. The archaeological evidence of Artemis' sanctuary at Brauron indicates that there was not room for every Athenian girl to be a bear for Artemis, and in fact the myths point to both Brauron and Mounychia as sites for the bear ritual in honour of Artemis. Other late sources note that Athenian girls acted as bears for Artemis, without commenting on any compulsory nature for this.[74]

Various fragments of vases – known as krateriskoi – discovered at Brauron show young girls running naked, as well as a bear chasing them. This is probably a mock ritual, in which the young girls fled before an attacking bear, real, imaginary or tame. Some of the girls appear quite young, but the Greeks had notorious difficulties depicting children in art, and, moreover, many 10-year-old Athenian girls will have been quite small. In myth, a young girl had teased a bear and it attacked and killed her; the myth is told of Brauron, but also of Mounychia; her brothers in turn killed the bear. Artemis, angered, sent a plague and had to be propitiated by the service of the young girls. This is a rite which girls participated in before puberty and marriage.[75] Krateriskoi are found not only at Brauron, but also at other Artemis sanctuaries in Attica, most notably at Mounychia, near the Piraeus, but also at Halai, and at the sanctuary of Artemis Brauronia on the acropolis and at Artemis Aristoboule's shrine in the city. Whether girls took part in arkteia-style ritual here (the rite of serving Artemis 'as bears'), or simply dedicated the vases in these places as part of a transition rite to marriage, is unknown.

However, in some states, certain rites were compulsory. An inscription from the sanctuary of Nike on the island of Kos refers to sacrifices to be made in the shrine on the occasion of a marriage.[76] Also from Kos, a third-century BC inscription specifies that all the free women of Kos, irrespective of their status, be they citizens or non-citizens, had to sacrifice to the goddess Aphrodite Pandamos within a year of marriage; the nature of the sacrifice is not made clear, except by the phrase 'in accordance with their means', indicating that the wealthier class of woman would be expected to make a more substantial offering than a poor woman.[77] Also on Kos, in a fourth-century BC cult of Demeter, rites were held for those who were marrying and for the betrothed.[78]

A similar but earlier regulation of the end of the fourth century BC from the Greek city of Cyrene in Africa provided that the bride (nymphe) was to make a sacrifice to Artemis, and that if she failed to do so she had to make another sacrifice in addition to the sacrifice she should originally have made.[79] Clearly the city in both cases, Kos and Cyrene, was concerned that all brides make due worship to the goddesses, with the expectation of engaging the goddesses' concern for childbirth resulting from marriage. Acting the bear was not a compulsory pre-nuptial ritual decreed for by the state at Athens: only Kos and Cyrene, as far as is known, made marriage offerings compulsory, but the proteleia itself seems to have been a customary rite throughout the Greek world, whether prescribed or not.

Kourotrophic deities and women

Worshipping kourotrophic deities will presumably have been largely the preserve of women. Deities such as Hera and Artemis could be invoked to protect and nourish children, and offerings made to appease them so that their children would not be harmed. Kourotrophic figurines are presumably dedicated mainly, if not solely, by women, and numerous examples of these are found throughout the Greek world.[80]

Ge, the earth goddess, was naturally seen as kourotrophic, and Hera – the divine consort – was the 'generator of all'.[81] Hera is particularly prominent in this respect. An isolated example of a kourotrophic figurine, an import from Argos, from Hera Akraia's sanctuary at Perachora near Corinth, is matched by numerous examples from the Argive Heraion. Here, the Argives celebrated the festival of 'Hera of the childbed', Hera Lecherna, and she was equated with Eileithyia.[82] In a late source, Homer was said on Samos to have come across women celebrating the Apatouria and sacrificing at a crossroad to Kourotrophos; they told him to go away from the sacrifice[83] – his masculine gender would affect the fertility being invoked.

At Athens, the cult of Ge Kourotrophos or simply Kourotrophos is attested, but she was not worshipped only by women: the ephebes, approaching marriageable age, sacrificed to Athena Polias, Pandrosos and Kourotrophos when their service was over. Kourotrophos also received sacrifices in the sacred calendar of the deme Erchia, and from the Salaminioi, and the Tetrapolis calendar prescribed sacrifices to her. One woman, Nikostrate, dedicated a Boeotian amphora, discovered in Mounychia, to Kourotrophos.[84]

The Lokrian pinakes (plaques)

In discussing the role of women in Greek religion, Lokri in Italy (Epizephyrii Lokri, i.e. western Lokris, as opposed to the Lokris in Greece itself) provides an amount of iconographic material which after Athens is rivalled only by Corinth. In the first half of the fifth century BC, at least several hundred terracotta plaques (pinakes, singular: pinax), most of them 26 to 28 centimetres square, were made from moulds and dedicated at Mannella, outside Lokris, at a sanctuary of Persephone.

It is clear that the same moulds were used frequently, and presumably the individual plaques were sold, and then dedicated by the purchaser in the sanctuary. The holes by which these pinakes were attached to walls of the temple are still clearly visible. There have been several interpretations of these pinakes;

FROM ADOLESCENT TO WOMAN, WIFE AND MOTHER

women worshipping a goddess appear on many of them, and there has been discussion as to whether this is the goddess Aphrodite or Persephone.

Few of the hundreds of discovered Lokrian pinakes appear in publications. One shows a veiled seated figure on the right, obviously a goddess, with an offering table in front of her, with a standing woman worshipper holding a round object, probably a ball, in one hand, and a rooster – symbol of fertility – in the other (Figure 7.1).[85] The circular offering is too spherical to be an apple or pomegranate as is sometimes suggested; Persephone is shown holding a ball in other depictions, and a ball was an item dedicated by at least one girl along with her childhood toys, and is found in the tombs of children at Lokris.[86] The

Figure 7.1 Woman presenting offerings to Persephone; terracotta plaque (pinax) from Lokris (Italy), sanctuary of Persephone in the Mannella district, Italy, 500–450 BC; height: 28 centimetres (courtesy, ©Ministero per i Beni e le Attività Culturali; Reggio Calabria, Museo Nazionale Archeologico, inv. 28272).

SACRIFICIAL AND DOMESTIC RITUALS

Figure 7.2 Procession scene; terracotta plaque (pinax) from Lokris (Italy), sanctuary of Persephone in the Mannella district, Italy, 500–450 BC; height: 25 centimetres (courtesy, ©Ministero per i Beni e le Attività Culturali; Reggio Calabria, Museo Nazionale Archeologico, inv. 57482).

goddess herself holds a bowl in her left hand: this is the type of bowl which women are shown carrying in processions (as in Figure 7.2),[87] and on the wall are a large jug (hydria) and two bowls (probably phialai for libations), which have been used for religious ceremonies. One of the items on the table is a folded piece of cloth, probably to be interpreted as the offering of a peplos; a small box (which can just be made out in Figure 7.1) on top of the peplos presumably contained other offerings, one suggestion being the bridal crown; in the pinax here illustrated the central part of the peplos is lost because of the fragmentary nature of the piece. The worshipper has presumably brought the peplos as an offering, probably a marriage offering in light of the other iconography on this and other plaques.

The rooster that is being offered to the goddess is seen on other pinakes, but especially on those which show Persephone being abducted by Hades, in which she carries a rooster.[88] It is also seen on the pinax in which Persephone and Hades are enthroned together: Persephone holds stalks of wheat in her left hand and a rooster nests in her right; under her throne is another rooster, while a tiny one perches atop the incense-burner in front of the two gods.[89] The goddess on the plaque discussed above (Figure 7.1) has been interpreted as both Aphrodite and Persephone. But the presence of the rooster and the number of plaques with a 'Persephone and Hades' theme indicates that this sanctuary was primarily concerned with Persephone as a deity of marriage. The rooster represents male sexuality and fertility, and the girl brings the offerings – peplos, box and ball – to the goddess in connection with marriage. The rooster while seen with Persephone and Hades is not shown in any depiction which is irrefutably Aphroditean in nature. Persephone, abducted by Hades and his consort in the afterlife, is an appropriate figure for girls undergoing the transition from virgins to married women, and the offerings of the young women at this shrine are made to the goddess before their marriage.

The bringing of the ball to Persephone is appropriate for young women: their childhood over, they dedicate the ball to the goddess who will oversee their transition to marriage. In a similar way, some of the pinakes show girls collecting pomegranates from trees and placing them in a kalathos basket (a basket with a narrow base and wide top). Significantly, abduction scenes show the horses of Hades' chariots overturning a kalathos full of fruit; in another pinax, a young woman presents her kalathos and a rooster before a low altar in a temple.[90] The kalathos is clearly a pre-nuptial symbol of the transition from virginity to marriage.

Other pre-nuptial scenes are shown on the Lokrian plaques. An adolescent girl sits on a chair, holding a small thin knife in one hand and her hair in another: she is clearly about to cut her hair to make a pre-nuptial offering. In another depiction, another young woman is shown within the house preening herself in a mirror while a small girl holds out an alabastron jar to her (the same kind as one of the winged Erotes figures holds as he pulls the chariot of Hermes and Persephone back to the upper world on another plaque). Mirrors are shown hanging on the walls of Persephone's temple: the young woman will presumably dedicate her childhood mirror to the goddess upon marriage, and the pinax conveys the preparations for marriage and the transition to it. On another pinax, two women stand at an altar before which there is a rooster on a stand; one holds an offering basket, the other has a rooster and a kalathos. The wall behind the altar has a mirror, bowls and vase. The figure closest to the altar bends over to place on the altar a very thin, thread-like, short item, which she holds curved between two fingers, which could well be, as has been suggested, a piece of hair, which the woman is dedicating as a pre-nuptial offering, obviously to Persephone judging by the rooster.

On another pinax, a bearded warrior presenting a rooster stands next to a young girl who is presumably his daughter. She holds a ball, which is her offering to the goddess, symbolising the end of her childhood; another fragment shows a girl with a rather large ball. A young girl stands next to a large water bowl on a pillar, a dove is on either side of it, and nearby is an upturned kalathos reminiscent of the scenes of girls collecting pomegranates and of the presence of this item in the scenes of dedications to Persephone.[91]

The goddess in Figure 7.1 holds the bowl and her right hand is outstretched, and she appears in fact to be reaching for the 'stick' which rests at an angle on the peplos: this, the so-called aspersion rod, is also carried by the second woman in the pinax of Figure 7.2, who carries the same type of bowl which the goddess has in one hand.[92] Clearly the rod and bowl are important attributes of the cult, but in particular the role of the rod is unclear and can only be a matter of conjecture. In Figure 7.2 the rooster who stands between the two taller figures can also be noted; one of the women carries a peplos on her head, while the other who follows has the bowl and rod; a girl child in front carries a thymiaterion. The peplos is a common offering brought to the goddess along with a rooster, and is almost certainly in most cases when it is depicted a marriage offering by a virgin or newly married woman. The rod is in some sense 'magical', perhaps used to tap the bowl or thought of as being held over the worshipper in a fertility ceremony.[93]

There are scenes of the offering of the peplos on other pinakes as well. A pinax akin to Figure 7.2 shows a small woman (the size possibly indicating her youth – perhaps she is an adolescent woman) with a peplos folded and carried on her head, while a taller woman (perhaps her mother) follows with a bowl and a rod; a stand on which a rooster sits is shown between the two figures.[94] A similar figure with bowl and rod leads a procession of four women, in two pairs, each pair carrying an unfolded cloth between them.[95] In another, a standing woman before a throne and a chest, such as appears in Figure 7.1, is placing the folded peplos into the chest: the goddess Persephone is imagined as putting away the peplos which has just been presented to her.[96] On the temple wall behind her, a kalathos and mirror hang.

Some have suggested that the goddess putting away the peplos should be interpreted as Aphrodite. One of the pinakes shows a small figure standing on a rock against which restored and conjectured waves break: she reaches out both hands to a female who also stretches out her hands to receive her. A female attendant on the left holds up a square cloth.[97] This scene is invariably connected with the birth of Aphrodite as depicted on the so-called Ludovisi Throne (Figure 6.3). This intrusion of an Aphroditean theme into the Persephone sanctuary requires some explanation, especially as such explicit Aphroditean iconography has encouraged some scholars to view the clearly Persephonine scenes as being Aphroditean. Actually, apart from this particular pinax, very few of the pinakes can be viewed as Aphroditean. In fact the pinax under discussion appears to depict a young girl embracing her mother, while another woman stands behind her with a marriage peplos: Persephone as a girl is being embraced by Demeter upon her return from Hades, with the peplos representing her union with this goddess.

Connected with this, other pinakes show a goddess in a chariot into which Hermes is ascending; it is pulled by a pair of winged Erotes; the first holding a dove, Aphrodite's bird, which for Prückner secures the identity of this goddess as Aphrodite, and the second an alabastron vase. But the theme of the chariot as part of Persephone's abduction runs through the Lokrian pinakes, and this pinax is also to be seen as part of the myth of Persephone. In fact, this is the theme of Persephone's return from Hades. In the *Homeric Hymn to Demeter*, Zeus sends Hermes to Hades to bring Persephone back to her mother; he succeeds in persuading Hades to do so; Hades yokes his chariot and horses for Hermes, who then drives them to the upper world where she is reunited with Demeter, as on the pinax discussed above in which the young maiden greets her mother. Another pinax shows the goddess Hekate with a torch coming upon a seated Demeter, which is part of the myth in which Demeter searches for Persephone. So there is almost a plaque series of the Persephone myth: abduction, search, her return by Hermes, and the reunion. Related to this are the plaques in which Hermes is seen offering a rooster to Persephone alone or to Hades and Persephone together: sent to bring Persephone back, he presents gifts in recognition of their union.[98]

A woman with the bowl and rod which Persephone holds or has with her in many depictions appears in several reliefs. This woman need not represent *the* woman priest of the cult, and there may have been more than one for the sanctuary. But she takes part in processions with the peplos, either leading it or at its end.[99] She is also shown following a two-wheeled cart, or chariot, drawn by two small horses;[100] the cart is very similar to the two-wheeled chariots, also usually drawn by two small horses, in which Hades abducts Persephone.[101] In this example, a winged Eros figure hovers over the horses. The woman priest is apparently taking part in a wedding procession in such depictions; carrying the goddess's bowl and wand she represents the role the goddess plays in the ceremony: the bride may be on her way to the temple. There, the women seen in the other plaques process with the marriage peplos, which the girl then presents to the goddess, who, when the worshippers leave, is imagined as putting the peplos in the chest which stands in front of her throne.[102]

What is interesting at Lokris, however, is that men appear also to be engaged in the peplophoria. Two pinakes, both fragmentary but apparently from the same mould, show four men carrying what can only be a large piece of cloth, fully unfolded, while a woman priest follows with a bowl and wand. Any attempted identification is pure speculation, but it is possible that these are cult officials who have received a peplos from the women who have woven it, and that they are about to present it to the goddess.[103]

All of the pinakes deal with Persephone as a goddess of marriage and as kourotrophic; none of them deal with Aphrodite.[104] The literary evidence of the vow made to Aphrodite at Lokris (see Chapter 6) has skewed the interpretation of the pinakes and made scholars see them as offerings to Aphrodite in connection with this vow. But Persephone had her own concerns: the various pinakes which show the abduction of Persephone by Hades are a reference to marriage, and Persephone at Lokris is clearly a nuptial deity. Cult activities in which the women appear to be engaged are not unusual: they bring peploi and offer other gifts (of balls, roosters and small boxes). Persephone is worshipped as a goddess of transition: the mothers and the girls themselves seek her assistance in this difficult – perhaps most difficult time – in a woman's life, marriage and loss of virginity, and her transition from a life of little or no responsibility to the cares and hazards of childbirth and child-rearing. Offerings and the dedications of plaques aim at winning the goodwill of Persephone, whose watchfulness and use of her aspersion wand will succour the girls in the separation from their mothers, and whose own experience enables her to empathise with them.

A pregnant woman sacrifices to the nymphs

Four painted wooden pinakes (offering tablets; they are all polychromatic) dating to 540–520 BC were discovered in a cave, where the nymphs were worshipped, at Pitsa near Sikyon in the Peloponnese. The best-preserved pinax, with the colouring and the entire tablet almost intact, depicts a sacrificial scene in which women are prominent (Figure 7.3).[105]

The names of the dedicators, the deities being honoured and the name of the painter are provided by the painted inscriptions on the pinax. On the far right is an altar of the nymphs, associated with childbirth, and a procession is shown which has just arrived in front of the altar. First in front of the altar is a woman; she holds an oinochoe in her right hand, from which she appears to be about to pour a libation. On her head she carries a large flat basket, on which are two vessels on either side of what appears to be a box. The box presumably contains sacrificial items, such as perhaps the knife. She is immediately followed by a boy who leads a sheep by a rope; like the other figures the boy is wreathed. He is followed by two males, also boys but larger, yet not adults. One strums a lyre while the other plays the flute. Two women follow carrying sprigs of vegetation, and behind the second woman is a shrouded figure, also clearly carrying a sprig of vegetation; she is taller than the other women, both in height and in girth: she appears to be pregnant (unfortunately the pinax is damaged and her face is lost); the last in the processional line and clearly the largest of the figures, she is the most important and the sacrifice of the sheep is for her benefit. At least two women are named on this pinax: Euthydika and Eupolis, and perhaps a third; these could refer to the three women depicted in the procession.[106]

FROM ADOLESCENT TO WOMAN, WIFE AND MOTHER

Figure 7.3 Pregnant woman and attendants sacrificing to the nymphs for a successful childbirth; painted wooden plaque discovered in a cave at Pitsa, Peloponnese (Greece); length: 30 centimetres; height: 15 centimetres; polychrome; 540–520 BC (courtesy, ©National Archaeological Museum Athens, inv. 16464).

The next best preserved pinax also shows a group of several women; the other two pinakes are each both much smaller fragments and show details of women's drapery, but one of these has an inscription indicating that it was dedicated to the nymphs.[107] Clearly all four pinakes depict women worshipping the nymphs and, if the main pinax is any guide, without important male worshippers: males only serve in subsidiary roles as musicians and bringers of the sacrificial animal. The nymphs are being worshipped in some aspect particularly appropriate for women: as deities of childbirth and as kourotrophoi.[108]

Leto, as mother of the divine twins Apollo and Artemis, is kourotrophic and could be invoked for the blessing of children.[109] In Italian Lokris at the sanctuary of the nymphs several hundred terracotta figurines of korai were discovered in the spring, clearly as dedications by adolescent girls – korai – to the nymphs, patrons of childbirth and children. Timarete, as noted above, dedicated her kore ('doll') to Artemis upon marriage, along with other childhood toys; Leonidas of Tarentum wrote an epigram to the nymphs referring to 'a thousand korai' lying in the nymphs' waters, while Plato refers to 'korai' and statues at a spring, and so associates it with Acheloos (the river god) and the nymphs. Such korai are also found in graves, apparently those of young girls, and like loutrophoroi on girls' graves bear witness to the marriage that will never take place.[110]

'Endure it, and don't give up'

So says a character in a play to a woman giving birth.[111] As seen in Chapter 5, midwives, with drugs and incantations, sought to alleviate the pangs of birth, which were considered to come from the goddess of birth, Eileithyia:[112]

> as when the sharp arrow pierces a woman who is giving birth,
> the painful one which is sent by the Eileithyiai, goddesses of labour,
> the daughters of Hera, who have the bitter pangs of childbirth as their charge.

Here the deity is pluralised, but otherwise she appears simply as Eileithyia. Her most famous mythical role was in attending Zeus when he gave birth to Athena from his head. The main Greek sanctuary of Eileithyia was at Amnisos in Crete, with evidence of her worship there from the Minoan period on.[113] At the sanctuary of Eileithyia at Tsoutsouros Inatos, Crete, a small terracotta figurine of a breastfeeding woman was found, and one of a pregnant woman, both dating to the seventh century BC.[114] The numerous temples, shrines, and cult statues to Eileithyia throughout the Greek world indicate that she had an extremely important role for pregnant women, and that they – and probably their women relatives and friends in particular – visited such shrines when the need arose.[115] Near the shrine of Artemis Orthia at Sparta was a sanctuary of Eileithyia, and two figurines from the sanctuary of Orthia probably originated in Eileithyia's: one shows a woman and child supported by two figures, probably birth daimones, and another a woman carrying a child.[116] Women could pray to Artemis-Hekate to 'watch over the child-bed of the Argives' women'.[117]

At Kaphyai in Arkadia there was an annual sacrifice to a group of heroised children which had been instituted on the advice of the Delphic oracle when the women there had been suffering from stillbirths. The children had been killed for hanging an image of Artemis from the trees; Artemis punished the women with stillbirths. King argues that Artemis is in fact a 'strangled' goddess, for death by hanging was one result of depression brought on by puberty, and was resorted to in myth by those who did not want to marry their chosen husbands: they could, through hanging, remain virgin for ever. Strangled Artemis was placated as a means of averting the death of young women through suicide. Similarly, at Corinth annual sacrifices were made to Medea's children to avert the death of the newly born.[118]

> Come once again, Eileithyia, when Lykainis calls you,
> You who help in childbirth and ease labour pains;
> This Lykainis gives to you now, Lady, in gratitude for a daughter, and in return for a son
> may your perfumed shrine receive some other thing.[119]

Eileithyia receives a gift, on which this epigram was inscribed, for the safe delivery of a girl, and while thanking the deity for the birth of her daughter the dedicant makes a promise of a further offering if the next child is a boy. Mothers often made dedications to kourotrophic deities by themselves.[120] In the fourth-century list of cures (iamata, singular: iama) attributed to Asklepios at Epidauros, women record how Asklepios assisted them to fall pregnant or to give birth. Kleo had had a long pregnancy (the five years of the iama are clearly an exaggeration), but after sleeping in the abaton, the god's healing building, she felt the birth-pangs coming on and went outside and gave birth successfully. Ithmonike thanked the god for his assistance both in falling pregnant and in the birth, Andromacha for becoming pregnant, and other women for falling pregnant.[121]

Presenting the child after birth: the Echinos relief

While there were various ceremonies associated with the birth of a new child, so far there has not been evidence for the actual presentation of a child in a temple. The superb relief, published in 1992 after its discovery in Echinos (modern Achinos) in 1979, now provides an important piece of evidence for such a procedure. This large relief, 1.21 metres long and 68 centimetres high (with a depth of 10 centimetres) has a frame with two pillars and a peristyle, indicating that the scene is taking place in a temple; the knob in the middle of the base of the piece indicates that, like other dedicatory reliefs, it stood on a small pillar or column for viewing (perhaps in fact the very pillar which the large female figure – a goddess – on the right is leaning against). The style places it toward the end of the fourth century BC (Figure 7.4).[122]

A tall goddess stands on the far right, with a long lighted torch in her right hand, and her left hand rests on a pillar; immediately before her is a small altar. A male figure whose short tunic and reduced scale must indicate servant status stands restraining the beast by the horn, with a sacrificial knife in his right hand. Behind the male stands a woman who is holding out an infant to the goddess; the child's hands extend towards the deity in a precocious display of piety. Behind this woman stands a smaller sized woman or girl, perhaps a slave, with a tray; on the tray are various fruits (an apple, pomegranate and bunch of grapes) and three tall conical pyramid cakes; there is a myrtle twig on top, on the left. The cakes and fruit are obviously part of the sacrifice; the servant also holds a small jug (an askos) in her right hand.

Behind the tray-bearer is the tallest of the mortal women, who has pulled her himation over her head, so that it is partially concealed from the viewer (the break in the stone unfortunately contributes to the obscurity here), unlike the faces of the other two women which are openly shown. Her right hand is raised in adoration, while in the left she carries a small bowl with something protruding from it; it might well be a small pot of incense for throwing onto the altar once lit. While the publishers of the relief, as well as van Straten and

231

Figure 7.4 A woman presenting a baby to the goddess Artemis in her temple, marble relief from Echinos (Greece); fourth century BC; height: 68 centimetres; length: 121 centimetres; thickness: 10 centimetres (courtesy, ©Archaeological Museum of Lamia: inv. AE 1041, and ©Ministry of Archaeological Receipt Funds, Greece).

Cole, interpret the woman holding the baby as the mother, it is this largest human figure, respectably veiled, who is the mother, with the two smaller female figures being her servants. This taller figure on the left is usually identified as a woman priest. But this relief has been a costly production, and the most prominent woman in it is also the one who is giving thanks. It is easy to imagine that the mother has brought assistance with her in the form of the nurse or attendant who carries the baby. The woman or her family who paid for this relief presumably would have dressed more formally than the woman who carries the baby, especially for an epiphany with the goddess in her temple, involving an expensive sacrifice. This figure on the far left is dressed in the style one would expect for someone who could pay for such a relief. The shape of her body could indicate that it is not long since she had her baby (while the woman who presents the baby does not seem to have recently given birth, judging by her figure). The woman on the far left is clearly the one who is dedicating the relief, and does so in thanks for her child. The uniqueness of such a scene could mean that it does not indicate a custom, even on a local scale, to dedicate such reliefs, but could well be a very individual expression of the mother's; the size of the relief points to some expense.

Who is the goddess? There are two clues to this. A child is being presented and a sacrifice made: this is a thanksgiving scene for the birth of a healthy child. From the wall behind the worshippers hang several items of clothing, including a pair of shoes. Items of clothing were dedicated to Artemis, and the long tapered torch also points (but not decisively) in her direction. Two other clues are the hole between her thumb and next finger of the left hand, in which something of bronze must have been added to the relief, and over her right shoulder, raised only slightly from the relief, is a projection which could well be the top of a quiver: this could then, as the original publishers argued, be Artemis.

The so-called Leukothea relief needs to be considered within the context of the Echinos relief. A woman sits on an elaborate chair, and an infant stands on her lap and extends its right hand in greeting towards her. Standing in front of the seated woman are a woman, and two girls, one a head taller than the other. The seated woman has been seen as the goddess Leukothea, and the woman as a mother presenting her child, along the same lines as the Echinos relief. Has the mother brought her child to a temple to thank the goddess for a safe delivery?

But this relief looks very much like a funerary one, and reliefs which are definitely funerary in nature often show scenes such as this: a mother farewelling the living, who may or may not include a young child. The standing woman, in fact, holds a tainia (ribbon) (partially restored), familiar from Attic lekythoi, which was used to decorate the tomb of the deceased. Under the seat, there is an object which could be interpreted as a wool basket, a domestic item which would be suitable to show with a deceased woman. The relief must clearly be disassociated from a thanksgiving context, and be seen as a funerary monument.[123]

However, in a damaged relief of the last quarter of the fifth century BC, a woman sits on a stool; behind her a woman holds a swaddled baby; the seated woman has just given birth, and this is clearly a relief in thanksgiving for a successful birth. There are two deities: immediately before the woman is a female figure, behind her a damaged figure of which nothing survives except the hand and arm. The damaged figure could well be Artemis and the other Eileithyia, or Asklepios and the figure in front Hygieia.[124]

Various ceremonies at Athens were associated with the birth of a child. On the fifth day, there was the amphidromia,[125] and on the seventh, a seventh-day festival, of which little is known. On the tenth day, the dekate ('tenth') took place, when the father named the child, and a celebration for it (whatever its gender) was held. It was also the occasion of a pannychis, an all-night festival, when a sacrifice was made in thanksgiving for the birth of the child. Such celebrations thanked the gods for the safe delivery and the survival, during the first difficult days, of the child. The women had a prominent part in the festivities: in a play by Euboulos they are called upon to dance all night long at the tenth-day feast for the child, and prizes were offered (ribbons, apples and kisses);[126] elsewhere we are told of prizes for those who stayed awake all night at pannychides,[127] and that the aim of pannychides was to stay up as long as possible dancing.[128] As it is the women who are called upon to celebrate, this seems to imply that they celebrated the dekate separately from and differently from the men.

The presentation of the child to Persephone in the Lokrian tablets

Some of the votive pinakes from Italian Lokris show a seated woman, wearing a diadem, opening a chest which rests on a table; within the chest there is a child. A mirror hangs on a wall, presumably a dedication on a temple wall. This pinax type has been identified as part of the Adonis myth. Aphrodite hid the baby Adonis when he was born in a chest, which she entrusted to Persephone; when the latter opened the chest and saw Adonis, she coveted him. Persephone is clearly the subject of other pinakes found at Lokris, and it is certain that it is she who is shown here. How this relates to any local Adonia festival is unclear, and there is probably no connection. Aphrodite and Persephone quarrelled over who should have Adonis; Zeus' arbitration gave him for a third of the year to each goddess, with Adonis given a third for himself, which he chose to spend with the goddess of love. The fact that these pinakes were dedicated indicates that the dedicators thought the myth important, and it is possible that, as with all the pinakes, they might have been presented at the time of a particular cult occasion. It must be noted, however, that other interpretations have been argued for, including the view that the two figures are Kore and Ploutos, Aphrodite and the child Dionysos, Persephone and Ploutos, Persephone and Dionysos, or Athena and Erichthonios. The child in the chest is generally of indeterminate sex.[129] Children in chests would suggest Erichthonios, Kypselos and Adonis in myth, but Erichthonios would be a strange choice for a city so far from and without connections to Athens, while the myth of Kypselos was centred on Corinth. On the other hand, there are no other indications that Adonis was worshipped at Lokris.

As noted, Aphrodite in myth entrusted the child Adonis to Persephone, who coveted him. This would be a suitable subject to represent on a plaque which would be dedicated when a child was born in a marriage union over which Persephone had presided: after this goddess has accepted gifts of balls, roosters and the marriage peplos from young brides, the child of such a union was presented to the goddess.[130]

The transition from girl to wife and mother was the most momentous in the life of a Greek woman. It was not something she undertook unassisted, but invoked various deities to come to her aid. So crucial was this transition that Kos and Cyrene regularised cult activities at this time. But they need not have bothered. Girls everywhere, taking the momentous step in their lives which would alter them forever (and perhaps fatally), voluntarily invoked deities – usually female ones – to assist them. It is a well-known phenomenon that it was the virgin goddess who has never experienced love, marriage or birth, namely Artemis, who was the most important deity in assisting girls through this part of their life. Similarly various heroines, and the hero Hippolytos, are in the same position, easing the anxiety and suffering of their worshippers without ever having experienced these sufferings themselves. But it is precisely this virginity of the goddess that is dangerous and must be controlled and appeased. Artemis will lose her coteries of young adherents, the virgins; they must placate her to ensure that when they lose their virginity in marriage, and particularly their status as parthenoi through childbirth, she will not take revenge on them.

Girls were expected to marry, and this is underscored by their very invocation of this virgin goddess. They are expected to take husbands, they cannot remain like Artemis, but they can and must seek her assistance through this period of change in their lives. Artemis is in a very real sense without gender, her biological potential is eternally unfulfilled, and she is invoked precisely to engender the virgins, to take them from their virgin status as asexual beings through to motherhood. But other deities were also seen as concerned in this transition. The nymphs are actively involved in pregnancy; so too Persephone, herself a maiden with no choice in her marriage and taken forcibly from her mother, can more than empathise with the young women of Lokris. This goddess's favour must be won by gifts, of course, of locks of hair, balls, dolls, roosters and the like. In the Lokrian reliefs Persephone readily received and accepted these gifts, even though she must have been offered hundreds of similar items. It is the contribution of each individual, however, which is important; the state does not supplicate the goddesses on behalf of girls collectively, but each individually seeks out the goddess for an individual benefit, to cross her own physiological and biological frontier and enter womanhood and motherhood, her allocated roles within society.

Athena might well have a son (Erichthonios) without the trauma of birth, but mortal women could not escape travail. Once the baby had safely arrived, thanks-offerings had to be made. For those with the means a magnificent relief such as the one from Echinos made a suitable offering. Others would have been content with a visit to the temple to present the child, and to celebrate the various day ceremonies. The dedicatory lists examined in Chapter 1 point to the gratitude women felt for their safe deliverance from childbirth, and their surviving the birth-pangs. Within the confines of the Greek city, these women with the birth of their first child were now assured of an identity and security: their marriages were cemented and now their husbands trusted them to a much greater extent than before.[131] The goddesses must be praised and thanked for confirming and consolidating their status and societal role as 'successful' women.

8

WOMEN, SACRIFICE AND IMPURITY

> 'My mother is going to sacrifice to some god – I don't know to which one – she does so every day; she goes around making sacrifices throughout the whole district.' . . . 'You see, if she dreams of Pan of Paiania, I know we'll immediately go to sacrifice to him there.'

One is the comment of her son, Sostratos, the other of her slave, Getas. The mother – unnamed of course – is a wealthy citizen woman, and in Menander's *Dyskolos* (260–3, 407–9) she goes to a rural shrine of Pan and the nymphs to sacrifice, at the behest of a dream; the play is set at Phyle in Attica, and Pan himself says of the nymphaion at Phyle that it is well known. An old man and his young daughter live near the shrine, and this daughter cares for it. The slave Getas, burdened with the items needed for the sacrifice, arrives with Sikon (who has the sacrificial sheep), complaining of all that the woman has made him carry, and that if Sostratos' mother has a dream of Pan of Paiania, then they will all be off there to make sacrifice too, some 30 kilometres away. Baskets, lustral water for washing the hands and thylemata ('things offered', such as cakes or incense), as well as the sheep, form part of the essentials (440). Sostratos' mother will clearly preside over the sacrifices, and the slave perform the butchery; it is inconceivable that she will not eat of the sacrificial meat.[1]

Recent scholarship has focused on the attendance of women at sacrifices, and whether they partook of the meat which was distributed to the worshippers present, and if so whether they did so only as relatives of the male participants. 'Just as women are without the political rights reserved for male citizens, they are kept apart from the altars, meat, and blood', writes Detienne, in a statement that in fact over-generalises even his own arguments.[2] While women might not have received meat at state festivals, they clearly had plenty of opportunity to do so at other festivals and sacrifices. That women could not only attend sacrifices but partake of them is important for assessing their role in religion. If they could attend sacrifices but did not eat any of the sacrificial meat, whether they were full participants becomes unclear. However, specific evidence indicates that women did receive sacrificial meat, not simply as adjuncts to their fathers and husbands at state festivals, but at other celebrations as well.

Women specifically barred from or included in sacrifices, cult activities and temples

Women, for whatever reason, were restricted from attending some sacrifices. On the island of Mykonos, the sacrifice to Poseidon Phykios excluded women, but the sacred calendar setting down this prohibition refers to various other sacrifices without excluding women; on the day before, at the sacrifice to Poseidon Temenites, they were not specifically excluded. On the same day as they were forbidden from Poseidon Phykios there was also a sacrifice to Demeter Chloe, and it would be hard to imagine women being excluded from this. Specific exclusion in one particular case and then lack of specific exclusion can only imply that women were attending the other sacrifices in the calendar. Later in the calendar foreigners (xenoi) are specifically debarred from the sacrifice to Zeus Chthonios and Ge Chthonia, which implies inclusion of non-citizens at other sacrifices. In fact, it is probable that without specific regulations, anyone could *attend* a sacrifice, but whether everyone also *received* a share in the sacrifice is unclear.[3]

When women were denied participation in cult activities, clearly they could not attend the sacrifices which were a part of these. At Elateia, women could not sacrifice to the hero Anakes at the Anakeion. Women could not participate in the sacrifice for the Agamemnonidai at Taras. On Lindos, three separate sacred laws excluded women from taking part in rites. They could not be present at sacrifices to Athena Apotropaia, Zeus Apotropaios and Zeus Amalos.[4] Prohibitions against women taking part in sacrifices clearly do not imply their restriction at a particular site, but rather segregate them out from the menfolk for certain religious observances. Examples of general prohibitions are not scarce but do seem to be comparatively few in number, suggesting that it took the combination of a particular site and a particular cult to ban women.

Women were forbidden entry to the temple of Aphrodite Akraia near the city of Karpasia in Cyprus. Aphrodite Akraia ('of the heights') had temples at both Athens and Corinth but no mention is made there of an exclusion of women. On Delos a sanctuary, possibly devoted to Egyptian gods, prohibited the entry of women and men wearing wool (a particularly Egyptian dislike, with their preference for linen in ritual contexts).[5]

The cult of Zeus Hypatos on the island of Paros excluded women, and uninitiated men. Also on Paros, ethnicity was the ground for excluding women in one case: it was 'not lawful' for Dorian women to participate in a cult of Kore there; Paros was Ionian. Similarly, all women except Thracian women were excluded from the sanctuary of Herakles at Erythrai. Only women initiated into the cult of Demeter participated in the sacrifice to her on Mykonos. At the shrine of Leukothea at Chaironeia in Boeotia, 'no male or female slave, nor male or female Aetolian' was permitted entry. Women, except for the woman priest and the prophetess, were not to enter the temple of a prophetic cult on Eresos.[6]

At Geronthrai in Lakonia there was a temple and grove of Ares; every year a festival was celebrated there from which women were excluded. No woman could enter the grove of Orpheus in Thrace, or the sanctuary of Hermotimos at Clazomenai. A sanctuary of Kronos warned off women, and dogs and flies as well.[7]

In Tanagra in Boeotia, the hero Eunostos ('good yield') had a hero-shrine and sacred grove which women were not permitted to enter. As he was the male agricultural deity, women were kept away lest his powers fade. The heroon and grove were tightly guarded to prevent women going in; earthquakes, droughts or signs caused the Tanagrans to worry that a woman had in fact entered the shrine. Diokles in his work *The Shrines of Heroes* quoted the decree of the Tanagrans concerning what one Kleidamos reported: he saw an epiphany of Eunostos who was going to the sea to bathe because a woman had gone into his sanctuary. The hero had to purify himself from the presence of the woman.[8]

Women were allowed, once a year only, into the Hippodameion at Olympia to honour Hippodameia, the wife of Pelops. A myth provides an aetiology for the exclusion of women at the Olympic contests. Pelops was angry with Hippodameia at the death of Chrysippos (his son), and she left Elis and settled in Argos, where she died; later because of an oracle the Eleans brought her bones back to Olympia. The withdrawing of women from Elis at the time of the Olympic festival, which centred so significantly on Pelops, found expression in the mythical withdrawal of Hippodameia from Olympia. At Olympia, only the woman priest could enter the inner part of the sanctuary of Eileithyia and (Zeus) Sosipolis, while the women worshippers waited in the outer part.[9]

This parallels cult practices from which men were permanently or temporarily excluded, such as the Thesmophoria rites. Only the women sacred to the goddess Rhea could enter her cave on Mt Thaumasion. At Megalopolis there was a shrine of Kore, which women could enter at any time, but men only once a year. As noted, only the basilinna, the wife of the basileus archon at Athens, could enter the shrine of Dionysos in Limnai, open only once a year, on 12 Anthesterion.[10] Each year a seven-day festival was celebrated at the Mysaion, a sanctuary of Demeter Mysia, near Pellene, and men participated but left the sanctuary on the third day and returned the next. The example at Methymna, where the gynaikonomos is to wait outside while the women celebrate their all-night festival, and make sure that no other man enters the shrine, has been noted already in the context of the Thesmophoria.[11]

At Hermion where the old women priests carry out a sacrifice of a cow (see below) there was a temple in which what was worshipped was unknown to any but the women priests themselves; and in another temple at Hermion, only the woman priest could see the cult image of Eileithyia. Similarly, at Aigion only the woman priest could look at the statue of Hera. At Bryseai in Lakonia, there was a temple of Dionysos where women performed rites in secret and there was an image in the temple which only they could see.[12]

Rites were performed by women and virgins for Demeter in Catana, Sicily, and there was a statue so secret and hidden from men's eyes that they did not even know about its existence.[13] The shrine of Aphrodite at Sikyon could only be entered by a woman who could never sleep with a man again, and a parthenos was chosen as priest for a year, who was called a loutrophoros. Everyone else saw the image only from outside the shrine and prayed outside.[14] While some cults specifically excluded men or women at specific times or generically, it must be assumed that in general temples and cults were open to both genders.

Herakles the misogynist? Women and Herakles

'A woman to Herakles does not go', went a Greek proverb.[15] An oracle of Apollo at Didyma forbade women in one particular cult of Herakles: 'On Herakles . . . the god [Apollo] said: Women may not enter.'[16] A cult law of Herakles on Thasos stated that it was not lawful for a woman to participate; other prohibitions were against sacrificing pigs or goats, priestly perquisites, and on athletic contests.[17] Another cult rule from Thasos can be restored to exclude women in an unspecified cult, perhaps one of Herakles'.[18] Aelian reports that in one sanctuary of Herakles and that of his wife Hebe, there were, respectively, roosters and hens which were kept separate except when the roosters went to mate with the hens, and afterwards the roosters purified themselves.[19]

Women in Greek cult and Herakles (most misogynistic of all Greek deities) might, therefore, at first seem an incongruous juxtaposition, but Herakles' aversion to women can be exaggerated, and the attitude of this masculine deity towards women varied from place to place and cult to cult. Plutarch relates that the shrine of Herakles Misogynist (the Woman-Hater) in Phokis had a priest who was not to have sexual intercourse with a woman for one year after his appointment. An old man was usually appointed as priest: those who had passed their sexual prime best fulfilled the prerequisite. However, Plutarch notes that 'just a few years ago', in his own lifetime, a young man who was in love was appointed as priest, and at first didn't have intercourse with the girl he was in love with, but one day after drinking and dancing did so. In fear, he consulted the Delphic oracle about how to placate Herakles or be released from his wrongdoing. The oracle replied, 'All necessary things the god yields to.'[20]

Herakles was, after all, also the patron of marriage. The sanctuary of Herakles, Hebe and Hera in the cult founded by Diomedon on Kos in about 300 BC could be used for marriage ceremonies, presumably by cult members. A couch would be provided for Herakles for a xenismos (visit), and he is therefore to be imagined as presiding over the ceremony. Weddings were not, however, to interfere with the regular sacrifices made to Herakles, so the sacrificial calendar was to remain in force. However, there is a reference to an andreia oikia and a gynaikeia oikia, that is, a men's and a women's house. These could refer to separate buildings for use in dining, or perhaps for men and women preparing for the wedding.[21] Clearly, Herakles was not inimical to marriage. Also from Kos is the rite in which the priest of Herakles at Antimacheia on Kos dressed as a woman when he sacrificed, just as Herakles did in order to escape the Meropes; similarly, bridegrooms on Kos dressed in women's clothing when receiving their brides.[22]

Iconographic evidence points to women's involvement in Herakles' cults. A fourth-century BC relief from Athens shows Herakles standing with his club on the right; in the centre appear a male attendant and a large bull; the worshippers are a man and a woman both with their right arm raised in adoration, with a young child (perhaps a girl), standing next to the man, followed by a woman servant with a large kiste covered with a cloth on her head. The dedicatory inscription reads: 'Panis (and) Aigirios, to Herakles', presumably the woman and man who are the chief worshippers shown.[23] This relief was discovered south of the Ilissos stream, perhaps near Kynosarges, where Herakles had a temple.

A similar relief from the late fourth century BC shows Herakles with club and lionskin touching a large head emerging from the ground, with worshippers to the left, a man, a woman, and their two children; the inscription indicates that Peithon dedicated it to Pankrates. The large head is Pankrates (a chthonic deity, hence his head appears from the earth), and this relief and others like it were found in the sanctuary of Pankrates on the Ilissos, which had dedications to Herakles, Pankrates and Palaimon, with one inscription referring to Herakles–Pankrates. In this particular relief, Herakles and Pankrates are both shown but the dedication is made to Pankrates alone. The assimilation between these two deities means that the relief is indicative of women's participation in the cult of Herakles–Pankrates.[24] A woman kneels before him and touches his knee in another relief,[25] while an inscription attests to a dedication by a woman Nikarete to Pankrates,[26] and other reliefs show women worshipping him, usually with men, and sometimes with men and children, but sometimes by themselves.[27] As in the healing cult of Asklepios, women were probably common amongst Pankrates' worshippers, thanking him for cures effected.

A dedication at Athens of 'Lysistrate on behalf of her children, dedicated to Herakles', in the late fourth century BC shows four worshippers (a couple and two children), and a boy with a pig. The inscription is only roughly inscribed on the dedication, so that perhaps it is the case that this, like presumably so many other votives, was produced in a generic form and then sold to the dedicant.[28] Family worship and Herakles were clearly not incompatible. A woman kneels before Herakles in another votive relief. Behind her are various body parts, a bust of a woman, a torso with thighs, a pair of arms and lower legs.[29] In this instance, Herakles, holding his horn of plenty, is to be seen as a healing deity, invoked by the kneeling woman. There was a koragogos, a 'leader of the korai (maidens)' in a cult of Herakles of the Mesogeioi genos in Attica.[30] Women were obviously debarred from some of Herakles' cults, but they also clearly participated in others as well. Perhaps no god could afford not to have the attentions of women worshippers.

Women present at sacrifices

> For the woman caught in the act of adultery he [Solon] does not permit to adorn herself, nor even to attend the public sacrifices, so she does not mix with guiltless women and corrupt them. But if she does attend, or adorn herself, he orders any man who meets her to tear off her clothes and strip off her ornaments, and beat her (only he cannot kill or maim her), his intention being to dishonour such a woman and make her life not worth living.[31]

> Another woman Zeus made from a ferret. . . . She does a lot of harm to her neighbours with her thieving, and often eats up sacrifices left unburned.[32]

An orator and a poet indicate in these two passages that women and sacrifices were not mutually exclusive. In addition to the general information provided by the Parthenon frieze and vases that women were present at sacrifices, their attendance at specific rites is vouched for by other evidence. Clearly the first passage above indicates that the presence of virtuous women at public as well as domestic sacrifices was taken for granted. Ischomachos sacrificed and prayed before commencing the task of instructing his young wife (not yet 15 years of age) in the art of house management, and his wife (who is of course not named) was present when he did so, as would be expected of a ritual performed in the home. Brides, of course, were present at the sacrifices made at their wedding.[33]

Public sacrifices at Athens were also attended by women. A citizen woman who had committed adultery was not allowed to attend any of the public sacrifices, but the law allowed a foreign woman or a slave woman to attend these, either simply to watch or to offer prayer. Male and female bastards (nothoi and nothai) were forbidden from participation in family cults at Athens. A certain slave woman who attempted to pass off her sons as citizens joined in the procession when a sacrifice was being performed for the goddesses in an unnamed shrine, although she should not have done so: only legitimate citizen wives were meant to participate.[34] In Aristophanes' *Lysistrata* the old women seize the acropolis; they have gone there on the pretext of a sacrifice (177–9).

Citizen women and slave women could sometimes – but clearly not always – fall into two different categories of worshippers. When the Persians invaded Greece in 480 BC both the citizen women of Corinth and the prostitutes were present at the sacrifices made to Aphrodite for the safety of the city. Philoneos took his pallake with him to make a sacrifice to Zeus Ktesios in the Piraeus; the pallake poured out the wine for the libation while Philoneos and a companion made their prayers. Sinope, a hetaira, brought to Eleusis a victim to be sacrificed, and the hierophant Archias sacrificed it for her.[35] Whether she was present for the sacrifice or not is not made absolutely clear, but her journey to Eleusis would seem pointless unless she was actually present at the sacrifice. Moreover, slaves and women were initiates at Eleusis, so Sinope's presence need cause no surprise.

Virgin and women priests attended sacrifices as a matter of course. A notable example is the basilinna, the wife of the basileus archon (an annual office); at the annual rites which were celebrated for Dionysos she administered the oath to the gerarai who supervised the sacrifices, and herself carried out the sacrifices 'which none may name' on behalf of the city. The gerarai who assisted her carried their baskets before the altar and touched the sacrificial victims.[36] The woman priest of Athena Polias is shown on several vases, near the altar, receiving the sacrificial victims and, as has been seen, young women before marriage wreathed the sacrificial animals, and took part in sacrificial processions as basket-bearers, carrying baskets holding the sacrificial knife and barley, as well as pouring libations on the burning altar. At Pitsa, they made sacrifices in which men performed only the role of the sacrificer, while in the cult of Hekate, women sacrificed the young puppies the goddess delighted in.[37] The woman priest of Athena Polias would have presided over both public and private sacrifices; according to Euripides, her presence was required at all sacrifices requiring a fire to be lit on Athena's altar.[38] The woman priest of Athena Nike was ordered to make a propitiatory sacrifice for the demos, and received perquisites from sacrifices, implying her presence;[39] the son of the woman priest of Aglauros, whose cult was on the slope of the Athenian acropolis, reported to the boule about the sacrifices which she had made to Aglauros and other gods.[40]

Women and the ritual sacrificial cry

Women when they prayed and at sacrifice made a ritual cry: the ololyge. Penelope, after bathing and putting on a clean garment, puts barley in a basket and prays to Athena that her son Telemachos return home safely, and then she cries out the ololyge. At the sacrifice over which Nestor presides, immediately the axe slices through the neck of the heifer, Nestor's wife, daughters, and daughters-in-law yell the ololyge. Klytaimnestra recalls the sacrifices and cries – just like the ololyge of women – that accompanied the news of the fall of Troy: women usually made this cry but in the excitement of the victory news the men join in also. As Thebes is attacked, Eteokles calls upon the women, cowering in the sanctuaries, to pray for the gods to fight on the Theban side, and to cry out the 'sacred ololygmos' to give heart to those fighting and to remove the fear of battle from the warriors. Similarly, women at Athens are called upon to make the ololyge so that Athena will come to the aid of the city.[41]

While Burkert sees the ololyge as screamed, 'whether in fear or triumph or both at once', Collins correctly argues on the basis of Hittite parallels of this cry that the ololyge is a 'jubilant' cry, to summon the deity to the sacrificial meal and to express joy at the sacrifice being made to honour the deity. Such a loud screaming is of course inappropriate for the men present at the sacrifice, but not for the women; what form, if any, the ololyge took at sacrifices at which only men were present is unknown.[42]

Sacrifices at which women are expressly included

Detienne argues that in the cases where women are allowed to have a share of the sacrificial meat, there are specific reasons for this deviance from what he argues is the norm, which is that women are excluded from eating the sacrificial meat. But not all of the evidence for women eating sacrificial meat can be explained in this way, and clearly it was normal for women to eat meat from the sacrificial altar.

The woman priest of Athena Nike at Athens was to receive the legs and hides from public sacrifices, and she was not at all unusual in this respect. The parthenoi who won their races at Olympia in the three age categories were awarded olive crowns and a portion of a cow sacrificed to Hera. Adolescent girls are shown so frequently as kanephoroi at sacrifices, bringing in this role the grain to toss on the beast's head to make it nod, as well as the sacrificial knife, that their presence, at least as virgin attendants at a great many sacrifices, is assured; women priests too, stand before the flaming altars and receive the animals for sacrifice. The young women who served as kanephoroi in the Panathenaic procession, if the relevant inscription is correctly restored, did in fact receive a share of the sacrifice at this the greatest of Athens' state festivals. Aristophanes has women giving their meat from the Apatouria to their panders; how they came by it is not indicated. During the Thesmophoria the women of Eretria cooked their meat by the heat of the sun rather than by fire, indicating that they did eat of sacrificial meat.[43]

A sacred law from Thasos, from the sanctuary of Demeter Thesmophoros at the end of the fifth century BC, expressly stated that Athena Patroia was to receive sacrifice every second year, with women to receive a portion thereof.[44] The woman priest of Artemis Pergaia at Halikarnassos, and the wives of the pytaneis, in the month Herakleion, were all to have equal shares in the sacrifice.[45] From the deme Erchia, in Attica, comes a sacred calendar of sacrifices which specifically included women as consumers of the sacrifice. On the sixteenth day of the month Elaphebolion, the goat sacrificed to Semele, and the one sacrificed to Dionysos, were to be consumed 'on the spot' by the women (of the deme), and the woman priest was to have the skin as a perquisite. This provision to consume the meat on the spot implies some sort of dining arrangements, however informal. Presumably the sacrifices to Dionysos and Semele are all-women ones, as it is the women who are specifically mentioned here, and the provision not to take the meat away but to eat it there and then probably indicates an all-women ritual dining group.[46]

The women of Tegea in the sixth-century BC war between Tegea and Sparta successfully ambushed the Spartans led by King Charillos. They sacrificed to Ares without their men, and did not share the sacrificial meat with them. For this reason the carving of Ares on a slab in the Tegean marketplace is called, 'He who entertains women' (gynaikothoinas). Whether the aetiology is credible, here women eat the meat.[47] Athenian women had prayed that the enemy be pursued, and they were pursued, all the way to Chalkis. A sacrifice, referred to as the 'Chalkidian Pursuit', by the women at the Thesmophoria commemorated the event, which may well have been the Chalcidian invasion of Athens in 508. The women had probably prayed to Demeter Thesmophoros, and perhaps Persephone–Kore, and rewarded the goddess at her main festival.[48]

A third-century BC decree of orgeones (members of a private religious association) at Athens meeting to worship the hero Echelos provides that the meat is to be given to the orgeones who are present at the sacrifice, with a half-share for their sons, a full share for the 'free' wives of the orgeones, a half-share for their daughters, and a share for one slave (a neat way of avoiding discrimination against the wealthier who had more than one slave). The decree provides that the share of the woman is to be handed over to the man, not necessarily implying that women were not present at the sacrifice, but rather that it is the men who come forward to receive the meat that is being given away – it is they who are citizens and whose identity is recognised; it is the men who can 'prove' their identity as members (and, incidentally, who could carry the heavy parcels of meat that were presumably involved).[49]

Women and entrails

The flesh of sacrificed animals could be consumed on the spot or taken away, depending on individual cult regulations. But the entrails were consumed at once, roasted straightaway on spits. If a woman priest was at a sacrifice, as the presider or one of the presiders she was clearly a full participant in the sacrifice, and she would presumably have shared in the entrails. But apparently this is explicitly stated only once. The purchaser of the woman priesthood of Artemis Pergaia was to have shares in both public and private sacrifices to the goddess. This amounted to, in the case of both public and private sacrifices, thighs from the victims, skins (not mentioned for the private sacrifices), and a fourth part of the entrails. Presumably she tasted the entrails as part of the sacrifice, but one-quarter of the entrails is a lot of sausage and presumably she did not have to eat it all then and there, though questions concerning the frequency with which the shrine was visited and sacrifices took place might then become of interest.[50]

A decree of around 400 BC from the island of Chios stipulates that the woman priest of the goddess of childbirth, Eileithyia, was to have perquisites from the sacrifice and apparently she was to consume these 'along with the women who made the sacrifice'. These perquisites of the contents of the liknon (the sacrificial basket, which could contain cakes and fruit) and tongue of the sacrifice could easily be consumed at the place of sacrifice by the women in a convivial setting. In most cases, given the nature of the perquisite, such as a thigh-bone and often the tongue, this would have been impractical because of the amount of meat involved. It is women who are the agents of the sacrifice here: what is particularly appropriate is that they are propitiating a goddess, perhaps praying for successful childbirths, giving thanks for them, or just participating in kourotrophic worship in general.[51]

In Herondas' *Mime* 4, two women visit an Asklepieion – the scene is probably Alexandria but perhaps Kos (site of an important Asklepieion) – and one of them has brought a cock which she says she is going to sacrifice to Asklepios. She would, she says, sacrifice a cow or pig in thanksgiving for the healing Asklepios has carried out if they were better off. The neokoros (guardian) will receive a leg of the bird, and an offering made to the snake; the rest of the bird will be taken home and eaten.

Women as sacrificers

As seen in the discussion of the Thesmophoria in Chapter 4, women at least in some Greek cities killed piglets as part of Demeter rites. A fragment of a relief from Athens shows a woman with a knife on the point of sacrificing a goat. The piece comes (according to the excavator) from a brothel, and it is suggested that this is a depiction of a sacrifice to Aphrodite; a prostitute in Lucian's *Dialogues of the Hetairai* speaks of sacrificing a white goat to Aphrodite, though of course this does not mean that she intends to do this personally.[52] On a vase from Apulia, the Ruvo amphora, a similar theme is shown. At an altar a woman holds a small goat under her arm, and has a knife in her right hand. There is a fire in the middle of the altar, and an image of Dionysos at its end, opposite the woman. Another woman brings fruit and cakes in a basket to a table attached to the altar. Women play the cymbals and drum, while others are waving the thyrsos and torches, and dance. No men are present.[53] Perhaps the vase is depicting an imaginery maenadic sacrifice. But perhaps women did, after all, kill small sacrificial animals in private rites.

Women appear as sacrificers in a rite at Hermion in the Argolid, which both Aelian and Pausanias describe as a contemporary event. At the Chthonia festival, held in honour of Demeter, the biggest cow of the herd ('that not even ten men can control') allows itself to be led by an old woman, the priest of Demeter, to the altar where it is sacrificed. There is a procession of priests, magistrates, women, men and children – both boys and girls. Outside the temple are statues of women priests of Demeter; near them are four raised chairs on which four old women, clearly also women priests, sit while waiting for the procession; they then go inside. The doors of the temple are closed and the cow's bonds are loosened at the same time; through the doors the cow meets its end at the hands of one of the four women priests within, who slits its throat; each woman priest has a sickle. This procedure is repeated another three times, with three more cows being brought to the temple for this purpose, until four cows are dispatched. Pausanias saw the procedure outside; no one but the women priests was inside.[54]

The comic poet Pherekrates noted that no one had ever seen a woman mageiros (a mageiraina) or a woman fish-seller, which Athenaeus explains as meaning that tasks needed to be appropriate to men and women: certainly no one would assume that women under normal circumstances would kill and butcher bulls and other animals.[55] Apparently selling fish was not considered a woman's task, presumably because they did not go out and catch the fish.

A woman priest presiding at a sacrifice would not herself generally slay the victim. Iphigeneia is the virgin priest of Artemis at her temple in Tauris, where Orestes and Pylades are to be slain as sacrifices. Orestes asks her whether she will sacrifice him, to which she replies yes, but to his further question whether she will kill him herself, she replies no, but she will sprinkle his hair with holy water (the chernips). She will sacrifice him but not deal the blow itself, but if it was absolutely certain that she would not be the sacrificer, it is worth wondering why he asks the question at all.[56]

Women, Hekate and puppy sacrifices

Hekate, as seen in Chapter 5, was the especial patron of magic and sorcery, and women sacrificed to her. A red-figure lekythos from Athens shows a woman holding a small animal (Figure 8.1). Deubner took this to be a piglet, as do Detienne and Keuls, and he connected it with the Skira and pig sacrifices to Demeter. Detienne considered it to be a piglet thrown alive into the megaron as part of the Thesmophoria rite. But the animal is clearly a dog, perhaps a puppy, as Rumpf, Beazley and Simon take it. The woman leans over, holding the dog towards the ground. In her left hand she has a sacrificial basket. Before her are three torches, which look to be thrust into the soil; the bottom border of the vase represents ground level, and the torches are protruding up out of a hole in the ground. Into this chasm or crevice the woman is about to throw the puppy. In the basket she may well have had a sacrificial knife with which to slay it first. A dog offering was appropriate to Hekate, goddess of the underworld. The three torches are significant, as Hekate was often represented in threefold shape.[57] In a women-only rite, the sacrificial dispatch of a small mammal can hardly have been difficult for a woman. This particular sacrifice might have occurred at the time of the new moon, when Hekate received other offerings.

Curses, oaths and prayer

> And because of these things the women priests and priests stood up facing west and cursed Andocides, and they shook out their purple garments, as is the ancient and time-honoured custom.[58]

Women priests join in the cursing here of Andocides (and are here mentioned before the priests), found guilty of profaning the Eleusinian Mysteries in

Figure 8.1 A woman with a basket sacrificing a puppy to the goddess Hekate; Athenian red-figure lekythos; fifth century BC; Group of Palermo 16 (courtesy, ©National Archaeological Museum, Athens, inv. 1695).

415 BC. Alkibiades, also condemned at this time, was similarly cursed by 'all priests and women priests', except that Plutarch mentions that Theano, daughter of Menon of the deme Agryle, refused to curse his name, saying that she was a priest of prayer not of curses. Women's involvement in public cursing is also found in the Cyrene decree, in which women and girls join the men and boys in calling down curses on those who do not abide by the agreement concerning the colonists to Libya; wax images were burnt; if anyone did not abide by the agreement, he and his descendants would melt away like the figures.[59]

In myth at least, women could curse in their own right, and raise the sceptre of the avenging Erinyes against those who had wronged them. Telemachos fears that if he forces his mother to leave their house, as she is departing she will invoke the Erinyes against him. Klytaimnestra sacrifices Agamemnon to the Erinyes of her daughter, whom her father sacrificed. But Klytaimnestra's other offerings, motivated by guilt towards the husband she has murdered, are inappropriate, Elektra argues. Medea curses the royal household of Corinth, into which Jason abandoning her is to marry. In the *Thesmophoriazousai*, the meeting of the women opens with a parody of the prayer said before meetings of the male ekklesia: the woman herald invokes Demeter, Kore, Ploutos, Kalligeneia and Kourotrophos Ge, and destruction is invoked on anyone guilty of various misdemeanours.[60]

Oaths taken by men routinely involved a curse on themselves and their family if they broke the oath, such as the oath taken by Athenian jurors which ended with such a provision.[61] Oaths could include provisions to curse land with barrenness, and wives with the birth of children which did not look like their parents but instead were terata, monsters. It was thought that the family of a perjurer would suffer along with him.[62] Oedipus curses those who will take no action in finding out who killed the previous king Laios (his own father, whom he had himself killed), with barrenness for their wives.[63]

Women, excluded from politics and most other worldly affairs, did not need to take oaths as frequently as men. But the speaker acting on behalf of a mother, who in one of Lysias' speeches is involved in the prosecution of her own father concerning her children's property, states that she often swore to the truth of her claims on the lives of her children; no curse is mentioned, and when women at Athens took oaths, they swore by Aglauros, one of the heroines associated with the acropolis.[64]

Women take oaths in literature and myth. The women in Euripides' *Hippolytos* swear by Artemis that they will not reveal that Phaidra loves her stepson (710–14). She is appropriate here not just as the especial goddess of women but also as the goddess whom Hippolytos particularly honours, to the exclusion of Aphrodite. Iphigeneia swears by Artemis – the goddess for whom she is priest – when making an oath with Pylades. Erechtheus' daughters swore an oath that if one of them was sacrificed, the rest would kill themselves.[65] Mothers could swear oaths to the legitimacy of their children in the Delphinion at Athens.[66]

Women would pray for their particular concerns, but often as part of their passive role in Greek society, as in the case of the Corinthian wives and prostitutes who prayed for victory in war for their menfolk while these were actually off fighting, or in literature when the Trojan women pray to and supplicate Athena for her aid against the Greeks. Women, as did men, prayed, but they adopted different postures: women are shown much more frequently kneeling in supplication to gods, whereas men are rarely so shown. Men are generally shown standing with one hand raised in supplication, though there are some exceptions. When Xenophon was making a speech about the army's safety someone sneezed, and the whole Ten Thousand fell to their knees at this propitious omen. The Superstitious Man when he passes a stone set up at a crossroad will anoint it with oil, and kneel down before passing. The kneeling of a woman might be considered an ungainly sight in public. Women could cling to statues, but this is not the same as kneeling before them.[67]

The kneeling woman is most conspicuous in iconography, mostly from Athens, which has been assembled by van Straten, with various reliefs showing women kneeling before a divinity. One example is a relief inscribed 'in thanks' to the healing deity Palaimon, in which a woman kneels before the god; she has her arms stretched out and takes the folds of his clothes in her hands. Behind her stands a second woman worshipper, and it appears that a third worshipper stood behind her.[68] Women are depicted kneeling before deities such as Zeus Meilichios, Artemis, Asklepios, Demeter, Leukothea, and the healing deity Palaimon; there are several representations for each of these deities but fewer for Demeter and Leukothea. The significance of these to women is immediately apparent, except in the case of Zeus Meilichios, apparently a god providing for household needs and so important to women.[69] Women kneel and men do not because in many ways it is a ridiculous posture, particularly when the woman is doubled over, i.e. is prostrate, and such a position of base entreaty is appropriate for women, but not for men. The kneeling attitude, however, allows for a closer and more intimate contact with the deity being supplicated, and a greater feeling of abasement before divinity. All women, including foreign women but excluding adulterous citizen women, could pray to the gods at festivals.[70] Plato makes it clear that women had shrines within the house where they could supplicate the gods – clearly wealthy women are meant, though most houses presumably had some centre of worship. Alkestis, on the point of death, goes to all the altars in her house and prays at them.[71] Both men and women prayed; their concerns differed to some extent and women, viewed and treated as inferior to men, could abase themselves before the gods to a degree which men would not.

Menstruation

Menstruation, a woman's monthly flow of blood, is readily explicable as a source of pollution, a cause of disquiet for men. The Judaic–Christian tradition indicates this quite clearly. But it is only several centuries after the classical period that specific Greek cult laws address the 'problem' of menstruation. In the cult regulations of Egyptian Isis and Sarapis at Megalopolis in the Peloponnese from the second century BC (the earliest century in which menstruation is dealt with in a Greek purity law) a woman was pure from menstruation on the seventh day, and could then enter the shrine and worship. In the cult of a Syrian deity or deities on Delos, likewise in the second century BC, the woman was pure on the ninth day. In Egypt at Ptolemais in the first century AD seven days were required in an unknown cult. The seventh day also brought purification in the cult of Men at Athens in the second century AD, but after the woman 'washed' herself. Similarly, a woman who had menstruated could enter the shrine (the deity's name is lost) at Lindos (Rhodes) in the third century AD after she had cleansed herself, but the restoration (of a reference to menstruation) is very insecure. One second- or third-century AD fragmentary purity inscription from Thera mentions menstruation. None of these cults belong to before the second century BC, and none belongs to a Greek as opposed to an exotic cult (e.g., Isis and Sarapis). In the classical period, menstruation was clearly not a cause for religious concern.[72]

In the temple inventories of Artemis Brauronia which record dedications of clothing to Artemis, the word rakos appears. Mommsen in 1899 first suggested that the word meant 'rag' and referred to the menstrual cloth used by a virgin for her first menstruation. Linders, however, has noted that some of the inventories are duplicates, lists made at different times of the holdings of the sanctuary and so containing the same items. Some of the items in one list do not have the word rakos appended to them, but in another list they do, and so she argues for the primary meaning of the word: that some of the dedicated clothes have deteriorated – become ragged – over time, and are described as such.[73] Clothing was dedicated after menarche according to the Hippocratic *Peri Parthenion*, but clearly clothing as opposed to cloths or rags is meant.[74] Puberty was an important transition for a girl, but it does seem, as Linders argues, that the physical proof of this was not offered, but rather something more fitting.

Pregnancy

Pregnant women were forbidden to participate in the cult of the Despoina at Lykosoura. The hill in Arkadia where Rhea gave birth to Zeus was sacred, and pregnant animals and women with 'need of Eileithyia' would not venture there.[75] But these are atypical regulations. Pregnant women were expected to visit temples,[76] invoking the aid of the gods to assist in the transition from pregnancy to childbirth, a dangerous passage in which women could succumb and die. In the Demeter procession described by Callimachus, pregnant women were encouraged to go as far in the procession to the temple as their legs would carry them.[77] Shrines to Artemis, Eileithyia, Demeter and kourotrophic deities would have been particularly favoured by pregnant women. The main worshipper of the nymphs on the best preserved of the wooden tablets from Pitsa, which depicts a small procession of women, appears to be pregnant (Figure 7.3).

Pregnant women might be particularly susceptible to contracting pollution: they are amongst the three categories (priests, pregnant women, those soon to marry) that Iphigeneia warns to keep away when she is about to bring the polluted Orestes through the streets.[78] The extent to which this proclamation represents a reality is unclear: it is difficult to think of any occasions when a public proclamation might be made that a source of pollution (and hence danger) was approaching; Orestes, in fact, is a particularly unusual case.

Pregnant women were generally not debarred from religious life – in fact, it was apparently particularly appropriate for them to take part in religious activities.

Miscarriage

Miscarriage is dealt with in several sacred laws, but it is in the fourth-century BC cathartic (purification) law of Cyrene that most detail is found. Here there is a distinction relating to the appearance of the aborted foetus. If a woman miscarries and the foetus is 'distinguishable' (has a human appearance) the pollution is as from death. If the foetus is not distinguishable, then the pollution is as from childbirth, which at Cyrene involved three days' pollution for anyone present at the birth.[79]

Elsewhere, on the island of Kos, another text equates birth and miscarriage (without the Cyrenian distinction of 'distinguishable'), with both resulting in three days of pollution.[80] Another text from Kos also dealt with pollution from miscarriage; the type of pollution incurred is subject to restoration.[81] These laws from Kos date to after the fourth-century BC synoikismos in which various villages and towns physically joined together. They may represent codifications of what had applied earlier in the fourth century, and so almost certainly represent classical ideas about pollution arising from miscarriage and childbirth.

As with menstruation, later laws have long periods of pollution for miscarriages; they do not equate the pollution with childbirth (or possibly death), but have a set period, usually forty days. A third-century AD purity law from Lindos reads: 'from a miscarriage of a woman or dog or donkey, forty days'. One third-century AD inscription gives a 44-day period.[82] It is not clear in most of these laws whether it was only the woman who incurred pollution or whether the circle spread more widely; the Cyrene regulation applies it to those in contact with her (under the same roof when the miscarriage occurred) and this was presumably usually the case.[83] Shorter periods are known, too: a second-century BC cult required a ten-day waiting period for those coming from a childbirth or miscarriage.[84] Miscarriage is not so much pollution by birth but by death, and such miasma affected both genders, of course, but originated only with women.

Miscarriage – and infertility – may in the popular imagination have been connected with religious factors, which presumably strengthened the notion of pollution. The city as a whole could be punished for the wrongs of one bad man: Zeus sends famine and plague, men perish, and women do not give birth. The birthrate amongst the Pelasgians on the island of Lemnos declined because their men had killed the Athenian women whom they had abducted, and the children which they had had by them. The parricide, regicide and incest of Oedipus combine to render the women of Thebes barren.[85]

A deliberate or induced miscarriage – artificial abortion of the foetus – might well have come under the same heading as miscarriage, but the terminology of the sacred laws concerning abortions is 'neutral', not distinguishing between natural and induced miscarriage. An exception would be a second-century AD purity inscription from Lindos which refers to 'drugs inducing abortions', stipulating a forty-day purification period (with the previous line indicating a one-day period for purification after eating cheese).[86] The first-century BC private cult law from Philadelphia in Lydia, with its strong moral tone so unlike that of Greek cults in general, instructs that those who enter the shrine of the cult are to promise that they will not administer abortive or contraceptive drugs.[87] It is possible, therefore, that there was no moral tone in Greek religious thought towards the practice of abortion, and it was not a concern in the classical period.

Evidence about the exposure of children is patchy, and in the classical period it does not seem to have been considered a pollution. At Sparta, the decision to expose an infant was taken by a council of male elders and does not seem to have had any religious connotation, with exposure of deformed infants being a duty and obligation. At Smyrna in the second century AD the purification period required for exposing a child was the same as for miscarriage, forty days; it was fourteen days at Ptolemais in Egypt.[88]

Childbirth and pollution

The woman who had just given birth was considered to pollute those around her. The earliest reference comes from the cathartic law of Cyrene of the fourth century BC:

> The woman in childbed shall pollute the house . . . she shall not pollute [the person who is outside the house (?)], unless he comes in. Any person who is inside shall be polluted for three days, but shall not pollute anyone else, not wherever this person goes.[89]

Childbirth might not seem a logical impurity, such as death; the birth of new life should surely be a celebration, rather than polluting. But birth is also about blood – on the baby, with the afterbirth (the expulsion of the placenta), and the cutting of the thick purple blood vessel of the umbilical cord. This is disturbing to men, and the Greek man, like his counterparts in many cultures, left the business of childbirth to women. Those who were polluted for three days by their contact with the woman were the women relatives and other women assistants who came to her aid, the midwives with their drugs and incantations. Pollution is incurred, but there is a common-sense approach, and it is not contagious.

Women went to healing sanctuaries for aid in becoming pregnant and for help with lengthy pregnancies, but could not actually give birth within the sacred precinct. A woman (Kleo) with a lengthy pregnancy who had travelled to Epidauros received a dream in the abaton that she would give birth; she immediately left the abaton and had her child. Pausanias notes that women at Epidauros were not allowed to give birth in the sanctuary itself and had to give birth outside in the open, until a building was built for their use (in the Roman period).[90]

Yet birth was an important occasion, and thanksgiving was appropriate. A first-century BC inscription from Miletos mentions 'women walking out the lochia (afterbirth) and girded up', making sacrifices to Asklepios. As seen, Asklepios as a god of healing was thought to take an especial interest in women falling pregnant and childbirth, and their post-parturient state did not disqualify them from making sacrifice to the god who had assisted them; in fact such sacrifices were probably expected. In the classical period, a fourth-century BC inscription at Delphi records a sacrifice by a lecho (a woman who has just given birth).[91]

After the Athenians had purified the island of Delos in the fifth century BC, women were no longer allowed to give birth there, and had to leave the island and travel to the nearby island of Rheneia in order to do so (death and burial were also prohibited).[92] A sacred law from Despoina's cult at Lykosoura in the second century BC mentions a waiting period before women could be initiated after childbirth.[93] An Athenian decree of the first century BC states that it is ancestral practice that no births or deaths take place in sanctuaries (temene).[94] Aristophanes in his *Frogs* complained about Euripides having women giving birth in temples:[95] Euripides in his *Auge* had a virgin girl priest of Athena, Auge, giving birth to Telephos in Athena's sanctuary at Tegea (having been raped or seduced by Herakles; see below). To escape from the acropolis in the *Lysistrata*, a woman pretends to be pregnant, and prays to Eileithyia to delay her birth-pains until she reaches a place where it is hosios – holy – to give birth: that is, it was not pious to do so on the acropolis.[96]

To go from the bed where childbirth or death had just occurred to a shrine had been prohibited without reason according to the Stoic philosopher Chrysippos: as the gods were not polluted by animals having intercourse, giving birth or dying in shrines, why should they be so in the case of humans?[97] But this was not the view commonly held: Theophrastos writes of his character, 'The Superstitious Man' (16.9), 'He won't step on a grave, or view a corpse or a woman in childbirth, but he says it is wiser for him not to incur pollution.'

Cult laws usually prescribed periods of pollution apo lechous, probably best interpreted as those coming from the childbed.[98] On Kos, priests could enter the house where birth or death had occurred three days later.[99] The period for which people were debarred from certain sanctuaries after coming from the birth bed varied: two, three, seven and ten days are all attested. An inscription from Eresos distinguishes two periods: ten days' wait before a woman who has given birth can participate in the cult, but only three days for those who have come into contact with her (as in the Cyrene text); at Lindos, it was twenty-one days for the woman, and three for whoever came into contact with her.[100] The days were usually few in number, sometimes fewer than those required if one came into contact with a corpse; what is interesting is that women in childbirth and the corpse are so routinely grouped together: these were the two most important categories of pollution for many cults and shrines.

In practice, women were confined to the house for several days as a matter of course after birth. The longer periods of ten and twenty-one days of pollution incurred by the woman herself probably reflect local concerns that a longer period of purification was required for her, and also that it was assumed that a woman could be abroad (but should not be) before the tenth or twenty-first day after delivery of her child. The only evidence from the classical period – from Cyrene – indicates a minimal pollution, of three days, for those coming into contact with the woman, and nothing about the woman herself; only the later cults specifically prescribe the lengthy periods of pollution for the woman. On the fifth day the amphidromia occurred, in which the child was ceremoniously carried around the hearth of the house, and on the same day there was a ceremony of purification for the women who had been present at the birth.[101] The later medical texts have long periods of purification after childbirth: thirty to forty days; surely these would not reflect actual practice, but one cannot be certain, and they presumably indicate medical opinion as to how long a woman should rest after giving birth. There was a tenth-day naming festival, which perhaps corresponded to the period of post-parturient pollution.[102]

In addition to pregnant women, the mysteries of the Despoina at Lykosoura also prohibited mothers who were breastfeeding from participation, and although the context is uncertain women had to wait a certain period after childbirth, perhaps before being initiated but more probably before entering the sanctuary. This was because of the 'logic of opposition': the rites of the Despoina concerned fertility, and women about to give birth, or who were breastfeeding, were in that sense 'afertile', having produced children from the fertility which the cult was celebrating and inducing.[103] Other cults presumably did not have such concerns.

Sexual intercourse, sexual purity and temples

In Aristophanes' *Lysistrata*, Myrrhine's anxious husband wants sexual intercourse straight away, and suggests that they have it in Pan's sanctuary, whereat she asks how she will purify herself for returning to the acropolis; he tells her to bathe in the Klepsydra, a nearby spring.[104] Of greater concern than women and birth – at least judging from the number of purity regulations and the references in literature – were women and sexual intercourse, a source of pollution for a variety of reasons. Shrines, temples and sanctuaries of the gods, and sexual intercourse, were generally incompatible.[105] Pan is a notable exception, a god of hoary lusts who did not shrink according to Aristophanes from allowing his sanctuary to be used for such a purpose. Even sacred prostitutes do not provide an exception, there being no evidence that they gave their favours in the temple of Aphrodite at Corinth, but they probably did so in the many subsidiary buildings on the Acrocorinth or in the city. But in addition, sexual purity was required in some cults. This took two forms: a period of abstinence from sexual activity of any kind, and/or intercourse only with one's marriage partner. Virginity, of course, was a requirement for some young female priests, as well as sexual abstinence. Herodotos notes that the Egyptians were the first to decide that it was wrong to have sexual intercourse with women in temples, or to go into temples after intercourse without having washed first; the Greeks took the custom from them.[106]

From Metropolis in Ionia from the cult of Mater Gallesia comes a fourth-century BC inscription which mentions a prohibition for which there are other examples of later date possibly reflecting earlier practice: a man could enter a shrine after intercourse with a woman after an interval of a certain number of days; this particular inscription states: 'pure from an ordinary woman after two days, from a hetaira after three days.' The apo gynaikos, 'from a woman' rule appears in several inscriptions. Three other texts simply read 'from sex' rather than 'from a woman', but the meaning was probably meant to be the same.[107] A very few inscriptions, and none of them classical, include women as polluted by sexual intercourse, and so it seems that sexual activity for a woman was not generally considered to be polluting.

The gerarai, the fourteen women assistants of the basilinna, the wife of the basileus archon at Athens, who together with her carried out sacred and secret rites in honour of Dionysos, swore that they were free from intercourse with a man. An oath involving sexual abstinence is sworn by Lysistrata and the women, and may be a parody of this and similar priestly oaths.[108] In Aristophanes' *Knights* vaginal secretions are said to pollute, but the context is comic, and a situation in which such secretions would come to one's intimate notice is simply being depicted as a disgusting type of sexual activity.[109]

A cult at Tegea of the fourth century BC forbade a male from entering if he had been with a woman; how long before he was considered pure is not noted.[110] On Kos, one had to be pure from a woman or man the previous night in order to enter one shrine.[111] The Cyrene cathartic law gives a more detailed indication of pollution from sexual intercourse. A man, if he had had sexual intercourse with a woman at night, could sacrifice on the following day; the intervening period clearly was thought of as overcoming the pollution of sexual activity which is clearly implied by the provision; if he had had sexual intercourse by day, he could sacrifice after washing.[112] This brings us to the two main methods of purification from sexual intercourse: washing in some cults purified the impurity of sexual intercourse with a woman. Washing could purify in several cults: the second-century AD cult of Men in Attica allowed entry on the same day after washing for men who had been in contact with garlic (?), pigs and women, an interesting combination.[113] Similarly at Eresos, washing on the same day as sexual intercourse allowed entry to the shrine, as in an Arkadian cult. Washing after intercourse purified on Lindos, as at Pergamon.[114]

Other cults were stricter. Three days' purity from a woman was required for a private cult on second-century BC Kos. Some cults made the nature of sexual intercourse an issue. Again, Lindos on Rhodes provides a provision for purity 'from lawful intercourse', presumably referring to marriage (a period was mentioned but does not survive on the stone). As at Philadelphia, it is not envisaged that the clientele of the cult would engage in extra-marital sex. The sanctuary of the Syrian gods on Delos provided for purity on the third day after intercourse with a woman.[115] Some cults were non-specific, not mentioning specific periods, simply noting that one had to be pure from sexual intercourse.[116] A cult from Egypt is interesting and underlines what is clear from the Greek inscriptions: in general, men were thought to be polluted by women, but not women by men. But in this cult men were polluted by women, and women by men, and two days was required after intercourse before either sex could enter the temple.[117]

Those wishing to sleep at the Asklepieion at Pergamon had to abstain from sexual intercourse, as well as goat's meat and cheese.[118] In healing cults such as this, men and women slept overnight in the healing building, the abaton. Here, concerns about sexual proprieties might be raised. At Oropos, these concerns were met with the provision that those seeking cures were segregated by gender: women slept on the western side of the altar and the men on the eastern side.[119]

The classical texts are not discriminatory in the nature of the sexual relationship which a man has entered into; it is not pollution through morality in the Judaeo-Christian sense but rather sex with a woman (wife or prostitute) or man. The Cyrene provision indicates heterosexual sex, but does not distinguish between matrimonial or extra-marital (if the man were married). Later texts, however, do make such a distinction.

In the Pergamene cult of Athena Nikephoros of the second half of the second century BC a man or woman could enter the sanctuary if they had had sex with their spouse on that day, but, if with someone other than their spouse, then they could enter on the second day; washing was required.[120] To put such restrictions into context, the rule also had the provisions that worshippers were not on the day before or the day of going to the sanctuary to have contact with a corpse or with a woman in childbirth; contact with a funeral procession and burial was not permitted on the same day. However, worshippers could avoid the need for these delays if they sprinkled themselves and entered the shrine at the gate where the hagisteria were, presumably sacred water containers, like the perirrhanteria.

The private cult in Philadelphia, Lydia, already mentioned, had a similar injunction, with a woman swearing that she had not had intercourse with anyone other than her husband, and the husband that he had slept only with his wife, before they could enter the shrine.[121] This is particularly severe and at odds with other purity laws which take it for granted that men will have extra-marital sex. In a similar way, it is only in fairly late texts that injunctions are found concerning the defloration of virgins. A second-century AD inscription, and another from the third century AD, both from Lindos, indicate that sexual intercourse was considered more polluting when performed with a virgin, with the third-century text – from the shrine of the virgin goddess Athena –

requiring a wait of forty-one days. The time itself has no sexual significance, being the same period required in the case of pollution incurred when a relative died, as the next line in the inscription indicates. The provision concerning virgins is unknown elsewhere. In the classical period a newly married man would not have found himself barred from the temples of the gods because of the virginity of his bride.[122] Newly married virgins, as the Cyrene cathartic law makes clear, were not considered polluted, but had in fact to make their way to the temple of Artemis.[123]

At least a few years earlier than the Pergamene injunction, Maionia (also in Asia Minor) had a cult rule that a prostitute (hetaira) had to abstain from intercourse for two days before entering the shrine, and had to 'purify herself all over', probably referring to an all-over dousing with water. The same inscription refers to a man being able if he had had intercourse with a woman to enter the shrine after washing on the same day.[124] This tallies with the reference to legitimate sex at Lindos.[125] One third-century AD inscription, from Lindos involving the cult of Athena, had the injunction that a man who had had sexual intercourse with a prostitute (here koine) was to wait for thirty days before entering the shrine, but was pure after sex with another woman simply by washing. The same cult stated categorically that there was no purification possible for 'unlawful' (paranomon) sexual activities.[126] Sexual intercourse with hetairai in such cases is seen as more polluting than with other women, but this probably indicates that generally this sort of distinction was not made and these exceptions prove the rule: it was simply sexual activity in a generic sense which was considered to be polluting and was prohibited in temples, and occasionally for a restricted period before worship.

Lesbianism is not an issue, and male homosexuality attracts little attention. The private cult at Lydia has the husband swearing that he has only had intercourse with his own wife, and not another man's wife, a free or slave woman, and may not have seduced a boy or parthenos. But this is very unusual. At Kos, the priest of Zeus Polieus had to make a formal announcement before sacrificing that he had not had sexual contact with a man or a woman on the previous night.[127]

The fourth-century Cyrene purification law shows that sexual intercourse could be thought to be polluting in the classical period and required purification, even simply for a short period of time. But only in later texts do items such as menstruation and defloration become an issue, and even here the examples seem to indicate that these were not widespread concerns. In the classical period Greeks generally had few problems concerning sexual activity in itself and worship. Difficulties with extra-marital sex arose when a wife engaged in such activity. That prostitutes were not barred from temples becomes understandable in the light of all of the above.

Sexual activity in a temple was of course taboo, as Herodotos notes. The Spartan king Agesilaos (lived: c. 445–359 BC) always stayed in temples when on campaign, in order to give no grounds for gossip about scandalous behaviour, as sexual intercourse was not possible in a temple, as his pious biographer Xenophon informs us. The Persian Artayktes took over the hero shrine of Protesileos at Elaious in the Chersonese during the Persian Wars (480–479 BC); whenever he came to Elaious he had intercourse with women in the shrine; for this and despoiling the shrine of its considerable treasures he was eventually crucified when the Athenians in the aftermath of the defeat of the Persians captured the area.[128] The fact that Artemis Hymnia (a virgin goddess) was attended by a woman priest 'who'd had enough of sex with men' was explained by the story of a virgin girl priest being raped in her sanctuary, after which virgins were no longer appointed as priests. A similar story was used at Delphi to explain why the Pythia, although an older woman, dressed as a virgin: a virgin girl priest had been raped, and so the practice was changed, though the dress remained the same.[129]

The myth of Komaitho and Melanippos relates how the woman priest of Artemis Triklaria in Achaea was a virgin until the time for marriage came around, when she ceased to serve the goddess. Komaitho, a virgin, was appointed, but consummated her love for Melanippos in the sanctuary, and the wrath of the goddess fell on the land: people died, the earth was infertile, and fatal diseases flourished until the Delphic oracle commanded that the two be sacrificed, to be followed by an annual sacrifice of a virgin boy and girl.[130] A myth explained how the practice came to an end. At Olympia, an inscription seems to refer to a sacrifice and purification being necessary in the case of intercourse in a shrine.[131]

Auge, a young girl and still a virgin, was the priest of Athena at Tegea; she was either raped by Herakles at the fountain near Athena's temple during Athena's festival, or in the temple itself, and in other versions willingly had intercourse with Herakles whenever he came to Tegea. Becoming pregnant, she hid in Athena's temple, until a famine arose in Tegea and Athena in an oracle disclosed that something was profaning her temple. According to different versions, she had kept the child in the temple where she had given birth to it, or her father, discovering Auge pregnant in the temple, dragged her away from it but she fell on her knees outside a temple of Eileithyia and gave birth. Eileithyia at Tegea had the epithet 'Auge on her knees' as a result.[132] A scene in the second-century BC Telephos frieze which ran around the interior court walls of the Great Altar at Pergamon (Telephos was the city's mythical founder) in Asia Minor shows her and other women worshipping in a temple. The statue of the goddess is now just visible on the left-hand side of the relief, where the shield of the goddess can be seen, and the statue base. This is usually taken to be Auge establishing a cult of Athena in Mysia, she and her son Telephos having been reunited there. However, the establishment of an Athena cult is not part of the extant myth cycle, and it is better to interpret this scene as belonging to the beginning of the frieze, illustrating the commencement of the Auge–Telephos myth cycle, when Herakles came to Tegea and saw Auge worshipping in the temple (Figure 8.2).[133]

Figure 8.2 Auge and other maidens worshipping before a statue of Athena; Telephos frieze from the Great Altar, Pergamon (Turkey); height: 180 centimetres; marble; work on the frieze commenced *c.* 165 BC (courtesy, ©Antikensammlung, Staatliche Museen zu Berlin, Preussischer Kulturbesitz, inv. Pergamonmuseum 7756).

Statue clingers

Sanctuaries, and particularly the altars and statues therein, were places of refuge, not just for women but also for men. But in mythological terms, it is mainly women and especially virgins who seek this refuge and are represented in iconography.[134] A temple could serve as a place of assignation: Polyxena arranged for Achilles to meet her in the temple of Thymbraian Apollo to negotiate a marriage between them – if only the story had had a happier ending. Kassandra sheltered at the statue of Athena in her temple when the Greeks sacked Troy, but Ajax dragged her from this, and she was raped by him according to some accounts.[135]

In the rape scene from the frieze of Apollo's temple at Bassai in Arkadia (c. 400 BC) in the Peloponnese, a woman, perhaps Hippodameia, clings to a statue of Artemis while a centaur who has ripped most of her clothes off is assaulted by a rescuing Lapith; another woman with outstretched hands stands in front of the statue (Figure 8.3).[136] Similarly, one of the south metopes of the Parthenon showed two women, one partly stripped (as in the Bassai relief), seeking sanctuary at a statue of a goddess, while a battle between centaurs and mortals (probably Lapiths) raged around them, with some women, as in the Bassai relief, being carried off.[137] Both friezes apparently represent the story of the centaurs, drunk, ruining Peirithöos' wedding to Hippodameia; while the human guests, the Lapiths, fight, women have no other recourse but to be abducted or cling to the statue of a goddess.

On a volute krater by the Sisyphus Painter, while the two daughters of Leukippos (the Leukippidai) are carried off, another woman, perhaps one of their servants, clasps a statue, while another sits next to it. One of the daughters, Phoebe, was a virgin priest of Athena, while the other daughter, Hilaeira, was a virgin priest of Artemis.[138] The fifty daughters of Danaos at Argos seeking refuge against marrying their fifty cousins took up suppliant boughs at an altar.[139] Helen took refuge at the Palladion of Athena to escape Menelaos' wrath at the fall of Troy.[140] When Thebes was attacked, the women threw themselves before the statues of the gods.[141]

The mythical or semi-mythical Spartan lawgiver Lykourgos apparently introduced the custom of whipping boys at the altar of Artemis Orthia instead of the traditional human sacrifice. The woman priest of Orthia carried the statue of the goddess, and if the whippers laid into any boys lightly because of their good looks or rank, the statue, not itself weighty, would become heavy in the woman priest's arms, and she would castigate the whippers. In Arkadia, at a festival of Dionysos, the Skiereia, women were flogged because of an oracle from Delphi.[142] Statues were not simply representations of the gods but in a sense were the gods; often they would be statues which men should not see or certainly not touch; reaching for them or clinging for them was a desperate attempt to gain a deity's protection. Like kneeling to a god, clinging to a statue was appropriate behaviour for women, but also indicates their passivity and helplessness, particularly in the face of sexual violence.

Women, ornamentation and clothing

> Periander issued a proclamation that every woman in Corinth should come to the temple of Hera. The women rushed to the temple in their best clothes as if to a festival, and Periander, who had secretly posted some of his guards, had them all stripped – every one of them – both freeborn women and

Figure 8.3 Hippodameia clings to a statue of Artemis, while a centaur, who has ripped most of her clothes off and is about to assault her sexually is attacked; another woman with outstretched hands stands in front of the statue; frieze from Apollo's temple at Bassai in Arkadia (*c.* 400 BC) in the Peloponnese; height of marble frieze: 64 centimetres (courtesy, ©The Trustees of the British Museum, inv. BM 524).

servants – and their clothes collected into a pit and burnt, while he prayed to Melissa.[143]

The ghost of Melissa had appeared to Periander, her husband, tyrant of Corinth, complaining that she was cold and naked as her clothes had not been burnt with her. Festivals and rites were clearly times when women felt that they had the opportunity to dress up. Vase-paintings from Athens in particular show women priests and kanephoroi in elaborate dresses, with patterns, layers and billowing garments in some cases. This would not simply have been feminine vanity, with clothing as in many societies being one avenue in which women could mitigate their powerlessness, but also would have seemed fitting for the gods. To wear one's best clothing to a special social event is, after all, a sociological phenomenon which still afflicts early twenty-first-century society. Dress divides the ordinary from the special occasion; in Greek religion, dress could be used to differentiate between the sacred and profane through the regulations setting down what could and could not be worn to certain rites. The regulators of Greek cults and temples – usually men – had much to say on this particular topic, but largely in Demeter cults in the Peloponnese. In cults where there were no such clothing regulations women presumably wore what they liked, but probably their best 'outfit', unless unwritten local conventions applied. It is possible to interpret such regulations as sumptuary in character, but also one should not underestimate the way in which this was just another way in which men sought to control women and to regulate their behaviour.

In the fifth-century BC cult of Demeter Thesmophoros, in Arkadia, if a woman wore ornamented clothing while attending the rites, it became sacred to the goddess, that is, was dedicated to the goddess in the temple. The woman was apparently punished for her transgression. The emphasis here on plain clothing finds parallels in other Demeter cults: she was a goddess apparently with an aversion to brightly coloured clothing and ornamentation, presumably because of her association with mourning. However, Kritylla in Aristophanes' *Thesmophoriazousai* says that Mnesilochos has come to the Thesmophoria to steal the gold of the women; clearly this Demeter rite did not forbid it.[144]

After the evidence of Periander and Demeter Thesmophoros, the information is post-classical, and one is then led to consider whether the later regulations reflect earlier practice or in fact indicate a determination by the cult authorities to change what women had been wearing to cults in the classical period: had women been 'dressing up' and now are to stop, or do these regulations reflect a continuing tradition being formalised, and along the same lines as the Arkadian cult of Demeter Thesmophoros?

The Pythagorean hellenistic woman writer Phintys wrote that women should wear white, undecorated, inexpensive garments, and not gold or emeralds. This reflects some sort of religious preoccupation and could well have a moral emphasis.[145] Women in the cult of Demeter at Patras were forbidden to wear gold worth more than 1 obol, embroidered or purple clothing, to use white lead to make up their face, or to play the aulos (double flute). A fragmentary inscription from Thasos has a prescription that purple should not be worn and could well be a cult prohibition.¹⁴⁶

In the third century BC, the mysteries of the Despoina ('Mistress') at Lykosoura in Arkadia forbade the wearing of gold in the temple – except when it was to be dedicated to the goddess; rings could not be worn. Clothing was regulated: purple, brightly coloured or black garments were prohibited, and shoes could not be worn. Women with braided hair were denied entry, and men had to be bare-headed. The clothing requirements are not specifically stated to apply to women, but clearly the reference to 'brightly coloured' is more likely to apply to them. Presumably white clothing would have been the most appropriate form of attire. Other cults also regulated footwear, and when they did so these were rites of liminality, stressing the difference between the sacred and profane worlds.¹⁴⁷

A purity regulation from third-century AD Lindos on Rhodes prescribed for all worshippers clean clothes, while no headdress was to be worn. Leather was proscribed: one had to enter barefoot or in white shoes which were not made of leather (some type of cloth shoe is being envisaged, probably for women), and nothing could be worn that was made of leather, not even a tied belt. The emphasis here is on non-animal products; women are not singled out; these are general regulations for all worshippers. But at Kos, the women priests of Demeter seem to be forbidden to wear clothing made from dead animals.¹⁴⁸

The third-century AD regulations from the Asklepieion in Pergamon are quite similar: rings, belts, gold, braided hair, shoes are all proscribed; the worshipper had to wear white clothing. Around 300 BC, the cult of Alektrone on Ialysos, Rhodes, forbade shoes and anything made of pigskin; if these were worn or any of the other forbidden things happened, the shrine and the temenos were to be purified. The funerary legislation from Gambreion stipulated that mourning women wore clean, grey clothes. An inscription from sixth-century BC Sparta apparently refers to a restriction on the types of clothing that could be dedicated; dedications had to be approved by an official known as the polianomos, an appropriate measure in a society opposed to public displays of luxury. At Brauron, where large amounts of clothing were dedicated by women, no such restriction seems to have applied.¹⁴⁹

But the most detailed and important of the regulations concerning dress come from Andania, where in 92 BC a private individual revived the mysteries and a long and detailed set of regulations was inscribed pertaining to numerous aspects of the cult's organisation. The sheer detail of the regulations concerning clothing are atypical, and, once again, are found in a Peloponnesian context. The cult inscription is quite specific, on categories both of clothing and of person.

Gold ornaments, rouge, white make-up, hairbands and braided hair were forbidden for women, both priests and initiates. The women did not have to go barefoot, as the men had to, but their shoes had to be made of felt or leather tanned from the hide of sacrificed animals. The woman priests during the mysteries wore either a kalasiris (a long garment with a fringe at the bottom) or a hypodyma (tunic), as well as a cloak worth not more than 2 minas (200 drachmas), which represents a good deal of money. In these regulations, daughters of both women priests and initiates are mentioned as a separate category. The daughters of women priests wore a kalasiris (cloak) or a robe worth not more than 100 drachmas. In the procession of the mysteries the women priests wore a hypodyma and a woollen cloak, with stripes not more than half a finger wide, and their daughters a kalasiris and a garment that was not see-through. The women priests wore a white felt cap, and the priests wore a garland; the board of ten (men) in charge of the mysteries wore a purple headband during the mysteries. For sitting on during the ceremonies, the women priests had wicker seats with either pillows or a white round cushion, with neither decoration nor a purple design, and so matching the requirements for their clothes. The priests were to specify what the women were to wear 'for the gods'. Apart from the requirement of a garland, the clothing of the priests is not a concern of the regulations. Similarly, the only requirements for male initiates is that they went barefoot (liminality, once again) and wore white clothing.

The first initiates (apparently both men and women) wore a stlengis, a tiara, which they had to take off when instructed to do so by the priests, replacing it with a wreath of laurel. The women being initiated wore a garment which was not transparent, with stripes not more than half a finger wide. They could wear a linen chiton and a cloak worth not more than 100 drachmas, while their daughters were to wear a kalasiris, or a sindonites, and a cloak, not worth more than 1 mina; women slaves dressed as the daughters did, except that the value of the clothes was to be no more than 50 drachmas. The sindonites was a garment of fine cloth, usually linen considered to be pure since it was not of animal origin. The gynaikonomos – supervisor of the women – is not to allow anyone to breach the clothing regulations; he is authorised to punish any woman who transgresses the regulations; the punishment is to be devoted to the gods: possibly a fine, or as elsewhere, the confiscation of the clothes is being alluded to here.[150]

Departing warriors, women and libations

The Kleophon Painter painted several scenes on stamnoi (singular: stamnos) vases of a warrior departing for war. One of his pieces, a red-figure stamnos of *c.* 430 BC, shows a woman holding an oinochoe (jug), while a warrior holds a phiale (libation bowl) at face level; presumably she has just poured the wine into the phiale for him. The husband directs his gaze at his young wife; he is about to pour out the libation from the phiale onto the ground. The identity of the figures seems clear: the departing warrior is carrying his shield, spear and wearing his helmet. He looks forward and at the young woman, who lowers her eyes and modestly holds her peplos at the shoulder; she is surely his wife, with her hair bound with a fillet, and an earring on the side of the face which is visible. Behind her stands an old man, with his hair and beard painted in white; he has a long cane for walking with: presumably he is the warrior's father. The woman behind the warrior will almost certainly be his mother, and so here the family has gathered to bid him farewell and to carry out a libation to the gods for his success and safety (Figure 8.4).[151] This particular vase was found in a tomb in Vulci (Italy); it is the most finely executed example of the Kleophon Painter's departure scenes, and is one that is frequently illustrated. Similarly, a scene on a red-figure stamnos by the Achilles Painter of *c.* 450 BC shows a

Figure 8.4 A warrior leaving home performing a libation ceremony to the gods; red-figure Athenian stamnos; 430 BC; Kleophon Painter; height: 43 centimetres (courtesy, ©Staatliche Antikensammlungen und Glyptothek, Munich: inv. 2415).

woman holding an oinochoe and phiale, while a warrior looks in the other direction, shaking hands with another man.[152] On the other side of this stamnos a woman holds the oinochoe and is in the act of pouring wine into a phiale which is held out by another warrior.[153] Such scenes are also played out in the mythological repertoire as well. Aithra is shown on a red-figure kalyx krater holding out two libation bowls – phialai – to her son Theseus.[154]

An amphora by the Kleophrades Painter at Athens in the last quarter of the sixth century BC depicts a slave boy presenting the entrails of a sacrificed animal to a warrior, who holds up the liver for examination. A woman behind the warrior has a phiale in her hand; a libation has presumably taken place before the sacrifice.[155] The warrior is about to go off to war; a sacrifice has been made and he is examining the omens.

Other examples of the libation theme are numerous; there are literally several hundred of them; this is the most frequently depicted of religious roles for women on vases, far outweighing the portrayal of maenads, either mythical ones or those before the mask of Dionysos at the Anthesteria. Men pour libations onto altars or the ground, but it is women who pour the wine from jugs into the libation bowls for them. In public, adolescent girls performed this task, but after marriage it is only in domestic contexts that they do so. And the duty is domestic in nature, in a sense, performed in the same way as she would fetch the water. These libations were accompanied by sacrifices to seek the omens, and attest yet again the presence of women at sacrifices.

Certain rites forbade the presence of women; many cults did not. Women clearly attended sacrifices, in their capacities as citizen wives, foreigners, slaves and prostitutes. In addition, they sometimes ate of the sacrificial meat at these sacrifices. Many of these sacrifices would have been conducted under the auspices of the state by citizen men, and at these women might have had little or no chance to partake in the sacrificial meat, though at some they clearly did. Similarly, men were excluded from various women-only rites and sacrifices, and then could not, of course, partake of the sacrificial meat; men, for example, did not eat piglets at the Thesmophoria for the simple reason that they were not present to do so. Women were present at public sacrifices as members of their community; sometimes they were there as wives and daughters of citizens, but at the same time, at the Thesmophoria and other Demeter festivals, and in Dionysiac rituals, they were primarily present as women, and it is their gender which accounts for their presence. Despite some scholarly views, women were not condemned to vegetarianism in an age without vitamin supplements or a knowledge of soya substitutes, and many women priests and wealthy women who presided over public and private sacrifices respectively must have had a rich meat diet. The sacrifice on behalf of the city could in fact require and demand the presence of young women in particular, in their roles as basket-bearers and the like. In addition, certain cults presupposed the participation of women priests who received the sacrificial victim on behalf of a goddess, and as such were entitled to a share of the entrails and the meat. Women priests generally came from an upper socio-economic class, but clearly ordinary women were present at sacrifices, and family groups were an important body of sacrificers. In private life, Sostratos' mother indicates that they could take the initiative for sacrifice, and the Pitsa pinax (Figure 7.3) confirms this. Their gender did not disqualify women from taking the initiative in organising sacrifices, and if Sostratos' mother has a dream requiring a sacrifice on the other side of the Athenian countryside, then she will go there with sacrificial beasts and the necessary equipment. Sacrifice was the most essential expression of piety in Greek religion, and one which many women not only participated in but could also initiate. In some cults they clearly even carried out sacrifices themselves.

Women conducted their own rites, shielded from the eyes of men, who also occasionally barred women from their rites. Women's own physiology excluded them from certain rites or for periods of time, through concepts of pollution regulated by men, but which may nevertheless have been important to women, for example, as a period of rest after birth. But it is only in the later period, and in certain exotic cults, that menstruation became an issue. Women themselves may have felt 'polluted' by their ordeals and experiences in childbirth. Certain aspects of a woman's physiological condition, such as giving birth and lactating, affected their access to temples. But on the whole, a woman's biology did not constitute a serious impediment to her religious practices. The main categories of pollution in the classical period were birth and death, and a man present at the birth would incur the same pollution as the woman who actually gave birth. Often what women could wear to sanctuaries could be quite expensive, but what was more important was that women not appear to have been dressed in an ostentatious fashion, and their menfolk decided what this constituted. What women wore and did at shrines could be closely regulated, but their presence was crucial and required: men could dictate that they not wear a dress with wide stripes to a religious rite, but no man would propose as a further lever of social control that women be prohibited from attending such rites altogether and made to stay at home.

9

WOMEN AND THE CORPSE
Mourning rituals

> Anyone who wishes, both citizens and foreigners, may attend the funeral, and the women who are related to those who have died are present and lament at the tomb.[1]

Thucydides is describing the public funeral in 431 BC for the war dead, in place of each individual having the normal private ceremony. The women relatives lament as was customary, but, by the time of this particular state funeral, the activities of mourning women had been long prescribed by Solonian legislation. The mourning will have been loud and keen, but some funerary behaviour, such as public laceration of the cheeks and breast, would not have taken place any longer at Athens and in some other cities. However, throughout most of Greece in the archaic and classical periods, women's mourning was energetic and spontaneous, and a normal accompaniment to funerary practices.

Mourning women in Homer

At Athens, as in Greece generally in the archaic and the classical periods, it was women who attended to the corpse.[2] But the world of mourning women in Greek literature starts with 'Homer', who articulated the archaic world of the eighth century BC within the framework of the myth of the Trojan War. At the death of the warrior Hektor, his father Priam and mother Hekabe grieve for him, along with the entire city of Troy. His mother tears her hair and throws off her gleaming veil, while Priam groans, and grovels in the dust (a very non-Greek reaction for a man). Hekabe leads the lamentation (goos) of the women; when Hektor's wife Andromache hears the news, she throws off all her ornamental head gear and wails, and the women join in her laments. Hekabe and Andromache throw themselves onto the wagon bearing his corpse, clasp his head, lament, and tear at their hair. With Hektor on his funeral bed, Priam brings in singers, '(male) leaders of the dirges', who commence the lamentations in which the women led by Andromache join. When she had finished her own lament, Hekabe led the women, and then Helen did so. While she lamented, Andromache held Hektor's

268

head in her hands, and women seen cradling the head of the corpse on vases can be imagined as the women leaders in the goos, the lamentation.[3] Similarly, when Patroklos' corpse was brought to Achilles' tent,[4]

> Briseis, resembling golden Aphrodite,
> when she saw Patroklos pierced by the sharp bronze,
> flung herself upon him and wailed loudly,
> and with her hands she lacerated
> her breasts and delicate neck and beautiful face.

The chorus of women with Elektra who are to pour libations at Agamemnon's grave also gouge their faces with their nails.[5] This must have been a common death ritual. When women are shown with their hands on their heads, this is a preliminary to rending their hair, which is depicted on lekythoi (tall narrow vases particularly associated with the grave). Beating the head with the hands by women was also a sign of great sorrow and took place at a death.[6] When Patroklos died at the hands of Hektor, Achilles poured dust on his head, hair and tunic, and tore his hair, while the women of Achilles and Patroklos, gained as war-booty, shrieked and beat their breasts.[7]

Compelled and hired mourners

As noted, Priam placed singers, leaders in the dirges (threnoi), beside Hektor on his funeral bed, and the women took up their laments from them. This must mean professional singers who sang dirges at the corpse, and presumably at the grave as well. Solon, in fact, as part of his funerary legislation, prohibited the singing of prepared dirges, which must be in opposition to spontaneous lament, and refer to the participation of professional singers. However, such a prohibition seems to have lapsed, or needs to be interpreted in another way, as Plato refers to corpses being accompanied by Carian music by Carian women hired to perform this. Aeschylus seems to refer to hired mourners when he writes 'grief is your *unhired* fellow traveller'. Lucian refers to professional male dirge singers being employed throughout Greece for funerals. Sometimes it is suggested that the women other than those closest to the bier in artistic depictions are hired mourners.[8]

Akin to this but without the remuneration of hire was the compelled mourning required of the helots of Sparta which will be discussed below. Whenever one of the clique of oligarchs who had ruled Erythrai died the citizens were compelled, along with their wives and children, to sing dirges for the dead, forcing the women to beat their breasts, to cry out sharply and with loud voices; a whip-bearer stood over them forcing them to do these things. The men and women of Megara were compelled to go to Corinth when any of the Bacchiadai died there, and mourn for them. Slaves had no choice but to join in laments for their masters; slaves who liked their masters might have done so willingly, and in the *Iliad* Briseis needs no encouragement to mourn Patroklos, whereas the other captured women added their laments to those of Briseis, but each one was in reality mourning her own troubles. In Aeschylus' play of this name, the choephoroi, 'bearers of choes' from which to pour libations, go with Elektra to Agamemnon's tomb, and lacerate their cheeks, but they (like Elektra) have been ordered to the task by Klytaimnestra, and have themselves been captured in war.[9]

Spartan mourning

Spartan mothers were given little opportunity to mourn their sons if these died in battle, for the Spartan battle-dead were buried where they fell,[10] and there could be no women mourning at the funeral bier or grave; the only exception was the two kings: if they died in battle they were brought back to Sparta. The Spartan exemplum of the mother who showed her son a shield and said, 'Son, either with this or on this' (i.e. come back carrying your shield or be carried back dead upon it), is therefore a misunderstanding by a later age. But it does point to the Spartan ethos reflected in another saying, of the mother who on being told that her son had been killed in position in battle said, 'Bury him and let his brother fill his place.'[11] Such a woman would not show public grief.

Among the various social measures of the semi-mythical Spartan reformer Lykourgos was the provision that the name of the deceased was not to be inscribed on the tomb, except in two circumstances: it could be engraved on the tombstone of a warrior who had fallen in war, or on that of a woman who had died in childbirth. Both had fulfilled their duty to the Spartan state.[12] Lykourgos did away with mourning and lamentation;[13] this presumably applied to Spartans who might otherwise have mourned for fellow citizens, for the helots and even the citizens had to mourn when a king died.

Spartan helots, including their wives, mourned for their masters when these died.[14] More impressive, however, was their role in the kings' funerals. When either of the two kings died, horseriders carried the news throughout Lakonia, while women went throughout the city of Sparta beating cauldrons; whether these were citizen women or not is unclear. This was the cue for two people from each household, a man and a woman, to 'become polluted' (with a heavy fine if they failed to do so); the Spartans were joined in their mourning by the forced presence of perioikoi (those living in the cities around Sparta) from all over Lakonia, and by helots. Many thousands assembled, both the men and women helots zealously striking their foreheads and wailing (and so de-masculinising the male helots and emphasising their inferior status); the mourning lasted for ten days. Pausanias states that when a king or a magistrate died, helots had to come from Messenia, wearing black clothes. It was important that women announced the death in the city and their cauldron-beating was not merely annunciatory or preliminary, but began the mourning process, of which the noise of wailing was an important element.[15]

The 'harsh and barbaric' practices of mourning Athenian women

In 341 BC a speaker in a lawsuit referred to funerary legislation passed by Solon, Athenian archon in 594 BC.[16] This law as summarised by the speaker provided that the circle of women who could participate in mourning was restricted to those within the range of cousins, who could also return to the house after the ekphora (the carrying out of the dead body from the house). Plutarch's *Solon* provides other details (hopefully reliable) about Solon's funerary legislation. Women when they went outdoors for any purpose, including funerals, could wear no more than three cloaks, which was to prevent ostentation of dress. No mourners were to lacerate their flesh, and set dirges were not to be used at the funeral. Nor was anyone to bewail anyone else other than the deceased at a funeral, a provision obviously aimed particularly at women, and which is of course even now a common enough practice, when one's individual sorrows find expression in mourning for another's death. This would help reduce the amount of mourning at the funeral. Moreover, no other graves except family ones were to be visited, except on the actual day of internment. The scope of funerals and the lamentation and commemoration of those already dead was limited.[17]

The basket which women carried when they went outside was to be no longer than 1 cubit (for the Greeks, the distance from the tip of the elbow to that of the middle finger), and this presumably applied to any basket that they took to graves. As lekythoi of the classical period in general depict offering baskets of ribbons and lekythoi being taken to the tomb which greatly exceed this in length, this rule was clearly not observed, or did not apply when women visited graves (unless these large baskets are simply an artistic convention).

Plutarch viewed Solon's legislation as doing away with women's undisciplined behaviour and licentiousness. Lacerating the cheeks, so that blood was drawn, was obviously spectacular as a method of mourning. When Epimenides of Phaistos in Crete was invited to Athens after the massacre (probably in 632 BC) of Kylon's supporters, he supposedly reformed various aspects of the religious life of the Athenians, making them 'well-behaved' in their rites, and milder in their funerary behaviour, putting a stop to the 'harsh and barbaric practices' in which most of their women had previously taken part.[18] This was perhaps to stop excessive mourning keeping alive old hatreds,[19] but the focus is clearly on the behaviour of women at funerals as part of a reorganisation of religious activity. Epimenides and Solon represent a strong tradition that in the archaic period the conduct of women at festivals and funerals became circumscribed.

Plutarch, writing as a Boeotian in the second century AD, notes that the various mourning practices forbidden by Solon were also prohibited 'by our laws', i.e. those of Boeotia. In addition the gynaikonomoi have the power to enforce these provisions, and he specifically states that this is because these are unmanly displays of mourning. He seems to be thinking of men who mourn as women do, and as such are punished for their 'womanish' behaviour by the supervisors of women, which agent of punishment must have been more humiliating than any other punishment.[20]

Cicero in referring to Roman funerary legislation writes that it was modelled on the Solonian: whether any credence can be attached to such a statement is doubtful, but at any rate he refers to women mourners being prohibited from lacerating their cheeks. Cicero also notes a Roman prohibition of Solonian origin that women were not to hold a lessum (presumably an ululation of some sort) at a funeral. Cicero is also the source of the information that Demetrios of Phaleron, ruling Athens from 317 to 307 BC, introduced legislation that the ekphora had to take place before dawn. Pre-dawn funeral rites would have had the effect of reducing the visibility of women's role in funerals, but in fact may have primarily been intended to ease traffic congestion on Athens' streets.[21]

Mourning in Plato's ideal state

In the ideal city-state envisaged in the *Laws*, Plato deals with the Euthynai, the 'Examiners' who occupied the highest place in the state, and who were to have distinctive funeral privileges; Plato might be thinking of the honours accorded to Spartan kings. A chorus of fifteen girls (korai) and fifteen boys (arrhenoi) was to sing in turns around the bier. In the funeral procession itself, the boys were to go in front of the bier and the girls behind with all the women who had passed the age of child-bearing, followed by the priests and women priests. The explanation for this is clear: young girls are not yet married, and women past child-bearing are no longer sexually desirable. The married women do not take part, as they have husbands and are not to make a public display, nor be seen by would-be seducers, as could happen at Athens.[22]

Women and funerary legislation at Iulis and Gambreion

On the Aegean island of Keos, the funerary legislation of the city of Iulis in the fifth century BC was largely sumptuary in nature: a 'showy' funeral was to be avoided. After a funeral, no women were to go to the house of the deceased other than those who were already polluted by the death, and the category of polluted women included only the mother, wife, sisters and daughters, and five more women, from the children of the daughters and cousins, but no one else. A gathering of family women only could take place, and the intent was to prevent a large gathering of women at the deceased's house. This is similar to the Solonian legislation and indicates that it was not only at Athens that large numbers of women became involved in funeral rites. Moreover, the pollution – miasma – involved in contact with a corpse is confined to only a few, and this must have been deliberate. At the place of burial itself, there seems to have been no restriction on the number of women present, but they were to leave the tomb before the men did: obviously an excessive length of mourning by women was not allowed. In addition, the deceased was to be taken to the burial place in silence, so there was no women's mourning *en route*.[23] But here, as elsewhere, while men could attempt to regulate the women's activities at a funeral, women had an important role to play at it, and their presence itself could not be challenged.

The funerary legislation from Gambreion (near the city of Pergamon in Asia Minor) dates from the third century BC but is worth examining because of the specific light it might shed on other states' funerary practices.[24]

> It is to be the law amongst the people of Gambreion that women in mourning are to wear grey clothing which is not dirty, and men and children in mourning are to wear grey clothes, but if they don't wish to, then white ones. Ceremonies for the dead are to be completed at the latest within three months, and in the fourth month the men are to complete their mourning, and the women in the fifth month. The women are then to stop their funerary rituals, and to participate in processions as laid down in the law. The gynaikonomos . . . at the purifications before the celebration of the Thesmophoria is to pray for the well-being of the women who have abided by the law and obeyed it . . . and to those who have not obeyed it or abided by it, the opposite, and those women are to be considered unholy, because they have been impious, and are not to sacrifice to any of the gods for ten years.

Grey clothing would not show up deliberate soiling as a sign of grief, and the law specifically provided that it was to be unsoiled. That men were to wear grey but white if they wished underscores this: men were seen as less likely or unlikely to rend and soil their clothes. The city required that women take part in processions because the presence of women was required when the city honoured the gods, who might otherwise be offended: the failure of the women to attend because of mourning becomes after the set period (in the fifth month) impious – a case of asebeia. As women would normally attend sacrifices, the exclusion from these for ten years was an extremely stiff penalty. The law was to be inscribed and displayed in two places, at the Thesmophorion and the shrine of Artemis Lochia (Artemis of Childbirth), places frequented by the women (and perhaps only by them).[25] All such legislation indicates that its authors considered that there was a problem which needed rectifying.

The Labyadai phratry at Delphi

The laws of Iulis and Gambreion were authored by the state, but the funerary legislation of about 400 BC of the Labyadai phratry at Delphi, however, concerns the efforts of a phratry – religious brotherhood – to regulate the behaviour of its members.[26] While the phratry was not important as a political institution in post-Kleisthenic Athens except in affirming the citizenship of its members, the phratries at Delphi had a religious significance which extended to prescribing various aspects of the behaviour of members of the phratry.

The Labyadai prescribed a limit of 35 drachmas for the value of items placed on the tomb. On an Attic white lekythos discussed below, women are shown taking ribbons out of a household chest for placing on a tomb. Here, too, at Delphi perhaps the provision relates to items to be placed on the tomb which would be seen by those who attended the funeral or who came to the cemetery afterwards. The funeral shroud according to the Labyadai rule was to be thick and grey. There was a 50-drachma fine at Delphi if these provisions were not observed. The provisions concerning lamenting at the tomb presumably had as their primary focus women mourners: the corpse was to be taken to the grave site in silence, and was not to be put down at a crossroads along the way (i.e. in order to strike up mourning for the deceased there, where traffic in either direction could see – and hear – the funeral). In addition, there was to be no wailing outside the house of the deceased until the body was actually at the grave (which would mean that the lamentations at the bier within the house were the last lamentations heard until the grave-site was reached). While there was no prohibition on the singing of dirges and wailing once the corpse had arrived at its final resting place, only the actual deceased could be mourned: there was to be no mourning for any of the past dead at their tombs. The rationale for this must have been so that funerals did not become commemorations of previously deceased members of the family, and moreover that women would not attend the funeral simply to bewail their own previous deceased, or current sufferings. Such legislation would limit women's mourning ritual at the tomb. Moreover, once the body had been laid to rest, only those directly related or those related by marriage were to remain. No mourning was to occur on the day after the funeral, or at the ten-day ceremonies or the annual rites for those who had died. The tone is restrictive and women's behaviour was clearly thought to need circumscribing, especially as their role was, even with these regulations, prominent and lengthy.

Mourning women in geometric art

Moving from the evidence of inscriptions to art, we can return to the Homeric period. Scenes of mourning women clustered around the bier, with men to one side, usually at the right and often with a mourning woman between them and the foot of the bier, are common, especially in Athens, where from geometric art to black-figure plaques and black-figure vases to lekythoi the mourning woman is central to the prothesis, the lying-in-wait of the deceased on her or his funeral bier.

The prothesis was a popular theme of geometric pottery, and while the ekphora (the carrying out of the dead, the funeral procession) is much less common, the appearance of numerous chariots in bands on the very vases showing prothesis scenes must point to the ekphora. The geometric amphora of c. 750 BC attributed to the so-called Dipylon master and standing some 155 centimetres tall depicts a prothesis between the handles of this massive vase.[27] Along the side of the bier two figures kneel and two are seated; at each end of the bier there is a line of worshippers. The sex of the kneeling figures is indeterminate, but they have both hands on their heads, beating them or preparing to tear their hair, and so are presumably women. This huge vase and its smaller cousins were used as grave monuments, as is shown clearly in a fifth-century BC black-figure loutrophoros, the body of which depicts the corpse being lowered into its grave at night, while on the neck women mourn either side of the grave mound which has a loutrophoros on its crest.[28]

But the geometric stick figures are later transformed into women. For example, on one side of the neck of a later Attic geometric amphora, two women stand at the end of a funeral bier, and one woman is shown kneeling alongside it, with two women acting similarly at the other end. Two of them have both their hands on their heads, and two have one hand on their head and touch the bier with the other; the other side of the neck shows six standing women in a line, presumably as part of a funeral procession, all with both hands on their heads. The body of the vase has a procession of two-horse chariots, possibly as part of a funeral procession.[29] A similar band of mourning women occurs on the neck of other vases, but with the deceased being mourned in a lower register.[30]

Athenian black-figure plaques and mourning women (c. 650–480 BC)

From Attica come terracotta black-figure plaques (pinakes) used to decorate tombs. Some of the plaques have moulded figures, while others are flat with painted figures. Many of these black-figure plaques are particularly fine, and are attributed to the same painter, Exekias, who produced fine, detailed work using a variety of colours (c. 540 BC). Funerary plaques in general show women at the prothesis and ekphora, mourning by tearing their hair and raising their hands, while the men shown on the plaques tend to be much more passive in their mourning. None of the plaques were actually discovered *in situ* on a tomb, but many clearly belong to a series of plaques relating to one specific funeral, and obviously come from a particular tomb. Such plaques are referred to as a plaque series. Plaques belonging to a series tend to be rectangular, being anything from 43 to 50 centimetres long with a height of 37 to 45 centimetres, and about 2.5 to 3.5 centimetres thick. Dating to the seventh and sixth centuries BC, plaque series were apparently no longer produced after c. 530 BC, but scenes of the prothesis are found after that date on single plaques, of similar size to the plaques of plaque series. No plaques appear to date to after 480 BC.[31]

On one terracotta plaque with moulded figures, earlier than Exekias and in a much cruder style, a dead woman lies on a bier, and at her head a woman tugs

SACRIFICIAL AND DOMESTIC RITUALS

at her own ponytail and has her other hand on the hair of her forehead, while beside her, alongside the chest of the corpse, another woman also has a hand on the hair of her forehead; there is a hand on the dead woman's chest; this seems to belong to either the second or the third woman, whose figure is damaged (Figure 9.1); another (fourth) woman, also damaged, is present. The women's hair remains neat on this and similar plaques, and is often shown as bound, so the intention might be to show the women preparing to rend their hair just as the mourning was beginning.[32] One early plaque shows a flight of three storks to the right, indicating by their direction a good omen for the deceased. At the foot of the bier a woman touches her forehead, as does the woman at the head, but she also has her mouth slightly opened and is probably singing a lamentation or simply wailing.[33]

Women on the plaques, as noted, strike their heads and their hair is generally tidy, though on one, thin stray locks of hair are shown.[34] But other scenes, such as on black-figure vases, show mourning women with dishevelled hair, with

Figure 9.1 Women rending their hair at the bier of a deceased woman; terracotta funerary plaque; *c.* 630–620 BC; provenance, Olympos in Attica? (courtesy, ©The Metropolitan Museum of Art, New York, Rogers Fund, 1914; inv: 14.146.3a).

locks falling over their faces,[35] and this is apparently a change in the iconography of women and death, to show women in this untidy state. Another plaque of wailing women also has a flight of birds heading right, and one of the mourners holds a baby, indicating how difficult it was for a woman to combine her role as mother and participant in ritual, unless the child represents an orphan of the deceased.[36] Girls join women at the bier, in some cases clearly mourning.[37]

But the funerary plaques of the sixth-century painter Exekias are the best known. Several fragments survive, discovered in the Kerameikos near the Dipylon Gate of Athens, and when reconstructed and arranged can be shown to belong to a single plaque series, from one tomb; each plaque is episodic, depicting some event of the funeral, with every plaque having an upper border of maeander style. The death of a young woman is depicted on one plaque; another plaque in the series shows a group of five seated and three standing women grouped around a central seated woman, who in this prominent position and with her head covered with her himation is obviously the chief mourner, around whom the women cluster. There is no bier in sight; the women are presumably gathered in their quarters, silently grieving, at the very beginning, or after the end of the funeral: theirs is perhaps the quiet resignation after the body has been buried and the physical acts of mourning (hair-rending and breast-beating) and the wailing, which must have been physically and emotionally exhausting, are over. A child (usually identified, but not securely, as a girl) is being taken from one woman by another. As it is a dead woman being mourned in this series (she is shown on another plaque), the child is perhaps hers; the seated figure in the middle is clearly the chief mourner, and perhaps the mother of the deceased woman (Figure 9.2).[38]

The contrast between men's and women's behaviour at the bier is shown by another plaque, not by Exekias. Of the four women mourners at the bier of a dead man, one has a hand on the man's neck (referred to sometimes as cradling the head) and with the other touches her forehead; the other women touch their hair and raise their hands. The two men at the foot of the bier keep one hand in their cloaks, and raise the other, with their faces turned upwards.[39] But another fragmentary plaque shows a man with his hand on his head, indicating that, although men did not give way to more demonstrative grief, they were not always passive.[40] Women's role in funerary rites did not end of course at the bier, and they are seen with the wagon and horses which are apparently stationary and about to take the deceased to the grave. Another plaque by Exekias, from the same grave as Figure 9.2, shows the women rending their hair beside the horses and chariot leading the ekphora (Figure 9.3);[41] they will continue this to the grave.

One plaque from Cape Kolias in Attica names various mourners according to their relationship with the deceased: a man; the mother, who holds her dead son's head; the woman at the head of the bier is named as grandmother; three women are designated aunts (one specifically referred to as paternal), and two as sisters. The father, at the foot of the bier, faces men who approach him, raising

Figure 9.2 Mourning women seated, probably within a house, with a small child; black-figure funerary plaque (pinax) originally part of a frieze of plaques on a tomb, Athens; by the painter Exekias; height: 37.4 centimetres, length: 44 centimetres; depth: 2.7–3.2 centimetres; date: 540 BC (courtesy, ©Antikensammlung, Staatliche Museen zu Berlin, Preussischer Kulturbesitz, inv. 1813; photo: Ingrid Geske).

Figure 9.3 Mourning women in a funeral procession; black-figure funerary plaque (pinax) originally part of a frieze (the same as 9.2) of plaques on a tomb, Athens; date: 540 BC; by the painter Exekias; height: 38.1 centimetres; length: 44.2 centimetres; thickness: 2.7–3.2 centimetres (courtesy, ©Antikensammlung, Staatliche Museen zu Berlin, Preussischer Kulturbesitz, inv. 1819; photo: Ingrid Geske).

their hands; among them is a brother of the deceased. The word oimoi, the cry 'alas', which appears twice in this scene vocalises the mourners.[42] But it is not to be thought that women alone uttered this cry, and a black-figure phormiskos ('bulbous') vase which depicts a prothesis names the dead woman as Myrrhine, and her father in approaching the bier which is surrounded by women mourning calls out, 'Alas, daughter'.[43] Women were routinely commemorated with gravestones in the classical period, as a quick inspection of the hundreds of examples in Clairmont's corpus of funerary reliefs reveals, and daughters were mourned by their parents just as dead sons were. Women descended from famous men had this mentioned on their tombstones: Archedike, the daughter of Hippias, tyrant of Athens, and Xanthippe, the great-great-grandchild of Periander, tyrant of Corinth, had their connections with their famous relatives mentioned. Sometimes the responsibility for erecting gravestones fell to a woman. At their mother's orders, sons erected a monument to their father.[44]

Black-figure vases and women mourning

Aside from the black-figure pinakes, black-figure vases also show similar themes. A loutrophoros shows five mourning women on its neck with their hands in their hair, but no prothesis below,[45] while other loutrophoroi throughout the sixth century BC show similar scenes on the neck above and a prothesis scene.[46] An Attic black-figure loutrophoros of *c.* 500 BC has a frieze of mourners, all dressed in black, on its main body, while around the neck four women mourners strike their foreheads and rend their hair (Figure 9.4; only one side of the vase and not all of the participants are shown here). In the main scene, six women (not all visible here) take priority around the bier of a deceased man; at the head and shoulder of the bier, two of the women rend their hair. The three bearded men in a line at the foot of the bier mourn stoically, raising one hand in greeting to the deceased (they are on the other side of the vase). Their calmness and serenity are clearly intended to be contrasted with the active, painful mourning of their women counterparts.[47]

Geometric vases show women accompanying the deceased to the tomb, and two black-figure Athenian kantharoi (cups) also do so. Four men carry the deceased and his bier on their shoulders, while two mourning women follow. Another example has two women in front of the wagon conveying the dead, and at its side, mourning as they process to the grave.[48]

In this same period as Athenian black-figure ware, a Corinthian black-figure hydria (water-jug) indicates that practice throughout Greece was the same as at Athens. When the Nereids (the sea nymphs with Thetis, Achilles' mother) are depicted as mourning for Achilles, some tear at their hair and one strikes her forehead; one has a white fillet in her hand, and another a 'ribbed' fillet, ready for use in adorning the grave. This represents the reality of contemporary sixth-century funeral practice, in which women were the most active of the mourners.[49] Trojan mourners also appear in Athenian art: two women mourn

Figure 9.4 Women mourners at the bier; loutrophoros, Athens (Greece), *c.* 500 BC; black-figure terracotta, height: 43.5 centimetres (courtesy, ©The Cleveland Museum of Art, 1999, The Charles W. Harkness Fund: inv. 1927.145).

WOMEN AND THE CORPSE: MOURNING RITUALS

on the walls of Troy,[50] and, as Achilles begins to drag Hektor behind his chariot, Priam and Hekabe within the porch make mourning gestures: he stretches out his right hand, while she has one hand on her forehead.[51]

Terracotta women mourners

Mourning women are not only shown on vases but actual small terracotta figures of mourning women were made, usually incorporated into a larger terracotta piece, presumably as funerary equipment to be left at the tomb. Two women sit mourning with their hands on their heads on the rim of a sixth-century BC black-figure bowl (a lekanis) which depicts sirens, and was found in the Kerameikos cemetery, Athens (Figure 9.5).[52] The women are in 'plank' form, made from flat strips of clay, with only their facial features defined, but they are expressionless and no real attempt has been made to express their grief. Although they are 'sitting' on the handles, this is only a structural arrangement

Figure 9.5 Two terracotta figurine women mourners, on an Athenian sixth-century BC black-figure cup (lekanis); Kerameikos cemetery, Athens, height of mourners: approx. 18.5 centimetres; height of cup itself: 11 centimetres; diameter of cup: 33 centimetres; Kerameikos Museum, Athens, inv. 41 (courtesy, ©Deutsches Archäologisches Institut, Athens, neg. Ker. 5856).

for the strength of the piece, and they are to be imagined as standing, and rending their hair as part of a mourning ritual.

Women mourners appear as figurines on a terracotta model of an Athenian cart of the first half of the seventh century BC which carries a bier and the deceased, with women mourners on the cart with hands on their heads.[53] Sitting on the handle of a sixth-century BC black-figure one-handled jug (an olpis) is a woman with both hands on her head, with blood clearly streaming from her forehead, which she must have lacerated in mourning,[54] while four mourning women stand on a black-figure early sixth-century BC game table found in a tomb in the same cemetery, some of whom smite the breast with one hand.[55] An oinochoe from the Dipylon area shows on its body a prothesis scene, while its trefoil (three-spouted) neck was supported by three women; with their hands raised to support the neck they are obviously mourners.[56] Two thymateria are each supported by a mourning woman; both mourning women are damaged, but one still has its face, with large red streaks to indicate laceration.[57] Terracotta figurines of single women mourners are found at the Kerameikos cemetery in Athens, on Thera and at Tanagra, and would have been grave offerings.[58] They are largely pre-classical. From Tanagra comes a terracotta of a woman sitting next to a funerary stele with a hydria at its base; she holds her head in her hands. After the dead are buried, the mourning is not yet over.[59]

Women depicted as mourners on funerary vases

The timing of visits to graves was at least to some extent dependent upon custom. At Athens, on the third, ninth and thirtieth days and one year after the funeral, visits would be made to the tomb.[60] Presumably many of the scenes on lekythoi show one of these commemorative visits to the tomb. At the annual Genesia festival, held by all the Greeks, the dead were honoured;[61] it was held on the fifth day of the month Boedromion at Athens.[62] Tomb-visits would also have occurred on this day; women shown on lekythoi as visiting a tomb might be imagined as doing so on the Genesia. The dead could also be remembered on other occasions: Elektra will bring libations to her father Agamemnon's grave on her wedding day, and the Athenians invoked the Tritopatores, ancestors, before marriage.[63]

Lekythoi were often placed on graves at Athens. A lekythos was simply a pottery oil vessel, and the majority of, but not all, lekythoi were used in funeral contexts. The main class of lekythoi were the white-ground, or white, lekythoi: the middle portion excluding the base and actual neck would be painted white and then scenes would be painted on this area; sometimes there would be simple pattern designs (the so-called 'pattern lekythoi') on the white 'ground' as it is referred to, and not only funeral scenes but mythological and other non-funerary scenes were depicted. In addition, there were black lekythoi, with red figures, which tended to be squat, unlike the more slender white lekythoi. Moreover, lekythoi which were entirely black are shown on some of the white lekythoi being placed at the tomb; it is the white lekythoi which in particular show funerary iconography. Small squat black lekythoi were placed on tombs in both the fifth and fourth centuries BC.[64] The Achilles Painter in particular painted numerous lekythoi.[65]

Lekythoi indicate that fillets (tainiai), or ribbons, were a common item placed on tombs; these were usually flat, like modern ribbons, but sometimes they were tubular, and could be shaped like a wreath; they were apparently heavy, in that they are shown lying at the foot of the tomb, and so were probably filled, perhaps with sand or earth, and not secured to the tomb with a tie, unlike flat fillets. Fillets could also be rolled up, in the same way that modern ribbons are sold. On several lekythoi, women are shown at tombs holding the rolled fillets above their heads, often with some length of the ribbon unfurled at one end. The next action would be for the woman to tie the fillet around the tomb. These representations are all by the Reed Painter, and seem to reflect his liking for showing numerous fillets at tombs.[66]

The grave relief of the young male Eupheros shows two rolled up ribbons from a side profile, which have been painted above the pediment; there are concentric rings at the visible end of each rolled fillet, indicating the rolling up of the ribbon, and a loose end on the outer roll.[67] When painted on lekythoi, the rolls of ribbon took the appearance of rectangular objects, but the loose end is usually shown. These rectangular objects have been interpreted as tablets, deltoi (singular: deltos), and seen as offerings with a written message for a dead person, or connected with Orphism and Pythagoreanism.[68] Kurtz has indicated, however, that these are quite clearly rolled up ribbons, so they lack any religious overtones of this nature.[69] Fillets were used not only in funerary contexts, but also were tied on animals about to be sacrificed, or on victorious athletes and chariot drivers.[70]

The oil from the lekythos would be poured as an offering to the dead; some lekythoi had a false chamber, so that the entire vase did not have to be filled with oil. Many lekythoi in fact depict offerings being brought to the grave, and it is significant how many times a woman is shown doing this. The lekythos would be placed on the grave at death, when the libation was poured. But they were also left at the grave on subsequent visits. Why these scenes of offerings are depicted on the lekythoi is difficult to say: they are perhaps partly in the nature of a promise, that mourners, particularly women, will continue to visit the grave and make offerings.

A husband clearly could visit the tomb of his dead wife, and the sons as well, offering sacrifices and libations,[71] but the lekythoi concentrate on the role of women in doing this (perhaps also indicating that they are the main purchasers of lekythoi, or have the main say over which ones will be purchased). Funerals are times to weep, but the visit to the grave can also be emotional. One white lekythos of 475–450 BC shows two women on either side of a tomb. The woman on the left is rubbing her eyes with her left hand, while in her right hand she has a fillet with wavy pattern which she will, in a moment, hang on the grave-stele (gravestone). The second woman carries a large basket of offerings, from which ribbons hang (only her basket and hand are visible here); the women will adorn the tomb stele with the various fillets and lekythoi that are in the basket (Figure 9.6). But it is surprising how restrained are the emotions of the men and women on the lekythoi in general, indicating that by and large these represent visits to the tomb after the actual funeral.[72]

One lekythos, of 450–425 BC, shows an older woman, to one side of the head of the bier, who has her left hand on the corpse, and seems perhaps to be propping the dead man up on the pillows behind his head. But she extends her right hand to the young man standing at the head of the bier who has a hand in his hair; her hand nearly touches his arm. This is apparently a gesture of

Figure 9.6 Two women, one weeping, and one (partly visible) carrying a basket of tomb offerings, at a tomb; 475–450 BC; The Inscription Painter; white Athenian funeral vase (lekythos); height: 36.5 centimetres; found in Eretria on the island of Euboia (courtesy, ©National Archaeological Museum Athens, inv. 1958).

restraint: the women rend the hair, but the young man, at the head of the bier and probably therefore the principal mourner (perhaps it is his father on the bier), must not do so.[73] The Trojans depicted on a vase mourning for Memnon tug at their hair at the front or back of their heads, but this seems non-Greek and might be deliberately so. Men, of course, had their own mourning rituals, wearing black and cutting their hair.[74]

Another Attic white lekythos, of 450–425 BC, shows a woman by herself standing in front of a funerary stele, which has a fillet tied around it. She carries a very large flat basket tray which has several fillets hanging from it; a small lekythos stands on the tray.[75] But her basket is easily outdone by the woman who is depicted on a white lekythos and who stands on one side of a large grave monument, with a bearded male, possibly her husband, on the other side. She carries a very large basket, from which numerous red and white fillets hang, and there are several lekythoi on the basket as well (Figure 9.7).[76] At this point it can be noted that the painters of the lekythoi often rendered the ribbons blue, red, violet, pink, red and white, with several colours often used for the same tomb, and this must reflect the practice of the time. On an earlier lekythos, a couple is shown in the process of adorning the grave monument: a man is placing another fillet on it, while a woman holds a large basket from which several fillets hang; there are also two large black lekythoi in her basket.[77] Lekythoi often show Athenian women going to visit graves to pour libations accompanied by another woman, perhaps a maidservant, as a servant figure is sometimes shown helping the mistress to choose fillets to take to the tomb. Sometimes the grieving woman wears black, but not always.[78]

Of particular interest is one Attic white lekythos which shows not one, but two grave-stelai, indicating that two dead people are being brought offerings; a woman stands to one side of the pair, while a youth stands on the other. The dark base which both stelai rise from might indicate that this is a family plot. Both stelai are already covered by a large number of fillets and some wreaths, but the woman is about to tie on another fillet.[79] In at least one example, a woman is shown handing a helmet to a figure on the other side of the grave who holds a spear; she has a shield poised on the other hand. He is the dead warrior and she is possibly his wife; she is shown bringing his weapons to show not only that he died in battle, but that he had done so valiantly.[80]

Women pour libations in some situations, and the funerary context, in which women are prominent, is no exception. An obviously grief-stricken woman with one foot on the lower step of the tomb pours a libation from a large hydria, while someone holds the libation bowl;[81] this libation-pouring theme appears on another lekythos as well, where the woman also has a hydria.[82] In a similar scene to those of the women who pour libations for departing hunters, one white lekythos shows a woman with an oinochoe in one hand and handing a libation bowl in her outstretched right hand to a young man with a spear in his left hand, a petasos (wide brimmed hat) over his shoulder and a cloak, but whose right hand stays by his side. He has passed to the realm of the

SACRIFICIAL AND DOMESTIC RITUALS

Figure 9.7 Man, and woman with tray of funeral offerings, at a tomb; lekythos (white-ground), Athens, about 450 BC; attributed to the Inscription Painter; height: 37 centimetres (courtesy, ©The Museum of Fine Arts, Boston: Harriet Otis Cruft Fund, inv. 1970.428. Reproduced with permission. ©1999 Museum of Fine Arts, Boston. All rights reserved).

dead, and can no longer receive the libations she poured for him when he set out hunting.[83]

Occasionally, women carry a pottery vessel, the exaleiptron (plural: exaleiptra), to the tomb; the exaleiptron had a cylindrical base, sometimes narrow and high in proportion to the bowl above, widening out into a wide flat bowl shape, with a bowl lid, from which there was often a thin, tower-like projection. This was an unguent vessel, and presumably the contents were used

286

to anoint the tomb, a task suited to women, who also used the vessel in the house to hold unguents for personal use.[84]

The reader should note that women on the lekythoi sometimes appear naked or semi-naked, but this does not point to a funerary practice. On one lekythos, the woman appears naked, but only her top half has survived; the rest has worn away, and her clothes were clearly originally painted on.[85] Similarly there is a fully 'naked' woman at a tomb on another white lekythos but it is simply a case of the painted clothing having worn off.[86]

Most of these lekythoi, when the provenance is known, were found in Athens. But numbers of them have been found elsewhere, in Sicily, southern Italy, Corinth, and especially in nearby Eretria. This raises the question of what sort of reality these lekythoi are representing. Are most of them custom made, and depict the actual tomb at which the offerings are being made? The way in which so many different tombs are rendered individually, with different scenes of fillet-placing, strongly suggests that many lekythoi were produced for individual patrons. But the numbers found in cemeteries elsewhere in Greece indicates that many of the scenes need to be considered as generic in nature. Corinth imported large numbers of Athenian lekythoi in the fifth century, until the outbreak of the Peloponnesian War (431–404 BC), after which the Corinthians produced their own (vastly inferior) versions. Presumably the scenes on the lekythoi, with the involvement of women, also took place at Corinth and elsewhere. Corinthian white lekythoi which appear in numbers following the cessation of the importation of Attic white lekythoi are disappointing from an iconographic perspective and reveal nothing about the role of women at the tomb, which could in fact suggest that Corinthian women did not play such a conspicuous role at Corinthian tombs. However, this seems unlikely and inferior craftsmanship might well explain why the detailed scenes on Athenian lekythoi are not reproduced at Corinth.[87]

It is also important to note that the white lekythoi with their scenes of tombs and mourners were common in the fifth century BC. But around 430 BC they begin to be replaced by stone lekythoi, more durable than pottery. By the turn of the century, the white lekythos was no longer fashionable. During the fifth century there is a marked absence of large monumental stone tombs in Attica, and the pottery lekythos is part of this phenomenon. When stone monuments came into fashion again, the durable stone lekythos, imitating but displacing the terracotta variety, also came into being. However, the iconography of these stone lekythoi is very different and the scenes on white lekythoi are reproduced only in small numbers. Stone lekythoi tend rather to show the type of relief on the actual monument itself, usually the farewell to the dead. Funerary customs did not change, and women will have continued to take their offerings to tombs, but a shift in fashion denies the historian an iconography of mourning women at Athens in the fourth century BC.[88]

Before taking hemlock in 399 BC, Socrates sent the women away, so that there would be no loud lamentation, and scolded his male friends when they broke down and grieved.[89] A speaker in a lawsuit who was carried home after being beaten by his enemies says that at the sight of him the women commenced wailing and shrieking as if someone had died, so much so that the neighbours came to see what was going on.[90] Mourning practices continued to be the same into the fourth century BC as always, despite the fact that a change in funerary iconography had taken place and mourning women no longer appeared in art.

Women and Charon

An Attic lekythos with white background, and striking polychrome decoration, mainly of browns and reds, shows the ferryman of Hades, Charon, who has come to shore where a woman stands and waits for him, with an object in her hand, which could be an aryballos vase (a vase, used for holding perfumed oil, sometimes globular), or as is sometimes suggested, perhaps the purse which contains the fare for her journey across the river Styx to Hades. But the shape seems to be a vase.[91] Moreover, on another Attic white lekythos Charon's ferry-boat is shown at one side of a grave-stele, on the other side of which stands a woman with what is definitely an aryballos, so this is obviously part of a woman's funerary equipment. There is also a lekythos on the base of the grave, and the woman in addition carries an offering tray with fillets. She is thus shown as bringing the fillets to Hades, to adorn her own tomb in the underworld.[92] Various lekythoi show Hermes leading the dead woman to Charon waiting in his boat.[93] In Euripides' play, Alkestis as she lies dying sees the two-oared skiff of Charon in the lake; he beckons to her to hasten.[94]

Antigone and the corpse of her brother Polyneikes

Sophocles' *Antigone* has as its central plot the burial of Polyneikes: Antigone and Ismene's two brothers have killed each other in battle outside Thebes. One brother, Eteokles, has been buried, according to justice and custom. But the other, Polyneikes, who has attacked the city as an enemy, has not. Kreon as king of Thebes has forbidden that anyone bury him: the corpse is to be unburied, unlamented, and a feast for the birds and dogs. Death by stoning will be the punishment for whoever mourns or buries him. But Antigone buries her brother with dust, performs the requisite rites, and when the guards undo her efforts, returns and recommences her mourning, puts dust over him again, adorns the grave, and pours a triple libation over her brother. These rites, she says, are holy. Kreon after a dire prophecy from the seer Teiresias, reverses his decision to kill the perpetrator, realising that it is better to obey the established laws, and not to bury Antigone alive, and orders the burial of Polyneikes, but is too late to prevent tragedy in his family. This situation is peculiar; as Antigone's parents are dead, it falls on her (her sister Ismene refuses to help) to bury the corpse. But what is important is that it is the woman's role to mourn for the dead and adorn the tomb, which is consonant with Greek practice in general.[95]

When he is on the point of dying, Oedipus' daughters Antigone and Ismene (in a different myth) brought water from a running stream to him for washing and pouring a libation. They bathed him and clothed him as was customary: they, as the women should, anoint and dress him in funerary garb, but here they do so before his actual death; this is necessary, as his body is to be taken away by Zeus. Falling to their father's knees, they wept without ceasing, beating their breasts and crying out without stopping. Sophocles has obviously seen the women in Athens act in this very fashion at the death bier and tomb. In the same way, Antigone asks Kreon if she might at least bathe her brother's corpse, even if it is denied burial. Socrates says that he will bathe before taking the hemlock, specifically so that the women will be saved the trouble of washing the corpse. Alkestis, on the point of death, bathes herself; Hekabe prepares to wash the corpse of Polyxena by sending a slave for sea-water.[96]

The chin-strap

Agamemnon in Hades calls Klytaimnestra 'dog-eyed' and complains bitterly that as he lay dying she did not pull down his eyelids or close his mouth.[97] Open-mouthed corpses were considered to be unsightly and the dead felt the insult. The women will, as one of their duties, no doubt have placed the chin-strap on the deceased; it ran from the chin, to above the ear and over the head, to prevent the unseemly opening of the mouth. The effect was otherwise achieved by carefully propping the dead on pillows, and the limited artistic depictions of the chin-strap suggest that its use was the less common method, or perhaps that it was simply considered to be artistically inappropriate. A loutrophoros shows a deceased man wearing his chin-strap on his bier; a krater shows a deceased adolescent girl arriving in Hades with her chin-strap on.[98] Krito closed Socrates' mouth and eyes when he had died from the hemlock (Socrates had sent the women away, who would normally have performed this duty).[99]

Heroised women

Women might help found a cult for a deity, or themselves, but might also be objects of deification (such as the wives of the ruling dynasty of the Ptolemies in hellenistic Egypt). But this is generally not a classical phenomenon. Kyniska, however, the first Spartan woman to own and breed horses, and send them to Olympia, where they won victories in chariot races in 396 and 392 BC, had a hero-shrine at the Platanista, the Plane-tree grove in Sparta. The mythical Helen also had a hero-cult at Sparta. Another exception might be an Athenian rhyton of 500–450 BC with the inscription, 'I am the sacred property of Elephantis'. Discovered in a tomb, this inscription could indicate that Elephantis was 'accorded heroic honors by her family or community' after her death. The rhyton vase was specifically used in connection with the cult of heroes, and apparently had no other use.[100] This phenomenon could be compared with the woman whom Peisistratos in *c*. 557/6 BC dressed up like Athena and placed in a chariot next to him. He drove into Athens, with messengers going before them, saying that Athena herself was appointing Peisistratos tyrant of Athens.[101]

Aristotle was charged, probably in 323 BC, with asebeia (impiety) for worshipping Hermeias, tyrant of Atarneus in the Troas, after his death by singing paeans in his honour and sacrificing to him. Moreover, Aristotle had married, according to different accounts, Hermeias' daughter, niece or concubine, and offered a sacrifice to her after her death in the same way as the Athenians did to Eleusinian Demeter. The problem here was perhaps not so much sacrificing to a woman, but parodying an aspect of Eleusinian rites.[102]

A woman might 'heroise herself', but not in the classical period. Epikteta of Thera founded an annual three-day festival for the Muses and the heroes, amongst whom was included herself, her husband, and their sons. To this end, she left a bequest for an association to carry out the rites.[103] This needs to be seen as part of a hellenistic phenomenon whereby individuals left money for the purpose of such commemorative cults, and is a logical extension of the 'herobanquet' reliefs. Poseidonios, also in the third century BC, set up a similar bequest at Halikarnassos for himself, his wife, and his mother and father, and various deities.[104]

The gynaikonomos

The main concern of the gynaikonomos – an official in charge of women and applying the relevant laws to their behaviour – in Greek cities was the behaviour of women at funerals and at religious festivals: the very times when women were abroad, and engaging in public behaviour.[105] There is no evidence for gynaikonomoi before the fourth century BC; the office continued into at least the second century BC. Garland suggests that the gynaikonomoi were part of a tendency towards a greater number of officials in the fourth century BC and illustrate the trend for the polis to safeguard its institutions and customs through official oversight of citizens' behaviour.[106] Aristotle notes that some cities had a gynaikonomos and paidonomos (an official overseeing the behaviour of boys and youths), but that the existence of the office of gynaikonomos was not a democratic one as the poor had to allow their wives to go out because they had no slaves: that is, women, out and about, were more likely to engage in improprieties. Plato in the ideal state of the *Laws* has women who disobey the marriage regulations excluded from exodoi, processions, which probably refers both to funeral processions and religious festivals.[107]

A law of fourth-century BC Thasos provides that no one perform funerary rituals for the agathoi (men killed in battle in this case) for more than five days and that there is to be no lamentation: if anyone does so, the gynaikonomoi, archons and polemarchs are to deal with it, according to the penalties laid down by law. Clearly the role of the gynaikonomoi is to punish any women who do lament the dead for longer than five days; the archons and polemarchs presumably dealt with other (male) offenders.[108]

Gynaikonomoi are also found in festival contexts. At Methymna on Lesbos, the gynaikonomos, who was to be no younger than forty years of age, was to remain outside the shrine during the pannychis (all-night festival), and was to make sure that no other man entered the shrine and that nothing else impious occurred. Mysteries and thyrsos-bearers are mentioned, so that it is to be imagined that the women were celebrating a festival of Dionysos. Magnesia had officials referred to as paidonomoi and gynaikonomoi: for the festival of Zeus Sosipolis, each had, respectively, to choose nine boys and nine girls all with their parents living to participate in the festival; they were to take part during the festival in the prayers on behalf of the city, and presumably took part in the procession (pompe) in the god's honour. Second-century BC inscriptions from Pergamon, as well as from Smyrna, mention an official 'in charge of the good behaviour (eukosmia) of the girls'.[109] There was a gynaikonomos at the Andanian Mysteries in the first century BC whose responsibility it was to ensure that the women involved in the cult all wore appropriate dress, and he was to punish women who did not do so; he swore an oath to uphold this and other requirements. He was also responsible for appointing the sacred women and virgins (who had specific functions in the cult), and for ensuring that they processed in the order assigned by lot.[110]

Two plays – by Timokles and Menander – mentioned gynaikonomoi at Athens and a 'new law' (obviously sumptuary in nature) that they count the guests at weddings. The gynaikonomoi at Athens had the power to fine women, and displayed the amounts of the fines on a plane tree in the Kerameikos; the public nature of this was clearly part of the punishment, a social stigma for the husband to add to the financial penalty.[111] The religious activities of women in connection with the Eleusinian Mysteries were of concern to Lykourgos, the Athenian reformer whose period of activity is usually dated to 338–324 BC, who carried a law that women could not go to Eleusis for the Mysteries in a cart, but that all women had to walk, so that poor and wealthy women would be on an equal footing. Apparently his own wife disobeyed the law and was fined.[112]

In rending their hair and occupying first place around the bier, Greek women maintained a Mycenaean tradition. The Mycenaean clay coffins (larnakes) discovered at Tanagra and now present in some numbers at the Thebes Museum, belong to the late Mycenaean period of the thirteenth century BC, still removed by some centuries from the first geometric depictions of the prothesis, but showing the same features: women mourners rend their hair and stretch out their hands to and touch the deceased.[113] For well over a thousand years, then, Greek girls and women mourned their dead in relatively unchanging rituals.

Funerary iconography and the scenes of death that were portrayed changed, but the rituals themselves were timeless.

Women did not perhaps mourn the dead to a greater extent than men because they were closer to them, but because women were allowed to give vent to their emotions to a greater degree (though sometimes restricted by law) than was permitted to men. Men had to conform to strict societal norms on how they should behave when mourning. Women were viewed as being more emotional, more prone to hysteria than men. Their more open mourning clearly provoked a response in some quarters, judging from the regulations which sought to restrict their funerary activities. But these attempts to regulate the behaviour of women in mourning did not extend to excluding them from funerary rites: their presence was too important for this. The restrictions in some places on the degree of relationship entitling a woman to go to a funeral illustrate that there must have existed extended kinship groups amongst women, and that in this wide group there was a strong tradition of women's participation in funerary activities for its members. Women naturally expected that they would be involved in mourning both their own close kin and also the wider family group and even relatives by marriage. Funerals served as an opportunity for women to mourn not just for the dead but for their own lost ones, effectively venting their grief at the tragedies in their lives. It was also women who clearly, to a greater degree than men, visited tombs and carried out tomb rituals, acting as the custodians of tomb-cults.

Men remained generally passive in mourning the dead. Despite the various funerary legislations, it is clear that men, themselves almost emotionally 'crippled' by excessive societal constraints, and unable to participate fully in the dynamics of a funeral, looked to women to provide an effective mourning for the dead, to give them their due, and provide a fitting public tribute for the deceased, to provide for the one being buried what men could not or were not willing to offer: a dramatic and fitting funeral which expressed the depths of feeling of those left behind. Spectacular if perhaps unsettling, these groups of women who, weeping, singing, beating their breasts, lacerating their faces and tearing at their hair, processed from the house of the deceased to the cemetery, made it their business to express their grief and sense of loss, effectively denied, if not at Athens then definitely elsewhere, Perikles' admonition to show quiet grief in the face of heroic, glorious bereavement. It was almost a duty for women to ensure that the most awful and unavoidable of consequences of human mortality would not pass off quietly. Women's grief was constantly celebrated in clay of various forms, emphasising the importance attached to it. There was not just the funeral but also the whole process of mourning before the women even arrived at the grave and there were also the commemorations after the funeral, with the various visits to the grave and offerings to be made. Lamenting women were essential to the funerary process: dangerous if out of hand and so subject to restriction, but crucial for the burial process and subsequent rites, ensuring that the dead were properly honoured.

EPILOGUE

On the east frieze of the Parthenon on the Athenian acropolis, the Olympian deities sit in two groups. In one of these groups, Eros leans against Aphrodite. Behind Aphrodite sits Artemis, and this goddess has her hand going through the crook of Aphrodite's arm, so that her left palm rests on Aphrodite's right arm below the elbow.[1] At first sight, this seems odd: the virgin goddess and the goddess of love and sensuality, arm in arm. But these deities are much more complex than this. Artemis is a goddess of virgins – but in the sense that she helps them pass from the state of virginity to that of motherhood, and women cried out to her to ease the labour of childbirth. She was not in that sense inimical to marriage, and in fact could be its patron. Similarly, Aphrodite can be seen simply as a goddess of sensual love, or of prostitutes. But in addition, she too had oversight of marriage, and is worshipped by the 'respectable' woman on the Ludovisi Throne. In many ways, these were not opposing deities – that would be a simplistic notion – rather they were in many ways complementary, both deities being worshipped by the citizen wives of classical Athens. When they were married, the dangers and difficulties of childbirth automatically 'directed' women towards deities such as Artemis and Asklepios.

Artemis was the goddess *par excellence* of the young virgin, and transition rites for young girls centred on her more than on any other goddess. But the sexual maturity which Aphrodite brought changed the lives of virgins in every sense. And this was particularly so in the religious sphere. As parthenoi, citizen girls at Athens and elsewhere served the gods as basket-bearers, pure and without the 'taint' of sexual experience, and brought offering baskets, as well as jugs and shallow bowls with which men poured libations to the gods. Once they were married, this very public and visible service to the gods, so well illustrated on the east frieze of the Parthenon, ceased. But their service to the gods now took on a more serious dimension as participants in festivals like the Thesmophoria: once married, and with children, women became important to the community in their role as worshippers of Demeter and Persephone. Their child-bearing fertility rendered them suitable as conduits of the agricultural fertility which was conveyed by another – divine – woman, Demeter.

Yet, is it possible to assess the significance of these girls and women in Greek religion? Euripides at least thought that their role could be presented as important. Numerous pieces of evidence, such as inscriptions, literature, vases, terracottas, stone votive reliefs, painted wooden tablets, and gravestones, attest to the fact that women did participate in Greek worship. But to what extent did they do so, and was their role seen as essential, or did they worship simply as adjuncts to their fathers or husbands? Is it possible to argue that women's role was as important as men's without undertaking a study entitled, 'Boys and Men in Classical Greek Religion'?

Should it be assumed that the role of women in religion was equivalent to their negligible role in the political life of ancient Greece? Clearly, differences existed between states, especially between the more restricted lives of Athenian women and those of their property-owning counterparts in Sparta. It may seem paradoxical that the most information about women's religious experiences comes from Athens, a city often viewed as hostile to this gender. But it is also clear that, while for women at Athens there were a number of occasions when they would be called upon in a mediatory capacity with the divine, women in other states participated in many religious events as well, perhaps with even more freedom, and less supervision, than at Athens. Every two years, for example, Theban women and those of other cities took to the hills to worship Dionysos. Athenian women did not do so *en masse*, but worshipped Dionysos in private rites. When women worshipped Dionysos in ecstatic fashion at Athens, they clearly did so indoors, drawing wine at the Anthesteria; they loosened their hair, made music, danced wildly and drank in the company of a close circle of women associates. Even in Athens, women drank and got drunk in sacred – and often secret – rites: within the four walls where the Haloa was celebrated, in front of the pillars of Dionysos, on their roofs for the Adonia; all in places where they could celebrate the sacred rites (and have a drink) away from the presence of men.

We should also consider the part played by women in cults and rituals in the context of their position in Greek society as a whole. In many ways, their roles in religion reflected the patriarchal nature of Greek society. To be born female was to be destined to a role as wife and mother – important duties, but without the same powers and privileges as were entailed in male birth, and the role of husband, father and citizen. Women's main duty, to be married and bear children, channelled them into particular 'religious directions'. Young girls had the special attribute of virginity which was lost to society when they married. There were no older virgin women, and there was no special caste of women eschewing their sexuality for the community's religious benefit. Roles requiring virginity tended to devolve, then, on to girls and young women, and when there was a particularly important role requiring purity but also adulthood, as in the case of the women priests who served Apollo at Delphi, a temporary purity was occasioned by a lapse in sexual activity. It is also clear that girls were seen as particular repositories of purity.

The girls on the Parthenon frieze, representing one form or another (mythical or historical) of the procession which was an integral part of the Panathenaic festival, are on public display. When citizen girls served the state in these capacities in the post-classical period, inscriptions articulated the pride which their fathers felt for them in this role. While it is difficult to read the emotions of the young women of the Parthenon frieze because of the damaged state of the marble, what can be seen when the carvings are preserved is that they are not stereotypes; each is an individual, somebody's sister, daughter, or granddaughter. Along the processional route, their proud fathers (and mothers) watched them in this public role, their girls serving the virgin goddess who protected the city. The faces of the girls on the frieze are serious and perhaps pensive; certainly not relaxed or casual as many of the male figures on other sides of the frieze are. But the role of basket-bearer was 'elitist', reserved by custom (and the necessity of having fine clothes) to the daughters of aristocratic families, just as the arrephoroi, bears and corn-grinders constituted only a small number of Athenian girls. For the majority of girls, their virginity was not required for mediatory purposes, and it was marriage and childbirth that fully opened up for them the religious life of the polis, not simply as spectators and worshippers at festivals, but as participants in various festivals, such as the Thesmophoria, Stenia, Haloa, Skira, in cults of Dionysos, Pan, Aphrodite, Hekate, Herakles–Pankrates, Asklepios, and in more marginal rites, such as those of the Great Mother–Cybele, Adonis and Sabazios. Adulthood also brought a fuller participation in mourning rituals, and however restricted this was by legislation, clearly women had the chief role in funerary practices, and one which was always to some degree a public one.

For many of these girls on the Parthenon frieze, serving the goddess must have been a rewarding role – but also a daunting one: public, on show before the entire polis, being organised into lines and instructed by men who were unknown to them. But once married, they attended festivals such as the Thesmophoria with members of their own sex. This and similar festivals provided an intimate religious experience, away from male eyes. The opportunity to spend a whole day with other women, or a night, or a succession of days (the three-day Thesmophoria at Athens), provided for a degree of immersion in women's culture and thoughts outside their everyday experience, when at Athens all they might manage ordinarily was a quick word exchanged with other women outside their own family group at the fountain before carrying home a large pottery jar full of water and attending to the day's tasks. The nocturnal revel on the roof of a friend was another intimate, 'personalised' religious event for them; dining together in cults which required the sacrifice to be consumed on the spot was of the same nature. Through their shared cult and ritual experiences, classical Greek women presumably gained assurance and confidence about themselves; groups of women worshipping together brought a particular security to the wife and mother, a positive affirmation of her identity as a woman. The woman who was priest for Athena Polias had a particular type of status in the public domain, but conversely an individual woman's perception of her own status and self-esteem benefited through participation as one of a number of women worshipping the gods in a particular rite. These roles were not adjunctive to male ones but independent of them; when they returned home from secret all-women's rites, it was unnecessary – even forbidden – to tell their husbands about their day's activities.

Menander's *Samia* must provide another important clue as to women's involvement in festivals. While women did sincerely venerate Aphrodite and Adonis in the celebration of the Adonia described by Menander (and which was clearly not a secret ritual), there was room for fun and games (as there was also at the Tauropolia). Even the festival of the Thesmophoria, which involved a denial of sexuality, and fasting, nevertheless involved drinking, and at the end of the three days of this festival the participants returned home with a sense of both achievement and enjoyment. What needs to be noted is that there were several all-women festivals and rites: the Thesmophoria, Stenia, Skira, Haloa, Tauropolia, Adonia, and statue-washing rites. In addition there were the Eleusinian Mysteries, at which women could and did participate (including prostitutes) along with men. There was also the healing cult of Asklepios at Athens, but Athenian women of means could even travel to Epidauros. They watched the Panathenaic procession, and also attended various local and state festivals, processions and sacrifices to the gods. Male citizens, such as the proboulos in Aristophanes, and Demosthenes, ridiculed the cult of Sabazios, but there must have been many men who at least tolerated, countenanced, or even encouraged their wives' involvement in 'exotic' cults. Instead of assuming that women became involved in all of these to escape a life of 'drudgery',[2] it is clear that there were two rival social structures, or systems, operating within Athens and other Greek cities. Religious practices and male ideas about women (at least as expressed in the literary sources) were in some sense in opposition to each other.

Women – and the less well-off were about in the streets more regularly than those who had slaves to fetch their water and did not have to work for a living – were 'out and about' in classical Athens and other cities, both because of the necessities of life, and also because of their religious duties. In opposition to this, there was a counter-'system', the attempts – political, judicial and sexual – of men to limit women's public appearances. These two social structures competed against and complemented each other; it was not simply the case that women were attracted to religion to escape from their patriarchally ordered lives. What is particularly important is the degree to which women seem to have had at least some measure of freedom conferred on them by their involvement in religious activity. A degree of autonomy was imparted: having to leave the house – even with the child – countered attempts to seclude women.

But what is also important is not to over-stress the way in which women's behaviour at rites was circumscribed (for example, through clothing regulations): it is also crucial to consider how men facilitated the religious behaviour of their wives. At the most simplistic level men tacitly accepted their wives' involvement in rites, such as the biennial celebrations for Dionysos in Boeotia, or the citizen wives lamenting Adonis on the rooftops. Men knew that there were festivals only for women. Herodotos sees Miltiades' gangrene and subsequent death as divine vengeance for attempting to penetrate the women-only mysteries on the island of Paros. The stories about Battos being castrated for intruding on the Thesmophoria might well have originated with women, but if so it was men who wrote down and transmitted them. (In a similar way, the myths in which women are sent mad if they do not participate in Bacchic rites could in fact originate with women, and could be told to men to justify maenadic behaviour and absence from home.) Decrees called for the gynaikonomos to make sure no men entered the Thesmophorion at Methymna, provided that men were to finance celebrations of the Thesmophoria at Athens, guaranteed women priests and women in general shares in sacrificial meat, took up women priests' concerns about the behaviour of women in shrines, called upon the women to celebrate festivals in accordance with 'ancestral custom', and actually ordered women to take part in festivals. This is not to say that women's participation in Greek religion was compulsory, but rather that men actively supported women's dealings with the gods. The husband who is shown bidding farewell to his deceased wife who carries her drum with her into the next life had surely seen his wife off at the door when she went to her 'exotic' celebrations.

But why were so many rites for women only? Why were men excluded from worship in festivals in honour of extremely important deities such as Demeter? After all, the hard work on the farm was done by men, and, even if wives helped out on the land, it was largely men who had direct contact with the earth itself. Why, then, did the men not supplicate the goddess for the fertility of their fields? Women in many cultures are seen as repositories of fertility, not just human, but of the wider cosmos as well. The phenomenon of this cosmological procreativity cannot be underestimated in the ancient Greek world. While men obviously worshipped Demeter in the Eleusinian Mysteries, other festivals – the Stenia, Thesmophoria and Haloa – were exclusively women's festivals. While some evidence, for example, from Athens might suggest that only a select group of women took part in the Thesmophoria on the acropolis, the various celebrations of the Thesmophoria and also of pre-ploughing ceremonies throughout the Athenian countryside do point to women's widespread participation, if only at the deme level.

Socio-economic distinctions appear clear and obviously impinged on the level of religious activity for the individual woman. The family which could sacrifice a large sow to Athena was obviously not normative. In a sense, these various costly dedications in fact skew the picture of women's involvement. Grateful while the historian must be for these representations, there is the possibility that they emphasise the material culture of religious practice at the expense of the women who had to be content with a simple prayer by way of thanksgiving. But these dedications are also crucial for revealing the importance attached to the family as a unit, where a husband and wife are shown worshipping as a couple. Women often went their own religious way, but there is plenty of evidence to indicate that families worshipped together; though, when they did so, the husband generally took priority of place over his wife.

There were women, too, outside the world of the citizen daughters and wives. Foreign women at Athens watched processions, and this was allowed and accepted; the daughters of foreigners (metics) had a set role in the Panathenaic procession, even if this was to carry parasols and stools for the citizen daughters. There might well have been a community of citizens, within a wider community, which kept certain rites to itself, but there was clearly also an expectation that 'outsiders' would join in the rites of the city, at least to some extent. Foreign women also made dedications, but on the other hand, they were excluded from various fertility rituals which were for citizen women only. This seems to have been a matter of custom rather than law, and the Athenian women themselves might have preferred it this way, and could in fact have even been the authors of this social convention.

Women slaves, who were without property, have left nothing to indicate their religious feelings. But they are seen in their dozens on Athenian votive reliefs, the best-represented women after the citizen women themselves: the woman slave is the figure, smaller than the others, usually at the end of a procession, with a large round kiste (chest) on her head, carrying the necessary items for the sacrifice, generally either for Asklepios or for Artemis. Hopefully she received a share of the sacrifice, just as the cult group at Athens worshipping the hero Echelos gave for each man present at the sacrifice a share of meat for one slave. Prostitutes were often slaves, but there was a significant number of them who were free, with more access to money than many an Athenian housewife, and who could and did dedicate items to the gods. Their sexual activities did not taint them in any way in the classical period: they entered temples, made sacrifices, and at Corinth prayed for the survival of the state.

Greek women and girls of the classical period are themselves largely silent, if literature is the criterion for text. But these girls and women speak over the centuries of their devotion to the gods and goddesses in another way. In dedicating statues and other votive offerings, an inscription identifying the dedicator, and perhaps the reasons for the votive, are generally given. So as we have seen in Chapter 1, Nikandre in the seventh century BC identifies herself as the dedicator of a massive statue on the island of Delos. But other dedications are nameless, with women simply placing items such as mirrors in the sanctuaries of goddesses. Otherwise, women do not reveal a construction of their own religiosity, and the sources are male. A sympathetic insight such as the one from Euripides' *Melanippe* with which this book opened is unique. But the role which women played in religion was too great to be ignored, and formed a vital part of the religious fabric of any Greek city – indeed it was seen as normal, expected and essential. This role was taken for granted by the various writers of the classical period, and those who later commented upon their works.

In addition, art reflected the religious traditions of society, and in iconography women's role in various rites and rituals finds expression; the women who drew wine for celebrations of Dionysos captured the attentions of artists, who painted them in their ecstatic states on red-figure vases, and provide a text that can be interpreted today.

For women, the period in the middle of their lives was the busiest from a religious point of view. Before marriage some had been aristocratic enough to become basket-bearers. Then childbirth brought them 'closer' to the gods, especially Artemis and other kourotrophic deities, and as wives and mothers they played important roles as worshippers at the Thesmophoria and other Demeter festivals. But the departure of their children obviously opened up new avenues for them. Old women are specifically referred to as one of the three groups worshipping the Eumenides in Aeschylus. It is the 'hags', or old women, whom Demosthenes derides Aeschines for leading in the worship of Sabazios. The granddaughter of Chairestrate shown on her tombstone with her tympanum sums up nicely the freedom of the older woman to pursue her religious career once her domestic duties were largely over (and here Chairestrate perhaps combined caring for her granddaughter with cult activities).

Men took charge of politics and finance, and placed various restrictions on women's behaviour. Men had their own opportunities to make private sacrifices with their friends, they held priesthoods, and even had a few cults from which they excluded women. But the range of religious possibilities which were open to women because of their physiology and biology, their ability to bring forth new life and their primary role as carers, is clear from the number of rites and cults in which they participated. Although any assessment of the degree to which men and women participated in religious activities might need qualification, it is evident that when it came to the number of individual cults, and opportunities for leaving their tasks for the purposes of worshipping the gods, women spent more time involved in rites than men did. Euripides has Melanippe make a similar assessment 2,500 years ago: in matters concerning the gods, 'women have the greatest share'. Citizen men's opportunities, in particular, for beating drums, dancing ecstatically, lamenting their dead and giving full vent to their religious and emotional needs were far fewer than for women. Societal norms – developed over time by men – determined this to a large degree. But in choosing the political assembly, lawcourts and finance as spheres from which they excluded women, these men also in a sense abrogated to them the bulk of the task of worshipping the gods. Many of the women's rituals must have had long histories, many probably devised by women, and were in place long before the archaic and classical periods began.

Men did not allow women these rituals because they recognised that women were otherwise 'oppressed' and needed some sort of 'safety-valve'. Women had their own rites, and, while these will always have been important as a means of escaping the 'humdrum' of domesticity, this was not their primary purpose.

And while men sought to control some aspects of women's cults, the husbands who, for example, allowed their wives and friends to take over the rooftop for the Adonia, and who ensured that their wives were depicted on their gravestones with their cult implements, including the noisy drums used in the worship of the Great Mother, clearly did not keep their wives to a 'bare minimum' of religious worship but were on the whole supportive of their veneration of the gods.

Women through their fertility festivals, drum-beating for Bacchus, Pan, Aphrodite Kolias and Genetyllis, their predisposition for founding shrines, their maenadic rituals, their involvement in foreign though partly assimilated cults such as those of Cybele, Adonis and Sabazios, not to mention the privileged few who served as arrephoroi, basket-bearers and women priests, had a variety of religious roles to fulfil. They undertook these not at the behest of their husbands: many were timeless rituals harking back to the first days of agriculture, when women left their menfolk to invoke their own fertility and that of the soil. Others rites, such as the Adonia, were of more recent origin, and it seems that women, with the tacit consent if not necessarily approval of their husbands, participated in these because they considered them relevant and found them satisfying. When domesticity ebbed and they had more time, Sabazios and various cults had an even greater call, and the separate identity accorded to old women as religious devotees by Aeschylus marks out the main phases of the religious life of a woman – as girl, wife and old woman in classical Athens and elsewhere:

> For the . . . whole land of Theseus (i.e. Athens) shall come forth, a glorious company of girls and wives, and a throng of elderly women.[3]

NOTES

INTRODUCTION

1 Eur. *Melanippe Desmotis*: Page 1941: F13, pp. 112–15; Henrichs 1991: 169–79; Collard et al. 1995: 255–7, 272–4; cf. Lefkowitz 1996: 78–9; see also Ar. *Thesm.* 785–845.
2 Ar. *Lys.* 1–3.
3 Chapter 8, p. 236.
4 Ar. *Clouds* 52.
5 Hesych. sv Genetyllis.
6 Plato *Laws* 909e–910a.
7 Theophr. *Char.* 16.4.
8 Dion. Halik. 2.19.2; cf. Bravo 1997: 11–14.
9 Platon *PCG* vii F9–14 (floreat *c.* 410–391 BC).
10 For heroines, see esp. Larson 1995; Lyons 1997.

1 WOMEN AS DEDICATORS

1 Lazzarini 169 nn. 1–2 (80 of 884); Ridgway 1987: 401; Kron 1996: 155–71.
2 *Figure 1.1*: *ID* 2 (NM 1; *IG* xii.5.2, p. xxiv n. 1425b; *SGDI* 5423; Friedländer 46; Guarducci 1967: i.1, 153–6, figs 38a–c; Buck 6; Lazzarini 157; *LSAG* 47, 291, 303 n. 2, 311; Richter 1968: 26, no. 1, figs 25–8; 1970a: pl. 277; 1987: fig. 57; *CEG* i.403; *SEG* 19.507; Boardman 1991a: fig. 71; *LIMC* ii Artemis 83; Ridgway 1987: 400; Sturgeon 1987: 32, pl. 82a; Powell 1989: 341–2; Fantham 1994: 36–7, fig. 1.10; Kron 1996: 155–6, figs 9–10; Spivey 1997: fig. 66; Osborne 1998: fig. 33; Fullerton 2000: 65, pl. 43). For the daedalic style of which this statue is an example, see Boardman 1991a: 13–15.
3 *LIMC* ii Artemis 83 lists the statue under 'probable representations' of Artemis.
4 See Chapter 7, p. 215.
5 However, the word for 'now' is largely restored and perhaps not too much should be made of this.
6 Powell 1989: 342.
7 *IG* xii 5.i.216 (Lazzarini 726; Friedländer 110; *LSAG* 295; *CEG* i.413; Kron 1996: 157, fig. 11; Fantham 1994: 36); findspot actually unknown (though sometimes said to be from Paros).
8 *IG* xii 5.i.215 (*SGDI* 5430; Lazzarini 803; Friedländer 144; *LSAG* 305 no. 34, pl. 56; *CEG* i.414; Kron 1996: 158, fig. 12); findspot: Paros. The expression, 'apo koinon' might not mean 'together' but from their common financial resources.
9 *IG* i³ 1261 (Friedländer 80; *SEG* 21.158; *LSAG* 73, 401 n. 29, pl. 3; *CEG* i.24; Fantham 1994: 19–21, fig. 1).

10 Nearchos: *IG* i³ 628 (*CEG* i.193; Richter 1968: 69–70; Fantham 1994: 19); Alkimachos: *IG* i³ 618 (Lazzarini 732; Raubitschek 6; Friedländer 48; *CEG* i.195).
11 Lazzarini 52, 71, 91, 194, 275b, 667.
12 Hippylla: Lazzarini 52; fifth century BC (*Ergon* 1961: 28 figs 28, 33; *BCH* 86, 1962: 676 fig. 11, 679; Guarducci 1967: fig. 26; Linders 1972: 14 n. 59; Fantham 1994: 36, 38, fig. 1.11; Kron 1996: 159). For dedications of mirrors, see Tod 1930: 33; Linders 4, 14 n. 59, 27–8, 46; Pingiatoglou 1981: 66–7; Ridgway 1987: 403; Kron 1996: 159–60.
13 *IG* ii² 1522.30; it has also been suggested that the group of 22 items in *IG* ii² 1522.35 whose description needs restoration were bronze mirrors (see Linders 27). For the 119 mirrors: Linders 28; Tod 34.
14 *IG* ii² 1514.23–4; the same entry occurs in subsequent lists: *IG* ii² 1515.15–16; 1516.3–4; cf. Tod 34; Linders 28.
15 *IG* i³ 548 bis, c. 480 BC (J. Empereur *BCH* 105, 1981: 565 no. 5, fig. 46; *SEG* 31: 41, 1581).
16 *IG* i³ 536; c. 480 BC (*NM* 6944; de Ridder 1896: 585; Lazzarini 667).
17 J. Empereur *BCH* 105, 1981: 564, fig. 45, 565 no. 4 (Athens, collection P. Kanellopoulos 22; *SEG* 31, 1981: 1586); unknown provenance and date; possibly fourth century BC; Ridgway 1987: 402; Kron 159.
18 *IG* i³ 549; 450 BC? (Lazzarini 27).
19 *LSAG* 159, 168 no. 11; middle of the sixth century BC (Lazzarini 117 fig. 1, no. 275b; Kron 159). The inscription survives on what is clearly a mirror handle.
20 G. Daux *BCH* 83, 1959: 471 fig. 7, 472 no. 5.
21 Lazzarini 71; first quarter of the fifth century BC (*LSAG* 129 no. 34).
22 Lazzarini 91; middle of the fifth century BC.
23 *IG* xiv.664 (Schwyzer 435.2; Friedländer 166; *LSAG* 253, 260 n. 7, pl. 50; Richter 1968: 196, figs 618–21; Lazzarini 702; *CEG* i.395; Kron 1996: 159). The statue itself is 11 centimetres high, and the whole piece 13.4 centimetres.
24 Lazzarini 194; second half of the sixth century BC (*LSAG* 285–6 no. 8; Tod 1930: 32). Mirrors, which are obviously dedications, feature prominently on the terracotta pinakes depicting the interior of the Persephone temple at Lokris: see Chapter 7, p. 225–6.
25 See esp. for the sanctuary of Hera Akraia at Perachora: Payne 1942; Payne and Dunbabin 1962; cf. Tomlinson 1976: 197–202; J. Salmon *ABSA* 67, 1972: 159–204; Salmon 1984: 88, 94–5, 97–8.
26 Spindle-whorls: Payne and Dunbabin 1962: 130–1, 331–3, pls 39, 56, 127, 129, 131; bobbins: 131; loom-weights: 330–1, pl. 131; 'spectacle-fibulae' and other fibulae: 433–41, pls 183–5. Johnston 1997: 51 n. 22 suggests that the pyxides found in some numbers (Payne and Dunbabin 99–124, 158–91, 226, 304–8) might represent women's dedications of pyxides which functioned as containers for cosmetics or 'trinkets' (Cook 1997: 223; pyxides were round glazed terracotta bowls with lids, often about 10 centimetres in diameter). Cf. Shepherd 1999: 280–1.
27 Payne 1942: 67–9, pl. 33.11, 16; Payne and Dunbabin 1962: 328–30; J. Salmon *ABSA* 67, 1972: pl. 38; see also Price 1978: 208; for kourotrophic Hera: Price 146, 192, cf. 152–3; cf. Johnston 55.
28 Strabo 9.1.16.
29 Raubitschek p. 465, cf. p. 473; he gave three uncertain cases: *IG* i³ 703, 766, 814. In six other cases, the name of the father or husband is given: p. 465.
30 *IG* i³ 615 (Raubitschek 232; 525–10 BC; Lazzarini 617).
31 *IG* i³ 683 (Raubitschek 3; Friedländer 13; Lazzarini 3; *CEG* i.198; Kron 1996: 161)

NOTES

32 *IG* i³ 656; 510–500 BC (Raubitschek 81; Lazzarini 210).
33 *IG* i³ 794; 490–480 BC (*NM* Acropolis Museum 607; Raubitschek 380, and p. 465; Lazzarini 666; Ridgway 1987: 402; Kron 1996: 162, 165).
34 *IG* i³ 700; 500–480 BC? (Raubitschek 93; Lazzarini 23).
35 *IG* i³ 767; 500–480 BC (Raubitschek 25; Friedländer 22c; Lazzarini 649b; *CEG* i.250).
36 *IG* i³ 921; 490–480 BC (Raubitschek 348; Lazzarini 609b; *CEG* i.259).
37 *IG* i³ 813; 480 BC? (Raubitschek 258; Lazzarini 227).
38 *IG* i³ 857; around 470–450 BC (Raubitschek 298; Lazzarini 678; Ridgway 1981: 401; *CEG* i.273; Kron 1996: 161). Agalma is restored, but reasonably.
39 *Figure 1.2*: *IG* i³ 540; (*NM* 6447; de Ridder 1896: 796; Niemeyer 1960: 30 no. 70, 51–3, pl. 4, fig. 13; *Ant. Pl.* 3: 21–2, pl. 11; Lazzarini 647; Simon 1969: 189, fig. 172; van Straten 1981: fig. 4; *LIMC* ii Athena 146; Boardman 1993: 63–4, no. 56b; Hurwit 1999: 24, fig. 22).
40 *NM* 6837; 500 BC; the shield has a diameter of 10.8 centimetres (A.G. Bather *JHS* 13, 1892–3: 128 n. 60; de Ridder 1896: 264, fig. 60; Lazzarini no. 46, pl. 1.2; *IG* i³ 546; van Straten 1981: 81, fig. 5; Ridgway 1987: 402; Kron 1996: 163; Hurwit 1999: 61 fig. 45). The dedication simply reads: 'Phrygia the breadseller dedicated me to Athena'.
41 Myrtia: Ar. *Wasps* 1388–98; Lysilla: *IG* i³ 547; 500–475 BC; diameter: 7 centimetres (Athens Acr. *Mus.* 5905; Lazzarini 632).
42 *IG* i³ 858; 470–450 BC (Raubitschek 297; Ridgway 1987: 401; Immerwahr 1990: 165 n. 3, 181 no. 1141; Hurwit 1999: 60); note Raubitschek's suggestion that Glaukinos may have died in the Battle of Tanagra, with Argos and Athens' allies, leaving two daughters behind in Athens.
43 *IG* i³ 934; 480–470? BC (Lazzarini 620; Raubitschek 369).
44 *IG* i³ 894; 430–420? BC (Raubitschek 194; Lazzarini 41).
45 *IG* i³ 888; 440 BC ? (Raubitschek 378; Lazzarini 251).
46 *IG* i³ 745; 500–480 BC ? (Lazarrini 802; Raubitschek 79; *CEG* i.228; Ridgway 1981: 401 n. 10).
47 Harris 1995: 236–7.
48 *IG* ii² 1393.31, 1400.51–2, 1401.37–8; Harris 1995: 142 v.156.
49 *IG* ii² 1492.46–57 (305/4 BC); Harris 1995: 140 v.141, 179 v.358, 234–5; Parker 1996: 222; Hurwit 1999: 60.
50 Granikos: Harris 1995: 235; Gaza: Plut. *Alex.* 25.6; Delphi: *SIG*³ 252 nos 5–8; Hygieia: Hyp. 4.19, 26; Paus. 1.23.4; Dodona: Hyp. 4.24–6.
51 For the inventories of Artemis Brauronia from the Athenian acropolis, see esp. their publication in Linders 1972.
52 The inscriptions excavated at Brauron remain largely unpublished after several decades. The excavators discovered several inventories which they claim are duplicates of those on the Athenian acropolis: Linders 4, 72–3. However, if this were to prove not the case, the inventories on the acropolis could belong solely to its sanctuary of Artemis, and represent dedications made there. For the acropolis sanctuary: Travlos 1971: 124–6.
53 *IG* ii² 1514.8–9; cf. Linders 1972: 9 with n. 10.
54 *IG* ii² 1514.34–6.
55 *Anth. Pal.* 6.271 (third century BC).
56 Eur. *Iph. Taur.* 1462–7; see also *Anth. Pal.* 6.271; see van Straten 1981: 99; Cole 1988: 37–8.
57 Hippokrates *Peri Parthenion* (*Concerning Virgins*) viii.468.13–14 (Littré); for discussion, see King 1998: 75–80.
58 Hippokrates *Peri Parthenion* (*Concerning Virgins*) viii.468.13–14 (Littré). On the

treatment of women in the Hippocratic corpus, the various Hippocratic treatises concerning women, and hysteria, see Simon 1978: 238–68 (esp. 242–3); Lloyd-Jones 1983: 58–111; King 1983: 109–27, esp. 113–15; for the wandering womb, see esp. the passages from Hippokrates in Lefkowitz and Fantham 1982: 233–40; Pl. *Tim.* 90e–91e.

59 *IG* ii^2 1514.34–6, 1515.26–8, 1516.13–14, 1517.140.
60 *IG* ii^2 1514.7–19.
61 *IG* ii^2 1514.62 = 1518.79 (but not 78: Linders 45), 1516.52, 1522.9, 12, 28; perhaps 1516.34, 36.
62 Boxes: *IG* ii^2 1514.15–16: 'Pheidylla, a white woman's himation, in a plaision [oblong box]'; Parthenon: Harris 1995: 112; Theano: *IG* ii^2 1514.35–6; Nikolea: *IG* ii^2 1514.22–3, 1515.14–15, 1516.2; other examples of clothes on statues: Linders 11; racks: *AD* 22, 1967: 173–5, pl. 106.
63 Osborne 1985: 159.
64 *IG* ii^2 1514.15, 18–19, 62 (=1515.7–8, 10–11, 1516.37–8, 1518.79); Osborne and Byrne 1994: ii.447 (2), listing all three dedications under the same Phile.
65 See Chapter 8, pp. 260–4.
66 The text usually cited is T. Reinarch *REG* 12, 1899: 71–6; on its date: D. Knoepfler *Chiron* 7, 1977: 67–87; a new text by P. Roesch is presented and translated by Roller 1989: i.100–8 no. 87 (*LSCG* 72 has the obverse side only of this inscription, concerning amounts of money contributed by women to the construction costs of the sanctuary of Demeter and Kore, but not the reverse, with the dedications of clothes by women); see also Schachter 1981: i.162–3; L. Migeotte 1985: 'Souscriptions publiques en Béotie' in *La Béotie Antique*, Paris: 311–13; *SEG* 27.68.
67 Pingiatoglou 1981: 69–76.
68 Cole 1998: 38–9 (translating the inventory published by Günther 1988).
69 *IG* xii.9.124 (*SGDI* 5303; Friedländer 20; *LSAG* 86, 88 no. 20; Lazzarini 262; Ridgway 1987: 401 n. 11).
70 *SEG* 10.321; Pritchett 1940: 96–7; van Straten 1981: 75.
71 The inscription: *IG* ii^2 4596 (350–20 BC; *CEG* ii.775), photograph of inscription and dove-frieze: *ASAA* 45–6 (ns 29–30): 525, fig. 7 (see also 521–6); Simon 1983: fig. 7, pl. 15.1; Hurwit 1999: 41 fig. 33; reconstruction of the aedicula: *ASAA* 45–6 (ns 29–30) 524, figs 8–9; Kron 1996: 154, fig. 8; Travlos 1971: 2, 4, 8, fig. 5 (6); Wycherley 1957: 224–5 no. 731; 1966: 286, 289–90; Shapiro 1989: 118–19; dedication of sanctuary: *IG* ii^2 659 (*LSCG* 39).
72 *IG* ii^2 4573; *c.* 350 BC (*CEG* ii.770).
73 *CEG* ii.860 (*I. Knidos* 131; Kron 1996: 150–3).
74 Figure 1.3: *IG* i^3 987, 405–400 BC?, often dated 410–400 BC (NM 2576; *LSCG Suppl.* 17a); the relief was mounted on a pillar; translation: van Straten 1981: 90; see also Hausmann 1960: 63–5, fig. 33; Mitropoulou 1977: no. 65, fig. 103; Neumann 1979: 66–7, fig. 27a; van Straten 1981: 90, fig. 23; Ridgway 1981: 132–4; *CEG* ii.744 (=320b); Kron 1996: 166–8; *LIMC* i Acheloos 197, ii Apollon 968, Artemis 1182, iii Eileithyia 88, v Ilisos 2, v Kallirrhoe ii.2, vi Kephisos i.2, vi Hekate 106.
75 Thucydides 2.45.2.
76 *IG* ii^2 4547, *c.* 400 BC (*LSCG Suppl.* 17b); the correspondence between the two is probably not exact, and there are some differences of opinion in identifying the deities of the relief.
77 *LIMC* iii.1 p. 694.
78 Kron 1996: 168 unnecessarily suggests that Xenokrateia was an epikleros (heiress); but to dedicate the relief and sanctuary she must at least have been a woman of some financial means.

NOTES

79 Plato *Laws* 909e–910a.
80 *IG* iv² 1.121 iama 31. For women and Asklepios, see Dillon 1994; 1997: 189–92, 270 n. 26; King 1998: 99–113; for a translation of several of the cure inscriptions from Epidauros: Edelstein and Edelstein 1945: 221–38; cf. Cotter 1999: 17–19.
81 Van Straten 1981: 99 n. 173 with references.
82 Van Straten 1981: 99 n. 174 with references.
83 The mother of three shown with her husband worshipping Athena (*NM* 581, discussed elsewhere) has been taken to be pregnant (see Palagia 1995: 495), but there is no reason to assume this.
84 Berlin 685; unknown provenance, but surely Athens; 325 BC; marble; Blümel 1966: no. 100, pl. 125; Hausmann 1948: 177, no. 139 pl. 11; *LIMC* ii Asklepios 69; Kunze 1992: pl. 41; van Straten 1995: 283 R35 pl. 69.
85 Athenian Asklepieion, inventory v.130d; Aleshire 1989: 260, 287.
86 *IG* ii² 4960 (*SEG* 25.226), now known as the Telemachos monument, after the individual who brought Asklepios to Athens from Epidauros. For the Asklepieion, see Travlos 1971: 127–37; Aleshire 1989; 1991; Garland 1992: 116–35; Parker 1996: 177–80; cf. Vikela 1997: 189–92. This Asklepieion seems essentially to have been a private foundation and remained so for some decades.
87 Aleshire 1992: 85: 1,377 dedications 'either complete or in part' in the inventories; nearly 80 per cent of the entries are from the third century BC. Below, the inventories are referred to by Aleshire's numeration.
88 Aleshire 1989: 43, 45–6.
89 Aleshire 1992: 92
90 Inventory v.119d–e, Aleshire 1989: 259, 286.
91 Inventory v.100b; Aleshire 1989: 257, 284.
92 Girard 1881: 83.
93 Aleshire 1992: 87.
94 Aleshire 1992: 91.
95 Inventory v.110d, silver female genitalia weighing 12 drachmas and 2 obols dedicated by Stratonike; see also v.130g. Dedication of female genitalia by a man: v.100d: presumably in thanks for curing his wife (or perhaps daughter?).
96 Aleshire 1989: 41; breasts, e.g. v.103c, 106g.
97 *IG* vii.303; 202/199 BC (*LSCG* 70): the gold and silver offerings are to be melted down.
98 Phile: *IG* ii² 4407; Amynos: see below; Artemis Kolainis: *IG* ii² 4860 (cf. 5057); van Straten 1981: 116, 6.1; Zeus Hypsistos: Boston 08.34b; BM 804; see van Straten 117–18; Forsén 1993: 515–16 (nos 6, 19); Artemis Kalliste: *IG* ii² 4667; Travlos 1971: 301–2.
99 Roebuck 1951; van Straten 1981: 100, 123.
100 Athens *NM* 1821 (*IG* ii² 4575), fourth century BC. The sanctuary (some 1,500 metres west of Daphni) has several niches, carved into a rock face, which would have held various offerings. Several vulvae were discovered here: see Travlos 1988: 185, fig. 234 (including *NM* 1821); Paus. 1.37.7.
101 *NM* 3690; cf. van Straten 1981: 115, 4.2.
102 Van Straten 1981: 124, 128, 132.
103 *IG* iv² 1.121 iama 39.
104 Aratos: Paus. 2.10.3, 4.14.8; cf. Plut. *Arat.* 2.4, 53.1–7, esp. 5–6; Dillon 1997: 190.
105 *IG* iv² 1.122 iama 31; Dillon 1997: 189.
106 Dillon 1997: 189–92.

107 Eur. *Ion* 303.
108 *FD* iii.1.560 (end of the fourth century BC).
109 Eur. *Ion* 220–9.
110 See Chapter 8, p. 240.
111 Travlos 1971: 569–72; Forsén 1993; *IG* ii² 4783 (Forsén 515 no. 12), second century AD.
112 Travlos 1971: 76–8; Hedeia: *IG* ii² 4422 (fourth century BC).
113 Piraeus 405 (Hausmann 1948: pl. K1; Mitropoulou 1977: no. 126; van Straten 1981: 98; Krug 1984: pl. 7; Garland 1987: pl. 20; Vikela 1997: pl. 31.3). Traces of a dedicatory inscription are clear but no sense can be made of it; dimensions: 41 centimetres high; length: 78 centimetres, width: 9 centimetres.
114 *Figure 1.4*: NM Akropolis Museum 581; 490–480 BC (Berger 1970: fig. 129; Brouskari 1974: pl. 94; Mitropoulou 1977: no. 21, fig. 39; Ridgway 1977: 309, pl. 66 (after 480 BC); Neumann 1979: pl. 18a; *LIMC* ii Athena 587; van Straten 1981: fig. 18; 1995: pl. 79; Floren 1987: pl. 26.2; Boardman 1988: 169, no. 221; 1991a: fig. 258; Palagia 1995: pl. 114 (suggesting – implausibly – that this is a sacrifice connected with the Apatouria festival); Vikela 1997: pl. 20.1; Hurwit 1999: 58 fig. 420).
115 Brauron Museum 5 (*AD* 1967: 22, 195 pl. 104a; van Straten 1981: 104, fig. 47; ii Artemis 974).
116 Samos, Vathy Museum; Ornithe's statue is in Berlin, inv. 1739; 560–550 BC; length of base: 608 centimetres; marble; *LSAG* pp. 73, 329, 341 no. 6; *LSAG Suppl.* 471 (Blümel 1963: no 36, figs 102–5; Richter 1968: nos 67–8, figs 217–24; Freyer-Schauenburg 1974: nos 58–63; Boardman 1978: pls 91–3; 1984: 238, no. 317; Robertson 1975: 73–4, pl. 17b; 1981: 25, pl. 31).
117 Berlin 805 K111 (Rouse 1902: 23–4, fig. 5; *BCH* 82, 1958: 455–6, pl. 14; Blümel 1966: 100, no. 118, pl. 200; Larson 1995: 53 fig. 7; Preston 1997: 143 pl. 35).
118 Van Straten R105 and 109 respectively.
119 Berlin 807 K112; *c.* 340–333 BC? (Rouse 1902: 24; Blümel 1966: 67–8, no. 77, pl. 113; Higgins 1986: 52 pl. 44; Larson 1995: 52).
120 Thebes *Archaeological Museum* 62 (Schild-Xenidou 1972: 67, no. 77; Mitropoulou 1975: 19 no. 8; van Straten 1995: 301, R106, fig. 102; there are also examples from Lakonia, Epirus, and Pergamon: van Straten R104, 107, 111 respectively).
121 Berlin 731; *c.* 550 BC (Tod and Wace 1906: 102 fig. 1; Hausmann 1948: 25, pl. 11; Richter 1949: 87, pl. 153; 1970a: pl. 507; Blümel 1963: 22–5, pls 42–4; Boardman 1978: pl. 253; Floren 1987: 218, pl. 17.5; Larson 1995: 51 fig. 6; Spivey 1996: pl. 88).
122 Tod and Wace 1906: 103 fig. 3; see 108–10 for a still useful discussion of this type of relief, cf. Larson 1995: 50–2.
123 Lesbos, Mytilene Museum 3223 (Dentzer 1982: 322, 604 R304, pl. 91, fig. 554; Larson 1995: 50 fig. 5).
124 Lesbos, Mytilene Museum 3582 (Dentzer 1982: 378, 604 R306, pl. 91, fig. 556).
125 *NM* 3873 (Mitropoulou 1976: 99, no. 31; Dentzer 1982: 590, R195, pl. 76, fig. 453; van Straten 1995: 306, R126, pl. 103; Larson 1995: 45 fig. 1).
126 Istanbul, Archaeological Museum 407 (Pfuhl 1935: 35–6, pl. 18; Thönges-Stringaris 1965: 85, no. 123; Dentzer 1982: 577, R77, pl. 61 fig. 341; van Straten 1995: R149, pl. 107; a horse's head and snake are part of the scene).
127 Blümel 1966: pls 102, 115–16, 131–4; Mitropoulou 1976; Dentzer 1982; van Straten 1995: 303–26, Larson 1995: 48 fig. 4.

NOTES

128 Bern, private collection: van Straten 1995: 321, R188, fig. 105; a woman leads three men towards the divine group.

2 THE PUBLIC RELIGIOUS ROLES OF GIRLS AND ADOLESCENT WOMEN IN ATHENS

1 Ar. *Lys.* 641–6; eugeneis: schol. Ar. *Ach.* 242a; Hesych. sv kanephoroi. For kanephoroi at Athens: Jacoby *FGH* 3b.i, 275–6; Roccos 1995: 641–66; Lefkowitz 1996: 79–80; Athens and elsewhere: Schelp 1975; Brulé 1987: 287–324; van Straten 1995: 10–12, 14–24, 31–43; Roccos 1995: 651–4.
2 Thuc. 6.56.1 (cf. 1.20.2); [Arist.] *Ath. Pol.* 18.2; Arist. *Pol.* 1311a36–9; Ael. *VH* 11.8; Max. Tyr. 18.2d; cf. Pl. *Symp.* 182c. Harmodios and his lover Aristogeiton were of the aristocratic Gephyraioi genos (clan) (see Hdt. 5.57.1).
3 Akousilaos *FGH* 2 F30; in some versions she is abducted while gathering flowers along the Kephissos or Ilissos rivers, see also: Simonides F534 (*PMG*); Aeschyl. F 281 (*TrGF* iii); Philochoros *FGH* 328 F11; Pl. *Phaedr.* 229c–d; cf. Gantz 1993: 243.
4 Philochoros *FGH* 328 F8 (Harp. sv kanephoroi).
5 Philochoros *FGH* 328 F8. Baskets: singular: kanoun at Athens, elsewhere, kaneon; plural: kana.
6 Ar. *Peace* 948.
7 Scheffer 1992: 118, table 1 lists seven examples on archaic Athenian vases.
8 Roccos 1995: 642 with examples at n. 3.
9 Ar. *Birds* 1550–2.
10 Ar. *Ekkles.* 730–4.
11 Ar. *Ach.* 242.
12 Hermippos *PCG* v F25. Hermippos' description refers specifically to how the powdered effect was obtained: the kanephoros in fact was 'daubed with white flour'. The kanephoros should be white-faced, her complexion unsullied by the sun, reflecting an aristocratic elitism.
13 In his *Encheirogastores* ('The Hand-belly-fillers'): Nikophon *PCG* vii F7.
14 See below p.45.
15 Anaxandrides *Kanephoros* (*PCG* ii F22); Men. *Kanephoros* F218–22 (Koerte), note also the mention of kanephoros in his *Epitrepontes* (*Arbitrators*) 438–40.
16 Private collection: 560–550 BC (Neumann 1979: 27 pl. 13 a–b; Burkert 1983: fig. 1; Simon 1983: 63, pls 16.2, 17.2; 1985: 193 pl. 176; *LIMC* ii Athena 574; Shapiro 1989: pl. 9a–b; Bérard 1989: 108 fig. 152; Boardman 1994: 136–7 no. 139; van Straten 1995: fig. 2; Berger and Gisler-Huwiler 1996, *Tafelband*: 125).
17 Ferrara, Spina Museum 44894 T57C VP; overall height 77 centimetres; 430 BC; rf volute–krater attributed to the Kleophon Painter; *ARV* 1143.1; *Add.* 334 (Sparkes 1975: 131 pl. 15b; Schelp 1975: 88 K59; Parke 1977: fig. 11; Simon 1983: 73, pl. 23.1; *LIMC* ii Apollon 303; Robertson 1992: 224 fig. 231; Roccos 1995: 649 fig. 3; van Straten 1995: 20–1, 207 V78, fig. 13; Sparkes 1996: fig. 1.13).
18 *Figure 2.1*: Toledo 1972.55 (*CVA* Toledo 1.34, pl. 53; previously unpublished; Rasmussen and Spivey 1991: 29 fig. 8; Roccos 1995: 647 fig. 2; Reeder 1995: 186 fig. 38; Kunisch 1997: 179, pl. 64; Keuls 1997: 393 fig. 35).
19 Panathenaia: *IG* ii² 3477 (second century BC); Epidauria: 3457 (fourth or third century BC), 3554 (first century BC); Dionysia: 3489 (first century BC); Mother of the Gods: 3489 (first century BC); Sarapis: 3498 (first century AD); Dionysos Lyaios: 3567 (first or second century AD); Isis and Sarapis: 3565 (first/second century AD); Eleusinia: 3554 (first century BC); Pythais: 3477 (second century

BC). See Geagan 1994: 167. *IG* ii² 668.31–3 of the early third century BC praises the father of a kanephoros at the Dionysia.
20 E.g.: *IG* ii² 3477, 3489, 3554.
21 Geagan 1994: 169; the two statues: *IG* ii² 3477; *Hesperia* 1983: 155–8, nos 1–2. The Pythais to Delphi, see esp.: *IG* ii² 2336; Tracy 1982.
22 Roccos 1995: passim, esp. 650, 654–66.
23 Ferrara, Spina Museum 44894 T57C; references above.
24 *Figure 2.2*: Copenhagen, National Museum 10780; Lindos (Rhodes); mid-fourth century BC (Blinkenberg 1931: 706–7, no. 3016; Higgins 1967: 62 pl. 25b; Schelp 1975: 89 K74 pl. 3.1; Roccos 1995: 649–50 fig. 4; cf. Blinkenberg 706–7, nos 3014–15; pl. 140).
25 *IG* ii² 334.11–16 (335/4); *IG* ii² 334 and a new fragment of this decree are now Woodhead 1997: 75 (line 40), pp. 114–16; see for *IG* ii² 334, Schwenk 1985: 81–94; cf. Herington 1955: 31–2; 'for the kanephoroi' in line 15 is heavily restored.
26 Paus. 1.29.16; Plut. *Mor.* 852b; cf. *IG* ii² 457 (307/6; decree praising Lykourgos but not mentioning kanephoroi); Mitchell 1973: 197; note too *IG* ii² 333b.15, c.10, for which see: Linders 1972: 74–5; Schwenk 1985: 108–26.
27 For these weights, and references to the inscriptions, see Aleshire 1989: 48 with n. 3, see also 45, 242, 292.
28 *IG* ii² 3457, c. 300 BC; for kanephoroi at the Asklepieion, see Aleshire 1989: 90–2, with references.
29 Philadelphia University Museum MS 552 (Jucker 1963: 53 pl. 23.2; Callipolitis-Feytmans 1970: 47–9, 48 no. 1; Schelp 1975: 87 K 24; *LIMC* i Alkinoos i.3; iv Demeter 469; vi Moirai 10; Amyx 1988: 311–12 A2, 494–5, 654; Roccos 1995: 650 fig. 5, 651; van Straten 1995: 22–3, 254 V329).
30 Oslo 6909 (Amyx 1988: 658.2; van Straten 1995: 23, 214 V117).
31 BM B80 (*CVA* London 2, pl. 7, 4b; *JHS* 49, 1929: 169; *JHS* 87, 1967: 121, pl. 17a; Schelp 1975: 87 K26; *BCH* 99, 1975: 432 no. 1; *LIMC* ii Athena 586; Simon 1969: 193 pl. 176; 1983: pls 16.2, 17.2; Scheffer 1992: 127–30, figs 7–8; van Straten 1995: 21–2, 212–13 V107, fig. 14; Roccos 1995: 651 fig. 7).
32 For plates of the Parthenon, see the standard Robertson and Frantz 1975, plates at East V; but also now, Berger and Gisler-Huwiler 1996 (a reconstruction of the frieze); see also Brommer 1977; 1979; Jenkins 1994; for the east frieze, see also Boardman 1994: 137–8 no. 140.
33 Individual marble slabs making up the frieze, upon which varying numbers of figures appear, are numbered with Roman numerals, by frieze. The numbering for the figures on the east frieze is standard.
34 *Figure 2.3*: east frieze (slab II); figures §§4–6; height: 105 centimetres; length: 79 centimetres; Acropolis Museum, Athens inv. 877.
35 *Figure 2.4*: east frieze (slab III); figures §§7–19; height: 105 centimetres; length: 308 centimetres; BM 109.161.
36 See Boardman 1977: 40–1 for a summary of views; cf. Robertson and Frantz 1975, commentary to east frieze; Jenkins 1994: 77; Berger and Gisler-Huwiler, *Text*: 152. The objects are not quite visible in the photographs. There is clearly a long, thin, cone-shaped object between §12 and §13; whether §15 is carrying a similar one could be debated, despite the position of her hand. Both objects are clear in Stuart's drawing (Berger and Gisler-Huwiler, *Tafelband* 143).
37 *ARV* 556.104; cf. *ARV* 307.17; 553.34.
38 Harris 1995: 114.
39 *Figure 2.5*: east frieze (slab V); figures §§31–35; height: 105 centimetres; length of slab V: 442 centimetres; length of illustrated section: 190 centimetres; BM 115.161.

NOTES

40 East frieze, slab V, figure nos 31–2, and 33 (third woman): Robertson and Frantz 1975: plates at East v; Berger and Gisler-Huwiler 1996, *Tafelband*: 128, 133; in *Textband*, they collect the testimonia for kanephoroi, diphrophoroi and skiadephoroi: 194–5, nos 178–88.
41 Boardman 1977: 41; Jenkins 1994: 79. The projection from the small object is clear, but not a paw.
42 *Pace* Younger 1997: 120, that they 'carry stools is not in doubt'; it is very much in doubt. The tendency in discussions to have the girls as diphrophoroi *and* arrephoroi *simultaneously* does not help the issue.
43 For diphroi, see Richter 1966: 38–52, pls 198–269; more generally: Robsjohn-Gibbings and Pullin 1963: 67–95; Siphnian treasury: Richter pl. 213.
44 Wesenberg 1995, with detailed photographs from several angles, line drawings, and the evidence of terracotta torches, conclusively shows that the girls are not carrying stools, but baskets on their heads, with §32 clearly having a torch in her hand.
45 See Berger and Gisler-Huwiler 1996: *Textband* 157–8.
46 Brommer 1977: *Text* 264 has a useful table summarising the views of several scholars on the identity of these five figures. I cannot accept Younger 1997: 138 that the woman priest of Athena (Figure 33) is merely some sort of 'filler' in the frieze; his arguments for §35 being a boy are not sound.
47 The figure *looks* like a male in Stuart's 1787 drawing, but his text describes it as a girl, but the stone will not have been in much better condition then than it is now (Stuart and Revett 1787: ii.12, pl. xxiii; and also in Berger and Gisler-Huwiler 1996: *Tafelband* 144).
48 Other examples of bare-buttocked children are: (1) NY 27.45; (2) Thebes Museum; Lokris, Boeotian grave-stele, *c.* 400 BC; Jenkins 1994: 36, fig. 18; (3) *NM* 126; Robertson 1975: 2 pl. 104a; (4) Boston 13.195 appears not to have entered the discussion: *ARV* 35.1; *Add.* 158 (Schelp 1975: 87; Roccos 1995: 642 fig. 1); (5) the so-called Giustiniani Stele: Berlin 1482 K19 (Blümel 1966: no. 2, pls 2, 4, 9; Boardman 1967: pl. 185b, 1994: 16 fig. 14; Preston 1997: 95 pl. 21).
49 Only late evidence suggests that there was a boy in charge of the sacred snake on the acropolis: Brommer 1977: 269; Simon 1983: 67.
50 Paus. 1.18.2; Apollod. 3.187–90; Philochoros *FGH* 328 F10, 105, 183; but Amelesagoras *FGH* 330 F1 has a version that it was Herse who was the obedient one; the various sources have different variants of the myth; cf. Eur. *Ion* 267–74, 492–502. For the three sisters, see Brulé 1987: 28–45; Kearns 1989: 139–40, 161–2, 192–3; Larson 1995: 39–41. For a single woman priest of Aglauros and Pandrosos (who also served Ge Kourotrophos), see the Salaminioi decree (363/2 BC): Ferguson 1938: 1–9, no. 1, lines 45–6; Garland 1984: 86–7; Kearns 1989: 139–40; Larson 1995: 169 n. 62.
51 Philochoros *FGH* 328 F10.
52 For the (unlikely) interpretation that the third girl is a daughter of Erechtheus, voluntarily sacrificed so that he could win the battle against an attack by Eumolpos (the Thracian king), receiving her death shroud, see Connelly 1993.
53 *Figure 2.6*: east frieze (slab VII); figures §§49–56; height: 105 centimetres; length: 207 centimetres; Louvre Ma 738.
54 The suggestion seems to go back to Michaelis 1871: 259; accepted by Rotroff 1977: 380; Schelp 1975: 55–6; Simon 1983: 60; Roccos 1995; cf. Brommer 1977: 266–7.
55 *Figure 2.7*: east frieze (slab VIII); figures §§57–61; height: 105 centimetres; length: 160 centimetres; BM 124.161.
56 Toledo 72.55 (*CVA* Toledo 1.34; by Makron), full references above. Note also the incense-burner on the Ludovisi Throne, *c.* 460 BC, Figure 6.3.

57 Liknophoros: Callim. *Demeter* 126; Lokrian phialephoros: Diod. 27.4.2; Livy 29.18; Polyb. 12.5.9–11; Walbank 1967: ii.336; *Lokrides*: Anaxandrides *PCG* ii F27; Poseidippos *PCG* vii F15; *Phialephoros*: Anaxandrides *PCG* ii F52.
58 *Figure 2.8*. Photographs of the Erechtheion caryatids are common; see recently, Rhodes 1995: 35 fig. 20, 37 fig. 21; Spivey 1997: fig. 164; Hurwit 1999: 201 fig. 173, and the accompanying discussions.
59 Erechtheion korai caryatids, marble, 420–415 BC; height: 231 centimetres; there are numerous discussions and illustrations of these caryatids, of which a few of the more useful follow: Boardman 1967: pl. 235; 1994: 10–11, pl. 7; Robertson 1975: 115b; *Ant. Pl.* 11, pp. 32–3, pl. 1; *Ant. Pl.* 16, p. 52+ figs 10–19, pls 1–56; Ridgway 1981: 105–8, pls 82–3. For caryatids, cf. duBois 1988: 97–106. Photographs of Erechtheion: Rhodes 1995: 35 fig. 20, 37 fig. 21; Hurwit 1999: 201 fig. 173. Korai a–b, d–f are in Athens, Acropolis Museum, to which they were removed in 1979; kore c is in the British Museum.
60 For a back view of an Erechtheion caryatid, showing the hair, see Rhodes 1995: 142 fig. 72.
61 *Figure 2.9*: kore caryatid c: BM 407; Ridgway 1981: pl. 83; Richter 1987: fig. 178; Boardman 1996: 153 fig. 142.
62 *Ant. Pl.* 13 p. 24+ figs 1–20, p. 52+ pls 1–5; phialai fragments: p. 24+ figs 7–8; reconstruction of caryatids: p. 52+ pls 1–2; Vermeule 1977: fig. 3; Hurwit 1999: 268 fig. 216.
63 *Figure 2.10*: Hadrian's Villa no. 2233. Hadrian's Villa nos 2233 and 2238 hold a phiale in their right hands and have a basket on their heads, while the korai Hadrian's Villa no. 2236 and 2239 have damaged hands and a basket on their heads; *c*. AD 125. Plates of all four at: *Ant. Pl.* 13 p. 24+ figs 23–44, p. 52+ pls 1–32; for the phialai held by 2233 and 2238, see esp. p. 24+ figs 25–6, p. 52+ pls 19–21, 26, 28; see also *Ant. Pl.* 16 p. 52 figs 1–9; Hanfmann 1967: pl. 148; Vermeule 1977: fig. 4; Bieber 1977: pl. 8 figs 43–6; Richter 1987: fig. 179; Kleiner 1992: 247 fig. 214 (2233). For photographs of the four reconstructed by the pool: *Ant. Pl.* 13, p. 24+ figs 23–34; Vermeule fig. 63.
64 Vatican Kore (Braccio Nuovo): *Ant. Pl.* 13, p. 52+ pls 42–5 (no inventory number); Bieber 1977: pl. 8 figs 41–2.
65 Florence, Museo Archeologico (no inv. no. given) *AK* 13, p. 52+ pls 38–41.
66 Actual caryatids as preserved: *FD* iv.2: 57–71 fig. 30, pls 4–5; Lawrence 1972: pl. 16a; Boardman 1991a: fig. 210; *BCH* 107, 1981: 860 fig. 9; Richter 1987: fig. 94; Boardman 1988: 105–6, no. 124; Picard 1991: 39–42, figs 6–7; Croissant 1983: 71–82; Bommelaer 1991: 123–6; reconstruction of caryatid porch: *FD* iv.2, fig. 33; *BCH* 77, 1953: 360–4; Boardman 1967: 28 fig. 27; 1988: 100, fig. 117a; 1993: 44 fig. 28; Lawrence and Tomlinson 1983: 169 fig. 132; *BCH* 109, 1985: 156 fig. 18; Picard 1991: 47 fig. 11; Osborne 1998: fig. 60; Fullerton 2000: 89 pl. 61; height of kalathos: 25.5 centimetres; for the treasury: Hdt. 3.57; Paus. 10.11.2.
67 Caryatids: *FD* iv.2: 1–18, figs 1–4, pls 1–2; *BCH* 1953, 77: 346–53; Boardman 1991a: fig. 209; Croissant 1983: 71–82; Picard 1991: 39–40, figs 5, 6a–b ('excnidienne'); height of kalathos: 30.5 centimetres; Bommelaer 1991: 141–3.
68 Delphi Museum inv. 7723; height of caryatid and stand: 26 centimetres; female figure: 16 centimetres; *c*. 470 BC (Robertson 1981: pl. 80; Walter 1985: 34 fig. 28; Boardman 1994: 47 fig. 52).
69 *Figure 2.11*: Berlin SK 1747 (Blümel 1963: 41–2, no. 33, pls 90–3; Richter 1968: no. 6, pls 38–40; Boardman 1978: 25–6, pls 74–5; 1996 73 fig. 60; Sturgeon 1987: pl. 81c–e; Kunze 1992: 87 no. 11). For a catalogue of Greek perirrhanteria, see Sturgeon 18–19 (possibly add Metaponto 292623 (Carratelli

NOTES

1996: 368, 677 pl. 81.1), but this might be an incense stand); and Richter 1968: nos 7, 8, 9, 11. Athens, Acropolis Museum 592: 575–500 BC; Naxian marble; six female figures lean inwards on a circular base; nothing above the neck line of one of the female figures survives (Raubitschek 403 no. 375; Sturgeon 19 no. 19; Hurwit 1999: 104 fig. 73).

70 Isthmia: Isthmian Museum IS 3, 161–5, 220, 270; largely restored; heights of the four korai: approximately 52.5 centimetres; height of perirrhanterion, without base: 126 centimetres; grey marble; 660–650 BC; possibly carved by Samian artists; traces of paint survive (Richter 1968: no. 5; Sturgeon 1987: 14–61 (the definitive discussion), pls 1–22; Boardman 1999: 73 fig. 62).

71 For the material in this paragraph, see Sturgeon 1987: 17–28.

72 Such as Ker. 141, 145, 146 (Kübler 1970: nos 46–8, pls 36–7, 46; Sturgeon 1987: pl. 82d).

73 'Balsam-containers': Carratelli 1996: 683 pls 95.xiv–xvi; Hellenkemper 1998: 123 pl. 53; thymiateria: Carratelli 720 pl. 259.i–iii; height: 14 to 22 centimetres; cf. 729 pl. 295.vii; Hellenkemper 1998: 231 pl. 173.

74 Ker. 149 (Kübler 1970: no 49, pls 39–40).

75 Porph. *Abst.* 2.30.1; cf. Ael. *VH* 8.3; for the festival, on Skirophorion 14, see Parke 1977: 162–7; Burkert 1983: 136–43; Simon 1985: 8–12. This was the rite of the bull-slaying – bouphonia – held for Zeus of the City. This annual slaying of the ox was seen as a murder, of which each of the participants was accused; the young women water-carriers, accused, passed the blame on to those who killed the ox, who in turn blamed the axe and knife. The north frieze of the Parthenon has four men (§§16–19) with large water jars; the best explanation for their presence, rather than young women, is the great number of sacrifices to be made and the need for a quantity of water.

76 Ar. *Peace* 956–61; cf. *Od.* 3.445; Thuc. 4.97.3; Dem. 20.158.

77 Ar. *Birds* 850, *Lys.* 1129.

78 Eur. *Iph. Taur.* 617–24.

79 Hesych. sv lykiades korai. See Travlos 1971: 345–7 for the Lykeion.

80 Ker. P1131 (Clairmont 1993: i.334, cf. no. i.157 showing a youth carrying a hydria on his shoulder, and another youth carrying a lagynos (flask), each on either side of a priest holding a kantharos; the priest is the deceased, depicted with his two attendants).

81 Museo Nazionale Romano; 470–460 BC; 43 centimetres high; Paribeni 1953: pl. 87.

82 One is in the Eleusis Museum (Mylonas 1961: 159 pl. 56; Kerényi 1967: 77 a–c; Robertson 1975, pl. 180c), the other at Cambridge, Fitzwilliam Museum inv. GR.i.1865 (Budde and Nicholls 1964: 46–9 no. 81, pl. 25.81; Spivey 1996: pl. 146).

83 Deubner 1932: pl. 34.2; Parke 1977: pl. 31; Simon 1983: pl. 3.

84 Ar. *Birds* 826–7.

85 For the arrephoroi, see Deubner 1932: 9–17; Burkert 1966a; Parke 1977: 140–3; Burkert 1983: 150–4; 1985: 228–9; Robertson 1983a: 241–88; Simon 1983: 39–46; cf. Larson 1995: 39–41.

86 Ar. *Lys.* 641.

87 Harp. (citing Deinarchos), EM, Suid. sv arre(ne)phorein; Suid., *EM*, sv Chalkeia; cf. *CAF* i, F263; schol. Eur. *Hek.* 467 (cf. schol. to 468–9) has the woman priest of Athena setting up the warp. Paus. 1.27.3 has two arrephoroi taking part in the nocturnal rite, without mentioning that there were four arrephoroi in total; what the other two did is unclear, but there is no reason to doubt that there were four, unless Pausanias is taken strictly literally.

88 Suid., EM sv Chalkeia.
89 Suid. sv epiopsato.
90 Jenkins 1994: 28 pl. 15; he suggests that the female is one of the arrephoroi, but she could be one of the ergastinai.
91 Lys. 21.5. There was also a play by Menander, *Arrephoros* or *Auletris*, F59–67 (Koerte).
92 Paus. 1.27.3 (near Athena Polias' temple); Plut. *Mor.* 839c (playground).
93 Travlos 1971: 70–1 for the arrephoroi building; for the Mycenaean well, see 73–5, esp. the line drawing of the fissure and well, 75 fig. 96.
94 *IG* ii^2 3461, 3466, 3470, 3471, 3472, 3473, 3488, 3496, 3497, 3515, 3528, 3554, 3555, 3556, 3634, restored as such: 3465, 3482, 3516 (late third century BC to second century AD); dedicated to Athena, but two (*IG* ii^2 3472, restored: 3515) dedicated to Athena and Pandrosos. See Geagan 1994: 168. The vase NY 1931.33.10 shows several women weaving, with two smaller female figures at the loom; but the suggestion that these are arrephoroi is untenable: they have clearly started work, and their size, smaller than the other women, does not represent a younger age but their servile status.
95 *IG* ii^2 1034 (98/7 BC; *SIG*^{3} 718).
96 *IG* ii^2 1034 (98/7 BC); 1036 (78/7 BC).
97 Hesych. sv ergastinai; Parke 1977: 38–9; Lefkowitz 1996: 79–80.
98 *EM* sv arrephoroi gives the month as Skirophorion; Robertson 1983a: 281; Larson 1995: 39; the precise date is unknown.
99 Paus. 1.27.3; schol. Ar. *Lys.* 641: they bore the secret things in kistai.
100 Paus. 1.19.2; see Travlos 1971: 291, fig. 379 no. 190.
101 Broneer 1932: 31–55, esp. 50–5 on the arrephoroi, followed by most scholars (e.g., Travlos 1971: 228); the accounts of Burkert 1983: 151; Simon 1983: 40–1, took the sanctuary of Eros and Aphrodite to be the one referred to by Pausanias as the destination of the arrephoroi.
102 Dontas 1983: 48–63, esp. 57–8 on arrephoroi.
103 For sources for the 'birth' of Erichthonios, his care by the three daughters of Kekrops, and vases depicting the basket: see Kearns 1989: 161, 192; Eur. *Ion* 268–74; 271 actually refers to the fact that Athena's entrusting of the infant to the three sisters is often depicted (see Brommer 1973: 258, 262–4). Basel BS 404 (*LIMC* i Aglauros, Herse, Pandrosos 19; Oakley 1990: pl. 84) shows Aglauros with hands raised in horror as a snake rears from a dropped basket at Athena's feet (see also *LIMC* iv Erechtheus 30). The wool thrown on the earth: Apollod. 3.188; Harp. sv autochthones.
104 Munich 2413 (J.345); rf stamnos, Painter of Munich 2413, 460 BC; *ARV* 495.1, 1656; *Para.* 380; *Add.* 250 (Alfieri 1962: 358, pls 182–3). This side of the vase is frequently illustrated: Simon 1969: 195 fig. 178; 1976: pls 175–7; Bérard 1974: pl. 5; Boardman 1975: fig. 350; Stumpfe 1978: 64 fig. 9; Keuls 1993: 43 fig. 21; Walter 1985: 44 fig. 39; Loraux 1993: pl. 4. Other examples: *ARV* 580.2; 585.35; 1268.2.
105 Schol. Luc. *Dial. Het.* 2.1 (Rabe 1906: 275–6); Robertson 1983: 255–65, esp. 255–6.
106 *Figure 2.12*: Boston 98.668; 450 BC; bronze (Lippold 1950: 170 fig. 7; Neugebauer 1951: 37; Comstock and Vermeule 1971: 54–5 no. 55: 'said to have been found at Corinth' (54); the piece is probably of Peloponnesian workmanship, perhaps from Argos or Kleonai).
107 *Figure 2.13*: Rome, Museo Nazionale Romano 596; 'Anzio Girl' (southern Italy), early Roman imperial, probably but not necessarily a copy of a Greek bronze original of the first half of the third century BC; Pliny *NH* 34.80

NOTES

(Lippold 1950: 332 pl. 119.3; Boardman 1967: pl. 284; Charbonneux 1970: 257–8, pl. 278–80; Richter 1970a: fig. 353; Robertson 1975: pl. 150d; 1981: pl. 232; Bieber 1981: figs 97–100; Havelock 1981: pl. 114; Rühfel 1984: 238 pl. 101; Pollitt 1986: 56 pl. 49, rejecting the equating of the Anzio Girl with the *Epithyousa*; Ridgway 1990: pls 111a–c; Smith 1991: pl. 110; Carratelli 1996: 78).

108 Ar. *Lys.* 643, with schol.; Hesych. sv aletrides.
109 Hesych. sv agretai; Sherwin-White 1978: 299. The term perhaps simply stems from the verb *agreo*: choose.
110 *LSCG* 156b.6–7 (third century BC); Sherwin-White 299 refers to an unpublished inscription apparently referring to a choros of girls, called Daliades, for Apollo Dalios on Kos.
111 *LSCG* Suppl. 96; third century BC; Hesych. sv anthesteriadas.
112 Eur. *Hel.* 1312–14; cf. *Hom. Hymn Dem.* 5–18, 417–33.
113 Kore: Poll. 1.37; Hera: Poll. 4.78; Hera Antheia had a temple in Argos: Paus. 2.22.1.
114 Ar. *Peace* 948.
115 *Figure 2.14*: BM E284; rf amphora; Nausicaa Painter; 450–425 BC (*CVA* BM 3, pl. 17.3a, 3b; *ARV* 1107.7; *Para.* 452; *Add.* 330; Pfuhl 1923: fig. 519; Webster 1972: 133; Kron 1976: 239–41, pl. 32.2; van Straten 1995: 208 V87).
116 BM F66; Apulian rf bell-krater, 375–340 BC (*RVAp* i, p. 195 no. 18; van Straten 1995: V384, fig. 43).
117 Lucerne Market (A.A.); 500–450 BC, by the Bowdoin Workshop; *ARV* 683.127 ter (interpreting this scene as Theseus and the bull); *Add.* 279; Kurtz 1975: pl. 14.6.
118 Rhodes 1995: 122 fig. 64; Hurwit 1999: 215 no. 187; Fullerton 2000: 106 pl. 76.
119 *ARV* 1036.5 (Munich 2412; 440–430 BC). The large tripod in the scene could indicate that the vase refers to a victory (possibly in a dithyrambic contest) for which a tripod was the prize.
120 Aen. 31.24.
121 Strabo 13.1.40. Other sources referring to an annual dispatch of maidens: Ael. F50a; Serv. 1.41; schol. Lykoph. 1141 (Timaios *FGH* 566 F146b).
122 Apollod. 6.22; Lykoph. 1168–71, schol. 1168–71 (Scheer p. 339).
123 Other sources provide further details: in addition to Aen. 31.24, see Polyb. 12.5.6–9 (citing Timaios *FGH* 566 F12); schol. Lykoph. 1155 (partly Timaios *FGH* 566 F146a); see also Scheer 1958: 2.335–7; Tzetzes Lykoph. 1141 (Timaios *FGH* 566 F146b, citing also Callim. F35 Pfeiffer); Strabo 13.1.40; Plut. *Mor.* 557d; Lykoph. 1141–73; Ael. *VH* F50; Apollod. 6.20–2; Iambl. *Vita Pyth.* 8.42; Serv. 1.41 (citing Aeneas Placidus); schol. *Il.* 13.66; Huxley 1966; Walbank 1967: ii.335; Sourvinou-Inwood 1974: 186–98; Fontenrose 1978: 131–7; Vidal-Naquet 1986: 189–204; Whitehead 1990: 188–9; Hughes 1991: 166–84. Agrionia: Chapter 5, pp. 152–3.
124 Parke and Wormell 1956: R332; Fontenrose 1978: L157.
125 Strabo 13.1.40–1.
126 Ael. *VH* F50d–g; Parke and Wormell 1956: R331; Fontenrose 1978: Q232 ('not genuine').
127 Antigonos the One-Eyed (306–301 BC), Antigonos Gonatas (276–239 BC), and Antigonos Doson (227–221 BC) are all candidates. The date of the inscription favours Gonatas, but Vidal-Naquet 1986: 194, points out that One-Eyed controlled the Troad and that this could explain his involvement.
128 Inscription: *IG* ix², 1 fasc. 3, no. 706 (Schwyzer no. 366; Buck no. 60; see A. Wilhelm 1911, *JOAI* 14: 163–5; W. Leaf 1914–16, *ABSA* 21: 148–54;

Fontenrose 1978: 134–5; Vidal-Naquet 1986: 190). For Fontenrose 1978: 135, cf. Vidal-Naquet 1986: 201 n. 25.
129 Lykoph. 1155–9.
130 Plut. *Mor.* 557d; Apollod. 6.21; schol. Lykoph. 1141 (Scheer p. 336).
131 Apollod. 6.22; schol. Lykoph. 1141 (Scheer p. 336).
132 Apollod. 6.22; Tzetzes on Lykoph. 1141 (Timaios *FGH* 566 F146b); schol. Lykoph. 1141 (Scheer p. 336); cf. Lykoph. 1153 (1000 years).
133 Aelian F50b; Lykoph. 1155–9.
134 Paestum 133156, 510–500 BC; height: 85 centimetres, length: 71.6 centimetres; sandstone: Carratelli 1996: 390, 674 pl. 69; Hellenkemper 1998: 113, pl. 37; this or one of the others are illustrated in: Richter 1949: fig. 291; Richter 1970: pl. 81; 1970a: fig. 439; 1987: 82 figs 110–11; Schoder 1960: pl. 21; von Matt 1962: 39–42; Langlotz 1963: pls 9, 30–1, pl. ii; Becattti 1967: 109 pl. 95; Boardman 1984: 284–6 no. 369; 1995, fig. 163.1; Floren 1987: pl. 38.5; Pedley 1990: 75 pl. 44. Tarquinia RC 4194, *c.* 550 BC (a cup), does show a ring of Nereids (the daughters of Nereus) dancing around a circular composition of Herakles wrestling with Triton (Simon 1976: 81, pl. 21; Schefold 1992: 139, fig. 165; *LIMC* vi Nereides 264). The earlier set of metopes from the previous temple (*c.* 530 BC) includes one with a pair of dancing girls, one of whom holds a phiale, pointing to a further ritual role once the dance is done (Boardman 1995: fig. 162.1). Alkman: see Chapter 7, p. 214.
135 Selinounte: 525–500 BC (Langlotz pl. 9; Robertson 1975: pl. 33b; Stewart 1990: pl. 209); Reggio 786c: 550–525 BC, terracotta (Langlotz 1963: ii; Robertson 1975: pl. 33a; 1981: pl. 25; Boardman 1995: fig. 165; Carratelli 1996: 672 pl. 54; Spivey 1996: pl. 42).
136 Geometric vases from Argos show women performing dances: Waldstein 1905: i.114.17; Foley 1988: 66; Calame 1997: 119–20.
137 Eur. *Elekt.* 173–4; Dion. Halik. 1.21.2.
138 Branchidai: Richter 1970a: fig. 505; Clazomenai: *CVA* BM 8: pl. 13.3–4; Lehmann and Spittle 1982: 227 fig. 196; cf. Boardman 1998, fig. 342.
139 Eur. *Herakl.* 781–3; Calame 1997: 130–1.
140 Boston 65.908; Lehmann and Spittle 1982: pl. 208; Cartledge 1998: 331. Compare Boston 14909, the lid of a bf pyxis for a similar scene but with more lively dancers (Lehmann and Spittle 1982: pl. 209); an Athenian bf lekythos has three groups of three dancing women, with two male seated musicians (NY 56.11.1).
141 One example: Berlin, East 1456 (K184), late fifth or early fourth century BC, 95 centimetres; Robertson 1975, 130c; line drawings of six and discussion at M.A. Tiverios 1981, *AE*: 25–37, pls 4b, 5a. Kalathiskos dance: Poll. 4.105; Athen. 629f; Kallimachos' Spartan dancers: Pliny *NH* 34.19.92.
142 Oakley and Sinos 1993: 24–5, who give the following references; young men dance as the bride is led to her home: *Il.* 18.494; women and girls: Eur. *Tro.* 328, and Men. *Dysk.* 950–3; rf lebes gamikos, 470 BC, *ARV* 261.19: Oakley and Sinos, figs 54–8 (Beazley *ARV* suggested, however, that the main figure is Apollo, as opposed to a bride); bf lekythos: NY 56.11.1; Berard 1989: fig. 137; Oakley and Sinos, fig. 59.
143 Samothrace, the propylon (gateway) of the Hall of the Choral Dancers; *c.* 330 BC; the dancers are about 25 centimetres high: Lehmann and Spittle 1982: 6–261, esp. 173–8, 201–2 (suggesting that the two lines of dancers converged on a central panel which, like the Parthenon frieze, might have had divine subjects), plates xxiii–xxv; Fullerton 2000: 133 pl. 97. For the Samothracian Mysteries, see Cole 1984a; Dillon 1997: 71–2.

NOTES

144 Dillon 1997: 104, 111.
145 Jeanmaire 1939: 300 argues for an initiatory character for the rite.
146 Eur. *Med.* 1378–83; Paus. 2.3.11; schol. Eur. *Med.* 264, 1382; Philostr. *Heroikos* 53.4 (laments); Diod. 4.54.7, 55.1; Apollod. 1.145; Ael. *VH* 5.21; Burkert 1966: 118–19; 1983: 153; Dunn 1994; Johnston 1997.
147 Delos: Callim. *Delos* 306–13; Dikaiarchos F85; Plut. *Thes.* 21; Paus. 9.40.3–4; Poll. 4.101; Knossos: *Il.* 18.590 with schol. AB; Bruneau 1970: 331–3, 341; Calame 1990: 158–60.
148 Pl. *Phaed.* 58a–b; Callim. *Delos* 314–15; Thuc. 3.104; Dillon 1997: 124–8; cf. Paus. 2.7.7, with Calame 1997: 111.
149 For this rite, see Deubner 1932: 118–21; Hani 1978; Burkert 1983: 241–3; examples collected by Burkert 1983: 241. Cf. Plut. *Mor.* 249b–d: the parthenoi of Miletos at some stage were afflicted with a hanging epidemic which was terminated by a decree that any parthenos hanging herself was to have her body carried naked through the market-place on its way to burial. The fear of such shame ended the epidemic.
150 Berlin 2394, rf hydria, Washing Painter; *ARV* 1131.172, *Add.* 333 (Robertson 1975: 85d; Kerényi 1976: pl. 94).
151 *Figure 2.15*: NY 75.2.11; rf oinochoe, *c.* 420–410 BC; Meidias Painter; *ARV* 1313.11 ('women perfuming clothes'); *Para.* 477; *Add.* 362 (Richter and Hall 1936: pl. 158; Hoorn 1951: 12; Simon 1963: pl. 6.3; 1969: 238, fig. 224; Richter 1970a: fig. 326; Kerényi 1976: pl. 96 ('festive preparations of a distinguished woman'); Rühfel 1984: 129, fig. 69; Burn 1987: pl. 52b; Boardman 1989: fig. 288).
152 Callim. F178.1–4 (Pfeiffer); also the sources at Burkert 1983: 241–2 nn. 11–13. For the Aoira, see Deubner 1932: 118–21; Parke 1977: 118; Hani 1978; Burkert 1983: 241–3; 1985: 241; Simon 1983: 99.
153 See Chapter 1, p. 20.
154 Athens, Vlasto; Eretria Painter, rf oinochoe; *ARV* 1249.14; *Add.* 354 (van Hoorn 1951: pl. 10; Pickard-Cambridge 1968: fig. 9; Kerényi 1976: 95; Simon 1983: pl. 31.2; Lezzi-Hafter 1988: pl. 214).
155 Figure 57 holds the burner, rather than it being a case of 56 holding it and appearing in a twisted pose with the burner 'behind' her. Compare too Carrey's drawings of figures §2 and §3 (Berger and Gisler-Huwiler, pl. 141); §3 is turning behind to §2, obviously to exchange words; Carrey made his drawings, probably in 1674, a few years before the explosion in the Parthenon in 1687; these drawings are not regarded as completely accurate.

3 WOMEN PRIESTS

1 Istanbul Museum: Hogarth 1908: pl. 21.6, 22.1 a–e; *JHS* 51, 1971: pl. 34 f–h; Akurgal 1961: figs 169–73; Richter 1968: no. 81, pls 259–62; 1987: fig. 273; Robertson 1975: 72, pl. 15a–b; 1981: pl. 27; Boardman 1978: 88; 1984: no. 287; Mantes 1990: pl. 1a.
2 For women priests, see: Martha 1882; Feaver 1957: 125, 132, 137–8, 140–2, 145–6, 153–4, 157; Jordan 1979: 28–36, 77–80; in general, Garland 1984: 76–7, 79, 86–7, 88–9, 90–101, 112; 1990a: 77–80; Turner 1983; 1988; Malkin 1987: 69–72; Mantes 1990; Sourvinou-Inwood 1990: 320–2; Zaidman 1992: 372–5; Kraemer 1992: 80–92; Aleshire 1994: 325–37; Dillon and Garland 1994; 2000: 12.34–7; Fantham 1994: 93–6; Dillon 1995: 65–6; 1997: 82–6, 150–1, 196–7; 1999a; Kron 1996: 140–55.

NOTES

3 Aeschylus: *TrGF* 3 F86–8; Men. F210–11 (Koerte); Hellanikos *FGH* 4 F74–84; cf. *FGH* 323a, 608a; Thuc. 2.2.1 (cf. 4.133.2–3).
4 Aristoboule: *SEG* 22.116.5 (the same method used of a priest: *SEG* 21.519.1); Kallisto: *IG* ii² 4638b, fourth century BC (Pouilloux 1954a: no. 40; Mantes 1990: pl. 48): 'In the woman priesthood of Kallisto. Sostratos dedicated (this) to Nemesis'.
5 Amphipolis: Eur. *Iph. Taur.* 1114 (also used of priests); melissa: Pind. *Pyth.* 4.60; peleiai: Paus. 7.21.2, 10.12.10 (Hdt. 2.55.1 calls them the promanties: prophetesses; cf. Strabo 7.7.12); gerarai: [Dem.] 59.73, 78.
6 *ED* 178, end of the third century BC.
7 E.g. *LSCG* 65.70, first century BC, Andania.
8 *ED* 216.7–8, end of third century BC, see also *LSCG* 166.8–10, second or first century BC. Male priests to be holokleros, e.g. *ED* 2a13–15, 180.15–16, 215.8–9, 182.5–7, cf. *LSCG* 162.14. Note also that on Kos the woman priest of Demeter, and the priest of Zeus Polieus, had to avoid pollution of various kinds (*LSCG* 154a 21–45, 156a 7–16 respectively). Cf. Isok. 2.6.
9 Anaxandrides *PCG* ii F40: apergmenoi, 'without scrotum'; Pl. *Laws* 759c (cf. 947d); *EM* sv apheles. For the religious duties of the basileus archon, see [Arist.] *Ath. Pol.* 57. On the physical soundness of priests, Garland 1995: 64; 1984: 85; Dillon 1995: 48 with n. 103; Kos: Dillon 1999a: 75–6.
10 Lys. 24.13; Dillon 1995: 38, 47.
11 Aesch. 1.19–21, 188; Dover 1978: 24–5.
12 Dem. 59.85–6.
13 Sikyon: Paus. 2.10.4; Kalaureia (modern Poros): 2.33.2; Artemis Triklaria (the story of Komaitho and Melanippos): 7.19.1–6 (Redfield 1990); Laphria: 7.18.11–12; Aigeira: 7.26.5; Tegea: 8.47.3; myth about a parthenos woman priest of Artemis in Crete: Paus. 3.18.4. Boys as priests (until puberty), Elateia: Paus. 10.34.8; Aigion: 7.24.4; Thebes: 9.10.4.
14 Paus. 8.5.11–13, 8.13.1, 5.
15 Paus. 8.42.12.
16 Paus. 6.6.7–10.
17 Eight: *ED* 215.8–9 (the priesthood of Zeus Alseios); 10: *ED* 109.10, *ED* 180.16, *LSCG* 166.8–10 (Kos); 12: *ED* 216.7–8 (the age of the woman priest in the cult of Dionysos Thallophoros is given as 10 in *ED* 216.7–8, but in the same cult as 12 in *LSCG* 166.8–10, indicating a change over the course of time, probably not to be viewed as due to problems experienced with a 10-year-old woman priest, as there were several pre-puberty priesthoods in ancient Greece); 20: *LSAM* 49A 6; or 40 years of age: *ED* 2A 14, *LSCG* 162.14–15 (Kos), depending on the individual cult; woman priest: *ED* 216.7–8 and *LSCG* 166; cf. *ED* 177.6. For pre-puberty priesthoods, see Paus. 2.33.2, 7.19.1, 8.47.3, 10.34.8; priesthoods requiring older priests: Paus. 6.20.2, Plut. *Mor.* 403f–404a (priest of Herakles Misogynos), and the case of the Pythia at Delphi: see the references at Dillon 1997: 247 n. 143. Pl. *Laws* 759d: priests and women priests in the ideal polis to be over 60 years of age.
18 *ED* 178.7–8; *ED* 180.15–16, 182.7, 216.7–8, cf. 109.11; *LSCG* 166.10; cf. *ED* 177.6; *LSAM* 56.9, 63.4, 73.8.
19 Pliny *NH* 34.19.76; cf. *IG* ii² 3453, *c.* 360 BC, where her name is restored; Lewis 1955: 4–7; Davies 1971: 169–71; Mantes 1990: 73–6.
20 Thuc. 2.2.1, 4.133.2–3; cf. Paus. 2.17.7, 3.5.6; Dillon 1997a: 124.
21 *IG* ii² 2874.
22 Epitaph: *SEG* 12.80; date: see Dillon 1999a: 66 n. 20, with bibliography. There was a cult of Athena Nike on the acropolis from the sixth century BC on (*IG* i³

NOTES

596: altar); but Myrrhine's appointment was the first time that the goddess received her own woman priest.
23 Athena Nike: *IG* i³ 35, *c.* 448 or *c.* 424/3 BC (Dillon and Garland 1994, 2000: doc. 12.36); *IG* i³ 36: 424/3 BC; Bendis: *IG* i³ 136.30, 413/2 BC? (*LSCG Suppl.* 6.16); cf. *IG* ii² 1361, fourth century BC (*LSCG* 45); cf. Parker 1996: 172.
24 Davies 1971: 169, notes of the branch of the Eteoboutadai from which the woman priest of Athena Polias came: 'For no member of this branch can even moderate wealth be attested'. The priesthood was a hereditary privilege, but this did not signify that the family was wealthy.
25 Theano: *Il.* 6.300 (that she helped Odysseus and Diomedes steal the statue of Athena – the Palladion – which was in her care: schol. *Il.* 6.311; Suid. sv palladion); inherited male priesthoods: references at Aleshire 1994: 326 n. 8.
26 *SIG*³ 823a (*FD* iii.5.5); chastity: Plut. *Mor.* 435d, 438c; a married Pythia: *BCH* 49, 1925: 83 no. 10; Diod. 16.26.6; Dillon 1997: 247 n. 143; old: Aeschyl. *Eum.* 38.
27 Plut. *Mor.* 404a.
28 Dem. 22.78.
29 Arr. *Epict.* 3.21.16; Hippol. *Ref.* 5.8.40; Serv. 6.661; Orig. *Cels.* 7.48; Jul. *Or.* 5.173d; cf. Pliny *NH* 25.95.154; Stobaios 4 (73); Paus. 2.14.1; Clinton 1974: 116; Burkert 1983: 284 n. 46; Dillon 1997: 65.
30 Sikyon: Paus. 2.10.4; Achaea: Paus. 7.25.13 (cf. Pliny *NH* 28.39.147); Elis: Paus. 6.20.2.
31 Paus. 9.27.6–8.
32 Eleusis: *SEG* 16.160 (*c.* 350 BC); Aglauros: *SEG* 32.115.10–11; Mother of the Gods: *IG* ii² 1316 (late third century BC); Brauron: Hyp. F199 (Jenson); Dein. 2.12 (discussed below); Rhamnous: *IG* ii² 3462 (late third century BC).
33 [Dem.] 59.78: the oath of the gerarai is a later insertion, and might not be historical; Ar. *Lys.* 212–36.
34 *IG* ii² 3453 (provided that it is her name which is correctly restored in the inscription on the base); Plin. *NH* 34.19.76; Lewis 1955: 4–7; cf. Feaver 1957: 156–7.
35 *IG* ii² 776.26–7; *c.* 240 BC.
36 Paus. 4.12.6.
37 Hdt. 1.31; Pind. *Nem.* 10.21–4. The Argives made statues of the two sons, which were dedicated at Delphi; a pair of statues there are frequently identified as the sons, Kleobis and Biton (Boardman 1978: pl. 70).
38 Eleusis: *IG* ii² 1672.17–18, 74, 127 ('the sacred house where the woman priest lives'), 293, 305; 329/8 BC; Clinton 1974: 71.
39 Paus. 1.27.3.
40 Jordan 1979: 30–1 with bibliography.
41 Dillon 1997: 163–4.
42 Cheese: Strabo 9.1.11; Athen. 375c; ewes: Athen. 375c. The women priests of Demeter on Kos were forbidden to eat meat 'slaughtered in a particular way' (perhaps strangled): *LSCG* 124.14, with Parker 1983: 52.
43 Jordan 1979: 29–30; Garland 1984: 92; sacrifices of sheep: *IG* i³ 246.26–7 (at the Plynteria, for Athena); *LSCG* 18d.15–17 (*SEG* 21.541): the sacrificial calendar of the deme Erchia prescribed a sheep sacrifice to Athena Polias on the acropolis in the city on the twelfth day of the month Metageitnion. Sheep are also depicted in the procession on the Parthenon frieze, but may have been for Pandrosos, rather than Athena.
44 *FHG* i.394 (Athen. 375c).
45 *LSAM* 73.4–8 (third century BC).

46 *LSCG* 174.13–14 (Halasarna); *LSCG* 138.14 (Rhodes).
47 [Dem.] 59.106; cf. Poll. 8.85.
48 Arist. *Pol.* 1329a 29–30; cf. Athen. 239d.
49 Dontas 1983: 52, lines 9–33 (*SEG* 33.115).
50 *IG* ii² 659.17 (*LSCG* 39).
51 Arkesine: *LSCG* 102; Dillon 1997: 151; Thesmophorion: *IG* ii² 1177; middle of the fourth century BC (*LSCG* 36); Mylasa: *LSAM* 61.
52 *LSCG* 175.2 (Antimacheia, cult of Demeter, end of the fourth century BC); see also *LSCG* 166.28 (Kos, cult of Dionysos Thyllophoros, second or first century BC).
53 Cf. the brief comments of Stears 1995: 123 (but *NM* 4485, the lekythos of Myrrhine, is not relevant).
54 *Figure 3.1*: Boston 01.7515; bronze (now green patina); fifth century BC; Arkadia. The inscription on the key reads: 'Of Artemis in Lousoi': *IG* v.2.399 (Schwyzer 670; *LSAG* 212, 215 no. 23). The eyes, now hollow, may well have been inlaid. See Comstock and Vermeule 1971: 435–6 no. 638.
55 *Figure 3.2*: Kerameikos Museum, Athens i.430, *c.* 380–370 BC; marble (*SEG* 22.199; *BCH* 86, 1962: 652; *AD* 17b, 1961/2: pl. 18b; Mantes 1990: 40, pl. 11a; Clairmont 1993: i.277–8, no. 1.248; Scholl 1996: no. 49, pl. 7).
56 *IG* ii² 13062; 370–360 BC (*SEG* 40.246; Clairmont 1993: i.329–30, no. 1.350a; Scholl 1996: no. 520, pl. 38).
57 Athens *NM* 2309 (Clairmont 1993: i.310–11, no. 1.316).
58 *IG* ii² 6288 (*c.* 350 BC); *SEG* 21.863; *CEG* ii.566; Clairmont 1970: 97–8 no. 26 pl. 13; 1993: i.495–6 no. 1.934; Pfisterer-Haas 1990: 194).
59 *IG* ii² 7244 (*c.* 300 BC); *IG* ii² 5271 (second century BC); *IG* ii² 7356 (first century BC).
60 (i) Habryllis, *c.* 150–130 BC, key: *IG* ii² 6398; woman priest of Athena: *IG* ii² 3477; (ii) Chrysis, 106/5 BC, *IG* ii² 1136, 3484, 3485, 3486. Cf. Aleshire 1994: 337 n. (j).
61 See Chapter 9, p. 283.
62 Illustrated examples in Clairmont 1993: nos 11, 1.186, 1.250, 2.412a.
63 Eur. *Iph. Taur.* 130–1; see also Aeschyl. *Suppl.* 291.
64 *Figure 3.3*: Berlin 1504, *c.* 420 BC? (Blümel 1966: 17–18 no. 6, pl. 12; Berger 1970: 144 fig. 155, 147; Schild-Xenidou 1972: no. K32, 31, 104, 116, pls 1, 142; Ridgway 1981: 148–9 pl. 108; Mantes 1990: 67–8, pl. 28); the lettering of her name is Boeotian.
65 Paus. 2.17.7, cf. 17.3.
66 *IG* i³ 7.6, 10–11, cf. 474.1.
67 Woman priest: Aesch. 2.147; Lykourgos F38 (11); Drakon *FGH* 344 F1; Apollod. 3.196; priest of Poseidon Erechtheus: Apollod. 3.196; Plut. *Mor.* 843e–f; Athena and Poseidon are paired as they so often are. Of the brothers Erechtheus and Boutes, the former took the kingship, and the latter these two priesthoods. For the woman priest of Athena Polias: Toepffer 1889: 128–30; Martha 1882: 147–8, no. 18; Lewis 1955: 1–12; Feaver 1957: 132; Jordan 1979: 29–32; Garland 1984: 91–4; Aleshire 1994: 332–5; Parker 1996: 290.
68 Lyk. F47 (20); Istros *FGH* 334 F9 (both Harp. sv trapezophoros); Hesych. sv Trapezo; Jordan 1979: 30; Garland 1984: 93; Parker 1996: 290.
69 *IG* ii² 776.10–14 (259/8 BC).
70 *IG* ii² 3464; perhaps this is the statue mentioned at Paus. 1.27.4.
71 At Athena's commmand: Eur. *Erechtheus* F65.96–7 (Austin).
72 Peisistratos: [Arist.] *Oikonomika* 2.2.4 (1347a); Nikomachos: *LSCG* 17c.1–3 (*IG* ii² 1357); cf. *IG* ii² 1363.20. Athena Nike: *IG* i³ 35.9–12 (Dillon and Garland 1994, 2000: doc. 12.36), 36.4–11.

73 *IG* ii² 1356 (*LSCG* 28; beginning of the fourth century BC).
74 Aphrodite Pandamos: *ED* 178b(a).12–16 (Dillon 1999a: 78 n. 88 for other examples of this procedure; *LSCG* 175.12, unlike the others, is classical but the relevant reference is largely restored); woman priest of Artemis: *LSAM* 45.8–11 (380/79 BC); woman priest of Demeter: *LSCG* 175 (note the similar second-century BC injunction concerning a woman priest from Ios: *LSCG* 107).
75 Lyk. F31 (4).
76 Aesch. 3.18.
77 *IG* ii² 1472.a7 (before 326/5 BC); cf. 1463a.10 (*c.* 330 BC?).
78 *IG* ii² 1456a.22–3 (after 341/0 BC); Alkibiades: see below, n. 111.
79 *IG* ii² 1524a.44–50, 112 (353/2, 336/5 BC).
80 *IG* ii² 1177 (*LSCG* 36; fourth century BC).
81 Kleomenes: Hdt. 5.72.3 (for exclusion from temples on grounds of ethnicity, cf. Dillon 1997: 113, 150); snake: Hdt. 8.41.2–3; Plut. *Them.* 10.1; Lysimache: see above.
82 *IG* ii² 3455, end fourth century BC (stating that the statue was made by Kephisodotos and Timarchos, the sons of the famous sculptor Praxiteles). Lewis connects her with the woman priest of the name Lysimache known from Paus. 1.27.4 and *IG* ii² 3464, but the date of 3464 is against this; Lewis 1955: 8; cf. Davies 1971: 171.
83 *IG* ii² 776; *c.* 240 BC.
84 *IG* ii² 928.10 (beginning of the second century BC); see also for her: *IG* ii² 3470, 3471.
85 Lewis 1955: 7–12; Aleshire 1994: 336. Three (Lewis 1955: 8) or perhaps four (Aleshire 1994: 336 n. c) of these are before the third century BC, the others after.
86 Turner 1983: 249–51; cf. Aleshire 1994: 332.
87 Lyk. F43 (16); Davies 1971: 171.
88 [Arist.] *Ath. Pol.* F2; discussed by Aleshire 1994: 328–34.
89 *IG* ii² 3453; cf. Feaver 1957: 156–7; Garland 1984: 93.
90 Poseidon Erechtheus: *IG* ii² 5058; Athena Polias: *IG* ii² 5063a (the woman priest Athenion; cf. *IG* ii² 2810, 3596); 5104 (Philippe; Plut. *Mor.* 843b); *IG* ii² 5105 and 5107 (if the woman priest Megiste of *IG* ii² 3173 and this Megiste are the same); Lewis 1955: 12 suggests *IG* ii² 5123 and 5159 as possibilities.
91 *IG* ii² 1078.16–18 (AD 221/2; *LSCG* 8); Clinton 1974: 95.
92 *Figure 3.4*: Berlin 1686; bf belly amphora, Painter of Berlin 1686, *c.* 540 BC; *ABV* 296.4; *Add.* 77 (Boardman 1974: fig. 135; Beazley 1974a: pl. 135; Parke 1977: fig. 67; Shapiro 1989: 30, 34, 36–7, 41, pl. 9c–d; Bérard 1989: 110 fig. 153; Neils 1992: 55 fig. 34; van Straten 1995: 197, pl. 4; *LIMC* ii Athena 575).
93 Plut. *Thes.* 23.2–5 (part Demon *FGH* 327 F6); Istros *FGH* 334 F8; Philochoros *FGH* 328 F16; Hyp. F87 (all three Harp. sv oschophoroi); Proklos *Chrestomathia* 87–92 (322a13–30); Suid. sv oschophoria; Phot. sv oschophorein; Hesych. sv oschophorion, oschophoroi; return on Pyanopsion 7: Plut. *Thes.* 22.4. See Deubner 1932: 142–7; Parke 1977: 77–80; Simon 1983: 90–2; Burkert 1985: 230; *FGH* 3b *Suppl.*, commentary to Philochoros *FGH* 328 F14–16; Vidal-Naquet 1986: 114–16; Hedreen 1992: 83–5; Robertson 1992: 120–33; Walker 1995: 98–101; Parker 1996: 57–8, 308–16; date: Mikalson 1975: 68–9; Robertson 1992: 122–3 (placing it in the month Boedromion); Parker 1996: 315–16. The greatest sacrifice to Theseus was on the 8th according to Plut. *Thes.* 36.4, the day on which he came back from Crete with the youths and maidens.
94 Plut. *Thes.* 18.2; Mikalson 1975: 140.
95 Inscription of 363/2 BC: Ferguson 1938: 1–9, no. 1, with translation (*LSCG Suppl.* 19; *SEG* 21.527; Lalonde et al. 1991: L4a, pp. 175–7; see also Taylor 1997:

47–50; S. Lambert *ZPE* 119, 1997: 85–106; third century (265/4 or 251/0 BC) arbitration: Ferguson 1938: 9–12, no. 2 (with translation); Lalonde et al. 1991: L4b, pp. 177–8; see also *IG* ii² 1232 (with Ferguson 1938: 63). The heptaphylai presumably claimed descent from the two groups of seven children (cf. Philochoros *FGH* 328 F183) who successfully, under Theseus' leadership, survived the trip to the Minotaur and returned to Athens.

96 Lines 8–16, 45–6 (45–6 gives the woman priest of these three deities a loaf of bread, and one to the kalathephoros, basket-bearer; cf. Euboulos *PCG* v F39); appointed by lot: 8–16. See too *IG* ii² 3458–9 (a woman priest of Aglauros, beginning of the third century); *EM* 12364 + *IG* ii² 3481 (A.E. Raubitschek, *AJA* 49, 1945: 434–5; *c*. 150 BC; a woman priest of Pandrosos); *IG* ii² 5152 (woman priest of Kourotrophos from the Aglauron); see also Martha 1882: 10–11, 173; Feaver 1957: 129; Ferguson 1938: 20–1; Price 1978: 101–32; Garland 1984: 86–7; Kearns 1989: 139, 192.

97 Lines 47–50.

98 Salaminioi decree: lines 47–50; see also Philochoros *FGH* 328 F183; Plut. *Thes.* 23.4; Hesych. sv deipnophoroi; Harp. sv deipnophoros (Hyp. F 88).

99 *IG* i³ 4b.13–17 (*LSCG* 3); Feaver 1957: 141–2; Jordan 1979: 21 (his translation is used here), 103–16.

100 *LSCG* 48.

101 Suid., *EM*, Phot., sv zakoros; Hesych. sv zakoroi; Philemon *Lexicon* sv zakoron; Men. F 257 (Koerte).

102 Hyp. F178.

103 For the woman priest of Demeter: Martha 1882: 71.7; Feaver 1957: 125; Clinton 1974: 68–76; Mylonas 1961: 231; Garland 1984: 100–1, cf. 96–9; women priests of Demeter and Kore: Mylonas: 231–2; 'women priests panageis' ('all-holy') at Eleusis: Mylonas 231–2; but cf. Clinton: 69, 98.

104 *IG* i³ 6C.6–20 (*c*. 460 BC?; Dillon and Garland 1994, 2000: doc. 12.5); the fee for the hierophant is lost; it would have been interesting to compare his with that of this woman priest; Dillon 1997: 266 n. 95.

105 *LSCG Suppl.* 10a.75–6 (403–399 BC); Clinton 1974: 70.

106 Grain: *IG* ii² 1672.255–8 (329/8 BC); Clinton 1974: 71.

107 [Dem.] 59.116.

108 Dein. F35 (Conomis).

109 Plut. *Mor.* 534c.

110 Aesch. 3.18; cf. *IG* ii² 1283.20–4, *c*. 250 BC (*LSCG* 46).

111 Plut. *Alk.* 22.5; *Mor.* 275d; there is no reason to doubt this account. Later, when Alkibiades was accepted back at Athens, the curses were revoked: Plut. *Alk.* 33.3. Cf. Chapter 8, pp. 246–7.

112 *IG* i³ 79.9–11 (422/1 BC).

113 Istros *FGH* 334 F29; see esp. Clinton 1974: 86–8.

114 *IG* ii² 204.57–60 (352/1 BC; Harding 1985: no. 78).

115 Cf. Garland 1984: 100.

116 Phot. sv Philleidai; Parker 1996: 317.

117 Clinton 1974: 69–76.

118 *IG* i³ 953 (*SEG* 10.321; Lazzarini 715; Immerwahr 1990: 168 n. 1167; *CEG* i.317); mid-fifth century BC; cf. Clinton 1974: 69; Garland 1984: 101.

119 Wycherley 1957: no. 224: Lysimache: *IG* ii² 3453, discussed above.

120 *IG* i³ 6d.24–6.

121 Choice and expense: Harp. sv aph hestias mueisthai; cf. Is. F21 (Thalheim); propitiate: Porph. *Abst.* 4.5.4; statues: Clinton 1974: 101–8; see in general: Mylonas 1961: 236–7; Clinton 1974: 98–116; Golden 1990: 44; quote: Clinton 113.

NOTES

122 *Hesperia* 49, 1980: 258–88; side a.41–2, with 285, at lines 41–2.
123 See also *IG* ii² 4077 (possible chorus of children), with Clinton 1974: 111.
124 Hom. *Hymn Dem.* 219–74; Apollod. 1.31; Orphic F49.100–1.
125 See Martha 1882: 152–3; Jordan 1979: 33–4; Garland 1984: 88–9; Rhodes 1993: 607–8.
126 Acropolis shrine: Paus. 1.23.7; Travlos 1971: 124–5; cf. Osborne 1985: 160.
127 *IG* ii² 1524.45, 1526.27.
128 Dein. 2.12; hypothesis (§1–2) to [Dem.] 25; cf. [Dem.] 25.87.
129 Father: Dem. 54.25; daughter: Hyp. F199.
130 *IG* i³ 403.69.
131 [Arist.] *Ath. Pol.* 54.7.
132 Aeschyl. *Eum.* 1021–47, cf. 854–7; Parker 1996: 299.
133 Apollodoros *FGH* 244 F101; Callim. F681 (Pfeiffer); *SEG* 26.98.9–10; schol. Aesch. 1.188; Hesych. sv leiteirai; Dem. 21.115; Dein. viii F2 (Conomis); Philo *Quod Omnis Probus Liber Sit*, 140 (from Parker 1996: 298); Phot. sv hieropoioi; Henrichs 1994a: 43–4; Parker 1996: 298–9; Mikalson 1991: 214–17; 1998: 182–3, 185.
134 *IG* ii² 112.6–9 (362/1 BC), cf. 114.6–8 (362/1 BC).
135 Introduction, p. 1.
136 See Introduction, p. 1.
137 Pl. *Rep.* 327a–328b, 354a; date (Thargelion 19): Mikalson 1975: 148; for the woman priest, see: Martha 1882: 155; Deubner 1932: 219–20; Feaver 1957: 138; Garland 1984: 94–5; for the festival, the Bendideia, see: Parke 1977: 149–52; Simon 1985: 53–4; Garland 1987: 72, 103, 109; 1992: 111–14; cf. Dillon 1997: 39.
138 *IG* i³ 136 (*SEG* 10.64). Much depends on the restoration of lines 29–30, for which see the app. crit. of *IG* i³ 136, p. 151. As Bendis is a goddess, a woman priest would be expected, and the restoration that would give a male priest (see app. crit.) seems unwarranted.
139 Garland 1984: 95–6.
140 *IG* ii² 6288; see above n. 58.
141 As opposed to the aegis which 'cries out with the hissing of myriad snakes': Pind. F70b *Dith.* 2.17–18 (Maehler).
142 The evidence for this practice is a proverb: *CPG Suppl.* i.65: aigis peri polin; Nilsson 1953: 511–12; 1960: 246–7; Robertson 1983: 162–3.
143 Nilsson 1953: 512; 1960: 247; Burkert 1985: 101.
144 Great Mother: *IG* ii² 1328.11 (c. 183/2 BC), 1329.15 (175/4 BC); Ferguson 1944: 111–12, 114; Parker 1996: 193. The metragyrtai, castrated priests, are evidenced in Greece from the fourth century BC on and took up collections for the Phrygian Mother Goddess (known as the Meter): Roller 1998: 120–2; Bendis: Phot. sv Bendis; cf. Parker 1996: 195 n. 155.
145 Esp. Burkert 1985: 102, cf. Parker 1996: 162.
146 Aeschyl. *Xantriai TrGF* 3 F168.16–28 (Robertson 1983: 153–62); cf. Burkert 1985: 101; Parker 1996: 162.
147 Hdt. 4.35.3–4.
148 *LSCG* 175.12 (end fourth century BC).
149 Robertson 1983: 164–9, note esp. 165 with n. 49.
150 *ED* 178.27, 29 (late third century BC); cf. *REG* 108, 1995: *BE* no. 448, p. 503.
151 *ED* 215a.23, 236.7.
152 *ED* 236.5–8. For other references to collections and ritual begging, see Sokolowski *LSAM* 47, p. 122.

153 *LSAM* 73.25–8, third century BC (*SIG*³ 1015); Nilsson 1953: 512; 1960: 247; Burkert 1985: 101; Parker 1996: 162 n. 32.
154 *LSAM* 47 (before 228/27 BC); Robertson 1983: 149; Fontenrose 1988: Response 8, 183–4. Not only women but boys and men also begged for ritual purposes. Athenian boys carried the eiresione, an olive branch, decorated with bread, fruit, small oil flasks, and cups of wine, in the month Pyanopsion. The eiresione was dedicated to Apollo, and would be placed by each householder outside his front door; the begging boys in conducting the eiresione branch around were promoting fertility, as they sang that the branch would bring forth the things that were on it: Plut. *Thes.* 22.6–7 (Diehl ii, *Carmina* 2, pp. 193–4 and the scholiasts there quoted); Ar. *Knights* 728; Lyk. F82 (2a–b; b); Parke 1977: 76–7, 80, 189; Simon 1983: 76–7, 83, 90; Robertson 1983: 157; Burkert 1985: 101; a boy with a branch, probably the eiresione, appears on the Hagios Eleutherios calendar relief in Athens (Parke pl. 32; Simon pl. 3). Boys on Rhodes begged cheeses, wine, fruit, and bread in the month Boedromion to ensure a continuation of prosperity for those begged from (Theognis *FGH* 526 F1 (=Athen. 360b–d; *PMG* 848)). On Rhodes the male koronistai begged for the Crow (korone); the blessing offered was of childbirth. The master of the house and his new bride were specifically asked to give (Athen. 359d–360b citing Phoenix of Colophon (Diehl iii, pp. 126–7), Pamphilos of Alexandria, Hagnokles of Rhodes, otherwise unknown, but there is no need to emend to Aristokles). For begging boys at Cumae (Italy): Plut. *Mor.* 261e; herdsmen in Sicily: Wendel 1914: 2–3, 7, 16–17, esp. 14; Burkert 1985: 101, 388 n. 26.
155 Paus. 2.10.3.
156 Strabo 4.1.4; Malkin 1987: 69–71; cf. Picard 1922: 239–76.
157 Eur. *Ion* 226–9.
158 Eur. *Ion* 303.
159 See for more detail on the Pythia: Dillon 1997: 82–6.
160 Three women priests: Plut. *Mor.* 414b; see also Diod. 16.26.4; Strabo 9.3.5; Paus. 10.5.7; virgin dress: Diod. 16.26.6; Aeschyl. *Eum.* 38; cf. Eur. *Ion* 1324.
161 Eur. *Ion* 1320–3; Plut. *Mor.* 405c.
162 Dillon 1997: 247 n. 145.
163 Parker 1985.
164 Lucan *Civil War* 5.165–74, 190–3; Dillon 1997: 82.
165 Aeschyl. *Eum.* 19: Apollo himself is Zeus' agent.
166 E.g., Hdt. 1.53–4.
167 Hdt. 7.140–3.
168 Kleomenes: Hdt. 6.66, 75.3, cf. 5.74.1–75.3, 6.48.1–51; Alkmeonidai: Hdt. 5.63.1, 5.66.1, 5.90.1; [Arist.] *Ath. Pol.* 19.4; Pleistoanax: Thuc. 5.16–17.1, cf. 1.114.2. Lysander's attempts to bribe the women priests at Delphi and Dodona: *FGH* Ephoros 70 F206.
169 Thuc. 1.118.3; cf. Plut. *Nik.* 13.6.
170 Xen. *Hell.* 4.7.2, cf. 3.2.22.
171 Parker 1985: 320.
172 [Arist.] *Ath. Pol.* 21.6.
173 *IG* ii² 204, 352/1 BC (Harding 1985: no. 78).
174 *FD* 3.1.560; cf. Paus. 9.37.4; Plut. *Thes.* 3.5 (Aegeus).
175 Famines, pestilence, drought: Parke and Wormell 1956, e.g.: Response 64, 150, 155, 389, 544, 569.
176 Hdt. 5.43.1; Thuc. 3.92.5.
177 Tyrtaeus 4, Plut. *Lyk.* 6.1
178 Plut. *Mor.* 408c.

NOTES

179 Dillon 1997: 95.
180 Hdt. 2.55.
181 Epirus: Ael. *Nat. An.* 11.2; the text reads a 'naked (gymne) virgin', which is emended to gyne by editors; this makes the text read a 'woman parthenos' (gyne parthenos), which makes no sense. Clearly the woman priest went into the enclosure naked: she went alone, and none saw her, so there is no need to doubt the nakedness. Cf. 11.16 for a similar practice (without nudity) at Lavinium in Latium. Pedasos and beard: Hdt. 1.175 ; Strabo 13.1.59.
182 *IG* ii^2 1136, 106/5 BC.
183 Heralds: Dillon 1997: 9–11; Thebes: Arr. *Anab.* 1.9.9; Plut. *Alex.* 11.12; another example: Plut. *Alk.* 29.3; cf. Paus. 10.28.6.
184 Alexander: Plut. *Alex.* 14.6–7; Philomelos (355/4 BC): Diod. 16.25.3.
185 [Dem.] 59.73.
186 Also basilissa, see Burkert 1983: 232 n. 9. For her and the sacred marriage, see: Deubner 1932: 100–1; Parke 1977: 111; Simon 1983: 96–8; Burkert 1983: 232–4; 1985: 239–40; Garland 1984: 112; Rhodes 1993: 104–5.
187 [Dem.] 59.75–76, 85.
188 Thuc. 2.15.4.
189 Samuel 1972: 284–5. For the Anthesteria, see: Harrison 1922: 32–74; 1927: 275–94; Deubner 1932: 93–123; van Hoorn 1951; Pickard-Cambridge 1968: 1–25; Parke 1977: 107–20; Simon 1983: 92–9; Burkert 1983: 213–43; 1985: 237–42; Golden 1990: 41–3; Hedreen 1992: 79–83; Hamilton 1992.
190 [Arist.] *Ath. Pol.* 3.5. For symmeixis, see Rhodes 1993: 104–5 noting Wilhelm's suggestion that symmeixis can hardly mean intercourse here and then be followed by marriage; it must refer to a 'ceremonial meeting of the partners before their marriage'.
191 [Dem.] 59.73. For the dates, Mikalson 1975: 113–14.
192 NY 06.1021.183; fourth century BC, early Kerch style (Hoorn 1951: no. 745, fig. 105a–c; Metzger 1965: pl. 27.2; see Simon 1963: 12–14; 1983: 97; Burkert 1983: 233–4 nn. 12–14; cf. Deubner 1932: 246; AJA 46, 1942: 64–7).
193 Burkert 1983: 233 suggests the night of the 12th. The woman who stands pensively behind her door while her obviously inebriated husband bangs on the door is not the basilinna awaiting her god–bridegroom: Tarquinia RC 4197; rf kalyx-crater, Group of Polygnotos; *ARV* 1057.96, *Add.* 322 (Simon 1963: 21; 1983: 97, pl. 31.1; Kerényi 1976: pl. 100; Burkert 1983: 233 n. 12; Keuls 1984: pl. 20.14; 1993: 374 pl. 316; *LIMC* iii Ariadne 110; iii Dionysos 320; Hedreen 1992: pl. 18). Cf. the similar NY 37.11.19; rf chous, *c.* 425 BC (Hoorn 1951: pl. 117; Richter 1970: pl. 157; Simon 1963: pl. 5.4; Robertson 1975: pl. 132e; Keuls 1993: 67 pl. 48, 1997: 388 fig. 25), which is inarguably a domestic scene.
194 Berlin 2589; rf skyphos, Penelope Painter; *ARV* 1301.7; *Add.* 360 (most of the following show both sides of the vase: Deubner 1932: 18.1–2; Marcadé 1962: 162–3; Simon 1963: pl. 3.1, 3.3; 1983: pl. 30.2; Charbonneux 1969: 254 pl. 288; Kerényi 1976: pl. 42a–b; Parke 1977: fig. 45; *LIMC* iii Chorillos 2; Hedreen 1992: pl. 20a–b). It has been suggested that NY 24.97.34 (Dionysos in a two wheeled cart with canopy, attended by boys), rf chous, fourth century BC, represents the sacred marriage of Dionysos, but this is unlikely; cf. Simon 1983: 98 (Deubner 1932: pl. 11.3–4; Pickard-Cambridge 1968: fig. 10; Keuls 1993: 378 pl. 325). NY 25.190 (*c.* 350 BC) is sometimes identified as showing the wife of the basileus archon with Dionysos (Schefold 1998: 303 fig. 82), sometimes as Dionysos with Pompe ('Procession'; Simon 1983: pl. 5.3; Richter 1987: fig. 473; *LIMC* iii Dionysos 849; vii Pompe 2).

195 Dillon and Garland 1994, 2000: doc. 8.10.
196 [Dem.] 59.80–4; Wallace 1989: 108–9. The points about the Areiopagos not punishing Theogenes sound rather suspicious.
197 [Dem.] 59.50.
198 An. Bekk. sv Geraradas, Gerairai; Poll. 8.108; *EM*, Hesych., Harp. sv Gerarai; see Deubner 1932: 100; Parke 1977: 111; Burkert 1983: 232, 234; Garland 1984: 112; for the gerarai at the Theoinia and Iobakcheia, see Deubner 1932: 148; Parke 1977: 111–12; cf. Parker 1996: 299. The Mother of the Gods in the Piraeus had a woman attendant called a geraira: *IG* ii^2 6288 (*c.* 350 BC).
199 Timaios *FGH* 566 F158; Phanodemos *FGH* 325 F11 (both Athen. 437d); see Ar. *Frogs* 211–19, with Burkert 1983: 231. Wreathed choes are depicted on some choes: Hamilton 1992: figs 3–4, 13.
200 Boys with toys: van Hoorn 1951, numerous pls; Hamilton 1992: figs 3, 5, 7, 9, 11, 15, 17; crawling towards a chous: van Hoorn 1951: 41 pls 285, 492–5 etc; Hamilton: fig. 16; wreaths: see Philostratos *Heroikos* 35.9; cf. Golden 1990: 41–2; amulets: Hamilton: pls 2–3, 7, 14; most of the scenes of boys show them wearing headbands.
201 Hdt. 6.134–5.
202 Hdt. 6.66.
203 Dem 19.281, with schol. to same (Dilts 1986: 495a, b, p. 83 = Dindorf 1851: 431.25 pp. 440–1); Menekles: Dem. 39.2, 40.9.
204 Josephus *Against Apion* 2.267–8; for the insertion of Nino's name into the text, see Versnel 1990: 115–17, 127–9; Garland 1992: 150; Parker 1996: 163 n. 34.
205 Sacred flame: Plut. *Numa* 9.11–12, cf. *Cam.* 20.5; Strabo 9.1.16; Kallimachos: Paus. 1.26.6.
206 Selinounte: Palermo 3892; height: 7.4 centimetres; diameter: 21.5 centimetres (Langlotz 1965: pl. 2; Carratelli 1996: 402, 670 pl. 43; Hellenkemper 1998: 98 pl. 21); Heraion: Paestum 48496; height: 17 centimetres; height of the four supporting women figures: 10.5 centimetres; diameter 17.5 centimetres; 580–570 BC (Pedley 1990: 73 pl. 43; Carratelli 1996: 375, 668 pl. 35); Athens: Athens, Acropolis Museum 190 (Hurwit 1999: 97 fig. 68).
207 Paus. 9.34.2.
208 Paus. 6.20.8–9.

4 WOMEN-ONLY FESTIVALS

1 *IG* ii^2 1177, middle of the fourth century BC (*LSCG* 36). The Kalamaia is also mentioned in *IG* ii^2 949.9 (Eleusis; second century BC) but otherwise is unknown; see Brumfield 1981: 151–3; perhaps it was concerned with the threshing of wheat.
2 Ar. *Thesm.* 834–5, with schol. 834; for the Stenia, see Deubner 1932: 52–3; Parke 1977: 88; Brumfield 1981: 79–81; Simon 1983: 20; date: Deubner 52; Dow and Healey 1965: 29–31; Mikalson 1975: 69–70.
3 *IG* ii^2 674.6–8; 277/6 BC.
4 Euboulos *PCG* v F146; Hesych., Phot. sv Stenia; Hesych. sv steniosai.
5 Aischrologia: abuse and ribaldry serving a cathartic quality, imitating the jests of Iambe in cheering up the depressed Demeter when Hades abducted her daughter; see Dillon 1997: 64–5.
6 For the Thesmophoria, see Harrison 1922: 120–62; Deubner 1932: 50–60; Pomeroy 1975: 77–8; Parke 1977: 82–8, 158–60; Brumfield 1981: 70–103; Parker 1983: 81–3; Simon 1983: 18–22; Burkert 1985: 242–6; duBois 1988: 60; Detienne 1989: 129–47; Winkler 1990: 193–200; Zaidman 1992: 349–53; Versnel 1994: 235–60; Robertson 1995: 194–5, 197.

NOTES

7 Aelian F47; Paus. 4.17.1.
8 Hdt. 6.134.1–135.3; Dillon and Garland 1994, 2000: doc. 12.34; see also Hdt. 2.171.
9 Ar. *Thesm.* 214–63, 472, 571–629, 1150, cf. 948: *semna*.
10 Ar. *Thesm.* 62–9.
11 Simon 1983: 18.
12 Xen. *Hell.* 5.2.29.
13 It might be useful to gather here all the evidence for the Thesmophoria in the demes: Pithos: Is. 8.19–20; unknown deme: Is. 3.80; Piraeus: *IG* ii^2 1177 (*LSCG* 36); Cholargos: *IG* ii^2 1184; Melite: *Hesperia* 1942, 11: 265–74, no. 51; Eleusis: *SEG* 23.80, lines 25–7; Halimous: next footnote. See Mikalson, 1975: 68, 71; 1977: 426; Whitehead 1986: 79–80, 127, 443 no. 293.
14 Halimous: schol. Ar. *Thesm.* 80 (Dindorf iii.312 at 86); Plut. *Sol.* 8.4–6, Polyain. *Strat.* 1.20.2; Whitehead 1986: 80; other sources, with variant details, including having the women at Eleusis at night sacrificing to Demeter: Aen. 4.8; Justin 2.8.1–4; Front. *Strat.* 2.9.9; cf. Paus. 1.31.1; Hesych. sv Kolias (a shrine of Demeter at Kolias); cf. Paus. 1.31.1; Hesych. sv Kolias.
15 Athens: Alkiphron 2.37.1; schol. Ar. *Thesm.* 80; Phot. sv Thesmophorion; Mikalson 1975: 71–3; on Plut. *Dem.* 30.5, see Mikalson 73; Syracuse: Diod. 5.4.7; Delos: *IG* xi 287a.67 (Bruneau 1970: 285). A meeting of the ekklesia at Athens on Pyanopsion 11 took place in 122/1 BC: *IG* ii^2 1006.50–1, but none are attested for Pyanopsion 9, 10, 12, 13, and this particular meeting might have been very unusual: Mikalson 1975: 71–3.
16 Is. 8.19–20; *IG* ii^2 1184, 334/3 BC, with Whitehead 1986: 80.
17 *LSAM* 61.5, third century BC, with Sokolowski's commentary, p. 153; cf. Detienne 1989: 143.
18 Finance: *IG* xi 287a, lines 67–70; *IG* ii^2 1177, 1184.
19 Is. 8.19–20.
20 Ar. *Thesm.* 293–4; Luc. *Dial. Het.* 2.1; Callim. F63 (Pfeiffer).
21 Hesych. sv Anodos: the women 'went up' to the Thesmophoria.
22 Procharisteria: Lyk. F50 1b; 1a (Suid. sv Procharisteria), and An. Bekk. sv Procharisteria, give a different explanation which seems incorrect in associating the festival with Athena; Thebes, on the Kadmeia (acropolis): Xen. *Hell.* 5.2.29.
23 Fasting: Ar. *Thesm.* 949, 984, *Birds* 1519; Athen. 307f; Plut. *Mor.* 378e, *Dem.* 30.5; *Hom. Hymn Dem.* 47–50, 200; see Arbesmann 1929: 90–2.
24 Plant, a type of willow: Ael. *Nat. An.* 9.26; Plin. *NH* 24.38.59 (agnus castus); Dioskorides 1.103.3; schol. Nikander *Theriaka* 71; Galen 11.807–8, esp. 808, lines 5–7; Eustathios commentary to *Od.* 9.453; Steph. Byz. sv Miletos (a pine twig placed under the pallet of agnos); cf. Fehrle 1910: 139–54; Detienne 1994: 79, 94. For the question asked of the Pythagorean woman Theano, concerning how many days without sexual intercourse had to be observed by a woman before she could 'go down to the Thesmophoreion', see Parker 1983: 82 n. 33 with references. Three days for 'Bailers': schol. Luc. *Dial. Het.* 2.1 (Rabe 1906: 275–6); bees: Apollodoros *FGH* 244 F89 (for the aetiology of the Thesmophoria on Paros); bees and chastity: Parker 1983: 83 n. 37; Detienne 1989: 145, 248 n. 109; Versnel 1994: 251–2.
25 Plut. *Mor.* 298b–c.
26 Diod. 5.4.7; Apollod. 1.30; Kleomedes *de motu circulari corporum caelestium* 2.1, 91; cf. Dillon 1997: 64–5.
27 Hesych. sv morotton. With it can be compared the Roman Lupercalia in which Roman youths ran through Rome striking women; barren women and married

women wishing for children would deliberately seek to be struck for fertility: Plut. *Rom.* 21.5; Ovid *Fasti* ii.451–2; Gelasius *Letter against the Lupercalia* 16.
28 Schol. Luc. *Dial. Het.* 2.1 (Rabe 1906: 275–6); for this scholiast, see Brumfield 1981: 73–4; Robertson 1983: 253, 255–6; 1995: 197; Burkert 1985: 242–3; Lowe 1998.
29 Clem. *Protrep.* 2.14 (ascribing the ritual to the Thesmophoria, Skirophoria and Arretophoria); for megara, see Burkert 1985: 243; Detienne 1989: 134, 244 n. 40; Robertson 1995: 197.
30 Rolley 1965: 470 fig. 30–1.
31 Demeter carrying a piglet: A. Bignasca 1992, *AK* 35: 18–53 pls 5.5, 13.1, 14.3–7 (Morgantina, Sicily); note the example from Bitalemi, near Gela (Sicily), where Demeter holds the pig by its hind legs, upside down, vertical against the front of her body: Gela Museum, inv. 23246: P. Orlandini 1966, *Kokalos* 12: pl. 10.2; U. Kron 1992, *AA*: 624 pl. 4 (examples from Sicily are very common); see too *LIMC* iv Demeter 102–3, 107, 211, 213; note Straten 1995: 56–7 nn. 150–4 on terracotta representations of women with piglets at various sites (not all from Demeter sanctuaries). Some examples show the pig held upside down by its hind legs, while others have it held in the crook of the arm. It is not clear whether the intention, in the case of the former as suggested by Detienne 1989: 135, is to convey that the piglet is on the point of being hurled alive into a megaron, but this is not impossible.
32 Paus. 9.8.1.
33 Robertson 1995: 197 suggests that the 'Bailers' did their mucking out just before the final ploughing, when the mix would be spread on the fields. Deubner 1932: 40–4, 51, suggested the Skira as the date when the pigs were thrown into the megara, to be retrieved at the Thesmophoria (accepted by Versnel 1994: 235); Simon 1983: 19–20 argues that they were thrown in at the Stenia, on 9 Pyanopsion, and retrieved during the Thesmophoria, 'during the night of the Kalligeneia', which seems too soon.
34 Battos: Ael. F47; Lakonia: Paus. 4.17.1. Detienne 1989: 130, concentrates on dismissing the Battos story as being impossible historically, and the Messenian story as being probably from 'the pages of a Messenian novel', and hence discounts the stories as evidence for women butchers. In Ar. *Lys.* 188–92 the women consider sacrificing a sheep or horse to swear their oath not to have sex until their husbands make peace, but instead decide to slay a wine jar.
35 Schol. Ar. *Frogs* 388.
36 Ar. *Thesm.* 692–755.
37 Robertson 1995: 198.
38 Paus. 2.17.1.
39 *IG* xi 287a.69; the expense of the mageiros is a drachma. See Bruneau 1970: 285–90, cf. 272–3.
40 *LSCG* 127, fourth century BC (Henrichs 1984: 81; Cole 1995: 184 n. 14); possibly concerning Dionysos given the reference to the thyrsoi.
41 *LSAM* 61.9–10, with Detienne 1989: 143. A 'man' is mentioned in one line, and the phrase 'depart from the rites' in the next but this need not have any reference to sacrifice; despite the restoration some sort of general prohibition against men at the rites is surely intended here.
42 Detienne 1989, esp. 144.
43 *SEG* 23.80, lines 25–7; local: Dow and Healey 1965: 36; state festival: Mikalson 1977: 426 (but see his 1975: 68 where he accepts this as a local festival); Whitehead 1986: 189–90. Note that the woman priest receives money to hold

NOTES

banquets for the Thesmophoroi, like the deme liturgy referred to above. Date: Robertson 1996a, after the Thesmophoria.
44 Whitehead 1986: 80, with nn. 57–8 for bibliography on different views of references to the Thesmophoria in deme contexts: 'With some of the data it seems frankly impossible to decide' whether deme celebrations, or arrangements by the demes to celebrate the Thesmophoria in the city, are being mentioned. However, the natural interpretation is that these are deme Thesmophoria celebrations, and Is. 3.80, 8.19–20 can have no other interpretation.
45 *IG* ii^2 1184.
46 Broneer 1942: 265–74 no. 51; Whitehead 1986: 79, 443 no. 293.
47 Is. 3.80.
48 Men. *Epitr.* 749–50. The second wife was a porne, prostitute, but the point seems to be that she will move in and be of the same status as the citizen wife (this is comedy, after all). The passage doesn't point to the possibility that concubines could attend the Thesmophoria.
49 *IG* ii^2 1177 (*LSCG* 36); Whitehead 80, 127 n. 39, 385 no. 85.
50 Ar. *Wasps* 690 (law-courts); Andoc. 1.36 (boule); Suid. sv semeion (ekklesia).
51 Harrison 1890: 106; H. Thompson 1936, *Hesperia* 5: 189, 'an entire village of tents'; cf. Simon 1983: 18; Zaidman 1992: 349–50.
52 Lys. 1.20.
53 Pnyx: Thompson 1936: 151–200, esp. 189–91; acropolis: Broneer 1942.
54 Paros: Hdt. 6.134.2; Thebes: Xen. *Hell.* 5.2.29; Aigila: Paus. 4.17.1.
55 Xen. *Hell.* 5.2.29.
56 Paus. 4.17.1; cf. Parker 1989: 151.
57 Paus. 1.14.3, cf. 1; cf. Travlos 1971: 198.
58 Schol. Ar. *Thesm.* 658.
59 Schol. Ar. *Thesm.* 658; for the pnyx, see esp. Broneer 1942: 252–3. Note schol. Ar. *Thesm.* 624, 631, where the scholiast actually gives as one of its glosses for syskenetria, syndiaitos, 'messmate'; graffito: Gela, Museum 17363; ritual dining in Demeter cults, see esp. Bookidis 1993: 45–61.
60 Hes. *WD* 465–7, cf. 379, 474, 485.
61 Eur. *Suppl.* 28–36; note 'bursts', in the present tense: at Eleusis before anywhere else the seed sprouts. The play suggests that aristocratic women would have come from Athens to Eleusis to celebrate the proerosia.
62 Plut. *Mor.* 144a–b.
63 Myrrhinous: *IG* ii^2 1183.33, after 340 BC (perhaps on the 5th: Mikalson 1975: 88); Eleusis: *SEG* 23.80.7–8, beginning of the third century BC (*IG* ii^2 1363); *IG* ii^2 1006.10; Suid. sv proerosia; cf. Hes. *WD* 465–7; Dow and Healey 1965: 14–17; Mikalson 1975: 67–8; Thorikos: G. Daux 1983, *AC* 52: 152–4, lines 5–6, 13 (*SEG* 33.147); Whitehead 1986: 197; Piraeus: *IG* ii^2 1177.9, middle of the fourth century BC (specific date of rite unknown); Paiania: *IG* i^3 250a.8, b.4, 450–430 BC (specific date of rite unknown); cf. Hesych. sv proerosia. For sacred ploughings, Mikalson 1977: 434; Whitehead 1986: 196–7; Robertson 1995: 197; esp. 1996a, dating the Eleusinian proerosia to after the Thesmophoria. Parian Marble *FGH* 239a 12–15 is restored to give a proerosia established at Eleusis.
64 Schol. Luc. 279–81; *IG* ii^2 1672.124, 329/8 BC; *FGH* 328 F83 (Harp. sv Haloa); Phot. sv Haloa; Deubner 1932: 60–7; Mikalson 1975: 94–5; Parker 1983: 83; Simon 1983: 35–7; Robertson 1984: 2–6; Winkler 1990: 194–5.
65 [Dem.] 59.116.
66 *IG* ii^2 949.7–8, c. 165/4 BC.
67 Agon: *IG* ii^2 1299, late third century BC: agon: 29, 77; sacrifice: 11–14, with Robertson 1984: 4.

68 Luc. *Dial. Het.* 1.7.4; Alkiphron *Letters* 4.6.3, cf. 4.18.4, 17; women in general: 2.37.1 (Haloa mentioned along with Apatouria, Dionysia and the Thesmophoria).
69 *Figure 4.1*: the lines which extend from her hands to the phalloi, and the shoots which are painted around them are not clear in all photographs. BM E819; rf pelike, Washing Painter, *c.* 430 BC; *ARV* 1137.25; *Para.* 454; *Add.* 333 (Deubner 1932: pl. 3.3; Johns 1982: 48 pl. 5; Boardman and la Rocca 1978: 48; Winkler 1990, title page; Dierichs 1993: 46 pl. 71). Simon argues that the 'Niinnion tablet' represents the Haloa, but there is no real ground for disassociating it from its traditional place in the iconography of the Eleusinian Mysteries: E. Simon 1966, *AK* 9: 86–92; 1983: 36; Niinnion tablet: Athens 11036, found at Eleusis; Simon 1983: pl. 11.
70 Rome, Villa Giulia 50404; rf cup, 490 BC; *ARV* 1565.1; *Add.* 388–9 (Deubner 1932: pl. 4.2; Johns 1982: 43 fig. 27; Keuls 1993: 85, fig. 78).
71 Berlin F2275; rf cup fragment, Near the Painter of the Agora Chairias Cups, 490–480 BC; *ARV* 177.2; *Para.* 339; *Add.* 185 (Deubner 1932: pl. 3.2; Johns 1982: 43 fig. 26; Dierichs 1993: 44 pl. 68).
72 Syracuse 20065; rf pelike, Myson, late archaic; *ARV* 238.5; *Para.* 349; *Add.* 201 (Keuls 1993: 84 fig. 76; Dierichs 1993: 100 pl. 179). Very similar is Paris, Petit Palace 307, rf amphora, Flying–Angel Painter, 500–470 BC; *ARV* 279.2; *Add.* 208 (Johns 1982: 67, fig. 50; Keuls 1993: 84 fig. 77; Dierichs 1993: 47 pl. 74). The other side shows a prostitute with a phallos in hand (Dierichs 1993: 100 pl. 178), and clearly is so similar to representations showing prostitutes using these that the whole vase obviously depicts prostitutes' activities.
73 Berlin 3206; rf column krater, Pan Painter, 475–450 BC; *ARV* 551.10; *Para.* 386; *Add.* 257 (Deubner 1932: pl. 4.2; Boardman 1975: fig. 342; Johns 1982: 146, fig. 120; Keuls 1993: frontispiece; Dierichs 1993: 46 pl. 72).
74 BM E815; rf cup, Nikosthenes Painter, 500 BC; *ARV* 125.15; *Add.* 176 (Keuls 1993: 86 pl. 80; Dierichs 1993: 100 pl. 177). Compare Leningrad, Hermitage 14611; rf cup, Epiktetos, 510–500 BC; *ARV* 75.60; *Add.* 168 (Keuls 1993: 83 pl. 73; Dierichs 1993: 99 pl. 176), where the prostitute is just about to make personal use of the dildo.
75 For the Skira, see: Deubner 1932: 40–50; Parke 1977: 158–62; Burkert 1983: 143–9; 1985: 230; Simon 1983: 22–4.
76 Ar. *Ekkl.* 18 (with schol.), 59, *Thesm.* 834, with schol. 834.
77 Philochoros *FGH* 328 F14; Lysimachides *FGH* 366 F3 (Harp. sv Skiron, cf. Suid. sv Skiron); Pherekrates *PCG* vii F265; Lyk. F46 (19); schol. Ar. *Eccl.* 18; cf. Plut. *Mor.* 350a with Mikalson 1975: 170.
78 Paus. 1.36.4. For the hero Skiron, see Kearns 1989: 197–8. There was a Skiros, an Eleusinian prophet, buried at Skiron, killed in the war between Eleusis and Erechtheus of Athens: Paus. 1.36.4, but also Skiros the king of Salamis and son of Poseidon, and Skiron, a Megarian brigand killed by Theseus.
79 Simon 1983: 24; cf. Burkert 1983: 144; cf. 1985: 230.
80 Philochoros *FGH* 328 F89.
81 Ar. *Thesm.* 493–6.
82 Nixon 1995: 104–5 rejects this interpretation, and sees it as a festival of plastering the threshing floors (in anticipation of the harvest).
83 Plut. *Mor.* 144a.
84 Cf. lines 121–3.
85 Quotation: Callim. *Demeter* 118–19. Scholiast quoted by Hopkinson 1984: 32; Callimachus' description is presumably inspired by processions which he has witnessed.

NOTES

86 Callim. *Demeter* 1–6; 'from above' is possibly a reference to the women's quarters of a house.
87 Callim. *Demeter* 124–5. For women barefoot and bareheaded in cult, see for example: *LSCG* 65.23, first century BC, Andania; *LSCG* 68.6–7, third century BC, Lykosoura; cf. *LSCG Suppl.* 59.10–16, Roman period, Delos; *LSAM* 6, first century AD, Cius, on the Propontis.
88 Callim. *Demeter* 128–38.
89 Paus. 2.4.6 for a description of the sanctuary.
90 Bookidis 1994: 90.
91 Bookidis 1993 and 1994; Bookidis and Stroud 1997: 393–421; cf. N. Bookidis 1969, *Hesperia* 38: 298–309; Bookidis 1972, *Hesperia* 41: 283–317; Bookidis and J.E. Fisher 1974, *Hesperia* 43: 272–8; Bookidis 1972; 1974; 1993; 1994 (for plans of the dining rooms); Merker 2000, for the terracotta figurines (cf. R. Stroud 1965, *Hesperia* 34: 22–4; 1968, *Hesperia* 37: 322–4); Bookidis 1999.
92 Dedication: Gela, Museum inv. 17363 (Orlandini 1966, *Kokalos* 12: 20, pl. 10.4; 1968–9, *Kokalos* 14–15 pl. 53.3; Kron 1992: 615 fig. 3; Lazzarini 586; duBois 1989: 175–6 no. 155); 'skana' as referring to participating in sacred meal: *LSCG* 82.
93 Sixth-century BC celebration at Agrigentum, also in Sicily: Polyain. 5.1.1.
94 *IG* v.1, 1498, second century BC, Messenia; for this and other inscriptions mentioning this official, see Tod 1912 (103 for *IG* v.1 1498), cf. 1905, *JHS* 25: 49–53.
95 *LSCG* 65; thoinarmostria: 30–1; sacred meal: 95–9; one hundred lambs: 68.
96 *LSAM* 72.41–2, third century BC; Cole 1992: 117 n. 25.
97 Bell 1991: 84–5, nos 85–94, pls 21–2 for reclining women diners at the Demeter sanctuary at Morgantina, Sicily.
98 Such night festivals, pannychides, seem to be particularly but not peculiarly associated with women: here at lines 432, 474; and see Men. *Dysk.* 857–8, *Samia* 46 (Adonia); cf. *Phasma* 195; Eur. *Hel.* 1365.
99 Men. *Epitr.* 451–2, 472, 474–9, 517, 863, 1119; in line 482 she refers to the women she played for; rape: 453, 527–9; psaltria: 621 (an instrument like a small harp); chorus: 1120; playfulness at the Adonia: see Chapter 5, p. 165. Note Habrotonon's appeal to Peitho, 'Persuasion', associated with Aphrodite and Eros.
100 Strabo 9.1.22; Hesych. sv Tauropolia. For the temple (at modern Loutsa), see Hollinshead 1985: 435–9; Travlos 1988: 211–15.
101 Steph. Byz. sv Halai Araphenides kai Halai Aixonides, states that Menander's play is set at Halai Araphenides.
102 *AE* 1925–6, pp. 168–77, with Whitehead 1986: 142 n. 129, 183 n. 36; see also *AE* 1932 *Chronika* pp. 30–2, lines 13–16, contests: line 16 (agones) (*SEG* 34.103) with Whitehead 222 n. 273. For the festival, see Deubner 1932: 208–9; Gomme and Sandbach 1973: 330.
103 Cf. Hollinshead 1985: 437.
104 Hollinshead 1985: 428 n. 46 suggests that Euripides attributes this rite to barbarian influence to explain 'a religious practice which was disturbing' to fifth-century BC Athenians (cf. Hdt. 4.103.1). But surely it was no more disturbing or bizarre than marrying the basileus archon's wife to a god (Dionysos) each year.
105 Hollinshead 1985: 430–2.
106 Paus. 2.35.1.
107 *Figure 4.2*: Baltimore 48.192. Jucker 1963: 51 no. 13, pl. 20.1 (the other side to that shown here); Amyx 1988: 229 A3, 654, pl. 98.1; Roccos 1995: 650 fig.

NOTES

6, 651. For *frauenfest* scenes, see Dohan 1934: 523–6; Jucker 47–61 (the standard discussion); Callipolitis-Feytmans 1970; Seeberg 1971: 65; Amyx 228–30, 653–7; Lehmann and Spittle 1982: pl 191.

108 BM 1865.7–20.20 (Jucker 51, pl. 20.2; Amyx 230, pl. 99.2). Another classic example is the Béziers Frauenfest Painter, Montpellier 127 (two friezes of women hold hands and wreaths, while others carry sacrificial baskets, play flutes, and also hold wreaths; small women figures are also present; Jucker pl. 17.2. 4; Amyx pl. 98.2).

109 For further examples, see Jucker pls 17, 19.5, 20, 21; Amyx 229–30, also 186–8 (the Patras Painter, who painted many *frauenfest* scenes).

110 E.g. Corinthian pyxis, Berlin 4856 (Juckers pls. 22.2, 4, 5, 7; Seeberg no. 220; Amyx 655); Taranto 20703 (Seeberg no. 222; Amyx 186, A1); Athens 536 (Seeberg no. 212; Amyx 188, A63, pl. 72.1), but in this case, the padded dancers and women are in two different zones of the vase and the painter need not have assumed any connection. For the padded dancers, see esp. Payne 1931: 118–24; Seeberg, *passim* (the standard discussion); Amyx 651–2, 654–5.

111 E.g. Corinth 2013, Corinth C–61–463 (Amyx 186 A22, 187 A31).

112 Coldstream 1968: pl. 11d, f; Amyx 656 n. 88.

113 Coldstream 1968: pl. 30a–b; Coldstream 1983: 23; Foley 1988: 66.

114 Sappho 59 (Campbell p. 49); Alcaeus 130b.17–20 (Voigt); Athen. 610a; Calame 1997: 122 n. 98.

115 Women and girls at Olympia: Paus. 5.6.7, 5.13.10, 6.20.9; des Bouvrie 1995; Dillon 1997: 194–5, 271 n. 44; Serwint 1993; women and Greek athletics: see Dillon 2000. For Kallipateira in the fourth century BC who (without retribution) defied the ban and dressed as a man in order to accompany her son to Olympia and watch him compete, see Paus. 5.6.7–8; Philostr. *Gymn.* 17; hypoth. *c.* Pind. *Olym.* 7; Ael. *Nat. An.* 5.7, 11.8; Dillon 1997: 194.

116 Dillon 2000.

117 Dillon 1997: 195.

118 *SIG*[3] 802 (*FD* iii.1.534; Dillon 1997: 195–6; sometime after AD 45 or 47). These competitions may have been recent innovations. Malalas 12.288 has women competing in the Olympic contests at Antioch in the second century AD.

119 Scanlon 1988; Dillon 2000.

120 Ar. *Lys.* 77–82.

121 Note for example (among others), the statuette found at Dodona of a girl with muscled legs, holding her skirt in her left hand as she strides along: Athens NM, Carapanos Collection 24; bronze; height: 11.7 centimetres; 550–540 BC; the holes in her feet indicate that it was originally riveted to another object (Charbonneux 1968: frontispiece; Richter 1970a: fig. 90; Rolley 1986: 108 fig. 79; Herfort-Koch 1986: 93–4 (with bibliography), pl. 6.5 (cf. 6.6); Boardman 1988: 166 no. 216; Dillon and Garland 1994, 2000: cover; des Bouvrie 1995: 61 fig. 3; Stewart 1997: fig. 16). See Scanlon 1988: 191–204 for the bronze statuettes of naked girls from Sparta or of Spartan workmanship.

122 Kaibel 1958: 155 (10); Cyrene: Pind. *Pyth.* 9.97–103.

123 Wives and children: Hom. *Hymn Apollo* 146–50; Thuc. 3.104.4; the Delian kourai (i.e. korai): 157–64; Dillon 1997: 126.

124 See Chapter 6, p. 193.

125 For this hymn, see esp. the commentary of Bulloch 1985; cf. Calame 1997: 128–30.

126 Lines 33–51.

127 Paus. 2.38.2–3; Hesych., *EM* sv Eresides; Hesych.: the Eresides were girls (korai).

NOTES

128 An. Bekk. sv Gerarades.
129 For the Plynteria at Athens: Herington 1955: 29–31; Parke 1977: 152–5; Simon 1983: 46–8; Parker 1996: 307–8; Ginouvès 1962: 283–98.
130 *IG* i³ 7 (*LSCG* 15); see Lewis 1954: 17–21; A.M. Woodward 1955, *ABSA* 50: 271; Parke 1977: 154; Ostwald 1986: 145–8; Garland 1992: 100–2 (with a translation). Lykourgos mentioned the Plynteria in his speech, 'Concerning the Woman Priest', Lyk. F43 (16). As Parker 1996: 307 notes, the Praxiergidai and the woman priest of Athena Polias were linked: *IG* ii² 776.18–20; 3678.
131 *IG* i³ 7.24–5.
132 Hesych., Phot. sv loutrides.
133 *EM*, An. Bekk. sv Kataniptes.
134 Phot. sv Kallynteria kai Plynteria; Hesych. sv Plynteria.
135 Xen. *Hell.* 1.4.12; Plut. *Alk.* 34.1. Hesych. sv Praxiergidai on the dressing of the ancient statue; date: Mikalson 1975: 160–1 on Phot. sv Kallynteria kai Plynteria.
136 Poll. 8.141.
137 *IG* i³ 7.20–3.
138 *IG* ii² 1006.11–12; 1011.10–11; ephebes and statue: Pélékidis 1962: 251.
139 Burkert 1970, argues that the two statues must be distinguished; accepted by Parker 1983: 27; Brulé 1987: 105–6; but not by: M. Christopoulos 1992: *Kernos* 5: 36–8; Parker 1996: 307–8 n. 63; cf. Nagy 1991: 288–306.
140 Hesych., Phot. sv hegeteria, repeated by *EM* sv hegetoria; cf. Athen. 74d.
141 Philochoros *FGH* 328 F64b; schol. Dem. 23.71; Burkert 1970: 364 n. 31. The ephebeia is usually thought to have come into existence in the fourth century BC.
142 *IG* ii² 1006.9–13, 1011.8–12; cf. Nagy 1991: 291–3.
143 [Arist.] *Ath. Pol.* 57.3; Rhodes 1993: 646.
144 Phot., *EM*, sv Kallynteria kai Plynteria; not on the nineteenth, contra Phot.: Mikalson 1975: 163–4. 'Old' temple: *IG* i³ 7.6.
145 *AC* 1983, 52: 152–4, lines 52–3; Whitehead 1986: 188 n. 63, 197.
146 *IG* ii² 659, c. 287/6 BC (*LSCG* 39); Paus. 1.22.3.
147 Eur. *Iph. Taur.* 1029–51, 1157–1233; pregnancy: 1228.
148 *LSCG* 154b.17–32, third century BC; Parker 1983: 53; Burkert 1985: 79.
149 Plut. F157.6 (Sandbach); Paus. 9.3.5–9; Dillon 1993; see also Chapter 7, p. 218.
150 Menodotos *FGH* 541 F1 (Athen. 672a–e). Carian pirates had attempted to steal the statue, but left it on the seaside with offerings of cakes to appease it; the Samians who found their statue tied it to a lygos bush, thinking that it had been trying to escape; Burkert 1979: 129–30.
151 *EM* sv Daitis; Burkert 1979: 130.
152 Samuel 1972: 295; cf. Nilsson 1957: 469; Ginouvès 1962: 294 n. 5.
153 Paus. 5.14.5; An. Bekk. sv Phaidryntes: cleaning the temple and the statues.
154 Clinton 1974: 95; Garland 1984: 104; see esp. the sixth-century BC inscription *IG* i³ 231a.14 (*LSCG Suppl.* 1); also *IG* ii² 1078.16, 1092.29, cf. 1079.11.
155 *IG* ii² 5064, 5072.
156 *LSAM* 79.14–15, first century BC.
157 *LSCG* 58.12–13, third century BC.
158 *Il.* 6.86–98, 269–78, 286–311; quotation: 301–4.
159 Elis: Paus. 5.16.2–8, 6.24.10; Sparta: Paus. 3.16.2.
160 Plut. *Mor.* 1134c; Thaletas F7 (Campbell 1988: p. 324).
161 Ar. *Lys.* 1–3.

5 WOMEN AT THE MARGINS OF GREEK RELIGION

1 He is referred to as such in an inscribed epigram from Thasos: Roux 1972: 2. 633; Merkelbach 1988: 19, 60; Henrichs 1993: 40 n. 73.
2 Eur. *Bacch.* 32–6.
3 *Figure 5.1*: Munich 2645; interior of Athenian rf cup (kylix), Brygos Painter, 480–470 BC (or 490–480); *ARV* 371.15; *Para.* 365; *Add.* 225 (Boardman 1967: pl. xxv; 1975: fig. 218; Charbonneux 1968: 347 pl. 398; Wegner 1973: pl. 39a; Boardman 1975: fig. 218; Simon 1976: pl. 145; M. Robertson 1992: 97 fig. 92; Keuls 1993: 361 fig. 297; *LIMC* iii Dionysos 333 (exterior scene, showing maenads and Dionysos), viii Mainades 7; Moraw 1998: no. 251).
4 See, from amongst the extensive literature for maenadism, Harrison 1922: 388–400; Rohde 1925: 255–89; Edwards 1960; Nilsson 1967: 569–78; Henrichs 1978; 1982: 143–7; 1987: 99–106; 1994; McNally 1978; Kraemer 1979; 1980; Seaford 1981; Bremmer 1984; Keuls 1984; 1993: 357–80; Versnel 1990: 137–50; Zaidman 1992: 355–60; Zaidman and Pantel 1992: 198–206; Carpenter and Faraone 1993; Seaford 1994: 257–75; Osborne 1997; Lyons 1997: 116–17. Schöne 1987, and Moraw 1998, are important works cataloguing the relevant vases depicting maenads.
5 Diod. 4.3.2–3; cf. for biennial celebrations: Hdt. 4.108.2; Ael. *VH* 13.2; Artemidoros *Oneirocritica* 4.39; Henrichs 1978: 137 n. 48.
6 The thyrsos with its ivy plaits: Anakreonta 43.
7 Of the numerous studies of the *Bacchae*, Dodds's 1960 commentary, whatever its flaws, is central; see also Roux 1972; Seaford 1996.
8 *Il.* 6.130–40; Andromache compared to a maenad: 6.389, 22.460.
9 Herakleitos F15 (Robinson 1987: 16–17).
10 Hes. F130–3 (MW); Callim. *Artemis* 233–6 (Proitos thanks Artemis for curing his daughters); Diod. 4.68.4; Hdt. 9.34; Gantz 1993: 311–13, esp. 312 on machlosyne. This is apparently depicted in the painted clay metope from the temple of Apollo at Thermon: *NM* 13413, *c.* 625 BC (Boardman 1967: 160 fig. 116; *LIMC* vii Proitides 1, showing two women with breasts exposed and taking off their cloaks), and in the carved ivory group NY 17.190.73, 13.7 centimetres high, 675–650 BC (Boardman 1967: pl. 81; 1991a: pl. 39; 1996: 53 fig. 39; Robertson 1975: 8b; *LIMC* vii Proitides 3). The placement of the feet indicates that they are dancing (as maenads do). Faraone 1999: 92 sees in the myth an example of female adolescent hysteria which is cured by marriage.
11 Bacchyl. 11.53–8, 92–112; Apollod. 2.26–9.
12 Plut. *Mor.* 299e; Ael. *VH* 3.42; Ovid *Metamorphoses* 4.1–42, 389–415; Antoninus Liberalis 10; *Xantriai*: see Gantz 1993: 737.
13 The tetralogy *Edonoi TrGF* 3 F57–67; Plut. *Alex.* 2.7 refers to the Edonian women of northern Greece and their attachment to Orphic and Dionysiac rites (orgia), the *Bassarai* or *Bassarides* (Thracian Bacchants) *TrGF* 3 F23–5, *Neaniskoi TrGF* 3 F146–9, and *Lykourgos TrGF* 3 F124–6; and his plays *Semele or Hydrophoroi TrGF* 3 F221–4, *Bakchai TrGF* 3 F22, *Pentheus TrGF* 3 F183, and *Trophoi* (*Nurses* (of Dionysos)) *TrGF* 3 F246a–d. Aristophanes of Byzantium in his hypothesis to Eur. *Bacch.* (*TrGF* 3, p. 299) stated that Aeschylus *Pentheus* dealt with the same myth as Eur. *Bacch.*; see too Aeschyl. *Eum.* 26, *Xantriai* (*TGrF* 3, p. 55).
14 Thespis *Pentheus TrGF* 1 F1c; Polyphrasmon, tetralogy: *Lykourgos TrGF* 1 T3; Iophon *Backhai* or *Pentheus TrGF* 1 F2; Xenokles *Bakchai TrGF* 1 F1; Spintharos *Semele Keraunoumene TrGF* 1 T1; Kleophon *Bakchai TrGF* 1 F1; Sophocles perhaps wrote a *Bakchai TrGF* 4, p. 170. Theokritos 26 also dealt with the Pentheus myth, including the sparagmos; cf. Ovid *Metamorphoses* 3.

NOTES

15 Eur. F472 (*TGF*), line 12 for the omophagia. For omophagia, Dodds 1951: 276; 1960: xvi–xx; Henrichs 1978: 144; 1981: 220–3; 1984a: 229–32; Seaford 1981: 266; Versnel 1990: 145; Obbink 1993: 68–72. Theories such as sacrificial communion with the god are too old-fashioned and bizarre to be treated here.
16 Alcaeus F129.9 (Voigt).
17 Plut. *Mor.* 417c.
18 Schol. Clem. *Protrep.* 12.119, 92P; Phot. sv nebrizein.
19 *LSAM* 48.2, 276/5 BC, with commentary.
20 Oakley 1997: 52.
21 Boston 10.221; rf psykter, Euphronios, 520–505 BC; *ARV* 16.14; *Para.* 322; *Add.* 153 (Boardman 1975: fig. 28; Schefold 1992: 84 fig. 92; Moraw 1998: no. 208, pl. 25).
22 Eur. *Bacch.* 1209–10.
23 Berlin 3223; rf pelike, unattributed; *ARV* 586.47 (Keuls 1984: pl. 17.3).
24 Nonn. *Dion.* 21.114–15 has the maddened women of Nysa chopping up their children 'with iron'; Argive women, one with a dagger, kill children and babies: Apollod. 2.28, 3.37; Nonn. *Dion.* 47.483–92. Nysa was an imaginary mountain of no fixed locale, special to Dionysos.
25 CdM 357; rf amphora; Achilles Painter; 450–445 BC; *ARV* 987.2; *Para.* 437; *Add.* 311 (Robertson 1975: 106b; Bérard 1989: 149 fig. 204; Oakley 1997: pls 2b–3a).
26 Warsaw 142465; rf stamnos; Phiale Painter; *c.* 450 BC; *ARV* 1019.82; *Add.* 315 (Frickenhaus 1912: no. 28; Pickard-Cambridge 1968: fig. 20b; Kerényi 1976: fig. 86; Frontisi-Ducroux 1991: figs 94–5; Oakley 1990: pl. 62a; Moraw 1998: no. 385).
27 Eur. *Bacch.* 33, 51, 116, 139–40, 164–5, 661, 945, 986, 1176, 1292, 1384–5; see also 191, 228, 445, 719, 726, 791, 811; cf. 55, 65, 86–7, 462.
28 Hom. *Hymn Demeter* 386; cf. Eur. *Bacch.* 218; *Il.* 22.460; Eur. *Hel.* 543, *Hippol.* 550–1, *Trojan Women* 349; Xenophon of Ephesos 5.13.2. On the mountain in the *Bacchae*, see R. Buxton 1992, *JHS* 112, 12–13.
29 Anakreon F357.5 (*PMG*); cf. Alkman F56.1 (*PMG*).
30 Text: A. Henrichs 1969, *ZPE* 4: 223–41; R. Merkelbach 1972, *ZPE* 9: 77–83; third or early second century BC; see also Henrichs 1978: 148–9.
31 NY 29.131.4; Brygos Painter; 490–480 BC; *ARV* 381.176, *Add.* 227 (Charbonneux 1968: 347 pl. 397; Moraw 1998: no. 254, pl. 31).
32 *LSCG* 181.16–7. This evidence is complicated by the presence of boukoloi, male worshippers of Dionysos, but the inscription is many centuries removed from classical maenadism.
33 Paus. 10.4.3, 10.6.4.
34 Diod. 4.3.2–3; Dodds 1951: 278 n. 2; *ZPE* 1975, 17: 107, line 16.
35 *LSAM* 48, esp. 18–20.
36 Ar. *Lys.* 1–3.
37 See Dodds 1951: 275; Bremmer 1984: 268.
38 Plut. *Alex.* 2.9, cf. 2.6 (a serpent lying next to Olympias as she slept); see also Athen. 659f; Duris *FGH* 76 F52 (Athen. 560f).
39 Bremmer 1984: 277; cf. Henrichs 1978: 157 n. 113.
40 Eur. *Bacch.* 59, cf. 513–14.
41 BM E424; rf pelike; Marsyas Painter, *c.* 340; *ARV* 1475.4, *Para.* 495; *Add.* 381 (Carpenter 1991: fig. 49).
42 Duris *FGH* 76 F52 (Athen. 560f).
43 Eur. *Bacch.* 24, 68, 689, 1034; Diod. 4.2.3.
44 Eur. *Bacch.* 21, 63, 184–5, 190, 205, 220, 240–1, 323–4, 379, 482, 511, 569–70, 862, 865, 930–1; other examples: Dodds 1960: 185.

45 Munich 2344; 500–490 BC; *ARV* 182.6, *Add.* 186 (Schöne 1987: pls 22–3; Boardman 1975: fig 132; 1996: 121 fig. 111; Moraw 1998: no. 231, pl. 28d; other scenes: Edwards 1960: 82 with n. 38).
46 Berlin F2290 (*ARV* 462.48).
47 See esp. Touchette 1995 for plates and drawings of the various maenad reliefs.
48 Paus. 10.4.3; cf. *Od.* 11.581.
49 Plut. *Mor.* 249e–f.
50 Plut. *Mor.* 953d.
51 Paus. 10.32.7.
52 See Henrichs 1984, on Eur. *Bacch.* 115, 135–6.
53 Eur. *Bacch.* 222, 225, 261, 314–15, 354, 453–4, 459, 675–6, 685–8, 814, cf. 236, 382–6, 421–31, 651, 773–4; Jameson 1993.
54 Eur. *Bacch.* 485–7, 862; Alkman F56.1–2 (*PMG*).
55 Plut. *Mor.* 249e.
56 Eur. *Bacch.* 680–2; *I. Magn.* 215.24–36 (third century BC). The translation is that of Henrichs 1978: 123–4; for the oracle, Parke and Wormell 1956: R338; Fontenrose 1978: L171.
57 Eur. *Bacch.* 23–5, 34, 109–10, 137, 175–7, 188, 205, 249, 308, 313, 323, 341–2, 363, 495, 543, 696, 821–35, 854–6, 915–17, 935–6, 980, 1156–8; Thespis *Pentheus TrGF* 1 F1c; Aeschyl. *Edonoi TrGF* 3 F59.
58 Some examples include: *ABV* 152.25 (*LIMC* iii Dionysos 294; Moraw 1998: no. 18, tafel 4, pl. 9); BM E75; a maenad wears a skin of a big cat of some kind on *ABV* 156.72 (Moore and Philippides 1986: pl. 11.95: 'panther'); *ARV* 186.47.
59 Munich 2344 (*ARV* 182.6).
60 Kallixeinos *FGH* 627 F2.27–35 (Athen. 197c–203b); see esp. Rice 1983; also Fraser 1972: i.202, 207, 231–2.
61 Polyain. 4.1; Plut. *Alex.* 2.7 calls the Macedonian maenads 'Klodones and Mimallones'; Olympias and Dionysiac cult in Macedonia: O'Brien 1992: 14–16.
62 Mimallones: *RE* 15.1713; Bassarai: Aeschyl. *Bassarai* or *Bassarides* (Thracian bacchants) *TrGF* 3 F23–5; Anakreon F411b (*PMG*); Artemidoros *Dreams* 2.37 (141); Nonn. *Dion.* 8.9–12, 14.219–20, 21.128; Propertius 3.17.30; Perseus 1.101 (referring to sparagmos); Hesych., An. Bekk. sv Bassarai; Poll. 7.59; *EM* sv Bassarides; Eustathios commentary to *Il.* 14.320; schol. Clem. Al. *Protr.* 23.3; schol. Horace *Ode* 1.18.11; *RE* 3.104; Lydai: Lucian *Dance* 3; Nonn. *Dion.* 14.217–18; *RE* 13.2119–20. For these three groups of maenads, see Rice 1983: 61–2.
63 Plut. *Mor.* 299e–f.
64 Plut. *Mor.* 364e; Klea was 'leader', archeis, for which title in Delphic inscriptions (and possibly this Klea herself), see *BCH* 1946, 70: 256–9; cf. *FD* iii.6, pp. 3–4.
65 But compare Bremmer 1984: 285–6.
66 *Pace* Dodds 1960: xxxv–xxxvi.
67 Berlin F2290 (*ARV* 462.48; full details below); Naples H2419 (*ARV* 1151.2; full details below).
68 Frickenhaus 1912, catalogued 29 such vases, arguing that they depicted the Lenaea; Frontisi-Ducroux 1991: 233–63 catalogues 73 vases which she identifies as Lenaean; other possibilities bring the total to about 100. For the details of this debate, with bibliography, see Burkert 1983: 236 n. 22; Frontisi-Ducroux 1991: 41–52. M.P. Nilsson disputed this identification: 1916, *JDAI* 31: 309–39; as does Burkert 1985: 236; accepted as the Lenaea by Deubner 1932: 127–32; Parke 1977: 105–6; Simon 1985: 100–1. Phanodemos *FGH* 325 F12 does not bear on the question.
69 *Figure 5.2*: rf stamnos; Villa Giulia Painter and his Group; 460–450 BC; Boston

NOTES

90.155; *ARV* 621.34, *Add.* 270 (Frickenhaus 1912: pl. 3.16; Burkert 1983: fig. 7; Bérard 1989, 123 fig. 166; Frontisi-Ducroux 1991: figs 10–11; Osborne 1997: pl.10; Moraw 1998: no. 334).

70 The theme was a favourite of the Villa Giulia Painter (460–450 BC); see the list at Frontisi-Ducroux 232–7 (several of the following are illustrated in Frickenhaus 1912, and Philippaki 1967): *ARV* 621.33 (Frontisi-Ducroux figs 7–8; Moraw 1998: no. 333 pl. 40a); *ARV* 621.35 (Frontisi-Ducroux figs 5–6); *ARV* 628.6 (Frontisi-Ducroux figs 17–18); *ARV* 621.37 (Frontisi-Ducroux figs 3–4; Jameson 1993: 52 fig. 6); *Para.* 399.37bis; *Add.* 270; *ARV* 621.39 (Schöne 1987: pl. 31.1; Frontisi-Ducroux fig. 9); *ARV* 621.40 (Frontisi-Ducroux L6 no fig.); *ARV* 621.36 (Frontisi-Ducroux fig. 16); Milan A224 (Frontisi-Ducroux figs 14–15).

71 Sion, Musée du Valais; rf stamnos, *c.* 450 BC (Frontisi-Ducroux fig. 21; Osborne 1997: pl. 8).

72 Naples H2419; Dinos Painter; *c.* 420 BC; *ARV* 1151.2; *Para.* 457; *Add.* 336 (frequently illustrated; Frickenhaus 1912: no. 29; Philippaki 1967: 135 no. 8; Boardman 1967: pl. 234; Simon 1969: 275 fig. 265; 1976: pls 212–15; Charbonneux 1969: 280 pl. 321; Parke 1977: fig. 36; Durand and Frontisi-Ducroux 1982: figs 8–9; Frontisi-Ducroux 1991: figs 1, 19–20; *LIMC* iii Dionysos 33; Osborne 1997: pl. 11; Moraw 1998: no. 442, tafel 20, pl. 51).

73 *Figures 5.3–4*: Berlin F2290; Makron, Athenian rf cup, *c.* 490–480 BC; discovered at Vulci (Italy); *ARV* 462.48; *Para.* 377; *Add.* 244 (Frickenhaus fig. 11; Charbonneux 1968: 351 pl. 404; Simon 1976: pls 168–9; 1983: pl. 32.2; Keuls 1993: fig. 299 ('ranting maenads'!); Boardman 1975: fig. 311; 1986: 270; 1988: fig. 223; Bérard 1989: figs 206–7 ('a ring of wild maenads'!); Lissarrague 1990: fig. 81; Frontisi-Ducroux: pls 76a–b; M. Robertson 1992: pls 97–8; Kunisch 1997: 197 no. 345, pls 116–17; Osborne 1997: pl. 9; 1998: fig. 81; Moraw 1998: no. 266 pl. 34).

74 Athens, Vlasto; rf oinochoe (chous); Eretria Painter; 430–420 BC; *ARV* 1249.13; *Para.* 522; *Add.* 354 (Hoorn 1951: p. 24 pl. 38; Kerényi 1976: fig. 89; Bérard 1989: 152 fig. 209; Frontisi-Ducroux, fig. 97; Lezzi-Hafter 1988: pl. 215; Boardman 1994: 143–4 no. 148; Moraw 1998: no. 456, pl. 54; cf. Burkert 1983: 236–7).

75 Warsaw 142351; *ARV* 499.10; *Add.* 251; rf stamnos; Deepdene Painter; 470–460 BC (Frickenhaus 1912: 14; *LIMC* iii Dionysos 38; Frontisi-Ducroux figs 81–2; Moraw 1998: no. 297). See the list of such depictions in Schöne 1987: 302–3; Boardman 1975: 137, fig. 380, for 'wing sleeves' as a preference of the Briseis Painter.

76 (1) PL G227; rf pelike; Painter of Louvre G238, *c.* 480–470 BC; *ARV* 283.2; *Add.* 208 (Frickenhaus no. 12; Bérard 1989: 122 fig. 167; *LIMC* iii Dionysos 37; Frontisi-Ducroux, fig. 88); (2) Palermo 2023; Painter of Gela; *c.* 490 BC (Haspels 1936: 206.3; Bérard: 154 fig. 212; Frontisi-Ducroux fig. 99); (3) PL G532; rf stamnos, unattributed, 450–440 BC (Frickenhaus no. 23; Philippaki pl. 58.3; Bérard 1989: 142 fig. 194; *LIMC* iii Dionysos 40; Frontisi-Ducroux fig. 85; Moraw 1998: no. 380).

77 Cf. S.M. Pierce 1986, *AJA* 90: 218.

78 See *ARV* 1249.13 above.

79 Theokitros 26 (title: 'Lenai or Bakchai'); Hesych. sv Lenai; Herakleitos F14 (Robinson 1987: 16) juxtaposes Bakchai and Lenai; and Dionysos Lenagetas (leader of the Lenai) is known from Halikarnassos (G. Hirschfeld 1916, *Ancient Greek Inscriptions in the British Museum*, Oxford: iv, no. 902.1; third century BC); see also Strabo 10.3.10; Dionysius Periegetes, lines 702, 1155.

80 Mikalson 1975: 109–10.

81 Parke 1977: 105.
82 Plut. *Mor.* 299e–300a; Hesych. sv Agrionia; Schachter 1981: 1.179–81; Burkert 1983: 175. There was also an Agrionia at Chaironeia: Plut. *Mor.* 716f–717a.
83 Apollodoros *FGH* 244 F338d, 339.
84 For Pythagoras and Pythagoreanism, see (a selection only): Vogel 1966; Philip 1966; Burkert 1972; 1982: 1–22; O'Meara 1989; Zhmud 1997; Dillon 1999. Important sources are: Aristoxenos F11–41; Timaios (*FGH* 566 F13–14, 16–17, 131–2) in the hellenistic period, and the three biographies by Diogenes Laertios (8.1–50), Porphyry (VP) and Iamblichos (VP), the last three drawing on earlier material. Aristotle wrote lost works about Pythagoreanism, note also Diodoros (10.3.1–11.2) and Justin (20.4), and various fragmentary authors: see Burkert 1972: 97–109; Zhmud 1997: 45–9; esp. Thesleff 1961, and 1965 (collecting the relevant hellenistic texts). For Iamblichus, see esp. O'Meara 1989: 30–52, 86–105.
85 Dikaiarchos F33; Philochoros *FGH* 328 T1; Justin 20.4.8; DL 8.41–2. Iambl. *VP* 267 (17 'famous' Pythagorean women), cf. 30, 54, 132.
86 Neanthes *FGH* 84 F31a (Porph. *VP* 61); F31b (Iambl. *VP* 189–94).
87 Alexis *PCG* ii F201–3; Kratinos (Junior) *PCG* iv F6.
88 Iambl. *VP* 50, 132, 195.
89 DL 8.43 (Theano), cf. 8.9; Iambl. *VP* 55, 132, cf. 48.
90 Hieronymos F42 (DL 8.21).
91 Iambl. *VP* 54; cf. Porph. *VP* 36.
92 Alexis *PCG* ii F201; see also Neanthes *FGH* 84 F31 (Iambl. *VP* 191); DL 8.39, cf. 40; Empedokles 31 B141 (Diels); DL 8.19; Iambl. *VP* 60–1; mullet was avoided: DL 8.19, 33; vegetarianism also in DL 8.13, 20; Iambl. *VP* 99, 186.
93 Xenophanes 21 B7 (Diels), cf. DL 8.36; Empedokles 31 B137 (Diels); see also Arist. *de Anima* 407b12–26, cf. 414a 24–5; DL 8.21; Ael. *VH* 4.17; Iambl. *VP* 63, 109, 143; cf. Hdt. 4.95.
94 Empedokles 31 B117 (Diels).
95 Pl. *Crat.* 400c; M.L. West 1982, *ZPE* 45: 18–19; Zhmud 1992; 1997, 119–20; Dillon 1999.
96 Plut. *Alex.* 2.7–8; cf. Eur. *Hippol.* 952–4.
97 Theophr. *Char.* 16.11.
98 For the 'Great Mother', see Ferguson 1944: 107–15, 137–40; Vermaseren 1977: 32–7, 110–12; Burkert 1979: 102–5; Gasparro 1985: esp. 1–19; Versnel 1990: 105–11; Parker 1996: 188–94. What appears to be the first evidence for her is from Lokri Epizephyrii, Lokris in southern Italy: *LSAG Suppl.* 464a, pl. 78.2; the first literary reference: Hipponax F127 (West). Oriental touches such as self-castration (Plut. *Nik.* 13.3–4) were unusual in her Greek cult.
99 The pedum is seen to best effect in *LIMC* iii Attis 248; see Roller 1994. For Attis and the Great Mother at Athens, see *IG* ii^2 1314 (213/12 BC), 1315.10 (211/0 BC), 1327 (178/7 BC), 1328 (*LSCG* 48; 183/2, 175/4 BC), 1329 (175/4 BC).
100 For clappers, see Figure 5.4: the second maenad on the left has a pair in each hand.
101 Pind. *Pyth.* 3.77–9 (cf. *Anth. Pal.* 6.281); statue: Paus. 9.25.3; see Vermaseren *CCCA* 2, no. 420; only late sources credit him with the building of a shrine to the Great Mother.
102 *TrGF* 1 F1.
103 Eur. *Hel.* 1301–68; cf. Hom. *Hymn to the Mother of the Gods* 2.
104 See Robertson 1996: 239–304.

105 Eur. *Cretans* (F79.13; Austin 1968; *TGF* 472), *Hippol.* 141–4, *Hel.* 1301–68, *Bacch.* 78–9, cf. 59), cf. *Palamedes* F586 (*TGF*); Ar. *Birds* 873–6; Soph. *Phil.* 391–402; Diogenes (*TrGF* 1 F1); and a fragment of unknown authorship (*TGrF* 2 F629); note too Sophocles' play *Tympanistai* (*TGrF* 4 F636–45). The first reference to collectors for the Mother–Cybele is Kratinos (*PCG* iv F66). Note that both Antiphanes (*PCG* ii F152–3) and Menander F274 (Koerte) wrote a *Metragyrtes* or *Menagyrtes*; and Philemon an *Agyrtes* (*PCG* vii F2).
106 Robertson 1996: 241–2.
107 Jul. *Or.* 5.159a; schol. Aesch. 3.187; schol. Ar. *Wealth* 431; Phot. sv metagyrtes, cf. Metroion; Suid. sv barathron; metragyrtes; Wycherley 1957: 150–60.
108 See Versnel 1990: 106 n. 37 for references; cf. Roller 1996: 314–19.
109 Naumann 1983: 145, 308 no. 111; Parker 1996: 191.
110 Paus. 1.3.5; Arrian *Periplous* 9; Pliny *NH* 36.4.17; Naumann 1983: 159–69; Pollitt 1990: 67. An early date for the Metroon might also establish her presence in the archaic period: see H.A. Thompson 1937: *Hesperia* 6: 135–40; Versnel 1990: 107; Parker 1996: 190 n. 139.
111 Moschato: Piraeus 3851–2 (Vermaseren *CCCA* 2, no. 307, pls 76–7; Naumann 1983: pl. 22.1; Travlos 1988: 288–97, pl. 372).
112 *IG* ii^2 6288, *c.* 360–340 BC (*SEG* 21.863; *CEG* ii.566; Clairmont 1970: 97–8 no. 26 pl. 13; 1993: i.495–6 no. 1.934; Scholl 1995: no. 295 pl. 38.3). Shrine: Garland 1987: 129–31; Parker 1996: 192.
113 *Figure 5.5*: Piraeus 217; Athenian; marble; 360–350 BC; *IG* ii^2 12292 (Clairmont 1970: 98; Clairmont 1993: ii.362; Mantes 1990: 50; Scholl 1996: no. 275 pl. 38.4).
114 *IG* ii^2 4609 (Ferguson 1944: 108 n. 52; Vermaseren *CCCA* 2, no. 267; Parker 1996: 192, with n. 45).
115 Paus. 8.37.2; Lykosoura: Dillon 1997: 73, 198–9.
116 *IG* ii^2 4671 (Vermaseren 1966: 22 pl. 11; 1977: 35, pl. 24, *CCCA* 2, no. 308, pl. 78; Gasparro 1985: 25 n. 24; *LIMC* iii Attis 416; Roller 1994: 246–8, pl. 55a; usually dated *c.* 300. Roller 248–9 suggests 350–325 on the basis of the letter shapes).
117 Cf. Gasparro 1985: 34–41.
118 Sandbach 1972: p. 146, line 20 (not Koerte); cf. Arnott ii: 68, line 50; see Gomme and Sandbach 1973: 405 at 20. Agdistis' cult met with opposition as late as the first century BC: Pouilloux 1954a: no. 24, pp. 139–41, esp. 141 (83–82 BC; Rhamnous, Attica); Vermaseren *CCCA* 2, no. 245, pl. 55, cf. no. 396.
119 *Figure 5.6*: Venice, Museo Nazionale Archeologico 17; 240–230 BC; Vermaseren 1966: 23, pl. 12.1; Vermaseren 1977: pl. 57; *CCCA* 7, no. 158, pl. 96 (suggesting that this is a mother and daughter); Havelock 1981: pl. 171; Naumann 1983: 242–6, 359, no. 553, pl. 40.2; Smith 1991: pl. 213.
120 Literary testimonia for his Greek cult: Lane 1985: 46–52; Sabazios at Athens: Bremmer 1984: 269; Lane 1989: 1–4; Versnel 1990: 114–18; Garland 1992: 4, 149–50; Parker 1996: 159–61, 191 n. 142; Johnson 1984.
121 See Versnel 1990: 114 n. 73.
122 Cic. *Laws* 2.15.37; this is perhaps a reference to the *Horai* (*PCG* iii.2 p. 296 (ii), no separate fragment number), which mentioned Sabazios in a derogatory manner: 'This Phrygian, this flute-player, this Sabazios' (*PCG* iii.2 F578); Sabazios is in a list of deities at Ar. *Birds* 873, cf. *Wasps* 9, *Lys.* 387–90 (referred to below).
123 But see Lane 1985: 52; 1989: 2–3; Strabo 10.3.18 connected the Demosthenes' passage with Sabazios (note too Plut. *Mor.* 671f).

124 Theophr. *Char.* 27.8, 16.4.
125 Dem. 18.259–60; Ar. *Wasps* 9–10.
126 'Orgiastic': Versnel 1990: 114; 'wantonness': Ar. *Lys.* 388 taking it as going with Sabazios in particular and not as a general comment upon women; cf. Garland 1992: 149–50: the cult 'was pilloried for its orgiastic practices in no fewer than four Aristophanic comedies'.
127 Dem. 18.259–60 (330 BC); cf. 18.265, 19.199, 249, 281; drums: Ar. *Lys.* 388. Note the comments of Johnston 1984: 1587; Versnel 1990: 114–15. The old women are the graidia, literally, 'hags'.
128 Dem. 19.199.
129 Dem. 19.199; Ar. *Wasps* 9–10; Johnson 1984: 1587.
130 Bremmer 1984: 269; Parker 1996: 159 (pointing to the resemblances with Dionysiac and Orphic rites). There is of course nothing unusual in itself in this saying, 'I have left evil, I have found the better'; in fact, it was a proverb said at weddings. When Aeschines, having cleansed the initiates told them to say this, the rites were borrowing from a marriage proverb, and so in the same way as the married couple, the initiates were entering a new life: Zenobios 3.98 (*CPG* i.82–3); Diogenianos 4.74 (*CPG* i.243); Plut. *Centuria i* (*CPG* i.323–4); Apostolios 8.16 (*CPG* ii.429); Porph. *Abst.* 1.1; Hesych., Suid. Phot. sv ephugon kakon, heuron ameinon; Eustathios' commentary to *Od.* 12.357.
131 Ar. *Lys.* 388 (tympanismos); Dem. 19.259–60; Iambl. *Myst.* 3.9–10.
132 Ferrara T128; Athenian rf volute krater; 440–430 BC; overall height of vase: 77 centimetres; Group of Polygnotos; *ARV* 1052.25; *Add.* 322 (Alfieri 1979: 69–70, pls 157–9; *LIMC* iii Dionysos 869, viii Kybele 66, viii Sabazios 1; Naumann 1983: 134; Bérard 1989: 22–30, figs 21a–f; Boardman 1989: fig. 157; Vermaseren *CCCA* iv 88–9 no. 213, pl. 83–5; Keuls 1993: 372 fig. 312: 'Girls learning how to become Maenads'!). The author was unable to obtain a photograph of this vase.
133 *IG* ii² 337 (333/2 BC; Tod *GHI* ii.189; *LSCG* 34), lines 43–5 for Isis.
134 Cf. Simms 1989: 216–21.
135 In *IG* ii² 1927.148–50 (Osborne and Bryne 1994: 239, Isigenes no. 23; also Matthews and Fraser 1987: 238, 1997: 224; see Dow 1937: 221–3).
136 For Isis and the Greeks: Witt 1971; 1997; Heyob 1975; Solmsen 1979; Walker 1979; Garland 1987: 126–8.
137 Vidman 1969: no. 269.
138 Walters 1985: esp. 1–3, 90.
139 *Figure 5.7*: Karlsruhe, Badisches Landesmuseum R8057; Athenian rf lekythos (aryballos), *c.* 390 BC, Circle of the Meidias Painter (*CVA* Karlsruhe 1 Deutschland 7, pl. 27.2; Deubner 1932: pl. 25.1; Metzger 1951: 92 no. 41 (listing nos 41–6 as 'gardens of Adonis'); Atallah 1966: 178–9 figs 39a–b; *LIMC* i Adonis 47; Bérard 1989: 97 fig. 131; Boardman 1994: 143–4, no. 150; Detienne 1994: opposite p. 73).
140 NY 22.139.26; rf lekythos, Kirch style, 350 BC (Deubner 1932: pl. 25.1; Richter and Hall 1936: 219–20 no. 173, pl. 168; Metzger 1951: 92–3 no. 42; Atallah 1966: 188 fig. 48; *LIMC* i Adonis 49: again, the ascending woman is probably Aphrodite herself).
141 Sappho F168, F140 (Voigt). Breast beating also at *Anth. Pal.* 5.53, 5.193.
142 Theok. 15, tapestry: 80–6, the song is at 100–44, see esp. 132–5 for the sea-side rite; Dover 1971: 197 dates the idyll to a year either side of 274 BC; for commentaries, see Gow 1952: ii.298–301 (dating it to *c.* 272 BC: p. 265); Atallah 1966: 105–35; Dover 209–10, 214; line 132, referring to the time of dew, presumably means dawn.

NOTES

143 For the Adonia, see esp. Detienne 1994; also Deubner 1932: 220–2; Nock 1934: 290–2; Weill 1966: 664–98; Burkert 1979: 99–101, 105–11; Winkler 1990: 189–93; Segel 1991: 64–85; Kramer 1992: 30–5; Simms 1998: 121–41; still important is Hauser 1909, who identified Adonis scenes on vases. For Theokritos 15, see Gow's commentary, 1952: ii.262–304; Griffiths 1981; Whitehorne 1995.
144 Paus. 2.20.6.
145 Praxilla 747 (*PMG*); Dillon and Garland 1994, 2000: doc. 13.6; see Snyder 1989: 57; proverb: Zenobios 4.21 (*CPG* i.89); Apostolios 8.53 (*CPG* ii.445).
146 Dover 1971: 209.
147 See Chapter 7, p. 234.
148 Apollod. 3.183, 185; for the boar: see *LIMC* i Adonis 32, 36, 38, 38a, 39a–d, 39e, 40.
149 Once a year: Theok. 15.103, 143, 149 (Gow ii.264); Bion *Adonidos Epitaphios* 98 (see Reed 1997: 194–251). Theophastos *Enquiry into Plants* 6.7.3, *de causis plantarum* 1.12.2, and Pl. *Phaedr.* 276b clearly assume a once a year celebration.
150 Plut. *Alk.* 18.5; Plut. *Nik.* 13.11; for the eidola, see also Phot., Suid., sv Adonia, Hesych. Adonidos kepoi; EM: Adoniasmos, Adonis.
151 *PCG* vii F181.
152 Photios sv Adonios, Adonia; Pherekrates: *PCG* vii F181, 213; Platon: *PCG* vii F4; Kratinos: *PCG* iv F404; Aristophanes: *PCG* iii.2 F759; cf. Eur. F514 (*TGF*).
153 Antiphanes *PCG* ii F14–16; Araros *PCG* ii F1–3; Nikophon: *PCG* vii p. 63 (without an F no.); Philippides *PCG* vii F1–4; Philiskos: *PCG* vii p. 356 (without an F no.); Platon: *PCG* vii F1–8; Kratinos *PCG* iv F17. Theokritos' *Fifteenth Idyll* describes the celebration of the Adonia at Alexandria, where Queen Arsinoe organised it as a state cult, and another poet at Alexandria, Sotades, also wrote an *Adonis*; Bion of Smryna (see above) wrote an *Adonidos Epitaphios*; see also the Anacreontean *On Dead Adonis* (Edmonds 1912: 480–3).
154 Ar. *Peace* 418–20. Dipolieia: Zeus.
155 Phot. sv Adonia.
156 Theok. 15. 103, 143, 149; Gow 1952: ii.264.
157 Burkert 1979: 105–11; Penglase 1994: 177–9; Reed 1995: 317–18.
158 Hesiod F139 (MW 1990); cf. Apollod. 3.183; Sappho: F140, 168 (Voigt); cf. Paus. 9. 29.8.
159 Ar. *Lys.* 387–98; for divination and the Sicilian expedition, see Dillon 1996a: 117. For Demostratos, see Weill 1966: 684–7.
160 Men. *Samia* 41–2. The same word, *paidia*, is used by Pl. *Euth.* 277d of the Corybantic rites.
161 Munich, Glyptothek 467; height: 92 centimetres; Roman copy of Greek original, sometimes ascribed to Myron of Thebes, of the third or second century BC (Boardman 1967: pl. 298; Robertson 1975: pl. 178b; Keuls 1993: 203 pl. 180; Pollitt 1986: 143 pl. 154; cf. Ridgway 1970: 131). Alexandria: Theok. 15.
162 Plut. *Nik.* 13.11 and *Alk.* 18.5 clearly refer to women, and he surely means at least a significant proportion of citizen women.
163 Men. *Samia* 38–46; for these lines, see Weill 1970: 591–3; and the introduction to the play in Gomme and Sandbach 1973: 540–2.
164 Cf. Deubner 1932: 220.
165 As Diogenianos 1.14 (*CPG* i.183) states, the seedlings 'wither quickly as they have not taken root'; cf. Plut. *Mor.* 560c.
166 Theok. 15, esp. 132–5; Sappho F211c (Voigt); Callimachus F478 (Pfeiffer); Kratinos *PCG* iv F370; Euboulos *PCG* v F13; Phot., Suid., sv Adonia; Phot.,

Hesych., Suid. sv Adonidos kepoi; Zenobios 1.49 (*CPG* i.19); Diogenianos 1.14 (*CPG* i.183), 1.12 (*CPG* ii.3); Jul. *Symp.* 329c–d; proverb: Zenobios 1.49 (*CPG* i.19).
167 Frazer 1913: i–ii, esp. i.223–59.
168 Detienne 1994, *passim*; cf. Atallah 1966: 325–7.
169 Winkler 1990 189–93.
170 Simms 1997.
171 Solon: Plut. *Sol.* 21; Funeral Oration: Thuc. 2.45.2.
172 Burkert 1979: 107 (cf. 187 n. 1 with earlier bibliography).
173 Reed 1995; cf. 1996.
174 Segel 1991.
175 Plut. *Nik.* 13.11, *Alk.* 18.5.
176 *PCG* v F49 (Theseus), F42 (Painter).
177 Festival: Alkiphron 14.8; devotees: 14.3; cf. 10.1.
178 Gomme and Sandbach 1973: 549; Winkler 1990: 200–1 shows that Detienne's characterisation (1994; accepted by Thornton 1997: 152–3) of the Thesmophoria and the Adonia as contrasting rites, with citizen wives at the Thesmophoria as against prostitutes at the Adonia, and fertility versus the futility of the gardens of Adonis, which never bear fruit, is not sustained by the evidence. Winkler correctly criticises this neat structuralist approach in which Detienne ignores the facts about who participated in the Adonia.
179 Discussions on the date of the Adonia include Walton 1938 (arguing for spring, but not accepted by scholars; he notes (66) the discrepancy between Aristophanes and Plutarch, but does not explain this), and most recently, Simms 1997 (Skirophorion 4); most scholars accept summer as the date: Kramer 1992: 30; Reed 1995: 319 (summer); Burkert 1979: 106 (beginning of summer); Winkler 189 (when the dog-star Sirius rose, 'the hottest time of the year'). Much later than the classical period, Adonis for John Lydus meant the season of spring (*de mensibus* 4.64), but he could be influenced by notions of the dying and reborn vegetation god (cf. Burkert, 100). Under the Roman Empire the Adonia was apparently celebrated to coincide with the rising of Sirius (Walton 65, with bibliography), which was certainly not at the height of summer. There is no ancient evidence for a summer dating for the Adonia, and scholars' statements about the withering of the gardens due to summer heat are simply imaginary.
180 Plut. *Nik.* 13.11, *Alk.* 18.5.
181 Theophrastos *de causis plantarum* 1.12.2, *Enquiry into Plants* 6.7.3. Pl. *Phaedr.* 276b: Socrates says that no farmer would plant seeds in summer in gardens of Adonis; what is relevant here is not the time of year but the container (cf. Reed 1995: 319 n. 12).
182 *Figure 5.8*: Paris, Louvre CA 1679; fragment of an Athenian rf lebes gamikos (marriage vase), Painter of Athens 1454, *c.* 425 BC; *ARV* 1179.3; *Para.* 460; *Add.* 340 (*AM* 32, 1907: pl. 5.2; Deubner pl. 25.2; Atallah 1966: 180 fig. 40; Weill 1966: 669 fig. 4; *LIMC* i Adonis 46; Bérard 1989: 97 fig. 132; Boardman 1989: fig. 299; cf. Oakley and Sinos 1993: 66 fig. 123). See Walton 1938: 65; Deubner 1932: 221; Nock 1934: 290–2; Weill 1966: 675–98; see Edwards 1984: 64–5 for the identification of the fragment as a wedding scene.
183 *IG* ii^2 1261.9–10, 30/1 BC (*SIG*^{3} 1098).
184 *IG* ii^2 1290.8–10, mid-third century BC; Parker 1996: 160–1 n. 29. The epimeletes is honoured in the month Posideion, which does not help with the date of the Adonia, as he is honoured for several duties which could have occurred over an extended period of time. A fifth-century BC metic had the

name Adonis (*IG* i³ 476.294–5, 301–2); perhaps this is to be connected with the Kitians granted the right to have their own temple of Aphrodite.
185 See Atallah 187; Bérard 1989: 96–8. Keuls 1993: 26 misinterprets the pots as gardens, which they are not.
186 *ARV* 1482.1; *Add.* 382 (*LIMC* i Adonis 48b; Metzger 1951: 93 no. 43; *Hesperia* 53, 1984, pl. 19b; Bérard 1989: 97 fig. 133; interpretation as an 'incense' scene: *ARV* 1482.1, Bérard 97; *CVA* p. 8; Edwards 1984: 61).
187 *ARV* 1482.5; *Add.* 382 (*LIMC* i Adonis 48; Metzger 1951: 93 no. 44; Atallah 1966: 185 fig. 45; Keuls 1993: 27, fig. 4).
188 *ARV* 1482.6; *Add.* 382 (Metzger 1951: 93 no. 45; Atallah 1966: 186 fig. 46a; *LIMC* i Adonis 48a; Bérard 1989: 98 fig. 134; Keuls 1993: 27 fig. 5). Two other examples are: (i) BM E721 (Metzger 94 no. 46; Atallah 1966: 187 fig. 47); (ii) Athens, Acropolis Museum 1960-NA K222 (Brouskari 1974: 119, figs 230–1; with two dancers).
189 Ar. *Clouds* 749; *LIMC* ii Astra 45 (an rf Athenian, or south Italian) krater, now lost, depicted two naked women, either side of the moon, one holding a sword and the other a wand. There was an inscription which apparently read, 'Hear us, Potnia Selene [the moon goddess]'. They could well be calling down the moon (some claim to see in the surviving drawing of the vase a chain linking the moon to the earth). The vase is usually interpreted in connection with Ar. *Clouds* 749; cf. *LIMC* ii Astra 43.
190 Pharmakeutria: Theok. 2 (title); pharmakis: [Dem.] 25.79; Ap. Rhod. 4.53; polypharmakos: Circe: *Od.* 10.276; Medea: Ap. Rhod. 3.27. See also Luc. *Dial. Het.* 4.4.
191 Hes. *Theog.* 450.
192 New moon *deipna* (dinners): Apollodoros *FGH* 244 F109; Ar. *Wealth* 594–7 with schol.; *PCG* iii.2 Ar. F209; washing and crowning: Theopompos *FGH* 115 F344; cakes were carried to temples of Artemis and crossroads: Philochoros *FGH* 328 F86a–b; in Philemon's *The Beggar-Woman* or *The Woman from Rhodes* a character, presumably the main protagonist as in the title, says, 'My beloved Mistress Artemis, I bear to you, O Lady, this amphiphon (cake) and libation' (*PCG* vii F70); see also for the amphiphon: Poll. 6.75; *EM* SV amphiphon. For Hekate at the crossroads, see esp. Johnston 1991.
193 *Figure 8.1* (sometimes the puppy is erroneously described as a piglet).
194 Dogs accompany her: Ap. Rhod. 3.1040; as deipnon for Hekate: Plut. *Mor.* 290d; sacrificed to her: Plut. *Mor.* 277b, 280c (the puppies are first rubbed onto those in need of purification); schol. Theok. 2.11–12d. For dogs sacrificed to the war god Enyalios at Sparta, and passing between a split dog as a ceremony of purification at Thebes: see Plut. *Mor.* 290d.
195 Lagina: Johnston 1990: 41–2; epigraphic evidence (from the first century BC to the third century AD) at 41 n. 31.
196 *Od.* 10.229–394; Luck 1985: no. 1; Scarborough 1991: 139.
197 *Od.* 4.220–6; see Faraone 1996: 89–90. The opium poppy is described at *Il.* 8.306–7. Helen is not described as a sorcerer, but Homer narrates that she had many drugs in her possession which had been given to her by a woman while she was in Egypt.
198 Scarborough 1991: 140. Pl. *Rep.* 364b–366b complains of the begging priests and diviners (agyrtai and manteis) who go to the doors of rich men persuading them that through sacrifices and spells they can expunge any wrongdoing not only of the rich man but also of his ancestors, and that if he wishes to harm an enemy they can persuade the gods to do this by means of spells and enchantments (epagogai and katadesmoi); cf. Pl. *Laws* 909a–d, 933a–b.

199 Winkler 1990: 81 = 1991: 221–2.
200 Such as Plut. *Mor.* 256c.
201 Jason: Pind. *Pyth.* 4.213–19 (the lines are clearly an agoge spell, to 'lead' the woman out to the man); the iynx (plural: iynges) is used by the woman sorcerer of Theok. 2; see also Pind. *Nem.* 4.35 (with schol); Xen. *Mem.* 3.11.17–18; Suid., Hesych. sv iynx; *Anth. Pal.* 5.205; cf. Aeschyl. *Pers.* 989 and Soph. *Oinomaos TrGF* 4 F474.1; Gow 1952: ii.41; Rühfel 1984: 234–5, fig. 99; Johnston 1990: 90–1; 1995; Faraone 1993; 1999: 55–69, esp. 63. For the use of apples in wedding ceremonies to ensure that the wife was attracted to her husband, see Faraone 1999: 69–78.
202 *Il.* 14.198–217, 313–28; see Faraone 1990; 1999: 97–110.
203 *Hymn Dem.* 227–30; Richardson 1974: 229–31; Foley 1994: 48; Faraone 1996: 87–8 (whose translation has been used here); Johnston 1999: 168, 187.
204 Zenobios 3.3 (*CPG* i.58; Sappho F168a; Voigt).
205 Johnston 1999: 161–99.
206 The lithica, written in Greek, are of the late hellenistic and early Roman period (Halleux and Schamp 1985); the *Cyranides*, written in Greek in the first or second centuries AD, contains magical material (Kaimakis 1976; *ICS* 1995, 20: 169 n. 4). Both the lithica and the *Cyranides* deal with love, and may well reflect classical material, but this is far from certain.
207 *LSAM* 20.17–20.
208 Soph. *Rhizotomoi* (*Rootcutters*) *TrGF* 4 F534–6, translation of F534 by Scarborough 1991: 144. Care needed in cutting roots: Theophrastus *Enquiry into Plants* 9.8.5, cf. 9.8.3. For 'rootcutters': Lloyd 1983: 119–35. The Danaids in Melanippides *Danaids* (*PMG* 757) hunt, drive chariots and collect herbs.
209 Soph. *Kolchides TrGF* 4 F337–49.
210 The drug to anoint himself with, and the Hekate sacrifice: Pind. *Pyth.* 4.221–2, 233; Ap. Rhod. 3.843–68, 1029–51, 1169, 1246–8 (the scene is clearly modelled on the nekuia, consultation of the dead, in *Od.* 11); Apollod. 1.129–30. The serpent and the Golden Fleece: Ap. Rhod. 4.87–163; Musaios 2 B2 (Diels); cf. Pind. *Pyth.* 4.230–2, 249; Diod. 4.47.3. Talos: Ap. Rhod. 4.1638–88; cf. Simonides 568 (*PMG*); Apollod. 1.132; Pelias: Pherekydes *FGH* 3 F105; Eur. *TGF* 150–1; Diod. 4.50–2; Apollod. 1.144; cf. Pind. *Pyth.* 4.250; Eur. *Med.* 9–10, 486; Euripides' play *Peliades* dealt with this myth: *TGF* F601–24. Aison (Jason's father) and Jason rejuvenated: *Nostoi* F7 (*PEG*); Simonides 548 (*PMG*); Pherekydes *FGH* 3 F113; Lykoph. 1315. Medea with a box, obviously containing drugs, is shown with Jason and the serpent on vases: *LIMC* v Iason 37–8, cf. 42; Jason rejuvenated: 59 (also at *LIMC* vii Pelias 16b, 62). Ram rejuvenated: *LIMC* v Iason 62; *LIMC* vii Pelias 10–12, 16c, 18–19; *LIMC* vii Peliades 5–8. Pelias being led to the cauldron: *LIMC* vii Pelias 19, 21, 23; Pelias watching the rejuvenation of the ram: *LIMC* vii Pelias 10.
211 *Figure 5.9*: BM E163; Copenhagen Painter; Athenian rf hydria; *c.* 470 BC; *ARV* 258.26; *Add.* 204 (Boardman 1975: fig. 200; *LIMC* v Iason 62; Meyer 1980: pl. 9.2; Grimal 1986: 242; Cartledge 1998: 183, where the vase is described inaccurately: the inscriptions indicate that the figures are Medea and Jason, not Medea and 'the elderly Pelias, father (sic) of Jason' to whom Medea 'promises the same results' as with the ram. Medea will return the elderly Jason to youth).
212 Vatican 9983; perhaps neo-Attic and a first-century AD copy of a fifth-century BC original, but it is sometimes suggested that this itself is in fact a fifth-century work, *c.* 420 BC (H.A. Thompson, *Hesperia* 21, 1952: fig. 8; Robertson 1975: 122c; Meyer 1980: pl. 14.1; Ridgway 1981: 206–7, pls 130–1; *LIMC* vii Peliades 11, noting vii.1 p. 272).

NOTES

213 *Figure 5.10*: Berlin SK 925 (*LIMC* vii Peliades 11a; Kunze 1992: 134–5, pl. 43); marble; *c.* AD 1550; height: 116.5 centimetres; width: 89–96 centimetres.
214 Page 1941: 328–31. As he notes, the participle *potibantes* is sometimes taken to indicate that the woman sorcerer is addressing both men and women, but the sense does seem to indicate women only.
215 Kaibel 1958: F3 (p. 154; Athen. 480b); the Page fragment is not in Kaibel. Cf. Theophr. *Char.* 16.7. Alkman F63 mentions Lampads, nymphs who carry torches with Hekate.
216 For this Idyll, see the standard commentary of Gow 1952: ii.33–63; cf. Griffiths 1981: 260–8. Hekate was particularly associated with sorcery, and is invoked at Soph. *Rhizotomoi TrGF* 4 F535; Eur. *Med.* 397; Ap. Rhod. 3.842, 1035, 4.147–8. Since antiquity Theokritos 2 has been thought to be modelled on Sophron's mime, but there is no real reason for this to be assumed.
217 Soph. *Trach.* 584–5, cf. 555–87, 600–15, 672–722, 756–812, 1138–40; see also Hes. F25.17–25 (MW); Aeschyl. *TrGF* 3 F73b (thought to be from his *Herakleidai*); Bacchyl. 16.20–35; Diod. 4.36, 38; Apollod. 2.151–2, 157–9; Faraone 1999: 110–19.
218 *Figure 5.11*: BM E370; Athenian rf pelike (jug); *c.* 440–430 BC; Manner of the Washing Painter (?); *ARV* 1134.7; *Add.* 333 (Vollkommer 1988: 31–2 no. 217, 34 fig. 42; Boardman 1989: fig. 212; Carpenter 1991: fig. 228); for the traditional interpretation of this vase: *LIMC* iv Herakles 1680, *LIMC* vi Lichas 7; *LIMC* vi Nessos 93 (none illustrating 1134.7); cf. Gantz 1993: 458 (cf. 434–5); Shapiro 1994: 155–60.
219 Quotation: Eur. *Med.* 1198–1202, see also 784–99, 806, 978–80, 1065–6, 1125–6, 1159–1219; Paus. 2.3.6; Diod. 4.545–6; Apollod. 1.145.
220 Hermione: Eur. *Andr.* 157–60, 205–8, 355–6; Aigeus: Plut. *Thes.* 12.3.
221 See Chapter 3, p. 104 for Nino.
222 Antiphon 1, discussed below.
223 Aesop 56.
224 [Dem.] 25.79–80; Plut. *Dem.* 14.6; Philochoros *FGH* 328 F60, cf. Eur. *Hippol.* 506–17; Dodds 1951: 205 n. 98; Versnel 1990: 118; Parker 1996: 163 n. 34.
225 Plut. *Mor.* 126a, 139a, 256c, e; Antiphon 1.
226 See esp. Preisendanz 1973–4; Graf 1986.
227 Sappho F1 (Voigt): Petropoulos 1993. Hipponax F172 (West) mentioned a pharmakon that would be drunk when the first swallow (sc. of the season) was seen, swallows being associated with love.
228 Gager 1992: 85 (his translation; the Greek text is apparently unpublished); Schmidt 1995: 60.
229 Plato *Theaetetus* 149b–d.
230 Cf. Pl. *Phaed.* 77e–78a (male singers of charms against *mormolukeiai*, women ghosts specialising in attacks on children), *Rep.* 381e; Johnston 1999: 168.
231 Scarborough 1991: 145.
232 Padel 1983: 12, 18 n. 19 (with references).
233 Men. *Theophoroumene* 20–57 (Arnott ii.63–9). The ancient commentaries on the play by Nikadios and Artios are lost: *EM* sv *euantetos* (the play and its theme clearly excited interest); cf. Alkiphron 4.19.21. For Corybantiontes (those worshipping the Corybantes), music, and dance: Pl. *Ion* 536c, cf. 533e; *Euth.* 277d–e; Plut. *Mor.* 758e; cure: Ar. *Wasps* 118–20.
234 Diktynna: a goddess of Crete, identified with Artemis. Alkman (in an unknown context) mentioned lettuce-cakes (*thridakiskai*) and pan-cakes (*kribanai*); Sosibios explained that the *kribanai* were cakes baked in the shape of breasts, and used by the Lakonians for the festivals of the women who carried them when

the followers in the chorus were about to sing the encomion which had been prepared for the 'Parthenos'; at Sparta, the Parthenos is presumably Artemis: Alkman F94 (*PMG*); Sosibios *FGH* 595 F6; Apollodoros *FGH* 244 F255.
235 They do not think of Athena, who is in fact responsible in this case: Soph. *Ajax* 172–86, 756–77; Pan: Eur. *Rhesos* 36.
236 Pl. *Phaedr.* 265a, cf. 244a–245a; see Plut. *Mor.* 758e–759b; see the classic discussion of Dodds 1951: 64–101, 270–82.
237 Kassandra and the Pythia in a state of being entheos: Aeschyl. *Ag.* 1209; Plut. *Mor.* 758e. Pl. *Phaedr.* 244b: the women priests at Delphi and Dodona prophesy through mania. An oracle in Thrace had a prophesying woman priest, but Dionysos provided the inspiration, and Herodotos compared the oracular procedure there with that at Delphi: Hdt. 7.111.2; cf. Eur. *Hek.* 1267; Plut. *Mor.* 623b.
238 Hippocrates *Epidemiai* 7.28 (Littré); Ar. *Wasps* 1019 with schol.; Pl. *Sophist* 252c with schol.; Plut. *Mor.* 414e; Lucian *Lexiphanes* 20; Philo *Mechanicus* 1.654; Poll. 2.168; Hesych., Suid. sv engastrimuthos; Soph. *Aichmalotides TrGF* 4 F59; Plut. *Mor.* 414e; Dodds 1951: 71, 88–9 n. 46. Sometimes the practice is referred to as ventriloquism but the evidence (including *Wasps* 1019) does not point in this direction; modern mediums can speak in a voice other than their own.
239 Apollod. 2.26–9; other versions had the madness sent by Hera, Apollodoros 2.26, citing Akousilaos (*FGH* 2 F28: they slighted Hera's statue); Bacchyl. 11.47–52 (they boasted that their father was wealthier than Hera); there was a tradition that there were two rather than three daughters (Pherekydes *FGH* 3 F114), which seems to be the one represented in art.
240 Apollod. 3.35.
241 Diod. 4.3.3.
242 Eur. *Bacch.* 32–6, 119, 305, 326, 665, 850.

6 PROSTITUTES, FOREIGN WOMEN AND THE GODS

1 [Dem.] 59.122.
2 Hetairai: Athen. 583f; pallake and brothel: Antiphon 1.14 (Dillon and Garland 1994, 2000: doc. 13.49).
3 See the collection of Gow 1965; Athen. 567a, 583d, 586a–b, 591d, 596f, 591d.
4 See Henry 1995: 57–64.
5 Athen. 567c.
6 Philemon *PCG* vii F3 ((Dillon and Garland 2000: doc. 13.88); Xenarchos *PCG* vii F4 (Dillon and Garland 2000: doc. 13.91); Nikander of Kolophon *FGH* 271–2 F9; cf. Euboulos *PCG* v F67 (Athen. 568f–569).
7 Evidence for male prostitutes: Aesch. 1, *Against Timarchos*, passim, but note §§3, 7–14, 19–21, 29, 40–1, 52, 70, 72, 74–5, 79, 130, 155, 158–9, 165, 184, 188; Ar. *Wealth* 149–59 (Dillon and Garland 2000: doc. 13.92); Dem. 22.58, 61; [Dem.] *Letter* 4.11; *Lys.* 3; Xen. *Mem.* 1.6.13; Eupolis *PCG* v 99.26; Alexis *PCG* ii F158 (Arnott 1996: F244); Kratinos *PCG* iv F3; Ephippos 20; Timaios *FGH* 566 F35b, cf. F124b (Demochares; see below); DL 2.9.105. Note for pederasty and homoeroticism: Pl. *Symp.* 181d–185b, 191c–192e. There was a tax on male and female prostitutes; the right to collect it was contracted out by the council (boule) to private individuals: Aesch. 1.119–20; Poll. 7.202. Select bibliography: Dover 1989: 19–42; Krenkel 1978: 49–55; Foucault 1984: 47–62; Reinsberg 1993: 201–12; Halperin 1989: 37–53; 1990: 88–104; Winkler 1990: 45–70;

1990a: 171–209, esp. 186–97; Cohen 1991: 171–202; Cantarella 1992: 48–53; Keuls 1993: 274–99; Kilmer 1993: 11–25; Thornton 1997: 110–20; Dillon and Garland 2000: docs 423–40; for pederasty, note Percy 1996; cf. Athen. 605d.
8 Solon F25 (West), cf. Aeschyl. *Myrmidons TrGF* 3 F135 (both Dillon and Garland 2000: docs 13.65–6); Ar. *Birds* 137–42; scenes of intercrural sex, genital fondling, and rejection: Dover 1989: pls B76, B250, 271, R59, R196a; Kilmer 1993: pls R142, R196, R371.
9 Aesch. 1.7–14.
10 Ar. *Wealth* 149–59.
11 Aesch. 1.3, 19–21, 29, 72, 188. Cowards also suffered restrictions on their religious activities: Aesch. 3.176.
12 Dem. 22.73.
13 Timaios *FGH* 566 F35b, cf. F124b (Polyb. 12.13.1, 12.15.4).
14 *Figure 6.1*: Lawrence Alma-Tadema, *Pheidias and the Frieze of the Parthenon*, 1869, Birmingham Museums and Art Gallery inv. 118.23 (Henry 1995: 103–4; Spivey 1997: fig. 248; Cartledge 1998: 278–9).
15 Note esp. Pl. *Menex.*; see Henry 1995: 29–56, for her appearance in Socratic discourses by Socrates' disciples Antisthenes, Plato, Xenophon and Aischines.
16 *Figure 6.2*: Vatican Museums 272 (Richter 1965: i.154–5, pls 875–6; Ridgway 1970: 65–8; 1981: 240–1; Henry 1995: 17). Her name is engraved at the base of the herm (*IG* xiv 1143). Richter considers the herm to be a Roman copy of a fifth-century BC original (it was found in Italy), but Ridgway argues that it is a commissioned Roman piece.
17 Law: *Ath. Pol.* 26.3; citizenship grant: Plut. *Per.* 37.3.
18 *IG* ii^2 7394; early fourth century BC; Bicknell 1982; accepted by Henry 1985: 10–11.
19 Antisthenes F142, Giannantoni 1990: 2.191 (= Athen. 220d); commentary on Antisthenes' *Aspasia*: Giannantoni 4.323–5.
20 Antisthenes F143 (Giannantoni p. 191 (= Athen. 589e; cf. Plut. *Per.* 24.9 (greeting)); Antisthenes F144 (Giannantoni p. 192 = Athen. 533c–d); or consult F34 = Athen. 220d, F35 = Athen. 589e in Caizzi 1966: p. 34.
21 Trial: Plut. *Per.* 32.1, 5 (Plut. *Per.* 32.5 = Aischines F67, Giannantoni p. 614), cf. F59–72 (Giannantoni pp. 611–18). Aischines, like Antisthenes (Athen. 220b–d), wrote an *Aspasia* (F59 Giannantoni p. 611); Hermippos *PCG* v T2; cf. Plut. *Per.* 13.15 (Pheidias and women).
22 Motivation: Ostwald 1986: 192; date: Mansfeld 1980: 76–80.
23 *Pace* Dover 1975: 28, cf. 24; Gomme 1956: 187; Henry 1985: 17; cf. de Ste Croix 1972: 236; Ostwald 1986: 194; Stone 1988: 233–5. For Aspasia's trial: Mansfeld 1980: 31–3, 76–7; Ostwald 192, 194–5; Bauman 1990: 38, 41; bibliography of those who accept or reject that she was tried: Mansfeld 32 n. 130; Baumann 181 n. 29; add: de Ste Croix 1972: 235.
24 *IG* ii^2 1409.14 (395/4 BC); with Harris 1995: 191, v.421.
25 Kratinos *PCG* iv 259 (the *Cheirones*; produced *c*. 440–430 BC?).
26 Duris of Samos *FGH* 76 F65; 340–260 BC; Harp. sv Aspasia (citing Duris, Ar. *Ach.* 524–9, and Theophrastos *Politics*); Plut. *Per.* 24.2, 25.1.
27 Ar. *Ach.* 524–9; 425 BC: the theft of three of Aspasia's prostitutes by Megarians caused the outbreak of the war; the tradition that she ran a brothel is also mentioned in Plut. *Per.* 24.5, but probably has no basis in reality, despite Aristophanes.
28 Eupolis *PCG* v F267. For women as causes of war, see especially the list in Athen. 560b–f, where Aspasia is not mentioned.
29 Thuc. 2.45.2 (Dillon and Garland 1994, 2000: doc. 13.27).

30 In Eupolis' *Demes*, produced 411: *PCG* v F110.
31 Philetairos *PCG* vii F8 (Athen. 559a, 572d); Apollodoros *FGH* 244 F112; Sappho F142, 160 (Voigt); Hesych. sv hetairas hieron.
32 Hegesander *FHG* iv F25 (Athen. 572de).
33 Eualkes *FGH* 418 F2 (Athen. 573a).
34 Neanthes *FGH* 84 F9 (Athen. 572e–f).
35 Baumann 1990: 38; Ostwald 1986: 195; Mansfeld 1980: 32 n. 131; Derenne 1930: 9; [Dem.] 59.85–6, 113–14; Is. 6.50.
36 Aesch. 1.183: Solon's law that adulterous women could not attend public sacrifices.
37 Is. 6.49–50.
38 [Dem.] 59.46; 'in the temple'; unfortunately, the speaker is not more precise.
39 Pallake: Antiphon 1.16–17; Maionia: *LSAM* 18.13–15 (147/6 BC), see below.
40 Plut. *Demet.* 12.1–7, 23.5–24.2, 26.1–5; Philippides *PCG* vii F25 (*Demet.* 26.5).
41 Theopompos *FGH* 115 F248, cf. F247 (Athen. 604f–605d); Plut. *Mor.* 397f.
42 Metropolis: *LSAM* 29.4–8 (fourth century BC); Lindos: *LSCG Suppl.*, 91.18, cf. 19: 'unlawful' (paranomon) sexual activities.
43 *LSAM* 18.13–15 (147/6 BC).
44 Dio Chrysostom 77/78.4, cf. 35.15; Dillon 1997: 189.
45 Ar. *Peace* 879–80, with Sommerstein 1985: 174–5.
46 Garland 1992: 111–14.
47 *IG* ii^2 334.
48 See Dillon and Garland 1994: 278–86; 2000: 284–93.
49 Athen. 251b; Ael. *VH* 5.12.
50 Plut. *Mor.* 389a; cf. Versnel 1990: 119.
51 *IG* ii^2 1177.3–4 (*LSCG* 36; middle of the fourth century BC).
52 Poseidippos *PCG* vii F13 (Athen. 591e–f).
53 Athen. 590d–e.
54 As Havelock 1995: 45 notes, the baring of breasts was not unusual, not only in funerary contexts, but also as a plea for compassion; later accretion: Cooper 1995: 312–16.
55 This was the well-known Poseidonia festival on Aegina, at the time of which Aristippos spent two months with the prostitute Lais on the island (Athen. 588e).
56 Luc. *Amores* 13–14; Pliny *NH* 36.4.20 (whose description differs and might refer to a previous building which housed the statue); Havelock 1995: 58–63; Spivey 1996: pl. 113. Aphrodite herself comes as a tourist, exclaiming in wonder, "Where did Praxiteles see me naked?": Plato xxv (Page 1976).
57 Havelock 1995: 4.
58 She was also said to be the model for Praxiteles' 'Smiling Courtesan': Pliny *NH* 34.70. Throughout Alexandria there were many images (eikones) of Ptolemy's woman cupbearer Kleino (Polyb. 14.11.2; cf. Ptolemy of Megalopolis *FGH* 161 F3; Athen. 576f).
59 Trial: Athen. 590d–f, citing: Hyp. 60 F171–80 (Jensen pp. 143–5); Hermippos *FHG* iii F66 (see also F67); Diodoros Periegetes *FHG* ii F5; Aristogeiton *Against Phryne* F4 (Müller 1858: 2.436); Herodikos *Komoidoumenoi* (Athen. 591c); other information on her: Athen. 590f–591f. Spengel 1853: i.455.8–11 records the specific charges, and this appears to have been either the epilogue of Euthias' charges or at least part of the speech. Cf. for Phryne, Athen. 558c; Timokles *PCG* vii F25; Amphis *PCG* ii F24 (Athen. 591d); Machon F18 (Gow 1965: 54 = Athen. 583c); Apollodoros *FGH* 244 F212 (Athen. 591c); Kallistratos *On Hetairai* (Athen. 591d); Propertius 2.5; Quintilian *Instituto Oratoria* 2.15.9 (that Phryne revealed herself, not Hypereides). See Versnel 1990: 118–19; Garland

1992: 150; Havelock 1995: 42–8; Cooper 1995; Parker 1996: 162–3, cf. 214–17. There was a tradition that there were two prostitutes called Phryne.
60 Statue at Delphi: Alketas *FGH* 405 F1 (Athen. 591b–c); Plut. *Mor.* 401a; Ael. *VH* 9.32; Paus. 9.27.3 (cf. 1.20.1–2); DL 6.60; epigram of Praxiteles' Knidian Aphrodite statue (modelled on Phryne) at Athens: Athen. 591a; *Anth. Pal.* 16.203–6. Praxiteles' statue of Eros dedicated at Thespiai: Athen. 591b.
61 [Dem.] 59.21–2 (the word mystagogos is not used). Lysias is described as a sophist in [Dem.] 59.21 and is sometimes connected with Lysias the orator, an attractive but not necessary assumption.
62 [Dem.] 59.24.
63 [Dem.] 59.116; Athen. 594ab.
64 Dein. 1.23.
65 Athen. 586c; Poseidonios *FGH* 87 F14 (Athen. 594e–595c); Dikaiarchos *FHG* ii F72 (a tomb monument which none other approaches in size; the remains of the foundations: Travlos 1988: 177, 181); Theopompos *FGH* 115 F253 (cf. F254); Philemon *PCG* vii F15; Alexis *PCG* ii F143 (Arnott 1996: F216); Paus. 1.37.5; Plut. *Phok.* 22.1–2; Diod. 17.108.5; Osborne and Byrne 1994: 386; Flower 1997: 258–62.
66 *TGF* pp. 810–11; *c.* 325 or 324 BC (Athen. 595e–f).
67 Theopompos *FGH* 115 F253; cf. Athen. 603d.
68 Athen. 586c, 595d–e citing: Theopompos *FGH* 115 F254a–b, and Kleitarchos *FGH* 137 F30, *TGF* pp. 810–11; Flower 1997: 261.
69 Ptolemy Euergetes *FGH* 234 F4 (Athen. 576f).
70 Athen. 588c–589b (cf. 587c); Paus. 2.2.4; Plut. *Mor.* 767f–768a; see the same story at Polemon F44 (Preller 1838: 75), from Athen. 589a–b, who has 'Anosia (Unholy) Aphrodite' rather than 'Androphonos', homicidal; schol. Ar. *Wealth* 179; see also for Lais: Plut. *Nik.* 15.4; Hyp. F13 (Jensen p. 116); Strattis *PCG* vii F27; Nymphodoros *FGH* 572 F1; Timaios *FGH* 566 F24; Steph. Byz. sv Eukarpeia (Timaios *FGH* 566 F24b), sv Krastos (Neanthes *FGH* 84 F13). Note also the case of Ptolemy, son of King Ptolemy II Philadelphos and a concubine, when he took refuge in the temple of Artemis in Ephesos and was killed there; his hetaira Eirene who had fled to the temple with him hung onto the door knockers of the temple and her blood was spilled on the altars, until she too was killed (Athen. 593a–b).
71 A prostitute in Luc. *Dial. Het.* 7.1 says that she will offer a goat to Aphrodite Pandemos, a young steer to Aphrodite Ourania, and a wreath to 'the giver of wealth', i.e. Demeter, if she and her daughter find another rich lover.
72 *Anth. Pal.* 6.283, 285.
73 Athen. 596c citing Kratinos, but the lines are missing from the manuscript; Hdt. 2.134–5. Herodotos notes that Sappho in her poetry abused her brother for his actions: see also Sappho F15.11, 252, 254 (Voigt). A stone base at Delphi can be restored to read: Rhod[opis] [dedicat]ed {this/these}: *LSAG* 102, 103 n. 7, pl. 12; *SEG* 13.364; Delphi Museum 7512.
74 Polemon F18 (Preller 1838: 48 = Athen. 574c–d).
75 Plut. *Lyk.* 9.5.
76 Alexis of Samos *FGH* 539 F1 (Athen. 572f).
77 Alexis *PCG* ii F255; methuein, to drink, was added into the text by Porson, probably unnecessarily (see app. crit. of *PCG*); 'to revel' presumably implies plenty of drinking.
78 Machon F16–17 (Gow 1965: 47–52; Athen. 579e, 581a, 582b–c).
79 Machon F16 (Gow 1965: 48–9; Athen. 580c, 580f).
80 Polemon *FHG* iii, F3 p. 116; she was mentioned by Hyp. F142 (Jensen p. 138);

Harp. sv Nemeas; Athen. 587c; other festival names: Athen. 586c, e, 587e, 593f, 594e; 592a–b for Theoris; [Dem.] 59.19: Isthmias. Harp. also cites Polemon but makes the prohibition specific to the names of penteteric (four-yearly) festivals (such as the Olympia).
81 Semos of Delos *FGH* 396 F24; Ar. *Ach.* 241–79; phallophoria (phallos-bearing): Krentz 1993; Cole 1993.
82 Babylon and Cyprus: Hdt. 1.199; cf. the alleged prostitution of the daughter of King Khufu (Cheops), Egypt: Hdt. 2.126.
83 Hdt. 1.93.4. See also Klearchos F43a (Athen. 516a–b). In a Greek inscription of the Roman period from Lydia, a woman (with a Roman name) records that she became a pallake and 'unwashed of feet' like her ancestors in accordance with an oracle (*BCH* 7, 1893: 276); presumably this is a reference to temple prostitution. The woman may well have consulted an oracle about a particular personal problem and been told to take up again the service of her women ancestors.
84 Justin 18.5.4.
85 Luc. *The Syrian Goddess* 6.
86 Thuc. 1.13.5. For sacred prostitutes at Corinth, see MacLachlan 1992; Pembroke 1996; Kurke 1996; Beard and Henderson 1998. For a possible prostitute kanephoros on a Corinthian vase, see Amyx 1988: 554–5, 563.
87 The proverb is found in: Ar. *PCG* iii.2 F928, p. 416; Strabo 8.6.20, 12.3.36; Hesych., Suid., Phot. sv ou pantos andros es Korinthon esth ho plous; Apostolios 13.60 (*CPG* ii.591); Zenobios 5.37 (*CPG* i.135); Diogenianos 7.16 (*CPG* i.289); Aulus Gellius 1.8.4; Eustathios commentary on *Il.* 2.570; cf. schol. Ar. *Wealth* 149; see *CPG* i.135–6 n. 37; expense: Ar. *Wealth* 149–52. Cf. for sailors and prostitutes: Strabo 8.6.20; Aristagoras *Mammakythos* (Athen. 571b; not in *PCG* ii).
88 Individual vows: Athen. 573e; Pindar: F122 (Maehler); Athen. 573f–574a. For this ode, see esp. Kurke 1996, with discussion of previous bibliography. For sacred prostitution in Corinth and elsewhere in the Greek world, see Licht 1932: 388–95; Yamauchi 1973; Salmon 1984: 398–400; Williams 1986: 19, 20–1; Cantarella 1987: 50; Powell 1988: 367–9; Vanoyeke 1990: 27–31; MacLachlan 1992; Blundell 1995: 35–6; Kurke 1996.
89 The translated phrase is that of Kurke 1996: 51.
90 Browsing: phorbadon; *LSJ*^{9} sv phorbadas suggests that this is metaphorical for women supporting themselves by prostitution; see esp. Kurke 1996: 57.
91 Strabo 8.6.20, 12.3.36. At 11.14.16 he discusses sacred prostitution in Armenia; see also 17.1.46. Pindar and Athenaeus do not mention the term hierodouloi in connection with Xenophon's vow.
92 Chamaileon of Herakleia F34 (Steffen 1964: 25; Athen. 573c).
93 Theopompos *FGH* 115 F285a; Timaios *FGH* 566 F10 (both Athen. 573d); Suid., Phot. sv ou pantos andros es Korinthon esth ho plous; Apostolios 13.60 (*CPG* ii.591).
94 Athen. 573d.
95 Simon. F104a–c (Diehl); Theopompos *FGH* 115 F285a (Athen. 573d–e), 285b (schol. Pind. *Olym.* 13.32b); Plut. *Mor.* 871b; Page 1981: 207–11, no. 14. The texts of the epigram in Athen., Plut., and schol. Pind. *Olym.* 13.32b all differ. The epigram need not necessarily be by Simonides (Plutarch alone makes this identification). The epigram is discussed by Page 1981: 207–11; Brown 1988; cf. Kurke 1996: 64–5. For daimoniai in line 2, see esp. Brown 1988, who argues that it is a special term for the hierodouloi of Corinth.
96 Plut. *Mor.* 871a; schol. Pind. *Olym.* 13.32b.
97 Athen. 573d; Plut. *Mor.* 871b; Page (1981: 209) preferred the idea that the women were painted on the pinax; Kurke 1996: 64–5.

NOTES

98 Theopompos *FGH* 115 F285b.
99 See Page 1981: 209; Brown 1988: 8; cf. Kurke 1996: 64.
100 Schol. Pind. *Olym.* 13.32b (Theopompos *FGH* 115 F285b).
101 Paus. 2.5.1; cf. 3.15.10, 3.23.1.
102 Williams 1986: 15–17.
103 Kurke 1996: 64–5, suggests that the word prodomen means betray, rather than simply 'hand over', and that the Corinthians were praying that Aphrodite, with her eastern connotations at Corinth as 'armed Aphrodite' and being akin to Ishtar the eastern goddess of love and war, might betray the city to the eastern Persians. But it is unlikely that the Corinthians saw Aphrodite in this way (modern scholars are the ones making the connection with eastern Ishtar – nothing suggests that the Corinthians thought similarly).
104 Strabo 6.2.6; Diod. 4.83.6 (perhaps a reference to sexual activity with women at the temple); Cic. *In Q. Caecilium Divinatio* 55. A cult of Aphrodite was imported to Rome from Eryx in the third century BC, and Venus (Aphrodite) had a temple near the Colline gate which took its name from Eryx; Roman prostitutes had an annual festival here to worship Venus: Ovid *Fasti* 4.865–76.
105 Strabo 11.14.16.
106 Strabo 12.3.36. Pembroke 1996: 1263–4, attempts to play down this aspect of Greek religion, obviously uncomfortable with the phenomenon, unrealistically seeing the term 'sacred' as referring to 'no more than manumission by fictive dedication of a kind . . . attested in a cult of Poseidon at Taenarum'. But this will not explain Xenophon's vow.
107 Pind. *Pyth.* 2.18–20.
108 Justin 21.2.9–3.8; Klearchos F43a (Athen. 516a–b). See Sourvinou-Inwood 1974: 186–7, 195–6; MacLachlan 1995: 208–9, 219.
109 Unlike Justin 21.3.3–8, Klearchos F 47 (Athen. 541c–e) clearly followed by Ael. *VH* 9.8, and Strabo 6.1.8, record a tradition that Dionysios violated the virgin daughters of the Lokrians, but not in connection with the vow or Aphrodite's temple.
110 *Figures 6.3–5*: Ludovisi Throne, Rome: Museo Nazionale 8570; marble; fifth century BC; discovered in Rome (Boardman 1967: pl. 184; 1973: 140 fig. 143; Prückner 1968: 89–91; Simon 1959: 12 pl. 3; 1969: pls 236–8; Ridgway 1970: pl. 71; 1990: 236 pl. 119; Richter 1970a: figs 513–15; 1987: figs 124, 127; Sourvinou-Inwood 1974a: pl. 13b; Robertson 1975: 203–9, pl. 66c; 1981: pl. 83; Schefold 1981: 76–7, figs 91–2; *LIMC* ii Aphrodite 1170; Stewart 1990: pls 306–8; Carpenter 1991: 83 fig. 90; Keuls 1993: 217 pls 191–3; Carratelli 1996: 70, 392–3, 705 pl. 189). Robertson 205 notes other possible identifications for the figure assisted by the attendants (Hera, Eileithyia, or Persephone), but these are unconvincing.
111 See Chapter 5, pp. 153–4.
112 *IG* ii^2 1534.27, 41 (301 BC). Castner 1982, has argued that these hetairai are the dedicators of the inscriptions, as all of the names are uncommon, and particularly because of the appearance of Mammarion and Hedeia together in *IG* ii^2 1534.27, 41 (especially sceptical of Castner's identifications is Aleshire 1989: 67; 1992: 89, 99). Castner 51, lists the literary evidence for the seven Epicurean hetairai; note also Athen. 588b.
113 *SEG* 16.300.6, 9, 12–13 (first half of the third century BC).
114 Girard 1881: 82–3, followed by many scholars, who argued that many of the dedicators were hetairai or slaves; Aleshire 1989: 67, 313, shows this not to have been the case.
115 *LSCG* 69.43–8.

NOTES

116 For numbers, see: fourth century BC: Ktesikles *FGH* 245 F1 (Athen. 272c); fifth century BC: Thuc. 2.13.6–7; archaic Athens: Arist. *Pol.* 1275b 34–8; [Arist.] *Ath. Pol.* 13.5, cf. 21.2; Plut. *Sol.* 24.4; see Whitehead 1977: 97–8, cf. 1986: 83–4; Duncan-Jones 1980; Dillon and Garland 1994: 330; 2000: 338–9.
117 For religion and the metics, see Gauthier 1972: 112–13; Whitehead 1977: 86–9.
118 [Dem.] 59.104–6, cf. 57.47–8.
119 Whitehead 1984: 58, for some examples.
120 *IG* i³ 244c.8–9; c. 460 BC (*LSCG* 10; Dillon and Garland 1994, 2000: doc. 5.20); Whitehead 1986: 205; cf. Mikalson 1977: 428, 430.
121 *IG* i³ 82.23; 421/0 BC (*LSCG* 13).
122 Demetrios *FGH* 228 F5 (Harp. sv skaphephoroi); Ael. *VH* 6.1; schol. Ar. *Birds* 1551. For the metics in the Panathenaic procession, see Whitehead 1977: 87; Rotroff 1977: 380–2; Simon 1983: 63, 65; Lefkowitz 1996: 80. The sources on the hydrophoroi, skiadephoroi, skaphephoroi and diphrophoroi are all lexicographical, but they mention as their own sources Deinarchos, Demetrios of Phaleron, Theophrastos, and the playwrights Hermippos, Nikophon and Menander, which give their statements some authority.
123 Schol. Ar. *Birds* 1551a (Hermippos *PCG* v F25, and Nikophon *PCG* vii F7); Hesych. sv diphrophoroi.
124 North frieze (three standing and one crouching): Robertson and Frantz 1975, North vi plate; Berger and Gisler-Huwiler 1996: *Tafelband* 42, 46–7.
125 Brommer 1977: 1.217.
126 Cf. Simon 1983: 64; Younger 1997: 151 n. 83.
127 Demetrios *FGH* 228 F5 (Harp. sv skaphephoroi); Poll. 3.55; Phot. sv skaphas; Phot. and Suid. sv systomoteron skaphes (see also the testimonia at Berger and Gisler-Huwiler 1996: *Textband* 195–6, nos 189–199). North frieze: v, fig. 13: Robertson and Frantz 1975: at North ii; Berger and Gisler-Huwiler *Tafelband* 42, 45–6; he was followed by two other skaphephoroi (figs 14–15).
128 Sanctuary: *IG* ii² 337; 333/2 BC (Tod *GHI* ii.189; *LSCG* 34), lines 43–5 for Isis; dedication: *IG* ii² 4636.
129 Berlin SK709; *IG* ii² 2934 (Blümel 1966: 77–8 no. 90, pls 123–4 (124 for the inscription); *LIMC* i Acheloos 202; Travlos 1971: 294 fig. 382; Neumann 1979: 74, pl. 47a; Kunze 1992: 130–1, no. 40; *BCH* 116, 1992: 156; Kron 1996: 163).
130 *IG* ii² 4609; Ferguson 1944: 108 n. 52; Vermaseren *CCCA* 2, no. 267; Parker 1996: 192, with n. 145.
131 [Dem.] 59.85; Is. 6.48–9.
132 Men. *Arbitrants* 477–8, cf. 517 (parthenos).

7 FROM ADOLESCENT GIRL TO WOMAN, WIFE AND MOTHER

1 Ar. *Lys.* 1296–1320; Dillon and Garland 1994, 2000: doc. 6.14.
2 Alkman, Pindar, Simonides and Bacchylides: Plut. *Mor.* 1136f; Anakreon: F500.
3 Theok. 18; Paus. 3.14.8, 3.15.3, cf. 3.19.10; Gow 1952: ii.358–9; Scanlon 1988: 187–8; Calame 1997: 191–202; cf. Eur. *Hel.* 1667.
4 Hdt. 6.61.2–5; Calame 1997: 196–9. At the Kopis ('Cleaver') festival, the nurses – titthai – took the male children to the sanctuary of Artemis Korythalia, and celebrated the Tithenidia 'for the children'; the name of the festival relates to nursing, and the rite was clearly kourotrophic (Polemon *FHG* iii.86; Hesych. sv korythalistriai ('the dancers for (Artemis) Korythalia'); cf. Plut. *Mor.* 657e; Parker 1989: 145; Calame 1997: 169–74.

5 Ar. *Lys.* 596–7.
6 Hellanikos *FGH* 323a F18; cf. *Il.* 16.179–86; Alkman F21 (*PMG*). Vases: *LIMC* iv Helene 30 (BM B310: *ABV* 361.12), 42 (Florence 82894: *ARV* 386.1).
7 Paus. 3.13.7, 3.16.1; Hesych. sv Dionysiades; Pettersson 1992: 34, 40; Larson 1995: 64–9; Calame 1997: 185–91.
8 Paus. 3.10.7, cf. 4.16.9–10; Luc. *Dance* 10; Plut. *Artox.* 18.2 (Klearchos' ring; Ktesias *FGH* 688 F28); Diomedes Grammaticus iii.486; Poll. 4.104; Steph. Byz. sv Karya; Statius *Thebaid* 4.225; Servius' commentary to Virgil *Eclogues* 8.30; cf. Vitruvius 1.1.5; Thuc. 5.55.3; Calame 1997: 149–56.
9 Paus. 4.16.9; Jerome 1.308 has the scene as the nocturnal Hyakinthia; Aigila: Paus. 4.17.1.
10 Karyai: Paus. 4.16.9–10, cf. 3.10.7; Thesmophoria: Paus. 4.17.1; Pelasgians: Hdt. 4.145, 6.138; Philochoros *FGH* 328 F101; Plut. *Mor.* 296b (Tyrrhenians). The Spartans in 382 BC took possession of the Kadmeia of Thebes during the Thesmophoria, which the women were celebrating on the Kadmeia: Xen. *Hell.* 5.2.29.
11 Paus. 4.4.2–3; Calame 1997: 143–9.
12 Leukothea: Alkman F4a (*PMG*); Keos: Plut. *Mor.* 249d.
13 Helen: Eur. *Hel.* 1465–70; Ar. *Lys.* 1298 (Dillon and Garland 1994, 2000: doc. 6.14); procession in chariots: Polykrates *FGH* 588 F1; Polemon *FHG* iii.86; Agesilaos: Xen. *Ages.* 8.7; Plut. *Ages.* 19.7–8; Athen. 139c–f, 173f; Hesych. sv kannai, kannathra; Pettersson 1992: 7–41; Calame 1997: 174–85; cf. Plut. *Mor.* 775c–e.
14 de Polignac 1995: 44–5; cf. Parker 1989: 149.
15 Alkman F1 (*PMG*; Dillon and Garland 1994, 2000: 13.14 (part); F3 is another shorter but important fragment). The scholiast interprets pharos as 'plough' (Calame 5), but its primary meaning, 'robe', would be more appropriate here. There are numerous difficulties of interpretation in F1: see esp. Calame 1997: 1–6. Sung at dawn: lines 41–3.
16 Alkman F1.98–9 (*PMG*; eleven girls); schol. quoted by Campbell 1988: 372; artistic evidence: Calame 1997: 21–5.
17 Delos: *Hom. Hymn Delos* 146–50, *Hom. Hymn Apollo* 169; Thuc. 3.104.5 (chorus of women); Pind. *Paian* 12; Eur. *Hek.* 462–4; cf. Callim. *Delos* 279; Delphi: Pind. *Paian* 2.96–102; Thebes: Proclus, from Photios *Bibliotheka* 321b 30.
18 Hdt. 3.48.
19 Autokrates *PCG* iv F1 (fifth–fourth century BC); Callim. *Artemis* 237–47 (Callimachus provides an aetiology: the Amazons established the dance in honour of the goddess at Ephesos); cf. *EM* sv Daitis; Calame 1997: 93–6. That these lines survive from a play called *Tympanistai*, women drum-beaters, might not be accidental.
20 *Anth. Pal.* 6.280 (a virgin, Timarete, dedicates her toys, a tambourine, ball, hairnet, and dolls with their dresses, to a virgin, Artemis Limnatis, at Sparta). For dedications of toys by parthenoi, see Rouse 1902: 249–51; Burkert 1985: 70; Golden 1990: 72, 75. For Greek marriage customs: Licht 1932: 38–53.
21 *Anth. Pal.* 6.276.
22 *Anth. Pal.* 6.276, 277; Poll. 3.38.
23 Cutting a lock of hair as a rite of passage: Larson 1995: 73, cf. 120; Tyrrell 1984: 74. The bride's hair would then be adorned for marriage: Sappho F194 (Voigt).
24 *Od.* 4.198; Hdt. 2.36.1 (see Lloyd 1994: 152–4, note 37.2), cf. 4.71.2; Aeschyl. *Choe.* 6; Soph. *Elekt.* 448–52, 901, *Ajax* 1173–5; Eur. *Tro.* 1182–4, *Iph. Taur.* 172, 703, *Elekt.* 90–1, 515, *Orest.* 96, *Phoen.* 322; Aesch. 3.211; Lys. 2.60; *Anth. Pal.* 7.181.

25 Megara: Paus. 1.43.4; Delos: Hdt. 4.34–5 (cf. 33.3); cf. Callim. *Delos* 296–9; Sparta: Plut. *Lyk.* 15.5.
26 Athena: *Anth. Pal.* 6.59; Hera: Archilochos 326 (West).
27 Hippolytos: Eur. *Hippol.* 1425–7; boys: Diod. 4.24.4–5; *Anth. Pal.* 6.155–6, 279; Paus. 8.41.3 (Arkadia); *Il.* 23.141–2, with Eustathios' commentary to same, 23.151 (Achilles); at the Koureotis, Athens: Hesych. sv koureotis; Suid. sv koureotes; Tyrrell 1984: 68–9; Strauss 1993: 95; Vidal-Naquet 1986: 140; Garland 1990: 179; Lambert 1998: 163; ephebes: Athen. 494f; Hesych. sv oinisteria; long hair at Sparta to make the warriors more terrifying in battle: Xen. *Lak. Pol.* 11.3, 13.8–9 (Dillon and Garland 1994, 2000: doc. 6.12; note Hdt. 1.82.8); see also for Sparta: Hdt. 7.208.3–209.1; Arist. *Rhet.* 1367a28–32; cf. Ar. *Birds* 1281–2, *Wasps* 466, 475–6, *Lys.* 279–80.
28 Xenophon of Ephesos 1.2.3, 6.
29 Duris *FGH* 76 F60; Asios F13 (*PEG* pp. 130–1) (both Athen. 525e–f); for Asios and Samian hairstyles: Bowra 1970: 122–33.
30 Xenophon of Ephesos 5.11.
31 For pre-nuptial rituals, and hair cutting other than in a pre-nuptial context, note: Eitrem 1915: 366–9; Licht 1932: 42–3; Price 1978: 211; King 1983: 120–2, cf. 114; Tyrrell 1984: 74, 77; Burkert 1985: 70; Dowden 1989: 2–3, 123; Zaidman and Pantel 1992: 186–8; Zaidman 1992: 361; Oakley and Sinos 1993: 15–21; Reinsberg 1993: 50–1; Rehm 1994: 12, 14.
32 Apostolios 10.96 (*CPG* ii.513); dedication of veil to Hera after wedding: Archilochos 326 (*Anth. Pal.* 6.133, perhaps dubious; Dillon and Garland 1994, 2000: doc. 13.41).
33 *Anth. Pal.* 7.182.
34 Plut. *Lyk.* 15.6.
35 Lekythos: *ARV* 993.80; *Add.* 312; Athenian rf; 450 BC (Kurtz 1975: pl. 34.2; *LIMC* ii Artemis 721a; Oakley and Sinos: 56 fig. 9; Oakley 1997: 57, pl. 73a–c); pyxis: Mainz University 116; Oakley and Sinos 1993: 53 figs 3–5. See Oakley and Sinos for numerous plates of Athenian vases depicting wedding ceremonies. For the pyxis, see p.302 n. 26.
36 Loutrophoros: Oakley and Sinos 1993: 32, 96 figs 82–4; Rehm 1994: 14–17.
37 Paus. 2.33.1.
38 *Anth. Pal.* 6.59, 200 (for twins), 201, 202, 272; King 1983: 121.
39 PL Cp11269 (krater; Bérard 1989: fig. 136).
40 [Arist]. *Oikonomika* 2.2.4 (1347a).
41 Proteleia: Men. F903 (= Phot. sv proteleia; Koerte); see also Poll. 3.38; Hesychius sv gamon ethe; Burkert 1983: 63 n. 20; Garland 1990: 219–20; Suid. sv proteleia; Apollod. 1.105 (Admetos); Phot., Suid., EM, sv Tritopatores; cf. *IG* i^3 1066–7 (445–410 BC; 500–480 BC respectively); Proclus *in Platonis Timaeum commentarii* iii.176.27–8.
42 *SEG* 41.182; Parker 1996: 196; Dillon 1999a: 73.
43 Statue of Aphrodite Ourania in Aphrodite sanctuary: Paus. 1.19.2; sanctuary of Aphrodite Ourania, and Aigeus myth: Paus. 1.14.7 (see Wycherley 1957: 49–50 no. 106; Travlos 1971: 79–80, 82 pl. 105); see also Paus. 1.27.3 (Travlos 1971: 228). To dream of Aphrodite Ourania was propitious for marriages and children, but not so a dream of Aphrodite Pandemos: Artemidoros *Dreams* 2.37.
44 Erinyes: Aeschyl. *Eum.* 834–6 (with schol.), cf. 854–7; Fates: Poll. 3.38; Praisos: Agathokles *FGH* 472 F1a, Neanthes *FGH* 84 F15; young men: *Anth. Pal.* 6.318; cf. Eur. *Iph. Taur.* 206–7.
45 Hermion: Paus. 2.34.12; Artemis Eukleia: Plut. *Arist.* 20.7–8; Haliartos: Plut. *Mor.* 772b; Zeus Teleios and Hera Teleia (Diod. 5.73.2–5); for Hera Teleia, see

also Poll. 3.38, and below; Plataea: Paus. 9.2.7; for the aetiological myth for this statue, see Dillon 1993: 327–9; Hera Gamelia: Plut. *Mor.* 141e–f; Hera Teleia: *LSAM* 25.157, 163; Zeus Teleios: *LSCG* 18c.39–40 (*SEG* 21.541). Cf. *Od.* 20.74; Pind. *Nem.* 10.18; Aeschyl. *Eum.* 214, F383 (*TGF*); Ar. *Thesm.* 973.
46 Ar. *Lys.* 976; cf. Aeschyl. *Eum.* 213–14.
47 Hes. *WD* 783–5, 788, 794, 813.
48 Paus. 9.3.1–9; Plut. F 157; Dillon 1993.
49 Aeschyl. *Ag.* 227; cf. 65; Eur. *Iph. Aulis* 432–9, 718–19; Foley 1982: 161; Seaford 1987: 109; Rehm 1994: 43.
50 Pl. *Laws* 774e–775a; Plut. *Mor.* 138b, 264b (cf. Poseidippos *PCG* vii F28.21).
51 Men. F265 (Koerte); Hesych. sv Gamelion; Mikalson 1975: 107, 189.
52 *LSCG* 18.b33–7, c39–41, d30–2; first half of the fourth century BC (*SEG* 21.541).
53 See Oakley and Sinos 1993: 10, 132 n. 12.
54 Suid. sv Kourotrophos.
55 Phanodemos *FGH* 325 F6.
56 Eur. *Alk.* 163–9.
57 *ARV* 899.146 (pyxis, white background); *c.* 400 BC (*Add.* 303; *LIMC* v Hestia 26).
58 For the pre-nuptial bath, see Ginouvès 1962: 265–82, esp. 267–9; cf. Cook 1940: iii.1.370–96; Rehm 1994: 14, 30–1.
59 For a definition of these terms and vases, see Oakley 1990: 41–2; Oakley and Sinos 1993: 6, note esp. 119 fig. 119; Dillon 1999a: 70.
60 Horos stone: *IG* i^3 1064 (*SEG* 17.10); end of the fifth century BC; for the shrine: Travlos 1971: 361–3, pl. 465; Oakley 1990: 41; Oakley and Sinos 1993: 6; Reinsberg 1993: 70; Dillon 1999a: 71.
61 Acropolis and Eleusis: Dillon 1999a: 71; Vari: Dillon 1997a: 119–20. *IG* ii^2 1485.54 mentions two nuptial footstools. Travlos 1971: 361, 417; Bell 1981: 108 n. 134; Connor 1988: 180; cf. Travlos 1988: 447–8.
62 Dem. 44.18, 30; Phot. sv loutra; Hesych. sv loutrophoros; Harp., Suid. sv loutrophoros kai loutrophorein; Poll. 8.66.
63 Thuc. 2.15.5; Hdt. 6.137.1–3 (*FGH* 1 Hekataios F127).
64 Aeschyl. *Prom.* 552–9; the groom having a bath is depicted on a hydria: Oakley and Sinos 1993: 56–8 figs 10–13.
65 Eur. *Phoen.* 346–9, with schol. 347; Plut. *Mor.* 606f.
66 Porphyry *The Cave of the Nymphs* 12; the water of the Imbrasos on Samos, however, was too sacred to be drawn: *LSCG Suppl.* 81, first century AD (Dillon 1997a: 122); cf. *LSCG Suppl.* 50, fifth century BC (Dillon and Garland 1994, 2000: doc. 12.28).
67 Ps. Aeschin. *Letter* 10.3.
68 See Dowden 1992: 118, 140–1.
69 Leitao 1995; Crete: Ephoros *FGH* 70 F 149.
70 Plut. *Lyk.* 15.5 (cf. *Mor.* 245e–f); Vidal-Naquet 1986: 150; Leitao 1995: 162. Plutarch mentions the Hybristika festival at Argos in which women dressed in men's tunics and cloaks and the men in women's dresses and headdresses: Plut. *Mor.* 245e–f; Paus. 2.20.8–10; Max. Tyr. 37.5. The historicity of the aetiological myth for this, that it celebrated the defeat of the Spartan king Kleomenes by the Argive woman poet Telesilla and the Argive women after Kleomenes had defeated the men in battle, is debated.
71 *ED* 178; early second century BC.
72 Suid. sv Arktos e Brauroniois; Ravenna scholium on Ar. *Lys.* 645.
73 Ar. *Lys.* 641–7; Dillon and Garland 1994, 2000: doc. 12.38.

74 Suid., Harp. (partly Krateros *FGH* 342 F9), An. Bekk. sv arkteusai; Hesych. sv arkteia; schol. Ar. *Lys.* 645 (Leiden); cf. Men. *Phasma* 194–8.
75 Kahil 1963; 1965; 1977; 1981; 1983; Perlman 1983; 1989; Osborne 1985: 154–72; Sourvinou-Inwood 1988; 1990a; Dowden 1989: 25–32; Hamilton 1989; Reeder 1995: 321–8; Dillon 1997: 201–2; 1999a: 74–5.
76 *LSCG* 163.1–2 (second century BC).
77 Dillon 1999a: 66–7.
78 *LSCG* 175.4–5 (*SGDI* 3721; *SIG*^{3} 1006; Dillon 1999a: 67).
79 *LSCG Suppl.* 115.15–23 (*SEG* 9.72; Buck 115); Parker 1983: 345; Dillon 1999a: 67.
80 Price 1978.
81 *Hom. Hymn to Ge* 5; Alcaeus F129.6–7 (Voigt).
82 Perachora: Price 1978: 21 no. 56; Lecherna: Hesych. sv lecherna; as Eileithyia: Hesych. sv Eileithyias. At Hermion, there were vast numbers of votives offered to Eileithyia: Paus. 2.35.11.
83 Price 1978: 152 (cf. 207), citing *Vita Herodotea, Hom. Vitae* 399.
84 Ge Kourotrophos: Paus. 1.22.3; esp. *IG* ii^2 4869, cf. 4756, 4757, 5131; Price 1978: 106; ephebes: *IG* ii^2 1039.58; Erchia: *LSCG* 18a.25–6, 59–60, b.7–8, 33–4, c3–4, d.3–4 (*SEG* 21.541); Salaminioi: *SEG* 21.527.12; tetrapolis: *LSCG* 20b.6, 14, 31, 37, 42, 46, 57 (*IG* ii^2 1358); Nikostrate: *AE* 1884: 194; Price 120; perhaps third century BC.
85 *Figure 7.1*: Reggio Calabria, Museo Nazionale 28272, 500–450 BC (Carratelli 1996: 700 pl. 166.iii; Hellenkemper 1998: 166 pl. 96); cf. Taranto *IG* 8327 (Matt 1962: 144; Prückner 1968: pl. 7.6; *LIMC* ii Aphrodite 810; MacLachlan 1995: 222 fig. 14); see also Prückner pl. 14; *Loc. Ep.* pl. 5. Some but by no means all the pinakes are published in: Higgins 1954: pls 167–8, nos 1215–25; Prückner 1968; *Loc. Ep.* pls 1–20, 66–80; MacLachlan 1995: 220–3; Montuoro 1961: 674–7, pls 803–6; Borelli 1995: 404–6, pls 483–5. For discussions, see also Atallah 1966: 160–8; Zuntz 1971: 164–8; Sourvinou-Inwood 1974a: 132–4; 1978.
86 Dedication: *Anth. Pal.* 6.280 (Timarete, discussed above); tombs: Sourvinou-Inwood 1978: 108; cf. MacLachlan 215 n. 70.
87 *Figure 7.2*: Reggio Calabria, Museo Nazionale 57482; 500–450 BC (Carratelli 1996: 700 pl. 166.ii; Borelli 1995: 405 fig. 484).
88 Reggio Calabria 28270 (Matt 1962: 140; Prückner pl. 14.4; MacLachlan 1995: fig. 2; Carratelli 701 pl. 166.i); cf. Boardman and la Rocca 1978: pl. 119.
89 Reggio Calabria (inv. no. unknown), *c.* 470 BC (Matt pl. 147; Montuoro 1961: 676 pl. 804; Langlotz 1963: pl. 72; Prückner pl. 14; Higgins 1967: pl. 38c; *LIMC* iv Hades 50 (cf. 58); MacLachlan 1995: fig. 13).
90 Kalathos scenes: *Loc. Ep.* pls 2, 3.1, 8, 11, 13, 67.2, 70, 78.2, 79.1; Prückner pls 10, 12; MacLachlan 1995: figs 3, 8; Langlotz 1963: 71.
91 Cutting hair: *Loc. Ep.* pl. 6.1; Prückner fig. 8; MacLachlan fig. 5; presenting hair: *Loc. Ep.* pl. 8.1; warrior and daughter: *Loc. Ep.* pl. 3.2, 4.1, 9.1.
92 Also in other examples, such as Prückner pl. 5 (MacLachlan 221 fig. 9), pl. 6 (MacLachlan 221 fig. 10).
93 Compare the morotton of the Thesmophoria: Chapter 4, p.114.
94 Prückner pl. 6; *Loc. Ep.* pl. 7.1; MacLachlan fig. 10.
95 Prückner pl. 5; *Loc. Ep.* pls 6.2, 68.2; MacLachlan fig. 9; cf. Matt 1962: 142; *Loc. Ep.* pl. 68.
96 Tarento *IG* 8332 (Prückner pl. 4.4; Langlotz pl. 75; MacLachlan fig. 11; Matt 145).
97 Prückner fig. 4; Simon 1959: 8 fig. 1, 11 fig. 2; 1969: 249 no. 240; *Loc. Ep.* 15; *LIMC* ii Aphrodite 1171; MacLachlan 223 fig. 19.

NOTES

98 Hermes in the chariot: Taranto *IG* 8326 (Prückner pl. 2.1; Matt 1962: pl. 11; Langlotz pl. ix; Montuoro 1961: 677 fig. 805; Simon 1959: pl. 22; *LIMC* ii Aphrodite 1329); Hekate and Demeter pinax: *Loc. Ep.* 15.1; Hermes offering a rooster: *Loc. Ep.* 71.1–2, 74, cf. 20; Dionysos makes offerings to Persephone and Hades: *Loc. Ep.* 75.2, 76; Higgins 1967: pl. 38d; this was the anakalypteria ceremony when the bride was unveiled and received gifts; Hermes brings Persephone back to her mother: *Hom. Hymn Dem.* 334–83.
99 *Loc. Ep.* pl. 6.2, 7.1, 68.2, 69.1, 69.2.
100 *Loc. Ep.* 1.1, 79.
101 *Loc. Ep.* note esp. *Loc. Ep.* 67.1; also 12.1–2, 13.1–2, 17.1, 66.1–2, 67.2, 68.1.
102 Taranto *IG* 8332: see above, n. 96 for full details.
103 *Loc. Ep.* pls 69.1–2.
104 *LIMC* ii Aphrodite 810, 1327, 1328, 1329 (the last two are also *LIMC* v Hermes 757–8): all of the Lokrian pinakes assigned to Aphrodite need to be reassigned to Persephone.
105 *Figure 7.3*: Pitsa painted wooden plaque, NM 16464; polychrome (mainly blue and red paint for the figures on a cream-brown background); the less well preserved ones are: 16465, 16466, 16467; see *SEG* 23.264 a–c (Hausmann 1960: 14 pl. 4; Schelp 1975: 86 K16; Robertson 1975: pl. 34d; 1981: pl. 45; Lorber 1979: 93, no. 154, pls 45.154, 46.154; Amyx 1988: 394–5, 543, 604–5; Boardman 1993: pl. vii.64; 1996: 122 fig. 112; van Straten 1995: 57–8, pl. 56; Carratelli 1996: 101; Schefold 1998: pl. 38).
106 A third group of letters could be interpreted as the name 'Ethelonche'.
107 Several women: Lorber 1979: 154d; smaller fragments: Lorber 154b ('to the nymphs'), 154c.
108 Eur. *Orest.* 624–6; Aeschyl. *TrGF* 3 F43.
109 Theok. 18.50–1.
110 Timarete: *Anth. Pal.* 6.280; Leonidas: *Anth. Pal.* 9.326, with Bell 1981: 94–7; Pl. *Phaedr.* 230b–c; graves: Bell 95.
111 Platon *PCG* vii F66.
112 *Il.* 11.269–71; cf. *Il.* 19.119, 188.
113 Amnisos: *Od.* 19.188; Strabo 10.4.8.
114 Price 1978: 18 (c) [14], 86–7, figs 2a–c. R. Olmos, 'Eileithyia', *LIMC* iii.1 p. 686, notes that Eileithyia's functions are also shared with other goddesses (Olmos' list: Artemis Hekate: Aeschyl. *Suppl.* 675–6; Artemis Lochia: Eur. *Hippol.* 166–8, *Suppl.* 958–9, *Iph. Taur.* 1097); Artemis Eileithyia: *Orphic Hymn* 2.12; cf. Hesych. sv Eileithyias. For kourotrophic Hekate: Hes. *Theog.* 450, 452.
115 Pingiatoglou 1981: 30–82; Olmos 694–5.
116 Paus. 3.14.6, cf. 3.17.1; Dawkins 1929: 50–1, fig. 29.
117 Aeschyl. *Suppl.* 676–7. Whether keys were offered 'to a goddess in order to facilitate parturition' is unclear: van Straten 1981: 100.
118 Kaphyai: Paus. 8.23.7 (see esp. King 1983: 118–19); Corinth: Paus. 2.3.6–7.
119 Callimachus *Anth. Pal.* 6.146.
120 See Kron 1996: n. 129 for examples.
121 *IG* iv^2 1.121–2 iamata 1–2, 31, 34, 39, 42.
122 *Figure 7.4*: Archaeological Museum of Lamia: inv. AE 1041; published in Dakoronia and Gounaropoulou 1992, dating it to *c.* 300 BC; an earlier date is preferable, about the middle of the fourth century BC; van Straten 1995: 82–4, 293 R75 bis; Cole 1998: 34–5, fig. 3.1; Echinos is between Malis and Achaea in the Malian Gulf region. The sex of the child is unclear but it is dressed in what appears to be a belted peplos with himation, and could be a girl.

123 Rome, Villa Albani; unknown provenance, but south Italian, from a Greek city; early fifth century BC, 135 centimetres high (Ridgway 1970: pl. 126; Robertson 1975: pl. 66a).
124 NY 24.97.92 (Mitropoulou 1977: no. 66; van Straten 1981: 100, fig. 43).
125 Amphidromia: see Chapter 8, p.254; seventh-day festival: Hesych. sv hebdomai; Harp. sv hebdomeuomenou; Suid. sv hebdomeuomena.
126 Euboulos *PCG* v F2; cf. Eur. *Elekt.* 1126, F2 (*TGF*); Ar. *Birds* 494–6, 922 with schol.; Dem. 39.22, 40.28; Is. 3.30, 70; Hesych. sv dekaten thuomen (cf. amphidromia); Suid. sv dekaten hestiasai, dekateuein; An. Bekk. sv dekaten hestiasai.
127 Athen. 647c, citing Iatrokles *On Cakes*.
128 Athen. 668c.
129 One fragment shows a long haired infant, but the dress is arranged in a fashion suitable for a male child, and the intention here might be to indicate the child Adonis (*pace* MacLachlan 1995: 216).
130 Women presenting their child to the goddess: Sourvinou-Inwood 1978: 116–18; MacLachlan 1995: 216–17; for the scenes as representing Kore and Ploutos: *Loc. Ep.* pl. 14.1–2; as Aphrodite and the child Dionysos: Prückner 29–31; myth of Adonis: Apollod. 3.183–5; votive reliefs (at Reggio Calabria museum): Higgins 1954: no. 1219; Atallah 1966: 160–2 figs 26–8; Prückner 31 fig. 3; *Loc. Ep.* pls 14, 77; Borelli 1995: pl. 485; Schefold 1981: 36 fig. 30; *LIMC* ii Aphrodite 1365b (*LIMC* i Adonis 58); MacLachlan 222 figs 16–17.
131 Lys. 1.6.

8 WOMEN, SACRIFICE AND IMPURITY

1 Men. *Dysk.* esp. 1–4, 11–12, 37–40, 51, 197, 408–18, 857–8 (a pannychis of women); quotations: Men. *Dysk.* 260–3, 407–9. See, for the nymphaion at Phyle: Travlos 1988: 319–20, 325–6, pls 408–9.
2 Detienne 1989: 131; cf. Zaidman 1992: 338–9. For women and their presence at sacrifices, see Detienne 1989; Osborne 1993; cf. Cole 1992: 105–7; 1995: 183–4.
3 *LSCG* 96.8–9, 24–26; *c.* 200 BC (*SIG*³ 1024). Chthonios refers to these gods' local associations or origins, from which xenoi are understandably restricted.
4 Elateia: *LSCG* 82; end of the fifth century BC (*SIG*³ 979). Taras: ([Arist.] *Mirabilia* 840 a8–10); Lindos: *LSCG Suppl.* 88a (fourth century BC), b (second century BC); 89 (fourth century BC). The last three use the formula gynaixi ouk hosia ('for women, not holy').
5 Cyprus: Strabo 14.6.3; Athens and Corinth: Paus. 1.1.3, 2.32.6; Delos: *LSCG Suppl.* 56, second century BC (*ID* 2180); linen: Hdt. 2.37.2.
6 Zeus Hypatos: *LSCG* 109 (end of the fifth century BC); Kore: *LSCG* 110 (fifth century BC); Erythrai: Paus. 7.5.8; Mykonos: *LSCG* 96.15–22, esp. 22 (*c.* 200 BC); Leukothea: Plut. *Mor.* 267d; Eresos: *LSCG* 124.18–20 (second century BC).
7 Geronthrai: Paus. 3.22.7; Orpheus: Konon *FGH* 26 F1.xlv; Hermotimos: Apollonios *Mirabilia* 3.4; Herakles on Thasos: see below; Kronos: Phylarchos *FGH* 81 F33. Lambert 1998: 347, cf. 186, rejects Wilhelm's suggestion that *IG* ii² 1240.5, a phratry inscription (Attica), is a reference to a prohibition against women 'from some religious event'.
8 Eunostos: Plut. *Mor.* 300d–301a; Diokles: *FHG* iii F4, *FGH* i.a.295; Plut. also cites Myrtis 716 (*PMG*); see Farnell 1921: 88; *AJA* 78, 1974: 156; Schachter 1981: i.222; Roller 1989: i.33–5, 153–4.
9 Hippodameion: Paus. 6.20.7; Eileithyia: Paus. 6.20.2–3.
10 Rhea: Paus. 8.36.3; Kore: Paus. 8.31.8; basilinna: see Chapter 3 pp.101–4.

NOTES

11 Mysia: Paus. 7.27.9–10; Methymna: *LSCG* 127, fourth century BC (Henrichs 1984: 81; Cole 1995: 184 n. 14); possibly concerning Dionysos given the reference to the thyrsos.
12 Hermion: Paus. 2.35.8; Eileithyia: 2.35.11; Aigion: Paus. 7.23.9; Bryseai: Paus. 3.20.3, cf. 2.4.6.
13 Cic. *Against Verres* ii.4.45.99–102.
14 Paus. 2.10.4.
15 *CPG* i.392: 88. For Herakles' cults excluding women, see Farnell 1921: 162–3; Cole 1992: 106–7; Osborne 1993: 392, 394, 397–8.
16 *LSAM* 42a, about 500 BC, the relevant lines require restoration (Fontenrose 1988: no. 3, pp. 180–1).
17 *LSCG Suppl.* 63.3–4, c. 440 BC; see Bergquist 1973: 30–2, 65–6, 70–80.
18 *LSCG Suppl.* 66, beginning of the fourth century BC; cf. *LSCG Suppl.* 68, fourth century BC, Thasos, where a provision against women might have been part of the inscription; Herakleia on the Pontos prohibited burial in the shrine but nothing else is mentioned: *LSAM* 83 (fourth century BC).
19 Ael. *Nat. An.* 17.46.
20 Plut. *Mor.* 403f–404a; Parke and Wormell R 464; Fontenrose 1978: H63.
21 *LSCG* 177.101–11 (PH 36); see the commentaries of *LSCG* 177 p. 313 and *PH* 36 p. 76; cf. Cole 1992: 107.
22 Plut. *Mor.* 304c–e.
23 Athens *EM* 3942; *LIMC* iv Herakles 1388; D.M. Robinson 1948, *Hesperia* 17: 137–40, pl. 34; M. Billot 1992, *BCH* 116: 137–8 fig. 4; van Straten 1995: 297 R90, fig. 93; Boardman 1995: fig. 145.
24 *LIMC* iv Herakles 1383 (*LIMC* vii Pankrates i.2); see also I. Meliades 1954, *Praktika*: 48 fig. 6; Meliades 1954, *Ergon*: 4 fig. 1; van Straten 1974: 171 fig. 21; *SEG* 22.164; Vollkommer 1988: 83 no. 553; Vikela 1994: B10, pl. 22.2; 1997: 214, pl. 28.1. For the shrine of Herakles Pankrates, see also Travlos 1971: 278–80.
25 Kneeling relief, 340–330 BC: *LIMC* vii Pankrates i.6; a male figure (her husband?) is directly behind her, there is no inscription; the relief could indicate thanks for a sucessful supplication; see also Travlos 1971: 279 fig. 358; van Straten 1974: 170 no. 16; Mitropoulou 1975: 26–7 no.2; Vikela 1994: A3 pl. 3. Similarly, a male figure kneels and touches Pankrates' robes, with a female figure standing behind: *LIMC* vi Melikertes 50 (Vikela A10 pl. 8).
26 *SEG* 16.182; I. Meliades 1953, *Praktika*: 55, 57 fig. 8; fourth century BC.
27 See *LIMC* vii.2 Pankrates i, pls 101–103; families: 102.i.7, 11, 13, 15; women only: i.14 (around 300 BC; van Straten 1974: 170 no. 17; Mitropoulou 1975: 35–7 no. 10 pl. 11; Vikela 1994: A12 pl. 10), perhaps 23 (340 BC); also Vikela: A13 (325–300 BC; a woman standing before the god; the dedicatory inscription reads: 'Agnothea dedicated (this)'.
28 *IG* ii² 4613 (Athens *EM* 8793; end of the fourth century BC); *LIMC* iv Herakles 1387; Hausmann 1948: 180, no. 164; van Straten 1981: 104; Kearns 1989: 35–6; Vikela 1994: 168.
29 *LIMC* iv Herakles 1386: fourth century BC, Athens (AM 7232); van Straten 1974: 168; Vollkommer 1988: 43 no. 283, 45, 85; Vikela 1994: pl. 37. For Herakles as a healing deity: Vollkommer 45, nos 85–6.
30 *IG* ii² 1247 (c. 250 BC); on the Mesogeioi as probably but not definitely a genos: Parker 1996: 306–7.
31 Aesch. 1.183.
32 Semonides F7.50, 55–6, with Lloyd-Jones 1975: 76–8.
33 Ischomachos: Xen. *Oik.* 7.8; brides: Theophr. *Char.* 22.4.
34 Adultery: [Dem.] 59.85; bastards: Is. 6.47, 51; slave woman: Is. 6.49–50.

35 Philoneos: Antiphon 1.16–19; Sinope: [Dem.] 59.116; Athen. 594a–b.
36 [Dem.] 59.73, 78.
37 Figures 2.1–2, 2.13–14, 3.4, 7.3 (Pitsa), 8.1 (Hekate).
38 Eur. F65.90–7 (Austin); Jordan 1979: 31–2.
39 *IG* ii² 403.15–19 (*c.* 350–320 BC); *IG* i³ 35.11–12.
40 *SEG* 33.115.9–25; Dontas 1983: 52.
41 Penelope: *Od.* 4.759–67; Nestor: *Od.* 3.450–1, cf. *Od.* 22.408, 411 (Eurykleia was about to make the ololyge over the corpses of the slaughtered suitors, but Odysseus stops her); Klytaimnestra: Aeschyl. *Ag.* 594–5, cf. 1118; Eteokles: Aeschyl. *Seven* 265–70; Athena: Eur. F351 (*TGF*); cf. Hdt. 4.189.2.
42 Burkert 1983: 5, 12; cf. 1985: 56; Collins 1995: esp. 325; Zaidman and Pantel 1992: 32, 35.
43 Athena Nike: *IG* i³ 35; Olympia: Paus. 5.16.3; kanephoroi: *IG* ii² 334.15; Apatouria: Ar. *Thesm.* 558–9 (the Apatouria celebrated the phratry, membership of which constituted proof of citizenship; phratry members upon marriage made an offering at the festival, presumably to indicate their intention to produce legitimate citizen heirs); Eretria: Plut. *Mor.* 298b–c.
44 *BCH* 89, 1965: 446–7, 462–3 no. 6; Detienne 1989: 131; Osborne 1993: 392.
45 *LSAM* 73; third century BC (*SIG*³ 1015); Detienne 1989: 131; Osborne 1993: 399; cf. Suid. sv He Pergaia Artemis.
46 *LSCG* 18.a44–51 (*SEG* 21.541); for the 'ou phora' provision (the meat was to be consumed on the spot and not taken away), see Dillon 1997: 160–1.
47 Paus. 8.48.4–5; Detienne 1989: 132–3.
48 Hesych., Suid. sv Chalkidikon diogma; Winkler 1990: 197.
49 *LSCG Suppl.* 20.17–23; Ferguson 1944; 1949: 130–1; Nock 1944: 141–74; Detienne 131–2; Osborne 1993: 400.
50 *LSAM* 73.8–14; Halikarnassos, third century BC (*SIG*³ 1015); entrails for a woman priest are restored in *LSCG* 120.1–2, 10 (fourth century BC). A share in the entrails was a common prerequisite for priests as well, of course; e.g. *LSCG* 119.3–9; Chios, priest of Herakles, fourth century BC; tongue and entrails (*SIG*³ 1013); *LSAM* 59.3; fourth century BC, Iasos; the priest of Zeus Megistos: head, feet, and a fourth share of the entrails; *LSAM* 72.39; Halikarnassos, third century BC: thigh, fourth share of entrails, an 'equal share' of everything else.
51 *SEG* 35.923a, *c.* 400 BC; esp. Osborne 1993: 402. Osborne comments that this seems to be the only occasion when a priest or woman priest was to consume their perquisites 'on the spot'. Presumably this rarity is explained by the fact that the perquisites were generally of a generous nature, more than a meal's worth.
52 *AM* 97, 1982: 153–70; cf. Osborne 1993: 403 n. 51; van Straten 1995: 107; Luc. *Dial. Het.* 7.1.
53 The 'Ruvo amphora', Apulian rf volute, *c.* 400 BC; Naples, Museo Nazionale 2411, inv. 82922 (*AJA* 37, 1933: 242, pl. 31.1; *LIMC* iii Dionysos 863; *RVAp* I no. 35, 8 (2); Detienne 1989: 140; van Straten 1995: 220 V149, pl. 111).
54 Ael. *Nat. An.* 11.4 (quoting Aristokles); Paus. 2.35.4–8; both accounts differ in some details; Bremmer 1987: 199.
55 Pherekrates *PCG* vii F70; cf. the gloss of Athen. 612a–b.
56 Eur. *Iph. Taur.* 617–24, with Cropp 1997: 32–3.
57 *Figure 8.1*: NM 1695; rf lekythos, connected with the Group of Palermo 16, fifth century BC; *ARV* 1204.2 (and 1704), *Para.* 463 (Deubner 1932: 44, pl. 2; A. Rumpf 1961, *Bonner Jahrbücher* 161: 208–9; Detienne 1989: 134; Simon 1983: 20; 1985: 273–4, pl. 49.3; Keuls 1993: 355–6 fig. 295 (piglet); see *OCD*³ 671). Three-faced Hekate representation, e.g.: Athens, Kerameikos 4961 (Simon 1985: pl. 49.1). Hesych. sv Genetyllis has women sacrificing dogs to Hekate.

58 Lys. 6.51.
59 Theano: Plut. *Alk.* 22.5; Cyrene: *SEG* 9.3; Dillon and Garland 1994, 2000: doc. 1.24.
60 Telemachos: *Od.* 2.135–6; Klytaimnestra: Aeschyl. *Ag.* 1433; Elektra: Soph. *Elektra* 431–63; Medea: Eur. *Med.* 607; Ar. *Thesm.* 295–351.
61 Dem. 24.151; see for references, Mikalson 1983: 125 n. 11; Parker 1983: 191 n. 3.
62 Aesch 3.111; Mikalson 1983: 125 n. 13; Parker 201 n. 65 for several references.
63 Lys. 32.13; Aglauros: Bion *FGH* 332 F 1; Ar. *Thesm.* 533.
64 Soph. *Oed. Tyr.* 269–72.
65 Iphigeneia: Eur. *Iph. Taur.* 735–58; daughters: *Erech.* F65[a], 68–70 (Austin).
66 Dem. 40.11; Is. 12.9.
67 Xenophon: Xen. *Anab.* 3.2.9; superstitious man: Theophr. *Char.* 16.5; cf. Pl. *Laws* 887e; unseemly: DL 6.37–8; statue clinging: see below; kneeling as womanly: Polyb. 32.15.8.
68 *SEG* 16.184 (van Straten 1974: 170 no. 15 fig. 22; Vikela 1994: 20–1 A10 pl. 8).
69 Van Straten 1974 collects the iconography of kneeling worshippers, and notes only one case of a kneeling male worshipper: 170, 175.
70 [Dem.] 59. 85.
71 Plato *Laws* 910a; Eur. *Alk.* 162–71.
72 Megalopolis: *BCH* 102, 1978: 326; Delos: *LSCG Suppl.* 54.7–8; Egypt: *LSCG Suppl.* 119.13; Athens: *LSCG* 55.5–6; Lindos: *LSCG Suppl.* 91.16; Thera: *Hesperia* 1971, 40: 237. For menstruation, see Wächter 1910: 36–9; Parker 1983: 100–3, 354; Cole 1992: 111. Arist. *Generation of Animals* 728a (*pace* Cole 1992: 111) does not indicate that menstruation was considered a source of impurity. The comment of Achilles Tatius 4.7.7 in the fourth century AD that it was 'not right' (ou themis, almost 'not holy') to have intercourse with a woman during menstruation, but that it was all right to 'kiss and cuddle', strikes one as a sexual preference rather than as an indication of impurity and pollution. Parker 1983: 346 raises the possibility that the 'involuntary pollution' of the Cyrene cathartic law (*LSCG Suppl.* 115b.3–8) might be menstruation only to discount it (probably correctly).
73 For Mommsen, see Linders 1972: 58, accepted by Robertson 1995: 201 (and 201 n. 26 for where the word occurs in *IG* ii^2 1514–18, 1523–4); Dillon 1997: 201–2; argued against by Linders 1972: 58–9. I am now persuaded that the word does not refer to menstrual cloths.
74 Hippokrates *Peri Parthenion* (*Concerning Virgins*) viii.468.13–14 (Littré).
75 Despoina: *LSCG* 68.11–13 (third or second century BC); Arkadia: Callim. *Zeus* 11–13.
76 Arist. *Pol.* 1335b12–16.
77 Callim. *Demeter* 130–3. For Censorinus in the third century AD who wrote that amongst the Greeks pregnant women do not go to a shrine before the fortieth day, see *De dei natali* 11.7; Parker 1983: 48; Garland 1990: 46–7.
78 Eur. *Iph. Taur.* 1226–9.
79 *LSCG Suppl.* 115b.24–7.
80 *LSCG* 154a.23–4, cf. 39 (first half of the third century BC).
81 *LSCG* 156a.13 (first half of the third century BC); Parker 1983: 50 n. 67 (see this note, and 353–5, for miscarriage).
82 *LSCG Suppl.* 91.11. Parker 1983: 50 n. 67 notes the analogy with *LSAM* 51.6–10, where a dog giving birth pollutes like a woman, 'no doubt because dogs share a roof with men'. Other post-classical laws concerning miscarriage are cited at Parker 355; these are: *LSCG Suppl.* 54.6, 119.10; *LSAM* 84.5; *LSCG* 55.7, 139.12, 171.17. Forty-four days: *BCH* 102, 1978: 325, lines 6–8.

NOTES

83 See esp. Parker 1983: 354.
84 *LSCG* 171.16–17.
85 Zeus: Hes. *WD* 238–45; Pelasgians: Hdt. 6.139.1; Thebes: Soph. *Oed. Tyr.* 25–7, 171–3; see Garland 1990: 38 giving the three above examples.
86 Lindos: *LSCG* 139.12. For abortion, see Parker 1983: 355–6; Garland 1990: 52–5; Cole 1992: 110.
87 Philadelphia: *LSAM* 20.20.
88 Sparta: Plut. *Lyk.* 16.1; Smyrna: *LSAM* 84.3–5 (cult of Dionysos Bromios); Ptolemais: *LSCG Suppl.* 119.7 ('if anyone should expose'; this text also mentions miscarriage (5) but the number of days' purification for this are missing from the stone). For exposure, see Garland 1990: 84–93, with references and bibliography.
89 *LSCG Suppl.* 115a.16–20; translation of Parker 1983: 336.
90 *IG* iv² 1.121 iama (cure) 1; Paus. 2.27.6.
91 Miletos: *LSAM* 52b.10 (first century BC); Delphi: *LSCG* 77d.13 (c. 400 BC).
92 *IG* iv² 1.121 iama 1 (Dillon 1997: 79, 169–70, 189, 219–20); Paus. 2.27.1, 6; Delos: Hdt. 1.64.2; Diod. 12.58.6–7; Plut. *Mor.* 230c–d; Thuc. 1.8.1, cf. 3.104.2, 5.32.1; Callim. *Delos* 277; Strabo 10.5.5.
93 A.P. Matthaiou and Y.A. Pikoulas 1986: *Horos* 4: 75–8 (second century BC); cf. Loucas and Loucas 1994; Dillon 1997: 181, 270 n. 15.
94 *IG* ii² 1035.10–11.
95 Eur. *Auge* F266 (*TGF*); Ar. *Frogs* 1080 (with schol., quoted at *TGF* p. 436); Wächter 1910: 31–2.
96 Ar. *Lys.* 742–3.
97 Chrysippos F753 (Arnim); cf. Eur. *Iphig. Taur.* 380–4; Parker 1983: 34.
98 For the problems involved in interpreting apo lechous, see Parker 1983: 352; other similar expressions are found: *LSCG Suppl.* 54.5; *LSAM* 12.7.
99 *LSCG* 154a.24, 39 (third century BC), 156a.12–13 (heavily restored); Cole 1992: 119 n. 68.
100 *LSAM* 12.7; Pergamon, after 133 BC, cult of Athena Nikephoros: the second day; *LSAM* 51.6–10, Miletos, end of the first century BC: the third day; *LSCG* 124.7–8, Eresos, second century BC; *LSCG Suppl.* 91.15, Lindos, third century AD; *LSCG Suppl.* 54.5, Delos, end of the second century BC; the sanctuary of the Syrian gods: the seventh day; *LSCG Suppl.* 119.6, Ptolemais, Egypt; the period is lost where the stone is broken; *LSCG* 171.16–17, Isthmos, second century BC, cult to Artemis, Zeus, and the ancestral gods: ten days (the same as for a miscarriage); *BCH* 102, 1978: 325–6, lines 5–6, Megalopolis, cult of Isis and Sarapis; second century BC: on the ninth day.
101 Parker 1983: 51, citing schol. Pl. *Theaet.* 160e; Hesych., Suid. sv amphidromia; Apostolios 2.56 (*CPG* ii.278); Garland 1990: 93–6.
102 Medical texts: Parker 1983: 55, with references; he suggests that as the heavy post-parturient bleeding normally lasts for ten days, with light discharges lasting anything up to three to four weeks, ten days was the period of impurity. But there is no firm evidence. Women were probably expected to stay inside after birth for at least these ten days. For the tenth-day naming festival: see Garland 1990: 94–5.
103 *LSCG* 68.11–13, third or second century BC; cf. Parker 1983: 49.
104 Ar. *Lys.* 910–13.
105 For chastity in general in cult, see Fehrle 1910.
106 Hdt. 2.64.1.
107 Metropolis: Metropolis: *LSAM* 29.4–7. 'From sex': *LSCG* 139.14: *apo synousias*; *LSCG Suppl.* 108.1: *apo aphrodision*. *BCH* 102, 1978: p. 325 lines 13–14: *apo aphrodision*.

NOTES

108 Gerarai: [Dem.] 59.73, 78; Lysistrata: Ar. *Lys.* 212–36.
109 Ar. *Knights* 1284–7; but cf. Parker 1983: 99 n. 101; Cole 1992: 118 n. 39.
110 *LSCG Suppl.* 31.6.
111 *LSCG* 151a.41–2, fourth century BC.
112 *LSCG Suppl.* 115a.11–13; Parker 1983: 74 n. 4, 335–6. Whether the provision related to simply one shrine or all of those in Cyrene is unclear; Parker argues against such a blanket provision and correctly considers it more likely to be a provision relating to one sanctuary (the text is fragmentary).
113 *LSCG* 55.3–4, second century AD.
114 Eresos: *LSCG* 124.9–10, second century BC; Arkadia: *BCH* 102, 1978: p. 325 lines 13–14; Lindos: *LSCG Suppl.* 91.17, third century AD; Pergamon: *LSAM* 12.4–9, after 133 BC.
115 Kos: *LSCG* 171.17; Lindos: *LSCG* 139.14; Syrian gods: *LSCG Suppl.* 54.4, end of the second century BC.
116 *LSCG Suppl.* 59.15–16, Roman era; 108.1, first century AD; *LSCG* 95.5, after 166 BC.
117 *LSCG Suppl.* 119.7–9, Egypt, first century BC.
118 *Alt. Perg.* 8.3, no. 161.13.
119 *LSCG* 69.43–8, fourth century BC, from the Amphiaraion, the healing shrine of the hero Amphiaraos, on the border between Attica and Boeotia.
120 *LSAM* 12.4–9, after 133 BC.
121 *LSAM* 20.25–32, Philadelphia, first century BC.
122 *LSCG Suppl.* 91.12–13, Lindos, third century AD (sanctuary of Athena); *LSCG* 139.18, second century AD (not necessarily the sanctuary of Athena).
123 See Chapter 7, p. 22.
124 *LSAM* 18, 147/6 BC; Parker 1983: 74 n. 4; Cole 1992: 108.
125 *LSCG* 139.14, Lindos, second century AD.
126 Lindos: *LSCG Suppl.* 91.18–19, third century AD; also Metropolis: *LSAM* 29.4–8, fourth century BC.
127 Lydia: *LSAM* 20.25–8; Kos: *LSCG* 151a.42.
128 Agesilaos: Xen. *Ages.* 5.7; Artayktes: Hdt. 9.116–20. Compare Demetrios Poliorketes: Chapter 6, p. 192.
129 Artemis Hymnia: Paus. 8.5.12; Delphi: see Chapter 3, p. 77.
130 Paus. 7.19.1–6.
131 Buck 64 (Dillon and Garland 1994, 2000: 10.29)
132 Hekataios *FGH* 1 F29a–b; Paus. 8.4.8–9, 47.4, 48.7; 10.28.8; Apoll. 2.7.4, 3.9.1; Soph. *Aleadai TrGF* 4 F77–91; Eur. *Auge* F265–81 (*TGF*), *Telephos* (Page 1941: 130–3); Hes. F165 (MW); Diod. 4.33.7–12; Strabo 13.1.69; Gantz 1993: 428–31. For Auge and Herakles, see *LIMC* iii Auge 6–24, iv.1 Herakles p. 823, v.1 Herakles pp. 114–15.
133 *Figure 8.2*: Pergamonmuseum 7756, Auge with women (possibly other maidens) worshipping; Telephos frieze from the Great Altar, Pergamon; marble; work on the frieze commenced *c.* 165 BC (*LIMC* iii Auge 7 = *LIMC* ii Athena 594 = *LIMC* vii Telephos i.11; Smith 1991: pl. 199.2; Heilmeyer 1997: 101 fig. 2, 140 fig. 38). *LIMC* iii Auge 7 (cf. *LIMC* vii Telephos i.11, and *LIMC* ii Athena 594) interprets the scene of Auge and other female worshippers on the Telephos frieze of the Pergamon altar not as her founding a cult of Athena in Pergamon but as worshipping in Athena's temple at Tegea, where Herakles sees Auge, and the Auge–Telephos cycle begins. If the fragment of the frieze *LIMC* vii Telephos i.2–3, which shows a standing Herakles, looking to the right (and hence in this arrangement at Auge in Athena's temple) is juxtaposed, with *LIMC* iii Auge 7 = *LIMC* vii Telephos i.11 = *LIMC* ii Athena 594, it can be

interpreted as Herakles in Tegea seeing Auge with the other women worshipping Athena. This juxtaposition occurs, for example, in *LIMC* vii.1, pp. 858–9, but not in the 1994–5 rearrangement of the frieze in the Pergamonmuseum in Berlin, for which see Heilmeyer 1997.

134 For Greek sanctuaries and suppliants, see Sinn 1993.
135 Polyxena: schol. Eur. *Hek.* 41; Cassandra: *LIMC* i Aias ii, esp. the very fine no. 44: Naples 2422 (Athenian rf hydria; Kleophrades Painter; *c.* 480 BC; *ARV* 189.74; *Add.* 189; Boardman 1984: 126–7 fig. 152; Shapiro 1994: fig. 117; Schefold 1998: 243, *LIMC* vii Kassandra i, esp. 104, 136).
136 *Figure 8.3*: Bassai, BM 524 (Hofkes-Brukker and Mallwitz 1975: 55–6, pls H4–524, H5–529; *LIMC* v Hippodameia ii.5, viii Kentauroi et Kentaurides 214 (p. 436); Ridgway 1981: 94–6; Boardman 1994: 11–12 no. 9; 1995: 35 fig. 5.5; Osborne 1994: 79 fig. 22; 1998: fig. 12; Rhodes 1995: 175 fig. 86; Spivey 1997: fig. 137; Cartledge 1998: 66).
137 South metope 21 (Brommer 1967: pl. 151; 1979: 26 fig. 13; Berger 1986: Textband 91–2; Castriota 1992: 152–65, fig. 15; Osborne 1994a: 69 fig. 18). The rectangular metopes, each 120 centimetres high and a separate piece of stone, rest on the architrave above the columns, and below the pediment, of the Parthenon. Many of the metopes, such as this one, are known only from the drawings of Carrey.
138 Volute krater (rf Apulian): Ruvo 1096, end of the fifth century BC (*LIMC* iii Dioskouroi 202, interpreting the statue as Aphrodite; she appears with Eros watching the abduction, in a corner of a vase); *RVAp* i.16 no. 1/52, pl. 5.1 (Trendall 1989: fig. 35, cf. fig. 208); see also *LIMC* iii Dioskouroi 189–214, Tinas Cliniar 79–82 (81 is a second-century BC relief from Volterra which shows each of the Leukippidai carrying statuettes, presumably of the goddesses), Castores 148–58; *LIMC* vi Lynkeus i et Idas 10–12.
139 Esp. Aeschyl. *The Suppliant Maidens (Hiketides)*; Gantz 1993: 204.
140 *ARV* 1173 (rf oinochoe; 430–425 BC; *LIMC* iv Helene 272bis; Brommer 1979: 31 fig. 16).
141 Aeschyl. *Seven* 94–5, 185, 258.
142 Paus. 3.16.10–11, 8.23.1; cf. Xen. *Lak. Pol.* 2.9; Plut. *Mor.* 239d, *Lyk.* 18.1–2, *Aristeid.* 17.10; Philostr. *Apoll.* 6.20; Brelich 1969: 134; Henrichs 1981: 205 n. 4; Burkert 1985: 152; Vernant 1991: 213, 237. Arkadia: Paus. 8.23.1.
143 Hdt. 5.92 η3. For clothing regulations in Greek cults, see Mills 1984; Culham 1986; Cole 1992: 114; Dillon 1997: 161–3, 196–8. Profane clothing regulations: Athens: Hdt. 5.87.2–88.3; Plut. *Sol.* 20.6, 21.6; Megara: Plut. *Mor.* 295a–b; Syracuse: Phylarchos *FGH* 81 F45 (women wearing gold, brightly coloured clothes, or purple bordered robes considered to be hetairai); Lokris (Epizephyrian): Diod. 12.21 (as at Syracuse); Massilia: Strabo 4.1.5.
144 Demeter Thesmophoros: *LSCG Suppl.* 32; Ar. *Thesm.* 894.
145 Phintys 591–2 (Thesleff 1965). Cf. Callim. *Demeter* 126–7, with Hopkinson 1984: 43.
146 Patras: *LSCG Suppl.* 33.1–8 (third century BC); Thasos: Pouilloux 1954: i.164 (possibly fourth or third century BC).
147 *LSCG* 68 (third century BC); Dillon 1997: 198–9.
148 Lindos: *LSCG Suppl.* 91; cf: *LSCG* 124.17; Kos: Parker 1983: 52.
149 Pergamon: *LSAM* 14. The requirement to dress in white at this sanctuary is also mentioned in *Alt. Perg.* 8.3, no. 161.2–14; and *IG* iv^2 1.128.2.18–19 (third century BC); Rhodes: *LSCG* 136.25–30; Gambreion: *LSAM* 16; Sparta: *LSCG Suppl.* 28.1–3; Osborne 1993: 398; Brauron: see Chapter 1 pp. 19–23.
150 *LSCG* 65.13–26; see on linen, Dillon 1997: 196–8.

NOTES

151 *Figure 8.4*: Munich 2415; rf Athenian stamnos; Kleophon Painter; *c*. 430 BC; height: 43 centimetres; *ARV* 1143.2; *Para*. 455; *Add*. 334 (*CVA* München 5: pl. 256.1; Pfuhl 1923: 218 fig. 558; Philippake 1967: pl. 60.1; Boardman 1967: pl. 231; 1973: fig. 176; 1989: fig. 172; Folsom 1976: pl. 54; Kasper 1976: 114 no. 163; Charbonneux 1969: 257, fig. 292; *AM* 1985: 100, pl. 47.1; Walter 1985: 37 fig. 31; M. Robertson 1992: 222 fig. 230; Dierichs 1993: 92, pl. 164; Cartledge 1998: 182; see esp. Simon 1976: pls 205–7).
152 BM E448 (*CVA* BM 3: pl. 22.3a, c; *ARV* 992.65, *Para*. 437, *Add*. 311–12; Philippake 1967: pl. 49.1–2; Charbonneux 1969: 249, fig. 281; *AJA* 1985, pl. 68 fig. 3; Ducrey 1986: 206, fig. 140; Boardman 1986: 143; Bérard 1989: 44 fig. 61; Oakley 1997: pl. 55).
153 BM E448 (see above note); *CVA* BM 3: pl. 22.3b, c; this side is not generally illustrated; they are two different warriors on each side.
154 Bologna, Museo Civico PU 285; rf kalyx krater, Methyse Painter, *c*.460 BC; *ARV* 633.6; *Add*. 272 (*CVA* Bologna 4: pls 77.1–2, 78.3–7; Schoder 1960: pl. 32; *LIMC* i Aithra i.47). The two are named by inscriptions on the vase.
155 Würzburg 507; rf amphora, Kleophrades (=Epiktetos ii) Painter; *CVA* Würzburg 2: pls 8.1, 9.1–2; *ARV* 181.1, *Para*. 340, *Add*. 186 (Boardman 1975: fig. 129.1; Ducrey 1986: 264 fig. 179; Bérard 1989: 48 fig. 68). Two of the six examples shown by Bérard 48, of warriors examining entrails, have a woman present, including the vase discussed here.

9 WOMEN AND THE CORPSE: MOURNING RITUALS

1 Thuc. 2.34.4, cf. 2.45.2. For Greek death, see Vermeule 1979; Garland 1985; 1989; Morris 1987; 1992–3; Sourvinou-Inwood 1995; Johnston 1999.
2 Is. 6.41.
3 *Il*. 22.405–15, 430–7, 468–72, 476, 515, 24.710–12; 720–3, 746–7, 760–1. While she lamented, Andromache held Hektor's head in her hands, 24.724 (cf. 18.71).
4 *Il*. 19.282–5.
5 Chorus of women: Aeschyl. *Choe*. 22–31 (cf. Eur. *Hek*. 650–6, *Hel*. 373); dirges sung by women: Eur. *Andr*. 1038–40; see also for breast beating and cheek laceration: Eur. *Suppl*. 71–7, 87–8, 826; women with heads covered in dust; Eur. *Hek*. 495–6, *Suppl*. 827.
6 *Il*. 22.33–4 (Priam); Eur. *Phoen*. 351, *Tro*. 794 (and breasts), *Hel*. 372; cf. Luc. *Funerals* 12.
7 *Il*. 18.23–32. For extending the right hand to the dead: Aeschyl. *Choe*. 9.
8 Priam: *Il*. 24.720–3; Solon: Plut. *Sol*. 21.6; for professional mourners, Plato: Pl. *Laws* 800e, with schol.; Hesych. sv *Karinai* (the women played dirge music); Poll. 4.75; cf. Aeschyl. *Pers*. 935–40, 1054: the Mariandynians and Mysians were famous mourners; Aeschylus: *Choe*. 733; Lucian: *Funerals* 20; Alexiou 1974: 10–12; Garland 1985: 30, 142; artistic depictions: Ahlberg 1971: 131–2; Alexiou 1974: 6.
9 Erythrai: Hippias *FGH* 421 F1; Megara: schol. Pind. *Nem*. 7.155 (105); Briseis: *Il*. 19.301–2; choephoroi: Aeschyl. *Choe*. 22–5.
10 Plut. *Ages*. 40.4.
11 Plut. *Mor*. 241f–242a; Dillon and Garland 1994, 2000: doc. 6.13.
12 Plut. *Lyk*. 27.3; other aspects of funerary legislation attributed to Lykourgos: Plut. *Lyk*. 27.1–2, 4, *Mor*. 238d; mourning was to last only eleven days, and on the twelfth a sacrifice was made to Demeter. At *Lyk*. 27.3 an acceptable emendation of the text, supported by epigraphic evidence, yields a woman dying in childbirth; see too Herakleides *FHG* ii.211.

NOTES

13 Plut. *Mor.* 238d.
14 Tyrtaeus F7 (Paus. 4.14.5); Ael. *VH* 6.1; cf. Xen. *Lak. Pol.* 15.9.
15 Hdt. 6.58; Paus. 4.14.4.
16 [Dem.] 43.62; Ruschenbusch 1966: F109. The speech contains these details. The law the speaker refers to was read out; in the speech itself this law, with details further to those given in the speech, was inserted by a later scribe; its authenticity cannot be vouched for. The extra detail includes that no woman under 60 except the cousins could enter the room where the deceased lay. For discussions of funerary legislation in Greek states, including references to restrictions placed on women, see Humphreys 1980: 99–101; Garland 1989; Takabatake 1992; Toher 1991; Morris 1992–3.
17 Plut. *Sol.* 21.5–7; Ruschenbusch 1966: F72c; cf. *Sol.* 12; Cic. *Laws* 2.23.59; Ruschenbusch F72b.
18 Plut. *Sol.* 12.1, 8.
19 Alexiou 1974: 21; Garland 1989: 4.
20 Plut. *Sol.* 21.7.
21 Cic. *Laws* 2.23.59 (Ruschenbusch 1966: F72b, Solon), 2.24.60 (Demetrios).
22 Pl. *Laws* 947b–e, 958d–960b, esp. 960a; cf. 873c–d; seducers: see n. 105 below.
23 *LSCG* 97, second half of the fifth century BC (Dareste no. 2).
24 *LSAM* 16, third century BC (Dareste no. 3).
25 Note also the funerary legislation of Mytilene: Cic. *Laws* 2.26.66; Catana: Stobaios 4.2.24; Gortyn: *LSAG* 315 no. 2 (*IC* iv.22).
26 *LSCG* 77 (Schwyzer 323; LGS ii.74; *SGDI* 2561; Solmsen-Fraenkel 49; *SIG*³ 1220; Dareste no. 28; Buck 52; *CID* i.9; translated in Zaidman and Pantel 1992: 75).
27 NM 804 (Boardman 1967: 123 fig. 98, and pl. 64; Coldstream 1968: pl. 6; Schweitzer 1969: pl. 30; Richter 1970: pl. 29; Ahlberg 1971: fig. 2; Beazley 1986: pl. 1). For geometric pottery and prothesis and ekphora scenes, see esp. Ahlberg with figures, also Coldstream 1968: 29–41 for the Dipylon workshop which produced NM 804; Garland 23–9; Ahlberg illustrates these scenes but see also the various plates of geometric mourning scenes in: Coldstream 1968: pls 6–8, 11–12, 14, 30; Schweitzer 1969: figs 29–50; Richter 1970: fig. 29; Rombos 1988 *passim*. Various geometric amphoras show the same sexless figures mourning at the bier: see Ahlberg 79 table 3.
28 NM 450; bf loutrophoros, fifth century BC; Sappho Painter (*CVA* Athens 1, pl. 8; K&B pl. 36; Vermeule 1979: 21 fig. 17).
29 Cleveland 27.6; Attic geometric amphora, 720–710 BC (*CVA* Cleveland 1, pls 2–3.1; Ahlberg 1971: fig. 36).
30 PL CA3283, 26 centimetres (Coldstream 1968: pl. 14d), and in the lower register figures, which are just identifiable as women, wail; cf. Rombos 1988: pl. 13a.
31 For a catalogue of these plaques, series and single, see *AM* 1928, 53: 39–40; Boardman 1955: 58–63; cf. Richter 1942–3; see for plaques: Vermeule 1979: 11–18; K&B 83; Garland 1985: 23–4; Beazley 1986: 65–6; Shapiro 1991: 633–4. For Exekias, see esp. Mommsen 1997.
32 *Figure 9.1*: NY 14.146.3a, *c.* 630–620 BC; provenance, Olympos, Attica? (Richter 1949: 8, pl. 8; 1968: fig. 85; 1987: fig. 333; Boardman 1955: 58.1; Vermeule 1979: 11 fig. 6).
33 Boston 27.146, *c.* 600 BC (Fairbanks 1928: pl. 66; *AJA* 1928, 32: 82; Richter 1949: p. 8 (no pl); Boardman 1955: 59.5; Vermeule 1979: 19 fig. 13).
34 NY 54.11.15.
35 Ker. 691, *c.* 510 BC (*ABV* 678 (under Naples RC187); K&B pl. 11; Shapiro 1991:

636–7 figs 7–9); Ker. 1687 (*ABV* 113.81, *Para.* 45, *Add.* 32; Shapiro 1991: 635 fig. 5).
36 Tübingen 1153 (*CVA* Tübingen 2, pl. 44; Boardman 1955: 59.4). A baby is also held by a mourner in Athens NM 12352 (Boardman 58.3), and a woman is taking a baby from another woman in another (Boardman 66.iii, but see further below); see also PL MNB905 (Boardman 62.28; 1988: 167 no. 217; K&B pl. 33), and a plaque of Exekias (Berlin F1813), discussed below.
37 Athens, Vlasto Collection (Boardman 1955: 59.8); NM 12697 (Boardman 60.12); PL MNB905 (Boardman 62.28); Athens, Vlasto Collection (Boardman 62.25); NY 54.11.15 (Boardman 62.23, pl. 4).
38 *Figure 9.2*: Berlin 1813, 540 BC (Pfuhl 1923: 73 fig. 278; Boardman 1955: 66(iii); Richter 1966: 34, pl. 166; Robertson 1975: 131 (for the suggestion that the central figure is the child's grandmother), pl. 37c; 1981: pl. 54; Rühfel 1984: 43–4, pl. 15; Beazley 1986: pl. 76; Kunze 1992: 265, pl. 143; Mommsen 1997: Farbtafel 4, pl. xv, arranging it at the very end of the plaque series, i.e. after the funeral procession).
39 NY 54.11.5 (bf sixth century; Vermeule 1979: 13 fig. 7; Shapiro 1991: 638 fig. 11). Cradling the neck with one hand is also seen on PL MNB905 (L4).
40 Berlin 1811, Exekias (Beazley 1986: pl. 74.2; Mommsen 1997: pl. i; the plaque shows two pillars, indicating mourning at the bier in the house, in the porch area, cf. Boardman 1955: 55).
41 *Figure 9.3*: Berlin 1819; 540 BC (Beazley 1986: pl. 75.1; Mommsen 1997: pl. 7); this is the best preserved example.
42 PL MNB905 (L4); bf Sappho Painter, c. 500 BC (Boardman 1955: 62.28; 1974: fig. 265; K&B pl. 33; Shapiro 1991: 630 fig. 1).
43 Ker. 691 (details above). The phormiskos has a bulbous body and a narrow neck, and presumably held oil to be poured onto the grave of the deceased.
44 Clairmont 1993; Archedike: Simonides 26a (Dillon and Garland 1994, 2000: 4.34); Xanthippe: Simonides 36 (Dillon and Garland 1994, 2000: 13.31); mother's orders: Friedländer 69a (*SEG* 15.66; Pfohl 1967: 52), mid-sixth century BC. See Humphreys 1980: 104 n. 18 for some further examples from the archaic period.
45 Boston 24.151; Polos Painter; 600–580 BC (*CVA* Boston 2, pl 67; Fairbanks 1928: pl. 65).
46 E.g. Keil B56 (*CVA* Keil 1, pl. 16.4–6; c. 500 BC); Tübingen S./10 1481 (*CVA* Tübingen 3, pls 11.2–8, 12.1–4, 13.1–5; c. 510 BC).
47 *Figure 9.4*: Cleveland 27.145, Attic bf loutrophoros, c. 500 BC (*CVA* Cleveland 1, pls 15–16; Folsom 1975: pl. 12a).
48 CdM 353; sixth century BC; *ABV* 346.7 (K&B pl. 34; Vermeule 1979: 20 fig. 15); CdM 355, sixth century BC (*ABV* 346.8; K&B pl. 35; Vermeule 20 fig. 16). However, these kantharoi copy an Etruscan shape, were discovered in Italy, and depict features (pyrrhic dancers and a flute-player) which were not Athenian funerary practices, and these vases may have been made in Athens for an Etruscan market: see Shapiro 1991: 633; Rasmussen and Spivey 1991: 146–7.
49 Corinth: PL E643; middle Corinthian bf hydria, Damon Painter, c. 570–550 BC (Richter 1970: pl. 64; Lorber 1979: pl. 32.111; Amyx 1988: 264–5, 577, 624; Schefold 1978: fig. 366; Barringer 1994: 183, pl. 61). For their mourning, see *Od.* 24.48–9, 58–9.
50 Munich 1700; bf hydria Antiope Group or close; *ABV* 362.27, 695 (Shapiro 1991: fig. 17).
51 Boston 63.473; bf hydria, Leagros Group?, 520 BC; *Para.* 164.31bis; *Add.* 96 (*CVA* Boston 2, pl. 82; Vermeule 1979: 111 fig. 27; Schefold 1978: fig. 312).

52 *Figure 9.5*: Ker. 41, *ABV* 19.5 (Kübler 1970: no. 106 pls 94–5; K&B pl. 15; Vermeule 1979: 63 fig. 19).
53 NM, no inv. known (K&B pl. 16; Vermeule 1979: 18 fig. 12; Garland 1985: fig. 9).
54 Ker. 40 (*ABV* 19.2; Kübler no. 107 pl. 93).
55 Ker. 45 (Kübler no. 129 pl. 102; Richter 1968: figs 171–2; K&B pl. 12; Vermeule 1979: 78 fig. 33); the women are about 12 centimetres high.
56 Ker. 149, mid-seventh century BC (Kübler no. 49 pls 38–40; Richter 1968: pl 6a–c, figs 31–2); the statuettes are 15.5 centimetres high.
57 Ker. 145, mid-seventh century, woman: 35 centimetres (Kübler no. 46 pls 36–7 (36, lower left corner photo clearly shows the streaks, not visible in Richter's photograph; Richter 1968: figs 33–4, 36)); Ker. 146, mid-seventh century BC (Kübler no. 47 pl 37); height of woman, about 30 centimetres.
58 Richter 1968: figs 86–102, 170–2; K&B pls 24, 43. They mainly have their hands on their heads; one beats her breast with a hand.
59 Athens NM (no inv. given); 12 centimetres high (K&B pl. 44).
60 K&B 120–1, 144–8; Alexiou 1974: 7, 207–8 with references.
61 Hdt. 4.26.
62 Philochoros *FGH* 328 F168.
63 Elektra: Aeschyl. *Choe.* 486–8; Tritopatores: Phanodemos *FGH* 325 F6.
64 Definition of lekythos: Cook 1997: 221–2. For white lekythoi, see Fairbanks 1907; 1914, both are still particularly useful; K&B 103–5, 124–7; Felten 1971: pls 85–116 (1–32); Kurtz 1975; see also Kardara 1960: 149–58; *AM* 1966, 81: pls 23–37. Mythological and other non-funerary scenes, and pattern and black lekythoi, are shown in Kurtz 1975: pls 1–17, 35.1–2, 55–72; see too K&B pl. 21. Black lekythoi at tombs, often on a tray carried by a woman, are depicted on white lekythoi: e.g. Kurtz 1975: pls 20.1–2, 23.3; cf. 25.2, 25.3, 28.3, 29.4, 30.1–2.
65 Oakley 1997: pls 91–175; see also the Phiale Painter, Oakley 1990: colour plates 1–4, pls 109–13; cf. Bérard 1989: figs 142–50.
66 Tubular fillets: see Kurtz 1975: 50–1, pls 25.3, 26.1, 35.3, 36.1; Felten 1971: pl. 98.2 (14.2). For rolled ribbons, see Kurtz 61–2.
67 Eupheros: Ker. P1169 (K&B pl. 30; Kurtz 1975: pl. 46.3; Clairmont 1993: 1.235–37, no. 1.081). The best example of a rolled fillet looking like a tablet is PL MNB616; last quarter of the fifth century BC, The Reed Painter; *ARV* 1378.44, *Add.* 371 (Fairbanks 1914: 144 no. 24, pl. 22.2, taking it as a tablet from which a ribbon 'floats'); Kurtz 1975: pl. 46.2. See also *ARV* 1377.12, 1380.80.
68 Fairbanks 1914: 235; Kardara 1960: 149–58, esp. 152.
69 Kurtz 1975: 62.
70 Animals: see Chapter 2, p. 63; victors: Dillon 1997: 114–15.
71 Is. 6.65.
72 *Figure 9.6*: NM 1958; white lekythos by the Inscription Painter, 475–450 BC; found in Eretria (Euboia); *ARV* 748.2, 1668 at pp. 748–9, *Para.* 413, *Add.* 284 (Fairbanks 1907: 203 no. 20 fig. 45; K&B pl. 27; Kurtz 1975: pl. 19.3).
73 BM D62; Sabouroff Painter, 450–25 BC; from Eretria; *ARV* 851.273, *Add.* 297 (Kurtz 1975, pl. 29.2).
74 Memnon: Ferrara NM T.18 CVP; rf cup, *ARV* 882.35 (M. Robertson 1992: fig. 169); mourning men: Xen. *Hell.* 1.7.8; Is. 4.7; cf. Hdt. 6.39.2.
75 Providence 06.050 (*CVA* Providence 1, pl. 25.4; 450–425 BC; *ARV* 759.9).
76 *Figure 9.7*: Boston 1970.428; 475–450 BC; lekythos (white-ground), attributed to the Inscription Painter; Athens (Kurtz: 1975, pl. 20.2).

NOTES

77 PL CA1640; Attic white lekythos, 475–450 BC; Kurtz 1975: pl. 20.1.
78 E.g., NM 12743; Achilles Painter, 460–450 BC; *ARV* 995.125 (Oakley 1997: pl. 96a–b).
79 NY 35.11.5; white Attic lekythos, Vouni Painter, second quarter of the fifth century BC; *ARV* 744.1, *Para.* 413, *Add.* 284 (Kurtz 1975: 207, pl. 26.2; Wehgartner 1985: 17 fig. 11).
80 Athens, Vlasto Collection (no inventory number); white lekythos, Sabouroff Painter; 475–450 BC (?); *ARV* 847.200, *Add.* 297 (Felten 1971: pl. 97.1–2 (13.1–2)); compare both (a) NM 12745, *ARV* 999.185, white lekythos, Achilles Painter, 450–425 BC, a woman and warrior at a tomb (Oakley 1997; pl. 131 c–d), and (b) NM 2021; *ARV* 854.1; white lekythos, Painter of Athens 2020, 450–425 BC (Kurtz 1975: pl. 29.3): a sword hangs in its scabbard on the stele, which is decorated with fillets; an old man and woman mourn at the tomb.
81 Karlsruhe 234; 450–400 BC; Woman Painter; *ARV* 1372.17, *Add.* 370 (Fairbanks 1914: 21.1; Kurtz 1975: pl. 43.2). Kurtz 219 notes of the women of this painter: 'Their gestures are grand; their spirit is grave.'
82 NY 34.32.2; 450–400 BC; Woman Painter; *ARV* 1168.131, *Add.* 338 (Kurtz 1975: pl. 42.2; *AJA* 1980, 84: pl. 64.4).
83 Meggen, Käppeli, now Basel 402; *ARV* 1227.3, *Add.* 350 (Felten 1971: 90.3–4 (6.3–4)).
84 For the exaleiptron, see esp. Scheibler 1964. Examples of white lekythoi showing exaleiptra being carried by women at tombs: *ARV* 1244.2, 1230.41, 750.2; see the index entry at Fairbanks 1914: 275, 'smegmatotheke'.
85 NY 34.32.2; full details above.
86 Boston 00.359; Thanatos Painter, 450–425 BC; *ARV* 1229.23, *Add.* 351 (Fairbank 1907: pl. 12 (as Boston 8440); Felten 1971: 93, figs 3–4; Kurtz 1975: pl. 32.1; *AJA* 1980: 84 pl. 64.2–3; Wehgartner 1985: 19, fig. 13).
87 Kurtz 1975: 136–43.
88 Kurtz 1975: xx, 73–4, cf. 68–72 (note the discussion of lekythoi as mentioned in Aristophanes).
89 Pl. *Phaed.* 116b, 117d.
90 Dem. 54.20.
91 Providence 25.082, *c.* 400 BC; *CVA* Providence, pls 25a, 25.5, suggesting it might be a purse; *ARV* 1376.5, *Add.* 371 (*LIMC* iii Charon i.36; Buitron 1972: 142–3 no. 78).
92 PL CA537, 425–400 BC; Group R; *ARV* 1384.18, *Add.* 372 (Fairbanks 1914: 162.1, pl. 24.3, cf. 24.1; Kurtz 223, pl. 50.1a–b; *LIMC* iii Charon i.41 (Charon only); the best plate is Felten 1975: pl. 31).
93 Two examples are: (a) NM 1926; *ARV* 846.193, *Add.* 297 (Felten 1975: pl. 30; *LIMC* iii Charon i.5; Vermeule 1979: 9 fig. 4; Bérard 1989: 107 fig. 150); (b) Munich 2777; *ARV* 1228.11, *Add.* 351 (Felten 1975: pl. 19; Vermeule 1979: 71 fig. 29 (Charon only); *LIMC* iii Charon i.10).
94 Eur. *Alk.* 252–7.
95 Soph. *Ant.* 23–5, 26–30, 34–6, 74, 205–6, 245–7, 255–8, 385, 395–6, 402, 404–5, 409–10, 429–31, 545, 697–8, 998–1090, 1017, 1021–2, 1040–1, 1081–3, 1100–14, 1192–1205, and *passim*. Necessity of burying the dead: Eur. *Suppl.* 538–41.
96 Oedipus: Soph. *Oed. Kol.* 1598–1603, 1607–10; Antigone: Eur. *Phoen.* 1667; Socrates: Pl. *Phaed.* 115a, 116a–b; Alkestis: Eur. *Alk.* 158–60; Hekabe: Eur. *Hek.* 609–13, cf. 780. Cf. for bathing, Luc. *Funerals* 11.
97 *Od.* 11.425–6.

98 NY 27.228; bf loutrophoros, early fifth century BC (no *ABV*; Vermeule 1979: 14 fig. 8a; Mommsen 1997: 70, no. 65); NY 08.258.21; rf kalyx krater, Nekyia Painter; *ARV* 1086.1, *Add.* 327 (Vermeule 1979: 15 fig. 8b). For chin-straps, see K&B 364; Vermeule 1979: 14.
99 Pl. *Phaed.* 118.
100 Kyniska: Paus. 3.8.1–2, 3.15.1, cf. 5.12.5, 6.1.6; Dillon 1997: 195, 271 n. 49; Elephantis: Berlin F4046, rf rhyton, Sabouroff Painter, 500–450 BC (no *ARV*; Hoffman 1962: no. 1, p. 7, pl. 1; interpretation: Hoffman 1989: 132–4, 165–6; fig. 1a–b (132) = *SEG* 39.53); the name Elephantis: Osborne and Byrne 1994: 141; rhyta specifically used in connection with the cult of heroes: Athen. 461b, 497e.
101 Hdt. 1.60.3–4; [Arist.] *Ath. Pol.* 14.4–15.1 (Dillon and Garland 1994, 2000: 4.6–4.7).
102 DL 5.3–4, 6, 8; Athen. 696a–697a; Luc. *Eunuch* 9; Eusebius *Praeparatio Evangelica* 15.2.5; see esp. Derenne 1930: 189–98.
103 *LSCG* 135, third century BC (*IG* xii.3.330; Dareste no. 24; Humphreys 1980: 122; Garland 1985: 110).
104 *LSAM* 72, third century BC (*SIG*³ 1044); Humphreys 1980: 122. For Epicurus, see DL 10.16–18.
105 See Plut. *Sol.* 21.7; the seducer of Euphiletos' wife first sees her at a funeral: *Lys.* 1.8.
106 Garland 1981: 178–87.
107 Arist. *Pol.* 1299a22–3, 1300a4–8, 1322b37–1323a6; Pl. *Laws* 784d.
108 Thasos: Pouilloux 1954 no. 141, p. 371, lines 4–7; date: late fifth or early fourth century BC; other lines at Dillon and Garland 1994, 2000: doc. 13.53. For dedications by gynaikonomoi on Thasos and elsewhere, see Garland 1981: 189–96.
109 Methymna: *LSCG* 127, fourth century (perhaps 340s); Magnesia: *LSAM* 32.18–21, 23; 197–196 BC (*I. Magn.* 98); Pergamon: Garland 1981: 4 n. 9.
110 *LSCG* 65.25–8, 32–3.
111 Timokles *PCG* vii F34; Men. F238 (Koerte); cf. Garland 1981: 29–34; Athen. 245a (thirty guests allowed); Philochoros *FGH* 328 F65; cf. Plut. *Mor.* 666d. Fines: Poll. 8.112; Hesych. sv Platanos.
112 Plut. *Mor.* 842a–b; *Comparison of Nikias and Crassus* 1.3; Ael. *VH* 13.24; Dillon 1997: 64, 212.
113 K&B 1971: 27–8; Ahlberg 1971: figs 67–8; Vermeule 1979: 63; *AM* 105, 1990: 127–8.

EPILOGUE

1 East frieze, slab VI, §§40–41. See Brommer 1977: pl. 179; Berger and Gisler-Huwiler 1996: Tafeln, pl. 136.
2 See for example, Burkert 1979: 107; Reed 1995: 346.
3 Aeschyl. *Eum.* 1025–7.

GLOSSARY

[ ] used to indicate that a work usually attributed to a particular author is not (necessarily) by that author (e.g. [Aristotle] *Athenaion Politeia*).
aparche 'first-fruits' offering to a deity.
arrephoroi four 7-year-old Athenian girls chosen each year to serve the goddess Athena; two took part in a nocturnal rite; see Figure 2.5.
aryballos a small unguent vase; see Figure 4.2.
Attica the countryside around the city of Athens.
black-figure a pottery vase on which the figures are painted in black; abbreviation: bf; see Figure 3.4 for an example.
chiton a tunic worn under a peplos or himation.
chous a small oinochoe (jug); plural: choes.
dekate 'a tenth', usually of proceeds from craftwork or other business, dedicated to a deity.
deme Attica was divided into 140 demes, and citizens (and their wives) were known by their own name, their father's name, and the name of the deme where their family originated; demes were small units, often centred on villages or towns; the city of Athens itself was divided into several demes.
ekphora the carrying out of a dead body from the house; see Figure 9.3.
epaulia the day after the wedding (gamos).
Erotes Eros figures, sometimes winged; see Figures 5.7–5.8.
gerarai citizen women who assisted the basilinna, the wife of the basileus archon at Athens, in rites at the Anthesteria.
gyne, gynaikos women, wife; plural: gynaikes.
hetaira a prostitute who could demand higher prices than an ordinary prostitute and be more selective in her choice of clientele because of her beauty, professional expertise or conversational skills.
himation robe or outer garment.
hypothesis an introduction to a piece of literature, such as lawsuit, ode or play, by an ancient commentator.
kalathos a basket with a narrow base.
kanephoroi adolescent women who prior to marriage carried baskets in processions or at sacrifices.

GLOSSARY

kanoun basket; plural: kana; it contained items needed for a sacrifice.
kantharos a broad cup, about 10–15 centimetres wide, with two vertical handles.
kiste cylindrical chest, containing sacrificial items or sacred objects; carried on head.
kore maiden or virgin; cf. parthenoi.
Kore plural: korai; Persephone, daughter of the goddess Demeter.
kourotrophic child-rearing; the nymphs and some goddesses were invoked to assist in bringing up children to be healthy.
krater a vase used for the mixing of wine; some could be quite large.
lekythos a cylindrical vase, usually narrow, often used as a grave offering; Figure 9.6 is an example.
loutrophoros a tall vase, often slender, used for the ritual wedding bath and often decorated with wedding scenes; a common offering to those who died unmarried; stone versions are common; Figure 9.4 is an example.
maenads women devotees of Dionysos, noted for their ecstatic behaviour; see Figures 5.1–5.4.
oinochoe plural: oinochoai; a small jug for pouring wine into a phiale, and then onto an altar or the ground, held by some of the parthenoi on the Parthenon frieze; see Figure 2.4.
parthenos plural: parthenoi; a girl or young woman not yet married, opposite of gyne (see above).
pelike a vase; an amphora with a bulbous, 'sagging' shape; Figure 5.11 is an example.
peplos plural: peploi; the standard dress for a woman in the classical period; see Figures 2.5, 7.2; often presented to goddesses, as in Figures 7.1–7.2.
petasos a broad-brimmed hat of felt.
phiale plural: phialai; a shallow bowl, of terracotta or metal, into which wine was poured for making a libation; see Figures 2.10, 8.4.
pinax plural: pinakes; tablets of terracotta (Figures 7.1–7.2) or wood (Figure 7.3).
prothesis the dead body laid out awaiting burial, accompanied by the lamenting of women; see Figures 9.1, 9.4.
red-figure a pottery vase on which the figures are painted in red; this technique followed that of black-figure ware; abbreviation: rf; see Figure 2.1 for an example; cf. black-figure, above.
satyrs mythical male attendants of Dionysos, usually sexually aroused and naked, with animal tails and bestial expressions.
stamnos a vase with a wide mouth and a very short neck; see Figure 5.2 for an example.
thiasos a group or band of cult members, which could be informal or formal (passing decrees and owning property); a group dedicated to the worship of a particular deity; used especially of followers of the god Dionysos.
thiasotoi the members of a thiasos.

thymiaterion plural: thymiateria; incense-burners on tall stands; see Figures 2.1, 6.5 for examples.

thyrsos a branch, sometimes of fennel; the end was wrapped with ivy usually with a pine cone – often stylised in artistic depictions – at one end; carried by maenads; see Figure 5.1.

tympanum drum; often translated as kettle-drum; it was shallow and usually circular or nearly so; sometimes with two handles. Beaten with the hand by women, particularly in the rites of Dionysos, the Great Mother–Cybele, and Sabazios; see Figures 5.5–5.6.

vase item of pottery, usually a container or drinking vessel, often decorated with mythical scenes or scenes of daily life.

ABBREVIATIONS

When a fragment (F) of an ancient author is referred to in the text, the edition used can be found here under the ancient author's name.

AA	*Archäologischer Anzeiger*
ABSA	*Annual of the British School of Athens*
ABV	Beazley, J.D. 1956, *Attic Black-Figure Vase-Painters*, Oxford
AC	*L'antiquité classique*
AD	*Archaiologikon Deltion*
Add.	Carpenter, T.H. 1989, *Beazley Addenda. Additional References to ABV, ARV² and Paralipomena*, 2nd edn, Oxford
AE	*Archaiologike Ephemeris*
Ael.	Aelian; *V(aria) H(istoria)* (fragments: Domingo-Forasté, D. 1994, *Claudius Aelianus. Epistulae et Fragmenta*, Stuttgart)
Ael. *Nat. An.*	Aelian *de natura animalium* (*On Animals*)
Aen.	Aeneias the Tactician (*How to Withstand a Siege*)
Aesch.	Aeschines (orator)
Aeschyl.	Aeschylus; *Ag(amemnon)*; *Choe(phoroi)*; *Eum(enides)*; *Pers(ai)* (*Persians*); *Prom(etheus Bound)*; *Seven (against Thebes)*; *Suppl(iant Maidens; Hiketides)*
AHB	*The Ancient History Bulletin*
AJA	*American Journal of Archaeology*
AJPh	*American Journal of Philology*
AK	*Antike Kunst*
Alcaeus	Voigt, E. 1971, *Sappho et Alcaeus: Fragmenta*, Amsterdam.
Alt. Perg.	Habicht, C. 1969, *Altertümer von Pergamon. Die Inschriften des Asklepieions*, Berlin
AM	*Mitteilungen des deutschen archäologischen Instituts athenische Abteilung*
An. Bekk.	Bekker, E. 1814–21, *Anecdota Graeca* i–iii, Berlin
AncSoc	*Ancient Society*
AncW	*Ancient World*

ABBREVIATIONS

Andoc.	Andocides
ANRW	Aufsteig und Niedergang der Römischen Welt ii: Principat 19–, Berlin
Ant. Pl.	Niemeyer, H.G. 1964, Antike Plastik 3, Berlin; Kabus-Jahn, R. 1972, Antike Plastik 11: Die Grimanische Figurengruppe in Venedig, Berlin; Schmidt, E.E. 1973, Antike Plastik 13: Die Kopien der Erechtheionkoren, Berlin; Lauter, H. 1976, Antike Plastik 16: Die Koren des Erechtheion, Berlin
Anth. Pal.	Anthologia Palatina (Greek Anthology)
Ap. Rhod.	Apollonios of Rhodes Argonautika
Apollod.	Apollod(oros) Bibl(iotheka) (Library of Greek Mythology)
Apollod. Epit.	Apollodoros Epitome (of Bibliotheka)
Ar.	Aristophanes; Ach(arnians); Ekkl(esiazousai); Lys(istrata); Thesm(ophoriazousai)
Arist.	Aristotle; Pol(itics); Rhet(oric)
[Arist.] Ath. Pol.	[Aristotle] Athenaion Politeia
Aristoxenos	Wehrli, F. 1967, Die Schule des Aristoteles ii: Aristoxenos, 2nd edn, Basel
Arnott	See Men.
Arr.	Arrian; Anab(asis); Epict(eti Dissertationes)
ARV	Beazley, J.D. 1963, Attic Red-Figure Vase-Painters i–iii, 2nd edn, Oxford
ASAA	Annuario della Scuola Archeologica di Atene e delle Missioni Italiane in Oriente
Athen.	Athenaeus Deipnosophistai
Austin 1968	See Eur. below
BABesch	Bulletin Antieke Beschaving
Bacchyl.	Bacchylides (Snell, B. and Maehler, H. 1970, Bacchylides, Leipzig)
Baltimore	Walters Art Gallery, Baltimore
BCH	Bulletin de correspondence hellénique
BE	Bulletin épigraphique; see also REG
Berlin	Staatliche Museen, Berlin (Pergamonmuseum and Altes Museum)
bf	black-figure vase
BICS	Bulletin of the Institute of Classical Studies
BM	British Museum, London
Boston	Museum of Fine Arts, Boston
Buck	Buck, C.D. 1955, Greek Dialects, 2nd edn, Chicago
c.	circa
CAF	Kock, T. 1880–8, Comicorum Atticorum Fragmenta i–iii, Leipzig
Callim.	Callimachus (Pfeiffer, R. 1949–53, Callimachus i–ii, Oxford)

373

ABBREVIATIONS

Campbell	See Sappho
CdM	Bibliothèque Nationale, Cabinet des Médailles, Paris
CEG i	Hansen, P.A. 1983, *Carmina Epigraphica Graeca Saeculorum viii–v A. Chr. N.*, Berlin
CEG ii	Hansen, P.A. 1989, *Carmina Epigraphica Graeca Saeculi iv A. Chr. N.*, Berlin
Chrysippos	Arnim, H. 1903, *Stoicorum veterum fragmenta* iii: Leipzig
Cic.	Cicero
CID	Rougemont, G. 1977, *Corpus des Inscriptions de Delphes. Lois sacrées et règlements religieux* i, Paris
CJ	*Classical Journal*
ClAnt	*Classical Antiquity*
Clem. *Protrep.*	Clement *Protreptikos pros Hellenas (Exhortation to the Greeks)*.
CPG	Leutsch, E.L. von and Schneidewin, F.G. 1958–61, *Corpus Paroemiographorum Graecorum* i–ii, *Suppl.*, Hildesheim
CQ	*Classical Quarterly*
CR	*Classical Review*
CVA	*Corpus Vasorum Antiquorum*
Dareste	Dareste, R., Haussoullier, B., Reinarch, T. 1892–1904, *Recueil des inscriptions juridiques grecques* i–ii, Paris
Dein.	Deinarchos (Conomis, N.C. 1975, *Dinarchus. Orationes cum fragmentis*, Leipzig)
Dem.	Demosthenes
Diehl	Diehl, E. 1949–52, *Anthologia Lyrica Graeca*, 3rd edn, Leipzig
Diels	Diels, H. 1961, *Die Fragmente der Vorsokratiker*, Berlin
Dikaiarchos	Wehrli, F. 1967, *Die Schule des Aristoteles i: Dikaiarchos*, 2nd edn, Basel
Dindorf	Dindorf, W. 1835–8, *Scholia graeca in Aristophanis* i–iii, Oxford
Diod.	Diodoros (Siculus)
Dion. Halik.	Dionysios of Halicarnassos *Roman Antiquities*
DL	Diogenes Laertius
DNP	*Der Neue Pauly*, 1996–, Stuttgart; cf. *RE*
ED	Segre, M. 1993, *Iscrizioni di Cos i: Testo, ii: Tavole*, Rome
edn	edition
EM	*Etymologicum Magnum* (Gaisford, T. 1848, *Etymologicum Magnum*, Oxford)
Eur.	Euripides; *Alk(estis)*; *Andr(omache)*; *Bacch(ae)*; *Elekt(ra)*; *Hek(abe)*; *Hel(en)*; *Herakl(eidai)*; *Hippol(ytos)*; *Iph(igeneia in) Aulis*; *Iph(igeneia in) Taur(is)*; *Med(ea)*; *Mel(anippe) Des(motis)*; *Orest(es)*; *Phoen(ician Women)*; *Suppl(iant Women)*; *Tro(jan Women)*; fragments: Austin, C. 1968, *Nova fragmenta Euripidea in papyris reperta*, Berlin, or *TGF* (see below)

F	Fragment
FD	*Fouilles de Delphes*; iii.1: Bourguet, E. 1910–29, *Inscriptions de l'entrée du Sanctuaire au Tresor des Atheniens*, Paris; iii.6: Valmin, N. 1939, *Les inscriptions du théâtre*, Paris; iv.2: Homolle, T. et al. 1909–77, *Monuments figures*, Paris
FGH	Jacoby, F. 1923–58, *Die Fragmente der griechischen Historiker*, Berlin; Fornara, C.W. 1994–, vol. iiic fasc. 1–, Leiden
FHG	Müller, C. 1841–70, *Fragmenta Historicorum Graecorum* i–v, Paris
fig., figs	figure, figures
Friedländer	Friedländer, P. and Hoffleit, H.B. 1948, *Epigrammata: Greek Inscriptions in Verse*, Chicago
Front. *Strat.*	Frontinus, *Strategemata*
GRBS	*Greek, Roman, and Byzantine Studies*
Harp.	Harpocration (Dindorf, W. 1853, *Harpocrationis lexicon in decem oratores atticos* i–ii, Oxford)
Hdt.	Herodotos
Hes.	Hesiod; *W(orks and) D(ays)*; *Theog(ony)*; MW: Merkelbach, R. and West, M.L. 1967, *Fragmenta Hesiodea*, Oxford; MW 1990: Merkelbach, R. and West, M.L. 1990, *Hesiodi Theogonia Opera et Dies Scutum*, 3rd edn, Oxford
Hesych.	Hesychius (Schmidt, M. 1858–68, *Hesychii Alexandrini Lexicon*, repr. 1965, Amsterdam)
Hieronymos	Wehrli, F. 1967, *Die Schule des Aristoteles x: Hieronymos*, 2nd edn, Basel
Hippol.	Hippol(ytus) *Ref(utatio Omnium Haeresium)*
Hom.	Homer; *Hymn (to) Aph(rodite)*; *Hymn (to) Apollo*; *Hymn (to) Dem(eter)*; *Il(iad)*; *Od(yssey)*
HSCPh	*Harvard Studies in Classical Philology*
HThR	*Harvard Theological Review*
Hyp.	Hypereides (Jensen, C. 1917, *Hyperidis Orationes Sex*, Leipzig)
Iambl.	Iamblichus, *Myst*: *de Mysteriis*; *VP*: *de Vita Pythagorica* (*On the Pythagorean Life*)
IC	Guarducci, M. 1935–50, *Inscriptiones Creticae* i–iv, Rome
ICS	*Illinois Classical Studies*
ID	Durrbach, F. 1921, *Choix d'inscriptions de Délos* i, Paris
IG	*Inscriptiones Graecae*
I. Knidos	Blümel, W. 1992, *Die Inschriften von Knidos*, Bonn
Il.	Homer *Iliad*
I. Magn.	Kern, O. 1900, *Die Inschriften von Magnesia am Maeander*, Berlin
inv.	inventory number
Is.	Isaeus (Thalheim, T. 1953, *Isaei orationes*, 2nd edn, Stuttgart)

Isok.	Isokrates
JDAI	*Jahrbuch des deutschen archäologischen Instituts*
JHS	*Journal of Hellenic Studies*
JOAI	*Jahrbuch des österreichischen archäologischen Instituts*
Jul.	Julian; *Or(ations)*; *Symp(osium)*
Justin	Seel, O. 1972, *M. Iuniani Iustini Epitoma Historiarum Philippicarum Pompei Trogi*, Stuttgart
K&B	Kurtz, D.C. and Boardman, J. 1971, *Greek Burial Customs*, London
Karlsruhe	Badisches Landesmuseum, Karlsruhe
Ker.	Kerameikos Museum of Kerameikos cemetery, Athens
Klearchos	Wehrli, F. 1948, *Die Schule des Aristoteles* iii, Basel
Lazzarini	Lazzarini, M.L. 1976, 'Le formule delle dediche votive nella Grecia arcaica' *Atti della Accademia Nazionale dei Lincei, Memorie, Classe di Scienze morali, storiche e filologiche*, ser. 8, vol. 19, fasc. 2, 1976, 47–354
LCM	*Liverpool Classical Monthly*
LGS	Prott, J. de and Ziehen, L. 1896–1906, *Leges Graecorum sacrae e titulis collectae*, Leipzig
LIMC	*Lexicon Iconographicum Mythologiae Classicae (LIMC)* i–viii, 1974–97, Zurich
Littré	Littré, E. 1846 and 1853, *Hippocrates Opera Omnia* v and viii, Paris
Loc. Ep.	No ed. 1977, *Locri Epizefirii. Atti del Sedicesimo Convegno di Studi sulla Magna Grecia, Taranto, 3–8 Ottobre 1976*, Naples
LSAG	Jeffery, L.H. 1961, *The Local Scripts of Archaic Greece: A Study of the Origin of the Greek Alphabet and its Development from the Eighth to the Fifth Centuries BC*, Oxford; and Johnstone, A.W. 1990, rev. edn, with suppl.
LSAM	Sokolowski, F. 1955, *Lois sacrées de l'Asie Mineure*, Paris
LSCG	Sokolowski, F. 1969, *Lois sacrées des cités grecques*, Paris
LSCG Suppl.	Sokolowski, F. 1962, *Lois sacrées des cités grecques: Supplément*, Paris
LSJ^9	Liddell, H.G., Scott, R., Jones, H.S. et al. 1996, *A Greek–English Lexicon, with a Revised Supplement*, Oxford
Luc.	Lucian, *Dial(ogues of the) Het(airai)*
Lyk.	Lykourgos (Conomis, N.C. 1970, *Lycurgus. Oratio in Leocratem, cum ceterarum Lycurgi orationum fragmentis*, Leipzig)
Lykoph.	Lykophron *Alex(andra)* (Scheer, E. 1958, *Lycophronis Alexandra ii: Scholia*, Berlin)
Lys.	Lysias
Maehler	Maehler, H. 1975, *Pindarus ii: Fragmenta*, Leipzig
Max. Tyr.	Koniaris, G.L. 1995, *Maximus Tyrius*, Berlin

ABBREVIATIONS

Men.	Menander; *Dysk(olos)*; *Epitr(epontes)*; fragments: Koerte, A. 1959, *Menander reliquiae* i–ii, Stuttgart; Sandbach, F.H. 1972, *Menandri reliquiae selectae*, Oxford; the edition of plays used is: Arnott, G. 1979–2000, *Menander* i–iii, Cambridge MA
Munich	Staatliche Antikensammlungen Museum, Munich
MW, MW 1990	See Hes.
neg.	photograph negative number
NM	National Archaeological Museum, Athens
Nonn. *Dion.*	Nonnos *Dionysiaka*
NY	The Metropolitan Museum of Art, New York
OCD^3	Hornblower, S. and Spawforth, A. (eds) 1996, *The Oxford Classical Dictionary*, Oxford, 3rd edn
Od.	Homer *Odyssey*
OJA	*Oxford Journal of Archaeology*
Orig.	Orig(enes) *(contra) Cels(um)*
Orphic F	Kern, O. 1922, *Orphicorum Fragmenta*, Berlin
P.	Painter
Para.	Beazley, J. 1971, *Paralipomena. Additions to Attic Black-Figure Vase-Painters and to Attic Red-Figure Vase-Painters*, Oxford; see *ABV*, *Add.*, *ARV*
Paus.	Pausanias
PCG	Kassel, R. and Austin, C. 1983–, *Poetae Comici Graeci*, Berlin
PEG	Bernabé, A. 1987, *Poetarum Epicorum Graecorum Testimonia et Fragmenta*, Pars i, Leipzig
PH	Paton, W.R. and Hicks, E.L. 1891, *The Inscriptions of Cos*, Oxford
Philostr.	Philostratos; *Apoll(onios)*; *Gymn(astikos)*
Phot.	Photios (Theodoridis, C. 1982, *Photii Patriarchae Lexicon* i: A–D, Berlin; Naber, S.A. 1864–5, *Photii Patriarchae Lexikon*, Leiden)
Pind.	Pindar; *Nem(ean Ode)*; *Olym(pian Ode)*; *Pyth(ian Ode)*; (scholiasts on Pindar: Drachmann, A.B. 1910–27, *Scholia vetera in Pindari carmina* i–iii, Leipzig; fragments: see Maehler)
Piraeus	Piraeus Archaeological Museum, Piraeus, Athens
pl., pls	plate, plates
Pl.	Plato; *Crat(ylus)*; *Euth(ydemus)*; *Menex(enus)*; *Phaed(o)*; *Phaedr(us)*; *Rep(ublic)*; *Symp(osium)*; *Theaet(etus)*; *Tim(aeus)*
PL	Louvre, Paris
Pliny *NH*	Pliny *Natural History*
Plut.	Plutarch; *Ages(ilaos)*; *Alex(ander)*; *Alk(ibiades)*; *Arat(os)*; *Arist(eides)*; *Artox(erxes)*; *Dem(osthenes)*; *Demet(rios)*; *Eum-*

ABBREVIATIONS

	(enes); Lyk(ourgos); Lys(ander); Mor(alia); Nik(ias); Per(ikles); Phok(ion); Rom(ulus); Them(istokles); Thes(eus); fragments: Sandbach, F.H. 1969, *Plutarch's Moralia* 15, London
PMG	Page, D.L. 1962, *Poetae Melici Graeci*, Oxford
Poll.	Pollux (Bethe, E. 1900–37, *Pollucis Onomasticon* i–iii, Leipzig)
Polyain.	Polyainos; *Strat(egmata)*
Polyb.	Polybius
Porph.	Porphyry; *Abst*.: *On Abstinence*; *VP*: *Vita Pythagorae*
PP	*La Parola del Passato*
ps.	pseudo
RA	*Revue Archéologique*
Raubitschek	Raubitschek, A.E., with the collaboration of Jeffery, L.H. 1949, *Dedications from the Athenian Akropolis. A Catalogue of the Inscriptions of the Sixth and Fifth Centuries BC*, Cambridge MA
RE	Paulys *Real Encyclopädie der classischen Altertumswissenschaft* 1894–, Stuttgart, cf. *DNP*
REG	*Revue des études grecques*
rf	red-figure vase
RVAp	Trendall, A.D. and Cambitoglou, A. 1978–82, *The Red-figured Vases of Apulia* i–ii, Oxford
Sappho	Voigt, E. 1971, *Sappho et Alcaeus: Fragmenta*, Amsterdam; Campbell, D.A. 1990, *Greek Lyric* i, Cambridge MA
Scheer	see Lykoph.
schol.	scholiast
Schwyzer	Schwyzer, E. 1923, *Dialectorum Graecarum Exempla Epigraphica Potiora*, Leipzig
SEG	*Supplementum Epigraphicum Graecum*
Semonides	West, M.L. 1972, *Iambi et Elegi Graeci ante Alexandrum Cantati* ii, Oxford
Serv.	Serv(ius) (*In Vergilii carmina commentarii: Aenead*)
SGDI	Bechtel, F. 1886, *Sammlung der griechischen Dialektinschriften*, Göttingen
SIG³	Dittenberger, W. (ed.) 1915–24, *Sylloge Inscriptionum Graecarum* i–iv, 3rd edn, Leipzig
Simon.	Simonides (see also Diehl)
Solmsen-Fraenkel	Solmsen, F. and Fraenkel, E. 1930, *Inscriptiones Graecae ad inlustrandas dialectos selectae*, 4th edn, Leipzig
Soph.	Sophokles; *Ant(igone)*; *Elekt(ra)*; *Oed(ipus at) Kol(onos)*; *Oed(ipus) Tyr(annus)* (*Oedipus the King*); *Phil(oktetes)*; *Trach-(iniai)* (*The Women of Trachis*)
Steph. Byz.	Stephan of Byzantium *Ethnika* (Meineke, A. 1848, *Stephan von Byzanz. Ethnika*, Berlin)

ABBREVIATIONS

Suid.	Suida (Adler, A. 1928–38, *Suidae Lexicon* i–v, Leipzig)
sv	sub vide (see under)
Syracuse	Museo Archeologico Regionale 'P. Orsi', Siracusa
TAPhA	*Transactions of the American Philological Association*
TGF	Nauck, A. and Snell, B. 1964, *Tragicorum Graecorum Fragmenta: Supplementum*, Hildesheim
Theok.	Theokritos *Idylls*
Theophr. *Char.*	Theophrastos, *Characters*
Thuc.	Thucydides
Tod *GHI*	Tod, M.N. 1948, *A Selection of Greek Historical Inscriptions* ii, Oxford
TrGF	*Tragicorum Graecorum Fragmenta*, Göttingen; 1: Snell, B. 1971; 2: Kannicht, R. and Snell, B. 1981; 3: Radt, S. 1985; 4: Radt, S. 1977
Vermaseren *CCCA*	Vermaseren, M.J. 1977–89, *Corpus Cultus Cybelae Attidisque (CCCA)*, Leiden
Voigt	See Alcaeus; Sappho
West	West, M.L. 1971–2, *Iambi et Elegi Graeci ante Alexandrum Cantati* i–ii, Oxford
Xen.	Xenophon; *Anab(asis)*; *Cyrop(aideia)*; *Hell(enika)*; *Lak(edaimonion) Pol(iteia) (Spartan Constitution)*; *Mem(orabilia)*; *Oik(onomikos)*
YCS	*Yale Classical Studies*
ZPE	*Zeitshrift für Papyrologie und Epigraphik*

BIBLIOGRAPHY

Ahlberg, G. 1971, *Prothesis and Ekphora in Greek Geometric Art*, Göteborg.
Akurgal, E. 1961, *Die Kunst Anatoliens*, Berlin.
Aleshire, S.B. 1989, *The Athenian Asklepieion*, Amsterdam.
—— 1991, *Asklepios at Athens*, Amsterdam.
—— 1992, 'The economics of dedication at the Athenian Asklepieion' in Linders, T. and Alroth, B. (eds) *Economics of Cult in the Ancient Greek World*, Uppsala: 85–99.
—— 1994, 'The demos and the priests: the selection of sacred officials at Athens from Cleisthenes to Augustus' in Osborne, R. and Hornblower, S. (eds) *Ritual, Finance, Politics. Athenian Democratic Accounts Presented to David Lewis*, Oxford: 325–37.
Alexiou, M. 1974, *The Ritual Lament in Greek Tradition*, Cambridge.
Alfieri, N. 1958, *Spina. Das antike Spina und seine Wiederentdeckung*, Munich.
—— 1962, *A History of 1000 Years of Greek Vase Painting*, New York.
—— 1979, *Spina. Museo Archeologico Nazionale di Ferrara* i, Bologna.
Amyx, D.A. 1988, *Corinthian Vase-Painting of the Archaic Period* i–iii, Berkeley.
Arbesmann, P.R. 1929, *Das Fasten bei den Griechen und Römern*, Giessen.
Arnott, W.G. 1996, *Alexis: The Fragments. A Commentary*, Cambridge.
Atallah, W. 1966, *Adonis dans la littérature et l'art grecs*, Paris.
Barringer, J.M. 1994, *Divine Escorts: Nereids in Archaic and Classical Greek Art*, Michigan.
Baumann, R.A. 1990, *Political Trials in Ancient Greece*, London.
Beard, M. and Henderson, J. 1998, 'With this body I thee worship: sacred prostitution in antiquity' in Wyke, M. (ed.) *Gender and the Body in the Ancient Mediterranean*, Oxford: 56–79.
Beazley, J.D. 1947, *The Berlin Painter*, Mainz.
—— 1947a, *The Pan Painter*, Mainz.
—— 1948, *The Kleophrades Painter*, 2nd edn, Mainz.
—— 1974, *The Pan Painter*, revised edn, Mainz.
—— 1974a, *Athenian Black Figure Vases: A Handbook*, London.
—— 1986, *The Development of Attic Black-Figure*, 2nd edn, Berkeley.
Bell, M. 1981, *Morgantina Studies i: The Terracottas*, Princeton.
Bérard, C. 1974, *Anodoi. Essai sur l'imagerie des passages chthoniens*, Rome.
Bérard, C. et al. 1989, *A City of Images*, Princeton.
Berger, E. 1970, *Das basler Arztrelief*, Basel.
—— 1986, *Der Parthenon in Basel. Dokumentation zu den Metopen. Textband, Tafelband*, Mainz.

Berger, E. and Gisler-Huwiler, M. 1996, *Der Parthenon in Basel: Dokumentation zum Fries. Teil 1: Tafelband, Teil 2: Textband*, Mainz.
Bergquist, B. 1973, *Herakles on Thasos*, Uppsala.
Bicknell, P.J. 1982, 'Axiochos Alkibiadou, Aspasia and Aspasios' *AC* 51: 240–50.
Bieber, M. 1977, *Ancient Copies. Contributions to the History of Greek and Roman Art*, New York.
—— 1981, *The Sculpture of the Hellenistic Age*, New York.
Blinkenberg, C.S. 1931, *Lindos* i, Berlin.
Blümel, C. 1963, *Die archaisch-griechischen Skulpturen der Staatlichen Museen zu Berlin*, Berlin.
—— 1966, *Die klassisch-griechischen Skulpturen der Staatlichen Museen zu Berlin*, Berlin.
Blundell, S. 1995, *Women in Ancient Greece*, Cambridge MA.
Boardman, J. 1955, 'Painted funerary plaques and some comments on prothesis' *ABSA* 50: 51–66.
—— 1973, *Greek Art*, 2nd edn, London; see also Boardman 1996.
—— 1974, *Athenian Black Figure Vases*, London.
—— 1975, *Athenian Red Figure Vases: The Archaic Period*, London.
—— 1977, 'The Parthenon frieze – another view' in Höckman, U. and Krug, A. (eds) *Festschrift für Frank Brommer*, Mainz: 39–49.
—— 1978, *Greek Sculpture. The Archaic Period*, London.
—— 1984 (ed.), *The Cambridge Ancient History. Plates to Volume iii. The Middle East, the Greek World and the Balkans to the Fifth Century B.C. New Edition*, Cambridge.
—— 1988 (ed.), *The Cambridge Ancient History. Plates to Volume iv. Persia, Greece and the Western Mediterranean, c. 525 to 479 B.C. New Edition*, Cambridge.
—— 1989, *Athenian Red Figure Vases. The Classical Period*, London.
—— 1991, 'The naked truth' *OJA* 10: 119–21.
—— 1991a, *Greek Sculpture: the Archaic Period*, 2nd edn, London.
—— (ed.) 1993, *The Oxford History of Classical Art*, Oxford.
—— (ed.) 1994, *The Cambridge Ancient History. Plates to Volumes v and vi. The Fifth and Fourth Centuries B.C. New Edition*, Cambridge.
—— 1995, *Greek Sculpture. The Late Classical Period*, London.
—— 1996, *Greek Art*, 4th edn, London.
—— 1998, *Early Greek Vase Painting*, London.
—— 1999, *The Greeks Overseas. Their Early Colonies and Trade*, 4th edn, London.
Boardman, J. and la Rocca, E. 1978, *Eros in Greece*, New York.
Boardman, J. et al. 1967, *The Art and Architecture of Ancient Greece*, London.
—— 1986, *The Oxford History of the Classical World*, Oxford.
Bommelaer, J. 1991, *Guide de Delphes. Le site*, Paris.
Bookidis, N. 1993, 'Ritual dining at Corinth' in Marinatos, N. and Hägg, R. (eds) *Greek Sanctuaries: New Approaches*, London: 45–61.
—— 1994, 'Ritual dining in the sanctuary of Demeter and Kore at Corinth: some questions' in Murray, O. (ed.) *Sympotica: A Symposium on the Symposium*, Oxford: 86–94.
Bookidis, N. and Stroud, R.S. 1997, *Corinth xviii.3: The Sanctuary of Demeter and Kore. Topography and Architecture*, Princeton.
Bookidis, N. et al. 1999, 'Dining in the sanctuary of Demeter and Kore at Corinth' *Hesperia* 68: 1–54.
Borelli, L.V. 1995, 'Locri Epizefirii: Pinakes Locresi' in Carratelli, G.P. (ed.) *Enciclopedia dell'arte antica. Classica e orientale*, Suppl. 2 iii, Rome: 404–6.

Bowra, C.M. 1970, *On Greek Margins*, Oxford.
Bravo, B. 1997, *Pannychis e Simposio*, Pisa.
Brelich, A. 1969, *Paides e Parthenoi*, Rome.
Bremen, R. van 1996, *The Limits of Participation. Women and Civic Life in the Greek East in the Hellenistic and Roman Periods*, Amsterdam.
Bremmer, J. 1984, 'Greek maenadism reconsidered' *ZPE* 55: 267–86.
—— 1987, 'The old women of ancient Greece' in Blok, J. and Mason, P. (eds) *Sexual Asymmetry. Studies in Ancient Society*, Amsterdam: 191–215.
—— 1994, *Greek Religion*, Oxford.
Brommer, F. 1967, *Die Metopen des Parthenon: Katalog und Untersuchung*, Mainz.
—— 1973, *Vasenlisten zur griechischen Heldensage*, 3rd edn, Marburg.
—— 1977, *Der Parthenonfries. Teil 1: Text, Teil 2: Tafeln*, Mainz.
—— 1979, *The Sculptures of the Parthenon*, London.
Broneer, O. 1932, 'Eros and Aphrodite on the north slope of the acropolis in Athens' *Hesperia* 1: 31–55.
—— 1942, 'The Thesmophorion in Athens' *Hesperia* 11: 250–64.
Brouskari, M.S. 1974, *The Acropolis Museum*, Athens.
Brown, C.G. 1988 'The prayers of the Corinthian women (Simonides, *Ep.* 14 Page *FGE*)' *GRBS* 32: 5–14.
Brulé, P. 1987, *La fille d'Athènes: La religion des filles à Athènes à l'époque classique. Mythes, cultes, et société*, Paris.
Brumfield, A.C. 1981, *The Attic Festivals of Demeter and their Relationship to the Agricultural Year*, Salem.
—— 1996, 'Aporreta: verbal and ritual obscenity in the cults of ancient women' in Hägg, R. (ed.) *The Role of Religion in the Early Greek Polis*, Stockholm: 67–74.
Bruneau, P. 1970, *Recherches sur les cultes de Délos à l'époque hellénistique et à l'époque impériale*, Paris.
Bryce, T. 1996, 'The gods and oracles of ancient Lycia' in Dillon, M.P.J. (ed.) *Religion in the Ancient World: New Themes and Approaches*, Amsterdam: 41–50.
Budde, L. and Nicholls, R. 1964, *A Catalogue of the Greek and Roman Sculpture in the Fitzwilliam Museum, Cambridge*, Cambridge.
Buitron, D.M. 1972, *Attic Vase Painting in New England Collections*, Harvard.
Bulloch, A.W. 1985, *Callimachus. The Fifth Hymn*, Cambridge.
Burkert, W. 1966, 'Greek tragedy and sacrificial myth' *GRBS* 7: 87–121.
—— 1966a, 'Kekropidensage und Arrhephoria' *Hermes* 94: 1–25.
—— 1970, 'Buzyge und Palladion', *Zeitschift für Religions- und Geistesgeschichte* 12: 356–68.
—— 1972, *Lore and Science in Ancient Pythagoreanism*, Cambridge MA.
—— 1979, *Structure and History in Greek Mythology and Ritual*, Berkeley.
—— 1982, 'Craft versus sect: the problem of the Orphics and Pythagoreans' in Meyer, B.F. and Sanders, E.P. (eds) *Jewish and Christian Self-Definition* 3, Philadelphia.
—— 1983, *Homo Necans: The Anthropology of Ancient Greek Sacrificial Ritual and Myth*: Berkeley.
—— 1985, *Greek Religion: Archaic and Classical*, Oxford.
Burn, L. 1987, *The Meidias Painter*, Oxford.
Caizzi, F.D. 1966, *Antisthenis Fragmenta*, Milan.
Calame, C. 1990, *Thésée et l'imaginaire athénien légende et culte en Grèce antique*, Lausanne.

—— 1997, *Choruses of Young Women in Ancient Greece. Their Morphology, Religious Role, and Social Functions*, Lanham.
Callipolitis-Feytmans, D. 1970, 'Déméter, Corè et les Moires sur des vases corinthiens' *BCH* 94: 45–65.
Cameron, A. and Kuhrt, A. (eds) 1983, *Images of Women in Antiquity*, London.
Campbell, D.A. 1988, *Greek Lyric* ii, Cambridge MA.
Cantarella, E. 1987, *Pandora's Daughters: The Role and Status of Women in Greek and Roman Antiquity*, Baltimore.
—— 1992, *Bisexuality in the Ancient World*, Yale.
Carpenter, T.H. 1986, *Dionysian Imagery in Archaic Greek Art: Its Development in Black-Figure Vase Painting*, Oxford.
—— 1991, *Art and Myth in Ancient Greece*, London.
—— 1993, 'On the beardless Dionysus' in Carpenter and Faraone 1993: 185–206.
Carpenter, T.H. and Faraone, C.A. (eds) 1993, *Masks of Dionysus*, Cornell.
Carratelli, G.P. (ed.) 1996, *The Western Greeks. Classical Civilisation in the Western Mediterranean*, London.
Cartledge, P. 1998 (ed.), *The Cambridge Illustrated History of Ancient Greece*, Cambridge.
Castner, C.J. 1982, 'Epicurean hetairai as dedicants to healing deities?' *GRBS* 23: 51–7.
Castriota, D. 1992, *Myth, Ethos, and Actuality. Official Art in Fifth-Century BC Athens*, Wisconsin.
Charbonneux, J. et al. 1968, *Grèce archaique (620–480 avant J.-C.)*, Paris.
—— 1969, *Grèce classique (480–330 avant J.-C.)*, Paris.
—— 1970, *Grèce hellénistique (330–50 avant J.-C.)*, Paris.
Clairmont, C.W. 1970, *Gravestone and Epigram*, Mainz.
—— 1993, *Classical Attic Tombstones*; 1995, *Supplementary Volume*, Kilchberg.
Clinton, K. 1974, *The Sacred Officials of the Eleusinian Mysteries*, Philadelphia.
—— 1996, 'The Thesmophorion in central Athens and the celebration of the Thesmophoria in Attica' in Hägg, R. (ed.) *The Role of Religion in the Early Greek Polis*, Stockholm: 111–25.
Cohen, D. 1991, *Law, Sexuality and Society: The Enforcement of Morals in Classical Athens*, Cambridge.
Coldstream, J.N. 1968, *Greek Geometric Pottery*, London.
—— 1983, 'The meaning of regional styles in the eighth century BC' in Hägg, R. (ed.) *The Greek Renaissance of the Eighth Century BC: Tradition and Innovation*: Stockholm: 17–25.
Cole, S.G. 1984, 'The social function of rituals of maturation: the Koureion and the Arkteia' *ZPE* 55: 233–44.
—— 1984a, *Theoi Megaloi: The Cult of the Great Gods at Samothrace*, Leiden.
—— 1992, '*Gynaiki ou themis*: gender difference in the Greek *Leges Sacrae*' *Helios* 19: 104–22.
—— 1993, 'Procession and celebration at the Dionysia' in Scodel, R. (ed.) *Theater and Society in the Classical World*, Michigan: 25–38.
—— 1995, 'Women, dogs and flies' *AncW* 26: 182–91.
—— 1998, 'Domesticating Artemis' in Blundell, S. and Williamson, M. (eds) *The Sacred and the Feminine in Ancient Greece*, London: 27–43.
Collard, C. et al. 1995, *Euripides: Selected Fragmentary Plays* i, Warminster.

Collins, B.J. 1995, 'Greek *ololyzo* and Hittite *palwai*-: exultation in the ritual slaughter of animals' *GRBS* 36: 319–25.
Comstock, M. and Vermeule, C. 1971, *Greek, Etruscan & Roman Bronzes in the Museum of Fine Arts Boston*, Boston.
Connelly, J.B. 1996, 'Parthenon and parthenoi: a mythological interpretation of the Parthenon frieze' *AJA* 100: 53–80.
Connor, W.R. 1988, 'Seized by the nymphs: nympholepsy and symbolic expression in classical Greece' *ClAnt* 7: 155–89.
Cook, A.B. 1940, *Zeus: A Study in Ancient Religion* iii, Cambridge.
Cook, R.M. 1997, *Greek Painted Pottery*, 3rd edn, London.
Cooper, C. 1995, 'Hyperides and the trial of Phryne' *Phoenix* 49: 303–18.
Cotter, W. 1999, *Miracles in Greco-Roman Antiquity*, London.
Croissant, F. 1983, *Les protomés féminines archaïques*, Paris.
Cropp, M. 1997, 'Notes on Euripides, Iphigenia in Tauris' *ICS* 22: 25–41.
Culham, P. 1986, 'Again, what meaning lies in colour!' *ZPE* 64: 235–45.
Dakoronia, F. and Gounaropoulou, L. 1992, 'Artemiskult auf einem Weihrelief aus Achinos bei Lamia' *AM* 107: 217–27.
Davies, J.K. 1971, *Athenian Propertied Families, 600–300 B.C.*, Oxford.
Dawkins, R.M. (ed.) 1929, *The Sanctuary of Artemis Orthia at Sparta*, London.
de Polignac, F. 1995, *Cults, Territory, and the Origins of the Greek City-State*, Chicago.
de Ste Croix, G.E.M. 1972, *The Origins of the Peloponnesian War*, London.
Demand, N. 1994, *Birth, Death, and Motherhood in Classical Greece*, Baltimore.
Dentzer, J. 1982, *Le motif du banquet couché dans le proche-orient et le monde grec du viie au ive siècle avant J.-C.*, Rome.
Derenne, E. 1930, *Les procès d'impiété*, Liège and Paris.
des Bouvrie, S. 1995, 'Gender and the games at Olympia' in Berggreen, B. and Marinatos, N. (eds) *Greece and Gender*, Bergen: 55–74.
Detienne, M. 1989, 'The violence of well-born ladies: women in the Thesmophoria' in Detienne, M. and Vernant, J.-P. *The Cuisine of Sacrifice among the Greeks*, Chicago: 129–47.
—— 1994, *The Gardens of Adonis: Spices in Greek Mythology*, 2nd edn (1977, 1st edn, Princeton = 1972, *Les Jardins d'Adonis*, Paris, 2nd edn 1992).
Deubner, L. 1932, *Attische Feste*, Berlin.
Dierichs, A. 1993, *Erotik in der Kunst Griechenlands*, Mainz.
Dillon, M.P.J. 1990, '"The house of the Thebans" (FD iii.1 357–58) and accommodation for Greek pilgrims' *ZPE* 83: 64–88.
—— 1993, 'Restoring a manuscript reading at Paus. 9.3.7' *CQ* 43: 327–9.
—— 1994, 'The didactic nature of the Epidaurian iamata' *ZPE* 101: 239–60.
—— 1995, 'Payments to the disabled at Athens: social justice or fear of aristocratic patronage?' *AncSoc* 26: 27–57.
—— 1995a, 'The Lakedaimonian dedication to Olympian Zeus' *ZPE* 107: 60–8.
—— 1996, 'The epimeletes ton krenon and the importance of the water-supply at Athens' *Hermes* 124: 192–204.
—— 1996a, 'Oionomanteia in Greek divination' in Dillon, M.P.J. (ed.) *Religion in the Ancient World: New Themes and Approaches*, Amsterdam: 99–121.
—— 1997, *Pilgrims and Pilgrimage in Ancient Greece*, London.
—— 1997a, 'The ecology of the Greek sanctuary' *ZPE* 118: 113–27.

—— 1999, Review of Zhmud, L. 1997, *Wissenschaft, Philosophie und Religion im frühen Pythagoreismus*, Berlin, in *CR* 49: 102–4.

—— 1999a, 'Post-nuptial sacrifices on Kos (Segre, *ED* 178) and ancient Greek marriage rites' *ZPE* 124: 63–80.

—— 2000, 'Did Parthenoi attend the Olympic Games? Girls and women competing, spectating, and carrying out cult roles at Greek religious festivals' *Hermes* 128: 457–80.

Dillon, M.P.J. and Garland, L. 1994, *Ancient Greece: Social and Historical Documents from Archaic Times to the Death of Socrates*, London; 2000, 2nd edn.

Dilts, M.R. 1986, *Scholia Demosthenica*, Leipzig.

Dindorf, W. 1851, *Demosthenes* viii, Oxford.

Dodds, E.R. 1951, *The Greeks and the Irrational*, Berkeley.

—— 1960, *Euripides Bacchae*, 2nd edn, Oxford.

Dohan, E.H. 1934, 'Some unpublished vases in the University Museum, Philadelphia' *AJA* 38: 523–32.

Dontas, G.S. 1983, 'The true Aglaurion' *Hesperia* 52: 48–63.

Dover, K.J. 1971, *Theocritus*, London.

—— 1975, 'The freedom of the intellectual in Greek society' *Talanta* 7: 24–54.

—— 1989, *Greek Homosexuality*, 2nd edn, London.

Dow, S. 1937, 'The Egyptian Cults in Athens' *HThR* 30: 183–232.

Dow, S. and Healey, R.F. 1965, *A Sacred Calendar of Eleusis*, Cambridge MA.

Dowden, K. 1989, *Death and the Maiden*, London.

—— 1992, *The Uses of Greek Mythology*, London.

duBois, L. 1989, *Inscriptions grecques dialectales de Sicile*, Rome.

duBois, P. 1988, *Sowing the Body. Psychoanalysis and Ancient Representations of Women*, Chicago.

Ducrey, P. 1986, *Warfare in Ancient Greece*, New York.

Duncan-Jones, R.P. 1980, 'Metic numbers in Periclean Athens' *Chiron* 10: 101–9.

Dunn, F.M. 1994, 'Euripides and the rites of Hera Akraia' *GRBS* 35: 103–15.

Durand, J.-L. and Frontisi-Ducroux, F. 1982, 'Idoles, figures, images: autour de Dionysos' *RA* 1: 81–108.

Edelstein, E.J. and Edelstein, L. 1945, *Asclepius: a Collection and Interpretation of the Testimonies* i–ii, Baltimore.

Edmonds, J.M. 1912, *The Greek Bucolic Poets*, London.

Edwards, C.M. 1984, 'Aphrodite on a Ladder' *Hesperia* 53: 59–72.

Edwards, M.W. 1960, 'Representation of maenads on archaic red-figured vases' *JHS* 80: 78–87.

Eitrem, S. 1915, *Opferritus und Voropfer der Griechen und Römer*, Kristiana.

Fairbanks, A. 1907, *Athenian Lekythoi: With Outline Drawing in Glaze Varnish on a White Ground*, New York.

—— 1914, *Athenian Lekythoi: With Outline Drawing in Matt Color on a White Ground*, New York.

—— 1928, *Catalogue of Greek and Etruscan Vases in the Museum of Fine Arts, Boston* i, Cambridge MA.

Fantham, E. et al. 1994, *Women in the Classical World: Image and Text*, Oxford.

Faraone, C.A. 1990, 'Aphrodite's kestos and apples for Atalanta: aphrodisiacs in early Greek myth and ritual' *Phoenix* 44: 219–43.

Faraone, C.A. 1993, 'The wheel, the whip, and other implements of torture: erotic magic in Pindar *Pythian* 4: 213–19' *CJ* 89: 1–19.

―― 1996, 'Taking the "Nestor's Cup Inscription" seriously: erotic magic and conditional curses in the earliest inscribed hexameters' *ClAnt* 15: 77–112.

―― 1999, *Ancient Greek Love Magic*, Cambridge MA.

Farnell, L.R. 1921, *Greek Hero Cults and Ideas of Immortality*, Oxford.

Feaver, D.D. 1957, 'Historical development in the priesthoods of Athens' *YCS* 15: 123–58.

Fehrle, E. 1910, *Die kultische Keuschheit im Alterum*, Giessen.

Felten, W. 1971, *Thanatos- und Kleophonmaler*, Munich.

―― 1975, *Attische Unterweltsdarstellungen des vi. und v. Jh. v. Chr.*, Munich.

Ferguson, W.S. 1938, 'The Salaminioi of Heptaphylai and Sounion' *Hesperia* 7: 1–74.

―― 1944, 'The Attic Orgeones' *HThR* 37: 61–140.

―― 1949, 'Orgeonika', in *Commemorative Studies in Honor of Theodore Leslie Shear*, Hesperia Supplement viii, Princeton: 130–63.

Floren, J. 1987, *Die griechische Plastik i: geometrische und archaische Plastik*, Munich.

Flower, M.A. 1997, *Theopompos of Chios*, 2nd edn, Oxford.

Foley, A. 1988, *The Argolid 800–600 BC: An Archaeological Survey*, Gotenburg.

Foley, H.P. 1982, 'Marriage and sacrifice in Euripides' *Iphigeneia in Aulis*' *Arethusa* 15: 159–80.

―― 1994, *The Homeric Hymn to Demeter. Translation, Commentary, and Interpretive Essays*, Princeton.

Folsom, R.S. 1975, *Attic Black-Figured Pottery*, Park Ridge.

―― 1976, *Attic Red-Figured Pottery*, Park Ridge.

Fontenrose, J. 1978, *The Delphic Oracle: Its Responses and Operations, with a Catalogue of Responses*, Berkeley.

―― 1988, *Didyma: Apollo's Oracle, Cult and Companions*, Berkeley.

Forsén, B. 1993, 'The Sanctuary of Zeus Hypsistos and the Assembly Place on the Pnyx' *Hesperia* 62: 507–21.

Foucault, M. 1984, *L'usage des Plaisirs*, Paris.

Foxhall, L. 1995, 'Women's ritual and men's work in ancient Athens' in Hawley, R. and Levick, B. (eds) *Women in Antiquity: New Assessments*, London: 97–110.

Franzmann, M. 2000, *Women and Religion*, New York.

Fraser, P.M. 1972, *Ptolemaic Alexandria* i–ii, Oxford.

Fraser, P.M. and Matthews, E. 1987, *A Lexicon of Greek Personal Names* i, Oxford.

Frazer, J.G. 1913, *The Golden Bough*, Part iv, vols i–ii, London.

Freyer-Schauenburg, B. 1974, *Bildwerke der archäischen Zeit und des strengen Stils* (*Samos* xi), Bonn.

Frickenhaus, A. 1912, *Lenäenvasen*, Berlin.

Frontisi-Ducroux, F. 1991, *Le dieu-masque. Une figure du Dionysos d'Athènes*, Paris.

―― 1997, 'Retour aux "vases des Lénéennes"' in Bravo, B. *Pannychis e simposio. Feste private notturne di donne e uomini nei testi letterari e nel culto*, Pisa: 123–32.

Fullerton, M.D. 2000, *Greek Art*, Cambridge.

Gager, J.G. 1992, *Curse Tablets and Binding Spells from the Ancient World*, New York.

Gantz, T. 1993, *Early Greek Myth: A Guide to Literary and Artistic Sources*, Baltimore.

Garland, B.J. 1981, 'Gynaikonomoi: An Investigation of Greek Censors of Women', unpublished PhD Maryland, Baltimore.

Garland, R.S.J. 1984, 'Religious authority in archaic and classical Athens' *ABSA* 79: 75–123.
—— 1985, *The Greek Way of Death*, Ithaca.
—— 1987, *The Piraeus: From the Fifth to the First Century B.C.*, Ithaca.
—— 1989, 'The well-ordered corpse: an investigation into the motives behind Greek funerary legislation' *BICS* 36: 1–15.
—— 1990, *The Greek Way of Life: From Conception to Old Age*, Ithaca.
—— 1990a, 'Priests and power in classical Athens', in Beard, M. and North, J. (eds) *Pagan Priests: Religion and Power in the Ancient World*, London: 73–91.
—— 1992, *Introducing New Gods*, London.
—— 1995, *The Eye of the Beholder. Deformity and Disability in the Greco-Roman World*, Ithaca.
Gasparro, G.S. 1985, *Soteriology and Mystic Aspects in the Cult of Cybele and Attis*, Leiden.
Gauthier, P. 1972, *Symbola. Les étrangers et la justice dans les cités grecques*, Nancy.
Geagan, D.J. 1994, 'Children in Athenian dedicatory monuments' in Fossey, J.M. (ed.) *Boeotia Antiqua* iv, Amsterdam: 163–73.
Giannantoni, G. 1990, *Socratis et Socraticorum Reliquiae* i–iv, Naples.
Ginouvès, R. 1962, *Balaneutikè. Recherches sur le bain dans l'antiquité grecque*, Paris.
Girard, P. 1881, *L'Asclépieion d'Athènes d'après de récentes découverts*, Paris.
Golden, M. 1990, *Children and Childhood in Classical Athens*, Baltimore.
Gomme, A.W. 1956, *A Historical Commentary on Thucydides* ii, Oxford.
Gomme, A.W. and Sandbach, F.H. 1973, *Menander: A Commentary*, Oxford.
Gow, A.S.F. 1952, *Theocritus* i–ii, 2nd edn, Cambridge.
—— 1965, *Machon: The Fragments*, Cambridge.
Graf, F. 1986, *The Greek Magical Papyri in Translation, Including the Demotic Spells*, Chicago.
—— 1996, '*Pompai* in Greece. Some considerations about space and ritual in the Greek *polis*' in Hägg, R. (ed.) *The Role of Religion in the Early Greek Polis*, Stockholm: 55–65.
—— 1997, *Magic in the Ancient World*, Cambridge MA.
Griffiths, F.T. 1981, 'Home before lunch: the emancipated woman in Theocritus' in Foley, H.P. (ed.) *Reflections of Women in Antiquity*, New York: 247–73.
Grimal, P. 1986, *The Dictionary of Classical Mythology*, Oxford.
Guarducci, M. 1967, *Epigrafia greca* i, Rome.
Guen-Pollet, B. le 1991, *La vie religieuse dans le monde grec du ve au iiie siècle avant notre ère. Choix de documents épigraphiques traduits et commentés*, Toulouse.
Günther, W. 1988, '"Vieux et inutilisable" dans un inventaire inédit de Milet' in Knoepfler, D. and Quellet, N. (eds) *Comptes et inventaires dans la cité grecque*, Geneva: 215–37.
Halleux, R. and Schamp, J. 1985, *Les lapidaires grecs*, Paris.
Halperin, D.M. 1989, 'Sex before sexuality: pederasty, politics, and power in classical Athens' in Deberman, M.B. et al. (eds), *Hidden from History. Reclaiming the Gay and Lesbian Past*, London: 37–53.
—— 1990, *One Hundred Years of Homosexuality and Other Essays on Greek Love*, London.
Hamilton, R. 1989, 'Alkman and the Athenian Arkteia' *Hesperia* 58: 449–53.
—— 1992, *Choes and Anthesteria: Athenian Iconography and Ritual*, Michigan.
Hanfmann, G.M.A. 1967, *Classical Sculpture*, London.

Hani, J. 1978, 'La fête athénienne de l'Aiora et le symbolisme de la balançoire' *REG* 91: 107–22.
Harding, P. 1985, *From the End of the Peloponnesian War to the Battle of Ipsus*, Cambridge.
Harris, D. 1995, *The Treasures of the Parthenon and the Erechtheion*, Oxford.
Harrison, J. 1890, *Mythology and the Monuments of Ancient Athens*, London.
—— 1922, *Prolegomena to the Study of Greek Religion*, 3rd edn, Cambridge.
—— 1927, *Themis: a Study of the Social Origins of Greek Religion*, 2nd edn, London.
Haspels, C.H.E. 1936, *Attic Black-Figured Lekythoi*, Paris.
Hauser, F. 1909, 'Aristophanes und Vasenbilder' *JOAI* 12: 90–9.
Hausmann, U. 1948, *Kunst und Heiltum. Untersuchungen zu den griechischen Asklepiosreliefs*, Potsdam.
—— 1960, *Griechische Weihreliefs*, Berlin.
Havelock, C.M. 1981, *Hellenistic Art*, New York.
—— 1995, *The Aphrodite of Knidos and her Successors*, Ann Arbor.
Hedreen, G.M. 1992, *Silens in Attic Black-Figure Vase-Painting*, Ann Arbor.
Heilmeyer, W. (ed.) 1997, *Der Pergamonaltar. Die neue Präsentation nach Restaurierung des Telephosfrieses*, Tübingen.
Hellenkemper, H. 1998, *Die Neue Welt der Griechen*, Cologne.
Henrichs, A. 1978, 'Greek maenadism from Olympias to Messalina' *HSCPh* 82: 121–60.
—— 1981, 'Human sacrifice in Greek religion: three case studies' *Entretiens Hardt* 27, *Le sacrifice dans l'antiquité*: 195–235.
—— 1982, 'Changing Dionysiac identities' in Meyer, B.F. and Sanders, E.P. (eds) *Jewish and Christian Self-Definition* 3, Philadelphia: 137–60.
—— 1984, 'Male intruders among the maenads: the so-called male celebrant' in Evjen, H.D. (ed.) *Mnemai: Classical Studies in Memory of Karl. K. Hulley*, Chico: 69–91.
—— 1984a, 'Loss of self, suffering, violence: the modern view of Dionysus from Nietzsche to Girard' *HSCPh* 88: 205–40.
—— 1987, 'Myth visualized: Dionysos and his circle in sixth-century vase-painting' in (no ed.) *Papers on the Amasis Painter and his World*, Malibu.
—— 1991, 'Namenlosigkeit und Euphemismus' in Hoffman, H. and Harder, A. (eds) *Fragmenta Dramatica*, Göttingen: 161–201.
—— 1993, '"He has a god in him": human and divine in the modern perception of Dionysus' in Carpenter and Faraone 1993: 13–43.
—— 1994, 'Der rasende Gott: zur Psychologie des Dionysos und des Dionysischen in Mythos und Literatur' *Antike und Abendland* 40: 31–58.
—— 1994a, 'Anonymity and polarity: unknown gods and nameless altars at the Areopagos' *ICS* 19: 27–58.
Henry, M. 1995, *Prisoner of History. Aspasia of Miletus and her Biographical Tradition*, New York.
Herfort-Koch, M. 1986, *Archaische Bronzeplastik Lakoniens*, Münster.
Herington, C.J. 1955, *Athena Parthenos and Athena Polias*, Manchester.
Heyob, S.K. 1975, *The Cult of Isis among Women in the Graeco-Roman World*, Leiden.
Higgins, R.A. 1954, *Catalogue of the Terracottas in the Department of Greek and Roman Antiquities, British Museum, i: Greek: 730–330 BC*, London.
—— 1967, *Greek Terracottas*, London.

—— 1986, *Tanagra and the Figurines*, Princeton.
Hoffman, H. 1962, *Attic Red-figured Rhyta*, Mainz.
—— 1989, 'Rhyta and kantharoi in Greek ritual', in *Greek Vases in the J. Paul Getty Museum: 4* (Occasional Papers on Antiquities, 5); Malibu: 132–66.
Hofkes-Brukker, C. and Mallwitz, A. 1975, *Der Bassai-Fries*, Munich.
Hogarth, D.G. 1908, *Excavations at Ephesus*, London.
Holladay, A.J. and Goodman, M.D. 1986, 'Religious scruples in ancient warfare' *CQ* 36: 151–71.
Hollinshead, M.B. 1985, 'Against Iphigeneia's adyton in three mainland temples' *AJA* 89: 419–40.
Hoorn, G. van 1951, *Choes and Anthesteria*, Leiden.
Hopkinson, N. 1984, *Callimachus. Hymn to Demeter*, Cambridge.
Hoppin, J.C. 1919, *A Handbook of Attic Red-Figured Vases* i–ii, Cambridge.
Hughes, D.D. 1991, *Human Sacrifice in Ancient Greece*, London.
Humphreys, S.C. 1980, 'Family tombs and tomb cult in ancient Athens: tradition or traditionalism?' *JHS* 100: 96–126.
Hurwit, J.M. 1999, *The Athenian Acropolis. History, Mythology, and Archaeology from the Neolithic Era to the Present*, Cambridge.
Huxley, G.L. 1966, 'Troy viii and the Lokrian Maidens' in Badian, E. (ed.) *Ancient Society and Institutions. Studies Presented to Victor Ehrenberg on his 75th Birthday*, Oxford: 147–64.
Immerwahr, H.R. 1990, *Attic Script: A Survey*, Oxford.
Jameson, M. 1993, 'The asexuality of Dionysus' in Carpenter and Faraone 1993: 44–64.
Jeanmaire, H. 1939, *Couroi et Courétes*, Lille.
Jenkins, I. 1994, *The Parthenon Frieze*, Austin.
Johns, C. 1982, *Sex or Symbol: Erotic Images of Greece and Rome*, Austin.
Johnson, S.E. 1984, 'The present state of Sabazios Research' *ANRW* 17.3: 1583–1613.
Johnston, S.I. 1990, *Hekate Soteira*, Atlanta.
—— 1991, 'Crossroads' *ZPE* 88: 217–24.
—— 1995, 'The song of the *iynx*: magic and rhetoric in *Pythian* 4' *TAPhA* 125: 177–206.
—— 1997, 'Corinthian Medea and the cult of Hera Akraia' in Clauss, J.J. and Johnston, S.I. (eds) *Medea. Essays on Medea in Myth, Literature, Philosophy, and Art*, Princeton: 44–70.
—— 1999, *The Restless Dead. Encounters between the Living and the Dead in Ancient Greece*, Berkeley.
Jordan, B. 1979, *Servants of the Gods. A Study in the Religion, History and Literature of Fifth-century Athens*, Göttingen.
Jucker, I. 1963, 'Frauenfest in Korinth' *AK* 6: 47–61.
Kahil, L. 1963, 'Quelques vases du sanctuaire d'Artemis à Brauron' *AK* 1: 5–29.
—— 1965, 'Autour del'Artémis attique' *AK* 8: 20–33.
—— 1977, 'L'Artémis de Brauron: Rites and Mystères' *AK* 20: 86–98.
—— 1981, 'Le "Cratérisque" d'Artemis et le Brauronion de l'acropole' *Hesperia* 50: 253–63.
—— 1983, 'Mythological repertoire of Brauron' in Moon 1983: 231–44.
Kaibel, G. 1958 (reprint), *Comicorum Graecorum Fragmenta* i, 2nd edn, Berlin.

Kaimakis, D. 1976, *Die Kyraniden*, Meisenheim.
Kardara, C.P. 1960, 'Four white lekythoi in the National Museum of Athens' *ABSA* 55: 149–58.
Karouzou, S. 1956, *The Amasis Painter*, Oxford.
Kasper, W. 1976, *Handbuch der antiken Kunst*, Munich.
Kearns, E. 1989, *The Heroes of Attica*, London.
Kerényi, C. 1967, *Eleusis. Archetypal Image of Mother and Daughter*, New York.
—— 1976, *Dionysos: Archetypal Image of Indestructible Life*, Princeton.
Keuls, E.C. 1984, 'Male–female interaction in fifth-century Dionysic ritual as shown in Attic Vase painting' *ZPE* 55: 287–97.
—— 1993, *The Reign of the Phallus. Sexual Politics in Ancient Athens*, 2nd edn, Berkeley.
—— 1997, *Painter and Poet in Ancient Greece: Iconography and the Literary Arts*, Stuttgart.
Kilmer, M.F. 1993, *Greek Erotica on Attic Red-Figure Vases*, London.
King, H. 1983, 'Bound to bleed: Artemis and Greek women' in Cameron, A. and Kuhrt, A. (eds) *Images of Women in Antiquity*, London: 109–27.
—— 1998, *Hippocrates' Woman: Reading the Female Body in Ancient Greece*, London.
Kleiner, D.E.E. 1992, *Roman Sculpture*, New Haven.
Kraemer, R.S. 1979, 'Ecstacy and possession: women of ancient Greece and the cult of Dionysus' *HThR* 72: 55–80 = 1980, 'Ecstacy and possession: women of ancient Greece and the cult of Dionysos' in Falk, N.A. and Gross, R.M. (eds) *Unspoken Worlds: Women's Religious Lives in Non-Western Cultures*, New York: 53–69.
—— 1992, *Her Share of the Blessings*, Oxford.
Krenkel, W.A. 1978, 'Männliche Prostitution in der Antike' *Das Altertum* 24: 49–55.
Krentz, P. 1993, 'Athens' allies and the phallophoria' *AHB* 7: 12–16.
Kron, U. 1976, *Die zehn attischen Phylenheroen*, Berlin.
—— 1992, 'Frauenfeste in Demeterheiligtümern: Das Thesmophorion von Biltemi' *AA*: 611–50.
—— 1996, 'Priesthoods, dedications, and euergetism. What part did religion play in the political and social status of Greek women?' in Hellström, P. and Alroth, B. (eds) *Religion and Power in the Ancient Greek World*, Uppsala: 39–82.
Krug, A. 1984, *Heilkunst und Heilkult. Medizin in der Antike*, Munich.
Kübler, K. 1970, *Kerameikos. Die Nekropole des späten 8. bis frühen 6. Jahrhunderts. 6.2: Tafelband*, Berlin.
Kunisch, N. 1997, *Makron i–ii*, Mainz.
Kunze, M. 1992, *Die Antikensammlung im Pergamonmuseum und in Charlottenburg*, Mainz.
Kurke, L. 1996, 'Pindar and the prostitutes, or reading ancient "pornography"' *Arion* 4: 49–75.
—— 1997, 'Inventing the *hetaira*: sex, politics and discursive conflict in archaic Greece' *ClAnt* 16: 106–50.
Kurtz, D.C. 1975, *Athenian White Lekythoi*, Oxford.
—— 1983, *The Berlin Painter*, Oxford.
Lacey, W.K. 1968, *The Family in Classical Greece*, London.
Lalonde, G.V., Langdon, M.K., and Walbank, M.B. 1991, *The Athenian Agora xix: Inscriptions. Horoi, Poletai Records, Leases of Public Lands*, Princeton.
Lambert, S.D. 1998, *The Phratries of Attica*, 2nd edn, Ann Arbor.

Lane, A. 1948, *Greek Pottery*, London.
Lane, E.N. 1985, *Corpus Cultus Iovis Sabazii (CCIS) ii. The Other Monuments and Literary Evidence*, Leiden.
—— 1989, *Corpus Cultus Iovis Sabazii (CCIS) iii. Conclusions*, Leiden.
—— (ed.) 1996, *Cybele, Attis and Related Cults: Essays in Memory of M.J. Vermaseren*, Leiden.
Langlotz, E. 1963, *Die Kunst der Westgriechen*, Munich.
Larson, J. 1995, *Greek Heroine Cults*, Madison.
Lawrence, A.W. 1972, *Greek and Roman Sculpture*, London.
Lawrence, A.W. and Tomlinson, R.A. 1983, *Greek Architecture*, 4th edn, London.
Lefkowitz, M.R. 1981, *Heroines and Hysterics*, London.
—— 1986, *Women in Greek Myth*, Baltimore.
—— 1996, 'Women in the Panathenaic and other festivals' in Neils, J. (ed.) *Worshipping Athena: Panathenaia and Parthenon*, Madison: 78–91.
Lefkowitz, M.R. and Fant, M.B. 1982, *Women's Life in Greece and Rome*, London.
Lehmann, P.W. and Spittle, D. 1982, *Samothrace. The Temenos*, Princeton.
Leitao, D. 1995, 'The perils of Leukippos: initiatory transvestism and male gender ideology in the Ekdusia at Phaistos' *ClAnt* 14: 130–63.
Lewis, D.M. 1954, 'Notes on Attic inscriptions' *ABSA* 49: 17–50.
—— 1955, 'Notes on Attic inscriptions, ii' *ABSA* 50: 1–36.
Lezzi-Hafter, A. 1988, *Der Eretria-Maler*, Mainz.
Licht, H. 1932, *Sexual Life in Ancient Greece*, London.
Linders, T. 1972, *Studies in the Treasure Records of Artemis Brauronia Found at Athens*, Stockholm.
Lippold, G. 1950, *Die griechische Plastik*, Munich.
Lissarrague, F. 1990, *The Aesthetics of the Greek Banquet. Images of Wine and Ritual*, Princeton.
—— 1993, 'On the wildness of satyrs' in Carpenter and Faraone 1993: 207–20.
Lloyd, A.B. 1994, *Herodotos Book ii*, Leiden.
Lloyd, G.E.R. 1983, *Science, Folklore and Ideology*, Cambridge.
Lloyd-Jones, H. 1975, *Females of the Species*, London.
—— 1983, 'Artemis and Iphigeneia' *JHS* 103: 87–102 = 1990, *Greek Comedy, Hellenistic Literature, Greeek Religion, and Miscellanea. The Academic Papers of Sir Hugh Lloyd-Jones*, Oxford: 306–30.
Lloyd-Jones, H. and Parsons, P. 1970, *Supplementum Hellenisticum*, Berlin.
Locri Epizefirii. Atti del Sedicesimo Convegno di Studi sulla Magna Grecia, Taranto, 3–8 Ottobre 1976, 1977, Naples.
Loraux, N. 1993, *The Children of Athena. Athenian Ideas about Citizenship and the Division between the Sexes*, Princeton.
—— 1995, *The Experiences of Tiresias: the Feminine and the Greek Man*, Princeton.
Lorber, F. 1979, *Inschriften auf korinthischen Vasen*, Berlin.
Loucas, I. and Loucas, E. 1994, 'The sacred laws of Lykosoura' in Hägg, R. (ed.) *Ancient Greek Cult Practice from the Epigraphical Evidence*, Stockholm: 97–9.
Lowe, N.J. 1998, 'Thesmophoria and Haloa: myth, physics and mysteries' in Blundell, S. and Williamson, M. (eds) *The Sacred and the Feminine in Ancient Greece*: 149–73.
Luck, G. 1985, *Arcana Mundi. Magic and the Occult in the Greek and Roman Worlds*, Baltimore.

Lyons, D. 1997, *Gender and Immortality. Heroines in Ancient Greek Myth and Cult*, Princeton.
MacLachlan, B.C. 1992, 'Sacred prostitution and Aphrodite' *Studies in Religion* 21: 145–62.
MacLachlan, B.C. 1995, 'Love, war and the goddess in fifth-century Locri' *AncW* 26: 205–23.
McNally, S. 1978, 'The maenad in early Greek art' *Arethusa* 11: 101–35.
Malkin, I. 1987, *Religion and Colonization in Ancient Greece*, Leiden.
Mansfeld, J. 1980, 'The chronology of Anaxagoras' Athenian period and the date of his trial, ii' *Mnemosyne* 33: 17–95.
Mantes, A.G. 1990, *Problemata tes Eikonographias ton Hiereion kai ton Hiereon sten Archaia Hellenike Techne*, Athens.
Marcadé, J. 1962, *Eros Kalos. Essai sur les representations érotiques dans l'art grec*, Geneva.
Martha, J. 1882, *Les sacerdoces athéniens*, Paris.
Martin, L.H. 1987, *Hellenistic Religions: An Introduction*, New York.
Matt, L. von 1962, *La grande Grèce*, Paris.
Merkelbach, R. 1988, *Die Hirten des Dionysos*, Stuttgart.
Merker, G. 2000, *Corinth xviii.4. The Sanctuary of Demeter and Kore: Terracotta Figurines of the Classical, Hellenistic, and Roman Periods*, Princeton.
Metzger, H. 1951, *Les représentations dans la céramique attique du ive siècle*, Paris.
Meyer, H. 1980, *Medeia und die Peliaden*, Rome.
Michaelis, A. 1871, *Der Parthenon*, Leipzig.
Mikalson, J.D. 1975, *The Sacred and Civil Calendar of the Athenian Civil Year*, Princeton.
—— 1977, 'Religion in the Attic demes' *AJPh* 98: 424–35.
—— 1983, *Athenian Popular Religion*, Chapel Hill.
—— 1991, *Honor Thy Gods: Popular Religion in Greek Tragedy*, Chapel Hill.
—— 1998, *Religion in Hellenistic Athens*, Berkeley.
Miller, M.C. 1992, 'The parasol: an oriental status-symbol in late archaic and classical Athens' *JHS* 112: 91–105.
Mills, H. 1984, 'Greek clothing regulations: sacred and profane?' *ZPE* 55: 255–65.
Mitchell, F. 1973, *Lykourgan Athens 338–322. Lectures in Memory of L. T. Semple*, Cincinnati.
Mitropoulou, E. 1975, *Libation Scenes with Oinochoe in Votive Reliefs*, Athens.
—— 1976, *Horses' Heads and Snakes in Banquet Reliefs and their Meaning*, Athens.
—— 1977, *Corpus i: Attic Votive Reliefs of the 6th and 5th Centuries BC*, Athens.
Mitsopoulos-Leon, V. 1993, 'The statue of Artemis at Lousoi: some thoughts' in Palagia, O. and Coulson, W. (eds) *Sculpture from Arcadia and Laconia*, Oxford: 33–9.
Mommsen, A. 1898, *Feste der Stadt Athen im Altertum*, Leipzig.
Mommsen, E. 1997, *Exekias i. Die Grabtafeln*, Mainz.
Montuoro, P.Z. 1961, 'Locri Epizefiri: i pìnakes di Locri' in Bandinelli, R.B. (ed.) *Enciclopedia dell'arte antica. Classica e orientale* iv, Rome: 674–7.
Moon, W.G. (ed.) 1983, *Ancient Greek Art and Iconography*, Madison.
Moore, M.B. and Philippides, M.Z.P. 1986, *The Athenian Agora xxiii: Attic Black-Figured Pottery*, Princeton.
Moraw, S. 1998, *Die Mänade in der attischen Vasenmalerei des 6. und 5. Jahrhunderts v. Chr.*, Mainz.

BIBLIOGRAPHY

Morris, I. 1987, *Burial and Ancient Society: The Rise of the Greek City-State*, Cambridge.
—— 1992–3, 'Law, culture and funerary art in Athens, 600–300 BC' *Hephaistos* 11–12: 35–50.
Müller, C. 1858, *Oratores Attici* ii, Paris.
Mylonas, G.E. 1961, *Eleusis and the Eleusinian Mysteries*, Princeton.
Nagy, B. 1991, 'The procession to Phaleron' *Historia* 40: 288–306.
Naumann, F. 1983, *Die Ikonographie der Kybele in der phrygischen und der griechischen Kunst*, Tübingen.
Neils, J. 1992 (ed.) *Goddess and Polis: The Panathenaic Festival in Ancient Athens*, Princeton.
—— 1996 (ed.) *Worshipping Athena: Panathenaia and Parthenon*, Madison.
Neugebauer, K.A. 1951, *Katalog der statuarischen Bronzen im Antiquarium* ii, Berlin.
Neumann, G. 1979, *Probleme des griechischen Weihreliefs*, Tübingen.
Niemeyer, H.G. 1960, *Promachos*, Waldsassen and Bayern.
Nilsson, M.P. 1953, 'Wedding rites in ancient Greece' *Prosphora eis St. Kyriakiden*, Athens: 508–15 = 1960, *Opuscula selecta* iii, Lund: 243–50.
—— 1955, *Geschichte der griechischen Religion*, 3rd edn, Munich.
—— 1957, *Griechische Feste von religiöser Bedeutung*, Stuttgart.
—— 1967, *Geschichte der griechischen religion*, 2nd edn, Munich.
Nixon, L. 1995, 'The cults of Demeter and Kore' in Hawley, R. and Levick, B. (eds) *Women in Antiquity: New Assessments*, London: 75–96.
Nock, A.D. 1934, Review of Deubner 1932, *Gnomon* 10: 289–95.
—— 1944, 'The cult of heroes' *HThR* 37: 141–74.
Oakley, J.H. 1990, *The Phiale Painter*, Mainz.
—— 1997, *The Achilles Painter*, Mainz.
Oakley, J.H. and Sinos, R.H. 1993, *The Wedding in Ancient Athens*, Madison.
Obbink, D. 1993, 'Dionysus poured out: ancient and modern theories of sacrifice and cultural formation' in Carpenter and Faraone 1993: 65–86.
O'Brien, J.M. 1992, *Alexander the Great; the Invisible Enemy*, London.
Oikonomides, A.N. 1964, *The Two Agoras in Ancient Athens*, Chicago.
O'Meara, D.J. 1989, *Pythagoras Revived. Mathematics and Philosophy in Late Antiquity*, Oxford.
Osborne, M.J. and Byrne, S.G. 1994, *A Lexicon of Greek Personal Names* ii, Oxford.
Osborne, R. 1985, *Demos: The Discovery of Classical Attika*, Cambridge.
—— 1993, 'Women and sacrifice in classical Greece' *CQ* 43: 392–405.
—— 1994, 'Looking on – Greek style. Does the sculpted girl speak to women too?' in Morris, I. (ed.) *Classical Greece. Ancient Histories and Modern Archaeologies*, Cambridge: 81–96.
—— 1994a, 'Framing the centaur: reading fifth-century architectural sculpture' in Goldhill, S. and Osborne, R. (eds) *Art and Text in Ancient Greek Culture*, Cambridge: 52–84.
—— 1997, 'The ecstasy and the tragedy: varieties of religious experience in art, drama, and society' in Pelling, C. (ed.) *Greek Tragedy and the Historian*, Oxford: 187–211.
—— 1998, *Archaic and Classical Greek Art*, Oxford.
Ostwald, M. 1986, *From Popular Sovereignty to the Sovereignty of Law*, Berkeley.
Padel, R. 1983, 'Women: model for possession by Greek daemons' in Cameron, A. and Kuhrt, A. (eds) *Images of Women in Antiquity*, London: 3–19.
Page, D.L. 1941, *Select Papyri iii. Literary Papyri: Poetry*, London.

—— 1973, *Lyrica Graeca Selecta*, Oxford.
—— 1976, *Epigrammata Graeca*, Oxford.
—— 1981, *Further Greek Epigrams*, Cambridge.
Palagia, O. 1995, 'Akropolis Museum 581. A family at the Apaturia' *Hesperia* 64: 493–501.
Paribeni, E. 1953, *Museo Nazionale Romano: Sculture greche del v secolo*, Rome.
Parke, H.W. 1967, *Greek Oracles*, London.
—— 1977, *Festivals of the Athenians*, London.
Parke, H.W. and Wormell, D.E.W. 1956, *The Delphic Oracle*, vol. 1: *The History*; vol. 2: *The Oracular Responses*, Oxford.
Parker, R. 1983, *Miasma: Pollution and Purification in Early Greek Religion*, Oxford.
—— 1985, 'Greek states and Greek oracles' in Cartledge, P.A. and Harvey, F.D. (eds) *Crux: Essays in Greek History Presented to G.E.M. de Ste Croix*, London (= *History of Political Thought* 6): 298–326.
—— 1987, 'Festivals of the Attic demes' in Linders, T. and Norquist, G. (eds) *Gifts to the Gods*, Stockholm: 137–47.
—— 1989, 'Spartan religion' in Powell, A. (ed.) *Classical Sparta: Techniques behind her Success*, London: 142–72.
—— 1996, *Athenian Religion: A History*, Oxford.
Payne, H. 1931, *Necrocorinthia*, Oxford.
—— 1942, *Perachora. The Sanctuaries of Hera Akraia and Limenia*, Oxford.
Payne, H. and Dunbabin, T.J. 1962, *Perachora. The Sanctuaries of Hera Akraia and Limenia* ii, Oxford.
Pedley, J.G. 1990, *Paestum: Greeks and Romans in Southern Italy*, London.
Pélékidis, C. 1962, *Histoire de l'éphébie attique*, Paris.
Pembroke, S.G. 1996, 'Prostitution, sacred' in Hornblower, S. and Spawforth, A. (eds) *The Oxford Classical Dictionary*, 3rd edn, Oxford: 1263–4.
Penglase, C. 1994, *Greek Myths and Mesopotamia*, London.
Percy, W.A. 1996, *Pederasty and Pedagogy in Archaic Greece*, Urbana.
Perlman, P. 1983, 'Plato *Laws* 833c–834d and the bears of Brauron' *GRBS* 24: 115–30.
—— 1989, 'Acting the she-bear for Artemis' *Arethusa* 22: 111–33.
Peschel, I. 1987, *Die Hetäre bei Symposion und Komos in der attisch-rotfigurigen Vasenmalerei des 6.–4. Jahrhunderts vor Christus*, Frankfurt.
Petropoulos, J.C.B. 1993, 'Sappho the sorceress – another look at fr. 1 (LP)' *ZPE* 97: 43–56.
Pettersson, M. 1992, *Cults of Apollo at Sparta. The Hyakinthia, the Gymnopaidiai and the Karneia*, Stockholm.
Pfisterer-Haas, S. 1990, 'Ältere Frauen auf attischen Grabdenkmälern' *AM* 105: 179–96.
Pfohl, G. 1967, *Greek Poems on Stone. 1: Epitaphs from the 7th to 5th Centuries BC*, Leiden.
Pfuhl, E. 1923, *Malerei und Zeichnung der Griechen* iii, Munich.
—— 1935, 'Spätionische Plastik' *JDAI* 50: 9–48.
Philip, J.A. 1966, *Pythagoras and Early Pythagoreanism*, Toronto.
Philippaki, B. 1967, *The Attic Stamnos*, Oxford.
Picard, C. 1922, *Éphèse et Claros*, Paris.
Picard, O. (ed.) 1991, *Guide de Delphes. Le Musée*, Paris.

Pickard-Cambridge, A. 1968, *The Dramatic Festivals of Athens*, 2nd edn, revised by Gould, J. and Lewis, D.M., Oxford.
Pingiatoglou, S. 1981, *Eileithyia*, Würzburg.
Pollitt, J.J. 1986, *Art in the Hellenistic Age*, Cambridge.
—— 1990, *The Art of Ancient Greece: Sources and Documents*, 2nd edn, Cambridge.
Pomeroy, S.B. 1975, *Goddesses, Whores, Wives, and Slaves*, New York.
—— (ed.) 1991, *Women's History and Ancient History*, Chapel Hill.
—— 1997, *Families in Classical and Hellenistic Greece: Representations and Realities*, Oxford.
Pouilloux, J. 1954, *Recherches sur l'histoire et les cultes de Thasos*, Paris.
—— 1954a, *La forteresse de Rhamnonte*, Paris.
Powell, A. 1988, *Athens and Sparta: Constructing Greek Political and Social History from 478 B.C.*, London.
Powell, B.B. 1989, 'Why was the Greek alphabet invented?' *ClAnt* 8: 321–50.
Preisendanz, K. et al. 1973–74, *Papyri Graecae Magicae: Die griechischen Zauberpapyri*, 2nd edn, Stuttgart.
Preller, L. 1838, *Polemonis Periegetae Fragmenta*, Leipzig.
Preston, P. 1997, *Antike Bildmotive*, Stuttgart.
Price, S. 1999, *Religions of the Ancient Greeks*, Cambridge.
Price, T.H. 1978, *Kourotrophos. Cults and Representations of the Greek Nursing Deities*, Leiden.
Pritchett, W.K. 1940, 'Greek inscriptions' *Hesperia* 9: 97–133.
Prückner, H. 1968, *Die lokrischen Tonreliefs*, Mainz.
Rabe, H. 1906, *Scholia in Lucianum*, Leipzig.
Rasmussen, T. and Spivey, N. 1991, *Looking at Greek Vases*, Cambridge.
Raubitschek, I.K. 1969, *The Hearst Hillsborough Vases*, Mainz.
Redfield, J. 1990, 'From sex to marriage: the rites of Artemis Triklaria and Dionysos Aisymnetes at Patras' in Halperin, D.M. et al. (eds) *Before Sexuality. The Construction of Erotic Experience in the Ancient Greek World*, Princeton: 115–34.
Reed, J.D. 1995, 'The Sexuality of Adonis' *ClAnt* 14: 317–47.
—— 1996, 'Antimachus on Adonis?' *Hermes* 124: 381–3.
—— 1997, *Bion of Smyrna: The Fragments and the Adonis*, Cambridge.
Reeder, E.D. 1988, *Hellenistic Art in the Walters Art Gallery*, Princeton.
—— 1995, *Pandora. Women in Classical Greece*, Princeton.
Rehm, R. 1994, *Marriage to Death. The Conflation of Wedding and Funeral Rituals in Greek Tragedy*, Princeton.
Reinsberg, C. 1993, *Ehe, Hetärentum und Knabenliebe im antiken Griechenland*, Munich.
Rhodes, P.J. 1993, *A Commentary on the Aristotelian Athenaion Politeia*, rev. edn, Oxford.
Rhodes, R.F. 1995, *Architecture and Meaning on the Athenian Acropolis*, Cambridge.
Rice, E.E. 1983, *The Grand Procession of Ptolemy Philadelphus*, Oxford.
Richardson, N.J. 1974, *The Homeric Hymn to Demeter*, Oxford.
Richter, G.M.A. 1942–3 'Terracotta plaques from early Attic tombs' *Bulletin of the Metropolitan Museum*, ns 1: 80–92.
—— 1949, *Archaic Greek Art*, Oxford.
—— 1954, *Catalogue of Greek Sculptures in the Metropolitan Museum of Art*, Oxford.
—— 1961, *The Archaic Gravestones of Attica*, London.
—— 1965, *The Portraits of the Greeks* i–iii, London.

—— 1966, *The Furniture of the Greeks, Etruscans and Romans*, London.
—— 1968, *Korai: Archaic Greek Maidens*, London.
—— 1970, *Perspective in Greek and Roman Art*, London.
—— 1970a, *The Sculpture and Sculptors of the Greeks*, 4th edn, New York.
—— 1987, *A Handbook of Greek Art*, 9th edn, London.
Richter, G.M.A. and Hall, L.F. 1936, *Red-Figured Athenian Vases in the Metropolitan Museum of Art* i–ii, New Haven.
Ridder, A. de 1896, *Catalogue des bronzes trouvés sur l'Acropole d'Athènes*, Paris.
Ridgway, B.S. 1970, *The Severe Style in Greek Sculpture*, Princeton.
—— 1977, *The Archaic Style in Greek Sculpture*, Princeton.
—— 1981, *Fifth Century Styles in Greek Sculpture*, Princeton.
—— 1987, 'Ancient Greek women and art: the material evidence' *AJA* 91: 399–409.
—— 1990, *Hellenistic Sculpture i. The Styles of ca. 331–200 BC*, Madison.
—— 1997, *Fourth-Century Styles in Greek Sculpture*, Madison.
Robbins, E. 1994, 'Alcman's *Partheneion*: legend and choral ceremony' *CQ* 44: 7–16.
Robertson, M. 1959, *Greek Painting*, Geneva.
—— 1975, *A History of Greek Art* i–ii, Cambridge.
—— 1981, *A Shorter History of Greek Art*, Cambridge.
—— 1992, *The Art of Vase-Painting in Classical Athens*, Cambridge.
Robertson, M. and Frantz, A. 1975, *The Parthenon Frieze*, London.
Robertson, N. 1983, 'Greek ritual begging in aid of women's fertility and childbirth' *TAPhA* 113: 143–69.
—— 1983a, 'The riddle of the arrhephoria at Athens' *HSCPh* 87: 241–88.
—— 1984, 'Poseidon's festival at the winter solstice' *CQ* 34: 1–16.
—— 1992, *Festivals and Legends: The Formation of Greek Cities in the Light of Public Ritual*, Toronto.
—— 1995, 'The magic properties of female age-groups in Greek ritual' *AncW* 26: 193–203.
—— 1996, 'The ancient Mother of the Gods: a missing chapter in the history of Greek religion' in Lane 1996: 239–304.
—— 1996a, 'New light on Demeter's Mysteries: the festival Proerosia' *GRBS* 37: 319–79.
Robinson, T.M. 1987, *Heraclitus. Fragments*, Toronto.
Robsjohn-Gibbings, T.H. and Pullin, C.W. 1963, *Furniture of Classical Greece*, New York.
Roccos, L.J. 1995, 'The kanephoros and her festival mantle in Greek art' *AJA* 99: 641–66.
Roebuck, C. 1951, *Corinth xiv. The Asklepieion and Lerna*, Princeton.
Rohde, E. 1925, *Psyche. The Cult of Souls and Belief in Immortality among the Greeks*, London.
Roller, D.W. 1989, *Tanagran Studies i: Sources and Documents on Tanagra in Boiotia, 2: The Prosopography of Tanagra in Boiotia*, Amsterdam.
Roller, L. 1994, 'Attis on Greek votive monuments. Greek god or Phrygian?' *Hesperia* 63: 245–62.
—— 1996, 'The Mother of the Gods in Attic tragedy' in Lane 1996: 305–21.
—— 1998, 'The ideology of the eunuch priest' in Wyke, M. (ed.) *Gender and the Body in the Ancient Mediterranean*, Oxford: 118–35.

Rolley, C. 1965, 'Dieux patrôoi et Thesmophorion de Thasos' *BCH* 89: 441–83.
—— 1986, *Greek Bronzes*, London.
Rombos, T. 1988, *The Iconography of Attic Late Geometric ii Pottery*, Sweden.
Rotroff, S.I. 1977, 'The Parthenon Frieze and the sacrifice to Athena' *AJA* 81: 379–82.
Rouse, W.H.D. 1902, *Greek Votive Offerings*, Cambridge.
Roux, J. 1972, *Euripide Les Bacchantes 1–2*, Paris.
Rühfel, H. 1984, *Das Kind in der griechischen Kunst*, Mainz.
Ruschenbusch, E. 1966, *Solonos Nomoi*, Wiesbaden.
Salmon, J.B. 1984, *Wealthy Corinth*, Oxford.
Samuel, A.E. 1972, *Greek and Roman Chronology. Calendars and Years in Classical Antiquity*, Munich.
Scanlon, T.F. 1988, 'Virgineum Gymnasium. Spartan females and early Greek athletics' in Raschke, W. (ed.) *The Archaeology of the Olympics*, Madison: 185–216.
Scarborough, J. 1991, 'The pharmacology of sacred plants, herbs, and roots' in Faraone, C.A. and Obbink, D. (eds) *Magika Hiera. Ancient Greek Magic and Religion*, New York: 138–74.
Schachter, A. 1981, *The Cults of Boiotia 1–4*, London.
Scheffer, C. 1992, 'Boeotian festival scenes. Competition, consumption and cult in the archaic and classical periods' in Hägg, R. (ed.) *The Iconography of Greek Cult in the Archaic and Classical Periods*, Athens: 117–41.
Schefold, K. 1981, *Die Göttersage in der klassischen und hellenistischen Kunst*, Munich.
—— 1992, *Gods and Heroes in Late Archaic Greek Art*, Cambridge.
—— 1998, *Der religiöse Gehalt der antiken Kunst und die Offenbarung*, Mainz.
Scheibler, I. 1964, 'Exaleiptra' *JDAI* 79: 72–108.
Schelp, J. 1975, *Das Kanoun: Der griechische Opferkorb*, Würzburg.
Schild-Xenidou, W. 1972, *Boiotische Grab- und Weihreliefs archaischer und klassischer Zeit*, Berlin.
Schmidt, M. 1995, 'Sorceresses' in Reeder 1995: 57–62.
Schnapp, A. 1997, 'Images of young people in the Greek city-state' in Levi, G. and J.-C. Schmitt (eds), *A History of Young People in the West, i: Ancient and Medieval Rites of Passage*, Cambridge MA: 12–50.
Schoder, R.V. 1960, *Masterpieces of Greek Art*, London.
Scholl, A. 1995, 'Choephoroi: Zur deutung der Korenhalle des Erechtheion' *JDAI* 110: 179–212.
—— 1996, *Die attischen Bildfeldstelen des 4. Jhs. v. Chr. Untersuchungen zu den kleinformatigen Grabreliefs im spätklassischen Athen*, Berlin.
Schöne, A. 1987, *Der Thiasos. Eine ikonographische Untersuchung über das Gefolge des Dionysos in der attischen Vasenmalerei des 6. und 5. Jhs. v. Chr.*, Göteborg.
Schweitzer, B. 1969, *Die geometrische Kunst Griechenlands*, Cologne.
Schwenk, C. 1985, *Athens in the Age of Alexander*, Chicago.
Seaford, R. 1981, 'Dionysiac drama and the Dionysiac mysteries' *CQ* 31: 252–75.
—— 1987, 'The tragic wedding' *JHS* 107: 106–30.
—— 1994, *Reciprocity and Ritual. Homer and Tragedy in the Developing City-State*, Oxford.
—— 1996, *Euripides' Bacchae*, Warminster.
Seeberg, A. 1971, *Corinthian Komos Vases*, London.
Segel, R. 1991, 'Adonis: a Greek eternal child' in Pozzi, D.C. and Wickersham, J.M. (eds), *Myth and the Polis*, Ithaca: 64–85.

Serematakis, C.N. (ed.) 1993, *Ritual, Power, and the Body. Historical Perspectives on the Representation of Greek Women*, New York.
Serwint, N. 1993, 'The female athletic costume at the Heraia and prenuptial initiation rites' *AJA* 97: 403–22.
Shapiro, H.A. 1989, *Art and Cult under the Tyrants*, Mainz.
Shapiro, H.A. 1991, 'The iconography of mourning in Athenian art' *AJA* 95: 629–56.
—— 1994, *Myth into Art. Poet and Painter in Classical Greece*, London.
—— 1996, 'Cults of Solonian Athens' in Hägg, R. (ed.) *The Role of Religion in the Early Greek Polis*, Stockholm: 127–33.
Shepherd, G. 1999, 'Fibulae and females: intermarriage in the western Greek colonies and the evidence from the cemeteries' in Tsetskhladze, G.R. (ed.) *Ancient Greeks: West and East*, Leiden: 267–300.
Sherwin-White, S.M. 1978, *Ancient Cos*, Göttingen.
Simms, R. 1989, 'Isis in Classical Athens' *CJ* 84: 216–21.
—— 1997, 'A date with Adonis' *Antichthon* 31: 45–53.
—— 1998, 'Mourning and community at the Athenian Adonia' *CJ* 93: 121–41.
Simon, B. 1978, *Mind and Madness in Ancient Greece*, Ithaca.
Simon, E. 1959, *Die Geburt der Aphrodite*, Berlin.
—— 1963, 'Ein Anthesterien-Skyphos des Polygnotos' *AK* 6: 6–22.
—— 1969, *Die Götter der Griechen*, Munich.
—— 1976, *Die griechischen Vasen*, Munich.
—— 1983, *Festivals of Attica: An Archaeological Commentary*, Madison.
—— 1985, 'Hekate in Athen' *AM* 100: 271–84.
Simon, S.J. 1991, 'The function of priestesses in Greek society' *Classical Bulletin* 67: 9–13.
Sinn, U. 1993, 'Greek sanctuaries as places of refuge' in Marinatos, N. and Hägg, R. (eds) *Greek Sanctuaries. New Approaches*, London: 88–109.
Smith, R.R.R. 1991, *Hellenistic Sculpture*, London.
Snyder, J.M. 1989, *The Woman and the Lyre. Women Writers in Classical Greece and Rome*, Carbondale.
Solmsen, F. 1979, *Isis among the Greeks and Romans*, Cambridge MA.
Sommerstein, A. 1985, *Aristophanes Peace*, Warminster.
Sourvinou-Inwood, C. 1974, 'The votum of 477/6 B.C. and the foundation legend of Locri Epizephyrii' *CQ* 24: 186–98.
—— 1974a, 'The Boston Relief and the religion of Locri Epizephyrii' *JHS* 94: 126–37.
—— 1978, 'Persephone and Aphrodite at Lokri' *JHS* 98: 101–21.
—— 1988, *Studies in Girls' Transitions*, Athens.
—— 1990, 'What is *polis*-religion?' in Murray, O. and Price, S. (eds), *The Greek City from Homer to Alexander*, Oxford: 295–322.
—— 1990a, 'Ancient rites and modern constructs: on the Brauronian bears again' *BICS* 37: 1–14.
—— 1995, *'Reading' Greek Death. To the End of the Classical Period*, Oxford.
Sparkes, B.A. 1975, 'Illustrating Aristophanes' *JHS* 95: 122–35.
—— 1996, *The Red and the Black. Studies in Greek Pottery*, London.
Specht, E. (ed.) 1994, *Frauenreichtum. Die Frau als Wirtschaftsfaktor im Altertum*, Wien.
Spengel, L. 1853, *Rhetores Graeci* i, Leipzig.
Spivey, N. 1996, *Understanding Greek Sculpture*, London.

—— 1997, *Greek Art*, London.
Stadter, P.A. 1989, *A Commentary on Plutarch's Perikles*, Chapel Hill.
Stears, K. 1995, 'Dead women's society: constructing female gender in classical Athenian funerary sculpture' in Spencer, N. (ed.) *Time, Tradition and Society in Greek Archaeology*, London: 109–31.
Steffen, V. 1964, *Chamaeleontis Fragmenta*, Warsaw.
Stewart, A. 1990, *Greek Sculpture. An Exploration* 1–2, New Haven.
—— 1997, *Art, Desire and the Body in Ancient Greece*, Cambridge.
Stone, I.F. 1988, *The Trial of Socrates*, London.
Strauss, B.S. 1993, *Fathers and Sons in Athens*, Princeton.
Stuart, J. and Revett, N. 1787, *The Antiquities of Athens* ii, London.
Stumpfe, O. 1978, *Die Heroen Griechenlands, Einübung des Denkens von Theseus bis Odysseus*, Münster.
Sturgeon, M.C. 1987, *Isthmia 4. Sculpture i: 1952–1967*, Princeton.
Takabatake, S. 1992, 'Funerary laws and Athens' *Kodai* 3: 1–13.
Taplin, O. 1993, *Comic Angels and Other Approaches to Greek Drama through Vase-Paintings*, Oxford.
Taylor, M.C. 1997, *Salamis and the Salaminioi. The History of an Unofficial Athenian Demos*, Amsterdam.
Thesleff, H. 1961, *An Introduction to the Pythagorean Writings of the Hellenistic Period*, Åbo.
—— 1965, *The Pythagorean Texts of the Hellenistic Period*, Åbo.
Thönges-Stringaris, R.N. 1965, 'Das griechische Totenmahl' *AM* 80: 1–99.
Thornton, B.S. 1997, *Eros. The Myth of Ancient Greek Sexuality*, Boulder.
Tod, M.N. 1912, 'Thoinarmostria' *JHS* 32: 100–4.
—— 1930, 'A bronze mirror in the Ashmolean Museum' *JHS* 50: 32–6.
Tod, M.N. and Wace, A.J.B. 1906, *A Catalogue of the Sparta Museum*, Oxford.
Toher, M. 1991, 'Greek funerary legislation and the two Spartan funerals' in Flower, M.A. and Toher, H. (eds) *Georgica. Greek Studies in Honour of George Cawkwell*, London.
Tomlinson, R.A. 1976, *Greek Sanctuaries*, London.
Touchette, L. 1995, *The Dancing Maenad Reliefs*, London.
Tracy, S.V. 1982, *I.G. ii^2 2336. Contribution of First Fruits for the Pythais*, Meisenheim am Glan.
Travlos, J. 1971, *Pictorial Dictionary of Ancient Athens*, London.
—— 1988, *Bildlexikon zur Topographie des antiken Attika*, Tübingen.
Trendall, A.D. 1989, *Red Figure Vases of South Italy and Sicily*, London.
Trendall, A.D. and Cambitoglou, A. 1978, *The Red-Figured Vases of Apulia* i, Oxford.
Turner, J.A. 1983, 'Heireiai: Acquisition of Feminine Priesthoods in Ancient Greece' (University of California, unpublished Ph.D.).
—— 1988, 'Greek priesthoods' in Grant, M. and Kitzinger, R. (eds) *Civilization of the Ancient Mediterranean: Greece and Rome*, New York: 925–31.
Tyrrell, W.B. 1984, *Amazons: A Study in Athenian Mythmaking*, Baltimore.
van Straten, F.T. 1974, 'Did the Greeks kneel before their gods?' *BABesch* 49: 159–89.
—— 1981, 'Gifts for the gods' in Versnel, H.S. (ed.) *Faith, Hope and Worship. Aspects of Religious Mentality in the Ancient World*, Leiden: 65–151.
—— 1995, *Hiera Kala: Images of Animal Sacrifice in Archaic and Classical Greece*, Leiden.

Vanoyeke, V. 1990, *La prostitution en Grèce et à Rome*, Paris.
Vermaseren, M.J. 1966, *The Legend of Attis in Greek and Roman Art*, Leiden.
—— 1977, *Cybele and Attis: the Myth and the Cult*, London.
Vermeule, C.C. 1977, *Greek Sculpture and Roman Taste*, Ann Arbor.
Vermeule, E. 1979, *Aspects of Death in Early Greek Art and Poetry*, Berkeley.
Vernant, J.-P. 1991, *Mortals and Immortals: Collected Essays*, Princeton.
Versnel, H.S. 1990, *Inconsistencies in Roman Religion i. Ter Unus, Isis, Dionysos, Hermes: Three Studies in Henotheism*, Leiden.
—— 1994, *Inconsistencies in Greek and Roman Religion ii. Transition and Reversal in Myth and Ritual*, Leiden.
Vidal-Naquet, P. 1986, *The Black Hunter. Forms of Thought and Forms of Society in the Greek World*, Baltimore.
Vidman, L. 1969, *Sylloge Inscriptionum Religionis Isiacae et Sarapiacae*, Berlin.
Vikela, E. 1994, *Die Weihreliefs aus dem Athener Pankrates-Heiligtum am Ilissos*, Berlin.
—— 1997, 'Attische Weihreliefs und die Kult-Topographie Attikas' *JDAI* 112: 167–246.
Vogel, C.J. de 1966, *Pythagoras and Early Pythagoreanism*, Assen.
Voigt, E. 1971, *Sappho et Alcaeus: Fragmenta*, Amsterdam.
Vollkommer, R. 1988, *Herakles in the Art of Classical Greece*, Oxford.
Wächter, T. 1910, *Reinheitsvorschriften im griechischen Kult*, Giessen.
Walbank, F.W. 1967, *A Historical Commentary on Polybius* ii, Oxford.
Waldstein, C. 1905, *The Argive Heraeum* i–ii, Boston.
Walker, H.J. 1995, *Theseus and Athens*, New York.
Walker, S. 1979, 'A sanctuary of Isis on the south slope of the Athenian acropolis' *ABSA* 74: 243–57.
Wallace, R.W. 1989, *The Areopagos Council, to 307 BC*, Baltimore.
Walter, H. 1985, *Die Gestalt der Frau*, Stuttgart.
Walters, E.J. 1985, *Attic Grave Reliefs that Represent Women in the Dress of Isis*, Michigan.
Walton, F.R. 1938, 'The date of the Adonia at Athens' *HThR* 31: 65–72.
Webster, T.B.L. 1972, *Potter and Patron in Classical Athens*, London.
Wegner, M. 1973, *Brygosmaler*, Berlin.
Wehgartner, I. 1985, *Ein Grabbild des Achilleusmalers*, Berlin.
Weill, N. 1966, 'Adôniazousai ou les Femmes sur le Toit' *BCH* 90: 664–98.
Wendel, C. 1914, *Scholia in Theocritum Vetera*, Leipzig.
Wesenberg, B. 1995, 'Panathenäische Peplosdedikation und Arrhephorie. Zur Thematik des Parthenonfrieses' *JDAI* 110: 149–78.
West, M.L. 1982, 'The Orphics of Olbia' *ZPE* 45: 17–29.
Whitehead, D. 1977, *The Ideology of the Athenian Metic*, Cambridge.
—— 1984, 'Immigrant communities in the classical polis' *AC* 53: 47–59.
—— 1986, *The Demes of Attica, 508/7–c.a. 250 B.C.*, Princeton.
—— 1990, *Aineas the Tactician. How to Survive under Siege*, Oxford.
Whitehorne, J. 1995, 'Women's Work in Theocritus, Idyll 15' *Hermes* 123: 63–75.
Williams, C.K. 1986, 'Corinth and the cult of Aphrodite' in del Chiaro, M.A. (ed.) *Corinthiaca. Studies in Honor of D.A. Amyx*, New York: 12–24.
Winkler, J.J. 1990, *The Constraints of Desire: the Anthropology of Sex and Desire in Ancient Greece*, London.

—— 1990a, 'Laying down the law: the oversight of men's sexual behaviour in Classical Athens' in Halperin, D. (ed.) *Before Sexuality: the Construction of Erotic Experience in the Ancient Greek World*, Princeton: 171–209.

—— 1991, 'The constraints of desire' in Faraone, C.A. and Obbink, D. (eds) *Magika Hiera. Ancient Greek Magic and Religion*, New York: 214–43 = Winkler 1990: 71–98, 226–30.

Witt, R.E. 1971, *Isis in the Graeco-Roman World*, Ithaca = 1997, *Isis in the Ancient World*, London.

Woodhead, A.G. 1997, *The Athenian Agora xvi. Inscriptions: the Decrees*, Princeton.

Wycherley, R.E. 1957, *The Athenian Agora iii: Literary and Epigraphical Testimonia*, Princeton.

—— 1970, 'Minor shrines in ancient Athens' *Phoenix* 24: 283–95.

Yamauchi, E.M. 1973, 'Cultic prostitution. A case study in cultural diffusion' in Hoffner, H.A. (ed.) *Orient and Occident*, Kevelaer, 213–22.

Younger, J.G. 1997, 'Gender and sexuality in the Parthenon Frieze' in Koloski-Ostrow, A.O. and Lyons, C.L. (eds) *Naked Truths. Women, Sexuality, and Gender in Classical Art and Archaeology*, London: 120–53.

Zaidman, L.B. 1992: 'Pandora's daughters and rituals in Grecian cities' in Pantel, P.S. (ed.) *History of Women in the West: i. From Ancient Goddesses to Christian Saints*, Cambridge MA: 338–76.

Zaidman, L.B. and Pantel, P.S. 1992, *Religion in the Ancient Greek City*, Cambridge.

Zeitlin, F.I. 1982, 'Cultic models of the female: rites of Dionysus and Demeter' *Arethusa* 15: 129–57.

Zhmud, L. 1992, 'Orphism and graffiti from Olbia' *Hermes* 120: 159–68.

—— 1997, *Wissenschaft, Philosophie und Religion im frühen Pythagoreismus*, Berlin.

Zuntz, G. 1971, *Persephone*, Oxford.

INDEX

abaton 231, 252, 256
abortion 172, 251–2
Abydos 190
Achaea, Achaeans 77, 86, 94
Acheloos 206, 229
Achilles 259, 269, 279, 281; transvestism of 220
Achilles Painter 265–6; painter of lekythoi 283
Acrocorinth 126, 130, 254
acropolis (Athens) 26, 29, 41, 42, 43, 47, 50, 57, 58, 59, 63, 71, 72, 78, 79, 84, 93, 133, 134, 136, 203, 205, 219, 220, 221, 242, 248; dedications by women to Athena on 14–19; childbirth on not permitted 253; dedications by women to Artemis Brauronia on 19–22; Demetrios Poliorketes and 192; Dorians not permitted on 86; family worshipping on 31–3, Figure 1.4; gossip about Perikles and citizen women on 186; korai dedicated on 12; location of Thesmophoria? 113, 118–19; Oreithyia in procession to 38; playground for arrephoroi on 58; procession of the Skira starts from 124; prohibitions for women priests and zakoroi 90; proteleia offered on 217; ritual ploughing under slope of 120, 125; sexual intercourse and 254; shrine of Aphrodite Pandemos on south-west slope 23, 134–5; snake guarding 86; statues of woman priests of Athena Polias on 78, 86, 87, 92; woman priest sets out from for ritual begging 95; women seize 124, 164, 241; *see* arrephoroi, Athena Nike, Athena Polias, Erechtheion,
inventories, Parthenon frieze
acropolis, Corinth (Acrocorinth): 89, 130, 200, 201, 203
Admete 135
Admetos 217
Adonia, Adonis 97, 109, 127, 139, 162–9, 182, 199, 234, 295, 296, 297, 300; *Adoniazousai*, play 164; *Adonis*, play 164; at Alexandria 163, 165; annual 163, 164; at Athens 162–3; 'Beat your breasts for Adonis' 164, 167; breast-beating at 163, 164, 165, 167; citizen women and 163, 164; date 163, 166, 167–8; death 163; dirge 163; explanations of purpose of 166–7; 'Gardens of Adonis' 162–3, 165; incense at? 169; korallion 167; ladder 165, 168, 169; on Lesbos 163; metics 165, 168–9; mock funerals 163–4, 165–6; Phoenician origin 164; prostitutes 165; rooftop rites 164; sexual intercourse at 165; 'Woe, Adonis' 163, 164, 167; Figures 5.7–8
adultery 74, 191, 212, 241
aegis 60, 95; shown on vase in wedding scene 216
Aelian 65, 245
Aeneias the Tactician 63–5
Aeschines (orator) 85, 104; *Against Timarchos* 184–5; involved in cult of Sabazios 158–60
Aeschylus 73, 218, 220, 269, 299; *Choephoroi* 270; *Eumenides* 94–5; *Xantriai* 96, 142
Aesop 177
Aetolians 237–8
Agameda 29
Agamemnon 94, 218, 248, 282, 289; mourned by Elektra 270

INDEX

Agamemnonidai 237
Agaue 141, 145
Agdistis: see Angdistis
agermos 96, 97
agerseis 97
Agesilaos 214, 257–8
Agesipolis 99
Aglaurion 59
Aglauros 47, 59, 77, 79, 89, 133, 134, 242; woman priest of 77, 79; women's oaths by 248
Aglauros, Pandrosos and Kourotrophos: joint priesthood of 89
Agrai 95
agretai 61
Agrionia 64, 147, 152–3
Agryle 247
Aias 65
Aigeira 75
Aigeus 177, 217
Aigila 110, 118
Aigion 238
Aigirios 240
Aiora, rite of the 69–71, Figure 2.15
Aischines (Socratic) 186, 189
aischrologia 109, 114, 122, 324n.5
Aison 172
Aithra 120, 266
Ajax 179, 260
Akestor 132
Akilisene 201
Akraia 68–9
alabastron 227
Alcaeus 142
Alektrone 263
aletrides, aletris (corn-grinders) 37, 60, 220, 295
Alexander the Great 19, 101, 194, 196
Alexandria 126, 146, 214, 245; Adonia at 163, 165; maenadism at 146–7
Aleximachos 34
Alexis 153; *Philouse* 198
Alkathoe 142
Alkestis 218, 249, 288, 289; see Euripides
Alkibiades 86, 91–2, 247; and the Plynteria 133–4
Alkibiades, the elder 186
Alkiphron 122, 167
Alkman 66, 145; partheneia of 211, 214
Alkmeonidai 100
Alkmeonis 143
Alma-Tadema 186, Figure 6.1

Alpeios 131
altar, altars 32, 34, 35, 41, 43, 63, 67, 69, 84, 86, 91, 116, 117, 156, 160, 197, 211, 217, 225, 226, 236, 242, 243, 249, 259, 266; of Artemis 231, Figure 7.4; dedicated by women 3, 23–5; dedicated to the deceased prostitute Pythionike 196; at Delphi 73, 98; fourteen altars of Dionysos 103; frankincense burned on 200; Great Altar at Pergamon 258, Figure 8.2; of Iodama 105; kanephoros pours libation onto 39, Figure 2.1; in Limnai, of Dionysos 102; Ludovisi throne as 202; maenads at 149, Figures 5.2–4; of nymphs 228, Figure 7.3; purified 56, 135; segregrates sexes at Amphiaraion 205, 256; and Thesmophoria 114; virgins as suppliants at 260; whipping of boys at 260; woman kills goat at 245; woman priest of Demeter sits on at Olympic festival 106, 131; woman priest stands at 39, 88–9, 242, 243, Figure 3.4; of Zeus 131
Amasis 197
Ammonios 183
Amnisos 230
Amorgos 34
Amphiaraion, Amphiaraos 29, 30, 31, 205, 256
amphidromia 233, 254
amphipolis 74
Amphissa 145, 149
amphora 41; dedicated to Kourotrophos 222
amphoriskos 43
amulets 104, 171; for childbirth 172
Amyklai 137
Amyklaion 214
Amynos 30–1
Anakreon 143, 147, 212
Anakeion 237
Anakes 237
anakalypteria 355n.98
Anaxagoras 188, 189
Anaxandrides 38, 50, 74
Andanian Mysteries 263–4, 291
Andocides, cursed by priests 246
Andromacha 25, 30, 230
Andromache 177, 268
Angdistis 156, 179
Anodos 113, 111

404

INDEX

Anonymous Goddesses: *see* Semnai Theai
Anthea 199
Anthesphoria 62
anthesphoroi 62
Anthesteria 69, 102, 121, 149, 152, 266, 294
anthesterides 61
Anthesterion 102, 103, 152, 238
Anthia 216
Anti-aphrodisiacism 113
Antigone 71; buries brother 288–9; laments father (Oedipus) 289
Antigonos, king 65
Antimacheia 96, 240
Antiphanes 183, 186
Antisthenes 186
'Anzio Girl' 60, Figure 2.13
aparche 15, 369
Apatouria 222, 243
Apelles: *Aphrodite Rising from the Sea* 194–5
Aphrodision 198
Aphrodisios 198
Aphrodite 2, 29, 31, 59, 75, 77, 105, 127, 130, 177, 180, 198, 199, 202, 207, 208, 215, 217, 234, 239, 245, 248, 254, 269, 293, 295; and Adonia 162; in Italian Lokris 222–8; love magic 170–1; Ludovisi throne 202–3; painting of 194–5; and prostitutes 191–2; receives dedications from Athenian prostitutes 198; sacred prostitutes 199–201; statue of 195; Figures 6.3–5; *see* Adonia; Mylitta
Aphrodite, cult epithets: Akraia 237; Anosia 347n.70; in the Gardens 59; Hera 218; Hetaira 189–90; Homicidal 196; Hoplismene 201; Kitian 194; Kolias 300; Kourotrophos 217; Melainis 196; Ourania 200, 206, 217; Pandamos (Kos): compulsory marriage sacrifice to 221; purchase of priesthood 75; sacrifices to 85, 96; woman priest to be 'healthy and sound' 74; woman priest to receive fines and treasury proceeds 85; Pandemos (Athens): purification of sanctuary 134–5; woman priest and sanctuary 23; sanctuary financed by brothels? 184; son of woman priest of reports to assembly 79; Porne 190; Pythionike 196; 'in Samos' 198
apo gynaikos 255

Apollo 1, 61, 74, 79, 104, 105, 180, 193, 197, 214, 229, 260, 294, 322; chiton presented to 137; prophetic women priests of, *see* Dodona, Pythia
Apollo, cult epithets: Amyklai 211, 212, 214; Lykeios 56; Nomios 179; Phoebus 98; Thymbraian 259
Apollodoros (1) *On the Gods* 189
Apollodoros (2) 113
Apollodoros (3) 184
apometra 91
apples 231, 233
Aratos 30
Archedike 279
Archias 121, 196, 241
Archidamos, King 195
Archinos 23
archons 20, 41, 79, 103, 121, 184, 205, 271, 291; *see* basileus archon
archousai 112, 117
Areiopagos 31, 103, 190
Ares 179, 238, 243; Ares Gynaikothoinas 244
Argaios 147
Arge 96
Argonauts 190
Argos 35, 73, 96, 128, 132, 136, 142, 180, 217, 222, 238, 245, 260; women priests at 73; *see* Chrysis (1); Heraion (Argos)
Ariadne 69
Aristarcha 97
Aristeia 13
Aristodama 30
Aristogeiton (prosecutor) 93
Aristomache 17
Aristomenes 110, 115, 116, 213
Aristonike 32
Aristophanes (1) 125, 164, 243, 296; *Acharnians* 38, 189; *Birds* 38; *Clouds* 169; *Ekklesiazousai* 38, 124; *Frogs* 253; *Knights* 255; *Lysistrata* 2, 37, 57, 60, 76, 78, 158, 164, 166, 167, 211, 212, 220, 241, 253, 254; *Thesmophoriazousai* 79, 110, 112, 118, 122, 124, 248, 262; *Wasps* 17
Aristophanes (2) of Byzantium 183
Aristophanes (3), son of woman priest 79
Aristotle 79, 84, 253, 290
Arkadia, Arkadians 142, 230, 250, 260, 262, 263
Arkesine 79

405

arkteia, arktoi (bears) 21, 37, 220–1,
  295; *see* Artemis Brauronia, Brauron
arrephoria, arrephoroi 12, 37, 46–8,
  57–60, 72, 85, 206, 220–1, 295, 300,
  369; age of 57; clothing 57; expenses
  58; gold of 57; house of 78; rite not
  initiatory 60; nocturnal rite 59;
  playground of 58; selection of 58;
  statues of 58; Figure 2.5; *see* ergastinai
arrhenoi (boys) at funerals 272
Arsinoe II 163
Arsippe 142
Artaneus 290
Artayktes 258
Artemis 35, 38, 67, 73, 77, 81, 85, 105,
  156, 179, 182, 220–1, 222, 229, 235,
  246, 248, 249, 260, 293, 298; and
  childbirth 218; child presented to
  231–4, Figure 7.4; and death of
  Adonis 163; dedications by women to
  9–13, 19–23; and *frauenfest* scenes
  129–30; girls sacrifice lamb to 61; and
  midwives 178; prayed to for husbands
  11; pre-marital offerings to 215–17;
  prostitutes swear oath by 198; statues
  of 10, Figure 1.1; 260, Figure 8.3;
  statue purified 135; virgin priests of
  75; *see* acropolis, altars, arkteia,
  Brauron, Brauronia, inventories,
  kanephoroi, parthenoi, priests:
  women, rakos, statues, torch
Artemis, cult epithets: Agrotera 23, 134;
  Archegetis 37; Aristoboule 73, 221;
  Artemis-Iphigeneia 128; Boulephoros
  Skiris 97; Brauronia 13, 19–23, 28,
  72, 86, 93–4, 95, 128; Ephesia 97;
  Eukleia 217; Hekate 230; Hymnia 75,
  258; Kalliste 29; Karyatis 213, 214;
  Kolainis 92; Korythalia 350; Limnatis
  213; Lochia 25, 273; Lousoi 80; Orthia
  212–13, 230, 260; Orthria 214;
  Pergaia 79, 96, 243, 244; 'strangled'
  230; Tauropolia 127; Tauropolos 128;
  Triklaria 75, 258; *see* Figures 1.1, 8.3
Artemision 215
Artimitios 96
aryballos vase 288, 369
Arybbas 30
asebeia 186, 191, 273, 290; *see* impiety
Asios 216
Asklepieion, Asklepios 9, 18, 20,
  25–31, 35, 41, 105, 114, 144, 203,
  231, 233, 240, 249, 293, 295, 298;

cult spread by women 97; cures at
  Epidauros 29–31; sacrifices to by
  women 253; *see* Epicurean hetairai,
  Epidauros, Hygieia, serpents, snakes
Asopos river 218
Aspasia 186–9, 190, Figures 6.1–2;
  brothel of? 345n.27; dedicated tiara
  189; as Helen 189; as pallake 189;
  and Perikles 186, 188–9; as porne
  189; Socratic dialogues about 186,
  189; trial for impiety 186, 188–9
aspersion rod 226, Figures 7.1–2
assembly: *see* ekklesia
asylia 101
Athena 9, 13, 15, 16–17, 31–2, 35, 42,
  65, 71, 94, 105, 124, 124, 134, 186,
  215, 234, 248, 253, 256, 257, 258,
  259, 260; abandons Athenian
  acropolis 86; participation of woman
  priest of in the Oschophoria festival
  89; peplos presented to 47, 48,
  57–60, 136–7; refuses to answer
  Trojan wives' prayer 137; succession
  to priesthood 89; washing of statues of
  132–5; Figure 3.4; *see* palladion,
  priest, woman: of Athena Polias
Athena, cult epithets: 84, 95, 242, 243;
  Alea 75; Apotropaia 237; of the
  Bronze House 13, 197–8, 211, 212;
  Chalkioikos, *see* Bronze House;
  'Deceitful'; Ergane 58; Itonia 105;
  Nike 76, 84–5, 95, 242, 243;
  Nikephoros 256; Pallas 132, 214;
  Patroia 243; of the Pedesans 101;
  Polias 58, 59, 73, 75, 75, 78, 88, 94,
  106, 124, shown on vases 87–8;
  Poliouchos 15; Promachos 39, 41;
  Skiras 76, 89–90
Athenaeus 79, 183, 189, 194, 195, 198,
  201, 216, 246
Athenians, Athens: *see* acropolis, Adonia,
  arrephoria, Athena, basileus archon,
  basilinna, boule, Bouphonia, demes,
  Erechtheion, gene, Haloa, kanephoroi,
  Panathenaia, Parthenon frieze,
  Phryne, Plynteria, Semnai Theai,
  Skira, Stenia, Tauropolia,
  Thesmophoria, priest, woman: of
  Athena Nike, priest, woman: of
  Athena Polias, priests: women
Attis 154–6, 160, 161; pedum of 155
Auge 253, 258, Figure 8.2
auletrides (flute-girls) 183

406

INDEX

aulos: *see* flute
Autonoe 145

baby 212, 277; presentation of 231–3, Figure 7.4
Babylon 196, 199
Bacchiadai 269
Bacchic, Bacchae, Bacchus: *see* Dionysos, Euripides *Bacchae*, maenads
Bacchylides 142
bakcheia (bacchic bands): *see* maenads
'Bailers' (Antletriai) 113, 114, 115
balls 58, 104 223, 225, 235
balsam-containers 56
bare feet 32, 39, 65, 82, 88, 140, 264, Figures 1.4, 2.1, 5.1
barley 242
barrenness 251, 248, 258
basileus archon (Athens) 46, 47, 58, 70, 74, 101–4, 134, 190, 238, 242, 255
baskets 34, 41, 56, 116, 160, 246, 247, 271; shapes of 38, 39, 41; dedicated 41; *see* kana, kanephoroi, likna
basket-bearer, *see* kanephoroi
Bassai 260, Figure 8.3
Bassarai, Bassarides 146, 147
bastards (nothai, nothoi) 74, 127, 135, 189, 241
Bate 86
bath: before prayer 242; marriage 135; *see* bridal bath, loutrophoroi
Battos 110, 115, 146, 297
Baubo 146
beard 213, 226, 265, 279; of woman priest 101; of serpent key 80, Figure 3.1
bears: *see* arkteia, arktoi
bed, bridal 96
begging rituals, of women 4, 95–7; of boys 322
belts 21, 22, 39, 263
'belly-talkers', women 180
Bendis 95–6, 158, 194
betrothal 96
bidiaioi 127
biscuits 116
black-figure 369; *see* vases
blouse 88
bobbins 14
body parts, dedications of models of 26–9; *see* typion, typoi
Boedromion 57, 87, 120, 134, 282, 322

Boeotia, Boeotians 81, 105, 111, 140, 237, 238; funerary laws and practices 271–2
Boidion 203
books, sacred 160, 283
Boreas, the North Wind 38
boughs, suppliant 260
Boukoleion 102
boule: Arkesine 79; Athens 79, 133, 242
Bouphonia 56
Bouzygai 134
bowl 72, 73; of Persephone 226; Figures 7.1–2; *see* libations, phialai
boys 69–70, 89, 104, 160–1, 185, 240, 245, 322; begging 322; hair cut as transition rite 215; sent to Minotaur 90
Branchidai 67
Brauron 13, 37, 77, 93–4, 128, 213, 220–1, 250, 263; *see* arkteia, Artemis Brauronia
Brauronia festival 37
bread 116, 322
breastfeeding 230, 254, 267; terracotta of woman 230
breasts 105, 156, 216; bare, on Ludovisi throne 203, Figure 6.4; beating for Adonis 163–4, 165, 167; beating of 3, 269, 277, 289; cakes in shape of 343–4n.234; clothing arranged over 66; dedication of representations of 26, 28–30; of Erechtheion parthenoi 50; immature, indicating young women 60, 72; laceration of 269; Phryne's exposed in court 194
bridal bath 135, 219–20
bride 112, 240, 241, 257; begged from 95; and bridegroom seen off by woman priest 216; cross-dresses 220; customary and compulsory marriage sacrifices 220–2; gifts for 168, 219, Figure 5.8; girdle released 216; hair shorn 215; hand grasped by groom 216; at Lokris presents peplos 234, cf. 225; leads dance 67; as Nymphe 219; ritual bath before wedding 135, 219–20; sacrifice before marriage 217; visits temple? 277; of Zeus 135, 218
bridegroom 22, 217, 240; cross-dresses 240; releases bride's girdle 216
Briseis 269, 270

407

INDEX

Bromias 193
brothel 167, 197, 183
Brygos Painter 140, 143, Figure 5.1
Bryseai 238
buttock-jumps 131
buttocks, bare 47
buttons 22
Byblos 199

cakes 126, 134, 149, 154, 159, 221, 231, 236, 244, 245; *see* pelanos
calendar frieze, from the church Hagios Eleutherios 57, 83, 322n.154
calendars, religious and sacrificial 87, 109, 239; of Eleusis 116, 120; of Kos 239; of Mykonos 237; of Nikomachos 85, 91; of Tetrapolis 222; *see* Erchia, Thorikos
Callimachus 69, 112, 132, 250; *Hymn to Demeter* 57, 125–6
canopies 124
Canopus pool, Tivoli 51
caps 264
Caria 112, 170; Carian women, hired for funerals 269
Carrey 43
carts, in funerary processions: 282, 291, cf. 268
caryatids 50; at Delphi 53–4
castanets 150, 160, 169, Figure 5.4
Castor 211
castration 74, 110
Catana 239
caves 219; cave of Aglauros 59
Centaurs 260, Figure 8.3
chains of dancing women, Corinth 128–30; Argos 130; Athens 130
Chairestrate (woman priest) 78, 80, 95, 155–6, 299
Chairigenes 23
Chaironeia 237
Chalkeia 58
Chalkis, Chalkidian 35, 243
Chamaileon of Herakleia 200, 201
charcoal 116
Charias 13
Charikleia 17
Charillos, king 243
chariots 227, 289; at funerals 275, 277, Figure 9.3
Charisios 127
charms, erotic 175; *see* magic
Charon 288

chastity, women priests 77–8, 255, 258, 260
chastity, male priests 77
cheese 79, 154, 252, 256, 322
chernips 56, 246, cf. 236
Chian altar 197
chickens, clay models of 114
child, children 32–4, 35, 68–9, 84, 104, 132, 171, 215, 248; ceremoniously carried around house 254; exposure of 252; legitimacy of 100; new born Corinthian killed by Medea's spirit 68–9; new-born presented to goddess 231–4; statues of 92–3
'child of the hearth' 92–3
childbirth 65, 98, 126, 131, 135, 156, 178, 182, 211, 215, 217, 218, 245, 251, 258, 267, 270, 293, 299; assistance of Eileithyia in 230–1; and Athenian acropolis 253; death in 20; forbidden on Delos 253; not permitted on acropolis 253; placenta 252; pollution of 252–4; ritual begging in aid of 95–7; thanksgiving for 19–20, 22, 24–5, 29, 32, 231–4; *see* abortion, Artemis, lecho, nymphs
childlessness 100, 177, 217
chin-strap 289
Chios 135, 244
chiton 21, 22, 39, 41, 60, 66, 68, 369; of maenads 147
Chiton, room in which chiton for Apollo was woven 137
chitoniskoi 194
Chloe 121
Choes festival 69–70, 102, 103, 152, 270
choes, chous (cup) 102, 369
Choirine 80
choirs: *see* choruses
cholargos (deme) 112, 117
chorus (in plays) 71
choruses 66, 67–8, 69, 211–15
chous: *see* choes
Chrysanthis 13
Chrysapha 34
Chrysina 24
Chrysippos (1) 238
Chrysippos (2) 253
Chrysis (1) in Menander 165, 182
Chrysis (2) woman priest 73, 75–6, 83
Chrysogone 24
Chthonia 245

408

INDEX

Chytroi 102
Cicero 158; on Roman funerals 272
Circe 170, 175
Circle of the Meidias Painter 162–3, Figure 5.7
circumcision 74
citizenship 101–4
clappers 4, 155
Clazomenai 67, 238
Clement of Alexandria 114
cloaks 264
clothes 3, 10, 58, 65, 66, 69–70, 73, 77, 88, 94, 112, 241, 242, 246, 258, 260, 262, Figures 1.1–9.7; of Aspasia 186; black for mourning 270; certain types forbidden in women's rites 262–3; clean 263; dedication of 13, 19–23, 93–4, 232–3, 250, 263; delineate sacred and profane 262; of male initiates 264; of oschophoroi 89; purple not to be worn 262–3; regulated in cults by men 262; regulations for women's at Andania 263–4; of women in cult of Isis 161; of women worshipping Nameless Goddesses 94, 95; *see* bare feet, chiton, feet (shod), himation, peplos, rakoi, sandals, tiara, women
cock 245; *see* rooster
coffins 291; *see* larnakes
colonisation: and Delphi 100
colonists 247
columns, dedications of 11–12
comb, golden, of Athena 132
compost 114
concubines 153; *see* pallakai
contraceptives 172, 251
Copenhagen Painter 172, Figure 5.9
Corinth 29, 35, 68, 126–7, 190, 192, 196, 202, 230, 241, 248, 254, 262, 269, 287, 298; proverb 199; sacred prostitutes 199–201; *see* Corinthian *frauenfest* scenes
Corinthian *frauenfest* scenes 126, 128–130, Figure 4.2; and Artemis 129–30; and Dionysos 129–30
corpse, pollution of 253
Corybantes 179; Corybantic rites 4
Crane Dance, the 69
Crete 89, 217, 220, 230
cripples 65
cross-dressing 220; by Herakles 240; *see* bride, bridegroom, oschophoroi, priests (men)
crown 176, 243; bridal 224; of olive for girl victors 131
crucifixion 258
Cumae 33
cures, of women 25–31; *see* Asklepios, Herakles-Pankrates, Palaimon
curse tablets 177–8; used by a woman 178
curses, of women 246–8; cf. Theano
cushions 264
Cybele 2, 67, 68, 96, 166, 179, 181, 300; as 'All-bearing Mother' 80; woman priest of 95; *see* Great Mother–Cybele
cymbals 245
Cypriots, Cyprus 54, 161, 164, 169, 199, 202, 206
Cyrene, Cyrene cathartic law 110, 132, 211, 221, 234, 247, 251, 252, 255, 256, 257; compulsory marriage sacrifice 221

dadouchos 92
Daidala 218
daimones 182; birth 230; *see* Corybantes
Dalios 61
Damuzi/ Damu 164
Danaos 260
dancing: of girls and women 66–7, 122, 132, 139, 140, 148, 149–52, 159, 160, 164, 169, 193, 211, 212, 213, 215, 245, 294, 299; public of parthenoi before marriage 213; women in thanksgiving for childbirth 233; *see* Corinthian *frauenfest* scenes, Crane Dance
Daphni 219
daughter, daughters 11, 12, 13, 17, 18, 19, 23, 24, 25, 30, 33, 36, 47, 57, 59, 69, 71, 77, 86, 87, 89, 101, 102, 103, 106, 109, 111, 112, 121, 125, 128, 132, 135, 136, 138, 140, 143, 145, 146, 147, 153, 156, 161, 170, 176, 180, 190, 195, 198, 211, 213, 215, 220, 230, 236, 242, 247, 248, 266, 289, 290, Figure 1.4; clothing of in Andanian Mysteries 264; father and daughter dedication 23; of Leukippos 260; maddened 67, 142; when marries, mother sacrifices for 218;

409

INDEX

mother and daughter dedication 92; mother thanks Eileithyia for birth of 230–1; mourned by father 279; of Peleus 172–4, Figure 5.10; polluted by death 272; prostituted 199, 201, 202; raped by Pelasgians 220; receive share of sacrifice 244; sacrificed 248; seized with mothers at festival 213; warrior father presents to Persephone 226; of woman priest steals dedications 94; see metic women

daughter-in-law 118, 242

dedications 183; for arrephoroi 58; of baskets 41; by kanephoroi 41, 58; of men 12, 19, 23, 26, 27, 28, 73, 86, 103, 155; of perirrhanteria 54; of phialai 50; Figure 7.1; of prostitutes, by Xenophon of Corinth 199–200, by men and women 201–2; of statues of kanephoroi 40; of statues of women priests 86; by tray-bearers 60; see hair, Manes, metic, Mika, peplos

dedications, of girls and women 9–36; to Angdistis and Attis for children 156; in cult of Asklepios 25–9, 297; on the Athenian acropolis 14–19; of altars 3, 23–5; of clothing 19–23; to Demeter 126; by Epicurean hetairai 203–5; of girls before marriage 212, 215, 219, 225 (of balls) (see girdle, hair, Lokrian pinakes, peplos); of girl victors in the Heraia 131; to Hera 14; of korai 9–13; of kourotrophic figurines 222; of mirrors 13–14; made by prostitutes 197–8; not mentioning husband or father 14–17, 18, 28; socio-economic status of women dedicators 22, 23, 25–8, 30, 297; of temples 23, 24–5; see Artemis, clothing, Echinos relief, Herakles, Herakles-Pankrates, metics, Palaimon, Pankrates, Pitsa pinax

deer 75, 143

Deianeira 175–6, Figure 5.11

Deinarchos 91

deipnophoroi 89, 90

dekate, tithe 13, 15, 369

dekate, child's naming day 233, cf. 254

Deliades 215

Delos 9–11, 35, 69, 96, 215, 237, 256, 298; clothing dedications by women at 22; purification of 253; Thesmophoria at 116

Delphi 19, 24, 39, 65, 69, 95, 104, 121, 133, 146, 163, 197, 213, 230, 258, 294; caryatids at 53–4; consulted by women 98; dedications by prostitutes at 197; funerary legislation at 273–4; sacred fire 105; women at 1, 30, 98; see Pythais, Pythia

Delphinion 89, 248

Delphis 175

deltoi, deltos 283

Demades 194

demarch 121

Demeas 167

demes, of Athens: see Agryle, Bate, Cholargos, Erchia, Halai Araphenides, Halimous, Ikarion, Melite, Myrrhinous, Paiania, Pithos, Skambonidai, Thorikos

Demeter 36, 68, 77, 79, 87, 91, 92, 93, 94, 104, 105, 109, 111, 112, 116, 119, 120, 121, 122, 130, 138, 178, 197, 198, 245, 248, 249, 263, 266, 290, 293, 297, 299; dining in cult 126–7; fasting in cult 125; figurines of 126; magic of 171; and marriage 95, 218, 221; obscenities in cult 113; and pregnancy 250; prohibitions on clothing in cult 262; secret statue of 239; statuettes of, carrying a piglet 114; statuettes of, dedicated at Corinth 14; women contribute to rebuilding sanctuary 22; woman dedicates house and statue to 24; women dedicate clothes to 22, 23; see Haloa, Hermion, Stenia, Thesmophoria, Timo

Demeter, cult epithets: Chamyne 131; Chloe 85, 237; Malophoros 66; Mysia 238; Thesmophoros 110, 126, 127, 243, 262

Demeter, woman priest of 90–2, 120, 245; choice of 92; impersonates Demeter? 92; law-suits 91; receives cult fees 91; sets up portrait in temple 92; see Thesmophoria

Demetria 26, 36

Demetrios of Phaleron 272

Demetrios Poliorketes 192

Demochares, male prostitute 185, 186

Demophon, king 134

Demophoon 93, 172

Demosthenes 79, 104, 181, 296; *Against Neaira* 101–4; ridicules Aeschines' involvement in cult of Sabazios

410

158–60
Demostratos 164
depression, during puberty 230
Despoina 250, 253, 254, 263
Detienne, on women and sacrifice 236, 243
Diadikasia 91
diakonos 101
diakonoumenai 137
Dictyanna of the wild beasts 179
Didyma 97, 180, 239
Dikaio 126
dildos 123–4, 199
dining rooms 126–7
Dinos Painter 148
diodoi 119
Diodoros 50, 140, 146, 180, 217
Diogenes 155
Diokles (1) *The Shrines of Heroes* 238
Diokles (2) wife of 117
Diomedes 136, 137, 201
Diomedon 239
Dion, king 213
Dione 19
Dionysia 39, 199
Dionysiades 213
Dionysios of Halikarnassos 3
Dionysios of Syracuse 153, 202
Dionysos (Bacchus) 3, 4, 31, 87, 101, 121, 122, 129–30, 139–53, 158, 160, 180, 181, 194, 197, 213, 234, 238, 242, 243, 255, 260, 266, 290, 294, 295, 297, 300; altar of, in Limnai 102; ambivalent sexuality 147; dressed as maenad 146; fourteen altars of 103; mask of 149–52, Figures 5.2–3; and Orphism 154; priest of 153
Dionysos, cult epithets: Anthios 85; Bakchios 144; in Limnai 102, 103, 238; Lenaios 152; Lenagetas 335; Lyaios; Omestas 142; Pseudaner 147; Thyllophoros 74
Diopeithes 188
Diphilos 166
diphroi, diphros (stool) 45, 46, 205, 298
diphrophoroi, diphrophoros 38, 45, 206
Dipolieia 56, 164
Dipylon Gate 43, 277
Dipylon Master 275
dirges, funerary 269, 271; *see* Adonia, mourning women
disabled, physically 74

discus, dedication of 17
divorce 103
Dodona 1, 19, 74, 95, 106, 115, 180; prophetic women priests of 100
dogs 238, 251, 288
dolls, dedicated 235; *see* korai
donkey 251
Dorians 86
Doriche 197
Dorieus 86
double flute: *see* aulos
doves 23, 106, 226, 227
dowry, earned through prostitution 199
dream 24, 25, 97, 156, 236
dried figs 153; necklace of 37
drought 100, 337
drugs: abortive 252; contraceptive 251; erotic 175; used in childbirth 252; *see* Medea, midwives, pharmaka, pharmakeia
drum 155, 159, 245, 351; *see* tympana
drunkenness: *see* women: wine
Duris of Samos 144, 189, 216

earrings 18, 203, 265, Figure 2.1; hole for Figure 6.4
earthquakes 238
Echelos 243, 298
Echinos relief 21, 231–4; Figure 7.4
ecstacy, of women 2, 3, 4, 159, 161, 179, 294
Egypt, Egyptian 54, 161, 183, 194, 206, 237, 249, 252, 255, 256; priests 74; *see* circumcision, linen
Eileithyia, Eileithyiai 13, 22, 25, 126, 222, 230–1, 233, 238, 244, 250, 253; 'Auge on her knees' 258; *lysizonos* 25
Eirene 347n.70
eiresione 322n.154
ekklesia (assembly) 93, 112, 118, 164, 248
ekphora 275, 277, 369; to take place before dawn 272
Elaious 258
Elaphebolion 134, 243
Elateia 237
Eleans 94, 131, 238
Elektra 248, 270, 282
Elephantis 289
Eleusinia 39, 194, 195
Eleusinian Lesser Propylon 56
Eleusinian Mysteries, Eleusis 56, 91–3, 105, 104, 111, 117, 124, 134, 138,

171, 196; arrival of cult objects in Athens 87; cult objects escorted by women priests 87, 92; loutrophoroi found in caves at 219; profanation of 91–2, 246–7; sacred ploughing 111, 120; Thesmophoria at Eleusis 116, 117; women priests receive fees from initiates in 91; women walk to 291; *see* 'child of the hearth', Demeter, Haloa, Kore, Persephone, Sinope, telesterion
Eleusinian women priests 77, 78, 90–2; escort Eleusinian sacred objects 92; receive cult fees 91; receive Eleusinian sacred objects at Athens 87
Eleusinion 87, 92, 119
Eleusis: sacred calendar of 116–17
Elis 131, 136, 137, 238
Elythia: *see* Eileithyia
emeralds 262
Empedia 15
Empedokles 154
Endymatia 137
engastrimanteis 180
engastrimuthoi 180
enneakrounos 220
Enodia 179
entheos 179, 180
Enyalios 179
epaulia 369
ephebes (Athens) 94, 134, 222
epheboi (Samos) 216
Ephesos 7, 35, 97, 135, 190, 215
Epicurean hetairai: cured by Asklepios 203, 205
Epicurus 113, 203
Epidauria (festival) 39
Epidauros 29–31, 163, 252, 296; *see* Asklepios, cures
Epikteta of Thera 290
epilepsy 179
Epimenides 271
epiphany 212, 232, 238
Epirus 25, 34, 100
epistatai 86
Epithyousa ('Woman making a sacrifice') 60
erastes 185; *see* pederasty, sodomy
Erchia 217, 218, 222, 243, 317n.34
Erechtheion 17, 18, 50–3, 71, 84, Figures 2.8–10
Erechtheus 248
Eresides 132
Eresos 238, 253

Eretria 23, 110, 113, 138, 243
ergastinai 58
Ergokleia 15
Erichthonios 43, 47, 59–60, 133, 216–17, 234, 235
Erigone 69–70
Erinyes: *see* Nameless Goddesses
eromenos 185
Eros, Erotes 59, 162, 163, 169, 180, 225, 227, 369; Figures 5.7–8
Erythrai 35, 217, 237
Eryx 201
Eteoboutadai 76, 84, 87; and Skira 124
Euamera 76
Euboea 217
Euboulos 233
Eudeine 23
eugeneis, 'well-born' 38, 60, 118
Eumelides 17
Eumenides: *see* Nameless Goddesses
Eumolpidai 85, 98, 91, 92
Eumolpos, king 309
Eunostos 238
eunuchs 170
'euoi' 140; 'Euoi Saboi' 158
Euonyma 13
Eupheros 283
Eupolis 189
Euripides 24, 62, 94, 100, 113, 118, 120, 214, 299; *Bacchae* 140–5, 146, 147, 148, 180; *Cretans* 142; *Helen* 155; *Hippolytos* 179, 248; *Medea* 179, 396; *Melanippe* 1–2, 95, 298, 299; *Iphigeneia in Aulis* 218; *Iphigeneia in Tauris* 81, 128, 135; *see* Alkestis
Eurotas river 211, 212, 214
Eurydike 144
Eurykleis 180
Eurysakes: priesthood of 89
Euthias 194
Euthynai 272
ewes 79
exaleiptra, exaleiptron 286–7
exegetai 92, 218
Exekias 275–7, Figures 9.2–3
eyes, silver 26; *see* typoi

families, at worship 26, 31–5, Figure 1.4
famine 100, 251
fasting 111, 125, 138; *see* spitting, Thesmophoria
Fates 1, 2, 94, 217; *see* Nameless

412

Goddesses
father, fathers 6, 11, 12, 15, 17, 18, 19, 22, 28, 30, 32, 35, 47, 67, 71, 84, 93, 94, 99, 165, 167, 170, 172, 173, 177, 186, 191, 195, 217, 237, 248, 258, 265, 268, 285, 289, 294, 295; has children initiated into Orphism 154; heroised 290; mourn daughters 279; name new child 233; parthenoi honoured at fathers' request 58; priests to have citizen fathers 79; presents daughter to Persephone 226; sons erect monument to 279; take children to Delos 154
fawns: and bacchic worship 143, 148, 150
fawn-skins: in dress of maenads 144, 146; in cult of Sabazios 159, 160
feet, shod 82, 203; *see* bare feet
fennel 165
Ferrara krater 160–1, 181
ferret 241
fertility 14, 30, 98, 109, 122, 293, 300; *see* childbirth, childlessness, Eileithyia, Haloa, kourotrophic power, Kourotrophos, Kourotrophos Ge, Thesmophoria
festivals: *see* Adonia, Agrionia, Anthesteria, Aphrodisios, Brauronia, Chalkeia, Choes, Chthonia, Daidala, Dionysia, Dipolieia, Eleusinia, Endymatia, Epidauria, Haloa, Hephaistia, Heraia (Olympia, Samos), Hetairideia, Hybristika, Iobakcheia, Isis and Sarapis, Isthmia, Kalamaia, Karneia, Kopis, Koureotis, Laphria, Lenaea, Nemea, Olympia, Oschophoria, Panathenaia, Pithoigia, Plynteria, Poseidonia, Procharisteria, Ptolemaia, Pyanopsia, Pyloi, Pythais, Pythia, Sebasteia, Skiereia, Skira, Stenia, Tauropolia, Thesmophoria, Tithenidia, Tonaia
figs, dried 37, 134
fillet, ribbon: Athena's aegis made of woollen 95; beast adorned with by young women before sacrifice 23, 38, 60, 63, Figure 2.14, 283; as prizes 233; women adorn tombs with 271, 274, 279, 283, 285, 287, 288, Figures 9.6–7; worn in hair 39, 56, 80, 71–2, 80, 211, 265, Figure 8.4; *see* stemma, tainiai

fine 85, 93, 127, 264, 274
fire, profane: prohibited on acropolis? 90
first-fruits 217
fish 154, 246
flies 238
Florence kore 51
florets, on dresses 89
flowers 62, 102, 104
flute (aulos) 68, 89, 149, 155, 160, 179, 203, 228, 263; auletai 89; flute girl 150, 193, Figures 5.3, 6.4
foetus 251
Forum of Augustus 50
fountain-house 219; *see* enneakrounos
fox-skins, of maenads 147
frankincense 200
frauenfest scenes: *see* Corinthian *frauenfest* scenes
frenzy: *see* mania
friezes, of young and older women: *see* Bassai, *frauenfest* scenes, Parthenon frieze, Samothrace frieze
fruit 116, 126, 156, 231, 245, 322, 244
funerals 166, 268–92; clothing worn at 263; legislation 263, 269, 271, 272–4; *see* chin-strap, dirges, exaleiptra, lekythoi, mourning men, mourning women
Furies: *see* Nameless Goddesses

Galatia 136
Gallipoli 35
Gambreion 263
game table 282
Gamelion 152, 218
Gardens of Adonis: *see* Adonia
garlic 125, 255
Ge 22, 59, 77, 105, 217
Ge Kourotrophos 222
Gela 126
Gello 171–2
gem: set in gold 18
gene, genos 84; *see* Bouzygai, Eteoboutadai, Eumolpidai, Gephyraioi, Hesychidai, Mesogeioi, Philleidai, Praxiergidai, Salaminioi
Geneleos group 32
Genesia 282
Genetyllis 2, 300
gennetai 134
genos: *see* gene
geometric art 130, 274–5, 291, 314n.316; *see* Dipylon Master

413

INDEX

Gephyraioi 307
gerarai 74, 48, 101, 103, 242, 324n.199, 369; oath concerning sexual abstinence 255
Geronthrai 238
Getas 236
girdle: dedication of before marriage 23, 216; depicted on vase 216; loosened by groom 25
'Girl from Antium': see 'Anzio Girl'
girls (korai) 69, 89, 90, 133, 135, 152, 155, 160, 185, 245, 300; athletic training 131; bands of worship Helen 212; carry water to Lykeion 56; choruses of 214; at funerals 272; hysteria 20; mourn at funerary biers with women 277; naked in rites 221; pray and make ritual cries 133; raped at festivals 127; sent to Minotaur 9; suicide 70; supplicate Apollo 89; swinging 69–71; ugly 212; young prostitutes referred to as 167, 199; see Heraia, koragogos, partheneia, parthenoi
Glauke 176–7, 179
Glaukothea 104, 158, 182
Glyke 13, 18
Glykera 196
Gnathaina 198
Gnathainion 198
goat 68, 239, 245, 256
goddesses (and heroines): see Aglauros, Alektrone, Aphrodite, Artemis, Athena, Bendis, Cybele, Demeter, Despoina, Dictyanna of the wild beasts, Eileithyia, Eileithyiai, Elythia, Enodia, Erinyes, Ge, Ge Kourotrophos, Genetyllis, Graces, Hekate, Hera, Herse, Hestia, Ishtar, Kalligeneia, Kore, Kourotrophos, Kourotrophos Ge, Leukothea, Mater Gallesia, Mother of the Gods, Mountain Mother, Muses, Nemesis, Nikai, Nymphe, Opis, Pandrosos, Peitho, Persephone, Potnia Selene, Potnia Theron, Rhea, Semnai Theai, Thesmophoroi (Demeter and Kore)
gods (and heroes): see Acheloos, Aleximachos, Apollo, Ares, Boreas, Charon, Damuzi/Damu, Echelos, Enyalios, Eunostos, Eurysakes, Hades, Helios, Hephaistos, Herakles, Herakles-Pankrates, Hermes, Hermotimos, Kronos, Men, Ouranos, Palaimon, Pankrates, Pollux (2), Poseidon, Protesileos, Sarapis, Sosipolis, Tammaz, Tritopatores, the 'Twelve Gods', Zagreos, Zeus
gold: arrephoroi not to wear 57; ornaments of for kanephoroi 41; presented to goddess 57; prohibited 263; of women in Demeter cults 262; worn by men 216
Golden Fleece, the 172
goos 268, 269
Gorgias of Athens 183
Graces, the 112
granddaughter 78, 80, 155, 198, 299
grandmothers 159, 277
Granikos 19
grapes 89, 146, 168
graves (tombs) 12, 229; hair dedicated on 215; impurity of 253; children's toys in 223, 229; of prostitutes 196–7; see fillets, lekythoi, mourning women
grave-stelai (grave-stele, tomb reliefs) 56, 143, 229, 233, 282, 284, 285, 288, 299, 309, Figures 3.2–3, 5.5; showing women with keys 80–1, Figure 3.2; see Chairestrate, Choirine, fillets, lekythoi, loutrophoroi, mourning women, Nikomache, Polystrate, Polyxena
Great Mother–Cybele 2, 80, 96, 154–7, 279, 295, 300, Figure 5.6; Athenian citizen women and 155–6; consort (Attis) 154–5, 160–1; and Ferrara krater 160–1; headdress 154; music 155; sanctuaries 155; statue at Athens 155; syncretism 154, 156
Group of Palermo 16: 170, 246, Figure 8.1
gynaikes 57, 70, 140, 369; see wives
gynaikonomoi, gynaikonomos 238, 264; and funerals 271–3; oversee funerary behaviour of women 290–1; at Methymna 116; punish women 273, 291
gyne 106, 369; see gynaikes, wives

Habrokomes 216
Habrotonon 127, 206
Hades 13, 62, 113, 114, 138, 143, 153, 218, 225, 227, 288
Hagesichora 214

INDEX

Hagios Eleutherios, *see* calendar frieze
hagisteria 256; cf. perirrhanteria
hair 10, 39, 50, 56, 60, 66, 68, 71–2, 73, 80, 125, 140, 142, 146, 211, 246, 265, 269; braided 263; dedicated to Persephone 225–6; dedication of 215, 235; dishevelled hair of women at funerals 276–7; of maenads 140, 144, 148, 150; women tear in mourning 269, 275, 277, Figures 9.1, 9.3–5
Halai 128, 221
Halai Araphenides 128
Halasarna 79
Haliartos 217
Halikarnassos 79, 96, 101, 127, 161, 243
Halimous 111
Haloa 78, 91, 111, 120–4, 191, 295, 296; adulterous jokes at 121, 122; genitalia at 121–2; prostitutes and 122, 123; scholiast on 121; secrecy of 121; threshing floors at 122; vases depicting 122, Figure 4.1; wine-drinking at 121
hanging 230
Harmodios 38
harp 207; *see* psaltria
Harpalos 196
hawk-priestess 73
headband, snake 140, 161, Figure 5.1
headdress 67, 154, 263, 264, Figure 5.6
healing deities: *see* Amphiaraos, Artemis Kalliste, Asklepios, Herakles-Pankrates, Palaimon, Pankrates, Zeus Hypsistos
Hebe, wife of Herakles 239
Hedeia (1) 203
Hedeia (2) 30
hegeteria 134
Hekabe 136, 137, 268, 281
Hekataia 170
Hekate 2, 139, 179, 182, 242, 246, 295, Figure 8.1; antidote against 175; dinners for 170; expulsion of 170, 174–5; kourotrophos 170; midnight sacrifice to 172; puppies and dogs sacrificed to 170, 246, Figure 8.1, cf. 174; women priests of 170
Hekatompedon inscription 90
Hektor 136, 268, 269, 281
Helen 170, 178, 178, 211–14, 260, 268; abducted 213, 289; cult at Sparta 212

Helenos 136
Helios 216; priest of 124
Hellanikos 73
hellanodikai 131, 137
helmet 264, 285
helots, forced to mourn like women 270
hemlock 288
Hephaistia 205
Hephaistos 58, 59
Heptaphylai 89
Hera 13, 32, 33, 44, 62, 66, 67, 75, 85, 96, 105, 230, 238, 243, 260; dedications to 14; grants blessing 78; hair dedicated to 215; image washed 135; kourotrophic 222; marriage to Zeus celebrated 218; on Lesbos 130; peplos presented to 137; seduces Zeus 171; sends Proitos' daughters mad 142; women priests of 132; *see* Chrysis (2), Daidala, Heraia, Perachora
Hera, cult epithets: Akraia 68, 222, 302; Gamelia 217; Lecherna 222; Nympheuomene 217; Teleia 217, 218; *see* Zeus Teleios
Heraia (Argos) 78
Heraia (Olympia) 131, 213, 243
Heraia (Samos) 216
Heraion (Argos) 13, 67, 78, 83, 222
Heraion (Foce Sele) 105
Heraion (Samos) 54, 216
Heroines, the 85
Herakleion 243
Herakleitos 142
Herakles 77, 237, 253, 258; dedications to 240; and marriage 239–40; misogynistic 239–40; at Porthmos, priesthood of 89; poisoned 175–6, Figure 5.11; worshipped by families 240
Herakles, cult epithets: Herakles Misogynes 77; Herakles-Pankrates 30, 31, 35, 240, 295; Herakles at Porthmos 89
herald 89, 185, 248; *see* Kerykes
Hermeias 290
Hermes 24, 112, 227, 288
Hermion 128, 217, 238, 245
Hermione 177
Hermippos 38, 186, 188–9
Hermos 196
Hermotimos 238
Herodotos 78, 96, 110, 197, 199, 201, 212, 255, 257, 297

INDEX

heroes 33–5, 179, 290; Athenian 44–5; cult of women heroes 289–90; dedications to 33–5; as transvestites 220; see Theseus
Herondas *Mime* 4, 245
hero-reliefs 33–5
Herse 47, 59, 133
Hesiod 120, 143, 164, 170, 217
Hestia 218, 219
hestiades 105
Hesychidai 94
Hesychides 94
Hesychios 60, 133, 190
hetairai: Epicurean 203, 205; see prostitutes
hetairai (friends) 189–90
Hetairideia 190
hetairoi 189–90
heterosexuality 185
hiereiai 74
hierodouloi gynikai 201
hierodouloi: see prostitutes: sacred
Hierokles 93
Hieron 202
hierophant 77, 92, 117, 241; guilty of impiety 91; see Archias, Sinope
hierophantides, Eleusinian women cult officials 92
hieropoioi 94
hierosylia 93
Hilaeira 260
himation 277, 304, 369; dedication of 61; worn by kanephoroi 39, 41, Figures 2.1–2; worn by Polystrate (woman-priest?) 80, Figure 3.2; worn by Polyxenos (woman priest?) 82, Figure 3.3; worn by woman in Echinos relief 231, Figure 7.4.
hipne(uesthai) 90
Hippasos 147, 152
Hippias 279
Hippocratic *Peri Parthenion* 20–1, 70, 179, 250
Hippodameia 137, 238, 260; Figure 8.3
Hippolytos 215, 235
Hippostratos of Thessaly 196
Hippylla 13
Hittites 242
Homer 222; see *Iliad*
Homeric Hymns: *Hymn to Apollo* 132; *Hymn to Demeter* 111, 113, 143, 171, 182, 227; *Hymn to the Great Mother* 155
homosexuality, male 257; see lesbianism, pederasty, sodomy
horos 219
horses 33–4
horses, sacred 132
human sacrifice 128, 135, 260, of virgin boy and girl 258
husband, husbands 10, 17, 19, 26, 94, 125, 127, 170, 191, 211, 235, 237, 248, 272, 290, 294; allow wives to participate in cults 30, 137–8, 148–9 (maenadic), 156 (Cybele), 181 (Sabazios); Cypriots prostitute virgin daughters to Aphrodite 199; farewell wife on gravestone 156, Figure 5.5; farewelled by wife 264–7, Figure 8.4; girls reject chosen 230; joint dedications with wives 12, 156, 161, 206; pay for wives' dedications? 9; pay for wives' Thesmophoria expenses 117, cf. 137; poisoned 177; and prostitutes 183; sex other than with wife polluting 256, 257; sex with wife not polluting 153, 257; sexual abstinence of while wives engage in rites 113, 118, 119, 254; sexual anxieties about wives' participation in maenadism 145; take wives and children to Delos for festival 141, 148; visits grave with wife? 286, Figure 9.7; visits dead wife's tomb; 283; wife dedicators do/don't mention 14, 15, 18, 23, 28; wives pray that they be filled with the lust for battle 201; wives use drugs and magic to ensure their love 171, 175; of women priests 77, 78; worship with families 31–5, Figure 1.4, 240; young women pray to obtain 10, 212, 215, 219; see Epikteta, Klytaimnestra
Hyakinthia 137, 214
Hyakinthos 214
hybris 196
Hybristika 353
hydria, hydriai 219, 282; carried by metic daughters in Panathenaic procession 205; Corinthian, with funerary scene 279; example of Figure 5.9; on Lokrian pinax 224, Figure 7.1; statuette of young women holding 56; used for funerary libations 285; young woman on grave stele shown with 56;

INDEX

see hydrophoroi
hydrophoroi, hydrophoros 56; male 205
'Hyes Attes Attes hyes' 159
Hyettos 34
Hygieia 19, 26, 31, 233; *see* Asklepios
Hymettos, Mt 220
hymns 95, 155; to Adonis 163; *see* Callimachus, *Homeric Hymns*, partheneia
Hyperboreans 215
Hypereides 19, 194
hypodyma 264
hypothoinarmostriai 127
hypozakoros 104, 110
hysteria 20, 292; *see* puberty

Ialysos 263
iamata 29, 31, 231; *see* Asklepios, Epidauros
Iamblichus 153
iconography 4, 81, 259, 283, 287, 292; *see* reliefs, vases
Ikarion 155
Ikarios 69, 121
Iliad 142, 201, 270
Ilion: *see* Lokrian maidens
Ilissos 23, 59, 95, 206, 240
impiety 192, 197, 207, 291; of Archias 91, 121; of Aspasia? 186–9; of Phryne 194–5; of Timarchos 184–6; women at Gambreion 273; of women priests 104–5; *see* asebeia
incantations 170, 171, 178; in childbirth 252
incense 203, 236; *see* thymiateria
initiates, initiation 57, 68, 69, 91, 127, 133, 134, 142, 159, 220, 238; clothing of 263–4; pay fees 91; prostitutes as 192, 195–6, 242; restrictions about 125–6, 253, 254; rites not initiatory 60, 68; of women into exotic cults 105, 155, 159; of women into Orphism 154; *see* 'child of the hearth'
Ino 145, 146
Inscription Painter 283–4, 285, Figures 9.6–7
inscriptions 4, 11, 12, 13, 14, 15, 16, 17, 22, 23, 24, 25–6, 29, 30, 31, 58, 65–6, 76, 93, 95, 134, 142, 144, 146, 168–9, 186, 193, 201, 203, 216, 217, 219, 221, 240, 243, 250, 251, 252, 253, 255, 256, 257, 258, 263, 274, 289, 291; on Pitsa pinakes 228–9; Gambreion 272–3; honouring maenads 146; Labyadai phratry 273–4; Lokrian maidens' 65; *see* Hekatompedon, inventories, Praxiergidai
inventories: of dedications 9; Amphiaraion 29, 31; Artemis Brauronia 13, 19–23, 28, 93; Asklepieion 26–9, 31; Delos 29; Erechtheion 17–18; Miletos 23; Parthenon 17–18, 19–20, 44, 189; Tanagra 22
Iobakcheia 103
Iodama 105
Ion 98
Ionia 102, 154, 193, 237, 255
Ios 135
Iphidike of Athens 9, 15
Iphigeneia 20, 81, 93, 246, 250; as a proteleia 218
Iphinoe 215
Isaeus 112, 117, 191
Isagoras 86
Ischomachos 241
Ishtar 105, 164, 201, 349n.103
Isigenes 161
Isis 161–2, 181, 206, 249, 250; attributes of 161; and Sarapis, festival of 39
Ismene 71, 288–9
Ismenos river 220
Isodaites 194
Isthmia 54–5; festival 69, 131, 132, 193; prostitute named after 199
Isthmias, prostitute 199
ivy 159, 160
iynx 170–1, 175

Jason 170–1, 176–7, 190, 248; uses iynx 171; is rejuvenated 172, Figure 5.9
jewellery 18, 27, 126, 202
Josephus 105
jug 72, 73
jurors 194
Justin 199, 202

Kadmeia 113, 119, 140, 145
Kalamaia 86, 120
kalasiris 264
kalathephoros 320n.96

kalathiskos dancers 67
kalathos 54, 125, 225, 226, 369; *see* baskets
Kalaureia 75
Kalikrite 15
Kalligeneia 111, 112, 113, 114, 248
Kallimachos (sculptor) 67, 105, 144
Kallisto (1) 17
Kallisto (2) 73
Kallistomache 27
Kallistratos 183
Kalliteles 34
Kamiros (Rhodes) 61
kana, kanoun 370; *see* baskets, kanephoroi
Kanathos, spring of 132
kanephoroi, kanephoros 37–42, 48, 60, 63, 74, 87, 205, 220–1, 243, 262, 293, 295, 299, 300, 369; Athena and Artemis as prototypes for 38; carry baskets on head, Figure 2.2; chosen from aristocratic girls 38; Corinthian kanephoros 39, 41; dress of 39; honoured by state 40; illustrations of Figures 2.1–2; male 38; not named or honoured in classical period 39–40; and Parthenon frieze 48 Figure 2.6; pours libation Figure 2.1; 'powdered' 38; receive shares of sacrificial meat 41; Rhodes' kanephoros 41; statues of 40; votive statuettes of 41 Figure 2.2; *see* diphrophoroi, metics
kannathra, kannathron 214
kantharoi, kantharos 34, 152, 279, 311, 370; *see* vases
Kaphyai 230
Karneia 67
Karpasia 237
Karyai 213
karyatides 213
Kassandra 65, 180, 259–60
Kastalian spring 98
Kataibates thiasos 146
kataniptes 133
Kathodos 111
Kekrops, king 47, 59
Keos 213, 272
Kephissia 24
Kephissos 24–5, 124, Figure 1.3
Kerameikos cemetery, Athens 56, 291
Kerykes 85, 89, 91, 92
keryx 117
kestos himas 171

key-bearer 20
keys 80–2, 82, 95, 195, Figures 3.1–2; temple guardians and 80
Kiron 112
Kissoessa spring 217
kistai, kiste 26, 32, 35, 56, 57, 112, 240, 298, 370; women carry sacred objects in 92
kistaphoroi 56
Kithairon, Mt 143
kithara 68, 89
Kitharion 218
Kitian merchants 161
Kition 206
kittophoros 159
Klaros 180
Klea 147
Klearchos (1) 202
Klearchos (2) 213
Kleidamos 238
kleidophoros 170; *see* key-bearer
kleidouchos 81
Kleisthenes (1) 110
Kleisthenes (2) 100
Kleo 231, 252
Kleomedes 113
Kleomenes 86
Kleophon Painter 264, 265, Figure 8.4
Kleophrades Painter 146, 266
Klodones 147
Klymene 135
Klytaimnestra 94, 242, 248, 270, 289
kneeling, by women, 240, 249, 260, cf. 248; at bier 275
Knidia: *see* Praxiteles *Knidian Aphrodite*
Knidian treasury 54
Knidos 24, 195
knife, sacrificial 38, 63, 68, 231, 242, 243, Figure 7.4; wielded by women 110, 115, 116, 213, 245; *see* Aristomenes, Battos, Thesmophoria
Knossos 69
Kolias 111, 120, 277; *see* Aphrodite
Kolone 197
Komaitho 258
Komana 202
Komasts: *see* 'padded dancers'
komoi 215
Kopis 350
koragogos 240
korai (girls): *see* girls
korai, kore (representations of girls): doll (kore), dedicated 229; statues,

dedications of 9–11, 12, 13, 32, Figure 1.1; of Erechtheion 50–1, Figures 2.8–10; Florence kore 51; from the Forum of Augustus, Rome 50; at Canopus pool 51, Figure 2.10; support perirrhanteria 54–6, Figure 2.11; terracotta figurines of, in girls' graves 229; Vatican kore 51
Kore (goddess) 22, 24, 36, 62, 87, 92, 91, 94, 109, 112, 113, 114, 116, 121, 122, 124, 125, 130, 234, 237, 238, 244, 248, 370; dining rooms at Corinth 126; *see* Persephone
koronistai 322
korythalistriai 350
Kos 30, 61, 79–80, 96, 211, 221, 234, 239, 240, 245, 251, 253, 255–6, 257, 263; compulsory marriage sacrifices at 221
Kosko 146
Kosmo 84
Kottina 197–8
koulouria 14
Koureotis 352
kouroi statues 12
kourotrophic power 2, 14, 25, 28, 135, 156, 170, 212, 214, 218, 219, 222, 228–9, 230–1, 245, 250, 299, 350, 370
Kourotrophos 89
Kourotrophos Ge 112, 248; *see* Ge Kourotrophos
krater 35, 71, 260, 266, 289, 370; *see* Ferrara krater, krateriskoi
krateriskoi 221
Krates 195
Kratinos 164, 189, 197
Kreon 288
Kreousa 98
Krito 289
Kritylla 110, 262
krokotoi, krokoton 21, 22
Kronos 198
Kroton 153
Ktesias 213
kylix 39, Figure 5.1; *see* vases
Kylon 271
Kynarbos 17
Kyniska 289
Kynosarges 240
kyrioi, kyrios 79–80

labour pains 230; *see* childbirth

Labyadai phratry 273–4
ladder 165, 168, 169, Figure 5.8
Lagina 170
lagynos 311; *see* vase
Laios, king 248
Lais 196
Lakonia: *see* Sparta
lambs 61, 127
Lampito 131
Lampsakos 193
Lapith 260, Figure 8.3
larnakes 291
laurel, branch of 60
lead tablets 100
Lebena (Crete) 30
lebes gamikos 67, 219
lecho 253
Leda: *see* Helen
legitimacy 101, 183, 248
Leiteirai 94
lekanis 281, Figure 9.5
lekythoi, lekythos 44, 63, 67, 152, 169, 170, 282–7; definition of 269, 370; depict Charon 288; depict commemorative visits to tombs 282–3, Figures 9.6–7; depict funerary practices 271, 274; depict women with hands on head 269; oil in 283; provenance 287; shows puppy sacrifice to Hekate 170, 246, Figure 8.1; taken to graves 233, 271, 282, Figures 9.6–7; use of ceases 287; *see* vases
Lemnos 213, 251
Lenaea 149, 152
'Lenaea vases' 149, 152, 165
Lenai 149–52
Leonidas of Tarentum 229
leopard 140, 146, Figure 5.1
Leophron 202
lesbianism 257
Lesbos 142, 163
lettuce 163, 165
Leuke 206
Leukippe 142, 147
Leukippidai 213, 260
Leukippos 213, 260
Leukothea 213, 233, 237, 249
libations 32, 48, 49, 50, 160, 215, 217; for departing warriors 264–6, Figure 8.4; at Panathenaia 43; poured by kanephoros 39, Figure 2.1; poured by men, usually but not always 18; poured by mourning women 269,

270, 282, 283, 285, 288, 289; poured by women 94, 228, 269, 270; poured by women to Dionysos 152; Spartan girls pour to Helen 212; wine for poured by pallake 241; wineless 94; *see* phialai, phialephoros
likna, liknon 57, 126, 152, 244
liknophoros 159, 310
lily petals 56
Lindos 193, 237, 250, 251, 253, 256, 257, 263
linen 237; *see* clothing
lion, of Cybele 154, 155, 160, Figure 5.6; of perirrhanteria 54, Figure 2.11
lionskin of Herakles 240
lithica 171–2
Lokrian maidens 63–6; choice of 65; clothing 65; inscription 65; length of service 65–66; sustenance money 65
Lokrian plaques 222–8, 234, Figures 7.1–2; depict Persephone 225, 226–7; pre-nuptial scenes 225–6; presentation of peplos 226; peplophoria 227
Lokrians, Lokris (Italy) 13, 50, 163, 202
loom, for Athena's peplos 43, 57, 58; abandoned by maenads 141
loom-weights 14, 126
lotrochooi 132, 133
Lousoi 80
loutrides 133
loutrophoroi, loutrophoros 219–20, 370; depicting funerals 275, 279; placed on the graves of dead virgins 220, 229, Figure 9.4
loutrophoros, cult official 239
love potions: *see* philtra
Loxias: *see* Apollo
Lucian 112, 269; *Dialogues of the Hetairai* 122, 245
Lucian scholiast 60, 114–15, 121
Ludovisi throne 202–3, 226, 293, Figures 6.3–5
Lydai 146, 147
Lydia, Lydians 172, 199, 202, 215, 230, 252
Lykeion 56
Lykophron *Alexandra* 65–6
Lykosoura 156, 250, 253, 254, 263
Lykourgos (1) Athenian orator 41, 87, 141, 161, 291; *On the Priesthood* 113
Lykourgos (2) mythical, attacks Dionysos 153, 180
Lykourgos (3) Spartan lawgiver 260, 270
lyre 149, 196, 228; *see* kithara
Lysias (1) speech writer 118, 248
Lysias (2) lover of Metaneira 195
Lysilla 17
Lysimache (1) woman priest of Athena Polias 106; served sixty-four years 75; statue of 78, 86, 87, 92
Lysimache (2) woman priest of Athena Polias 84
Lysimache (3) woman priest of Athena Polias 91
Lysimache (4) woman priest of Athena Polias, statue of 86
Lysimache? (5) woman priest of Athena Polias, statue of 86
Lysippos 60
Lysistrata 144, 255; *see* Aristophanes *Lysistrata*
Lysistrate (1) 23, 92
Lysistrate (2) 240

Macedonia 147, 154, 178, 190
machlosyne 142
Machon 192, 198; *Chreiai* 183
maenadism, maenads 4, 139–53, 370; accused of alcoholic and sexual excesses 145, cf. 148; artistic depictions of 140, Figures 5.1–4; at Athens 149–52; bacchic bands 140; biennial festivals 144, 147, 181; carved reliefs of 144; dance 149–51; desert husbands and children 141; dress of 140, Figures 5.1–4; driven out of doors 140, 141, 147; 'euoi' cry 140; extent of participation in maenadic activity 147; head tossing by 144, 148; honoured 146; kill children 142; male cult leader? 145; mania of 139, 140, 148, 149; nocturnal 145, 147; at Orchomenos 142; oreibasia 143; participation in rites as social release? 148; and raw meat 142; ritual cry of 143; snakes 140, 144; sparagmos 141, 142, 143, 144, 147; at Thebes 145–9; thiasoi 144, 145–9; tympana 144; ululation 144, 148; use daggers and swords for dismemberment 143, 145, 146; vase paintings of 140, 143, 144, 146, 148, Figures 5.1–4; and wine 145, 148, 149, 152; *see* Bassarai, Dionysos,

INDEX

Klodones, 'Lenaea vases', Lenai, Mimallones, mountains, Parnassos, Pentheus, Thyiades
mageiraina 246
mageiros 116, 246
magic: *see* charms, curse tablets, iynx, Medea, Nino, pharmaka, pharmakeia, pharmakeus, pharmakeutria, pharmakia, pharmakides, philtra, sorcery, spells, Theoris
Magnesia 146, 190, 220, 290
magoi 196
Maionia 192, 192, 257
Maketai 146
make-up: forbidden 262–3; of kanephoroi 38
Makron 39, 148, 149, Figures 2.1, 5.3–4; *see* vases
Mammarion 203
Manes 156, 206
mania (frenzy) 139, 140, 148, 149–52, 179–80; definition of 180
Mannella 222
manteis (diviners) 20, 180, 193; *see* 'belly-talkers'
Mantineia 75
mantle 39
marble basin 15, 17
marriage 14, 18, 20, 31, 43, 44, 61, 67, 68, 71, 96, 166, 168, 171, 178, 189, 203, 211, 257, 259, 260, 266, 272, 282, 291, 293; Aphrodite and 202; bathing for 219–20; compulsory rites of 220–2; customary rites of 215–20; death instead of 12; dedications by young women upon 23; girls' priesthood before 75, 258; girls pray for 212; priesthoods after 77–8; prostitution before 199, 201; purity laws and 255, 256; religious roles before marriage 37–72, 74; sacred 75, 101–4; sacrifices for 217–18; go to temple for 135; thanksgiving for 11; wedding scenes 216, 219 Figure 5.8; *see* choruses, girdle, priests, women: begging
marshals, of Panathenaic procession 48
Massilia (Marseilles) 97
Mater Gallesia 255
Medea 68, 170, 172, 175, 182, 230, 248; and iynx 170–1; and Peliades 173–4, Figure 5.10; poisons Jason's new wife 176–7; rejuvenates Jason

172, Figure 5.9
Megalopolis 238, 249
Megara, Megarians 35, 92, 215, 269
megara, megaron 114, 115, 246
Meidias Painter Figure 2.15
Melanippe: *see* Euripides *Melanippe*
Melanippos 258
Meleso 16, Figure 1.2
Melissa 260, 262
melissonomoi 74
Melite 117
Melos 35
Men (god) 249, 255
men: absent from sacrifices 245; dedications by 12, 19, 23, 26, 27, 28; forced to mourn at funerals 269, 270; not present at festivals or rites 109–38; not to enter shrines 237–8; as professional mourners 269; unemotional at funerals 284–5, 292; versus women dedicators 26–7; *see* fathers, sons
Menander 38, 73, 156, 291; *Dyskolos* 217, 236; *Epitrepontes* 127, 128, 206–7; *Leukadia* 90; *Samia* 127, 165, 167, 296; *Theophoroumene* 179
menarche 20; *see* puberty
Menekles 104
Menekrateia 23
Menelaos 212, 260
menstruation 249–50, 251
Meropes 240
Mese 111, 118
Mesogeioi 240
Messenia 78, 213, 270
Metageitnion 111, 195, 317n.43
Metaneira 93, 195
Metapontion 193
metempsychosis 154
Methymna 116, 238, 290
metic men 161; celebrate Adonia 165; share in sacrifices 205; *see* Manes, Stephanos (2)
metic women 5, 17, 18, 189, 298, cf. 28; daughters carry parasol and chair for kanephoroi 38, 45, 205, 298; joint dedication with citizens at Athens 206; make dedications at Athens 17, 206; in religious rites 205–7; attend sacrifices 191, 241; *see* Mika (3)
metopes 42, 66–7
metragyrtes 155
Metroon 95, 155

421

Metropolis 193, 255
miasma 191
midwives 178, 182
Mika (1), in Ar. *Thesm.* 116, 120
Mika (2), woman dedicator to Asklepios 27
Mika (3), woman dedicator to the 'Mother of the Gods' 156, 206
Mikythe 15
Miletos 85, 186, 189, 253; and Dionysos 142–3, 143; and maenads 144
Miltiades 104, 110, 297
Mimallones 146, 147
Minotaur 69, 89
Minyas 142, 145, 147, 152–3
mirrors, dedications of 9, 13, 19, 126, 225, cf. 226
miscarriage 178; pollution of 251–2
Mnesilochos 110, 112, 113, 116, 118, 119
Moirai: *see* Fates
molones 60
monsters: women give birth to 65
months: *see* Artimitios, Boedromion, Dalios, Demetrios, Elaphebolion, Gamelion, Herakleion, Metageitnion, Mounychion, Plynterion, Posideion, Pyanopsion, Skiraphorion, Thargelion
moon, new 170, 246
Morgantina 127
mormolukeiai 343n.230
morotton 114
Moschato 95, 155
Moschion 165, 167
Mother of the Gods 39, 154, 179, 206; *see* Great Mother-Cybele
mother, mothers, motherhood 4, 19, 30, 32, 35, 36, 72, 90, 93, 94, 98, 104, 112, 117, 118, 120, 131, 135, 136, 138, 140, 143, 144, 158, 159, 161, 167, 170, 171, 189, 190, 226, 227, 229, 231, 234, 235, 265, 268, 279; and bride 216; cult for 290; cult involvement after role as mother has ended 159; dedication for birth of son 19; dedication for upbringing of son 24–5; in Demeter cults 125–6; and Erinyes 248; maenadism underlines role as 181; mourning 268, 270, 272, 277; orders sons to erect their father's gravestone 279; prayer of 78; sacrifice when daughter marries 218; sacrifices for marriage of son 2, 236, 267; shown in dedications 32, Figures 1.4, 7.3; and son dedications 23, 134; Spartan, did not mourn sons 270; swear oaths 248; transition to 96, 211–35; unable to leave baby at home for maenad rites 143; women define themselves as in inscriptions 12, 23, 24; *see* abortion, breastfeeding, childbirth, Echinos relief, lecho, miscarriage, Pitsa pinax, stepmother
Mountain Mother 179
mountains 155; maenads flee to 140, 141, 142, 143–5
Mounychia 221, 222
Mounychion 89
mourning men 269, 270 (helots), 271–2, 273, 277, 279, 284–5, Figure 9.7; passive role 292
mourning women: anoint tombs with unguent 286–7; in bands on vases 275, 279, Figure 9.4; baskets of 271, 284, Figures 9.6–7; beat cauldrons at Sparta 270; beat their breasts 269, 277, 289; behave differently from mourning men 271–2, 277, 285; behaviour circumscribed 271; on black-figure vases 279–81; and Charon 288; clothing 271, 273; cradle head of deceased 269; cry at tomb 283, Figure 9.6; dressed in black 270, 279, Figure 9.4; dressed in grey 273; forbidden by Solonian legislation to lacerate themselves 271, 272; forced to mourn 269–70; on funerary plaques 275–9; at Gambreion 273; on geometric pottery 274–5; gouge their faces to draw blood 269, 270; grave offerings of 271, 274; hired for funerals 269; in Homer 268–9; at Iulis 272–3; lacerate breasts 269; lacerate foreheads 282; leave grave before men 273; length of mourning 273; lamentations of 269, 270, 282, 283, 285, 288, 289; look after child 277; make commemorative visits to tombs 283–7, Figures 9.6–7; naked or semi-naked? 287; not to bewail anyone other than the deceased 271; number to be polluted by a death limited 272; number who could mourn a death limited 272, 274;

INDEX

prepare corpse 289; raise hands 275; rend hair 269, 275, 277, 279, 281; required to be silent on way to grave 273, 274; shriek and wail 269, 270, 271, 273, 274, 277, 288; silent grieving 277; Solonian legislation concerning 269, 271; strike their heads 269, 270, 275; terracotta 281, Figure 9.5; tug ponytail 276, Figure 9.1; Figures 9.3–7
Muses 68, 180, 290
music, and Corybantes 179
musical instruments 68, Figures 5.3–6, 6.4, 7.3; *see* aulos, castanets, clappers, drums, kithara, psaltria, tympana
Mykonos 237
Mylasa 79, 112, 116
Mylitta 199
Myrrhine (1) woman priest 76
Myrrhine (2) in Ar. *Lys.* 76, 254
Myrrhine (3) metic woman dedicator 206
Myrrhine (4) dead woman 279
Myrrhinous 120
Myrtia 17
Mysaion 238
mystai: *see* initiates
Mytilene 34, 35

Nameless Goddesses (Erinyes, Eumenides, Furies, Semnai Theai) 1, 2, 71, 94–5, 217, 247, 248, 299
Naryka 65
Naukratis 183, 197
Nausicaa Painter 63, Figure 2.14
Naxos 114
Neaira 101–4, 121, 183, 190
Nearchos 12
necklaces, gold 18
Nemea festival 69, 131, 132; prostitute named after 198
Nemeas 198
Nemesis 73, 77
Neo-Hittite lions 54
neokoros 77, 90, 245
Neoptolemos 177
Nereids 66, 279
Nessos 175–6
Nesteia 111, 113
Nestor 242
Niinnion tablet 328n.69
Nikagora of Sikyon 97
Nikai, Nike 44, 63, 146, 221

Nikander of Kolophon 183
Nikandre of Naxos 9–11, 35, 298, Figure 1.1
Nikarete (1) 195
Nikatere (2) 240
Nikidion 203
Nikoklea 21
Nikomache 156, Figure 5.5
Nikomachos 85, 91
Nikophon 38
Nikostrate 222
Nino 104–5, 177, 182, 194
nocturnal rites 4, 116, 122; Adonia 165; of the Great Mother 155; Hyakinthia 214; maenadic 145, 147; of parthenoi 212; of Sabazios 158; *see* arrephoria, Semnai Theai, Tauropolia
nomophylakes 134
nothai, nothoi: *see* bastards
nurse 212
nymphaion at Phyle 236
Nymphe: as bride 221; as bride-deity and shrine of 219, 221
nympheutria 215, 218, 220
nymphs 133, 136, 202, 235, 343n.215, Figure 6.3; aid sought in childbirth 25, 96, 228–9, Figure 7.3; caves of 219 (*see also* Pan); dedication to 206; Inachid 96; and marriage 2, 96, 217; pre-marriage sacrifices to 217; Samothracian 68; Tritoneian 135, 218; *see* Nereids (sea-nymphs)

oaths: of men 248; of women 198, 242, 248
Odyssey 170
Oedipus 71, 248, 251, 289
oil 105, 116, 249; oil lamps 105
oimoi 279
oinochoai, oinochoe 34, 39, 63, 102, 152, 228 Figure 7.3, 264 Figure 8.4, 266, 282, 285, 370; carried by parthenoi on Parthenon frieze: 43, 49, Figures 2.3–4, 2.7
Olbia 154
old women: *see* women
Oleiai 147, 152–3
olive branch 322
olives 153
ololyge, ololygai 133, 136, 159, 179, 242–3, cf. 146, 148
ololygma, ololygmata 67
ololygmos 243

423

olpis 282
Olympia 54, 136, 199, 200, 238, 258, 289; festival 106; oracle at 99; stadium 131; *see* Heraia
Olympias 19, 144, 154
Olympiodoros 218
omens 212, 217, 248, 266; funerary 276
omophagion embalein 142
omophagos charis 142
Onomarchos 192–3
Opis, heroised virgin 96
opisthodomon 192
Orchomenos: maenads at 142, 145, 147, 153
Oreithyia 38
Orestes 56, 94, 135, 246, 250
orge 179
orgeones 243
orgia 140
Ornithe 32
Oropos 256
Orpheotelestai 154
Orpheus, Orphism 153–4, 238, 283
Oschophoria 89
oschophoroi 89–90
Ouranos 217
outdoor religious activities of women 3

padded dancers 129
Paestum 56, 66
Paiania 120
paidia 165
paidonomoi 290
Painter of Athens 1454 168, Figure 5.8
Palaimon 240, 249
palladion 65, 134, 260
pallakai, pallake 167, 177, 183, 189, 241; goes to sacrifice with lover 192
Pallas (Athena) 132, 214; *see* Athena
Pamphile 127
Pan 2, 155, 179, 206, 217, 219, 236, 254, 295, 300
Panathenaia 38, 39, 41, 43, 47, 58, 59, 67, 72, 164, 195, 243, 295; participation of metic daughters and sons in 45, 205–6
Pandrosos 47, 89, 222, 312, 317n.43
panhellenic festivals 131–2, 193; *see* Olympia, Nemea, Isthmia, Pythian festival
Panis 240
Pankrates 240
pannychis 165, 233; *see* nocturnal

panther 140, 146, Figure 5.1
parasol 38, 102, 149, 186, 298
parents 35, 47, 58, 65, 72, 78, 79, 102, 104, 186, 212, 248, 279, 288; basilinna to have two citizen 102; make marriage sacrifices for daughter 217; rendered impure by death of their child 78, cf. 291; *see* childbirth, father, mother
Paris 136, 212
Parnassos Mt, and maenads 143, 145, 147
Parnes Mt 219
paroikoi, *see* metics
Paros 11–12, 104, 110, 135, 138, 237, 297
partheneia, partheneion 66, 211–12, 214
parthenoi, parthenos (virgins) 37–72, 106, 127, 133, 172, 211–19, 257, 293, 370; abduction of 213; aristocratic 214, 201; in athletic contests 131–2, 243, attacked at rites 213, cf. 220; basileus archon had to marry 102; choruses of 211–15; dedicate girdle before marriage 216; dedicate hair before marriage 215–16; find marriage partners 216, cf. 213; ineligible to attend the Thesmophoria 112; as maenads 140, 147; as priests 75, 77, 239; prostituted before marriage 201; serve woman priest of Artemis 81; special role in statue washing 133; suicidal tendencies of 20; watch athletic competitions 132; *see* agretai, anthesphoroi, arrephoroi, caryatids, Erechtheion, Gello, Heraia, kanephoroi, Lokrian maidens, metopes, Minotaur, Parthenon frieze, perirrhanteria, swinging girls, tray-bearers
Parthenon 42, 43, 45, 46, 47, 50, 57, 71; Athena's statue in 133; dedications in 18, 19 (see inventories, Parthenon); prostitutes in 189, 192; metopes 260
Parthenon frieze 5, 17, 42–50, 71, 84, 186, 189, 205, 206, 241, 293, 295; Aspasia admires 186, Figure 6.1; girls' facial expressions on 71–2; no kanephoroi shown on 40, 48; Figures 2.3–7
Patras 75, 262–3

Patroklos 269, 270
Pausanias 59, 77, 83, 105, 110, 115, 131, 135, 196, 201, 213, 245, 252, 270
pederasty 185, 220; *see* homosexuality, sodomy
pedum 155
Peirithöos 260
Peisistratos 84, 93, 290
Peitho 135, 199, 218
Peithon, dedicator 240
pelanos 30, 98, 179
Pelasgians 213, 220, 251
peleiai 74
Pelias, daughters of 172–4, Figure 5.10
pelike 144, 175, 370, Figures 4.1, 5.11
Pella 178
Pellene 238
Peloponnesian War 73, 75, 166, 189, 205, 249, 263, 283, 287
Pelops 238
Penelope 242
pennyroyal 178
pentathlon 199
Penteteris, woman priest 86
Pentheus 145, 146, 180; dismembered 141, 142, 143
Peplophoria: of men, 227
peplos 264, 370; of kanephoros 41, Figure 2.1; of korai of Erechtheion 50; marriage 227, 234; of parthenoi on Parthenon frieze 47, 71; poisoned 176–7; presented to goddesses 43, 47, 48, 57–60, 136–7, 214, 224–5, 226, 234; washing of goddesses' 133–4; worn by goddesses 10, 25, Figure 1.1; worn by woman priests 80, 81, 82
Perachora 13, 68, 222
perfuming: of clothes 69, Figure 2.15
Pergamon 30, 34, 35, 104, 256, 260, 262, 263, 279, 290
Periallos 104
Periander 260–2
Perikles 166, 292; and Aspasia 186, 188–9
Perikles, Junior 186
Perimede 175
perirrhanteria 54–7, 256
perquisites of priests 79, forbidden 239; *see* priests, men and women: perquisites
Persephone 3, 4, 87, 91, 109, 122, 138, 293; children presented to 234;

disappearance of 62, 111, 113, 114, 125, 143, 170; goddess of marriage 222–8, esp. 228; in Italian Lokris 202, 222–8, 234, 235; prostitutes swear by 198; return to Demeter shown on Lokrian pinakes 226–7; sanctuary on Paros 104, cf. 110, 297; *see* Kore
Persephone-Kore 243
Persian Invasions 65, 86, 99, 149, 200, 241, 258
Persuasion: *see* Peitho
pestilence 100
Phaidra 179, 248
Phaidryntai 136
Phaidyntes 92, 136
Phaleron 89, 134, 155
phalloi: models of 60, 121, 123, 199
phallophoria 122, 123, cf. 121
Phanis 60
Phano 103, 190–1
pharmaka, pharmakon 104, 169, 170, 172, 172, 177; *see* magic
pharmakeia 169
pharmakeus 175
pharmakeutria 169, 175
pharmakia 178
pharmakides, pharmakis 169, 177
Pharsalia 193
Phayllos 192–3
Pheidias 84, 133, 136, 186, 188
Pherekrates 164, 246
phialai, phiale 35, 212, 266, 370; dedications of 18, 50, 58, 67; on Lokrian pinakes 224, Figure 7.1; boy holds? 32, Figure 1.4; carried by goddesses 154, 160; held by warrior 264, Figure 8.4, cf. 265–6; Olympias dedicates 19; young women carry in processions 18, 43, 48, 49, 50, 51, Figures 2.6, 8–10
phialephoros 50
Phila 13
Philadelphia, purity law 172, 252, 256
Phile 22, 29
Phileia 32
Philemon 183
Philetairos 189–90
Philip II of Macedon 99, 195
Philippe 32
Philippides 192
Philleidai 92
Philomelos 101, 193

INDEX

Philoneos 241
Philoumene 29
philtra, philtron 175, 177, 178; lethal 177
Phintys 262
Phleiasians 94
Phoebe 260
Phoenicia 164
Phokaians 97, 193
Phokians, Phokis 145, 192, 193, 239; Phokian War 66
phormiskos 279, 365 n. 43; *see* vases
Photios 92, 133, 164, 216
Phrastor 190
phratries 205, 356; Labyadai at Delphi 273–4
Phrygia, Phrygian 16–17, 154–6, 206
Phryne 90, 194–5, 197; cries in court 194; stripped in court 194; *see* impiety, prostitutes
Phryne, Athenian dedicator: 15
Phrynion 192
Phyle 217, 236
[Ph]sakythe 15
Physkoa 136
Physkos 144
piety 4, 17, 18, 19, 22, 35, 102, 197, 207, 231, 253; *see* asebeia, impiety
pigs 110, 114–15, 116, 137, 239, 240, 245, 255, 263; preliminary sacrifice before marriage 217; symbol of fecundity 114; terracotta models of 114; thrown into pits to rot 114; *see* Demeter, Thesmophoria
pinakes, pinax 163, 200; *see* plaques
Pindar 78, 132, 155, 171, 202, 211; and sacred prostitutes 199–200
pins, dedication by women 9
Piraeus 25, 35, 95, 156, 206, 221, 241, 109, 120, 134, 155, 156, 168, 169, 198
Pithoigia 102, 152
Pithos (deme) 112, 117
pithos (jar) 69
Pitsa pinax 38, 228, 242, 250, 267, Figure 7.3
placenta 252
plague 65, 69, 155, 251
Plangon 167
plants, purifying 113
plaques, funerary: 275–9; series of 277; Figures 9.1–3

plaques: *see* Pitsa pinax, Lokrian pinakes, mourning women, on funerary plaques
Plataea 135, 217; Daidala at 218
Plataeans and priesthoods 79, 205
Platanista 289
Plato 3, 25, 74, 180, 182, 218, 229, 249, 269, 290; and midwives 178; and mourning 272
Platon (comic poet) 4, 164
Pleiades 214
plerosia 86, 109, 120
Pliny 60
ploughing ceremonies 120; *see* plerosia, prerosia, proerosia
Ploutos 112, 234, 248
Plutarch 65, 89, 91, 100, 111, 120, 125, 134, 153, 154, 167–8, 192, 201, 218, 239, 247; *Solon* 271
Plynteria: 87; at Athens: 133–4; in Athenian deme Thorikos 134; *see* Plynterion
Plynterion 135
plyntrides 133
Pnyx, location of Athenian Thesmophoria? 113, 118
polemarchs 290
Polemon the Periegete 14, 197, 199
pollution 250; of childbirth 252–4; of corpse 135; of grave 253
Pollux (1) 62
Pollux (2) 211
polos 67–8, 83, 154; of Cybele 156
Polybios 66
Polykrates 153
Polyneikes 288
polypharmakos 169
Polystrate 80
Polyxena 81–3, 259, Figure 3.3
pomegranate 34, 223, 231
pornai 183, 184; *see* prostitutes
Porphyry 220
Poseidippos 50, 194
Poseidon 54, 75, 87, 105, 179, 218; Poseidon Erechtheus priest of 84, 87, 124; statue purified 136
Poseidon, cult epithets: Erechtheus, priest of 84, 87, 124; Phykios 237; Poseidon Temenites 237
Poseidonia (1) festival 194
Poseidonia (2) city: *see* Paestum
Poseidonios 127
Poseidonios: founds cult 127, 290

INDEX

Posideion 120
Potnia Selene 341
Potnia Theron 54
Praisos 217
Praxiergidai, and Plynteria 84, 133–4
Praxilla 163
Praxiteles' *Knidian Aphrodite* 195
Praxithea 47
prayer, prayers, praying 71, 99, 100, 105, 112, 119, 120, 133, 155, 182, 184, 241, 242, 245, 248, 249, 262, 291, 297; for children 218; of foreign women 191, 241; gynaikonomos prays for women 273; Jason's 171; married couple for family 12; mother's prayer for her sons 78; of nurse for ugly baby 212; ololyge and 133, 243; outside shrine 75, 239; at presentation of peplos 136–7; priests (men and women) for Athens 85, 91, 246–7; of prostitutes 187, 192, 200–1, 298, cf. 241; for safe childbirth 230; Sappho's 177; before wedding 217; of women in war 242, 244 (cf. of prostitutes); women for husbands 11, 213
pregnancy 26, 172, 211, 228–9, 231, 250–1, Figure 7.3; pregnant women warned off 135; terracotta of 230; *see* Auge
Prepis, wife of 17
prerosia 120
Priam 136, 268, 269, 281
priest, woman: of Athena Nike 84–5, 90, 95, 242; perquisites 243
priest, woman: of Athena Polias 45, 46, 59, 76, 78, 84–9, 90, 95; aristocratic 85; arrival of hiera announced to 87; assistants 85; in charge of arrephoroi 46, 47, 57, 59; method of choice 87; presides over proteleia 216; and sacrifices 79, 84, 85, 87–9, 106, 242, Figure 3.4; signs registers 85; Skira procession 85, 124; and sacred snake 86; speaks 86; transmission through female line? 87; *see* Lysimache, Syeris
priests, men 76; attend funerals in Plato's ideal state 272; auctioned priesthoods 76; audit of 85; choice of 153; citizenship 79; cross-dressing 240; curse 86, 92, 246–7; death of child 78; at Delphi 98; disputes about priesthood of Salaminioi 89; dress 264; gravestones 81; of Hekate 170; of Herakles 239; holokleros 185; honoured with crowns 87; houses of 78; iconography of 81; inherited priesthoods 76; male prostitutes could not serve as 185; metragyrtes 155; non-citizens excluded from 205; perquisites 85, 89, 127, 239; of Poseidon Erechtheus 84; reserved seats in theatre of Dionysos, Athens 87; of Sabazios 159; sale of priesthoods 85; sexual abstinence 77, 78, 239, 255, 257; shown with sacrificial knife 63, 81; succession to 89; susceptible to pollution 250, 253; *see* Archias, Zoilos
priests, women: 1, 11, 33, 39, 73–108, 120, 207, 295, 297, 300; age of 75–6; aristocratic/gentilician 84, 87; of Artemis Brauronia 93–4; of Artemis Orthia 260; assistants 84; of Athena Skiras 89–90; attend funerals in Plato's ideal state 272; audit of 85–6; bare feet of 82, 88, Figure 3.4; begging in aid of childbirth 95–97; of Bendis 95; carry out sacrifices at Thesmophoria 110; children of 77, 78; choice of 76, 80, 92; chosen democratically 84–5; citizen status 79; clothing 69, 71, 169, 263, 264, Figures 2.15, 3.14; complain about women worshippers 79; curses 86, 92, 246–7; of Cybele 95; death of children 78; of Demeter 23, 24; of Demeter Chamyne 131; diet 77, 79; of Dionysos 142, 143, 146; disputes about priesthood of Salaminioi 89; dress 80, 81–2, 88, 169, 262, 263; drink bull's blood 77; in Echinos relief? 231–2; of Eleusis 90–2; eligibility for 205; executed 104; fined 90; general lack of public honours for 87; gentilician (gentile) 76; on grave reliefs 80, Figures 3.2–3; greed checked 85; guardianship 79; 'healthy and sound' 74; of Hekate 170; holokleros 185; houses 78; impious 104–5; incite women to adultery 121; have keys to temples 80–1; on Lokrian pinakes 227; marriage rites 216, 218; method of choice 87; named women priests 86–7; Nikandre as? 11; non-citizens excluded from 205; do not slay victim

427

246; only ones to see rite 238, 245; pay for priesthoods in instalments 75; parthenoi as 75, 239, 253, 255, 258; perquisites 79, 85, 89, 116, 144, 244; plays about 73; pray 91–2; preside over sacrifices 56, 75, 79, 84, 88, 90, 91, 92, 110, 116, 216, 243, 266–7, Figure 3.4; processions and 85, 89–90, 92, 94; prohibitions for women priests and zakoroi 90; prosecutes hierophant 91, 121; receive shares of sacrifice 243; receive treasury proceeds 85; represented by relatives 79; reserved seats in theatre of Dionysos, Athens 87; revenues 85; sacred fire 105; sale of priesthoods 74, 75, 85; seats of 263; sexual abstinence 77–8, 255, 258, 260; sexual and marital status 75, 76, 77, 78; shod feet of 82, Figure 3.3; slaughter cows 238, 245; speak in public 79, 86; statues of 84, 86; stipend 85; succession to 89; tenure 75–6, 84; of Thesmophoria 112, 117; titles of 74; upper socio-economic class 267; used for dating 73; *see* Alkmeonis, Anthesteria, Artemis Agrotera, Artemis Pergaia, basilinna, Chairestrate, Chyrsis (1), Dodona, gerarai, Glaukothea, Iphigeneia, Lykourgos *On the Priesthood*, Menekrateia, Nino, Polystrate, Polyxena, propolos, Pythia, Satyra, Timo, priest, woman: of Athena Polias, zakoroi

proagoreusis 111

processions 4, 32, 37, 38, 41, 50, 89, 132, 137, 196, 212, 221, 228, 241, 242, 250, 290, 295, 298; Adonia 163, 165, 167, 168; at Andania 127, 264; of Aphrodite Pandemos 134; at Argive Heraion 78; for Athena Promachos 39; of Brauronia 94; deer cart 75; for Demeter 57, 125–6, 245, 250; for Dionysos 143, 146; Eleusinian 57, 92, 291; of *frauenfest* scenes 129–30; funeral 256, 272, 275; for Hekate 170; Hera 216; Hyakinthia 214; at Lokris 224, 226, 227; of Oschophoria 89–90; Panathenaic 38, 42–50, 58, 71, 72, 205, 243, 296, Figures 2.3–7; phallic 122, 199; of Plynteria 134; of Pythais

39; of the Semnai Theai 94–5, cf. 300; of Skira 85, 124; wedding 219, 220

Procharisteria 113

proedria 87, 124

proerosia 111, 117, 120, 134

Proitides 67

Proitos 67, 142, 146, 180

propolos 92, 155

proselytisation 97

prostitutes (hetairai, pornai) 5, 39, 112, 123, 127, 256, 293, 362n.143; to abstain from sexual intercourse before entering temple 257; accepted in Greece 183; altar and shrine dedicated to the deceased prostitute Pythionike 196; ancient works on 183; celebrate Haloa 122; dedications of 197–8, 207; expensive 199; at festivals 132, 193, 198–9; impious female: *see* Phryne; impious male: *see* Demochares, Timarchos; initiated into Eleusinian Mysteries 195–6; and looted temple treasures 192–3; in Parthenon 192; plays about 183; prayers 200–1; present at sacrifices 241; presence in temples 183, 190–2, 198; sacred 199–202, 207, 241, 254; sacred laws dealing with 192, 193–4; sacrifice goats 245; secular 101–4; at Sparta 198; tax on 344; terms for 183, 184; tombs of 196–7; *see* Adonia, Anthea, Aspasia, Boidion, Doriche, Eirene, Glykera, Gnathaina, Gnathainion, Hedeia, Isthmias, Kottina, Lais, Mammarion, Metaneira, Neaira, Nemeas, Nikidion, Phryne, Pythionike, Rhodopis, Sinope, Stratonike

proteleia 216–17, 218, 222

Protesileos 258

prothesis 274–5, 279, 282, 370

prytaneion 102, 125

psaltria 127

Ptolemaia 146

Ptolemaies 249, 252

Ptolemies 289

Ptolemy II Philadelphos 125, 146, 147, 163, 196

puberty 47, 93, 250; of boys 72, 185; dangers of for girls 70, 230; dedication of representations of 26, 28–9; girdle of 216; virgin girl served

as priest until 75; *see* arkteia, menarche, *rakos*
puppies 154, 242
purifications, purity 37, 38, 39, 54, 65, 71, 86, 103, 114, 116, 134–5, 211, 238, 239, 273, 294; of clothes 69–70, Figure 2.15; of Delos 253; fasting as 113; with a pig 137, 195; of priests 74, 77; purifiers from entheos 179; purity regulations 172, 192, 193, 249–50, 251–2, 253–4, 263–4; in Sabazios' cult 159; sexual purity and temples 254–8; of temples 130, 134–5; *see* gerarai, Philadelphia, sexual intercourse: abstinence, statue washing
purple gowns 205–6; *see* clothes
Pyanopsia 117
Pyanopsion 57, 58, 89, 109, 110, 111, 120, 322
Pylades 135, 246, 248
Pyloi 193
pyramids 197
Pythagoras, Pythagoreanism 139, 153–4, 203, 262, 283; *Pythagorizousai* play 153
Pythais 39, 40, 101
Pythia 77, 98–100, 105, 106, 180, 258; ambiguous answers 99; answers questions on childbirth 98, childlessness 100, colonisation 100, crops 100, herds 100, health 100; bathes 98; bribed 99, 104; choice of 98; and Delphic priests 98; forced to prophecy 101; house of 77, 78; inspiration 98, 99; mouthpiece of Apollo 99; number of 98; prescriptions of 99; sexual abstinence 75, 77; war 99; *see* tripod
Pythian festival 54, 93, 131, 132, 199
Pythionike 196, 198
Pythones 180

rakos 250; *see* Artemis Brauronia, clothes
rams 105
rape 59, 65, 175, 220, 258, 260, Figure 8.3
Rarian plain 91, 120, 125
Reed Painter 283
reliefs 24–5, 31–2, 231–4, 279; dedicated and expensive 232; stone dedicated to Herakles 240; Figures 1.3–4, 7.4; *see* Echinos relief, grave stelai, hero-reliefs, maenadism (carved reliefs)
Rhamnous 77, 80
Rhea 238, 250
Rhegion 202
Rheitoi 92
Rheneia 253
Rhodes 54, 61, 79, 196, 216, 250, 256, 263, 322
Rhodopis 197
Rhossos 196
rhyton 18, 289
ribbon: *see* fillet
rites of passage: *see* transition rites
robes (of women) 21, 22, 88, 159, 160, 163, 175, 176; perfuming 69–71, Figure 2.15; robed pillar of Dionysos 4, Figures 5.2–3, cf. 152
Roman coins 201
rooster 34, 223–5, 239, Figures 7.1–2
Roxane 18–19
running competitions, for maidens 212, 213; *see* Heraia
Ruvo amphora 245

Sabazios 97, 139, 158–61, 164, 166, 181, 295, 296, 300; drunkenness in cult 160; ecstatic cult? 159, 160; exotic cult? 160; hostility to cult 158–9, 160; old women in cult 158–9; sexual activity in cult 159; slaves 159; thiasoi 159–60; women prominent in cult 158–9
sacred fire 105
sacred ploughings 125
Sacred Way (Athens) 43, 196
Sacred Way (Delphi) 54
sacrifices 35, 37, 39, 41, 47, 49, 57, 60, 61, 72, 79, 85, 89, 96, 103, 109, 110, 120, 121, 127, 132, 134, 136, 137, 140, 169, 172, 183, 190, 199, 205, 266, 273, 283, 290, 295, 296, 297, 298, 299; adulterous women debarred from 190, 191; of basilinna 101, 102, 103, 190; after birth 253; bloodless 153; 'Chalkidian Pursuit' 244; compulsory marriage 221; to be consumed on the spot 126, 243; for dead children 69–70; of Delphi consultants 98; distribution of meat from 127, 131, 205; expenses of 85, 116, 117; by family 31–2, Figure 1.4; foreign women and slaves can attend

190, 191; human 128, 135, 258, 260; impious women debarred from at Gambreion 273; implements for 38, 56, 60, 63, 67, 68, 74, 78, 81, 90, 110, 112, 115, 236, Figure 2.13; not to be made without presence of woman priest 86; by parthenoi before marriage 216–19; perquisites from 85, 89, 91, 127; pre-marital 217–19; prescriptions for 98, 100; presence of women at 236, 241–6; of puppies 170, 246, Figure 8.1; of raw meat 142–3; sacrificial fire 90, 185; transition 62; by women to nymphs for childbirth 228–9, Figure 7.3; women excluded from 237–40; women participate in 236, 237, 241–6; women slay victims at 110, 116, 115–16, 238, 245; *see* Echinos relief, hydrophoroi, knife, mothers, Sinope, sphageion, Thesmophoria, women
Salaminioi 76, 89, 169, 222
Samian temple water basin 54–5, Figure 2.11
Samians, Samos 32, 35, 135, 153, 215, 222
Samothrace frieze 67–8
Samothracian Mysteries 68
sanctuary of Eros and Aphrodite 59
sandals 19, 203
Sappho 163, 164, 171, 177, 190, 197
Sarapis 39, 161, 249, 250
Satyra 117
satyrs 69, 102, 140, 143, 145, 146, 370
sausages 244
Sebasteia 131
Sele 66
Selinounte 54, 67, 105, 140, 243
Semnai Theai: *see* Nameless Goddesses
Semonides 113
serpents 80, 100–1; *see* snakes
servants: *see* slaves
seven boys and seven girls 68–9
sexual intercourse: abstinence from 75, 77, 103, 113, 118, 125, 137, 159, 239, 255–6, 256, 294; oath of abstinence 255; jokes about in women-only rites 109, 113, 122; with prostitutes 39, 183, 184, 257; purification from before entering temples 255–7, cf. 153; Pythagorean attitudes to 153; sexual penetration, cultural norm of 185; in temples 90, 94, 153, 192, 193–4, 254–8; washing purifies from 255, 257; woman priest finished with 75, 258, cf. 105; women mock men's sexuality at the Adonia? 166; of Zeus and Hera 171; *see* aischrologia, maenads, satyrs
shamrock 102
shawls 21, 22, 68
shield 264, 270, 285; dedication of 16
shoes 232, 263
Sicilian expedition 167
Sicilians, Sicily 62, 110, 126, 167, 201, 202, 239; *see* Gela, Selinounte, Syracuse
sickle 245
Sidon 136
Sikyon 35, 75, 97, 228, 239
Sikyonian festival 131
silenoi 146
silversmiths 26
Simaitha 175
Simonides 200, 201
sindonites 264
singing 199, 220; for Adonis 163, 164, 167; funerary 269, 274, 276, cf. 290; of girls and women, 67, 128, 132, 140, 214, 215; of maenads 140, 143; *see* hymns
Sinope 121, 122, 192, 196, 241–2
Siphnian treasury 45, 53
Sirius 214
Sisyphus Painter 260
Sixteen Women, the 137
Skamander river 220
Skambonidai 205
skana 126
Skating Painter Figure 4.2
skenai 119
skiadia 205
skiadophoroi 206
Skiereia 260
Skira 295, 296
Skira: 85, 86, 109, 120, 124–5, 191, 295–6; date 124, 125; procession at 124; sexual abstinence at 125
Skiraphoria: *see* Skira
Skiron (hero) 124, 125
Skiron (place) 120, 124
Skirophorion 85
skirt 88, 122
slaves (and servants) 5, 26, 28, 31, 32, 35, 65, 99, 153, 156, Figure 5.6, 159,

161, 179, 183, 185, 198, 199, 206, 207, 231–2, Figure 7.4, 236, 240, 241, 257, 260, 266, 289, 285, 290, 296, 298; attend public sacrifices at Athens 191, 241; girl and women slaves dedicated to Aphrodite 200, 201, 202; girl slave plays music at Tauropolia 127, 206; initiates in Eleusinian Mysteries 195, 242; Ion as temple servant 98; Phryne as Aphrodite's servant 90; priests spared enslavement 101; receive sacrificial meat 244; women slaves not permitted in certain festivals and rites 132, 191, 206, 237–8, 241 (see Thesmophoria); women slaves not permitted at Thesmophoria 112, 120; temple boy servant on acropolis? 47; women slaves, dress at Andanian Mysteries 264; women slaves and Hera's temple 260, 262; women slaves as mourners 270; *see* diakonoumenai, prostitutes (sacred), Thratta
smegmatotheke 367n.84
Smikythe 15
Smyrna 290
snake, snakes 34; of Asklepios 29–30, 97, 144; on Athenian acropolis 86; brandishing of 159, 160; causes pregnancies 29–30; of dough 60; headband 146, 161; maenads and 140, 143, 144, Figure 5.1; squeezing 159; red 159
sneeze 248
Socrates 95, 194, 287–8, 289
sodomy 184, 185
Solon 166, 183, 18, 241, 268, 269
son, sons 2, 19, 86, 134, 136, 137, 140, 168, 169, 170, 177, 189, 235, 236, 238, 242, 258, 266, 277, 294; Alkestis prays for to marry 218; charged with hierosylia 93; co-dedicant with mother 23, 134; dead, on funerary plaque 277–8; dedication for birth of 19; dedication for upbringing of 24–5, Figure 1.3; dedication promised for future birth of 230; iama for birth of 26; mothers mention in dedications 12, 24–5; reports to boule on mother's priesthood 79, 242; Spartan 270; torn apart in sparagmos rite 141, 142, 147, 152; useful 124; *see* step-son

Sophocles 142, 180; *Ajax* 179; *Antigone* 288; *Kolchian Women* 172; *Oedipus at Kolonos* 71; *Root-cutters* 172
Sophron 132, 170, 174–5
sorcerers, male 170
sorcerers, women 2, 5, 139, 169–78, 182; Circe 170; historical 177–8; Medea 172–4, 176–7; Thessalian 169; Figures 5.9–10
Sosipolis 77
Sostratos 73, 236, 267
Sounion 89
sparagmos, rite of 141, 142, 143, 147
Sparta (Lakonia) 13, 34, 54, 99, 118, 127, 137, 213, 238, 243, 257, 263; choruses of parthenoi at 211–15; exposure of children 252; Spartan women dancing 67; Thesmophoria at 115; *see* Kyniska, helots, Lakonia
spectacle-fibulae 14
spells 170; erotic 171, 177; *see* magic
sphageion 116
spindle 215
spindle-whorls 14
spitting 125
stade 199
stamnos, stamnoi 59, 149; definition 370; depict departing warriors 264–6, Figure 8.4; and maenads 149–52, 181, Figure 5.2
statues 21, 32, 35, 36, 61, 80, 82, 97, 103, 106, 135, 136, 146, 148, 155, 170, 201, 212, 213, 216, 217, 218, 230, 298; Aphrodite in Samos, dedicated by prostitutes 198; of arrephoroi 58; of Artemis Orthia and whipping rite 260; of Artemis, bathed 135; of Athena bathed 132–3, 134; of Athena in Telephos frieze 258; of Athena of the Bronze House 197; of Athena Parthenos 43; of Athena Polias 84, 87, 88, Figure 3.4; bronze of the prostitute Glykera 196; of the 'child of the hearth' 92; clung to by women 249, 259–60, Figure 8.3; dedicated by women 9–12, 15, 17, 19, 23, 24; of Demeter priests at Hermion 245; of drunken festival woman 165; of Eros, dedicated by Phryne 195; of the hetaira Kottina 197; of Hera, purified 135; of kanephoroi 40; of themselves dedicated by girl victors in Heraia

431

INDEX

131; only seen by sacred women 238, 239; peplos presented to at Olympia 137; Praxiteles' *Knidian Aphrodite* (the *Knidia*) 195; washing of 132–6, 215: by aristocratic women 133; at Argos 132–3, at Athens 133–5; of women priests at Argive Heraion 83; of women priests of Athena Polias 86; women cling to 259–60, Figure 8.3; women throw themselves before 260; Figure 1.1; *see* Anzio Girl, Erechtheion, Lysimache (1), (4), (5), Nikandre, Palladion, Syeris
statuettes 41, 60, 73; dedicated by women 14, 16, 17, 32–3 (?); of girl athletes 131–2; of goddess 81, Figure 3.3; of korai 229; of women carrying piglets 114; of young girls running 131; Figures 1.2, 2.12; *see* hawk-priestess, terracottas
stelai, stele, funerary: *see* grave-stelai
stemma, stemmata 38, 63, Figure 2.14; cf. fillet
Stenia 109, 111, 117, 124, 191, 295, 296
step-son 248
Stephanos (1) 101, 190, 192
Stephanos (2), metic 168
stepmother 177, 248
sternomanteis 180
stillbirths 230, 251–2
stools: *see* diphroi
Strabo 64, 65, 97, 201; on sacred prostitutes 200
Stratonike 196
Strybele 103
Stuart 49
Styx, river 288
suicide, by pubescent girls 70
Suida 65, 66, 217, 218
sumptuary legislation 22
Superstitious Man 249, 253
swinging girls 69–71, Figure 2.15
Syeris 84
symmeixis 102
Syracuse 56, 132, 153; Thesmophoria at 111, 113, 114, 138
Syria, Syrian 54, 249, 256

tainiai 80, 233, 283; *see* fillet
Tammaz 164
Tanagra 34, 36, 238, 291; clothing dedications by women at 22–3
Taras 237
Tarsos 196
Tauris 128, 246
Tauropolia 127–8, 138, 207, 296
Tauropolion 128
Taygetos Mt 211
Tegea 75, 83, 243–4, 255, 258
Teiresias 133, 288
Telemachos (1) Homeric 242, 247–8
Telemachos (2) Athenian 97, 305
Telephos 253; Telephos frieze 258, Figure 8.2
Telesilla 353
telesterion (Eleusis) 192
Telestodike of Paros 9, 11–12
temples (including sanctuaries and shrines) 1, 4, 10, 13, 14, 19, 22, 23, 26, 29, 30, 31, 33, 34, 50, 54, 56, 57, 59, 61, 63, 64, 65, 67, 68, 72, 73, 75, 78, 84, 87, 89, 90, 92, 93, 95, 97, 98, 102, 103, 105, 106, 114, 116, 117, 118, 119, 120, 122, 124, 125, 126, 131, 132, 133, 134, 137, 139, 144, 147, 156, 170, 181, 183, 190, 198, 199, 212, 214, 215, 216, 217, 221, 222, 225, 226, 227, 230, 235, 236, 238, 240, 245, 246, 253, 258, 259, 260, 262, 267, 273, 291, 297, 298, 300; of Aphrodite the Whore 190; Argive Heraion burns down 76; of Athena, Ilion 63–6; no births in 252–4; dedication of by women 3, 23–5; dedications of prostitutes in 197–8; Demeter's on the Acrocorinth 126–7, 130; Dorians not permitted 86; of Eileithyia 230; entry without woman priest forbidden 79; erected to prostitutes 196; female prostitutes could enter 190–2, 193, 198, 199–202, 207; hero-shrine of Kyniska 289; male prostitutes not to enter 185, 190; no men 116; of Nymphe 219; of Semnai Theai 94–5; parthenoi watched by suitors at 213; Plato criticises women's establishment of 3; pollution of 135; Poseidon's at Isthmia 54; pregnant women and 125–6, 230, 250; presentation of a child in 231–4; prostitute stoned in 196; purification of 134–5; robbery of 93–4, 192–3; roped off 133, 136; shrine of the Eumenides, Kolonos 71; shrines in house 249; women banned

from or allowed in 237–41; *see* Aglaurion, Amphiaraion, Aphrodite Pandemos, Asklepieion, Athena Nike, Delphinion, Erechtheion, gold, Heraion (Argos, Foce Sele, Samos), inventories, Isis, keys, Metroon, Parthenon, Perachora, sexual intercourse (temples), Tauropolion, Thesmophorion
Ten Thousand, the 248
Tenos 35
terata, monsters 248
terracotta, terracottas: Adonis Gardens 162, 163, 165; of Demeter (?) 91; figurine of a breastfeeding woman 230; figurine of kanephoros 39, 41, Figure 2.2; figurines of korai dedicated 229; figurines of reclining women diners 127; figurines of women in labour 26; figurines of young women suggestive of cult roles 56, 57, 105; of girls dancing 67; *koulouria* dedicated 14; lekythos 287; of likna 126; of mourning women 281–2, Figure 9.5; phialai 18; phalloi 121; piglets 114; spindles dedicated 14; of women carrying piglets 114, 326 n. 31; *see* Lokrian plaques, pinakes, plaques (funerary), statuettes
Tetrapolis 222
thanksgiving: *see* dedications
Thargelion 133, 134
Thasos 135, 138, 239, 243, 263
Thaumasion Mt 238
Theano (1) of Troy 76, 136, 137
Theano (2) Athenian woman dedicator 19, 20
Theano (3) Athenian woman priest, 92, 247, cf. 86
Theano (4) Pythagoras' wife 153
Thebes 34, 35, 101, 111, 119, 180, 205, 220, 242, 251, 260, 294; maenads at 140, esp. 145–9; Thesmophoria at 113
thelktra; *see* charms
Themistios 196
Themistokles 86, 99
Theogamia 218
Theogenes 101, 103, 190
Theoinia 103
Theokritos 214; *Idyll* 2, 175; *Idyll* 15, 163, 165; *Idyll* 18, 212;
Theophrastos (1) 3, 154, 159, 253

Theophrastos (2) 168, 172
Theopompos 201
theoria 61, 69
Theoris 177, 182
Thera 250
Therapne 212
thesauros 217
Theseus 69, 89, 94, 102, 120, 266, 300
Thesmophoria 1, 57, 60, 72, 86, 105, 109, 166, 199, 238, 243, 145, 213, 246, 273, 293, 295, 296, 299; aischrologia at 113–14; aristocratic women and 111, 118; celebrated in Athenian demes 111–12, 117; date 110–11; dawn start for 118; fasting at 113; fertility rites at 114; invokes fertility 112; as a liturgy 117; lewd jokes at 113; location of celebration 118–19; Lucian scholiast on 114; mageiros at 116; megara, megaron at 114; mother and daughter-in-law at 118; number of women celebrating 119; sexual abstinence at 112; slaves and prostitutes not admitted to 112, 120; at Syracuse 111; women-only 110; women kill pigs at 115–16; women strike each other at 114; *see* Aristophanes *Thesmophoriazousai*; Thesmophorion
Thesmophorion: Athens 109, 112, 116, 118; Gambreion 273; Paros 104, 118; Piraeus 79, 86, 112, 117, 194
Thesmophoroi (Demeter and Kore) 112, 116, 117, 118
Thespiai (Boeotia) 35, 77, 194, 195
Thessaly 193, 196
Thestios' daughters 77
Thestylis 175
Thetima 178
Thetis 279
Thettale 146
thiasoi, thiasos 86, 104, 105, 144, 145–9, 158, 159, 160, 168, 169, 177, 182, 194, 370
Third Sacred War 192
Thoas, king 135
thoinarmostria 127
Thorikos 120, 134
Thrace 238
Thracian women 237
Thratta 112, 118
threnoi 269
Thucydides 25, 73, 75, 102, 189, 268

INDEX

Thyiades 144–5, 147, 181; *see* maenads
thylemata 236
thymiateria, thymiaterion (incense-burners) 39, 43–4, 49, 56, 60, 71, 72, 146, 156, 203, 212, 226, 231, 236, 371, Figure 2.1; at Adonia? 169; in shape of women 54, 56; incense burned by woman for Aphrodite, Figure 6.5; incense burned by prostitutes for Aphrodite 200; at Lokris 225; and magic 175; on Parthenon frieze 43–4, 49, Figure 2.4, 2.7; with mourning women 282
thyrsoi, thyrsos 140, 144, 146, 147, 148, 150, 245, 371, Figures 5.1, 5.3–4
tiara 189, 264
Timaios 185
Timarchos 184–5, 186
Timarete 229
Timo 104, 110
Timokles 291
Timothea 156
Timycha 153
Tiryns 142
Titans 142
Tithenidia 350
Tonaia 135
tongue, of sacrifice 244
torch 25, 46, 51, 114, 118, 219, 245; of Artemis 25, 232; in nocturnal rituals 134; Figures 1.3, 7.4; of Hekate 246
torture 153
toys 104, 223; dedicated before marriage 215
Tralleis 35
transition rites 60, 62, 199, 212, 293
transvestism: *see* cross-dressing
Trapezo: *see* Trapezophoros
Trapezophoros 84
tray, for sacrificial items 38, 60, 156
tray-bearers 60, 231; Figures 2.12–13
treasurers 18, 90
tripod 39, 63, 106, Figure 2.14; of Pythia 74, 98, 101, 106
Triton, river 135
Tritopatores 218, 282
Trojan War, Troy 65, 66, 116, 218, 248, 259, 260, 268; *see* Lokrian maidens
trophe 116
Tsoutsouros Inatos 230
Twelve Gods, the 94

tympana, tympanum 2, 68, 80, 144, 146, 154, 156, 160, 299, 371
Tyndaridai 211, 212
Typaion, Mt 131
typion 203
typoi 27

umbilical cord 252
Undercutter, the 171, 182
uteri, dedication of representations of 26, 28–9

Vari 219
vases: *see* Figures 2.1, 2.14–15, 3.4, 4.1–2, 5.1–4, 5.7–9, 5.11, 8.1, 8.4, 9.6–7, with discussion; *see* Achilles P., Adonia, alabastron, amphora, aryballos, Brygos P., Circle of the Meidias P., Copenhagen P., Dinos P., Dipylon Master, Corinthian *frauenfest* scenes, geometric art, Group of Palermo 16, hydria, kantharoi, Kleophon P., Kleophrades P., krateriskoi, lagynos, lebes gamikos, lekanis, lekythoi, loutrophoroi, lebes gamikos, Makron, Meidias P., Nausicaa P., olpis, P. of Athens 1454, phormiskos, Reed P., Ruvo amphora, Sisyphus P., Skating P., Villa Giulia P., Washing P., Manner of the
Vatican kore 51
vegetarianism 153–4, cf. 142
veil 34, 44, 82, 83, 156, 222; of bride 218; dedicated to Hera 352
Venice 156
Venus rings 50
Vestal Virgins 79
Villa Giulia Painter 149, Figure 5.2
virgin goddesses 12, 38, 42, 58, 71, 186, 189, 192, 256
virgins, virginity 33, 37, 38, 39, 47, 50, 56, 57, 58, 60, 66, 67, 71, 72, 102, 106, 215, 225, 226, 228, 234, 243, 259, 260, 291 102, 106; of boys 72; dead 220; heroised 96, 215; of Hera renewed 132; midwives as 178; *Peri Parthenion* 20, 250; prostituted 199, cf. 202; required for cult purposes 75, 77–8, 102, 105, 132, 190, 239, 246, 253, 255, 257, 258; sacrificed in myth 218, 258; *see* Auge, Gello, hanging, Komaitho, Opis, parthenoi
vows 3; of Xenophon of Corinth 200

434

INDEX

Vulci 265
vulva, vulvae 29

wagons: in funerary processions 277, 279; see chariots
warriors 220, 285; departing 264–6, Figure 8.4; presents daughter to Persephone 226
Washing Painter, Manner of the 175-6, Figure 5.11
washers, the 206
water 25, 35, 63, 122, 172, 205, 236; to bathe statues 132, 135; for purifications 72, 116, 255, 289; purifies from sexual intercourse 257; sacrificial victims heads doused with 49; for wedding baths 135, 219, 220; see chernips, enneakrounos, hagisteria, hydria, hydrophoroi, perirrhanteria
wax images 175, 247
weddings: see marriage
widows 159, 217
wife, wives 5, 11, 18, 31, 32, 33, 34, 47, 101, 118, 127, 132, 136, 152, 155, 156, 161, 163, 165, 167, 171, 175, 176, 177, 178, 181, 182, 183, 184, 186, 189, 190, 191, 193, 195, 201, 205, 206, 207, 211, 212, 213, 218, 234, 238, 239, 241, 242, 243, 244, 248, 255, 256, 264, 266, 270, 283, 290, 291, 294, 295, 297, 298, 300; attend Orphic rites 154; celebrate Adonia with hetairai? 165, 167, 181–2; deified 289, 290; of Dionysos 101–4; Dodona consulted on choice of 100; farewell husbands 264–6, Figure 8.4; mourn husbands 268, 285; not to attend funerals in Plato's ideal state 272; preside over Thesmophoria 112, 117; purity laws and 193, 256, 257; share in sacrifices 243, 244; unfaithful husbands of tortured 153; use erotic magic 175–6, 177, 178; women finish with role as 159; women identify themselves as 13, 17, 19, 24, 30; worship Aphrodite 200, 201, 202–3, Figure 6.5 (see Adonia); see husbands
wine 2, 34, 69, 112, 129, 137, 139, 170, 207, 241, 322; drunken festival woman 165; at Haloa 121, 122; in Sabazios cult 159; at Thesmophoria 116; tipsy woman at Adonia 164–5; see Anthesteria, Choes, libations, maenads, swinging girls, warriors (departing), Figures 5.2–3
wing-sleeves 152, Figure 2.7
women: abuse each other 109; attend panhellenic games 131–2; adulterous 191; adulterous, not permitted to attend sacrifices 241–6; Alexandrian 146; blasphemous 109; captured while celebrating a festival 110, 213; cult cries of 143 (see Adonia, 'Beat your breasts for Adonis', 'Woe, Adonis', 'euoi', 'Euoi Saboi', 'Hyes Attes Attes hyes', ololyge, ololygma, ololygmos); cult dining of 126–7; cult proselytisers 97; curse tablets 178; decision-making in cults 112; excluded from political and legal life of polis 299; extent of participation in maenadic activity 147; flogged at festival 260; guardianship of 79–80; heroised 289–90; kill sacrificial victims 115–6, 238, 245; old 94–5, 126, 158, 159, 172, 299, 300, 338n.127; old can attend funerals in Plato's ideal state 272; old, in exotic cults 158–9, 300; Orphic 154; religious decisions made by 79; return to domesticity after festivals 296; rights limited 296; rites as a safety valve for 148, 299–300; rooftop wailing 164; sacrifice on their own initiative 236; tipsy 164–5; uninitiated women forbidden 125; walk to Eleusinian Mysteries 291; see esp. bare feet, clothes, dining rooms, dancing, dedications, ecstacy, kneeling, mourning women, pregnancy, priests (women), Pythagoras, sacrifices, statues, wine
Woodcutter, the 171
wreaths 49, 103, 128, 185, 193, 212, 242; see fillets

Xanthippe 279
Xanthippos 186
Xenarchos 183
xene, xenoi 190, 191, 237
xenismos, of Herakles 239
Xenodoka 13
Xenokrateia 24–5
Xenophanes 154, 134, 248, 258
Xenophon of Corinth 199–200
Xenophon of Ephesos 216

435

youths: dressed as girls 213

Zagreos 142
zakoroi 90
Zea 134
Zeus 1, 12, 99, 105, 135, 136, 142, 171, 180, 217, 218, 227, 230, 234, 250, 251, 289
Zeus, cult epithets: Amalos 237; Apotropaios 237; Chthonia 237; Chthonios 120, 237; Eubuleus 116; 'from Perses' 136; Hetaireios 190; Hypatos 237; Hypsistos 29–31; Ktesios 241; Meilichios 249; Olympios 'in the city' 136; Olympios 94; Polieus 257; Sosipolis 238, 291; Teleios 217, 218
Zoilos 153